OXFORD WORLD'S CI

THE OXFORD SHAK

D0208061

General Editor · Stanley Wells

The Oxford Shakespeare offers new and authoritative editions of Shakespeare's plays in which the early printings have been scrupulously re-examined and interpreted. An introductory essay provides all relevant background information together with an appraisal of critical views and of the play's effects in performance. The detailed commentaries pay particular attention to language and staging. Reprints of sources, music for songs, genealogical tables, maps, etc. are included where necessary; many of the volumes are illustrated, and all contain an index.

Hamlet was edited by G. R. Hibbard, who was Emeritus Professor of English at the University of Waterloo in Ontario, Canada. He edited *Love's Labours Lost* in the Oxford Shakespeare and *Coriolanus, The Taming of the Shrew, Timon of Athens,* and *The Merry Wives of Windsor* for the New Penguin Shakespeare.

THE OXFORD SHAKESPEARE

Currently available in paperback

The rest of the plays are forthcoming

OXFORD WORLD'S CLASSICS

WILLIAM SHAKESPEARE

Hamlet

Edited by
G. R. HIBBARD

OXFORD
UNIVERSITY PRESS

OXFORD

UNIVERSITY PRESS

Great Clarendon Street, Oxford OX2 6DP

Oxford University Press is a department of the University of Oxford.
It furthers the University's objective of excellence in research, scholarship,
and education by publishing worldwide in

Oxford New York

Athens Auckland Bangkok Bogotá Buenos Aires Cape Town
Chennai Dar es Salaam Delhi Florence Hong Kong Istanbul Karachi
Kolkata Kuala Lumpur Madrid Melbourne Mexico City Mumbai Nairobi
Paris São Paulo Shanghai Singapore Taipei Tokyo Toronto Warsaw

with associated companies in Berlin Ibadan

Oxford is a registered trade mark of Oxford University Press
in the UK and in certain other countries

First published by the Clarendon Press 1987
First published as a World's Classics paperback 1994
Reissued as an Oxford World's Classics paperback 1998
Reissued 2008

British Library Cataloguing in Publication Data

Data available

Library of Congress Cataloging in Publication Data
Shakespeare, William, 1564–1616.
Hamlet.
(The Oxford Shakespeare)
Includes index.
I. Hibbard, G. R. (George Richard), 1915– .
II. Title. III. Series: Shakespeare, William, 1564–1616.
Works. 1982.
PR2807.A2H7 1987 822.3′3 86–2533

ISBN 978–0–19–953581–1

1

Printed in Great Britain by
Clays Ltd, St Ives plc

PREFACE

I AM DEEPLY GRATEFUL to the Social Sciences and Humanities Research Council of Canada for the grant it made me in 1981, thus enabling me to work uninterruptedly on this edition for a period of eight months in 1982–3.

I also owe a large debt of another kind to the General Editor, Stanley Wells, and to the Associate Editor, Gary Taylor. Their many suggestions and criticisms have been invaluable, and their patience exemplary.

G. R. HIBBARD

CONTENTS

LIST OF ILLUSTRATIONS

GENERAL INTRODUCTION

UP to the end of the First World War and for some time thereafter, *Hamlet* was generally regarded as the greatest of all Shakespeare's plays, the most exciting, absorbing, and profound drama
ever written. Since then the balance of academic judgement, as
distinct from interest, has tipped somewhat in favour of *King Lear*;
but the theatre-going public remains unconvinced; so does 'the
common reader'; and so do the actors. *Hamlet* is still the most often
produced of the plays, as well as the most widely read; and the role
of the Prince continues to be the ultimate goal to which actors
aspire. Moreover, Hamlet himself is part of the consciousness of the
modern world in a more intimate and familiar way than *King Lear*
has ever been or seems likely to become. Of all Shakespeare's tragic
heroes, the Prince of Denmark, his rank notwithstanding, is the
one whose experience comes closest to and impinges most
intimately on that of men in general. It has, despite its highly
unusual and, at times, almost bizarre nature, a representative
quality about it. Spectators and readers alike feel drawn to identify
themselves with Hamlet.

   Yet, while it has this universal appeal, *Hamlet* is also for many
the most personal of the plays, conveying, as does no other, a sense
of the playwright's involvement with his own creation. In part this
is due, no doubt, to the remarkable similarities between the great
central soliloquy in it, 'To be, or not to be', and Sonnet 66, 'Tired
with all these, for restful death I cry', which may well lead one to
think that at this point in the action Hamlet's sentiments are very
close to Shakespeare's own. But this is by no means the end of the
connection. There is a strong temptation to take the Prince's views
on the art of acting as a faithful reflection of his author's; and,
still more fascinating, the very length of the tragedy, even in the
Folio version, almost invites one to speculate that Shakespeare
composed it, at the compulsive urging of his *daimon*, for his own
satisfaction. The last act in particular cries out for some such
explanation; for into it he brings three entirely new figures: two
Clowns, for one of whom death is simply a means of livelihood; and
the empty-headed fop Osric. It is almost as though the creative
impulse refuses, for once, to heed the practical limitations and

demands of the theatre. In the very process of bringing his play to an end Shakespeare expands its reach and significance. He cannot let go of it; and it will not let go of him.

Universal, yet with pronounced overtones of the personal and the private about it, *Hamlet* is timeless in its preoccupation with the dilemmas and the uncertainties that are at the heart of life, and, simultaneously, very much of its own time. It belongs to that period in the history of England—and of Europe—when the assurances of the Elizabethan world, which had so much in common with the mediaeval world, were being invaded and eroded by 'the new doubt', as D. G. James calls it,[1] which is so characteristic of the modern world. Similarly, within the framework of its author's career as a practising dramatist, it comes as the climax to three or four years of extraordinary fertility and achievement. During the course of them he had written at least two comic masterpieces, *Much Ado About Nothing* and *As You Like It*, and probably, though its exact date is uncertain, yet a third in the form of *Twelfth Night*. He had also revolutionized the English history play by composing the two Parts of *Henry IV*, completed his dramatization of the fifteenth century with the making of *Henry V*; and then, as though to demonstrate his versatility yet further, turned his attention from celebrating the success of the English king who conquered France to the downfall and death of the Roman dictator who conquered Gaul, Julius Caesar. The resultant tragedy is a Janus. In so far as its hero is Caesar, it looks to the past. His tragedy is in his fall, in his being brought to 'lie so low'. But, in so far as its hero is Brutus, it looks to the future. His tragedy is an altogether more inward thing than Caesar's. In the end it is not what is done to him by others that matters, but what he does to himself. *Hamlet* belongs to this newer kind, and belongs to it with an assured confidence that *Julius Caesar* lacks. There is no doubt at any time in *Hamlet*, as there is for so much of the time in *Julius Caesar*, about the centrality of the character who gives the play its title. 'Like *Hamlet* without the Prince of Denmark' has been proverbial since the end of the eighteenth century. This tragedy asks insistently to be placed with, and compared to, those that were to follow it, rather than those that preceded it, in the Shakespearian *œuvre*. It is most fitting therefore that it should have been composed at almost the exact mid-point of its author's career as a playwright, and very soon after the com-

---

[1] *The Dream of Learning* (Oxford, 1951), 33–68.

pany for which he wrote and in which he was both an actor and a sharer had begun to occupy its new theatre the Globe, to which Rosencrantz probably refers at 2.2.357–8.

Date

Exactly when *Hamlet* was composed depends in part on which *Hamlet* is under consideration, for the play exists in three different forms. The relationships between the First Quarto, published in 1603, the Second Quarto, published in 1604–5, and the text of the tragedy that appeared in the First Folio of 1623 are complicated and controversial. They are discussed in detail in the Textual Introduction to this edition, where reasons are given for thinking that the Second Quarto represents Shakespeare's first draft of his play; that the Folio text is essentially his revision of that first draft, together with some additions to it; and that the First Quarto is a reported version of an abridgement of this revised text. This said, it can be stated that a Shakespearian *Hamlet* must have been written and performed by 26 July 1602, for on that day James Roberts entered it on the Stationers' Register as

A booke called the Revenge of Hamlett Prince Denmarke as yt was latelie Acted by the Lord Chamberleyne his servantes.[1]

On the other hand, however, *Hamlet* is not included by Francis Meres in the well known list of Shakespeare's plays that he gives in his *Palladis Tamia: Wits Treasury*, published in the autumn of 1598. Its absence from that list amounts to strong presumptive evidence that it had not yet been staged, and goes far towards establishing a *terminus a quo*. Allusions within the tragedy itself suggest that a further refinement is possible. Julius Caesar is named twice: first at Appendix A, i. 7, where Horatio describes the omens that preceded his assassination; and then again at 3.2.96–7. There Polonius, after admitting with pride that he did some acting in his student days, replies to the Prince's question, 'And what did you enact?', with the words: 'I did enact Julius Caesar. I was killed i'th' Capitol. Brutus killed me.' The answer appears to serve three different purposes at one and the same time. Like the previous reference, it acts as an advertisement for *Julius Caesar*, either still in

[1] Edward Arber, *A Transcript of the Registers of the Company of Stationers of London, 1554–1640* (1875–94), iii. 212.

3

repertory or newly revived. It also reminds the audience that the actor—probably John Heminges—now playing Polonius also played Caesar to the Brutus of Richard Burbage, now playing Hamlet. Furthermore, it hints that, just as Burbage/Brutus killed Heminges/Caesar, so Burbage/Hamlet will, in due course, kill Heminges/Polonius. From all this it seems reasonable to infer that *Hamlet* was written after, but not long after, *Julius Caesar*, which can be dated with unusual accuracy as having been composed in the late summer of 1599. The Swiss traveller Thomas Platter saw a performance of it at the Globe on 21 September of that year.[1]

The other crucial piece of evidence bearing on the date of *Hamlet* is a manuscript note written by Gabriel Harvey in his copy of Speght's *Chaucer*, published in 1598. Harvey signed his name, and added the date 1598, on the title-page and on the last page of his copy. This does not mean, however, that he made all the notes and marginalia it contains in that year; for it has been shown that he sometimes made fresh observations when rereading.[2] Occurring in the middle of a long paragraph dealing with literary taste, the relevant passage reads:

The Earl of Essex much commends *Albion's England* . . . The Lord Mountjoy makes the like account of Daniel's piece of the Chronicle . . . The younger sort takes much delight in Shakespeare's *Venus and Adonis*; but his *Lucrece* and his *Tragedy of Hamlet, Prince of Denmark* have it in them to please the wiser sort.[3]

The natural implication of the present tense used in connection with the Earl of Essex is that Essex was still alive when the note was written. He was executed on 25 February 1601. It therefore follows that *Hamlet* had been composed and, presumably, acted before that date, and, in all likelihood, before the Earl's abortive rebellion on 8 February 1601, which led to his condemnation and death, since it seems improbable that Harvey would have quoted his opinion of Warner's poem after that time. The two terminal dates for the composition of *Hamlet* would, then, be the late autumn of 1599 on the one side, and the beginning of February 1601 on the other. There is, however, a difficulty for some in the

[1] E. K. Chambers, *William Shakespeare* (Oxford, 1930), i. 397 and ii. 322.
[2] L. Kirschbaum, 'The Date of Shakespeare's *Hamlet*', *Studies in Philology*, 34 (1937), 168–75.
[3] *Gabriel Harvey's Marginalia*, ed. G. C. Moore Smith (Stratford-upon-Avon, 1913), 232.

way of this dating: the topical reference to the 'little eyases' at
2.2.335–58. The 'little eyases' in question are, it is generally
agreed, the Children of the Chapel, the boys' company playing at
the Blackfriars Theatre in 1600 and 1601 with such success as to
make them formidable rivals to the adult companies. The so-called
'War of the Theatres', caused by the ensuing competition for
public favour, began with the acting of Ben Jonson's *Cynthia's
Revels* by the Children late in 1600. Then, in the spring of 1601,
came Jonson's *Poetaster*, provoking a reply, *Satiromastix*, the joint
work of Dekker and Marston, performed by Shakespeare's company in the summer of that year. Consequently, the 'little eyases'
passage was probably written at much the same time. The relevant
lines are, however, peculiar to the Folio text of *Hamlet*, though the
First Quarto has a much abbreviated and typically garbled version
of them. They do not appear at all in the Second Quarto, generally
considered to have been set from Shakespeare's autograph. The
most natural and plausible explanation of their absence from it is
that they were not part of the play as originally written and then
revised, but were a later addition to the revised version which, it
will be argued (pp. 105–30), provided the copy for the Folio text.
This passage set apart, it seems safe to say that *Hamlet* was indeed
written in or about the year 1600.[1]

Sources

It has already been suggested in this introduction that *Hamlet*
belongs to a time when old certainties and long established ways of
thinking began to collide with new doubts and revolutionary
modes of thinking. The story that lies behind the play, and to
which its action ultimately goes back, might have been designed to
produce just such a collision when transferred, as Shakespeare
transferred it, to a Renaissance setting. The court where *Hamlet*
unfolds is a Renaissance court, the seat of a centralized personal
government. Indubitably Danish in its explicit references to Elsinore, in its close relations with Norway, and in its conformity
to the popular notion of the Danes, current in the England of the
later sixteenth century, as a nation much given to drinking, it is,
simultaneously, in its preoccupation with statecraft, intrigue,

[1] E. A. J. Honigmann, 'The Date of *Hamlet*', *Shakespeare Survey* 9 (1956),
24–34.

assassination, poisoning, and lechery, decidedly in keeping with the mental picture that many in the original audience for the play appear to have had of Italy. Moreover, the Prince himself, a student of the University of Wittenberg, the home of his illustrious predecessor among tragic heroes, Marlowe's Dr Faustus, is in many ways the embodiment of the Renaissance ideal of *l'huomo universale*. To quote Ophelia's description of him as he was before his father's death, he had 'The courtier's, soldier's, scholar's eye, tongue, sword'; and was indeed

> Th'expectancy and rose of the fair state,
> The glass of fashion and the mould of form.
>
> (3.1.153–4)

This is not the world in which the story of Hamlet first took shape, nor is this prince the prince of that story. Briefly mentioned by Snorri Sturlason in his *Prose Edda* (c.1230), a redaction of a work originally composed, it is thought, between 1140 and 1160, Amleth, as he is called, becomes a legendary hero in the *Historiae Danicae* of Saxo Grammaticus, compiled at the end of the twelfth century. The tale Saxo tells conforms to the pattern of blood revenge so common in Norse saga. But it also resembles, in its hero's assumption of 'an antic disposition' to further his revenge, Livy's account of the legendary Lucius Junius Brutus, who organized the expulsion of the Tarquins from Rome after the rape of Lucretia. This Roman element, already implicit in Saxo, becomes fully explicit in François de Belleforest's retelling of the story in the fifth volume of his *Histoires tragiques*, first published in 1570, reissued on seven further occasions by 1601, and ultimately translated into English as *The Hystorie of Hamblet* (1608), where it has been affected by Shakespeare's play. It is quite possible that this similarity between Amleth and Lucius Junius Brutus may have helped to attract Shakespeare to the story. He had already made use of the Roman hero twice: first in the final part of *The Rape of Lucrece*; and then by making him a shadowy yet potent force from the past, almost the ghost of republicanism, in *Julius Caesar*, where he exerts a strong influence on his descendant, Marcus Junius Brutus. Moreover, the playwright had even found a place for him in *Henry V* (1599), where the Constable of France draws a parallel between his behaviour in 'Covering discretion with a coat of folly' (2.4.37) and that of Prince Hal.

In Saxo's account two brothers, Horwendil and Feng, are appointed governors of Jutland by Rorik, King of Denmark. Horwendil wins great fame as a Viking, and sets the seal on that fame by killing Koll, the King of Norway, in single combat. Rorik rewards him by giving him the hand of his daughter Gerutha in marriage. Gerutha bears Horwendil a son, Amleth. But Horwendil's success arouses the envy of his brother Feng, who treacherously waylays and murders him, and then marries his widow, thus 'capping unnatural murder with incest' (Gollancz, p. 101).[1] Feng glosses over the murder, which is public knowledge, with smooth words and a hypocritical show of concern for Gerutha that find a ready acceptance in the sycophantic court.

Young Amleth, alone and almost friendless but fully aware of Feng's guilt, dedicates himself to revenge. First, however, he must grow up. He therefore seeks to give Feng the impression that he is harmless by pretending to have lost his wits. Filthy and in rags, he talks seeming nonsense which, nonetheless, has its point for those percipient enough to see it. For instance, he spends much of his time in making wooden crooks armed with sharp barbs, and, when asked what he is doing, replies that he is preparing javelins to be used in avenging his father. The answer is greeted with scoffs. All the same, some of the acuter courtiers have their suspicions. Two traps are laid. A beautiful girl, whom Amleth has known from childhood, is ordered to seduce him and worm his secret out of him. The plot fails because Amleth's foster-brother warns him of it. Then a counsellor of Feng's has a bright idea. He suggests that Feng absent himself from court for a short time, and that, during his absence, Amleth and his mother be brought together in the Queen's chamber, where, he is sure, Amleth will speak with complete candour. Before the interview begins, however, the counsellor will have concealed himself in the chamber, and later will reveal to Feng whatever he discovers. The Queen knows no more of this plan than does Amleth. But the wily counsellor has badly underrated the Prince's caution and cunning. On entering the chamber, Amleth, putting on his usual show of madness, crows like a cock, flaps his arms as though they were wings, and eventually jumps on the straw mattress under which the spy is hiding. Feeling the eavesdropper under his feet, the Prince promptly runs him through, pulls him out, finishes him off, chops the body into

[1] Sir Israel Gollancz, *The Sources of 'Hamlet'* (1926).

pieces, boils them, and then sends them down the sewer for the swine to eat. Going back to his mother, whom he finds wailing and grieving over what she sees as her son's folly, he upbraids her bitterly for her disloyalty to his dead father, and reveals the purpose behind his seemingly mad behaviour. His words pierce Gerutha's heart and lead her to 'walk in the ways of virtue' (Gollancz, p. 117).

Feng, on returning to the court, is surprised by the absence of his agent, and asks Amleth, among others, whether he knows what has become of the man. Thereupon the Prince, who always tells the truth after his own riddling fashion, replies that the counsellor went to the sewer, fell in, was stifled by the filth, and then eaten by the pigs. These words, though Feng can make nothing of them, increase his suspicions. He therefore decides that Amleth must be done away with. But he is deterred from taking direct action himself by his fear of offending Rorik, the Prince's grandfather, and of displeasing Gerutha. So he hits on the plan of making the King of England—the time is that of the Danelaw—do his dirty work for him, and sends Amleth off to that country, under the escort of two retainers. The retainers carry a letter with them containing the order that Amleth be put to death on his arrival. Before he sets off, however, the Prince, divining what is likely to happen, has a word in secret with his mother. He asks her to hang the hall with knotted tapestry, and to hold a funeral for him exactly a year after his departure, adding that he will return at the year's end. Then, during the voyage, he searches the luggage of the retainers while they are asleep, finds the letter, which is carved in runic characters on a piece of wood, erases the original order, and replaces it with another of his own devising calling for the execution of the retainers. To it he adds the entreaty that the King of England grant his daughter in marriage to a youth of great judgement whom Feng is sending to him. The plot works. Deeply impressed, as well he might be, by the preternatural acuteness of Amleth's mind and senses, which the Prince amply displays as soon as he reaches England, the King of that country bestows his daughter on the newcomer, and has the retainers hanged. At this point Amleth, pretending to be offended by the summary execution of his companions, demands wergeld for them, receives the appropriate sum in gold, melts it down in secret, and pours it into hollow sticks carefully prepared to hold it.

Arriving back in Jutland on the very day when the funeral rites are being carried out for his supposed death, Amleth puts on his old filthy attire, and enters the banqueting hall. At first his coming creates awe; but this soon changes to mirth, especially when, having been asked what has become of the two retainers, he points to the sticks, and says, 'Here they are.' This strange answer confirms the courtiers in their view that he is a harmless lunatic. Nevertheless, to make their assurance doubly sure, Amleth takes one further step. As he moves about the hall, he fidgets with his sword and pricks his fingers with it. To save him from himself, the courtiers have his sword firmly riveted to the scabbard. Secure in their knowledge that the Prince is unarmed as well as harmless, the courtiers allow him to egg them on to eat and drink until they all lie in a drunken stupor. Then, pulling down upon them the knotted hangings prepared by his mother, Amleth uses the barbed crooks he made long ago to fasten the hangings tightly about them, and sets fire to the hall. Thence he moves on to Feng's own apartment, takes the King's sword from the place where it is hanging by his bed, and substitutes his own useless sword for it. Arousing the sleeping Feng, he tells him the hour of vengeance has come. Feng leaps from his couch and seizes the sword hanging by it, but while he tries in vain to wrench it from the scabbard, Amleth kills him with the King's own sword. On the following day the Prince makes a speech to his countrymen, explaining what he has done and why he has done it. They greet the speech with unrestrained enthusiasm, and make Amleth their new king.

Saxo does not conclude his story here. He goes on to relate further exploits of Amleth—some of them very like his earlier exploits—down to his death in battle. In the course of them Amleth acquires a second wife; and she, after expressing her undying devotion to him and her determination to die in battle with him, promptly marries his conqueror. So far as Shakespeare is concerned, however, Amleth's later adventures are of no account, except that they exemplify yet again the perfidy of women. It is the revenge story that matters, and that story is all of a piece, a heroic tale of the heroic age in Northern Europe. Single-mindedly and single-handedly, the Prince does his duty in avenging his father's murder. Every stratagem he devises is held up to admiration; and he himself is not subjected to the slightest breath of censure. Never in doubt as to what he must do, he moves inexorably to the accomplishment of his purpose.

Belleforest's version of this tale is, in so far as its action goes, in essence the same as Saxo's. But he does make some additions to it that leave their mark on Shakespeare's tragedy. Three of these are most important. First, having related how Fengon, as he calls him, killed his brother, Belleforest goes on to say that before resorting to parricide Fengon had already incestuously sullied his brother's bed (*incestueusement souillé la couche fraternelle*) by corrupting the honour of that brother's wife (Gollancz, p. 186). There is plainly a close connection between this statement and the order the Ghost in *Hamlet* gives his son:

> Let not the royal bed of Denmark be
> A couch for luxury and damnèd incest.
>   (1.5.82-3)

Secondly, Belleforest remarks that Geruthe's subsequent marriage to Fengon led many to conclude that she might well have inspired the murder in order to enjoy the pleasures of her adulterous relationship with Fengon without restriction or restraint (p. 188). Amleth repeats this charge in his passionate harangue to his mother after his discovery of the spy, and draws an absolute denial of it from her. She begs him never to harbour the suspicion that she gave consent to the murder (p. 220). Thirdly, Belleforest is much troubled by the powers of divination his hero shows, especially after his arrival in England. Reluctantly he is forced to conclude that in pre-Christian times the North was full of enchanters, and, in the words of the English translator, that the Prince 'while his father lived, had been instructed in that devilish art whereby the wicked spirit abuseth mankind' (p. 237). However, having said this, he finds a partial excuse for his hero in the notion that Amleth could well have been rendered highly sensitive to impressions from without 'by reason of his over-great melancholy'. Here, surely, is the origin of Hamlet's lines:

> The spirit that I have seen
> May be the devil, and the devil hath power
> T'assume a pleasing shape; yea, and perhaps
> Out of my weakness and my melancholy,
> As he is very potent with such spirits,
> Abuses me to damn me.
>   (2.2.587-92)

It is Belleforest, not Saxo, who is responsible for the idea of Amleth as a victim of melancholy.

The French writer's unease about Amleth's powers of divination is typical of his attitude towards Saxo's story as a whole. He is not happy with it. As a good Christian, he disapproves of private revenge, especially when the object of it is a king; and his reservations on this score lead him into a great deal of special pleading and moralizing. For a solution to his difficulties he falls back on the providential idea of history which was so dominant at the time when he was writing. He prefaces his account with an 'Argument' justifying the writing of history on moral and religious grounds. The great lesson to be drawn from the past is that though God's vengeance may be slow it is absolutely sure. Amleth, the author of 'the most exquisite revenge imaginable, the most carefully planned and skilfully carried out' (p. 172), was, Belleforest implies, acting throughout as heaven's 'scourge and minister' (3.4.164).

Here, then, in the pages of Belleforest whose account Shakespeare seems to have read—it appears unlikely that he knew Saxo's version—are many of the essential elements of the tragedy: the single combat between old Hamlet and the King of Norway; the seduction of Gertrude by Claudius; the murder of old Hamlet; Claudius's marriage to Gertrude; the son's duty to avenge his father; his counterfeiting madness; his delay, if delay it can be called, since Hamlet has to grow up before he can act; his killing of Polonius; his upbraiding of his mother; his sea voyage; his forging of the letter that sends Rosencrantz and Guildenstern to their deaths; his return to Denmark; and his killing of the King. Here too are the bare bones of many of the characters—Gertrude, Claudius, Ophelia, Polonius, Rosencrantz and Guildenstern, and, in the foster-brother, Horatio. To the central figure Belleforest contributed far more than bare bones. He offered Shakespeare the ruthlessly efficient avenger of Saxo's story made more complex by a streak of melancholy in his nature; and Shakespeare added to that complexity by transferring the French writer's reservations about some of his hero's actions to that hero himself.

But, while the resemblances between the story and the play are evident enough, so are the differences. In Belleforest the fratricide is no secret; and the reason for the Prince's taking a long time over the accomplishment of his task is simple and natural, not problematic. The Hamlet of the story reaches England and marries the King's daughter. The Hamlet of the play does neither of these things. Cunningly planned and skilfully carried out in the story, Hamlet's revenge has nothing of the casual improvised quality it takes on in the play. More striking still, there is much in the play to which the story can provide no counterpart: the Ghost, made necessary by the murder being a poisoning done in secret; the coming of the actors to Elsinore; the play-within-the-play; the madness of Ophelia; her death by drowning; Laertes and the counter-revenge plot; the pirates who intercept the ship taking Hamlet to England; the grave-digger and his acquaintance; Ophelia's funeral; Osric; and, finally, Fortinbras.

How are these differences to be accounted for? In most cases we do not know; for at this point the stream that flows from Saxo to Shakespeare becomes muddied. Just as Hamlet is haunted by the ghost of his father, so his tragedy is haunted by the ghost of an earlier play, the *Ur-Hamlet*, as it is called, of which no text survives. The first reference to it occurs, appropriately enough, in the most tantalizingly allusive piece of Elizabethan literary criticism that we have, the address 'To the Gentlemen Students of Both Universities' which Thomas Nashe wrote as a preface to Robert Greene's prose romance, *Menaphon*, published in 1589. In the course of a rather erratic and rambling survey of the state of English literature at the time, Nashe turns his attention to 'a few of our trivial translators', as he calls them, and then continues thus:

It is a common practice nowadays amongst a sort of shifting companions, that run through every art and thrive by none, to leave the trade of *Noverint*, whereto they were born, and busy themselves with the endeavours of art, that could scarcely Latinize their neck-verse if they should have need. Yet English *Seneca* read by candlelight yields many good sentences, as *Blood is a beggar* and so forth; and if you entreat him fair in a frosty morning, he will afford you whole *Hamlets*—I should say handfuls —of tragical speeches. But O grief! *Tempus edax rerum!* What's that will last always? The sea exhaled by drops will in continuance be dry, and *Seneca*, let blood line by line and page by page, at length must needs die to our stage; which makes his famished followers to imitate the Kid in *Aesop* who, enamoured with the Fox's newfangles, forsook all hopes of life to leap into a new occupation, and these men, renouncing all possibilities of credit or estimation, to intermeddle with Italian translations.[1]

---

[1] *The Works of Thomas Nashe*, ed. R. B. McKerrow (1904–10) *With supplementary notes ... by* F. P. Wilson (Oxford, 1958), iii. 315–16.

These cryptic comments have led to a long drawn out and inconclusive conflict between those who hold that they identify Thomas
Kyd as the author of the *Ur-Hamlet* and those who think they do
not; but what factual information do they give? It seems to
amount to this: that there was a play called *Hamlet*; that it was
probably a tragedy, since it contained 'tragical speeches'; that it
was heavily indebted to 'English *Seneca*', meaning, one imagines,
translations óf Seneca into English; that it was, on the strength of
Blood is a beggar, in all likelihood a revenge play; and that it appears to have been written for the popular stage.

Five years later Philip Henslowe records a performance of 'hamlet' by the Lord Admiral's Men and the Lord Chamberlain's Men,
apparently playing together, at Newington Butts on 9 June 1594.[1]
The performance brought him the sum of eight shillings, which is
about average for his receipts from a play at Newington at that
time. He does not mention *Hamlet* again; but as the two companies
ceased to play together after 15 June, it looks as though the Lord
Chamberlain's Men took it with them to the Theatre, for it was
there that Thomas Lodge saw a performance of it which he refers
to in his *Wit's Misery and the World's Madness* (1596). There he
writes of a devil looking 'as pale as the vizard of the ghost, which
cried so miserably at the Theatre, like an oyster-wife, "Hamlet,
revenge"' (Bullough, vii. 24).[2] This is much the most helpful
information about the *Ur-Hamlet* that we have, since it shows that
the play departed from Belleforest's narrative by introducing a
ghost; and, as that ghost calls on Hamlet to take revenge, it follows
that the murder must have been done in secret, not during the
course of a banquet, as it is in Belleforest (Gollancz, p. 186).
Whether Shakespeare's tragedy owed anything else to its
predecessor it is impossible to say.

The tone in which Nashe and Lodge write of the *Ur-Hamlet*
suggests that both found it rather ridiculous. It may well have been
so; but one aspect of Shakespeare's genius was his ability to take
an old-fashioned drama and utterly transform it. Not long before
he wrote *Hamlet* he had made extensive use of the ramshackle *The
Famous Victories of Henry V* (*c.*1586) in composing the Two Parts
of *Henry IV* as well as *Henry V*, combining material from that old
anonymous piece with other material taken from Holinshed and

[1] *Henslowe's Diary*, ed. R. A. Foakes and R. T. Rickert (Cambridge, 1961), 21.
[2] Geoffrey Bullough, *Narrative and Dramatic Sources of Shakespeare* (1957–75).

from his own direct observation of the world he was living in. He seems to have followed the precedent he had set for himself in those three plays when he came to write *Hamlet*; annexing from the *Ur-Hamlet*, one presumes, whatever he found useful in it; going back to Belleforest where necessary, and, indeed, borrowing from him the unusual description of the play on the title-pages of both the First and Second Quarto as a 'Tragicall Historie'; recalling scenes or incidents from earlier plays, such as Marlowe's *The Tragedy of Dido* and the anonymous *A Warning for Fair Women* (recently performed by the company to which he belonged); drawing, it would seem, on accounts of the murder of Francesco Maria, Duke of Urbino, in 1538; capitalizing on the contemporary interest in the Danes; and, once again, of course, introducing matter that appears to spring out of immediate personal experience —a company of players arriving in a town or at the court, squabbles among the London theatres, legal quibbles about the definition of suicide, and a grave-digger plying his trade. This last, in particular, so marvellously apropos in a play where so many of the characters have been busy in digging graves for one another, and where even the Ghost has fully earned the right to be addressed as 'A worthy pioneer', does not smack, any more than does his crony, of a Senecan tragedy full of 'good sentences' and 'tragical speeches', nor is he to be found in the pages of Belleforest. The quite extraordinary richness and variety of *Hamlet* owe much to the number and diversity of the sources that have contributed to its making.[1]

From Stage to Study

From the outset *Hamlet* was an unqualified success in the theatre. It is true that no record has come to light of its being put on at the Globe, and that we have but two references to its being staged at Court, in 1619 and 1637 (Chambers, *William Shakespeare*, ii. 346, 353); but there is no shortage of other evidence. The publication of the bad quarto in 1603 tells one much. The stationers of the day were interested only in the manuscripts of plays that had proved popular on the stage; and, while the title-page of this version issued by Nicholas Ling and John Trundle is a typical publishers' blurb, there is no reason to doubt the substance, as distinct from

---

[1] See Bullough, vii. 3–189.

1. Richard Burbage

the detail, of its statement that the tragedy had been acted by Shakespeare's company 'in the City of London, as also in the two universities of Cambridge and Oxford, and elsewhere' (see p. 68). The anonymous author of an elegy on Richard Burbage, who died on 20 May 1619, is especially informative. Having said that Burbage is 'gone', he continues:

> young Hamlet, old Hieronimo,
> King Lear, the grievèd Moor, and more beside
> That lived in him have now for ever died.
> Oft have I seen him leap into the grave,
> Suiting the person which he seemed to have
> Of a sad lover with so true an eye
> That there, I would have sworn, he meant to die.[1]

We do not know exactly when one of the troupes of English actors who toured in Germany, and then established themselves there, took with them to that country a version of *Hamlet* that would eventually be transformed into the play known as *Der bestrafte Brudermord* or *Fratricide Punished*. It could have been as early as

[1] E. K. Chambers, *The Elizabethan Stage* (Oxford, 1923), ii. 309.

15

1603–4 (see Appendix C). What is certain is that a *Tragoedia von Hamlet einen Printzen in Dennemarck* was played by John Greene's company in Dresden in 1626.[1] Moreover, performances of *Hamlet* were not confined to the professional theatre, or even to Europe. William Keeling, captain of the East India Company's ship the Dragon, records two productions of it aboard his vessel while he lay off Sierra Leone: one on 5 September 1607, and the other on 31 March 1608. The entry he made in his journal on the second occasion is a remarkable tribute to the play's capacity to entertain. He permitted the performance, he says, 'to keep my people from idleness and unlawful games, or sleep' (Chambers, *William Shakespeare*, ii. 334–5). A tragedy that distracts sailors from dice, and supercargoes from slumber, clearly belongs with Sidney's tale 'which holdeth children from play, and old men from the chimney corner'. The captain's trust in *Hamlet* bears out Anthony Scoloker's testimony in the address 'To the Reader' which he prefixed to his strange poem *Daiphantus, or the Passions of Love*, published in 1604, where he expresses the wish that he may 'please all, like Prince *Hamlet*' (Chambers, *William Shakespeare*, ii. 215).

More proof of the tragedy's popularity in its own day is provided by the powerful influence it evidently exerted on the writings of other dramatists.[2] At the time when it was composed the tradition, going back to Kyd's *The Spanish Tragedy* (*c*.1587), of tragedy motivated solely by revenge was moribund or seemingly so. *Hamlet* gave that tradition not only a new lease of life but also, in the work of some playwrights, a new kind of life. *The Revenger's Tragedy* (1606), whether its author be Cyril Tourneur or Thomas Middleton, is, though deeply indebted to *Hamlet*, no mere imitation of it. It has its own narrow yet intense vision, its own peculiar metallic timbre. To the Chapman of *The Revenge of Bussy D'Ambois* (1610), as to the Tourneur who wrote *The Atheist's Tragedy* (1609), Shakespeare's play served as a challenge no less than as a model, spurring them on to find expression for different attitudes to revenge. Ophelia's mad scenes and songs were imitated time after time.

The greatest tribute of all, however, to *Hamlet*'s success with the theatre-going public is the frequency with which playwrights of

---

[1] Albert Cohn, *Shakespeare in Germany* (1865), p. cxv.
[2] See David L. Frost, *The School of Shakespeare* (Cambridge, 1968), 167–208.

the early seventeenth century make allusions to it in full confidence, it seems, that such allusions will be immediately recognized and applied by their audiences. In Act 3, Scene 2 of *Eastward Ho!* (1605), by Jonson, Chapman and Marston, for instance, there are no fewer than four allusions of this kind in the first eighty lines: one to the hero's sardonic comment about the 'funeral baked meats', another to his assumed madness, and two to Ophelia's remarks and songs when she comes on 'distracted' in 4.5.[1]

Unlike so many of Shakespeare's other plays, *Hamlet* underwent no radical alteration after the Restoration. It was not 'adapted'; its story line was left untouched. It was, however, very heavily cut; 'improved', in that many of its 'coarser' expressions were 'refined'; and 'modernized'. Reserved to Sir William Davenant and his company by an edict of the Lord Chamberlain dated 12 December 1660, it retained its wide appeal. John Downes, who acted as bookkeeper and prompter to that company from 1662 to 1706, tells us in his *Roscius Anglicanus* (1708) that Davenant's third production, following the opening of his new theatre in Lincoln's-Inn-Fields in the spring of 1662, was

The Tragedy of *Hamlet*; Hamlet being performed by Mr. Betterton. Sir William (having seen Mr. Taylor of the Black-Friars Company act it, who being instructed by the author Mr. Shakespeare) taught Mr. Betterton in every particle of it; which by his exact performance of it, gained him esteem and reputation, superlative to all other plays … No succeeding tragedy for several years got more reputation or money to the company than this.[2]

Some two years later the Earl of Shaftesbury describes *Hamlet* in his *Characteristics* as 'That piece of [Shakespeare's] which appears to have most affected English hearts, and has perhaps been oftenest acted of any which have come upon our stage'.[3]

Part at least of the play's success during the later seventeenth century can safely be attributed to Betterton. Downes is wrong when he says that Joseph Taylor was 'instructed' in the role of Hamlet by Shakespeare himself, since Taylor did not join the King's Men until 1619, three years after Shakespeare died. But it does seem highly likely that as Burbage's successor he learned from

---

[1] See Donald J. McGinn, *Shakespeare's Influence on the Drama of his Age Studied in 'Hamlet'* (1938, repr. New York, 1973), 149–50.

[2] *Roscius Anglicanus*, ed. M. Summers (1928), 21.

[3] Brian Vickers, *Shakespeare, The Critical Heritage*, 6 vols. (1974–81), ii. 264.

other members of the company how Burbage had played the part. There could, then, have been, and probably was, a certain continuity in the rendering of the title-role from the beginning of the seventeenth century to the end of it and beyond, for Betterton made the part his own for well over forty years. Steele, writing in the *Tatler* of 20 September 1709, has this to say about one of his last performances:

Mr. Betterton behaved himself so well that though now about seventy he acted youth; and by the prevalent power of proper manner, gesture and voice, appeared through the whole drama a youth of great expectation, vivacity and enterprise. (Vickers, ii. 207)

Betterton's was clearly an uncomplicated Hamlet of the kind George Bernard Shaw would have approved of, for Shaw wrote in 1918:

the most successful Hamlet of my day was Barry Sullivan, an actor of superb physical vigour, who excelled in the impersonation of proud, noble and violent characters. All the sentimental Hamlets have been bores. Forbes Robertson's gallant, alert Hamlet, thoughtful but not in the least sentimental, is *the* Hamlet of today.[1]

How, then, and when did *Hamlet* the puzzle, and Hamlet the puzzled and puzzling, both apparently unknown to the seventeenth century, come into being? The death of Betterton in 1710 coincides, as near as makes no difference, with the publication of the first edited Shakespeare, Nicholas Rowe's, which came out in 1709. Up to that time the plays were available only in the four folios (1623, 1632, 1663, and 1685) and, in some cases, as quartos. Most of those who knew them did so from having seen them acted; and this means that, prior to the closing of the theatres in 1642, the *Hamlet* they were familiar with was either that represented by the text of the First Folio or the abridged version of it that lies behind the First Quarto of 1603. There is no evidence that the longest version of the tragedy, that offered by the Second Quarto of 1604–5, was ever played at all during this time. Referring to the passages in it for which neither the First Folio nor the First Quarto give any equivalent, W. W. Greg remarks: 'It is, indeed, on general grounds probable that the passages in question never figured in the

---

[1] *Shaw on Shakespeare*, ed. Edwin Wilson (1961, repr. Harmondsworth, 1969), 99.

prompt-book.'[1] Confirmation, or at least something very close to it, of the accuracy of this deduction is provided by the allusions made to the play up to 1642. Of the large number—not all equally convincing—gathered together by Donald McGinn, only two (see pp. 159, 180) may refer to passages peculiar to the Second Quarto. Moreover, neither of them is an allusion in the proper sense of that word, since a knowledge of the Shakespearian context adds nothing of significance to what is being said. The first merely picks up the word *impostume*, and the second the word *pleurisy*, neither of them a Shakespearian invention.

By 1660, when the theatres reopened, the Globe prompt-book had, presumably, disappeared. Davenant therefore based his version of the play on the most recent of the quartos, the Fifth, dated 1637.[2] Eventually published in 1676, this 'Players' Quarto', as it fittingly came to be called, was prefaced by an address 'To the reader', running as follows:

This play being too long to be conveniently Acted, such places as might be least prejudicial to the Plot or Sense, are left out upon the Stage: but that we may no way wrong the incomparable author, are here inserted according to the Original Copy with this mark ''

According to Hazelton Spencer's count, '816 lines and parts of lines were left out on the stage' (191, note 49). Among the casualties are the entire roles of Voltemand and Cornelius; the whole of the dialogue between Polonius and Reynaldo at the opening of 2.1; Hamlet's advice to the Players; and all of the Fortinbras scene, 4.4. In addition, most of Laertes cautioning of Ophelia disappears, together with Polonius's advice to his son. Other cuts, such as one that halves the length of the Prince's soliloquy at the end of 2.2, dispose between them of hundreds of lines found in the Fifth Quarto. In fact, the only speech of more than thirty lines to survive intact is 'To be, or not to be', already, it would appear, too familiar to playgoers and readers alike to be sacrificed. For the rest, the emphasis falls on action and dialogue.

The cutting, although it includes nearly everything that was excised from the Second Quarto during the making of the Folio text, was evidently done without reference to that text. For instance, while Horatio's speech about the omens foreshadowing

---

[1] *The Shakespeare First Folio* (Oxford, 1955), 318.
[2] Hazelton Spencer, *Shakespeare Improved* (Cambridge, Mass., 1927), 174–5.

Caesar's death (Appendix A, i) goes, Barnardo's four lines preceding it are retained, as, rather surprisingly, is that part of the
dialogue between Hamlet and Osric in 5.2 (Appendix A, xvii)
which the Folio reduces to one brief sentence. Perhaps the Restoration interest in the figure of the fop ensured its survival. However
that may be, the principle behind Davenant's cutting is not exactly
that stated in the publishers' address 'To the Reader'. The first
scene of Act 5 loses a mere seven lines in all, yet prior to the entry
of Ophelia's funeral it contributes nothing at all to the plot. The
business of the grave-digger and his fellow clown was obviously
kept because it was extremely popular with audiences and, it seems
likely, because no speech in it runs to more than a dozen lines.

The Players' Quarto recognizes that by 1676 there were two
Hamlets not one. On the one hand, there was the play script, a kind
of quarry from which the theatre manager might extract whatever
he thought most suitable to make up an evening's entertainment,
provided, of course, that he included in that entertainment those
scenes, such as that in the graveyard, which no audience would
forgo. This attitude to the text was to remain the theatre tradition
for the next two hundred years, and has not, for sound practical
reasons, been completely superseded even now. *Hamlet* is a very
long play, especially when one recognizes that laconic stage directions, such as '*They play*' in the duel scene, may cover actions that
last for minutes. On the other hand, however, there was the
Shakespearian text, already establishing itself as a literary masterpiece, which no reader of the play would forgo.

Now, it was very naturally the interests of the reader that were
uppermost in the minds of Nicholas Rowe and of his publisher
Jacob Tonson when Rowe came to put together the first edited
version of Shakespeare's *Works*; and in the case of *Hamlet*, the
consequences were far-reaching and influential. His copy text, for
the edition as a whole, was the Fourth Folio of 1685; but when he
came to deal with *Hamlet* he deviated from his normal practice by
including in his text some passages that are not to be found in the
Fourth Folio but which belong to the tradition of the quartos going
back ultimately to the Second Quarto of 1604–5. It is not clear
why Rowe chose to treat *Hamlet* in a different way from that in
which he treated the other plays of Shakespeare which had appeared in quarto form before being printed in the First Folio; but a
probable reason is that it was the only one for which a quarto was

readily available. The edition of 1676 was followed by three others, appearing in 1683, 1695, and 1703. Their number not only bears witness to the play's popularity but also means that an editor whose eyes were open, as Rowe's evidently were, could not but be aware that there was another textual tradition apart from that of the Folio. It was from the Players' Quarto or from one of its three descendants that Rowe took the passage (Appendix A, i) he included in his version of the play's first scene. Proof is supplied by his reading, 'In the most high and flourishing state of *Rome*' instead of 'In the most high and palmy state of Rome', the form the line takes in the Fifth Quarto of 1637 and its predecessors.

But, while Rowe must have had a copy of one of the Four Players' Quartos by him as he did his work, there is no consistency in the use he made of it. He incorporates some passages peculiar to the quarto tradition but not others. Having found a place for the lines given in Appendix A, i, he rejects those given in Appendix A, ii. Similarly, he includes all the lines from the Fortinbras scene that are cut from the Folio, but not the lines from the dialogue between Hamlet and Osric (Appendix A, xvii). It is not at all clear what he thought he was doing, beyond giving his readers more Shakespeare than the Fourth Folio had to offer, and, perhaps, sparing them from the perplexity that the 'dram of eale' and the Prince's parody of Osric's fashionable twaddle might have caused them.

Pope, whose *Hamlet* came out in volume VI of his edition of Shakespeare, published in 1725, follows Rowe in general, but with some differences. Like Rowe, he includes Horatio's speech about the omens, giving it in the form it takes in Rowe, which is not exactly that of the quartos; but, unlike Rowe, he also finds a place, albeit a hesitant one, for Hamlet's lines about the drunkenness of the Danes, which he relegates to a footnote that completely ignores the 'dram of eale' passage with which they conclude. Likewise, he agrees with Rowe in accepting the Folio tradition when dealing with most of the dialogue between Hamlet and his mother in 3.4, but then parts company with Rowe and the Folio by including the nine lines from the quarto tradition in which the Prince looks forward with zest to his forthcoming battle of wits with Rosencrantz and Guildenstern. He treats the rest of the play in the same erratic fashion. With Pope, as with Rowe, it is hard to discover any consistent policy or principle behind the decisions that lead to an acceptance of quarto passages at some points and a rejection of them at others; but a tendency to acceptance is becoming more discernible.

That tendency triumphs completely in the *Hamlet* Lewis Theobald put together for his edition of Shakespeare that came out in 1733. Every one of the passages found in the Second Quarto but excluded from the Folio is incorporated into Theobald's text, along with those other passages—2.2.238–67, 2.2.333–58, and 5.2.69–81—that appear only in the Folio. There is nothing inconsistent about Theobald's procedure. His policy is to include all of *Hamlet* that he could find, irrespective of which of the two texts it comes from. Fortunately for him, he did not know of the existence of the First Quarto which might have complicated his task immeasurably. He justifies his inclusion of the passages peculiar to the Second Quarto and its successors in his note to the lines given in Appendix A, vi of the present edition, where he writes as follows:

Mr. *Pope* has left out the Quantity of about eight Verses here, which I have taken care to replace. They are not, indeed, to be found in the two elder *Folio's*, but they carry the Style, Expression, and Cast of Thought, peculiar to our Author; and that they were not an Interpolation from another Hand needs no better proof, than that they are in all the oldest *Quarto's*. The first Motive of their being left out, I am perswaded, was to shorten *Hamlet's* Speech, and consult the Ease of the Actor; and the Reason, why they find no Place in the *Folio* Impressions, is, that they were printed from the *Playhouse* castrated Copies. But, surely, this can be no Authority for a modern Editor to conspire in mutilating his Author: such *Omissions*, rather, must betray a want of *Diligence*, in *Collating*; or a Want of *Justice*, in the *voluntary stifling*.

It is a fascinating note, for although it begins and ends by taking Pope to task for his shortcomings, it nevertheless rests on an acceptance of his view, set out in the Preface to his edition, that it was the actors, meaning Shakespeare's fellow actors, who were responsible both for the 'castrations' some of the plays had suffered before they were printed in the Folio and also for the 'interpolations' that had somehow wormed their way into the text. Had Theobald been completely logical in his procedure, he would have excluded the three passages found only in the Folio text from his version of *Hamlet*. In fact, however, logic had to give way to his overriding compulsion 'to get it all in'.

The result of Theobald's diligence was by far and away the best edition of Shakespeare and of *Hamlet* that had yet appeared. It was consistent; it had a good knowledge of Shakespeare's reading behind it; and an equally good knowledge of Elizabethan English. Editors, who were now beginning to proliferate, paid Theobald the sincerest of compliments: while disagreeing with him, and with one another, over specific readings, they were in complete accord with him in thinking that there was one 'true' text of the play, the 'full' text, that would include all the passages peculiar to the Second Quarto and all those peculiar to the First Folio. They have continued to hold this view down to the present day. The most recent scholarly edition of *Hamlet*, Harold Jenkins's of 1982, still contains all the passages in question. Theobald's was indeed a massive and enduring achievement.[1]

Endurance alone, however, is no criterion of rightness; error too can persist. And so, Theobald having received his due, it now has to be said of his edition, and said with conviction, that it offers a *Hamlet* such as—with apologies to the shade of William Wordsworth—

> At Blackfriars or the Globe was never seen,
> A full conflation and a critic's dream.

There is no evidence that Shakespeare ever envisaged, much less wrote as one piece, a *Hamlet* such as Theobald's is, and none to show that such a *Hamlet* was ever staged prior to the closing of the theatres in 1642. Nor is this all. The kind of *Hamlet* Theobald provides would never be seen on any stage, either in England or elsewhere, until over a hundred and sixty years after his edition came out, for, according to Harold Child,[2] 'a composite text of the Second Quarto and the First Folio', which is, of course, what Theobald was the first to produce, was not acted *in toto* until 1899, when Sir Frank Benson eventually put it on the boards at the Memorial Theatre in Stratford-upon-Avon. Conservative by tradition, shrewd and practical from experience, the men of the theatre had up to this time either ignored or fought shy of the *Hamlet* that Theobald had, to use his own word for it, 'restored'.

---

[1] Since these words were written an important new edition of *Hamlet* by Philip Edwards has been published by Cambridge University Press (1985). It, too, includes the passages peculiar to the Second Quarto, but, very significantly, encloses them in square brackets to show that in the editor's opinion they had been excised by Shakespeare himself from his final version of the play.

[2] 'The Stage-History of *Hamlet*' in *Hamlet*, ed. John Dover Wilson (Cambridge, 1934, second edition 1948), p. xcvi.

And, it should be added, most of them, even today, still remain wary of the 'full' text, though they no longer have to allow time for scene changes as their predecessors in the eighteenth and nineteenth centuries did.

But, while the 'full' text had little or no effect on the theatre and its practices, it did have a profound effect on those who read their Shakespeare and thought about what they read. The rapidity with which editions of the *Works* followed one another throughout the eighteenth century testifies to an ever-growing interest in the plays; and that interest naturally took the form of criticism. It was at this point that *Hamlet* began to assume puzzling and problematic proportions, for the printed texts raised crucial issues that either did not exist at all for those who knew the play only in the theatre, or, if they did exist, did so in a much less acute manner. The first substantial piece of criticism on *Hamlet* that we have is an extended essay by George Stubbes, published in 1736, only three years after the appearance of Theobald's edition, to which it refers and from which it quotes. Stubbes thinks highly of Theobald who, he says, 'is generally thought to have understood our author best, and certainly deserves the Applause of all his Countrymen for the great pains he has been at to give us the best Edition of this Poet which has yet appear'd' (Vickers, iii. 41). The essay is very appreciative of Shakespeare's achievement in *Hamlet*, but it also asks two related questions: why does the Prince feign madness; and why does he delay his revenge? Stubbes sums up his position thus:

Had *Hamlet* gone naturally to work [instead of pretending to be mad, and thus making his task more difficult], as we could suppose such a Prince to do in parallel Circumstances, there would have been an End of our Play. The poet therefore was obliged to delay his Hero's Revenge; but then he should have contrived some good Reason for it. (Vickers, iii. 55)

However, when in his commentary on the action he reaches 4.4, he remarks:

Fortinbras's Troops are here brought in, I believe, to give Occasion for his appearing in the last Scene, and also to give Rise to *Hamlet*'s Reflections thereon, which tend to give some Reasons for his deferring the Punishment of the Usurper. (Vickers, iii. 61)

Stubbes's remarks have a bearing on two matters that are of particular importance for *Hamlet*: the effect of reading plays written to be seen; and the misconceptions generated by a conflated text. The reader sets his own pace. If something catches his interest in an unexpected way or, alternatively, puzzles him, he can pause and think, perhaps turn back to verify an impression. In the theatre he cannot do this. There the pace at which he responds is set by the production. It will not stop for his benefit and start again when he is ready. It presses forward carrying the spectator with it. Stubbes, when he raises the issue of 'delay', is thinking of Hamlet's soliloquy at the end of Act 2, in which the Prince, having listened to the First Player reciting the lines about Hecuba, accuses himself of inaction, or, to be more specific, of not having 'fatted all the region kites' with Claudius's 'offal'. He does not say, it is worth noting, that he has ever had the chance to do so. The audience has seen none. Hamlet and the King have never been on stage together since the King made his exit in 1.2, except for that fleeting moment in 2.2 when the King goes out as Hamlet comes in. What, then, is the function of the soliloquy in the theatre? It serves three purposes: it allows Hamlet to express his sense of frustration; to reveal that he has been thinking about the Ghost and its command; and, above all, to acquaint the audience with his plan to 'catch the conscience of the King'. The final effect of the soliloquy is to set an audience agog. While the studious reader is still mulling over the question of why Hamlet has not yet carried out his task, the theatre waits in suspense to see whether 'The Mousetrap' will work.

Let us turn now to Stubbes's second point, concerning the matter in Act 4, scene 4, that is to be found only in the Second Quarto. It is not clear, at least it is not to me, that Hamlet's soliloquy does provide any reasons for the Prince's failure to act. All that Hamlet does is to suggest some possible reasons, none of which he finds adequate. The eight lines that make up the entire scene in the Folio have their value. They serve to remind the audience of Fortinbras's existence and thus prepare the way for his reappearance at the end. But, more than that, they offer a pointed contrast to what we have just witnessed: a Hamlet ignominiously submitting, albeit in his usual riddling manner on such occasions, to the King's order that he go to England; whereas Fortinbras is doing exactly what he planned to do: marching to Poland at the head of an army. The rest of the scene, preserved in the Second Quarto, is, as Shakespeare had come to realize by the time he revised his foul papers, a mistake. It does nothing whatever to advance the action; nor does it tell us anything about the Prince himself that we do not know already. It is, in effect, a replay of the last part of 2.2, 'Aeneas' tale to Dido' and the soliloquy that follows it. As that 'tale' and the Player's rendering of it triggered off Hamlet's examination of himself and his conduct, so his dialogue with the Norwegian Captain has a similar effect. The only difference is in the circumstances. Then Hamlet had the initiative over the King, and could decide on a plan. Now he has lost that initiative. He has forgone the opportunity to kill Claudius that was his in the prayer scene. He has killed Polonius, and thus put himself in the wrong and in the King's power. He is a prisoner under escort, on his way to what looks like certain death. Yet here he is still using another occasion for self-reproach and for saying

> I do not know
> Why yet I live to say this thing's to do,
> Sith I have cause, and will, and strength, and means
> To do't.
>
> (Appendix A, xiii. 35–8)

He has indeed 'cause', even more than he previously had; but the will seems lacking; so does the strength; and the means are, so far as one can see, non-existent. The soliloquy at the end of 2.2 issued in a plan which was carried out. This one leads to nothing more positive than self-incitement (my emphasis):

> O, from this time forth,
> My *thoughts* be bloody, or be nothing worth.

In the light of what we have seen and heard already, this sounds unnecessary and unrealistic. Its only effect is to increase our doubts about the Prince's ever fulfilling his task. Even Betterton, though a great actor can do much with recalcitrant lines, would have been hard put to it to preserve Hamlet as a 'youth of great expectation, vivacity and enterprise' had he been burdened, as he was not, by these.

Hamlet's 'delay', whatever the reason for it, is undeniably an important element in the play, which would come to a premature end without it; but the attention devoted to it in this passage, and at this stage in the action, gives it a much greater prominence than it has in the revised text represented by the Folio. A *Hamlet* in which 4.4 is reduced to the seven and a half lines it occupies in the Folio is a different *Hamlet* from that found in the 'full' text. So is a

Hamlet unclogged of the Prince's disquisition on the drunkenness of the Danes (Appendix A, ii) which has provided such a convenient handle for those who have sought to pull the play into the Aristotelian pattern of tragedy, despite the fact that Hamlet says not a word about himself during the course of it but simply repeats, admittedly in Shakespearian phrasing, a stock piece of Elizabethan satire. Conveniently shorn, as Peter Alexander points out,[1] of the enigmatic 'dram of eale' crux with which it ends, this passage was used as the Prologue to the Olivier film version of *Hamlet* in which the most complex drama Shakespeare ever wrote was presented to millions as 'the tragedy of a man who could not make up his mind' — a 'dram of eale' surely, if ever there was one.

As to the matter of Hamlet's assumed madness which so troubles Stubbes and many a critic since, it was, as Stubbes notices, part of the original story, and, probably, part of the old Hamlet play. But there are other justifications for it. Shakespeare may well have seen in it a great opportunity for Burbage to show his versatility, much as he had been able to in *Richard III*, where the actor playing Richard must also play the various roles Richard adopts to deceive his victims—kind brother to Clarence, ardent lover to Anne Neville, benevolent uncle to his young nephews, and so on. Hamlet, 'but mad north-north-west', is, for much of the play's course, a variation on the court jester, the bitter fool, telling the truth about the King, the Queen, and the courtiers, especially Polonius, and doing it to their faces. There are also good practical reasons for his assumption of the 'antic disposition'. Even before he has so much as heard of the Ghost, much less seen it and listened to it, Hamlet evidently has great difficulty in restraining his sense of outrage and disgust at his mother's incestuous marriage, together with his instinctive loathing of Claudius, from speaking out. It surfaces in the first words he utters: 'A little more than kin, and less than kind.' It runs through everything he goes on to say to the King and Queen, and, finally, it erupts in his first soliloquy, which ends with the pregnant words: 'But break, my heart, for I must hold my tongue.' Recognizing the impossibility of his holding his tongue after he has heard the Ghost's story, he adopts the role of fool and madman, in order to attract the King's attention and lead him to show his hand. At the same time this role-playing will also

---

[1] *Hamlet Father and Son* (Oxford, 1955), 40.

serve to lure the King away from any suspicion of the great secret Hamlet has learnt from the Ghost.

This seems to be the right point at which to turn to the play itself. In what follows the *Hamlet* under consideration will be the *Hamlet* of this edition, substantially the *Hamlet* of the First Folio.

The Play

Full of riddles and paradoxical enigmatic statements, *Hamlet* is an even greater paradox than any of those it contains. As its popularity in the theatre so amply demonstrates, it appeals to all sorts and conditions of men. Yet, at the same time, much in it seems designed for a rather select audience, 'for spectators who were', as J. M. Nosworthy puts it,[1] 'disposed to consider curiously and had time in which to do so'. Closely connected with this paradox is another. *Hamlet* is, as we all know, a play in which the soliloquy is exceptionally prominent. Time after time, the action pauses while the hero gives vent to his feelings, works out a plan, or speculates on the human condition in general. Nevertheless, its basic appeal is to the curiosity of its audience, to the elementary desire to find out what will happen next in the unremitting battle of wits between the two 'mighty opposites', Hamlet and the King, as the advantage shifts from one to the other and back again. Nor is this all. The play's main concern is with death. The story it tells, as distinct from the action it dramatizes, begins with a single combat between the old King of Denmark and the old King of Norway, in which the latter is killed. It moves thence to the murder of the old King of Denmark by his brother Claudius. And only when all this has happened does the play proper start. As it reaches its end, Horatio, with four bodies lying at his feet and five other corpses, including that of old Hamlet, at the back of his mind, summarizes the main events in Hamlet's story. That story, he says, is made up

> Of carnal, bloody, and unnatural acts,
> Of accidental judgements, casual slaughters,
> Of deaths put on by cunning and forced cause;
> And, in this upshot, purposes mistook
> Fallen on the inventors' heads.
>
> (5.2.334–8)

---

[1] *Shakespeare's Occasional Plays* (1965), 166.

2. Fortune's wheel

It all sounds like a dismal, dreary, senseless chain of activity, nothing more than yet another instance of the wickedness and folly of mankind with which we are all too familiar. Yet none of these adjectives applies to the tragedy Shakespeare has made out of it all. Instead, that tragedy comes over to us as an intensely exciting, significant, and positive experience. It means something, even though, or perhaps because, that 'something' admits of no ready or simple definition.

Hamlet, despite its concern with death, is bursting with life. Doctor Johnson's final verdict on it recognizes this. He writes:

If the dramas of *Shakespeare* were to be characterised, each by the particular excellence which distinguishes it from the rest, we must allow to the tragedy of *Hamlet* the praise of variety. The incidents are so numerous, that the argument of the play would make a long tale. The scenes are interchangeably diversified with merriment and solemnity; with merriment that includes judicious and instructive observations, and solemnity, not strained by poetical violence above the natural sentiments of man. New characters appear from time to time in continual succession, exhibiting various forms of life and particular modes of conversation. The pretended madness of *Hamlet* causes much mirth, the mournful distraction of *Ophelia* fills the heart with tenderness, and every personage produces the effect intended, from the apparition that in the first act chills the blood with horror, to the fop in the last, that exposes affectation to just contempt.

It would be hard to think of anything less like a classical tragedy than *Hamlet*. In it the Elizabethan tendency to all-inclusiveness is pushed to the limit by a playwright who is fully conscious that he is doing just that. Polonius's systematic and unrelenting attempt to define the categories into which plays can be slotted culminates in the absurdity of 'tragical-comical-historical-pastoral'; yet even this critical portmanteau is not big enough to hold the play in which it so appropriately occurs, since it makes no mention of satire, epic, parody, and burlesque, nor does it find room for a critique of acting styles and an extended topical reference to 'the War of the Theatres'. Moreover, Polonius takes no account of the pronounced lyrical element in the play to which he belongs, although Ophelia's songs in Act 4 go far towards anticipating the ballad operas of the eighteenth century.[1] Hamlet himself may question whether life is worth living, and reject love because it leads only to the breeding of sinners; but the play in which he does this bears eloquent witness to its author's fertility of invention and to his exuberant delight in the sheer variety of human nature. There may or may not be more than meets the eye in the Prince's answer to the 'fishing' Polonius, 'You're a fishmonger.' What is certain is that in the theatre it is hilariously funny. The merriment Johnson finds in this tragedy is demonstrably there; and the tragic hero contributes greatly to it. His mastery of what Touchstone might have called 'the Retort Disconcerting' is complete.

Coming to *Hamlet* by way of the plays Shakespeare had written before it, one cannot but be struck by the extent to which it is a new development in his art. There is a sense of adventure about it all. It conveys the same feeling of excitement at moving into the unknown and the unexplored that Keats experienced 'On first looking into Chapman's Homer'. The clearest index of both the newness of what the playwright was now doing and of the effort he put into doing it is to be found in the tragedy's language; and here I take into account both the version of the First Folio and that of the Second Quarto, because both are, of course, Shakespeare's. According to Alfred Hart,[2] Shakespeare used more new words— 'new' in the sense that he had not employed them before—in the composition of *Hamlet* than he did in the composition of any other of his plays, over six hundred of them. Furthermore, many of them were new not only in the context of Shakespeare's work but also in the context of the English language as a whole. Hart's findings

---

[1] See F. W. Sternfeld, *Music in Shakespearean Tragedy* (1963), 60–3.
[2] 'The Growth of Shakespeare's Vocabulary' and 'Vocabularies of Shakespeare's Plays', *RES* 19 (1943), 128–40 and 242–54.

have since been confirmed and extended by Elliot Slater in his unpublished London Ph.D Thesis (1981): 'The Problem of *The Reign of King Edward III*, 1596: A Statistical Investigation'. In it he counts the occurrence in each of Shakespeare's plays of words that appear between twice and ten times only in the plays normally regarded as making up the canon. Once again *Hamlet* emerges with the largest number of such words, both absolutely and as a percentage of the different words Shakespeare employed in writing it.

This linguistic inventiveness is more than a matter of vocabulary alone. Phrases and even whole sentences from *Hamlet* have become indispensable parts of the language we speak. The first act —to go no further—has given us: 'Frailty, thy name is woman'; 'the apparel oft proclaims the man'; 'to thine own self be true'; 'a custom | More honoured in the breach than the observance'; 'thoughts beyond the reaches of our souls'; 'There are more things in heaven and earth, Horatio, | Than are dreamt of in our philosophy'; and 'The time is out of joint'. Even the cruxes that engage and tax the ingenuity of scholars are intelligible enough to serve as common currency—'the dram of eale', for example, or 'I know a hawk from a handsaw'. Drawing heavily on traditional proverb lore, *Hamlet* also contributed richly to it. What was it, then, in the *Ur-Hamlet* that caught Shakespeare's imagination and set it so vigorously to work? The issue of revenge alone seems an improbable answer. It was, after all, something he had handled already more than once. It is the main theme, almost the only theme, of *Titus Andronicus*; it has its place in *2* and *3 Henry VI*; it looms very large in *Richard III*, where Queen Margaret, the vindictive voice of the past, comes close to being the embodiment of it, and where the ghosts of Richard's many victims appear to bid him 'despair, and die'. It is also a motive of some importance in *Romeo and Juliet*, and it is a powerful shaping force in *Julius Caesar*, linking the deaths of Pompey, of Caesar himself, and of Brutus and Cassius in an iron chain of cause and consequence, crime and punishment. He had even found a place for it in comedy: notably so in *The Merchant of Venice* and in *The Merry Wives of Windsor*, if that play was written before *Hamlet*, as seems likely.

The novel interest the Hamlet story held out to Shakespeare was, surely, not its concern with the duty of revenge as such, but the situation within which that duty arises: that of the dutiful son who idealizes his dead father, the fratricidal usurping uncle, and the adulterous incestuous mother. Born of political ambition coupled with unbridled sexual passion, rich in its potential for conflict, and involving moral decisions of an extremely difficult and distressing kind for the son, this was a far more complex situation than any Shakespeare had dramatized hitherto. It offered a challenge to his art as well as an opportunity. He responded to that challenge by making the complex situation even more complex. He took over the Ghost from the *Ur-Hamlet*; and then, either from that source, or by independently developing Belleforest's account, he created Polonius and Ophelia. To them he added Laertes and young Fortinbras, who both appear to be his own inventions, serving as contrasts to Hamlet as well as taking part in the action. There is now a girl for Hamlet to love, distrust, and reject; her father for him to kill by accident, and thus drive her into madness; and her brother to take revenge on him, so making the chief revenger a victim of revenge. Thus the play ends, as H. D. F. Kitto well says, 'in the complete destruction of the two houses that are concerned',[1] and not simply in the deaths of the villain and the hero. Provision has, however, been made to ensure that Denmark, now purged of the rottenness that has plagued it ever since Claudius seduced Gertrude and poisoned old Hamlet, is not left without a ruler. Fortinbras is there, ready and eager to take over the business of government. The original Hamlet story has been transformed into something very different from, and much bigger than, what it was. Revenge still provides the basic structure; but the heart of the play is in the intense human relationships it creates and explores, and, above all, in the hero's struggle with, and reflections on, the world in which he finds himself.

The additions and the alterations Shakespeare makes, together with his shifting of the focus, go far towards solving the most difficult technical problem that revenge tragedy posed for every playwright who sought to write it: that of how to fill in the interval between the commission of the crime that calls for revenge, with which such a play begins, and the carrying out of that revenge, with which it will end. An extremely complicated situation demands a full and detailed exposition. Shakespeare provides one, and in doing so copes, at least in part, with that central difficulty by postponing the revelation of the crime to the last scene of his first

---

[1] *Form and Meaning in Drama* (1956), 329.

act, which is entirely expository. Yet, despite its length and the sheer mass of information it contains, that first act remains consistently dramatic, holding the interest of an audience riveted throughout its course. It is a demonstration of the art that conceals art.

In one respect, however, the first act can be misleading, especially for a modern audience or reader. It is very tightly organized in a manner that leads one to think of 'the well-made play'. Beginning just after midnight, the first scene ends with the coming of dawn. As it reaches its close, Horatio proposes that he and the two soldiers with him tell the story of their night's experience to 'young Hamlet'—the play's first mention of its hero—and Marcellus, approving of the idea, says: 'I this morning know | Where we shall find him most conveniently.' In the second scene they do find him. After taking part in the big scene at court, he is 'most conveniently' alone, listens eagerly to what they have to relate, and decides to join them on guard the coming night. When he exclaims 'Would the night were come' as the scene ends, he speaks for the audience as well as for himself. But, while Hamlet finds the enforced interval of inaction irksome, the playwright makes good use of it to work in more expository matter through a scene that is essentially domestic in nature and that moves to a different tempo from that of its predecessors. In the course of it Laertes sets off on his journey to Paris, after warning Ophelia not to allow herself to be taken in by Hamlet's professions of love for her, and Polonius, going much further, explicitly orders her to have nothing more to do with the Prince. By the time this scene is over the action can plausibly shift to the platform where Hamlet, Horatio, and Marcellus wait for the Ghost to appear. The Ghost does so, tells Hamlet its story, and imposes the duty of revenge on him. As dawn comes, it disappears, leaving the Prince to face a task of appalling magnitude and complexity.

The exposition, extending over five closely concatenated scenes, and dealing with the events of thirty hours or thereabouts, is now complete. It leaves its audience expecting an action that will be as closely knit together as its five scenes have been, and in which Act 2 will follow on from where Act 1 left off. We think we know the kind of play we are about to see, as it develops out of these beginnings. In fact, we are wrong, and we soon discover it. The scene between Polonius and Reynoldo that opens the second act is quite

different from any we have seen hitherto. Some time has obviously
elapsed since Polonius said farewell to Laertes, for he is now sending his son money; and this impression is endorsed by the return,
in 2.2 which follows immediately on 2.1, of the ambassadors
whom Claudius dispatched to Norway in 1.2. But, while there is
this unobtrusive yet clear insistence on the passage of time, the
scene has no effect whatever on the play's action. Reynoldo we
have never seen before, and shall never see again. When he sets off
for Paris, he goes out of the tragedy. This is not to say, however,
that the scene is pointless or irrelevant, though ever since 1676 it
has been an obvious candidate for deletion by any producer seeking to shorten the play. It has at least three clear functions. First,
it confirms our recognition that Polonius is, as we have already
seen in 1.3, both authoritarian and suspicious in his attitude to his
offspring; so much so that he has no hesitation in sending a servant to spy on his absent son. It thus prepares the way for his
deputing himself to spy on Hamlet in order to curry favour with the
King. Secondly, Polonius gives Reynoldo detailed instructions
about how he is to act, in the sense of playing a role, in order to find
out how Laertes is acting, in the sense of behaving himself. Thirdly,
it reveals his love of, and trust in, 'indirections', thus permitting his
characteristic idiom to come into full flower. His fondness for
laboured quibbling, already audible in the one brief speech he
makes in 1.2, and his sententiousness, so prominent in 1.3, are
now linked to a circumlocution so elaborate as to cause him to lose
all sense of direction and founder in mid-sentence. He has become
the perfect target for the arrows of Hamlet's wit. Contributing
nothing to the causal sequence of events, the scene, nevertheless,
announces two of the tragedy's major themes—spying and role-
playing—and is, moreover, broadly and richly comic in its own
right. It conveys a sense of the dramatist kicking up his heels, as it
were, because he has rid himself for the moment of the burden of
plotting and is free to indulge in the pleasure of writing an enter-
taining yet still significant bit of lively improvisation.

The same kind of deviation from the main 'business' of the
tragedy, and the same impression of a Shakespeare forsaking his
prepared scenario to improvise on significant themes and emphasize patterns, are to be found in other passages and episodes:
Hamlet's discourse on the art of acting and the abuses to which it
is prone, for instance; his baiting of Osric; and the whole matter of

the two Clowns in the graveyard. Furthermore, accident plays an unusually large part in *Hamlet*, as compared with the role it is allowed in the other major tragedies. The Players turn up in Elsinore at exactly the time when the hero can put their talents to use for his own purposes. The pirates most opportunely attack the vessel that is carrying him to England, and so ensure that he is already back in Denmark by the time when the funeral of Ophelia, herself a victim of accident, takes place. The world of this tragedy is not the self-contained world of the tragedies that were to follow, such as *Othello* and *King Lear*, where practically every character introduced is affected in some way by the events in which he is caught up. It is, instead, a very open world. Figures come into it unheralded and unexpectedly, and make their exits from it unobtrusively and often unnoticed. They touch the action at some particular point, but are themselves untouched by it. The result is a tragedy that has something of the same truth to life as we know it that W. H. Auden sees in Brueghel's painting of the Fall of Icarus:

> About suffering they were never wrong,
> The Old Masters: how well they understood
> Its human position; how it takes place
> While someone else is eating or opening a window or just
>   walking dully along. . . .[1]

Yet much as *Hamlet* depends for its structure on connections that are thematic rather than causal, the action does take place in time and is carefully organized. It falls into three large movements, as Granville-Barker aptly calls them, of roughly equal duration in the imagined time each covers, and separated from one another by two intervals in which a considerable amount of time is supposed to elapse. The first of these movements is the exposition, occupying the first act and dramatizing the events of about thirty hours. Then comes a long break of between two and three months, though we only discover this gradually. Final confirmation of it does not come until 3.2.119, where Ophelia assures the Prince that it is 'twice two months' since his father died. When the action does resume it deals with the events of about two days. The long second scene of Act 2 follows straight on from the first. Towards the end of it Hamlet asks the First Player to stage *The Murder of Gonzago* 'tomorrow night' (2.2.528). By the opening of Act 3, 'tomorrow night'

---

[1] 'Musée des Beaux Arts', in *Another Time* (1940), 47.

has become 'This night' (3.1.22). The play-within-the-play is performed on the evening of the same day; and all that follows on it
happens within the next few hours. It is tempting to think—
though there is no warrant in the text for doing so—that when the
Ghost appears to Hamlet, but not to his mother, at 3.4.95, the time
is just after midnight, its usual hour. The rest of the act would then
take place in the small hours, and be concluded by the entrance of
Fortinbras and his army, on their way to Poland, not long after
dawn. The break that ensues is not clearly defined; but during its
course Polonius is buried 'in hugger-mugger'; Ophelia goes mad;
Laertes comes back from Paris, and organizes an uprising against
Claudius; while Hamlet sails part of the way to England before
making his unexpected and, for the King, very disconcerting
return to Denmark. The remaining events of Act 4, beginning with
Ophelia's request to see the Queen and ending with the Queen's
account of her death by drowning, are continuous. In the middle
of them the King receives Hamlet's letter announcing his intention
to see the King 'tomorrow' (4.7.44). By the opening of Act 5,
'tomorrow' has come. Ophelia is buried; Hamlet and Laertes fight
at her grave; and Claudius tells Laertes:

> Strengthen your patience in our last night's speech.
> We'll put the matter to the present push.
>
> (5.1.284–5)

The final scene takes place later on the same day. Like the first
movement, the last deals with the events of about thirty hours at
the most.

The three clearly defined movements—beginning, middle, and
end—in each of which there are enough references to time to give
what happens in it an air of verisimilitude, leave little doubt that
Shakespeare had the main outlines of his tragedy, presumably in
the form of a scenario, before him as he wrote. But what I have
called the improvisations suggest that he had no hesitation about
pursuing new possibilities and interests as they opened up before
him during the act of composition. Indeed, when Hamlet says to
Horatio, 'Ere I could make a prologue to my brains, | They had
begun the play' (5.2.31–2), we may well be as close to Shakespeare actually working on *Hamlet* as we are ever likely to come. As
for the two intervals in the action, they are filled in for us solely, in
the case of the first, and mainly, in the case of the second, by

Hamlet himself. He alone can tell us, in his soliloquy at the end of Act 2, that he is ashamed because he has not yet carried out the task the Ghost set him, and only he can relate the story of his adventures at sea.

The Prince's consciousness is obviously the play's centre. And, because this is so, some important motives and concerns, which have been obscurely nagging away at him, as it were, for much of the time, do not receive their full and explicit formulation until they become clear to him as the action nears its end. Having told Horatio how he got hold of the King's letter ordering his death, Hamlet continues:

> Does it not, thinkst thee, stand me now upon—
> He that hath killed my king and whored my mother,
> Popped in between th'election and my hopes,
> Thrown out his angle for my proper life,
> And with such cozenage—is't not perfect conscience
> To quit him with this arm? And is't not to be damned
> To let this canker of our nature come
> In further evil?
>
> (5.2.64–71)

The third line there makes it evident that Hamlet had some hope of being chosen king after the death of his father, that the Danish constitution provides for the monarch to be elected, and that the Prince thinks Claudius used some sharp practice in getting himself elected to that position.[1] It thus throws light on Hamlet's earlier reference to his uncle as 'A cutpurse of the empire and the rule' (3.4.91) and on his description of himself as 'Hamlet the Dane' (5.1.248). At the same time, however, the trivial associations of 'Popped', in contrast to the powerful sense of outrage present in 'killed my king and whored my mother', make it plain that the loss of the kingship still is and always has been of far less consequence to Hamlet than the murder and the seduction.

The most remarkable thing about this speech is, however, the question it asks: 'is't not perfect conscience | To quit him with this arm?' Why, one feels impelled to inquire, should Hamlet need Horatio's assurance that Claudius deserves to be killed, when, in addition to all the other evidence Horatio has of the King's guilt, he

---

[1] On the nature of the Danish monarchy, see E. A. J. Honigmann, 'The Politics in *Hamlet* and "The World of the Play"' in *Hamlet*, ed. J. R. Brown and Bernard Harris (1963), 129–47.

is actually holding the royal commission ordering Hamlet's execution in his hand? The only possible answer is that conscience, distinguishing between what is right and what is wrong, has become a matter of overriding concern to the Prince, whose most urgent desire at the moment of his death is that his story should be reported correctly, so that his actions will be universally recognized as just and right, and his name—which is as important to Hamlet as it is to Coriolanus—will remain untarnished by any charge of treason, the accusation the courtiers level at him when he stabs the King (5.2.276). Whether conscience has or has not exerted any influence on Hamlet during the central movement, there can be no doubt about its having an effect on him in the final phase of the action; and this fact alone is sufficient to invite speculation about its possible effect earlier in hindering the Prince from taking the action the Ghost requires of him.

It may well be objected that to import a deep concern for conscience and justice, so much to the fore in the play's conclusion but not elsewhere in it, into a consideration of its central movement is to read *Hamlet* backwards. Yet the fact remains that having seen or read this play for the first time, one feels driven to go back to the beginning and to read it over again. Indeed, its conclusion positively suggests that one should. Forced by the Prince to live on 'in this harsh world' to tell his story, Horatio promptly sets about his task. It can be carried out in one way only: he must return to the opening, and have the whole thing re-enacted. For the best part of four centuries now, audiences and readers alike have been following Horatio's example.

Hamlet, I have said, invites speculation. It does so from the very outset before we have so much as heard of its hero who will, when the time for it comes, speak the most speculative soliloquy that Shakespeare ever wrote. The Ghost, difficult and even embarrassing though the modern producer may find him, is, for most of the time in which he is present, a masterpiece of ambiguity. There is no ghost at all like him in earlier Elizabethan drama, where ghosts are plentiful enough, or in any of Shakespeare's own plays written before *Hamlet*; and he had but one worthy rival and successor, the Ghost of Banquo in *Macbeth*. Much of the conviction he carries derives from the setting and circumstances in which he appears —the cold night, the sentinels whose nerves are on edge, the

4. David Garrick starts on seeing the ghost

3. The ghost appears to Hamlet (from Rowe's edition, 1709)

39

presence of the sceptical Horatio—and from the care with which he is introduced. First mentioned as 'this thing' (1.1.21), he quickly becomes 'this dreaded sight', and then 'this apparition'. When he appears, Horatio and the two soldiers consistently refer to him as 'it', emphasizing 'its' remarkable likeness to 'the King that's dead'. Challenging it, Horatio takes the orthodox Protestant position about ghosts. He accuses it of having 'usurped' the body of the dead king, thus implying that it is an evil spirit. Its response is to give a clear sign that it is offended and to stalk away. It does so, I think, not because Horatio concludes his challenge with the words: 'By heaven, I charge thee speak' (1.1.49), as Eleanor Prosser contends,[1] but because it was itself the victim of a multiple usurpation, 'Of life, of crown, of queen at once dispatched' (1.5.75). On its second appearance, Horatio bravely steps into its path. It does not 'blast' him. Instead, it listens to the three suggestions he makes about possible reasons—none of them offensive and none of them relevant—for its coming, and seems on the point of answering. But then the cock crows. Thereupon it starts 'like a guilty thing', and vanishes.

The reality of the Ghost has been firmly established; but its nature is left in doubt. The dialogue between the Prince, Horatio, and the two soldiers in 1.2 does nothing to clear up that doubt. When Hamlet says:

> If it assume my noble father's person,
> I'll speak to it though hell itself should gape
> And bid me hold my peace
>
> (1.2.246–8)

his position is very much that of Horatio when he accused the Ghost of usurping old Hamlet's form. But in his closing words, as he stands alone on the stage, his attitude is a more positive one as he divines the reason for the Ghost's coming:

> My father's spirit, in arms! All is not well;
> I doubt some foul play.

The uncertainty continues when the Prince confronts the Ghost. Is it, he asks it, 'a spirit of health or goblin damned' (1.4.19)? Does it come from heaven or hell, or simply from the grave, as Hamlet, increasingly impressed by its resemblance to his dead father,

---

[1] *Hamlet and Revenge* (Stanford, Calif., 1967), 98–9.

eventually assumes (1.4.23–30) and Horatio asserts when he remarks, 'There needs no ghost, my lord, come from the grave | To tell us this' (1.5.130–1)? The Ghost gives no answer to any of these questions until, alone with Hamlet, about six hundred lines after its initial entry, it speaks for the first time, saying that it is indeed his father's spirit, and that it comes from purgatory or somewhere closely resembling it, for it does not, perhaps significantly, use the actual word *purgatory*. Is it to be trusted? Purgatory would certainly seem the appropriate place, at least to a Catholic way of thinking, since old Hamlet died 'Unhouseled, disappointed, unaneled' (1.5.77). But, if it does come from a place of purification, why does it cry for revenge, something expressly forbidden by Christian teaching? Dr Prosser, who asks this question, has no doubt about the right answer to it: for her the Ghost is a devil (p. 138). Such a verdict not only goes against the instinctive reaction to the Ghost of many generations of playgoers and readers but it is also much too categorical and explicit.[1] It takes no proper account of the way in which, as J. C. Maxwell pointed out nearly thirty years ago,[2] Shakespeare subtly combines learned theological ideas about ghosts and their place of origin with popular beliefs and superstitions concerning them. Ideas and beliefs, it may be worth adding, which would have had their adherents and proponents in various sections of an average audience at the Globe—many of them Protestants; some of them Catholics; and most of them, in all probability, sharing memories, derived from ballads and stories heard in childhood, of ghosts as *revenants* from the tomb. Nor does this end the ambiguities. The coming of Horatio and the soldiers to recount their night's adventures to the Prince follows immediately on Hamlet's impassioned recollections of his father in his first soliloquy; and the Ghost's final appearance takes place in the course of the hero's even more impassioned evocation of his dead father in his upbraiding of Gertrude in 3.4. There is at least a hint here, reinforced by Gertrude's inability to see the apparition, that the Ghost could be a creation of the Prince's imagination, as the 'air-drawn dagger' is of Macbeth's.

The Ghost's precise nature is left mysterious and uncertain

---

[1] For a succinct statement of further objections to it, see Kenneth Muir, *Shakespeare's Tragic Sequence* (1972), 57–60.

[2] 'The Ghost from the Grave: A Note on Shakespeare's Apparitions', *Durham University Journal*, NS 17 (1956), 55–9.

because its main function in the play is to tell Hamlet the great
secret of the murder, but to do it in such a way and in such
circumstances as to lead him, in due course, to question its reliability and therefore to stage 'The Murder of Gonzago' as a test of its
truthfulness and of Claudius's guilt. The King's response to that
test puts the Ghost's honesty (i.e. *genuineness* as well as *truthfulness*) beyond question. It cannot be a devil. This does not mean,
however, that it is a regenerate spirit. The quality in it that comes
out in its dialogue with Hamlet in 1.5 is its essential humanity,
especially in the more discreditable senses of that word, though it
does show real concern for the Queen both here and again in 3.4.
This ghost, treacherously and in the most cowardly fashion
deprived by its brother 'Of life, of crown, of queen', and of any
opportunity to repent its sins, has a very natural feeling of bitter
resentment and grievance. Its insistence on a proper revenge is not
merely understandable but also something to which one reacts
with sympathy. Vindictive and unchristian though its call is, it
belongs to a cleaner and more wholesome world than the Denmark
of King Claudius. Old Hamlet, one recalls, fought old Fortinbras in
single combat and according to the rules governing such encounters, in striking contrast to the way in which he himself was
poisoned and to the treachery Laertes practises on Hamlet in the
murderous travesty of a friendly duel set up by Claudius.

Our first view of the King and his court should be sufficient to
establish their unwholesome nature, though there have been
those who have thought otherwise.[1] The play's second scene
presents a state occasion; and the King begins the proceedings
with a long formal speech. Admirably ordered, that speech falls
into three separate but related parts. Claudius clearly has a logical,
businesslike mind. He sounds—provided one does not listen closely to what he says and how he says it—reasonable, persuasive,
and efficient. Yet hearing his first sixteen lines, one has an uneasy
sense of having heard them, or at least something very like them,
before. 'Though yet ... Yet ... Therefore', the words that supply
the structure of the first part of the speech, are strongly reminiscent
of the 'Now ... But I ... And therefore' that serve the same struc-
tural purpose in Richard of Gloucester's soliloquy that opens

[1] See, for instance, G. Wilson Knight, *The Wheel of Fire* (1930, repr.
1954), 32–4.

Richard III and 'justifies' his determination to be a villain; and the more carefully one looks at the lines in question the more suspect they appear. What, one asks, is 'wisest sorrow' (1.2.6), especially when linked, as it is here, with 'remembrance of ourselves'? Can true grief be measured in the scales of prudence and self-interest? And what does that seemingly conclusive 'Therefore' imply? That 'wisest sorrow' and 'remembrance of ourselves' have led the King to marry his dead brother's widow, a union prohibited by the Church? It would seem so; for Claudius now goes on to remind his courtiers that this strange match has had their full approval. His language is the language not only of art but also of artfulness in its clever balancing of 'discretion' against 'nature', 'delight' against 'dole', and the oxymoronic 'mirth in funeral' against the no less oxymoronic 'dirge in marriage'. It is double-talk. It out-Richards Richard. Yet it is accepted without demur by the sycophantic court.

Eventually Claudius turns ingratiatingly to Laertes, using his name no fewer than four times in the course of nine lines, and grants him leave to return to France, much as he will calm the same young man down, later in the play, by asking him:

> What is the cause, Laertes,
> That thy rebellion looks so giant-like? ...
> Tell me, Laertes,
> Why thou art thus incensed.
>
> (4.5.118–24)

In fact, the King's methods, based on the assumption that all around him are eager for royal favour and will do anything to win it, work perfectly. Rosencrantz and Guildenstern, when they arrive on the scene in 2.2, show no hesitation whatever in agreeing to spy on their old school-fellow Hamlet, and continue faithfully though unsuccessfully in that course until the Prince sends them to their deaths. The court is as bad as the King.

Believing that every man has his price, Claudius turns at last to the one discordant figure in the otherwise colourful and complacently harmonious scene, Hamlet clad in black. His purpose in doing so is, when it ultimately emerges, a double one: to win the Prince's cooperation, or at least his acquiescence, in the new state of affairs by pronouncing him heir to the throne; and also to forbid him from returning to the University of Wittenberg. He does not reveal it, however, until some fifty lines later. The prohibition, if it came now, would be altogether too sharp a contrast to the gracious and ready permission he has just given Laertes to go back to Paris. He therefore approaches the matter indirectly. 'But now, my cousin Hamlet, and my son', he begins, only to have his overture interrupted by the Prince's bitter riddling rejection of it and of the strange unnatural relationship it takes for granted. 'A little more than kin, and less than kind', interjects Hamlet. A new voice has made itself heard. Sharp, uncooperative, and relying as Hamlet so often does, especially when speaking to Claudius, on monosyllabic Anglo-Saxon words, it jars harshly against the prevailing smoothness. Claudius refuses to be put out of his stride. As though Hamlet had not spoken, he completes his sentence by asking 'How is it that the clouds still hang on you?' It is the first of many such questions. From now on the King will make one attempt after another, either personally or through his agents, to probe into Hamlet's mind, only to find each probe frustrated, as this is by the Prince's punning riposte: 'Not so, my lord, I am too much i' th' sun.' A duel of wits has begun that will continue for the rest of the play.

The Queen adds her voice to the King's. Fond of her son, after her own unthinking fashion, she asks him to be more cheerful and to cease mourning for his father as—though she does not say it—she herself has done. This uncomprehending and, to Hamlet, incomprehensible request triggers off Hamlet's first speech of more than one line. Picking up her use of 'seems', he hurls it back at her in three curt sentences, and then goes on to accuse her and the entire court of having put on a mere show of grief for his father. His speech may be negative in its attitude to life; but what he says has, nevertheless, the accent and the virtue of sincerity.

The King responds with a large admonitory dose of verbal soothing-syrup, appealing to common experience, and backing up that appeal with the prescriptions and consolations of moral philosophy and religion, which roll glibly off his tongue with unctuous facility. He even refers to 'the first corpse', that of Abel murdered by his brother Cain, as an instance of the inevitability of death. We do not yet know that he himself has committed Cain's crime, but we ought to recognize the inconsistency of this fluent moralizer who, it appears, makes no distinction between natural death and murder. This spate of commonplaces is essentially an exercise in rhetoric, moving from sympathetic concession at the beginning to the veiled yet quite definite prohibition with which it ends:

> For your intent
> In going back to school in Wittenberg,
> It is most retrograde to our desire,
> And we beseech you bend you to remain
> Here in the cheer and comfort of our eye,
> Our chiefest courtier, cousin, and our son.
> (1.2.112–17)

Why, one may well ask, is the King who was so willing to allow Laertes to return to France so strongly opposed to his own nephew's wish to return to Wittenberg? As is the case with so many other questions that *Hamlet* raises in the minds of its audience, this one receives no direct answer in the play. One can, however, easily be deduced: Claudius has no intention of letting the Prince, who makes no secret of his hostility, out of the range and scrutiny, rather than 'the cheer and comfort', of his eye. So long as Hamlet remains in Denmark he can be watched. The Queen adds her obviously genuine request to the King's; and Hamlet, pointedly ignoring Claudius and implicitly refusing his bribe, replies: 'I shall in all my best obey you, madam' (1.2.120). Doing his best to save face by calling this a 'loving and a fair reply', the King makes his exit, leaving no doubt behind him that he and Hamlet are indeed antagonists, and well matched antagonists at that.

'I have that within which passeth show': so Hamlet has told his mother. Hitherto we have thought of 'that within' as profound sorrow for his father. Now, when he is alone, we are made to realize that it is not grief alone that is tormenting him. His first soliloquy (1.2.129–59) is of a kind and an intensity such as no English dramatist, not even Shakespeare himself, had ever written before. Made up of exclamations, parenthetical interjections, and that lacerating question which is also a protest, 'Must I remember?', it finds utterance, within the disciplined and disciplining framework of the blank verse line, for a chaos of emotions whose ultimate cause is not completely defined until the twenty-third line: 'married with my uncle, | My father's brother'. Driven on by the compulsion to remember; fighting against it—'Let me not think on't'—obsessed by memories of what was—'so loving to my mother'—and appalled yet fascinated by images of what is—'incestuous sheets'—Hamlet unpacks his heart with words that explain his longing for total dissolution as a way of escape from a world that the monstrous and outrageously hasty union of his mother and his uncle has made meaningless and intolerable to him. Worship of his dead father whom he sees as the epitome of all that is godlike in man, loathing of his uncle, the satyr, half man and half beast, and disillusioned disgust with his mother—'O God, a beast that wants discourse of reason | Would have mourned longer'—mingle inextricably with one another. One may, perhaps, regard these feelings, especially in an age when the marriage of a man to his brother's widow is no longer considered incestuous, as morbid, excessive, and immature, though what Hamlet says here anticipates to a remarkable degree what the Ghost will say to him at 1.5.42–57; but what matters for the play is that they are indubitably there in all their turmoil, made present and urgent by a power of expression that renders the chaotic without itself degenerating into chaos, and that is as ready to make use of a homely pair of shoes for its purpose as it is to resort to classical mythology. By the time the soliloquy ends, we know how deeply the Prince is involved in a tangled situation which is emphatically not of his own making, and from which there seems to be no way out, since suicide, ·which he contemplates, is forbidden by the dictates of religion and therefore has to be rejected. His position appears to be one in which, as Matthew Arnold says of his own *Empedocles on Etna*, 'there is everything to be endured, nothing to be done'.[1]

Expressing bewilderment and ending in frustration, the soliloquy is, nevertheless, packed with energy. The arrival of Horatio and the soldiers gives that energy something to expend itself on. Greeting Horatio with manifest pleasure, Hamlet asks him why he has left Wittenberg—which the Prince evidently looks on as his own spiritual home—for Elsinore, whose sole contribution to learning he sardonically sums up by saying, 'We'll teach you to drink deep ere you depart.' More irony at the expense of the royal marriage follows. This tragic hero, unlike the other tragic heroes of Shakespeare's maturity, is, we begin to realize, witty. And then

[1] *The Poems of Matthew Arnold*, ed. Sir A. T. Quiller-Couch (Oxford, 1913), 3.

Horatio tells him of the Ghost. The effect is electric. His *taedium vitae* forgotten, the Prince puts one purposeful question after another in the course of a superbly naturalistic dialogue in which the rhythms of prose and blank verse mingle easily and unobtrusively with one another. At the end of it he makes his decision: to join the guard that very night. Fully aware of the risk he may be running, he does not haver. Adjuring his companions to remain silent about their experience, he dismisses them, and then voices his suspicion that there has been 'foul play' and his conviction that 'foul deeds will rise'. Life, he now seems to be saying, is not futile and meaningless after all. A universal law is at work, seeing to it that crime is brought to light and that justice is done.

It is already clear from the evidence of this one scene that there are two sides to Hamlet. With Horatio and the soldiers he is all that the Renaissance prince or aristocrat should be, the paragon so eloquently described by Ophelia at 3.1.151–5, gracious in manner, curious and precise as befits a scholar, soldierly in his resolution and readiness to make a decision. In the environment of the court, on the other hand, where the *seeming* that he pounces on in his first speech of any length is so dominant, he is bitter, suspicious, and above all, disillusioned. Both sides of the man are apparent in his encounter with the Ghost. At first the determined Hamlet is uppermost. He even becomes ruthless when Horatio and Marcellus try to restrain him from following the apparition. There is real unmistakable menace in his cry: 'By heaven, I'll make a ghost of him that lets me' (1.4.60); and a consuming desire to take action informs his response to the Ghost's demand that he revenge his father's murder:

> Haste, haste me to know it, that I with wings as swift
> As meditation or the thoughts of love
> May sweep to my revenge.

> (1.5.29–31)

It is the answer we expect from the Hamlet we have seen since that moment in 1.2 when Horatio said, 'My lord, I think I saw him yesternight.' But Hamlet, when he makes it, does not yet know who the murderer is. The Ghost's revelation that 'The serpent that did sting thy father's life | Now wears his crown' comes as a shocking surprise to him but also as an endorsement of his deep-rooted intuition that Claudius is wicked, and hence leads to his exclamation, 'O, my prophetic soul! | My uncle!' An even more shattering surprise follows as the Ghost goes on to relate how his brother seduced Gertrude, who now stands accused of adultery as well as incest. Then comes the Ghost's final request (1.5.81–91). The first part of it seems intelligible enough; but how, after hearing of his mother's infidelity to his father, is the Prince to keep his mind untainted; and what sign has Gertrude shown of being pricked and stung by the thorns of conscience? It is no wonder that Hamlet feels the weight of his new knowledge and the duty it brings with it as a physical burden under which his knees sag. Already trapped in the past when he spoke his first soliloquy, he is now more firmly enmeshed in it than ever as he makes the Ghost's 'Remember me' his watchword. As the scene closes, the fine *élan* with which he responded to the initial cry for revenge has given way to a sober and daunting recognition of the true nature of the task that faces him:

> The time is out of joint. O cursèd spite,
> That ever I was born to set it right.
> (1.5.196–7)

The couplet is a pregnant one, rounding off the act as well as the scene; but what exactly does it mean? Even before he speaks it Hamlet's expressed intention to 'put an antic disposition on' implies that he has abandoned the idea of sweeping to his revenge. Now we begin to see why. The rottenness that infects Denmark is not confined to Claudius, though he is its source and centre. It has spread to Gertrude, to the court, and to the nation. The country cannot be healthy and wholesome while its king, who should be the fountain-head of justice, is guilty of fratricide, adultery, and incest. And how will the act of killing the King, who caused this dislocation of things by killing the previous king, serve to remedy matters? It does not seem a very convincing solution. Moreover, there is an obvious practical difficulty: how can the Prince, if he kills Claudius forthwith, justify his doing so? The only evidence of the King's guilt that he has is a tale told by a ghost; and that ghost has disappeared into thin air.

In fact, Hamlet's troubles at this point in the action are worse than he realizes. We first hear of his love for Ophelia in 1.3 when Laertes, saying farewell to his sister, bids her treat the Prince's advances with caution. His advice, though well meant, no doubt, is long-winded, heavily weighted with prudential considerations that are not well founded, and shows little trust in her ability to look after herself. Polonius shows none whatever. Regarding the double standard of sexual morality as the norm, he takes it for granted that Hamlet is trying to seduce his daughter—such being the way of young princes—and that Ophelia is acting like a fool in listening to his professions of love. Like Laertes, he makes assumptions that have no basis in fact. His worldly wisdom falls like a blight on the growing relationship of Hamlet and Ophelia, condemning it to frustration, bitterness, and sterility. The 'contagious blastments' Laertes feared have taken a form he did not anticipate. He and his father have, before the scene is over, gone far towards destroying the one positive force making for life, not death, that has appeared so far; and they have done it not out of malice but out of a misplaced and mistaken confidence in the validity of their own cynicism. Arrogant ignorance masquerading as knowledge derived from experience has its place in the tragedy.

Hamlet is a tragedy of thwarted love as well as a tragedy of revenge. Our first glimpse of the Prince and Ophelia together is an indirect one coming to us through Ophelia's account, in the latter part of 2.1, of how Hamlet came to her while she was sewing in her closet. His behaviour is indeed strange, as is his appearance, conforming to that of the distraught lover of convention. He has plainly adopted an antic disposition. But more than mere play-acting seems to be involved. It is hard to listen to Ophelia's story without being reminded of Sonnet 23 in which Shakespeare compares himself to an actor so overcome by stage fright that he forgets his part. He then goes on to say to the friend:

> O, let my looks be then the eloquence
> And dumb presagers of my speaking breast;
> Who plead for love, and look for recompense,
> More than that tongue that more hath more expressed.
> O, learn to read what silent love hath writ!
> To hear with eyes belongs to love's fine wit.

Has Ophelia learned, as a true lover would have done, to hear with eyes? The deep concern for the Prince that she voices to her father tells the audience that she has; but to Hamlet she offers neither word nor gesture. Timid by nature—she has been 'affrighted' by the whole incident—and in obedience to her father's orders, she fails to respond to Hamlet's dumb plea for love, understanding, and help. Her silence confirms him in his rash generalization, drawn from his mother's behaviour and, perhaps, from his reading of misogynistic satire and complaint: 'frailty, thy name is woman' (1.2.146).

As his letter to her shows, especially in the unexpected naïvety of its conventional phrasing, she has been his 'soul's idol' (2.2.109). But now that she has, as he thinks, failed him, he turns against her. The corruption of an idealist is the generation of a cynic. His rejection of her is in keeping with his changed vision of Denmark—Eden transformed into 'an unweeded garden' (1.2.135)—of the universe—'this brave o'erhanging firmament' become 'a foul and pestilent congregation of vapours'—and of man—'the beauty of the world, the paragon of animals' reduced to a 'quintessence of dust' (2.2.298–306). Already, when Polonius waylays him in 2.2, Hamlet is quite prepared to use Ophelia and his relationship with her as a means of disconcerting and disturbing the old fool, whom he regards with evident dislike and contempt, by obliquely hinting that he himself feels tempted to corrupt her. 'Let her not walk i'th' sun' is the kind of enigmatic remark that bears the Prince's own peculiar stamp. No other character that Shakespeare created makes anything like such constant and consistent use of teasingly pregnant and disquietingly ominous innuendo.

In fact, this particular remark leads straight into the Nunnery Scene of 3.1, the first occasion on which we actually see Hamlet and Ophelia on stage together, for when Hamlet eventually notices her presence as he concludes his 'To be, or not to be' soliloquy, Ophelia is walking in the sun. She is in a public place all by herself, and she seems to have come there with the express intention of meeting him, the 'son/sun' of the dead king, since she has brought along his presents to her in order to return them. It is all highly suspicious. Respectable young women did not go about unaccompanied in Shakespeare's world, as Polonius obligingly reminds us when he provides his daughter with a devotional work and tells her:

> Read on this book,
> That show of such an exercise may colour
> Your loneliness.

(3.1.45–7)

The precaution does not work. Ophelia's 'loneliness' prompts Hamlet's query, 'Are you honest?', and leads on in due course to his further query, 'Where's your father?' He seems to suspect her of trying to compromise him in some way, and comes increasingly, as a consequence, to direct his bitter feelings about his mother and about women in general at her. He gives vent to much that he has kept bottled up, as it were, ever since he said, 'But break, my heart, for I must hold my tongue', and that he will reveal in full to Gertrude herself in 3.4. The similarity between the endings of the two scenes is very striking. Here, in 3.1, Hamlet says farewell to Ophelia, but then, instead of going, continues his injunction that she enter a nunnery; says farewell twice more, but still fails to go; and does not depart until he has branded all women as wanton deceivers. In 3.4 he says good night to Gertrude no fewer than four times before he finally makes his exit after saying it once more. The 'antic disposition' Hamlet has assumed will not account for behaviour such as this. Woman's sexuality has evidently become an obsession with him; and to this extent at least he is genuinely mad.

It is Ophelia's tragic fate to pay the price in pain and suffering for Gertrude's sins and for the corrosive cynicism those sins have engendered in Hamlet. In 3.2, the last scene in which she and the Prince appear together, he treats her as though she were a common harlot; and his cruel bawdry becomes so outrageous and intolerable that even Ophelia, gentle though she is, is driven to protest. Then the man she loves kills the father she loves, and thus tears her apart. In her ensuing madness she confuses the one with the other and comes to identify herself with the betrayed and forsaken woman of popular song and ballad. Her tragedy is, as Harold Jenkins so perceptively and persuasively demonstrates, 'that Hamlet has left her treasure with her',[1] so that all she can do is 'to bewail her viginity' (p. 151). Like Hamlet himself who would, in the words of Fortinbras, have been 'likely, had he been put on | To have proved most royally' (5.2.350–1), Ophelia dies unfulfilled.

Yet in keeping with the paradoxical nature of *Hamlet* as a whole Ophelia's contribution to the tragedy is a positive one. The songs she sings are the effusions of a diseased mind, but there is no

---

[1] *Hamlet*, ed. Harold Jenkins (1982), 152. See also his 'Hamlet and Ophelia', *Shakespeare Jahrbuch* (West) (1975), 109–20.

5. Ophelia 'playing on a Lute'
(Royal Shakespeare Theatre, 1970)

madness in them. Probably written, among other reasons, to take advantage of the talents of a boy actor with a good singing voice and the ability to play on a lute—the Lucius of *Julius Caesar* ?— they bring a breath of fresh air into the close, overheated atmosphere of the Danish court. There is something wholesome about them. They belong to the world of common experience. Many if not all of the original audience for the play probably knew the tunes to which they were sung, and, perhaps, the words as well. Moreover, their poignant lyricism serves as a kind of counterpoint to the harsh satire of the Prince because it appeals to and relies on man's capacity for sympathy and understanding, as distinct from his readiness to accuse and condemn. They do much to widen the whole scope of the tragedy. As indeed, do her love of flowers and her knowledge of their traditional significances.

It has often been said that in the interval between the first two acts Hamlet has 'done absolutely nothing'. Bradley, whose words these are, goes even further by suggesting that the Prince has, in fact, done less than nothing, because through his 'transformation' he has excited 'the apprehensions of his enemy' and thus weakened

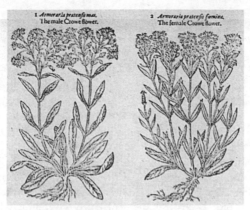

6. Crow-flowers, from Gerard's *Herbal* (1597)

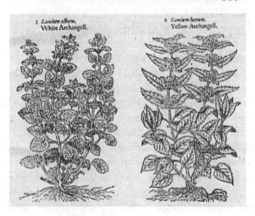

7. Nettles, from Gerard's *Herbal*

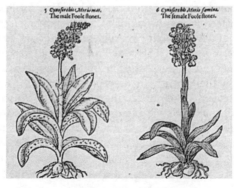

8. 'Long-purples', from Gerard's *Herbal*

his own position.[1] This interpretation of what has happened seems to me badly mistaken. Hamlet, having no case against the King that can be publicly stated and sustained, has skilfully adopted the 'antic disposition' for the prime purpose of exciting Claudius's suspicions and thus provoking him into action, into showing something of his true nature so carefully hidden behind the smiling face. And he has succeeded. Rosencrantz and Guildenstern have been sent for, and in 2.2 they duly appear to add their efforts to those of Polonius who, wrongly, attributes Hamlet's condition to thwarted love. Their amateurish attempts to pluck out the heart of his mystery merely arouse his scorn and contempt while also providing him with a grim kind of amusement. Before the scene is over he has warned all three of them not to interfere in matters which are no concern of theirs, by including Polonius among the 'tedious old fools' of this world and by telling his two old school-fellows that he is 'but mad north-north-west'.

All three spies bring out a characteristic quality of Hamlet that is too often ignored. He has all the *hauteur* of the Renaissance monarch or aristocrat. Sure of his own standing in the world, he can talk easily and familiarly with those who know their places —the soldiers, the actors, the clown in the graveyard—but he will not tolerate any word or action that breaches the rules of decorum. There is no missing the cold anger with which he reproves Guildenstern for trying to play on him as though he were a pipe (3.2.346–54) or the withering scorn he directs at the Rosencrantz who has presumed to address him in the imperative: 'Besides, to be demanded of a sponge—what replication should be made by the son of a king?' (4.2.11–12). True to his breeding, he feels no compassion for Polonius whom he has killed, or for Rosencrantz and Guildenstern whom he sends to their deaths. All three have deliberately and knowingly intervened in matters that are no proper concern of theirs. The dead Polonius is a 'wretched, rash, *intruding* fool' (3.4.32); and the fate of Rosencrantz and Guildenstern 'Doth by their own *insinuation* grow' (5.2.60). Sir Laurence Olivier had evidently not noticed this aspect of the Prince when he wrote: 'I feel that my style of acting is more suited to stronger character roles, such as Hotspur and Henry V, rather than to the lyrical, poetical role of Hamlet.'[2]

---

[1] *Shakespearean Tragedy* (1904, repr. 1957), 103.
[2] Quoted from Roger Manvell, *Shakespeare and the Film* (1971), 40.

To return to 2.2 : Hamlet's soliloquy at the end of it reveals that far from doing 'absolutely nothing' he has been doing something of the utmost importance—he has been thinking, and thinking to some purpose. It is precisely what Laertes will so signally and disastrously fail to do later in similar circumstances. Hamlet's thinking has led him to the conclusion that he must test the reliability of the Ghost and find confirmation of his own conviction, which has never really wavered, that Claudius is guilty.

The arrival of the Players in Elsinore provides him with the opportunity to do both. The final sequence in the scene is a superb demonstration of the way in which the skills of the man of the theatre, bent on whetting the curiosity of his audience, and those of the dramatic artist, intent on preserving and developing his hero's character, can be linked to reinforce one another. It all seems to occur casually and spontaneously as the Prince feels his way forward from one thing to another, much as he will do again when he steals the letter Rosencrantz and Guildenstern are carrying to England. His mind and his emotional responses go together as his initial request for 'a passionate speech' leads on to the account of the slaughter of Priam by Pyrrhus, another son set on avenging his dead father, thence to Hecuba, and so, finally, to the plan for staging *The Murder of Gonzago*, together with the 'dozen or sixteen lines' the Prince will add to it. When the Players leave the stage and Hamlet dismisses Rosencrantz and Guildenstern, the audience still does not know what the point of it all is. They discover it as the Prince, in his characteristic manner, looks back in soliloquy over what has been happening and seeks to understand the complex process of thought and feeling that has led him to evolve his scheme of action.

The play-within-the-play, which is, incidentally, a refined and subtle piece of revenge in itself, succeeds. It gives the Prince the proof of the King's guilt that he needs, and it certainly catches the conscience of its victim, literally bringing him to his knees. It is in these circumstances that Hamlet, on his way to his mother's closet, accidentally comes across the praying King—and spares him. Why? The only adequate reason is the one the Prince gives: his determination to ensure the King's damnation. Nothing short of that determination could possibly withhold him ; for the success of the playlet has left him wildly elated, confident, perhaps over-confident, in his own power, and ready, as he puts it in his soliloquy that closes 3.2, to

> drink hot blood,
> And do such bitter business as the day
> Would quake to look on.

Moreover, the distinct echoes of the Ghost's story heard in the lines

> He took my father grossly, full of bread,
> With all his crimes broad blown, as flush as May;
> And how his audit stands who knows save heaven?
>
> (3.3.80–2)

show that he is, indeed, remembering his dead father and his injunctions, and that the justice he has in mind is the *lex talionis*.

The speech deeply shocked Doctor Johnson, who found it 'too horrible to be read or to be uttered', and it has continued to shock and horrify many since, leading to the view, first expounded by William Richardson in the late eighteenth century and still widely current, that the Prince does not really mean what he says but is simply devising a plausible excuse for not doing a deed that he finds utterly repellent. There is not a shred of evidence in the text to support such an interpretation; and the theory would never have arisen had critics not ignored the theatrical dimensions and impact of the scene. In the theatre what we see, especially in a highly exciting episode such as this, counts for far more than what we hear. Behind the stage picture of Hamlet standing with drawn sword over the kneeling King are our memories of four other stage pictures already presented to our eyes or imaginations. The first is the scene so vividly conjured up by the Ghost of Claudius bending over his sleeping brother and pouring the poison into his ear. The second, again narrated but also, perhaps, mimed by the Player, shows another killer, Pyrrhus, standing motionless, with sword uplifted, over the prostrate and defenceless Priam, whose limbs he will soon 'mince'. Then come two re-enactments of the murder in the garden: one in dumb show, the other fully dramatized. The resemblance between the five stage pictures is deliberate and unmistakable. So is the difference. Hamlet, unlike Claudius and Pyrrhus, does not kill the man who is at his mercy, and so does not sink to their level in our eyes. His reason for refraining may be deplorable; but it is in perfect keeping with the paradoxical nature of the tragedy as a whole that his determination to see Claudius damned should have the positive effect of preserving him as a tragic hero.

The main part of 3.3, from the exit of Polonius at line 35 to the

10. Hamlet upbraids his mother
(Shakespeare Memorial Theatre, 1958)

9. Claudius attempts to pray
(Royal Shakespeare Theatre, 1965)

end of the scene, is a masterpiece of dramatic irony. Hamlet, as-sured of the King's guilt and given the perfect opportunity to carry out the Ghost's request, spares the King out of the mistaken belief that his enemy is in a state of grace. Claudius, stung into a recog-nition of his guilt by the play-within-the-play, and given the oppor-tunity to repent by Hamlet's desire to see him damned, finds himself unable to pay the price that true repentance demands.

The Prayer Scene is the still centre of the tragedy; but the stalemate it presents is soon broken. Early in 3.4 Hamlet inadvertently kills the eavesdropping Polonius and so loses the initiative that has been his since the end of the first act. This passes to the King who retains it to the final scene. The Prince recognizes what the consequences of the killing may be for him when he says:

> For this same lord,
> I do repent. But heaven hath pleased it so,
> To punish me with this, and this with me,
> That I must be their scourge and minister.
>   (3.4.161–4)

But this realization comes late in the scene which is, for Hamlet, concerned with more important and urgent matters than the fate of an over-busy spy. In effect, 3.4, the first and only occasion when he is alone with his mother, carries on from where his first soli-loquy ended with the words, 'But break, my heart, for I must hold my tongue.' Since then he has learned of Gertrude's adultery and of the murder of old Hamlet by Claudius. This new knowledge has led him to suspect, as we now discover, that his mother was in some way privy to the murder. Up to this point he has held his tongue, but not quite. He has most unfairly and cruelly made Ophelia a kind of whipping-girl for Gertrude, and, in 3.2, he has aimed some barbs at the Queen herself both through *The Murder of Gonzago*, which is designed to catch her conscience as well as the King's, and through such remarks to Ophelia as 'look you how cheerfully my mother looks, and my father died within's two hours' (3.2.117–18). His attacks have, however, left Gertrude quite unaffected, and they have done nothing to relieve the com-pulsive need to have it out with her that has been building in him ever since she married Claudius. Now, at last, the inner pressure finds its outlet, giving the scene an emotional intensity that sur-passes even that of the Prince's first soliloquy.

The links between this scene and the first soliloquy are firm and close: 'married to my uncle, | My father's brother' (1.2.151–2) reappears as 'You are the Queen, your husband's brother's wife' (3.4.16); 'So excellent a king, that was to this | Hyperion to a satyr' (1.2.139–40) is expanded into 'Look here upon this picture . . . hoodman-blind' (3.4.54–73); and the 'incestuous sheets' (1.2.157) become 'the rank sweat of an enseamèd bed' (3.4.84).

To hear a son upbraiding his mother in these terms and preaching to her thus is still deeply shocking. The effect of Hamlet's tirade on an Elizabethan audience, brought up to respect the fifth commandment, defies the imagination. Within the play, however, the Prince accomplishes his purpose. Pierced by her son's dagger-like words, the Queen who has hitherto seemed devoid of all moral sense—kind by nature, easygoing, and obviously sensual, she appears to be actuated in all she does by a dislike of being made to feel uncomfortable herself and of seeing others made uncomfortable—begins to realize something of what she has done and to see herself as she is. A new and more trusting relationship develops between her and her son. He confides in her that he is only 'mad in craft' (3.4.177); and she, for her part, promises not to reveal this secret. She keeps that promise later by 'covering up' for him in the account she gives the King of how Polonius came to be killed. But she does not become his firm ally until the very end. Whether she refrains from Claudius's bed or not, she loyally intervenes to prevent Laertes from attacking her husband in 4.5. It is not until she has drunk from the poisoned cup that she sees the truth and knows where she stands. Her last words are a rejection and an accusation of the King, coupled with a warning to her son whom she addresses as 'my dear Hamlet'.

On Hamlet the effect of the scene is profound. He undergoes a kind of catharsis. The horrible suspicion festering in his mind, that his mother could well have been involved in and privy to the murder of his father, is laid to rest in one brief exchange with her. Her four incredulous monosyllables, 'As kill a king?' (3.4.31), are enough to convince him of her innocence on that score. His obsession with her infidelity to his father, and with the perverse and incomprehensible, as it seems to him, sexual appetite which has united her with Claudius, the satyr, is less easily disposed of. He returns to the subject time after time, despite the Queen's repeated requests that he 'speak no more' and long after she has recognized and admitted her guilt. Even the intervention of the Ghost fails to halt his irrepressible outbursts of fascinated loathing for more than a moment. As though determined to purge his imagination, he continues on his course until he has cleansed his bosom of the poisonous stuff which has for so long weighed upon his heart.

Hamlet leaves his mother's closet a saner and more mature man than he was when he entered it. From this point onwards he is no longer preoccupied with the frailty of woman, and ultimately, by the side of Ophelia's grave, he comes to acknowledge his own love for her and to see it as something positive and good. That consequence of this climactic scene lies, however, in the future. The more immediate effect of his dialogue with his mother is to be seen in the Prince's behaviour in the next brief scenes in which he appears. The Hamlet we meet in 4.2 is very reminiscent of the Hamlet we saw after the Ghost left him in 1.5. The sense of release and exhilaration he felt then recurs here as he expresses his contempt for the King's lackeys, as well as for the King himself, before leading his pursuers in a wild chase round the palace. Brought under guard into the presence of the King, Hamlet, in no wise intimidated by the desperate situation he is in, uses the fate of Polonius as a means of putting Claudius in his place by reminding him of the end to which all men, including kings, must come. Some have found his dwelling on maggots, ingestion, and excretion 'disgusting'. The word is Wilson Knight's, and it leads up to his verdict on what has happened and is happening: 'The horror of humanity doomed to death and decay has disintegrated Hamlet's mind.'[1] It is, surely, a badly mistaken conclusion. Far from having been disintegrated, Hamlet's mind has been sharpened. He employs his wit, as though it were a rapier, to give what is, in effect, a most devastating answer to the platitudes about death that Claudius so glibly mouthed in 1.2. Sir John Gielgud appears to have caught the essence of the scene in his London production of the tragedy in 1934–5 and in his New York production of 1936–7. Rosamond Gilder writes:

Hamlet drops back . . . looking from the King on his right to the King's men on his left. The chase is closing in but the danger only stirs his blood and sharpens his tongue. A few more bandarillos for the bull-neck of the King.

---

[1] *The Wheel of Fire*, 27–8.

He throws his darts with malicious joy: first, 'your fat king'—a gesture to the right; and 'your lean beggar', left, to the two young men; then again the talk of heaven and hell. Hamlet walks over to the King and stands below him, twisting the point around—'seek him i' the other place yourself.'[1]

The Prince wins the encounter hands down. He sees the threat behind the King's reference to 'our purposes'; he firmly rejects, much as he did in 1.2, the same king's hypocritical and offensive claim to be his 'loving father'; and he leaves the stage unperturbed, apparently relishing the prospect of a voyage to England. Claudius, on the other hand, who seems to have Hamlet in his power and who now reveals to the audience that the letter Rosencrantz and Guildenstern are bearing to England contains the order for Hamlet's execution, makes his exit in a fever of anxiety and impatience. His last words are:

> Do it, England;
> For like the hectic in my blood he rages,
> And thou must cure me. Till I know 'tis done,
> Howe'er my haps, my joys were ne'er begun.
> (4.3.67–70)

Claudius, with every material advantage on his side, is desperately afraid. Hamlet, whose position seems hopeless, is confident and assured. Why? The reason, in the King's case, is not that he lacks physical courage. When Laertes bursts in on him in 4.5, he stands up manfully to the intruder, shows great presence of mind, and very quickly reasserts his royal authority. Nor is it because he feels himself illegitimate in his role as King, for on the same occasion he actually invokes the divine right of kings as his safeguard, telling the anxious Queen and the furious Laertes:

> There's such divinity doth hedge a king
> That treason can but peep to what it would,
> Acts little of his will.
> (4.5.121–3)

It is a truly astonishing statement, since it so accurately re-creates the original murder when Claudius himself did not stop at merely peeping through the hedge surrounding old Hamlet's garden. Yet, despite the unconscious irony, the King obviously believes what he

[1] *John Gielgud's Hamlet* (1957, repr. Freeport, NY 1971), 191–2.

says. Hypocrisy has grown to be a habit of mind with him, and it persists to the end. His last line in the play is 'O, yet defend me, friends. I am but hurt.' And he means it, even though he knows full well that the rapier with which the Prince has stabbed him is tipped with mortal poison. But neither animal courage nor his capacity for believing what he wants to believe can protect the King from the fear engendered in him by the Play Scene with its revelation that Hamlet knows his guilty secret. Only the death of the Prince will serve. The reasons Claudius gives Laertes for his failure to bring Hamlet 'to a public count' (4.7.17) for his killing of Polonius —the Queen's love for her son and that son's popularity with the people at large—may have their validity and even their influence, but they are not his prime reasons; and those who take them at their face value are being led astray as Laertes is. We are never told what the King says to Laertes in the interval between the end of 4.5 and the opening of 4.7. It can hardly have been an unbiased account of how Polonius met his death.

It is his fear of exposure and of the loss of the things for which he did the murder that dictates the King's subsequent behaviour. There is a brief moment in which he imagines himself safe and comes close to boasting about his own adroitness in disposing of the troublesome Prince; but it is brought to an abrupt end by the arrival of Hamlet's letter announcing his safe return to Denmark. For the first and only time in the play Claudius is at a loss as to what to do next, and admits it. His puzzlement is short-lived. Recognizing that he has the perfect instrument to hand in the shape of Laertes thirsting for revenge, he skilfully devises his final plot, and then, in his frantic compulsion to make all safe, he overdoes it. When Gertrude picks up the poisoned cup, he tries to dissuade her by saying 'do not drink', but he does not add 'There's poison in the cup', nor does he knock it out of her hand as he might so easily have done. His fear of the truth is, in the end, stronger than any love he may still feel for her. The lie by which he lives must be preserved at all costs. Only thirty lines or so later Hamlet, mortally wounded and on the point of death, musters up the strength to wrest the same poisoned cup from the hand of Horatio, in order that his friend may live on to tell the truth.

These two highly dramatic moments, so like one another and so unlike, lead, I think, to the very heart of the tragedy, and, incidentally, explain why the Hamlet of 4.3 is so unafraid and confident in a situation that looks quite hopeless for him. The King is, from the first speech he utters right down to his last words, enslaved to the lie, the 'forgèd process' (1.5.37) of old Hamlet's death, that has made him King, kept him King, and spread its poison through the land. His one serious effort to escape from its bondage, the Prayer Scene, ends in failure. His dependence on it kills Gertrude and, soon thereafter, Laertes and Hamlet as well. The Prince, on the other hand, is passionately devoted to the truth, and at the end, his attachment to it leads him to save Horatio's life and, perhaps, his soul as well, since it prevents Horatio from committing the deadly sin of suicide.

Looking back over the play from the vantage point of the final scene, and especially in the light of these two so tellingly contrasted episodes in it, one begins to see a pattern emerging. It would be hard to find a drama of the time that seems more remote from the world of the morality play than *Hamlet*. Yet, underneath the richly varied and realistic image it presents of highly individualized characters living and moving in the ambience of a Renaissance court, there is perceptible, as there so often is in Shakespeare's plays, a skeleton of allegory. The conflict the tragedy deals with can be seen as a struggle between Falsehood and Deception, embodied in the King, and Truth, embodied in the Prince.

There is no need to say more about Claudius's submission to lies and his reliance on deception, since it is evident enough. He sets the tragedy in motion by deceiving his own brother in seducing that brother's wife. At the end of it he tries to deceive the world by saying that Gertrude has merely fainted when he knows full well that she is dying and, albeit accidentally, by his hand. The Prince's concern for truth merits more attention, for it is total and goes far towards accounting for much in his behaviour and for the hold he has taken on the imaginations of audiences and readers alike. Many-sided in his activities and multifarious in his interests, Hamlet is powered, so to speak, by his consuming urge to know and to understand. It remains with him to the end. On his last day on earth, he stops to talk and question 'curiously' with the Gravedigger in an effort to glean what he can from one so familiar with death. He does not, as Marlowe's Dr Faustus does, sell that urge for an insubstantial mess of diabolical pottage.

Hamlet's love of truth and his respect for facts manifest themselves in his almost infallible capacity for recognizing and rejecting that which is not true. In his first words he refuses to accept the King's reference to him as 'my son'. As the play nears its close he toys with the pretensions of Osric to expose the courtier for the bubble that he is. Moving in a world given over to lies, he is ruthless and unsparing in his readiness to tell others that he sees them for what they are. In the case of his mother he goes much further. In the climactic scene, 3.4, he not only tells her what he thinks of her conduct but also forces her to confess that the picture he paints of her is substantially true. When he says to her 'I must be cruel only to be kind' (3.4.167), he is stating what is, for him, almost an article of faith. There is something almost fanatical in his insistence that one must seek to know oneself.

He would be an intolerable prig were it not that he is as honest with himself as he is with others. In his first soliloquy he describes his feelings, in all their rawness, in an effort to understand them. By the end of the second act he is accusing himself of cowardice and of behaving 'like a very drab, | A scullion!' (2.2.575–6). Soon thereafter he will tell Ophelia:

I am very proud, revengeful, ambitious, with more offences at my beck than I have thoughts to put them in, imagination to give them shape, or time to act them in.

(3.1.125–8)

They are not idle charges. Of his ambition, in the sense of ambition for place and power, we see little; but his pride certainly plays its part in his dealings with Polonius, Rosencrantz, and Guildenstern; and the accent of the traditional revenger is unmistakably there in his soliloquy ending 3.2. Hamlet does not spare himself any more than he spares others.

For Hamlet, however, knowing himself involves more than knowing himself in relation to other men. He seeks to understand himself within the context of human life as a whole. And that, in turn, implies coming to terms with death. The thought of it is with him from the outset; and he does not die until after he has discovered that 'The readiness is all' (5.2.169). That conclusion, following closely on his specific reference to Matthew 10:29: 'There's a special providence in the fall of a sparrow', and preceded, as it is, by statements such as 'There's a divinity that shapes our ends, | Rough-hew them how we will' (5.2.10–11), and 'even in that was heaven ordinant' (5.2.49), suggests that

11. The duel (Royal Shakespeare Theatre, 1961)

Hamlet has reached a state of Christian resignation. But has he? Subsequent events belie the notion. When Laertes wounds him with the unbated rapier and the truth begins to emerge, Hamlet takes complete control of the situation and metes out retributive justice, wounding the King with the poisoned sword and then killing him by forcing the poisoned potion down his throat. In doing so he obtains the revenge for the sake of which he spared the praying Claudius in 3.3.

Hamlet's readiness is a readiness to act as well as a readiness to die if necessary. The question he asks himself in his central soliloquy is:

> Whether 'tis nobler in the mind to suffer
> The slings and arrows of outrageous fortune,
> Or to take arms against a sea of troubles,
> And by opposing end them?
>
> (3.1.58–61)

His concern here is not with which of the two courses is the more virtuous, in the Christian sense, but with which of them is the nobler. The man who has chosen the first alternative is Horatio, who, as Hamlet says, has been

65

As one, in suff'ring all, that suffers nothing,
A man that Fortune's buffets and rewards
Hath ta'en with equal thanks.

(3.2.61–3)

Hamlet himself, however, without making any conscious decision about the matter, almost instinctively adopts the second course. When he speaks of it here, he seems to envisage it as having only one possible outcome: he who takes it will end his troubles by being overwhelmed by them. But at the end of *Hamlet* the hero ends them as well as being ended by them. His resistance to the King and to all that the King stands for is crowned with success. He accomplishes his task at the cost of his own life. Having already satisfied himself that killing the King is consonant with 'perfect conscience', he is concerned at the last not with the fate of his soul but with the clearing of his 'name'.

It is Horatio who calls on 'flights of angels' to sing Hamlet to his rest. Hamlet's own request is, characteristically, more modest and more realistic. He asks only that he be given his rightful place in history, in the minds of men. It is a request that has been granted him in ample measure. The Prince who greets the Ghost's revelation with the cry, 'O my prophetic soul! My uncle!', has become an integral part of 'the prophetic soul | Of the wide world dreaming on things to come'.

TEXTUAL INTRODUCTION

THERE are no fewer than three substantive texts of *Hamlet*: the First Quarto (Q1), published in 1603 and generally recognized as a 'bad' quarto; the Second Quarto (Q2), some copies of which are dated 1604 and some 1605, generally recognized as a 'good' quarto; and the First Folio (F) of 1623. The connections between them are tangled, and can best be dealt with by taking each text in turn, and attempting to determine its origin, its nature, its authority, and its relation to the other two.

The First Quarto

Q1, the earliest text of *Hamlet* that we have, survives in two copies only: one in the British Library, and the other in the Huntington Library. Both are imperfect, but fortunately they complement one another. That in the British Library contains the final leaf, I4, which is missing from the Huntington copy; while the Huntington copy has the title-page missing from the copy in the British Library. That title-page is reproduced as Fig. 12 on page 68. The device in that of N[icholas] L[ing] (McKerrow 301). The printer has been identified as Valentine Simmes on the evidence of the headpiece at the beginning of the text (see Fig. 13), with its two elaborate capital *As*, which was his property.[1]

There is, significantly, no mention of the name of James Roberts on this title-page, although it was he who had entered the play on the Stationers' Register on 26 July 1602. The entry reads:

James Robertes, Entred for his Copie vnder the handes of master Pasfeild and master Waterson warden A booke called the Revenge of Hamlett Prince Denmarke as yt was latelie Acted by the Lord Chamberleyne his servantes. vj^d. (Arber, iii. 212)

The reasons for Roberts's entry are not altogether clear. A. W. Pollard took the view that he was acting on behalf of the company, and that the entry was deliberately designed to block the

---

[1] A. W. Pollard, *Shakespeare's Folios and Quartos* (1909), 74–5.

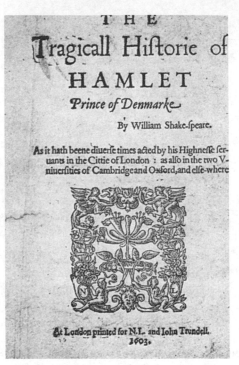

THE
Tragicall Hiſtorie of
HAMLET
Prince of Denmarke

By William Shake-ſpeare.

As it hath beene diuerſe times acted by his Highneſſe ſer-
uants in the Cittie of London : as alſo in the two V-
niuerſities of Cambridge and Oxford, and elſe-where

At London printed for N.L. and Iohn Trundell.
1603.

12. The title-page of Q1 (1603)

publication of the play by anyone else.[1] E. K. Chambers, on the other hand, thought that Roberts's object was more probably, since he was a printer rather than a publisher, to acquire the right to the play by making the entry, and then to turn that right over to another stationer in return for being commissioned to do the printing.[2] In the light of a recent article by Gerald D. Johnson,[3] Chambers seems to come nearer to the truth than does Pollard. Johnson shows that Ling was in the habit of benefiting 'from other stationers who located copy and brought it to him for help in publishing the editions. Or, similarly, he bought or assumed copyrights that had been entered by and in some cases published by other stationers' (p. 203). In the case of *Hamlet*, Johnson thinks it likely 'that John Trundle provided the copy for the first quarto' (p. 211); and then, after pointing out that Roberts was Ling's

[1] Pollard, op cit. 63–75.
[2] *William Shakespeare* (Oxford, 1930), i. 146.
[3] 'Nicholas Ling, Publisher 1580–1607', *Studies in Bibliography*, 38 (1985), 203–14.

favourite printer, goes on to suggest that Ling and Roberts might well have had a private agreement allowing Ling to go ahead with the publication of Q1 on condition that if 'Roberts had a better manuscript in hand or had access to one, both could hope to profit from the publication of a new edition that could correctly be advertised as "enlarged to almost as much againe as it was . . ."' (p. 212). This theory of collusion accords best with the incontrovertible fact that Roberts did eventually print the good quarto of 1604–5, something he could only have done with the consent of the players, since the copy for it must have come from the Globe or from the hands of Shakespeare himself.

Moreover, even if Roberts's entry was indeed meant to block the publication of Q1, it did not have the desired effect. Q1 came out in spite of it in 1603, at some date after 19 May, for it was on that day that the Lord Chamberlain's Men, referred to in that entry, became the King's Men, or, as the title-page of Q1 has it, 'his Highnesse seruants'. Its nature amply demonstrates that the company had every reason for seeking to prevent its appearance. In the first place, they did not as a general rule approve of their plays being printed; but in the case of Q1 there was another powerful objection operating: printed in seemingly open defiance of Roberts's entry of it, it is 'the only "bad" quarto [of any of Shakespeare's plays] that can strictly be called piratical'.[1] No matter how Ling and Trundle came by the text they put out, they had no right whatever to it. As for that text itself, it is a completely illegitimate and unreliable one, having no direct contact with any Shakespearian manuscript, or with any transcript of such a manuscript. It runs, according to Greg's count, to a mere 2,200 type lines, whereas there are nearly 3,800 in Q2 which claims on its title-page, with every justification in so far as length is concerned, that in it the play has been 'Newly imprinted and enlarged to almost as much againe as it was [in Q1], according to the true and perfect [i.e. complete] Coppie.' Moreover, very little care seems to have been exercised over the actual printing, for passages of sheer nonsense abound. The only signs of proof-reading the two extant copies afford are to be found in sheet B, with the Huntington copy showing the uncorrected state in each case.[2] The corrections made are few and obvious; the corrections

[1] W. W. Greg, *The Shakespeare First Folio* (Oxford, 1955), 52.

[2] The variants are listed in Greg's introductory note to Shakespeare Quarto Facsimile, No. 7 (Oxford, 1951).

that should have been made, but were not, are many and mostly equally obvious. In the following speech, corresponding to 1.2.196–212 in the present edition, the press corrector, confronted by bad grammar and senseless punctuation, made but one alteration in the first eight lines, removing the full stop after 'eies' at the end of the seventh:

> Two nights together had these Gentlemen,
> *Marcellus* and *Bernardo*, on their watch,
> In the dead vast and middle of the night.
> Beene thus incountered by a figure like your father,
> Armed to poynt, exactly *Capapea*
> Appeeres before them thrise, he walkes
> Before their weake and feare oppressed eies.
> Within his tronchions length,
> While they distilled almost to gelly.
> With the act of feare stands dumbe,
> And speake not to him: this to mee
> In dreadfull secresie impart they did.
> And I with them the third night kept the watch,
> Where as they had deliuered forme of the thing.
> Each part made true and good,
> The Apparition comes: I knew your father,
> These handes are not more like.
>
> (B4ᵛ–C1ʳ)

It is hard to understand how a man who could see the pointlessness of the full stop at the end of line 7 could have failed to notice its similar irrelevance at the end of line 3; and it would evidently be asking far too much of him to expect him to realize that the intrusive 'by' in line 4 results in nonsense, and should be replaced by a full stop. Since corrected and uncorrected sheets were bound up indiscriminately by the printers of the time, it is impossible to say whether the last nine lines of the passage, which belong to sheet C, represent a corrected or an uncorrected state. What is clear, however, is that the full stops at the ends of lines 9 and 14 are wrong and misleading. It certainly seems more than likely, in the light of his treatment of sheet B, where he also accepts 'invelmorable' (B2ᵛ) for 'invulnerable' (1.1.127) and 'impudent' (B3ʳ) for 'impotent' (1.2.29), that Simmes—or his man—would have found nothing to boggle at in 'dreames' (C3ʳ) for 'drains' (1.4.10), '*Plato*' (E3ᵛ) for '*Plautus*' (2.2.395), 'calagulate' (E4ʳ) for 'coagulate' (2.2.453), and the like. Nor would he have realized the strange oddity of 'honor' (H4ᵛ) when the word intended must be 'owner', used as a synonym for 'inheritor' (5.1.105), the reading of the two good texts.

There is no way of determining how far the blame for errors of the kind just cited should be laid at the door of the compositor, though it does seem highly likely that he was responsible for the intrusive and sense-destroying 'by' in line 4 of the passage quoted, because interpolation was, as we now know, one of his besetting sins.[1] On the other hand, no blame attaches to him for the metamorphosis of 'owner' into 'honor'. That mistake cannot be a result of misreading; the word 'honor' must have appeared in the manuscript he was working from; and it got there because whoever wrote that manuscript misheard the word 'owner'.

There are other features of Q1, of a much more general kind, which suggest that the copy Simmes's compositor had the task of setting up was both peculiar and defective. At a first glance, the play appears to be written almost entirely in verse. Only a few brief passages, amounting in all to a mere thirty lines or so, are set as prose, and some of those should have been set as verse. Nevertheless, much of the text is prose, but prose made to look like verse by the use of a capital at the beginning of each line of it. This capitalization must be the work of the compositor; but the manuscript he was working from was, one is driven to assume, set out in such a manner as to mislead him into thinking he was dealing with verse. The same phenomenon is, interestingly enough, also to be found in two other bad quartos of much the same date: *Henry V* of 1600, printed by Thomas Creede, and *The Merry Wives of Windsor* of 1602, again printed by Creede. Along with this form of error goes another of a similar kind: persistent mislineation of verse passages. Starting early, at the top of B1ᵛ, where Marcellus says:

> Therefore I haue intreated him a long with vs
> To watch the minutes of this night
>
> (1.1.26–7)

it continues thereafter almost to the end of the play.

One other immediately striking characteristic of Q1 deserves

---

[1] See Alan E. Craven, 'Simmes' Compositor A and Five Shakespeare Quartos', *Studies in Bibliography*, 26 (1973), 56.

mention at this point: the extreme inequality of the writing. There are passages, in the first act especially, which are almost as good as their counterparts in the other two substantive texts. There are others which can only be described as badly mangled relics of their counterparts, full of synonyms, halting in metre, shaky in grammar, and deficient in sense. And, finally, there are yet others, usually cast in a mechanical pedestrian blank verse, such as Shakespeare never wrote elsewhere at any stage in his career, that have little or no readily perceptible verbal connection with their counterparts.

In keeping with the unevenness of the writing, there are loose ends and inconsistencies in the conduct of the action and in the nomenclature of some of the characters. Q1 fails to explain how Hamlet escapes from the custody of Rosencrantz and Guildenstern, and from the ship that is carrying him to England—he is merely 'set ashore' (H2ᵛ) at some unspecified place; and while it promises a fuller account of how it all happened, it never keeps that promise. At a point corresponding to 3.2.48 in this edition, it has Horatio, without the benefit of a stage direction to signal his coming, appear out of nowhere to say 'Heere my Lord' (F2ᵛ) to a Hamlet who has not called him. In the Dumb Show that precedes the play-within-the-play, the first two figures to enter are '*the King and the Queene*' (F3ʳ). But, when 'The Murder of Gonzago' begins, these same two figures come on again as '*the Duke and Dutchesse*' and are designated *Duke* and *Dutchesse* in their speech prefixes. Furthermore, although Hamlet, when he asks the Players for the play, calls it 'the murder of *Gonsago*' (E4ᵛ), he now tells Claudius: 'this play is | The image of a murder done in *guyana, Albertus* | Was the Dukes name, his wife *Baptista*' (F4ʳ); and then, to add to the confusion, he goes on to say that the character now entering 'is one | *Lucianus* nephew to the King'. Even the First Clown, that most precise and dogmatic of characters, lapses into muddle. He ruins his own riddle by posing the question wrongly: 'tell me one thing,' he asks the Second Clown at 5.1.40–1, 'who buildes strongest, | Of [*instead of* stronger than] a Mason, a Shipwright, or a Carpenter?' (H4ʳ). Fittingly enough, muddle persists to the end. In the closing lines the Ambassadors from England turn up, along with Fortinbras, just as they do in the good texts. There can be only one reason for their coming: to announce the deaths of Rosencrantz and Guildenstern. In fact, however, they do no such thing. All

their spokesman has to offer is a piece of uninformative incon-
sequential nonsense:

> Our ambassie that we haue brought from *England*,
> Where be these Princes that should heare vs speake?
> O most most vnlooked for time! vnhappy country.
>
> (I4ʳ)

Their long journey has served no useful purpose.

Taken by and large, Q1 presents much the same action as that
of Q2 and F, but with some striking differences of detail. At one
point it alters the sequence of events. The 'To be, or not to be'
soliloquy and the 'Nunnery Scene' that follows it occur, not in 3.1,
as they do in those texts, but in what corresponds to 2.2, coming
immediately after Polonius broaches his plan for an 'accidentul'
meeting between Hamlet and Ophelia to the King. Secondly, Q1
contains an entire scene between Gertrude and Horatio for which
there is no parallel in either of the good texts. Taking place after the
scene in which Ophelia's madness is shown, it has Horatio relate to
the Queen the contents of a letter he has received from Hamlet. In
this letter the Prince tells how he circumvented Claudius's plot
against his life by finding 'the Packet sent to the king of *England*'
(H2ᵛ) and changing its order for his death into an order for the
execution of Rosencrantz and Guildenstern. Horatio also informs
Gertrude that Hamlet, already back in Denmark, has asked Horatio

> To meete him on the east side of the Cittie
> To morrow morning.

Gertrude, for her part, now recognizes Claudius's 'villanie'; states
her intention to 'soothe and please him for a time' in order not to
rouse his suspicions; and then proceeds to express her concern for
her son and, with it, her earnest desire that Hamlet not 'Faile in
that he goes about', namely, his revenge. She thus sustains the
role—and this is the third significant difference between Q1 and
the good texts—that she has already taken on in the 'Closet
Scene'. There the Prince makes a request of her:

> And mother, but assist mee in reuenge,
> And in his [Claudius's] death your infamy shall die.
>
> (G3ʳ)

73

To it Gertrude replies:

> *Hamlet*, I vow by that maiesty,
> That knowes our thoughts, and looks into our hearts,
> I will conceale, consent, and doe my best,
> What stratagem soe're thou shalt deuise.
>
> (G3ʳ–G3ᵛ)

Her character has thus acquired a much more positive cast than it has in either Q2 or F, in keeping with the strong assertion of innocence she makes in the same scene, where she assures Hamlet, swearing by heaven as she does so, 'I neuer knew of this most horride murder' (G3ʳ), meaning the murder of old Hamlet. It also has to be said, however, that part at least of Gertrude's new found resolution is the result of accident. The last two lines of the passage in which she promises to help her son are a recollection of four lines in *The Spanish Tragedy*. There Bel-Imperia tells Hieronimo:

> I will consent, conceal,
> And aught that may effect for thine avail,
> Join with thee to revenge Horatio's death.

Whereupon Hieronimo answers:

> On then, whatsoever I devise ... (4.1.46–9)

In the event Gertrude gives her son no more assistance in carrying out his task than she does in the two good texts, and, as in them, she stands by Claudius when Laertes makes his violent incursion into the palace.

The fourth marked difference between Q1 and the two other texts is that in Q1 Polonius appears as Corambis, and Reynoldo as Montano. The reason for this change has not been satisfactorily explained; but it is possible to hazard a guess. It would have been unwise for any company taking a play to Oxford at some time between 1600 and 1603, as the title-page of Q1 informs us the King's Men had done, to retain these two names in close association with one another. Polonius is perilously near to Polenius; and Polenius is the Latin version of Pullen, the founder of Oxford University, who died about 1147. He is mentioned admiringly by Samuel Lewkenor in his *A Discourse ... of all those Cities wherein doe flourishe at this day priuiledged Vniuersities*, a work that was published in 1600. After stating that the University began to thrive about 1130, Lewkenor goes on to say:

for the which much doth this noble university remain indebted to the worthy memory of *Robert Polenius*, a learned man, by whose only laborious and painful industry it hath recovered [i.e. won] the place and dignity which at this day it holdeth among other academies in our Christian world. ... (69ʳ)

As for Reynoldo (F)/Reynaldo (Q2), the name is much too close for safety to that of John Rainolds/Reynolds (1549–1607), the President of Corpus Christi College, an inveterate enemy of the theatre, who had recently published, in 1599, *Th'overthrow of Stage Plays*, etc. In these circumstances, the juxtaposition of Polonius and Reynoldo might well have been interpreted as a slighting reflection on the University, and so have caused trouble for the players, trouble which could be easily avoided by the simple expedient of altering the names.

   The copy of Q1 now in the Huntington Library was discovered by Sir Henry Bunbury in 1823; that now in the British Library is said to have been taken from Nottinghamshire to Dublin by a student of Trinity College there, who then proceeded to sell it to a Dublin bookseller for one shilling. It was bought by J. O. Halliwell in 1856; and he sold it to the British Museum in 1858. Bunbury's find aroused great interest. A reprint of it was made in 1825, with a prefatory note in which the text is described as the one 'originally written by Shakespeare, which he afterwards altered and enlarged'.[1] Further reprints and facsimiles followed; and, as these became available and were studied, controversy developed over the provenance and authority of Q1. One view of its origins was, of course, that expressed in the reprint of 1825: that it is Shakespeare's first draft of the play, a draft which he subsequently revised, expanded, and remodelled to give *Hamlet* the form it takes in Q2. The other view, first put forward by John Payne Collier in his edition of Shakespeare published in 1843, rejected this notion in favour of the idea that Q1 is simply a bad version, either taken down in shorthand by a spectator, or reconstructed from memory by an actor, of the Q2 text, or rather of the acting copy of that text preserved in F, and that it is a typical example of the kind of publication Heminges and Condell had in mind when, in their

---

[1] Quoted from G. I. Duthie, *The 'Bad' Quarto of 'Hamlet'* (Cambridge, 1941).

address 'To the Great Variety of Readers' prefixed to the First Folio, they wrote of 'diuerse stolne, and surreptitious copies, maimed, and deformed by the frauds and stealthes of iniurious impostors, that expos'd them'.

Nothing is to be gained from following the controversy in detail. It is sufficient to say that in the first three decades of this century the second view won more and more support, so that eventually E. K. Chambers, in his *William Shakespeare: A Study of Facts and Problems* (Oxford, 1930), was able to write: 'It is generally accepted that many of [Q1's] features are due to a reporter, introducing, as in *2, 3 Henry VI, Romeo and Juliet, Henry V,* and *Merry Wives of Windsor,* "gross corruption, constant mutilation, meaningless inversion and clumsy transposition"' (i. 415). Chambers backs up this statement with a tellingly lucid and succinct account of the text's errors and deficiencies, and thus prepares the way for the most careful and thorough-going examination Q1 has ever been subjected to, G. I. Duthie's *The 'Bad' Quarto of 'Hamlet'* (Cambridge, 1941). In it Duthie showed, beyond all reasonable doubt, that the quarto of 1603 is a reported text put together by a process of memorial reconstruction to provide a prompt copy for, in all probability, a band of actors playing outside London. In the course of his enquiry, Duthie accepted the hypothesis, first advanced by H. D. Gray in 1915,[1] that the man who vamped up Q1 from memory was an actor who had played the parts of Marcellus and Lucianus. The basis for this theory is the demonstrable fact that these two parts are rendered with considerable fidelity to the authentic text—Lucianus being almost word perfect—and that the dialogue as a whole is markedly better when Marcellus is on stage in Act 1 than it is when he is not. One other part, that of Voltemar (Voltemand in F) is also very accurately reproduced; but Duthie found himself unable to accept the idea that this was yet another of the reporter's roles because the final stage direction in Q1 reads: '*Enter Voltemar and the Ambassadors from England. enter Fortenbrasse with his traine.*' Noticing that Voltemar has no business in this scene, Duthie concluded that the actor who played the role would have been fully aware of this, would not, therefore, have made such a mistake, and so cannot have been the reporter. Greg, however, regards this deduction as wrong. He argues:

---

[1] *Modern Language Review,* 10 (1915), 171–80.

someone may have written [Voltemar's] name in the margin as a reminder that the actor who played a Danish ambassador in I. ii and II. ii was here available to play an English one. The wording of the stage-direction rather suggests that 'Voltemar' is an insertion, and the prefix is 'Ambass.' In fact, it is almost certain that the parts of Marcellus and Voltemand were doubled in the performance upon a recollection of which the reporter relied, for Q1 omits the beginning of I. ii down to the point at which the latter enters in F. Shakespeare seems to have intended Voltemand and Cornelius to be present from the beginning of the scene, for they have no separate entry in Q2; but the book-keeper had to consider the resources of the company, and the twenty-five lines before Voltemand is required would have given Marcellus time for a quick change of costume.[1]

Greg would seem to be in the right here, thus making the reporter an actor who played two small parts and one larger part, that of Marcellus, in some early performances of *Hamlet*.

The hypothesis acquires added support of an indirect kind from the work of T. J. King, who has shown that it was the practice of Shakespeare's company to give the major roles in a play to its permanent members, most of whom were also sharers in it, and to assign the 'bit' parts to journeymen actors. A hired player, who was eventually discharged after serving the purpose for which he had been engaged, would be exactly the sort of man to join another company, and to concoct a version of *Hamlet* for that company to put on.[2]

An examination of the first two pages of Q1 will serve to demonstrate how well grounded this Marcellus theory is. (See Figs. 13–16.) The first six lines, spoken while Marcellus and Horatio are still off stage, are, though evidently based on the authentic text, something of a muddle. Unable, it seems, to recall the names Francisco and Barnardo at the outset, though 'Barnardo' comes back to him by the time he reaches line 10, the reporter plays safe by making the initial stage direction read: '*Enter two Centinels*', and by giving them the non-committal speech prefixes '1' and '2'. But, as it is '1' who says at line 10, '*Barnardo* hath my place', '1' must, then, be Francisco. The sentry who gives the challenge is, therefore, in this version, the sentry on duty, not his relief. The effect of Shakespeare's surprise opening, inverting the normal and expected order of events, and so suggesting that Barnardo is jittery,

[1] *SFF*, 330, note C.
[2] 'The King's Men on Stage: Actors and Their Parts, 1611–1632', *The Elizabethan Theatre IX*, ed. G. R. Hibbard (Port Credit, Ontario, 1986).

14. B1 recto of Q2 (1604)

13. B1 recto of Q1 (1603)

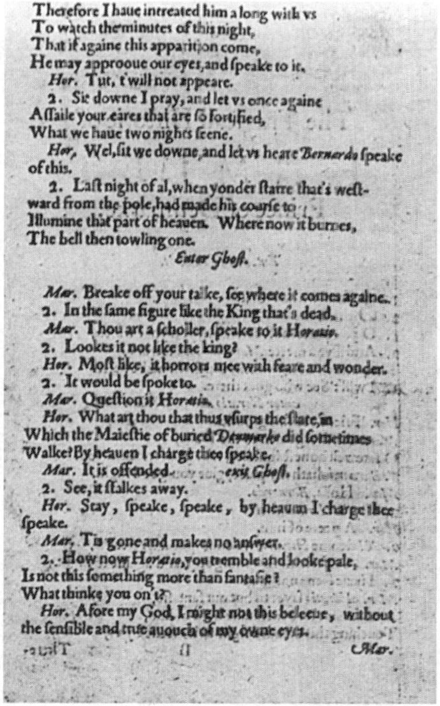

Therefore I haue intreated him a long with vs
To watch the minutes of this night,
That if againe this apparition come,
He may approoue our eyes, and ſpeake to it.
Hor. Tut, t'will not appeare.
2. Sit downe I pray, and let vs once againe
Aſſaile your eares that are ſo fortified,
What we haue two nights ſeene.
Hor, Wel, ſit we downe, and let vs heare *Bernardo* ſpeake of this.
2. Laſt night of al, when yonder ſtarre that's weſtward from the pole, had made his courſe to
Illumine that part of heauen. Where now it burnes,
The bell then towling one.

Enter Ghoſt.

Mar. Breake off your talke, ſee where it comes againe.
2. In the ſame figure like the King that's dead.
Mar. Thou art a ſcholler, ſpeake to it *Horatio.*
2. Lookes it not like the king?
Hor. Moſt like, it horrors mee with feare and wonder.
2. It would be ſpoke to.
Mar. Queſtion it *Horatio.*
Hor. What art thou that thus vſurps the ſtate, in
Which the Maieſtie of buried *Denmarke* did ſometimes
Walke? By heauen I charge thee ſpeake.
Mar. It is offended. *exit Ghoſt.*
2. See, it ſtalkes away.
Hor. Stay, ſpeake, ſpeake, by heauen I charge thee ſpeake.
Mar, Tis gone and makes no anſwer.
2. How now *Horatio,* you tremble and looke pale,
Is not this ſomething more than fantaſie?
What thinke you on't?
Hor. Afore my God, I might not this beleeue, without the ſenſible and true auouch of my owne eyes.
Mar.

15. B1 verso of Q1

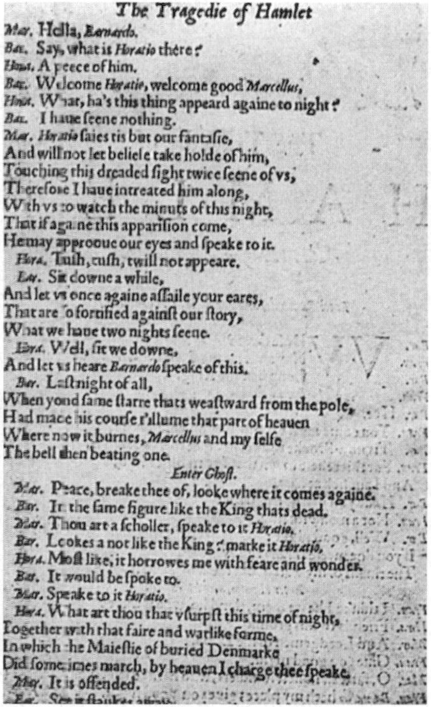

The Tragedie of Hamlet

Mar. Holla, *Barnardo.*
Bar. Say, what is *Horatio* there?
Hora. A peece of him.
Bar. Welcome *Horatio,* welcome good *Marcellus,*
Hora. What, ha's this thing appeard againe to night?
Bar. I haue ſeene nothing.
Mar. Horatio ſaies tis but our fantaſie,
And will not let beliefe take holde of him,
Touching this dreaded ſight twice ſeene of vs,
Therefore I haue intreated him along,
With vs to watch the minuts of this night,
That if againe this apparition come,
He may approoue our eyes and ſpeake to it.
Hora. Tush, tush, twill not appeare.
Bar. Sit downe a while,
And let vs once againe aſſaile your eares,
That are ſo fortified againſt our ſtory,
What we haue two nights ſeene.
Hora. Well, ſit we downe,
And let vs heare *Barnardo* ſpeake of this.
Bar. Laſt night of all,
When yond ſame ſtarre thats weaſtward from the pole,
Had made his courſe t'illume that part of heauen
Where now it burnes, *Marcellus* and my ſelfe
The bell then beating one.

Enter Ghoſt.

Mar. Peace, breake thee of, looke where it comes againe.
Bar. In the ſame figure like the King thats dead.
Mar. Thou art a ſcholler, ſpeake to it *Horatio.*
Bar. Lookes a not like the King? marke it *Horatio.*
Hora. Moſt like, it horrowes me with feare and wonder.
Bar. It would be ſpoke to.
Mar. Speake to it *Horatio.*
Hora. What art thou that vſurpſt this time of night,
Together with that faire and warlike forme,
In which the Maieſtie of buried Denmarke
Did ſometimes march, by heauen I charge thee ſpeake.
Mar. It is offended.
Bar. See it ſtalkes away.

16. B1 verso of Q2 (1604)

has been destroyed. 'Stand: who is that' looks as though it has been picked up from line 14 of the authentic text; and ' 'Tis I' is a feeble makeshift for the right password, 'Long live the King!' The next line, 'O you come most carefully upon your watch', begins with an intrusive and hypermetrical 'O', and ends with the substitution of 'watch', from line 13, for 'hour'. 'If you do meet Horatio and Marcellus' is converted into 'And if you meete *Marcellus* and *Horatio*', with an unnecessary 'And' taking the place of 'do' and the word order 'Horatio and Marcellus' reversed. In the line that follows the Shakespearian sense of 'rivals'—cf. 'And now both rivals, to mock Helena' (*A Midsummer Night's Dream*, 3.2.156)—is replaced by the synonymous but more commonplace 'partners'. The cautious and tentative 'I think I hear them' (l. 14), so suggestive of the night scene, becomes a flat 'I will'; and the imperative 'Stand! Who's there?' (F) loses its challenge by being reduced to 'See who goes there', where the 'See' has no particular force or significance. Furthermore, lines 7 to 10 of the genuine text, ' 'Tis now struck twelve . . . Not a mouse stirring', which do so much to create the right atmosphere of midnight, cold, sickness, and stillness, have disappeared without so much as a trace. The subtlety and imaginative force of Shakespeare's brilliant opening have been wrecked. All that remains of it is a dim memory, a confused blur.

With the entry of Horatio and Marcellus, the quality of the report improves immeasurably. At this point one begins to see why Q1 came to be regarded as a first draft. It is true that Marcellus conflates two speeches of his own into one, squeezing out Francisco's 'Give you good night' (l. 16) in the process; but one can also see how this has come about: Francisco says 'Give you good night' twice, once at line 16, and then again at line 18. It is true also that the word 'What' is omitted from Barnardo's 'Say— | What, is Horatio there?' (ll. 18–19), but the sense remains unimpaired, and the omission of 'What' allows Barnardo's question to make up a sound line of blank verse when joined to Horatio's answer. In what follows, down to the foot of B1^v, all three characters, including Marcellus, make mistakes, omitting short phrases and even, in Horatio's 'What art thou . . . speak' (ll. 46–9), almost a line and a half, with consequent damage to metre and lineation. They also have recourse to synonyms, substituting 'Illumine' for 'illume' (l. 37); 'towling' [i.e. 'tolling'] for 'beating' (l. 39); and 'Walke' for 'march' (l. 49). There is an evident loss of precision, rhythmic ease, and poetic richness; but the general sense of the dialogue does not suffer unduly. Moreover, there is at least one occasion when Marcellus, in agreement with F, offers a reading which seems preferable to that of Q2, by calling out, 'Question it *Horatio*', instead of 'Speake to it *Horatio*', where the Q2 compositor seems to have been influenced by 'spoke to' at the end of the previous line.

By this stage in the development of the first scene, it is already clear that the text of Q1 improves greatly with the advent of Horatio and Marcellus, but it is also equally clear that the text is, nevertheless, the product of a faulty memory. The mislineation that plagues it is a direct consequence of its departures, especially in the form of omissions, from the genuine text; and, by the same token, the omissions, since they have this effect, are indeed omissions, the results of lapses of memory.

There is, however, one obvious exception to this statement: Marcellus's lines

> Therefore I haue intreated him a long with vs
> To watch the minutes of this night . . .
>
> (ll. 26–7)

There is no omission here, no intrusive addition; the lines are word perfect; and yet they are misaligned. How has this come about? Q2 provides a clue. In it there is a comma after 'along' at the end of the first line, as there is not in F, which also divides the two lines correctly; and that comma alters the sense slightly. It looks as though the actor playing Marcellus was accustomed to speaking the lines as they are in F with no pause after 'along'. His mislineation here fits in with his marked propensity for remembering in speech units rather than lines; and it may well be this propensity which led the compositor into printing so much of the prose as verse. The great majority of the lines so printed are fairly short, each consisting of one or two speech units only. They almost certainly appeared thus in the reporter's manuscript, and for a good reason: he left himself space to insert bits that had eluded him on his first attempt at reconstruction. In the following speech, botched up out of two separate speeches of Hamlet's, 'He that plays the king . . . shall halt for't' (2.2.317–23) and 'It is not strange . . . picture in little' (2.2.359–62) which are given in reverse order, the words 'or the blanke verse shall halt for't' look very like a late addition:

> I doe not greatly wonder of it,
> For those that would make mops and moes
> At my uncle, when my father liued,
> Now giue a hundred, two hundred pounds
> For his picture : but they shall be welcome,
> He that playes the King shall haue tribute of me,
> The ventrous Knight shall vse his foyle and target,
> The louer shall sigh gratis,
> The clowne shall make them laugh
> That are tickled in the lungs, or the blanke verse shall halt for't,
> And the Lady shall haue leaue to speake her minde freely.

$(E3^r)$

The fact that the inserted clause comes at the wrong place—it should conclude the speech—makes it all the more likely that it was an afterthought.

While it is already apparent by the end of B1^v that Q1 is a reported text, it is not, as yet, clear who the reporter is. Barnardo has ruled himself out by the utter inadequacy of his opening exchanges with Francisco; but Horatio and Marcellus are candidates still. The rest of the scene settles the issue, for while Marcellus's divagations from the authentic text are few and slight, Horatio's are many and serious. Not surprisingly, Marcellus knows his own part better than he knows Horatio's; and his competence in recalling it identifies the actor who undertook this role as the man responsible for vamping up the text which was used as copy for Q1. If, however, as the excellence of Voltemar's speech in the equivalent of 2.2 seems to indicate, this same actor played that role also, the opening of 1.2 was bound to give him trouble, for he would then be off stage, busy changing rapidly into his Ambassador's costume. It plainly did. Q1 cuts the first twenty-five lines of the scene, beginning it at the point where F calls for the entry of Cornelius and Voltemand. All that is left of Claudius's initial speech is the last fourteen lines, here reduced to ten. There is some muddle and confusion at the outset, with mis-lineation occurring once more; but as Claudius turns directly to the two Ambassadors, the quality of the report improves, and it remains good, though not word perfect, down to the point at which the King says, while Cornelius and Voltemar are already on their way out but still within hearing distance :

> And now *Leartes* what's the newes with you ?
> You said you had a sute what i'st *Leartes*?

$(B3^r)$

The second of these lines is not entirely accurate, but it is certainly good enough and well in keeping with the general level of the report so far.

Now, however, the quality and nature of that report undergo an abrupt change. The rest of the King's speech, as it appears in the good texts, seven lines of ingratiating and orotund expansiveness, disappears without so much as a trace; and Laertes' reply to the question marks a fresh departure in the kind of writing Q1 has to offer. It takes the following form:

> My gratious Lord, your fauorable licence,
> Now that the funerall rites are all performed,
> I may haue leaue to go againe to *France*,
> For though the fauour of your grace might stay mee,
> Yet something is there whispers in my hart,
> Which makes my minde and spirits bend all for *France*.
>
> (B3^r–B3^v)

There is no mislineation here; no metrical irregularity; the general sense of the speech is the same as that of its counterpart in the good texts; and even some of the words are the same. Yet not a single line in it corresponds to any authentic line, though the last comes fairly close to doing so, as does the third. Moreover, two complete lines, the second and the fifth, have no verbal connection whatever with the text of Q2 and F. It looks as though the reporter, no longer on stage and occupied in getting ready to resume his role as Marcellus, but aware of the tenor of what Laertes says and of some of the words he uses, has resorted, either consciously or unconsciously, to paraphrase. In the process he has replaced Laertes' reason for returning to Denmark—'To show my duty in your coronation' —which he has forgotten, with one he knows far better, Horatio's reason for doing the same thing—'to see your [Hamlet's] father's funeral' (1.2.176). As for the fifth line, there is nothing like it in the text of *Hamlet* provided by Q2 and F. This impression of paraphrase is endorsed by what follows in the much shortened version Q1 offers of the ensuing dialogue between Claudius, Hamlet, and Gertrude, in which three lines only are correctly rendered. Laertes' little speech is, in fact, a foretaste of the sort of writing that will, once the first act is over, become the staple of the play: speeches that rest ultimately on a recollection of their general drift in the authentic text, eked out, as Duthie has so convincingly demonstrated, with lines and phrases culled from other parts of the play, and also, on some occasions, from other plays, not all of them Shakespeare's.[1]

It could well be argued that the absence of the last seven lines (1.2.44–50) from the King's speech to Laertes is a deliberate cut, designed to speed up the action, rather than the result of forgetfulness; but that reason will not hold for the reporter's treatment of Hamlet's first soliloquy. Able to make something of speeches and dialogue bearing fairly closely on the action, he is badly at sea when confronted by the Prince's passionate outburst, as he will be again when he has to deal with 'To be, or not to be'. Some phrases, and even some lines, stick in his head; but he has no idea of the order in which they occur or of the way in which they are related to one another. The outcome of his effort to recall what he heard is, to use his own words, 'a Chaos'. It runs thus:

> O that this too much grieu'd and sallied flesh
> Would melt to nothing, or that the vniuersall
> Globe of heauen would turne al to a Chaos!
> O God within two moneths; no not two: maried,
> Mine vncle: O let me not thinke of it,
> My fathers brother: but no more like
> My father, then I to *Hercules*.
> Within two months, ere yet the salt of most
> Vnrighteous teates had left their flushing
> In her galled eyes: she married, O God, a beast
> Deuoyd of reason would not haue made
> Such speede: Frailtie, thy name is Woman,
> Why she would hang on him, as if increase
> Of appetite had growne by what it looked on.
> O wicked wicked speede, to make such
> Dexteritie to incestuous sheetes,
> Ere yet the shooes were olde,
> The which she followed my dead fathers corse
> Like *Nyobe*, all teares: married, well it is not,
> Nor it cannot come to good:
> But breake my heart, for I must holde my tongue.
>
>   (B4^r)[2]

---

[1] 90–131.

[2] The text used here is the uncorrected version preserved in the Huntington copy. The press corrector made the following alterations to l. 4: 'God,' for 'God'; 'months' for 'moneths'; 'married' for 'maried'. He failed to notice the obvious errors 'teates' for 'teares' (l. 9) and 'The' for 'With' (l. 18).

The cry 'O God' at the beginning of the fourth line, corresponding to 'O God, God' in Q2, and 'O God, O God!' in F, shows clearly that the reporter was trying to recover the five lines that follow on from it in the good texts; but they obviously eluded him completely, as did so much else in the soliloquy, including the right sequence of the ideas. By no stretch of the imagination can the Q1 version be regarded as a first draft. We know what a Shakespearian first draft looked like from the examples that have survived by accident, and especially from the twenty-three lines, 4.3.292–314, of *Love's Labour's Lost* which should have been deleted but were not. They end in incoherence, or something very like it, but there is no incoherence in their evolution up to the last three lines, where its appearance seems to have led Shakespeare into deciding to begin the whole passage afresh. Nor can the soliloquy as we find it in Q1 be defended as a deliberately shortened version of its counterpart in the good texts. Starting with the substitution of 'the vniuersall | Globe of heauen' for 'the euerlasting', which throws everything wrong, muddle is written all over it. The reporter could not reconstruct the speech because he had never properly understood it. A failure to comprehend compounds the errors due to a failure to remember.

Critics prior to Duthie, forcibly struck, as well they might be, by the marked contrast between the confusion so evident in this first soliloquy and again in Q1's rendering of 'To be, or not to be' and the coherence and metrical regularity of the passages of non-Shakespearian verse that make their initial appearance in the speech of Laertes quoted at page 83, had sought to account for the latter in various ways. One hypothesis was that Q1 represents a partial revision by Shakespeare of the *Ur-Hamlet*, and that the passages in question are survivals from the old play. Another, espoused by those who looked on Q1 as an early draft, was that these same passages are simply pieces of early Shakespearian verse which he later revised so extensively as to render them unrecognizable. The third was that the reporter, incapable of writing competent verse of his own, made use in them of the services of a hack-poet. Duthie disposed of all three theories at one fell swoop by showing, to quote W. W. Greg, that the passages of un-Shakespearian verse

are largely a mosaic of words and phrases recollected from other parts of the existing play, or even from other Shakespearian or non-Shakespearian plays, and strung together after the fashion of the hooked atoms that dance along the road to Xanadu ... it is now evident that they were

85

written by someone whose mind was steeped in the language of the play, as the reporter's must have been, and there seems no reason why the reporter should not have been capable of writing them once his mind was freed from the shackles of verbal reproduction. So long as the reporter imagined that he could in any way recover Shakespeare's own words he toiled painfully and conscientiously along the broken paths of memory, but when all that memory retained was the general significance of a scene he was free to reconstruct it in his own pedestrian fashion, and the words and phrases of the original that he wove into his verse rose unbidden from the subconscious depths.[1]

Given, then, that Q1 is indeed a reported text, the crucial question arises as to what version of *Hamlet* the reporter acted in, knew, and relied on. Before that question can be properly dealt with, however, it is essential to decide how far the major differences between Q1 and the other two texts are the result of accident or of design. It has been suggested already that the change in Gertrude's character owes much, if not everything, to the reporter's recollection of *The Spanish Tragedy*. The alteration in the placing of the 'Nunnery Scene' also looks to be accidental; and the prime mover of the accident to be Shakespeare himself. At the close of 2.1, he has Polonius say to Ophelia, 'Come, go we to the King', words which the reporter almost recalled in rendering them as 'Let's to the King' (D3^r). But Shakespeare then changed his mind, so that Polonius arrives at the court, not accompanied by his daughter, as one would naturally expect, but bringing with him instead Hamlet's letter to her. It is the kind of inconsistency which is not uncommon in the plays and which an audience readily overlooks; but for a reporter trying to reconstruct the action it is a booby-trap. Fulfilling, as Shakespeare does not, the expectations he has raised, the reporter has Polonius arrive with Ophelia, and thus quite unwittingly finds himself in 3.1, instead of in 2.2, where he should be. To his credit, he remembers that the exchanges between the Prince and Ophelia are preceded by Hamlet's greatest soliloquy; but, to his shame, in attempting to reproduce it he reduces it to gibberish. The first eight lines are a fair measure of its quality:

> To be, or not to be, I there's the point,
> To Die, to sleepe, is that all? I all:
> No, to sleepe, to dreame, I mary there it goes,
> For in that dreame of death, when wee awake,

---

[1] *SFF*, 301.

> And borne before an euerlasting Iudge,
> From whence no passenger euer retur'nd,
> The vndiscouered country, at whose sight
> The happy smile, and the accursed damn'd.
>
> (D4ᵛ)

This display of uncomprehending effort to remember leaves little
room for doubt that the reporter was responsible for the misplacing
of the soliloquy and of the dialogue between Hamlet and Ophelia,
especially as Hamlet makes his entry 'poring vppon a booke' (D4ᵛ)
which he needs for his dialogue with Polonius in the 'Fishmonger
Scene', but not here in the 'Nunnery Scene'. In the performance
the reporter vainly sought to recall, both scenes almost certainly
occurred where they should, as did Hamlet's comparison of Rosencrantz to a sponge (4.2.11–19), which in Q1 has been attracted to
and follows immediately on the Prince's attack on the two courtiers for trying to play on him as though he were a recorder
(3.2.333–54).

The scene peculiar to Q1 in which Horatio tells Gertrude of
Hamlet's return to Denmark is another thing altogether. It not
only compresses the essential matter of 4.6, the scene involving
Horatio and the Sailors, and of 5.2.1–81, the dialogue in which
Hamlet recounts his adventures at sea to Horatio, into some thirty
five lines, but it also dispenses with some supernumerary characters, as well as acquainting the audience with the fate that awaits
Rosencrantz and Guildenstern in England. Moreover, it allows
Gertrude to express her continued support for her son. In brief, it
does exactly what a good piece of abridgement should: it simultaneously conflates and simplifies.

Suppose one now restores the misplaced scenes and passages to
their rightful places, excises the ten and a half lines tacked on at the
end of Hamlet's advice to the Players (3.2.1–42) in which he gives
examples of the Clown's interpolations, a passage for which there
is no warrant in the good texts, and, above all, replaces the reporter's muddles, borrowings from elsewhere, and paraphrases with
the words Shakespeare wrote? Suppose, further, one accepts
Hart's suggestion that between two hundred and three hundred
lines of the play as performed have been irretrievably lost through
the reporter's lapses of memory?[1] What then emerges from the
mess of Q1 is a fast-moving, coherent drama that is not without

[1] *Shakespeare and the Homilies* (1934), 24.

some, at any rate, of the overtones and resonances of the good texts, since, like F, it retains all the Prince's soliloquies except 'How all occasions do inform against me' (Appendix A, xiii. 24–58). In short, what we now have could very well be 'The Tragicall Historie of Hamlet Prince of Denmarke . . . As it hath beene diuerse times acted by his Highnesse seruants in the Cittie of London: as also in the two Vniuersities of Cambridge and Oxford, and else-where', even, perhaps, the *Hamlet* referred to by Gabriel Harvey.

From which of the two good texts does the abridged acting version that the reporter tried to recall derive? The evidence is overwhelmingly in favour of the view that it stems from the text behind F. It makes the same cuts as F does, while adding more of its own; and it reproduces, in a much truncated form, one (2.2.333–58) of the three passages of some length that are peculiar to F, passages which are, it will be argued (pp. 110–12), additions to that text, not accidental omissions from the text of Q2. Moreover, Q1 agrees with F in not perpetuating Q2's blunder of giving an entry to the Queen at 4.1.0 when she is already on stage; and, again like F, it dispenses entirely with the superfluous Lord of Q2 who makes a fleeting appearance after 5.2.155.

As Q1 is a reported text, it is hard to be sure how far passages in the good texts that have left no mark on it have been omitted through sheer forgetfulness or have been deliberately excised from it. The latter explanation should be the right one in the case of the omissions it shares with F; but what of the passages which it ignores but F retains? There are eight of them. The first, twenty-five lines at the opening of 1.2, can be accounted for: the reporter, busy transforming himself from Marcellus into Voltemand, was in no position to hear it. The omission of the others looks like part of a definite policy designed to do more than simply shorten the play, for the passages in question share a common feature: they do not contribute to the action. Three—Laertes' discourse on the reasons of state standing in the way of a marriage between Hamlet and Ophelia (1.3.16–28); the dialogue on 'the cease of majesty' (3.3.8–23); and Claudius's reasons for not taking legal action against the Prince (4.7.1–35)—are argumentative. Three more are purely descriptive—the last twenty-three lines of the Player's speech about Pyrrhus before he turns to the subject of Hecuba (2.2.465–88); Hamlet's praise of Horatio's fortitude (3.2.58–69); and the King's account of Lamord (4.7.69–88). As for the eighth, some twenty-four lines of the Player King's penultimate speech (3.2.176–99), it is the most extended piece of moralizing in the entire play. In sum, what disappears without trace is matter that a popular audience might well have found somewhat tedious.

Q1 is, as it stands, a sorry thing, and, from the editor's point of view, an extremely unreliable one, since it owes its existence to a faulty memory and much of its waywardness to sheer incomprehension. Any reading, especially in the first act, in which it agrees with Q2 must, for reasons that will appear later (pp. 99–100), be regarded with suspicion but also with care and respect, for there is always the possibility that the reporter heard and recalled aright. Its main value, however, lies in this: that through the fog, growing thicker as the play goes on and recollection becomes fainter, one catches glimpses of an acting version of the tragedy current in the early seventeenth century.

The Second Quarto

Having entered *Hamlet* in the Stationers' Register on 26 July 1602, Roberts took no action, so far as we know, against Ling and Trundle when Q1 came out, in defiance of his entry, a year or so later. Instead, he seems to have reached some kind of agreement with Ling, no longer in alliance with Trundle, which allowed Ling to publish Q2 in 1604–5 (see Fig. 17). The printing was done by Roberts; and it seems plausible that Roberts reserved the printing rights for himself as part of the bargain he made with Ling. The device on the title-page was again Ling's (McKerrow 301). There is, it is worth notice, no statement that the play had been acted. Seven copies of this edition are extant. Three, all dated 1604, are in the United States; three others, all dated 1605, are in England; and the seventh, also dated 1605, is in Poland.[1]

The claim that the text has been 'enlarged to almost as much againe as it was' in Q1 is, as has been shown (p. 69), substantially true; and its accuracy leads one to think that the words 'according to the true and perfect Coppie' ought to be equally reliable in their plain implication that the text faithfully follows an authentic

[1] The Library of the Elizabethan Club, New Haven; the Huntington Library; the Folger Library; the British Library; the Bodleian Library; Trinity College Library, Cambridge; and the Library of Wrocław University.

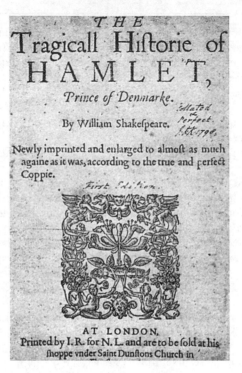

THE
Tragicall Historie of
HAMLET,
Prince of Denmarke.

By William Shakespeare.

Newly imprinted and enlarged to almost as much
againe as it was, according to the true and perfect
Coppie.

AT LONDON.
Printed by I. R. for N. L. and are to be sold at his
shoppe vnder Saint Dunstons Church in

17. The title-page of Q2 (1604)

manuscript giving a complete version of the play as Shakespeare
first wrote it. The hope those words engender is, however, short
lived. The text Roberts produced has been described by Dover Wilson, who did more than any other man to rehabilitate Q2 and to
establish its authority, as 'one of the worst printed of all the original Shakespearian texts' (*MSH*, p. 93), teeming 'with misprints,
with strange spellings, with missing letters, and with omitted
words, lines and passages' (p. 88). Convinced that the bad state of
Q2 was mainly, though not entirely, the fault of the printing
house, Wilson imagines the compositor concerned as a bundle of
contradictions: 'a learner or a young journeyman ... who *cannot*
work quickly because he has not mastered his craft', he is 'a
plodder, reproducing his copy letter by letter' (p. 100), yet when he
was pressed for time, his eye 'skipped words and phrases in his
copy, while his fingers leaped the boxes in his case' (p. 96). At the

same time, however, Wilson also noticed that oddly enough, despite its many shortcomings, Q2 'is surprisingly free from what may be called normal compositors' slips' (p. 94), meaning literals, transposed letters, and the like, and so appears, in one respect at any rate, to be the product of a competent workman. What, then, is the root of the trouble? Wilson's answer is that the compositor was 'driven to exceed his proper speed in the setting up of a very difficult manuscript' (p. 95).

The Manuscript of Shakespeare's 'Hamlet' was published in 1934. Twenty-one years later, some of its chief findings were challenged and controverted by John Russell Brown in his article 'The Compositors of *Hamlet* Q2 and *The Merchant of Venice*'.[1] Using variant spellings as a means of identifying compositors, Brown showed that Q2 was the work of two compositors, not one, as Wilson had thought; and that the two men involved were neither learners nor incompetent workmen, since they had also set *The Merchant of Venice*, and set it well, some four years previously when it was printed by Roberts in 1600 for Thomas Hayes. Moreover, neither of them, to judge from their work in general, was prone to omit words and phrases on the scale that Wilson finds them doing. It therefore follows, says Brown, that

Until it is proved that they were both guilty of such incompetence, or that they were rushed in setting Q2 *Hamlet*, we must presume that they were both defeated by a peculiar illegibility of their copy, or else that the Folio *Hamlet* contains additions to Shakespeare's original foul papers. A glance at Professor Wilson's lists of "omissions" [*MSH*, pp. 244–54] will show how likely the latter explanation is; few of them contain any hard words which do not occur in neighbouring lines, and many of them involve mere repetition or the addition of particles. In the present state of knowledge, it seems possible that the "omissions," accepted as authoritative by Professor Wilson, have no stronger authority than that of a scribe or the players' prompt-book. (p. 31)

These challenging observations open up afresh the much debated question of the nature and authority of the copy behind F, and so require careful examination. Before that can be undertaken, however, it is necessary to set out Brown's analysis of the printing process used to produce Q2. It divides the work between the two compositors, whom he labels X and Y, as follows:

[1] *Studies in Bibliography*, 7 (1955), 17–40.

X	1.1.1–1.5.191	X	4.5.86–4.5.119
Y	1.5.192–2.2.161a	Y	4.5.120–4.7.87
X	2.2.161b–2.2.565	X	4.7.88–4.7.111
Y	2.2.566–3.3.20	Y	4.7.112–5.1.272
X	3.3.21–Appendix A, x. 9	X	5.1.273–end.[1]
Y	3.4.191–4.5.85		

How do the two compositors compare as workmen? One thing can be said at once: Y is far less prone to what Dover Wilson calls 'normal compositors' slips' than is X. He is responsible for the one literal—'thrre' for 'there' 4.3.34—but that is all. It is X who transposes letters to give 'rehume' for 'rheume' (2.2.497), and 'spend thirfts' for 'spend-thrift' (Appendix A, xvi. 9); and it is he who inserts superfluous letters to produce 'imploratotors' (1.3.129) and 'againgst' (5.2.113). Both are, however, guilty of eye-skip—a sign of inattention or haste, but hardly of illegible copy. X, in the course of his second stint, makes two omissions which can certainly be ascribed to this cause, and a third that almost certainly can. At 2.2.210–11, instead of setting 'I will leaue him, and sodainely contriue the meanes of meeting between him, and my daughter', the obviously right reading of F, he allows his eye to jump from the first 'him, and' to the second, and thus reduces the sentence to 'I will leaue him and my daughter', which makes no sense at all in this context. A similar error, caused by the recurrence of 'Historicall Pastorall', leads to the elimination of the last two items, 'Tragicall-Historicall' and 'Tragicall-Comicall-Historicall-Pastorall', from Polonius's pedantic catalogue of dramatic 'kinds' at 2.2.393–4. Then, at 2.2.320–2, Hamlet, describing the stock roles he would expect to find represented in any company of travelling players, remarks in F: 'the humorous man shall end his part in peace: the Clowne shall make those laugh whose lungs are tickled a'th'sere; and the Lady shall say her minde freely . . .' There is no sign of 'the Clowne . . . sere' in Q2; and the likeliest explanation of its absence is that X missed it because 'sere', if spelled 'seare', could look rather like 'peace' in a careless secretary hand. X has, it would appear, made the same sort of mistake three times within the space of two hundred lines.

Y also falls a victim to eye-skip. His first slip of this kind occurs

---

[1] In terms of signatures the division is:

X $B1^r–D4^v, F1^r–4^v, I1^r–4^v, L1^r, L4^v, N1^r–o2^r$
Y $E1^r–4^v, G1^r–H4^v, K1^r–4^v, L1^v–4^r, M1^r–4^v$

at 3.2.104–7, and it is a venial one, for the passage in which he goes astray might have been designed as a test piece for compositors. In the Folio it runs:

> *Ham.* Ladie, shall I lye in your Lap?
> *Ophe.* No my Lord.
> *Ham.* I meane, my Head vpon your Lap?
> *Ophe.* I my Lord.

Confronted by this insidious pattern of line lengths and line endings, Y, not surprisingly, overlooked the last two lines. Not quite so venial, but still understandable, are his omission of 'Is this the fine of his Fines, and the recouery of his Recoueries' at 5.1.100–101 where he was evidently misled by 'his Recoucries' at the end of the previous sentence; and his confusion of 'Armes', at the end of 5.1.32, with 'Armes' in the middle of the First Clown's next speech, leading to the loss of four lines of dialogue.

When every possible allowance has been made for what may well be additions made in the Folio text, the number of omissions, in the form of lines, parts of lines, phrases, and words, from the text of Q2 remains a formidable one. It certainly does not inspire confidence in the reliability of the compositors concerned. Nor does their readiness to print what they should have recognized as unadulterated nonsense. X perpetrates such absurdities as—to give a small sample—the following, where the correct reading is placed in brackets: 'chapes [shapes] of griefe' (1.2.82.); 'So but [lust] though to a radiant Angle linckt, | Will sorte [sate] it selfe in a Celestiall bed' (1.5.55–6); 'a heaue, a kissing [heauen-kissing] hill' (3.4.60); and 'trennowed [winnowed] opinions' (5.2.154). Y's contribution includes, among other improbabilities, 'fingers, & the vmber [thumbe]' (3.2.341); 'she is so concliue [coniunctiue] to my life and soule' (4.7.14); 'so loued Arm'd [so loud a Winde]' (4.7.22); and 'As the King [As checking] at his voyage' (4.7.63). At the same time, however, the very nature of errors such as these does make it clear that the handwriting of the manuscript that served as copy for Q2 could be very misleading, and misleading in ways that we have every reason for thinking were characteristic of Shakespeare's hand.

The press-corrector in Roberts's shop, with such a rich harvest of mistakes awaiting his gathering, should have had a field day. Instead, he missed his opportunity badly. Overlooking gross and palpable errors, he concentrated his attention on minutiae, failed to consult the copy, and relying wholly on guesswork, succeeded in making things worse not better. Dover Wilson, when he examined the variants in the six copies of Q2 known to him, discovered seventeen definite corrections (*MSH*, pp. 123–4); and, according to Harold Jenkins, the copy at Wrocław University does not add to that number.[1] Fourteen of those corrections are of some significance for the text. Five are right, three make what was right wrong, three replace one error with another, two are questionable, and one is half-right. The final item in this list, the half-right correction, is accounted for by the substitution of 'be might hangers' for the uncorrected 'be hangers' at 5.2.123–4. Realizing that 'might be hangers' was what was required, the press-corrector supplied the missing word 'might' in, one assumes, the margin, whence compositor X transferred it to the wrong place in the text. There is, of course, no way of determining whether the corrector's interventions extended beyond the sheets which show variants; but, from the evidence these sheets supply, it becomes plain that the unsatisfactory state of Q2 cannot be blamed entirely on illegibility in the manuscript, though it was undoubtedly a contributing factor. Had the press-corrector taken the trouble to consult that manuscript before using his pen, he would not, for instance, have changed the erroneous 'thirtie' in 'An houre of quiet thirtie shall we see' (5.1.288) into 'thereby', instead of into 'shortly', as he should have done.

In the light of the nature and the number of the errors for which the two compositors and the press-corrector are responsible, it is hard to resist the conclusion that, no matter how well they had acquitted themselves when putting *The Merchant of Venice* (Q1, 1600) into print, working from manuscript, or the Second Quarto of *Titus Andronicus* (1600), using the First Quarto as their copy, they were not at their best or most conscientious when dealing with *Hamlet*. Moreover, even if they were not the same men as those Roberts employed four years earlier, it still looks very much as though there was a lack of proper supervision and discipline in Roberts's shop at the time when Q2 was going through the press; and there is a possibility at least that this slackness may have been deliberate. The availability of one copy, if not more, of Q1, and the compositors' recourse to it for assistance—a matter that will be treated later—raises the suspicion that Roberts, having, presum-

[1] *Hamlet*, ed. Harold Jenkins (1982), 53 n. 1.

ably, agreed with Ling on a price before starting the printing, cared little about whether the work was done well or ill. It could be that his one concern was to push it through as quickly, and so as cheaply, as possible. The heavy incidence of eye-skip certainly smacks of haste, and so does the printing of nonsense, with its suggestion that neither compositor had the time he needed to work out precisely what the words in front of him were and said. But, whatever the reason for the compositors' poor performance may have been, it seems plain that not all the shortcomings of Q2 can be attributed to the state of the copy from which it was printed.

This said, there are indeed signs that the manuscript used as copy had its rough edges. The nonsense readings cited at page 93 are sufficient to show that the hand in which it was written was far from a model of clarity, and so can hardly have been that of a professional scribe. Furthermore, the speech headings in it would appear, in several cases, to have been rather carelessly aligned with the text, and, in one instance, perhaps omitted altogether, for at 3.2.368, Polonius's little speech, 'I will say so', is caught up into and becomes part of the two speeches of Hamlet that lie on either side of it. Then, at 3.4.53, the speech prefix *Ham.* is placed one line too early, with the result that the Prince takes over the line with which Gertrude concludes her question: 'Ay me, what act, | That roars so loud and thunders in the index?'

This evidence alone is sufficient to show that the manuscript behind Q2 cannot have been the prompt-book or a transcript of it. Performance will not tolerate any uncertainty about who says what; and, for this same reason, it demands reasonable uniformity in the speech headings themselves. In Q2, however, there are some, though not many, inconsistencies in this matter. Introduced at 1.2.0.2 as '*Gertrud the Queene*', Gertrard—for this is the form her name invariably takes when it occurs in the dialogue—is *Queene.* when she makes her first speech at 1.2.68, and thereafter *Quee.* in all her speech prefixes up to the opening of 3.4. At this point she comes in as Gertrard; and all her speeches, with the one exception of that at line 52, where she reverts to *Quee.*, are headed *Ger.*, as they are in 4.1. In 4.5 she enters as *Gertrard*; but her speech headings become *Quee.* once more, and *Quee.* they remain to the end. It is almost as though Shakespeare is, perhaps subconsciously, emphasizing the personal and private nature of 3.4 and 4.1, in which Gertrude is essentially the mother and the wife, as distinct from the Queen. The case of Osric is especially interesting. Making his initial entrance at 5.2.81, he does so as '*a Courtier*', and is *Cour.* in his speech prefixes until he goes off at line 144. Some ten lines later, a *Lord* arrives on the scene, and promptly refers to him—a name being required at this point—as 'young *Ostricke*' (Appendix A, xviii.1). Not named as one of the Court party when they come in to watch the fencing match, Osric is nevertheless present, and, having been addressed by the King as 'young *Ostricke*' (5.2.206), he becomes *Ostr.* in his speech headings until he makes an unrecorded exit at line 265. He returns, this time as *Osrick*, at line 302; and his last brief speech is headed *Osr.* The shift from the generic '*a Courtier*' to the specific '*Ostricke*', and thence to '*Osrick*', enables us to observe Shakespeare at work, envisaging the character clearly from the outset, but not bothering to find a name for him until one becomes necessary, and then altering that name slightly to give it its final form, which will appear consistently in F as 'Osricke'. The inconsistencies in Q2 point unequivocally to its being based on Shakespeare's foul papers, his draft of *Hamlet* as he submitted it to the company, or, perhaps, read it to them.

The 'double false start', as Greg calls it (*SFF*, p. 314), at 3.2.157–8, adds further weight to the hypothesis that Q2 was set from Shakespeare's foul papers. Giving voice to her fears for the Player King's health, while simultaneously begging him not to be unduly disturbed by her natural womanly misgivings, the Player Queen explains her position thus:

> yet though I distrust,
> Discomfort you my Lord it nothing must.
> For women feare too much, euen as they loue,
> And womens feare and loue hold quantitie,
> Eyther none, in neither ought, or in extremitie.

Occurring in a passage conducted for the rest of its course in rigid heroic couplets, the line 'For women feare too much, euen as they loue', having no corresponding line to rhyme with it, sticks out clumsily, as does the last, since it begins with three redundant syllables. Moreover, the fourth line is plainly a revised version of the third, saying much the same thing but saying it differently, just as 'in neither ought' is a revised version of 'Eyther none'. F puts everything right by reading:

> For womens Feare and Loue, holds quantitie,
> In neither ought, or in extremitie.

Revising during the process of composition, Shakespeare either forgot to delete the matter he was discarding, or he made the deletion so inadequately that the compositor, possibly unfamiliar with theatrical markings, failed to notice it.

More signs indicative of foul papers are to be found in the stage directions of Q2. A considerable number of them are vague and permissive. Typical examples are: '*Enter Hamlet, Rosencraus, and others*' (4.2.0); '*Enter King, and two or three*' (4.3.0); '*Enter Rosencraus and all the rest*' (4.3.11); '*They enter*' (4.3.16); '*Enter Laertes with others*' (4.5.108); and '*Enter Horatio and others*' (4.6.0). Either undecided about how many 'others' he would like, or, more probably, realistically recognizing that he does not know how many might be available on any given occasion, Shakespeare has left things flexible. But performance demands that this flexible indeterminacy be replaced by precision. Someone, in all likelihood the bookkeeper, has to make up his mind as to whether '*all the rest*' at 4.3.11, for instance, includes Guildenstern or not, and about just how many of the guards it covers. It cannot mean all of them, since some are needed to remain 'Without' watching over Hamlet and ready to escort him in when '*They enter*'. The Folio solves the problem and seemingly economizes on actors by having Rosencrantz enter alone, by changing the order he gives in Q2, 'How, bring in the Lord' (4.3.16), into 'Hoa, *Guildensterne*? Bring in my Lord', and then by substituting '*Enter Hamlet and Guildensterne*' for '*They enter*'. It is a thoroughly workmanlike and practical solution to the uncertainties left by the permissiveness of Q2; it could be Shakespeare's own way of clearing up the difficulties he had created for the players; but it is not what he seems to have envisaged when he first wrote the scene. The desirable has been forced into a compromise with the possible, or at least with what someone regarded as the limits of the possible.

At this point the difference between a text that has been substantially prepared for performance and one that has not is particularly plain. So it is again at the climax of the duel scene. All Q2 can offer is this:

> *Laer.* Haue at you now.
> *King.* Part them, they are incenst.
> *Ham.* Nay come againe.
> *Ostr.* Looke to the Queene there howe.
> *Hora.* They bleed on both sides . . .
>
> (5.2.254–8)

No reader and, more to the point, no producer can possibly gather from these cryptic exchanges precisely what is supposed to be happening on stage. And when some ten lines or so later enlightenment should come at last, confusion takes its place, for compositor X has Laertes say to Hamlet: 'The treacherous instrument is in my hand'—instead of 'in thy hand'—'Vnbated and enuenom'd.' F, on the other hand, inserts between line 254 and line 255 the indispensable direction: '*In scuffling they change* [i.e. *exchange*] *Rapiers*', and, of course, reads 'thy' for 'my'. Without the assistance it, together with Q1, provides, *Hamlet* would be unactable at this catastrophic moment towards which the action has from the outset been moving. Nowhere else in the play are stage directions more badly needed than they are between 5.2.228, where the duel begins, and 5.2.311, where Hamlet dies; yet the only help Q2 has to offer is a curious double direction: '*Drums, trumpets and shot*' at line 232, followed immediately by '*Florish, a peece goes off*' on the next line; '*A march a farre off*' at line 301; and '*Enter Osrick*' at line 302. Gertrude, Claudius, Laertes, and Hamlet are all killed, yet the exact point at which each dies is left unmarked.

Taking all this into account, one cannot but be sceptical about Dover Wilson's view (*MSH*, p. 91), supported by Greg (*SFF*, p. 311) and Jenkins (p. 42), that '*Drums, trumpets and shot*' is an addition made by the bookkeeper to give greater precision to the authorial '*Florish, a peece goes off*'. It seems more plausible to regard both directions as the work of the playwright: the first intended to follow, as it does, Hamlet's success in the first bout; and the second, placed earlier than it should be, to signal his success in the second. It is almost inconceivable that any responsible bookkeeper would waste his time on a trivial adjustment when matters of the first importance positively cried out for his attention. It is highly questionable whether the manuscript behind Q2 ever came into the bookkeeper's hands. Jenkins, who thinks it did, cites with more caution than conviction some three or four directions which might be his (pp. 42–3), but pins his case mainly on two instances of what he regards as indications of cuts made by the bookkeeper. Accepting the ingenious suggestion of Dover Wilson (*MSH*, p. 30), he takes the hiatus at 4.1.39 in Q2, which coincides exactly with the beginning of a very neat cut in the Folio text, to be the result of the compositor's misinterpreting the mark, a horizontal line immediately above the first words to be omitted, designed to show where the cut is to start, and treating it as a deletion sign, while ignoring or not realizing the significance of the vertical line in the left-hand margin, intended to mark the lines beside it for cutting. To this piece of evidence he adds another of a similar kind, ascribing the absence from Q2 of the words 'Then senseless Illium' at 2.2.465 to yet another cut meant to begin at this point. In this instance, however, as he notes, the cut can only have been a temporary one, since the 23 lines that follow these words, though they have left no mark on Q1, and so were probably not represented in the performances to which it goes back, are found in F. He is almost certainly right about the reason for both the hiatuses in Q2, but he fails to offer any justification for his assumption that the cutting must be the work of the bookkeeper, as distinct from the work of Shakespeare. Yet both *Love's Labour's Lost* and *Romeo and Juliet* show clearly that the playwright did, on occasions, mark a first shot for deletion during the course of composition, but did it in such a way, probably using the theatrical bracket, that the printer failed to recognize it and, consequently, set both first and second shots.

A handwriting that could be difficult and misleading in ways that, other Shakespearian texts suggest, Shakespeare's often was; carelessly aligned speech headings; inconsistent speech headings; a double false start; a considerable number of imprecise stage directions; the total absence of stage directions at places where they are badly needed; and the general impression Q2 gives of a text that has not been properly prepared for performance—all these signs point in the same direction: to authorial foul papers as the copy from which Q2 was set. Unfortunately, however, these foul papers were not the sole copy available in Roberts's printing house. There was also at least one exemplar of Q1, and it was used by compositor X when he set the first act of *Hamlet*, or rather the first act minus the last seven lines of 1.5. The decisive evidence for some dependence of Q2 on Q1 comes at the play's opening (see Figs. 13–16). It is conveniently summarized by Greg, the first to notice it, as follows:

The first thirteen lines of Q2 differ widely from the briefer dialogue of Q1 … and offer no general typographical resemblance. After the entry of Horatio and Marcellus, however, the texts become closely parallel, and at once a typographical correspondence is observable likewise. Q1, continuing the practice with which it started, prints speakers' names and text level on the left as far as Horatio's speech ['Tush, tush, 'twill not appear'] at l. 30, where for the first time it indents the speaker. Q2, on the other hand, begins by indenting the text (setting the speakers full out) but after the entrance of Horatio and Marcellus it switches into agreement with Q1, printing ll. 24–29 level with the speakers, and then from l. 30 indents the speakers, again as in Q1 ... Moreover, Q2 ends two speeches erroneously with commas, l. 6 'houre,' and l. 15 'Dane,'. The first is one of the few lines before the entry that is closely rendered by Q1, and in Q1 it also ends with an erroneous comma, 'watch,': in Q1 l. 15 correctly ends with a comma, because the speech is continued. It is difficult to believe that these agreements are accidental or that they can have resulted from a merely casual consultation of Q1. (*SFF*, pp. 331–2)

Some confirmation of an intimate connection between Q1 and Q2 in the first act is provided by other features they share. First, they concur in some unusual spellings, though there are fewer of these than some recent textual studies would lead one to believe.[1] There is, for example, nothing uncommon about 'studient' (1.2.177). It is a recognized Elizabethan form of 'student' that is also to be found at *Twelfth Night*, 4.2.8, and at *Merry Wives*, 3.1.35. Similarly 'gelly' (1.2.205) appears again in F *King Lear* (3.7.82) and in *Winter's Tale* (1.2.418); while 'selleri(d)ge/ selleredge' (1.5.159) is the only form of 'cellarage', meaning 'cellars collectively', cited by *OED* before the early eighteenth century. Nevertheless there is a significant residue of rare spellings, 'strikt' (1.1.71), 'ship-writes' (1.1.75), and 'glimses' (1.4.32) being the most remarkable. Secondly, the two texts agree in printing 'cost' for 'cast' (1.1.73). Thirdly, as Jenkins points out (p. 47), there are correspondences in capitalization, with 'Gentlemen', 'Mole', and 'Pioner'—'Anticke', which he also cites was often capitalized even as an adjective—all occurring in the course of seven lines (1.5.165–71).

These coincidences in spelling and capitalization might not amount to much by themselves, but taken in conjunction with the bibliographical evidence cited by Greg, which is crucial, they leave little room for doubt that compositor X had a copy of Q1 to hand and referred to it when setting his first stint that accounts for practically the whole of what is now Act 1. How, then, did he come

[1] See my 'Common Errors and Unusual Spellings in *Hamlet* Q2 and F', *RES*, NS 37 (1986), 55–61.

to make mistakes it should have saved him from making? They are fairly numerous; 'souldiers' (1.1.16) for Q1's correct 'souldier'; 'with' (1.1.73) for 'why'; 'these' (1.1.88) for 'those'; 'Whereas' (1.2.209) for 'Where as'; 'fonde deedes' (1.2.259) for 'foule deeds'; 'Withall' (1.5.79) for 'With all'; and, most puzzling but, perhaps, also most illuminating,

> So but though to a radiant Angle linckt,
> Will sort it selfe in a celestiall bed
>
> (1.5.55–6)

where Q1 reads:

> So Lust, though to a radiant angle linckt,
> Would fate it selfe from a celestiall bedde . . .
>
> (C4ᵛ)

In all these instances, except the last, X must, one is driven to assume, have been working from the foul papers alone because he could see no difficulty in them, though he was, in fact, misreading them. In the last, however, although Q2 capitalizes the initial *a* in 'angle' whereas Q1 does not, it is hard to see whence its 'Angle linckt' can have come except from Q1. 'Angle' as a spelling of 'angel' was current in the early seventeenth century, as was 'linckt' for 'linked'; but 'angle' appears at only one other place in Shakespeare, *All's Well*, 3.2.125, and 'linckt' at no other place. Why, then, with Q1 to hand, did X print his nonsensical 'but' in place of its obviously correct 'Lust'? At first sight the error seems incomprehensible; but on thinking it over one can hazard a guess as to how it might have come about. Working from his manuscript copy, X probably printed 'but though' because he had just set 'but vertue as it neuer will be mooued, | Though' (ll. 53–4) and the two words 'but' and 'though' were still running through his head. Then, having difficulty with the manuscript, he turned to Q1, found what he wanted there, and carried on with his eye on both copies. His substitution of 'sort' for the 'fate' of Q1 and the 'sate' of the manuscript is not unintelligent. He evidently saw that the compositor of Q1 had mistaken long *s* for *f*, perhaps the commonest of all errors in the printing houses of the time, but he did not print 'sate', as he should have done, because he did not know of the word's existence, except as the past tense of 'to sit'. Shakespeare's use of it here is, according to *OED*, its first appearance in English.

Moreover, 'sorte', which is probably what X thought he was looking at in the manuscript, would be an understandable misreading
of 'sate', since there are good reasons for assuming that in Shakespeare's handwriting *a* often resembled *o* or even *or*; and, taken in
conjunction with QI's 'from', 'sorte', meaning 'separate', would
make tolerable sense. However, by the time he came to set 'from'
his eye was back on the manuscript, and he rightly replaced 'from'
with 'in', thus inadvertently turning sense, albeit the wrong sense,
into nonsense. Q2's muddle here is a nice illustration of the hazards
created by the availability of two divergent pieces of copy and also
by Shakespeare's fertility in neologism, nowhere more to the fore
than in *Hamlet*.

The avoidable errors just cited have a twofold implication : they
show that X did not make use of QI in any systematic fashion ; and
they prove that a corrected exemplar of QI cannot have been, as
Alice Walker argues it was,[1] the copy from which Act I was set in
Q2. She rests her case partly on the coincidences of unusual spellings and the like in the two quartos, but mainly on the typographical similarities, especially in speech headings, that Greg first
noticed in the thirty lines with which the play begins. What she
fails to take properly into account is that, to quote Greg once more,
'The first thirteen lines of Q2 . . . offer no general typographical
resemblance' to their counterparts in QI, because Q2 indents the
text, whereas QI does not. Compositor X began by setting the text
in his own way, which was not the way of the QI compositor,
because he was working from manuscript. He must have been,
since there is not the space available in QI to fit in the corrections
and the amplifications required to bring its first six lines into conformity with their thirteen-line equivalent in Q2. The only possible
annotation of QI here would be a cancelling of its first six lines and
a marginal note referring the compositor to the manuscript, unless
the hypothetical corrector took the trouble to copy those thirteen
lines on to a separate sheet, a curiously pointless exercise when a
reliable manuscript was already to hand. More pointless activities
of the same kind would have been necessary after l. 107 of the first
scene, since the eighteen lines that follow are not represented at all
in QI ; at the opening of 1.2, where there is no trace in QI of the
first twenty-six and a half lines of Q2 ; and again in 1.3, where Q2's
141 type lines have been reduced to a mere 73 in QI. Furthermore,

[1] 'The Textual Problem of *Hamlet*', *RES*, NS 2 (1951), 328–38.

even where corrections might have been feasible, their number and variety would have resulted in pages so difficult to work from as to make Shakespeare's manuscript, messy though it may have been, look pellucid by comparison. The inescapable conclusion is that Act I was set from that manuscript; but that X, while setting it, also had an eye, or perhaps half an eye might be more accurate, on QI.[1] That half eye would, incidentally, go far towards accounting for the anomalous commas noticed by Greg; for, if the pointing of the *Hamlet* foul papers was as light as that of the pages of *Sir Thomas More* generally attributed to Shakespeare, the compositor would, one imagines, have grasped eagerly at any assistance with it that he could find.

Did QI continue to exert some influence on Q2 after the end of Act I? If it did, that influence could hardly be expected to be of much consequence after 2.2.170, the point at which QI mistakenly introduces the 'To be, or not to be' soliloquy and the 'Nunnery Scene' that follows it, because the mere business of finding the corresponding passages would surely have been far more trouble than it was worth. One thing can be said with assurance: there was no consistent consultation, for the errors from which it would have saved both compositors of Q2 are many and serious. They include, for example, 'friendly Fankners' (2.2.422) for 'French Falconers'; '*Aeneas* talke to *Dido*' (2.2.437–8) for '*Aeneas* tale to *Dido*'; 'Considerat season' (3.2.240) for 'Confederate season'; 'my Ladies table' (5.1.183–4) for 'my Ladies chamber'. But while there was, as these examples show, some help to be had from QI, the persistent labour and exercise of judgement needed to distil it out was far beyond any that could be reasonably expected of two compositors. Roberts, it seems clear, made a very bad mistake in bringing one or more copies of QI into his printing shop, and thus saddling his men with a task for which they were not equipped.

In 1607 *Hamlet*, along with some other works, including *Love's Labour's Lost* and *Romeo and Juliet*, of which Nicholas Ling held the copyright, was transferred from him to John Smethwick (Arber, iii. 365). Four years later, in 1611, Smethwick published a Third Quarto (Q3) of it. He followed it with a Fourth Quarto (Q4), which is undated but which Jenkins (pp. 17–18) very plausibly assigns to 1622; and that, in turn, was succeeded by a Fifth Quarto (Q5),

---

[1] Fredson Bowers reaches a similar conclusion in his 'The Textual Relations of Q2 to QI *Hamlet* (I)', *Studies in Bibliography*, 8 (1956), 39–66.

published in 1637. However, as each of these later quartos was printed from its predecessor, with no reference to any other authority, none of them has any textual validity.

The First Folio

As well as being the publisher of three quarto versions of *Hamlet*, John Smethwick was a member of the syndicate of stationers that brought out the First Folio edition of Shakespeare's 'Comedies, Histories, & Tragedies' in 1623. His name appears, in a rather unusual spelling of it, in the colophon to that work which reads: 'Printed at the Charges of W. Jaggard, Ed. Blount, I. Smithweeke, and W. Aspley, 1623.' The most likely reason for his being included in the syndicate is that he held the copyright of no fewer than four of the plays in the collection: *The Taming of the Shrew*, *Love's Labour's Lost*, *Romeo and Juliet*, and *Hamlet*. The matter is of some importance, for it means that the syndicate would have run into no trouble about copyright in the case of *Hamlet* had they followed their usual practice, presumably agreed on with Heminges and Condell who supplied them with copy, of employing a 'good' quarto, or one of its descendants, as the copy text for such plays as were available in that form. *Love's Labour's Lost* and *Romeo and Juliet* are particularly significant in this connection, for their printing history is, up to a point, very similar to that of *Hamlet*. It is true that no edition of *Love's Labour's Lost* earlier than the quarto of 1598 has ever come to light; but the words 'Newly corrected and augmented', which appear on the title-page of that quarto, strongly suggest that there had been such an edition. As for *Romeo and Juliet*, it offers a closer parallel to *Hamlet* than does any other of the plays. A bad quarto of it appeared in 1597 from the press of John Danter. It was followed two years later by a good quarto 'Printed by Thomas Creede, for Cuthbert Burby', and announcing on its title-page that it had been 'Newly corrected, augmented, and amended'. Furthermore, this edition (Q2) of *Romeo and Juliet*, like Q2 of *Hamlet*, seems to have been based on authorial foul papers and yet carries some marks of having been affected by the bad quarto it sought to replace. Both the *Love's Labour's Lost* of 1598 and the *Romeo and Juliet* of 1599 also contain 'false starts' like those in Q2 *Hamlet*. But no attempt was made to get rid of these before a copy of the *Love's Labour's Lost* of 1598 and a copy of the

1609 edition (Q3) of *Romeo and Juliet*, a reprint of Q2, were sent off to Jaggard. Consequently, both the 'false starts' and the revisions intended to replace them are reproduced in the Folio versions of the two plays. Heminges and Condell were, it has to be remembered, professional actors not professional editors.

Such being the general practice of Shakespeare's fellow-actors-cum-editors, they would, had they followed it, have made Q2, or Smethwick's own Q3, or his Q4, if it was already in print, their choice as copy-text for the Folio *Hamlet*, annotating it somewhat, perhaps, but not interfering with it or altering it in any substantial way. In the event, however, they did not. Significantly, Shakespeare's 'false starts' at 3.2.157 and 158 are not reproduced in F; and this is but one of the numerous and very substantial differences between the two texts. This radical departure from a normal and, by the time F *Hamlet* was printed, well established procedure asks for an explanation. It is just possible that they rejected the idea of setting F directly from a copy of Q2, or Q3, or Q4 because they were aware of the multiplicity of printers' errors in them. This, however, seems most unlikely in the light of their readiness to use quartos that were far from models of accuracy as copy-texts for the Folio *Love's Labour's Lost* and *Romeo and Juliet*. A more plausible reason is that they found Q2, Q3, and Q4 quite unacceptable as proper representations of the play they had known and acted in for the best part of twenty years before they began to put the collection together. For them the 'true' text of *Hamlet* was that contained in the prompt-book at the Globe; and, in providing the copy for F that they did, they were, to the best of their knowledge, keeping the promise they had made 'To the great Variety of Readers' to publish the plays 'absolute in their numbers, as he [Shakespeare] conceived them'. It must be emphasized further that their knowledge was, by the time the printing of the Folio began in the middle of 1621, almost certainly unique; for, after the death of Burbage in 1619, they were the sole survivors among the King's Men of the leading actors in the Lord Chamberlain's Company for whom *Hamlet* was written. If anyone knew the play's history, it was they. Moreover, as the tragedy was very popular and widely known, it would be reasonable to assume that they would take special care to see that the text they published corresponded to that with which audiences were familiar.

What Heminges and Condell offered the reader was something

distinctly different from that offered by Q2 and the later quartos that stem from it. The major divergences are two: approximately 230 lines (the figures are Greg's, *SFF*, p. 316) found in Q2 do not appear in F; and some 70 lines not found in Q2 do appear in F. The 230 lines missing from F are almost entirely accounted for by what are quite evidently a series of cuts, varying in length from a single line to 58 lines. Beginning in the first scene, where a passage of 18 lines disappears, leaving no trace behind it, they continue through the play right down to the final scene, where three such cuts dispose between them of some 54 lines. Moreover, these cuts are remarkably deft, being carried out in a way that damages neither sense nor metre. Two of them, occurring in close proximity to one another, will serve, as Dover Wilson demonstrated (*MSH*, p. 28), to show the skill and understanding with which the surgery was done. The words excised to produce the text of F are italicized.

> Have you eyes?
> You cannot call it love; for at your age
> The heyday in the blood is tame, it's humble,
> And waits upon the judgement; and what judgement
> Would step from this to this? *Sense, sure, you have,*
> *Else you could not have motion. But sure that sense*
> *Is apoplexed; for madness would not err,*
> *Nor sense to ecstasy was ne'er so, thralled*
> *But it reserved some quantity of choice*
> *To serve in such a difference.* What devil was't
> That thus hath cozened you at hoodman-blind?
> *Eyes without feeling, feeling without sight,*
> *Ears without hands or eyes, smelling sans all,*
> *Or but a sickly part of one true sense*
> *Could not so mope.* O shame, where is thy blush?
> Rebellious hell,
> If thou canst mutine in a matron's bones,
> To flaming youth let virtue be as wax
> And melt in her own fire.
>
> (3.4.68–77)

Here line 72, left metrically incomplete by the beginning of the first cut, is made whole again by the tacking-on to it of 'What devil was't' from line 77, while the short line, 'Rebellious hell', is moved up, as it were, to fill out line 82. The metrical assurance and felicity with which the whole thing is managed is matched by the grasp on essentials that dictates the matter to be cut. The main concern of the passage is with Gertrude's lack of judgement in her choice of a second husband, which her son finds utterly incomprehensible, since she has reached an age when, in his opinion, sexual passion is on the wane. The lines that disappear expatiate on and amplify the connections between the judgement and the senses in a rather academic fashion that comes close to being something of a catalogue, but do nothing to alter or modify that central concern. The speech gains in strength and directness from their excision.

The cuts just considered, like most of the others of any length, can hardly be the work of the bookkeeper, as Dover Wilson thought they were when he examined them some fifty years ago (*MSH*, pp. 22–33). The informed understanding of matter that is far from easy, the critical sense that distinguishes between what is dramatically indispensable and what is not, together with the unerring ear for the rhythm of the line—all these abilities, so evident in the cutting, forbid any such deduction and point, instead, to Shakespeare himself as the exciser. Indeed, Dover Wilson comes close to making such an admission. As he proceeds with his analysis of the cutting, he gradually changes his position. Initially he pictures the 'abridger', to use his own term, as 'a man of the theatre with notions of stage-craft that are conventional, downright, a little crude' (p. 26). By the time he comes to consider the cuts made in the play-within-the-play, however, he is prepared to concede that they 'may indeed have been intended by Shakespeare' (p. 27); and he then goes on to express positive admiration for some of those made in 3.4. 'Shakespeare himself', he remarks, 'could hardly have pruned his own verse more tenderly' (p. 29). His final impression of the 'abridger' moves even nearer to an identification of him with the playwright: 'In short, (if he was not Shakespeare himself) he must have been a competent person' (p. 32). The bathetic phrase, 'a competent person', makes it pretty clear that by this time Wilson had lost all faith in his own alternative, the bookkeeper. Greg, it should be added, is more definite about the issue. Making an exception of the long cut in the scene where Fortinbras appears on stage for the first time, 4.4, he then remarks: 'as regards the other cuts we have some reasons to believe that they were made by [Shakespeare's] own hand' (*SFF*, p. 318).

To attribute the cuts in F to an 'abridger' is to beg the crucial question of why they were made. It is true that as *Hamlet* is the longest play in the whole Shakespeare canon, a need to abbreviate it in production seems, on the face of things, the most obvious and sensible answer to that question; but then comes the realization that, as Greg points out, 'the omission of 225 lines out of nearly 4,000 is not very much and does not suggest any serious attempt to shorten the play' (*SFF*, p. 317). But, while the cuts have little effect on the play's length, they do alter its pace. Their main effect is to tighten and speed up the action by removing from the text matter that can fairly be described in the Prince's own words as 'caviare to the general'. One can well imagine some members of the audience at the Globe becoming restive as Horatio gives his account of the omens that preceded the assassination of Julius Caesar in the first passage to disappear (Appendix A, i), or when Hamlet discourses on the unhappy consequences 'one defect' can have for both men and nations (Appendix A, ii). And the least sign of restiveness would be fatal to the primary dramatic purpose each passage is designed to serve: to hold the interest of the spectators so fixed on the speaker that they fail to observe the entry of the Ghost. As for Osric's eulogy of Laertes and Hamlet's parody of it, since both evidently called for a better acquaintance with courtly affectations of speech than either Roberts's Compositor X or his press-corrector could muster, it is not surprising that Appendix A, xvii should have gone the same way as the superfluous Lord who makes his entry after 5.2.155 to report that Osric has succeeded in conveying Hamlet's message to the King.

In the latter part of the play, from Act 4, Scene 5 onwards, the major casualty caused by the increased emphasis on action is characterization. In Q2 the orotund rhetoric in which Claudius cloaks his deviousness from the moment he first speaks at the opening of 1.2 is admirably sustained; but in F Shakespeare, now bent on pushing things forward to their conclusion, reduces it considerably. In 4.7, the scene in which the King receives Hamlet's letter and adroitly makes use of it to mould Laertes to his purpose, his characteristically roundabout introduction of the subject of fencing, by way of flattery of Laertes and the suggestion that the latter's skill in the art has aroused Hamlet's envy (Appendix A, xiv) is excised completely. Similarly, much, though not all, of his clever needling of Laertes also disappears.

These cuts are, however, no more than minor alterations by

comparison with what happens to 4.4, which is ruthlessly slashed from 66 lines to 8. Its main purpose in Q2 is to reveal through the last of Hamlet's soliloquies, 'How all occasions do inform against me', triggered off by his dialogue with the Norwegian Captain, that he is still the Hamlet who could speak a similar soliloquy, 'O what a rogue and peasant slave am I', in a very similar situation at the end of 2.2. In spite of all that has happened since then, he is fundamentally unchanged; he still does not know

> Why yet I live to say this thing's to do,
> Sith I have cause, and will, and strength, and means
> To do't.
>
> (Appendix A, xiii. 36–8)

The soliloquy, for all its felicity of phrasing, is redundant. It tells us nothing we do not know already, except that the Prince has become unrealistic. A prisoner under guard and on his way to England, he clearly does not have the means he speaks of. For an audience eager to learn whether he will find those means and thus avoid the ignominious fate Claudius has planned for him, the soliloquy is anticlimactic and disappointing. F therefore reduces the scene drastically, and thus makes a rapid transition from the old matter of Hamlet's failure to the new interests created by Ophelia's madness and Laertes' rebellion. At the same time, it also gives the actor playing Hamlet a much needed rest. He has been on stage almost continuously since he entered, '*reading on a book*', about a third of the way through 2.2. Greg's note on the cut is to the point. 'The most surprising thing about it', he remarks, 'is that it did not include the whole scene, for there seems no point whatever in retaining the eight lines of Fortinbras's rather otiose speech. Perhaps it was thought necessary that the audience should at least be on bowing acquaintance with him before his appearance at the end of the play' (*SFF*, p. 317 n. 37).

The cutting of Q2 is, then, the most important part of a logical and coherent process of revision designed to make a better acting version with a wide appeal. The excisions leave the action untouched but free the dialogue from some intricate and unnecessary elaborations, as well as from some matter that is rather tangential to the play's main concerns. A typical instance of the former is the King's discourse, after 4.7.99, on the way in which time eats into the essence of love, which is, in any case, self-destructive.

Before he finishes with the subject, even Claudius seems to feel that he is overworking it, since he cuts himself short with the words 'But to the quick of th'ulcer'. Moreover, the discourse itself is distinctly repetitive of the Player King's lucubrations on the same topic at 3.2.176–99, a passage that has significantly left no mark whatever on Q1, suggesting that it had been cut from the acting version of *Hamlet* on which the reporter relied. Typical instances of the tangential matter are Appendix A, i and ii, the first describing the omens that preceded the killing of Julius Caesar, and the second regretting the notoriety of the Danes as habitual drunkards.

But, as well as making cuts in the Q2 text, F also makes additions to it. Amounting to about seventy lines in all, these additions are substantially accounted for by three passages: 2.2.238–67, 2.2.333–58, and 5.2.69–81. They are described as 'additions' here because this seems the obvious answer to the question of why they appear in F only. But this is not the answer that commended itself to Dover Wilson and to those who have followed him. They regard all three passages as belonging originally to the manuscript behind Q2, and their failure to appear in that text as a consequence of either compositorial carelessness or of deliberate excision prompted by a concern not to give offence to Anne of Denmark, whose native land Hamlet calls a prison. Jenkins is quite categorical about the matter. He writes of the first two:

Both certainly are omissions from Q2 and not additions in F. The excision of the first has left unmistakable clues in the adjacent *buts*, an anomalous capital and a false presumption of continuity: 'but your newes is not true; But in the beaten way of friendship . . .' As for the second, the missing account of the boy actors is being led up to and reflected on in what remains in Q2: it explains the transition from the players who have lost popularity to the new king who has gained it. (p. 44)

However, as he agrees with most critics of recent times that *Hamlet* was written in 1600, whereas it was not until the middle of 1601 that the War of the Theatres, alluded to in the second passage, came to a head, he has to hypothesize that the matter in question was added to the version behind Q2 months after the rest of it had been completed, and then either excised from it before it went to the printer or inadvertently dropped from it during the course of the printing. Not quite so assured about a Q2 omission at 5.2.69–81, he eventually concludes that 'the incomplete sense and sentence (whereby "'is't not perfect conscience?" lacks its necessary complement)' is decisively in its favour.

The obstinate fact remains, however, that in each case Q2 makes good sense as it stands, and apparently did so to the adapter —almost certainly Davenant[1]—responsible for the preparation of the acting version that lies behind the influential Players' Quarto of 1676, who evidently found no difficulty in these Q2 readings, since he preserves them substantially unaltered. Had he considered them in any way obscure, he would not have hesitated for a moment to change Shakespeare's wording. Adjacent *buts* are by no means uncommon in Shakespeare. In Q2 *Hamlet*, to go no further, we have 'but you may say, not well, | But y'ft be he I meane' (2.1.17–18); 'What ist but to be nothing els but mad, | But let that go' (2.2.94–5); and 'It is but foolery, but it is such a kinde of gaingiuing' (5.2.162). Nor, within the context in which it occurs, is there anything particularly anomalous about the capitalization of the second *But*. Signatures F1 and F1^v of Q2 are so full of capitalized words coming after a comma and at the beginning of a line of print as to suggest that Compositor X thought he was setting verse. Some examples are: 'I sir to be honest as this world goes | Is to be one man pickt out of tenne thousand' (2.2.178–9). 'Conception is a blessing, | But as your daughter may conceaue' (2.2.184–5); 'on Fortunes lap, | We are not the very button' (2.2.227), and 'she is a strumpet, | What newes?' (2.2.233–4). As for the lack of continuity, Hamlet's sudden changes of direction are one of the most marked features of the scene. He has, for example, already said to Polonius: 'For if the sunne breede maggots in a dead dogge, being a good kissing carrion. Have you a daughter?' (2.2.181–2). It is a leap of the mind such as this which takes him from the fickleness of public favour in its treatment of actors to its fickleness in its attitude to his uncle. It is undeniable that 'is't not perfect conscience' lacks its necessary complement, but Hamlet has said enough to leave one in no doubt as to what that complement would have been had his speech not been interrupted by the entry of Osric. The question mark following 'conscience' was probably supplied by Compositor X.

Why, then, since Q2 makes good sense in all three cases, did Shakespeare make additions to it? The additions have at least one

---

[1] See Hazelton Spencer, *Shakespeare Improved* (1927, repr. New York, 1963), 174–83.

thing in common : they provide more explanation, making it easier for an audience to understand what follows, because Q2's transitions, though intelligible, are also abrupt. The first of them brings out more fully the evasiveness of Rosencrantz and Guildenstern, which the Prince, fresh from his encounter with Polonius, so quickly detects in Q2. In the second Shakespeare seizes on the War of the Theatres as a means of strengthening the analogy Hamlet draws between the public reaction to the new players, the Children of the Blackfriars, and to the new king, Claudius. As for the third, its evident purpose is to provide more reasons than does Q2 for Hamlet's readiness to take part in the fencing match: Horatio's reminder to him that he has little time left in which to accomplish his purpose; and the Prince's expressed intention to treat Laertes better than he has done hitherto, which makes it virtually impossible for him to reject Laertes' challenge when it comes a few moments later.

At this point another peculiarity of F comes into focus: the numerous brief additions it makes to the text of Q2, ranging, in the words of Harold Jenkins who has made a careful study of them,[1] 'from single words to passages no more than a line in length' (p. 31). It is not certain that all the instances he cites are in fact additions, because the Q2 compositors were prone to omit single words and short phrases, but in many cases there can be little doubt, since the addition disturbs the metre. It has this effect at 1.2.135, where F replaces Q2's 'Fie on't, ah fie, 'tis an unweeded garden' with 'Fie on't Oh fie, fie, 'tis an unweeded garden'; at 1.5.29, where Q2's 'Haste me to know't, that I with wings as swift' becomes in F 'Haste, haste me to know it, | That with wings as swift', with an omission of the essential word 'I' covering the metrical lapse at the expense of sense and grammar; and again at 1.5.107, where F reads: 'My Tables, my Tables; meet it is I set it down' in place of Q2's 'My tables, meet it is I set it down'. Jenkins lists sixty-five instances of these 'playhouse interpolations', as he calls them, most, though by no means all, of them occurring in the part of Hamlet. Sometimes referred to as 'actors' additions', they are not all of the same kind. The majority take the form of repeated words or phrases, like those quoted above, which do indeed have the appearance of the sort of thing actors are easily tempted into

[1] 'Playhouse Interpolations in the Folio Text of *Hamlet*', *Studies in Bibliography*, 13 (1961), 31–47.

doing, especially when given the cue provided by such bits of repetition in Q2 itself as 'Words, words, words' (2.2.192) and 'except my life, except my life, except my life' (2.2.215–16). Others, however, such as Hamlet's cry 'Mother, mother, mother', spoken from *within* before Gertrude tells Polonius, 'withdraw, I hear him coming' (3.4.8), seem designed to give the audience a stronger signal than Q2 has to offer. Jenkins sums up the effect of these 'playhouse interpolations' thus:

They never add to the sense nor introduce any significant word which the surrounding context does not supply. Many of them will no doubt seem harmless: perhaps we need not grieve if some continue in performance. A producer will do small damage to the play if he permits the gravedigger to make an extra reference to the skull or Polonius to shriek for help three times instead of once. But their cumulative effect is to modify the dialogue in a direction which is not towards subtlety. (p. 42)

It is a just verdict, though a decidedly austere one in its reluctance to make any concession to the popular theatre's fondness for broad and explicit effects; but the most fascinating feature of it is that it applies equally well both to the cuts F makes in the Q2 text and to the three long passages it adds to that text, for their 'cumulative effect' is also 'to modify the dialogue in a direction which is not towards subtlety'. No matter what the source of the playhouse interpolations may have been—and proof that they were not Shakespeare's is still lacking—they are so much in keeping with the general character of F as a whole that the playwright could hardly have objected to their inclusion in it, even had he felt like doing so. It is significant that a considerable number of them were introduced into the text at an early stage in the play's history when Shakespeare must have been taking a very active interest in it still, for they also appear in Q1. It has to be remembered that he was himself an actor, and that, as such, he would value and take into account the opinions and suggestions of the leading actors in the company, who were, in all probability, better equipped than anyone else in England at the time to recognize what would work on the stage and what would not. It is too often overlooked that when Shakespeare made Richard Burbage famous by writing the role of Richard III for him, Burbage repaid him by acting that part in a way that helped to make *Richard III* and its author famous.

The features of F considered so far—the cuts it makes, the

additions it makes, and the 'playhouse interpolations' it finds a place for—are, then, consistent with one another and serve the same purpose in that they lead to a more direct and a more readily intelligible action than that of Q2. Moreover, A. C. Bradley was emphatically of the opinion that Hamlet's habit of repeating himself—and the illustrations he chooses include some of the stigmatized 'interpolations'—goes far towards individualizing him (pp. 118–20). Other characteristics of F seem to be parts of the same general trend towards a greater concern with performance. The most obvious of them is, as one might expect, its treatment of stage directions. It improves on Q2 in naming characters as they come on. The earlier text makes no mention, for example, of the two ambassadors, Voltemand and Cornelius, in the direction that opens 1.2, though they must be present under one or the other of the two umbrellas '*Counsaile*' and '*Alijs*'. F, however, postponing their entry to line 25, names them in it. Similarly it has '*Enter young Osricke*' at 5.2.81, instead of Q2's '*Enter a Courtier*'. In the same scene it provides the indispensable piece of clarification, '*In scuffling they change Rapiers*', at a point where Q2 leaves actors as well as readers completely in the dark about what is happening; and it specifies that there be '*Flagons of Wine*' on the table that is brought in at line 170. It pays far more attention to the need for *Guards*, *Attendants*, and the like, with their *Torches*, *Trumpets*, and so forth than does Q2. Furthermore, it represents accurately, as the corresponding direction in Q1 shows, what happens at the beginning of 1.2, with Hamlet, 'the most immediate' to the throne of Denmark, coming in after Claudius and Gertrude, not at the tail-end of the procession as he does in Q2, where this initial direction is, in effect, a scenario, in which the characters are mentioned in the order in which they will speak and come to take part in the action (see note to 1.2.0). It is also remarkable for the care it shows in providing a single speech heading, that is almost invariably adhered to throughout, for each character.

Yet, heedful though it is of the demands of performance, F is not wholly systematic about them; and some rather strange and puzzling consequences follow from what Greg, echoing Dover Wilson, describes as its 'general urge to reduce the number of supers' (*SFF*, p. 319), though in fact it affects some speaking parts as well. At the opening of 3.2, for example, it replaces the precise stage direction of Q2, '*Enter Hamlet, and three of the Players*', with the imprecise direction, '*Enter Hamlet, and two or three of the Players*', thus introducing into the text the kind of permissiveness that performance cannot tolerate. Later in the same scene when Q2 calls for '*some three or foure*' to carry off the body of the Player King at the end of the dumb show (3.2.126.10), F reduces that requirement to the equally indefinite '*some two or three Mutes*'. Later still, at line 275, Hamlet calls for some music and specifies 'The recorders'. In response to this request, which takes the same form in both texts, Q2 very properly reads: '*Enter the Players with Recorders*'. F, however, changes this direction into '*Enter one with a Recorder*', and proceeds to modify the dialogue to fit the singular form. A subsequent alteration of the same kind has larger consequences. The direction in Q2 at 4.3.0 is '*Enter King, and two or three*', a perfect example of the imprecision so often found in foul papers. It is followed by a speech in Claudius's best diplomatic vein, justifying his conduct since he learned of Hamlet's killing of Polonius and especially his plan to send the Prince off to England. F manages things rather differently. Taking account of the failure of the 'two or three' to reply—they have no chance to, as the speech is interrupted by the arrival of Rosencrantz '*and all the rest*'—it drops them entirely, and thus turns Claudius's speech into a soliloquy of the informative plot-forwarding kind so common in *Richard III*.

These changes can hardly be the work of the bookkeeper. The last of them makes a radical change that would, one imagines, be out of his province; and the others signally fail to substitute exact for inexact requirements. Moreover, the whole procedure, if it is designed to economize on actors, seems pointless, because it does no such thing. Scene 2 of Act 3, the most demanding scene in the entire play for speaking as well as non-speaking parts, needs, even in Q2, a minimum of eleven actors who speak, and four who do not. In F, which becomes quite prodigal in its requirements at this stage, still more supers are called for, as it adds to those taking part in the royal entry at line 86 '*other Lords attendant with his [Claudius's] Guard*'. A company having the resources to cope with this scene will have no trouble in dealing with any other, especially after the end of 3.4, which leaves Polonius free for other roles—to return resurrected and rejuvenated as Osric?—and even less after the end of 4.3 in F and of 4.4 in Q2, for then Rosencrantz and Guildenstern become available for other duties—to continue their former association, perhaps, as the Two Clowns of 5.1.

How, then, did these alterations make their way into the play, and who was responsible for them? The general impression they give is that of an author tinkering with his work as he copies it fair or revises it, though tinkering is not the right word to describe the change at the beginning of 4.3. Still less will it do to describe the alteration F makes to the opening of 4.5. Here the initial stage direction in Q2 is '*Enter Horatio, Gertrard, and a Gentleman*', a distinctly anomalous direction, since it breaks the rule of precedence by naming Horatio before it names the Queen. Unwilling to admit Ophelia, who is now distracted, Gertrude nevertheless listens to the Gentleman's account of her wild behaviour, and then to Horatio's suggestion, ending with the request 'Let her come in', that it would be wise to hear what Ophelia has to say. But before the Queen has any opportunity to answer that request Ophelia makes her entry unbidden. The whole incident is messy; it does not hang together as it should. It looks as though Horatio is a late addition to the initial direction, and as though the speech heading for the Queen, to whom 'Let her come in' should rightly belong, has been misplaced. F puts things right. Almost predictably by now it dispenses with the redundant Gentleman, and, at the same time, restores the rule of precedence by reading '*Enter Queene and Horatio*'. It then proceeds to give the Gentleman's two speeches to Horatio; and the words 'Let her come in', together with the two lines that precede them, to the Queen. This is as neat a bit of revision as one could wish to see, since it has the further virtue of providing Gertrude with the opportunity for addressing four gnomic lines to the audience while Horatio is busy admitting Ophelia, instead of having to speak them as a rather clumsy aside after Ophelia has come in, which is what happens in Q2.

The differences between F and Q2 discussed so far raise the central issue concerning F: what precisely was the nature of the copy for it that Heminges and Condell handed to Jaggard? At this point it becomes necessary to examine F more closely, starting from what we know of the printing process. The work of Charlton Hinman, Trevor Howard-Hill, and Gary Taylor[1] has shown that F

---

[1] Charlton Hinman, *The Printing and Proof-Reading of the First Folio of Shakespeare*, 2 vols. (Oxford, 1963); Trevor Howard-Hill, *Compositors B and E . . . and Some Recent Studies* (1976), and *A Reassessment of Compositors in the First Folio Tragedies* (1977), both privately circulated; and Gary Taylor, 'The Shrinking Compositor A of the Shakespeare First Folio', *Studies in Bibliography*, 34 (1981), 96–107.

Hamlet was set by three compositors, B, E, and I, who divided the task between them as shown in Table 1.

Table 1

Compositor	Signatures	Pages	Text
B	nn4^v–5^v	152–4	1.1.0–1.2.164
I	nn6–oo1	155–257	1.2.165–1.5.21
B	oo1	257	1.5.22–57[1]
I	oo1^v–2	258–9	1.5.58–2.1.104
B	oo2^v–3	260–1	2.1.105–2.2.213
I	oo3^v	262	2.2.214–2.2.337
B	oo4–pp4	263–75	2.2.337–4.7.51
I	pp4–pp4^v	275–6	4.7.51–5.1.21
E	pp5–pp5^v	277–8	5.1.22–5.1.266
B	pp6–qq1^v	279–82	5.1.267–end

The two pages, 277 and 278, set by Compositor E are of special interest, because much can be deduced from them about the kind of copy he was using. E seems to have been the least experienced and least skilled of the workmen employed in setting the Folio; and his contributions to it are marked by a painstaking doggedness. In the course of his two pages of *Hamlet* E makes good no fewer than seven omissions from Q2: four single words—'frame' (5.1.42), 'all' (136), 'nowadays' (157), and 'Shards' (221)—one phrase —'to Yaughan' (58–9)—and two longer passages—'Why, he had none . . . without arms' (33–6) and 'is this . . . recoveries' (100–101). These invaluable corrections of Q2 omissions make it plain that the copy E was working from was either manuscript or an exemplar of Q2 that had been carefully annotated. But, as well as supplying words and passages missing from Q2, E also introduces some strange mistakes of his own which take one further towards a definition of his copy; for it seems most unlikely that anyone working from Q2 could have turned its 'sexton [Sexten]' (5.1.153) into 'sixteen [sixteene]' or its 'treble woe' (5.1.236) into 'terrible woer'. These errors are explicable only on the assumption that E was relying on manuscript copy that he had difficulty in deciphering.

---

[1] B set the last 35 lines on oo1, and I the last 20 lines on pp4.

Confirmation that E's copy was indeed manuscript has been provided by Gary Taylor.[1] He notes that in the plays set from printed copy and preceding *Hamlet* in which E is known to have had a hand—*Titus Andronicus*, *Romeo and Juliet*, and *Troilus and Cressida* (the pre-cancellation pages)—E's treatment of the punctuation of his copy is extremely conservative. In not one of the sample pages from these plays that Taylor has examined 'does the proportion of retained to altered punctuation fall below 3-to-1, and it occasionally rises as high as 6-to-1' (p. 45). Furthermore, the same pattern persists in the pages of *King Lear* which E set after finishing his work on *Hamlet*. It is not to be found, however, in his two pages of *Hamlet*; for in them, if one accepts Alice Walker's view that an annotated exemplar of Q2 served as copy, 'then the proportion of retained to altered punctuation is 53/82 (pp5) and 65/99 (pp5ᵛ). In other words, for these two pages the ratio of retention to variation is 2-to-3, whereas in the pages from the three plays where E is known to have set from printed copy it ranges from 3-to-1 to 6-to-1' (p. 46). Taylor therefore concludes that E did not set his pages of *Hamlet* from printed copy; and, further, that if E was not using such copy, then neither were the other two compositors concerned in the setting of *Hamlet*, since they were both more experienced workmen than E and, consequently, better equipped to cope with manuscript.

There is other evidence to show that B and I were using manuscript copy. Both repeatedly make mistakes which are intelligible as misreadings of handwriting but not of print. B has, for example, 'talkes' for 'takes' (1.1.145); '*Pons Chanson*' for 'pious chanson' (2.2.412); 'to take' for 'totall' (2.2.448); 'inobled' for 'mobled' (2.2.493, 494, and 495); and, to go no further, 'surge' for 'sugar' (3.1.49). Compositor I, for his part, prints 'wake' for 'walke' (1.2.244); 'treble' for 'tenable' (1.2.250); 'eye' for 'die [= dye]' (1.3.128); 'bak'd' for 'barckt [= barked]' (1.5.71); and the like. Moreover, both frequently employ a punctuation which, as Dover Wilson illustrates at length (*MSH*, pp. 192–215), makes nonsense of passages that are perfectly straightforward in Q2. Typical instances from B's stints are:

---

[1] 'The Folio copy for *Hamlet*, *King Lear*, and *Othello*', *Shakespeare Quarterly*, 34 (1983), 44–61.

F   Which done, she tooke the Fruites of my Aduice,
      And he repulsed. A short Tale to make,

Q2   Which done, she tooke the fruites of my aduise:
      And he repell'd, a short tale to make

(2.2.144–5)

and

F   I do beleeue you. Think what now you speake:

Q2   I do belieue you thinke what now you speake,

(3.2.174)

Among I's unhappier pointings, combined in the first instance with muddle and omission, are the following:

F   A Violet in the youth of Primy Nature;
      Froward, not permanent; sweet not lasting
      The suppliance of a minute? No more.

Q2   A Violet in the youth of primy nature,
      Forward, not permanent, sweete, not lasting,
      The perfume and suppliance of a minute
      No more.

(1.3.7–10)

and

F   Hauing euer seene. In the prenominate crimes,
      The youth you breath of guilty,

Q2   Hauing euer seene in the prenominat crimes
      The youth you breath of guiltie,

(2.1.42–3)

It is hard to believe that any compositor setting directly from a copy of Q2 could have distorted its plain meaning to the extent that it has been distorted in these and similar passages of F. A mere glance at Q3, printed for John Smethwick in 1611 from a copy of Q2, is sufficient to confirm this impression. Q3 makes its mistakes. It omits some short speeches; it has its misprints; and it emends wrongly; but, while using a heavier punctuation than Q2 does, it never makes the crass errors in pointing which so disfigure F. The discrepancies between the two primary texts in this matter of punctuation alone are too many and too great to allow of the notion that F was printed from a copy of Q2, even from a very extensively annotated copy of it.

Those who have espoused the theory that the text of F depends to some degree on that of Q2—and they make a formidable and influential group, since it includes Alice Walker, J. M. Nosworthy, W. W. Greg, and Harold Jenkins—attach great importance to a number of minutiae which, though not significant individually, nevertheless have, if the interpretation placed on them is correct, a certain cumulative cogency. The pointers to such a dependence consist of common errors in the two texts, unusual spellings of the same word, agreements in capitalization, identical abbreviations in stage directions, and, to quote Jenkins, 'the retention in F of small anomalous details when Q2 appears already to have taken them from Q1' (p. 67).

At first sight the argument built on these details appears a strong one; but a closer scrutiny of it reveals its vulnerability. Some of the weaknesses in it were exposed by J. K. Walton in 1971; and the present editor has found many more.[1] To repeat these criticisms *in extenso* would merely invite tedium; but a few salient points will serve to illustrate the shaky nature of the hypothesis. The first of the 'common errors' cited by Jenkins is Q2 'desseigne'/F 'designe' (1.1.94), instead of 'designd' as Shakespeare presumably wrote it. This is indeed a 'common error' in another sense, for the misreading of *d* as *e* is frequent in both texts; but there is no necessary dependence of the one wrong reading on the other, and the marked difference in spelling argues strongly against it. Nor is the appearance of Q2 'somnet'/F 'Somnet', meaning 'summit', at 3.3.18 a reliable indication of such dependence. The word occurs on two other occasions in Shakespeare: at *Hamlet*, 1.4.49, where it is again 'Somnet' in Q2 but 'Sonnet' in F; and at *Lear*, 4.6.57, where it is 'Somnet' in F, 'sommons' in Q1, and 'summons' in Q2. From all this it would seem likely that the peculiar form 'somnet' is an idiosyncratic Shakespearian spelling faithfully reproduced from manuscript copy by the various compositors concerned.

The same observation applies to many of the agreements of the two texts in unexpected capitalization. To take but one striking example, Q2 'Choples'/F 'Chaplesse' (5.1.84), in contrast to the normal use of the lower case in both for 'chopfalne' (5.1.183), is probably a consequence of Shakespeare's well known tendency, amply demonstrated in *Sir Thomas More* D and in *Coriolanus*, to

---

[1] J. K. Walton, *The Quarto Copy for the First Folio of Shakespeare* (Dublin, 1971), 175–83 and 208–10; see also n. at p. 100.

employ 'a capital *C* initially, for no apparent reason save that it was an easy letter to form' (*Coriolanus*, ed. Dover Wilson, p. 133). It is, perhaps, no accident that of the twenty-seven examples of more or less unexpected capitalization listed by Nosworthy (p. 148), the largest number, six in all, is made up of words beginning with the letter *c*.

The evidence of stage directions which are 'sometimes identically abbreviated even where F was under no pressure of space' (Jenkins, p. 67) is far from conclusive, since such abbreviation is common in F. It reads, for example, '*Exit Laer.*' at 1.3.87, where Q2 has '*Exit Laertes.*', and '*Exit Ambass.*' at 2.2.85, where Q2 has '*Exeunt Embassadors.*' In both cases there is ample room for the unabbreviated form, had the F compositors seen fit to use it.

Perhaps the most important of Jenkins's categories for textual purposes is the anomalous bits of detail in which F, he argues, follows Q2, which, in its turn, originally picked them up from Q1. The first of them is 'smot' (1.1.63) in all three texts. It looks impressive at first sight, but is it? *OED* recognizes it as a sixteenth- and seventeenth-century form of the past tense of 'smite'. Shakespeare uses that past tense five times. In *The Tempest*, where the spelling is probably Ralph Crane's, it is 'smote' (4.1.172); in *Othello* it is 'smoate' in F and 'smote' in Q1 (5.2.356); but in *Love's Labour's Lost* Q1 and F at 4.3.27, and in *Coriolanus* at 3.1.317, it is 'smot', exactly as it is in *Hamlet*. Still less reason is there for assuming that Q2 'allies'/F 'Allies' (1.5.67) must have its roots in Q1. There is nothing in the least unusual or anomalous about this plural of 'alley'. It is 'allies' in *The Comedy of Errors* (4.2.58), its only other appearance in the canon; Dekker writes it 'Allies' in *The Magnificent Entertainment* (l. 1038); and even more significantly *OED* states explicitly that the plural was 'formerly often *allies*'. It might well do so, since five of the six illustrations it gives for the years 1594 to 1625 take precisely this form.

Since so many of the spellings and the like just examined need not have come into F by way of Q2, but admit of alternative explanations, their combined evidence seems anything but decisive. It would be foolish to contend that whoever was responsible for selecting and preparing the copy for F that went to Jaggard's printing house never consulted Q2; but the signs of his having done so are at best ambiguous and fall far short of proof.

There are, then, good and sufficient reasons for thinking that F

was set from manuscript copy; and that copy plainly has its own
authority, since time after time F gives what is obviously a right
reading where Q2 gives a wrong reading. That said, however, the
precise nature and extent of that authority still has to be determined, for F, like Q2, is full of manifest errors, though they are not
usually—and most fortunately not—the same errors as those of
Q2. An index to their frequency is provided by a list compiled by
Gary Taylor. It is made up of readings, occurring in Compositor B's
stints in the plays he helped to set from either manuscript copy or
heavily annotated quarto copy, that have been unanimously rejected by the following editions: old Cambridge, New Cambridge,
New Penguin, Signet, New Arden, Alexander, Riverside, Sisson,
and the forthcoming Oxford Complete Works (where available).
Twenty-six plays are involved; and *Hamlet* easily tops the list. In it
B, who set no fewer than twenty-one and a half of the thirty and
a half pages it takes up in the Folio, perpetrated 38 literal and 130
substantive errors, an average of 6 substantive errors a page. The
nearest approach to these figures among the other plays Taylor
examines was in *Antony and Cleopatra*, generally thought to have
been printed from Shakespeare's foul papers (Greg, *SFF*, pp.
398–403). B set twenty and a half of its twenty-eight and a half
pages, making 76 substantive errors in the process, for an average
of 3.7 a page, as compared with his overall average of 2 a page.

Two deductions, that do not necessarily exclude one another,
can be made from these figures. First, that the manuscript copy B,
along with his fellow-compositors, used when setting *Hamlet* was
quite exceptionally difficult to cope with; and, secondly, that it was
in some way corrupt. It is plain that the handwriting was
troublesome, since over fifty of B's mistakes are due to misreading.
Furthermore—and this applies to the other F compositors as well
—many of his misreadings are similar to those which affect the text
of Q2. Four sets of parallel readings tell one much.

Q2	F	
No fairy takes	No Faiery talkes	(1.1.145)
Perchaunce twill walke againe	perchance 'twill wake againe	(1.2.244)
Aeneas talke to *Dido*	*Aeneas* Tale to *Dido*	(2.2.437–8)
Now is he totall Gules	Now is he to take Geulles	(2.2.448)

The letters *a*, *l*, *k*, and *e* in combination have defeated three different compositors here. X, who set all the examples from Q2, has three right and one, 'talke' for 'Tale', wrong. Compositor B supplies the correct reading at this point, but goes astray with 'talkes' for 'takes', and with 'to take' for 'totall'. Compositor I reads 'wake' instead of 'walke'. It looks very much as though all three men were faced with the same handwriting; and, as X was setting from foul papers, the handwriting in question should be that of Shakespeare himself. The likelihood that it was is strengthened by the fact that the same sort of pattern as that which appears above is apparent again in misreadings caused by the playwright's failure to discriminate clearly enough between *a* and *o*, and between *e* and *o*, as well as in those created by his inaccuracy in counting his minim strokes.

Perhaps the most obvious sign of corruption in the manuscript behind F is the marks F bears of what Dover Wilson, the first editor to notice it and recognize its significance, calls 'an active memory' (*MSH*, p. 59). As he sets out the evidence in detail (pp. 50–67), no more than a brief summary of it seems necessary. He observes that in Q2 there are five patent misreadings—the true reading being given by F—resulting from repetition. Typical of them is the following at 2.2.367–8 in which the repeated phrase is italicized:

Q2   Let mee comply with you in this garb: *let me* extent to the
       players ...

F   Let me comply with you in the Garbe, lest my extent to the
       players ...

In F, however, there are no fewer than fifteen instances of exactly the same kind of error, a discrepancy which suggests that since the repetitions in Q2 are probably compositorial, some other factor or agent must have intervened in F to account for their much higher frequency there. Wilson then goes on to say, very justifiably: 'Compositors may repeat words, but they are extremely unlikely to anticipate' (p. 54). Yet in F he detects some twenty-three examples of anticipation, whereas Q2 can provide two only. In fact, it is doubtful whether his two instances from Q2 and his first six from F, in all of which the 'anticipation' occurs within the line, are true illustrations of the phenomenon. When, for example, Compositor I set 'The vertue of his *feare*: but you must feare', instead of Q2's 'The vertue of his will, but you must feare' (1.3.16), he had probably sought to memorize the entire line and then allowed his memory of the last part of it to influence his setting of the first. But even if one discounts Wilson's first six instances, seventeen still remain, including such impressive examples as the following, in which the misreading and the anticipated words that gave rise to it lie as much as ten lines apart (3.2.342 and 350–1):

Q2   it wil discourse most eloquent musique
F   it will discourse most *excellent Musicke*
     there is much *Musicke, excellent* Voice, in this little Organe . . .

More striking still is Hamlet's substitution in F of 'Satyricall slaue' for Q2's 'satericall rogue' at 2.2.196, an anticipation of 'O what a rogue and pesant slaue am I' at 2.2.538.

From this evidence Wilson deduces that the 'agent responsible for the preparation of the F1 *Hamlet* must have been a copyist possessed of a pretty thorough knowledge of the play, upon which he relied over-much in the preparation of his transcript' (p. 64). As for the identity of this copyist, 'He was', says Wilson, 'a player or theatrical scrivener thoroughly familiar with the play upon the stage, and (since the whole Folio bears the endorsement of Heminge and Condell) he must assuredly have belonged to their company and to the Globe theatre' (pp. 64–5). Jenkins, on the other hand, thinks it 'more likely that the confusion arose in the memory of the actors' (p. 63), but he fails to explain why so many of them were prone both to repeat and to anticipate; for the double malady is not confined to one or two of the roles. Seven of the repetitions occur in Hamlet's part; two in Polonius's; and the remaining six are shared by Ophelia, the Player King, Rosencrantz, Horatio, Claudius, and Laertes. Similarly, Hamlet leads the way with anticipations, but Polonius, Horatio, Marcellus, Fortinbras, the Ghost, and Claudius all contribute to them. A single source of these two kinds of corruption seems far more credible than ten such sources; and, as Jenkins admits, it is very hard to see how actors' mistakes could make their way into a playhouse manuscript. No such difficulty arises if the author of the errors was the copyist himself.

Who, then, was this copyist 'possessed of a pretty thorough knowledge of the play', and belonging to Shakespeare's company at the Globe? The simplest and most obvious answer to that question is William Shakespeare himself. The whole matter of repetition combined with anticipation fits in perfectly with what we know of the behaviour and practice of other authors when copying out their own writings, and especially of authors who wrote rapidly, as Shakespeare is supposed to have done. E. A. J. Honigmann, in his *The Stability of Shakespeare's Text* (1965), has shown convincingly (pp. 200–3) how common both these phenomena are in Thomas Heywood's *The Escapes of Jupiter*, a work in which the most prolific of all Shakespeare's fellow dramatists copied out and incorporated whole passages from his own *Golden Age* and *Silver Age*.

There is no inherent improbability in the theory that Shakespeare made a fair copy of *Hamlet*. As Fredson Bowers has remarked, 'there is no evidence whatever . . . in Henslowe that an author ever submitted for payment anything but a fair copy' (*On Editing Shakespeare and the Elizabethan Dramatists*, p. 15); and while it is true that Henslowe's dealings were mainly with the Admiral's Men, not with the Lord Chamberlain's Men, there is no good reason for thinking that the latter adopted a different practice in this matter from that of their rivals, though they may, of course, have had some special arrangement with their own regular playwright. Moreover, there is a wide measure of agreement that *Julius Caesar* was indeed set from a fair copy. In the case of *Hamlet*, if the author's foul papers were anything like as messy and difficult as the state of Q2 suggests they were, a fair copy would, one imagines, have been an absolute desideratum; and the making of it would have the further advantage of giving Shakespeare the opportunity of taking into account criticisms and suggestions from the leading actors in the company.

Assuming that this, or something like it, is what happened, it seems reasonable to speculate further. Shakespeare probably set about his task with the intention of doing no more than tidying up what he had written and freeing it from some of its more peripheral content. But then, like most writers who copy out their own work, he was impelled to make improvements, or what seemed to be improvements, in it, and, almost without realizing it, was soon busy revising his earlier draft in ways that he had not contemplated. It has already been argued (pp. 105–10) that the cuts in F show every sign of his hand, and that the three long passages peculiar to F are additions to the foul papers text, not accidental omissions from it (pp. 110–12). Indeed, the three passages in question conform admirably to what we know was Shakespeare's practice. When dissatisfied with something he had written, he rewrote it from the beginning and, at the same time, expanded it (see *Love's Labour's Lost*, 4.3.292–313 and 314–61; and 5.2.805–10 and 825–42). But his revision of Q2 did not stop at these two complementary activities, it extended to matters of detail. There seems little room for doubt that it was he who removed from F the false starts, preserved in Q2, that he made at 3.2.157 and 158. At least two other F readings look like authorial corrections: its 'three thousand Crownes' (2.2.73) for Q2's 'threescore thousand crownes', and its 'some dosen or sixteene lines' (2.2.529) for Q2's 'some dosen lines, or sixteene lines'. These small revisions are, of course, part of the process of tidying-up; but their larger significance lies elsewhere. Once they are recognized as revisions, who can say where revision ends? Other readings in which F differs from Q2 can no longer be brushed aside lightly as compositors' errors or actors' interpolations. The crucial question to be asked about them is whether they serve some general end or ends that are in keeping with the character of F as a whole.

The major alterations in F—the cuts and the additions—seem to be parts of a definite policy designed to make the play more accessible to theatre-goers in general by giving it a more direct and unimpeded action, pruning away some of its verbal elaborations, and smoothing out its more abrupt transitions. The dominant trend in its minor alterations leads in the same direction, since it is towards modernization or what might be better described in some cases as normalization. The trend is at its clearest in F's treatment of the pronoun 'a', the unemphatic form of 'he'. In Q2 'a' is very common, occurring forty-one times and in the work of both compositors. In F, on the other hand, it appears but once. E sets 'a pour'd' at 5.1.170; but everywhere else it is normalized to 'he'. Less systematic but still noticeable is F's tendency to replace older forms with more modern ones: 'hath' with 'has'; 'sith' with 'since'; and 'whiles' with 'while' or 'whilst'. The spelling 'someuer' is found four times in Q2. In F three of them are altered to read 'howsoeuer', 'whatsoeuer', and 'so ere'; but 'someuer' survives at 3.2.381. Similarly, Q2's use of 'conuenient' (1.1.157), 'like' (2.2.152), and 'royall' (5.2.351) as adverbs gives way in F to the normal adverbial forms 'conueniently', 'likely', and 'royally'. In much the same way a number of unusual words and usages in Q2 are replaced in F with commoner words and usages. For instance, Q2's 'jump' (1.1.65), found at two other places only in the canon —5.2.328 and *Othello*, 2.3.374—becomes 'just'; and 'inquire' (2.1.4) as a noun becomes 'inquiry'. And so the process goes on through the play. Some particularly striking examples of it from the latter part of the tragedy are F's 'tunes' (4.7.152) for Q2's 'laudes', and its 'Rites' (5.1.222) for Q2's 'Crants'. Neither 'laudes' nor 'Crants' is to be found anywhere else in Shakespeare.

But while this trend is observable in F, it soon becomes clear that Shakespeare, once embarked on this course of revision, did precisely what revising poets do: forgetting or ignoring any predetermined course, he sought the best words in the best order irrespective of whether those words were usual or unusual. Consequently, the disappearance from F of some of Q2's rarer words is accompanied in it by the appearance of some rare words of its own replacing commoner words in the earlier text. Q2's 'interr'd' (1.4.28) becomes 'enurn'd'; its 'expectation' (3.1.153) 'expectansie'; its 'heated' (3.4.51) 'tristfull'; its 'criminall' (4.7.7) 'crimefull'; and its 'wisedome' (5.1.253) 'wisenesse'.

Greg, who in his British Academy lecture of 1928, *Principles of Emendation in Shakespeare*, espoused the view that some readings in F are indeed revisions of Q2, 'second thoughts' as he called them, subsequently allowed himself to be won over by Dover Wilson, and wrote in 1955: 'it is absurd to suppose that Shakespeare, when dissatisfied with a word in his text, commonly replaced it by another of generally similar appearance' (*SFF*, p. 315). Since then, however, Honigmann has brought together a great deal of impressive evidence demonstrating that this is in fact exactly what some authors do in the course of revision (pp. 67–77). And, even more to the point, there is at least one incontrovertible instance of Shakespeare's doing it. Q1 of *Love's Labour's Lost* prints, by a happy accident, both the first draft, some twenty-three lines, and the revised version of Berowne's praise of women's eyes. In the first draft three lines run thus:

> From womens eyes this doctrine I deriue,
> They are the Ground, the Bookes, the Achadems,
> From whence doth spring the true *Promethean* fire.
> (4.3.298–300)

In the revised version these lines become:

> From womens eyes this doctrine I deriue,
> They sparcle still the right promethean fier,
> They are the Bookes, the Artes, the Achademes ...
>
> (4.3.346–8)

The words 'spring' and 'sparcle' have a 'generally similar apearance', but there can be no question about the superiority of the second in this context.

These two versions of the same idea also serve to bring out two other common features of revision which Honigmann documents in some detail. The first is the substitution, as in 'Artes' for 'Ground' and 'right' for 'true', of one word for another to which it is not obviously superior. This too is characteristic of F *Hamlet*. It reads 'See thou Character' (1.3.59), instead of Q2's 'Looke thou character'; 'Be somewhat scanter' (1.3.121), instead of 'Be something scanter'; 'It wafts' (1.4.40, 54), instead of 'It waues'; and so the process continues right down to 5.2.269, where F has 'halfe an houre of life' in place of Q2's 'halfe an houres life'. The second mark of the author's revising hand in the three lines from *Love's Labour's Lost* is its transposition of the last two lines and its shifting of the word 'Bookes' from the second to the first place in the list (see Honigmann, pp. 65, 92, 111). In *Hamlet* there are at least seven instances of the same sort of transposition, beginning with F's 'What we two Nights haue seene' (1.1.33) for Q2's 'What we haue two nights seene'. Yet only once, when Laertes says in F 'Alas then, is she drown'd?' (4.7.158), instead of, as in Q2, 'Alas, then she is drownd.', does the transposition affect the sense; and even here the placing of the comma and the addition of the question mark, almost certainly signifying an exclamation, are probably the compositor's, imposing a spurious meaning on what was intended to read: 'Alas, then is she drown'd.'

Greg took the view that the rather half-hearted and inconsistent efforts made to purge the F text of profanity might have been made 'in the prompt-book in 1606 or later, or else in the course of printing' (*SFF*, p. 329). But Gary Taylor[1] has since shown that the Folio *Hamlet* bears little resemblance to other texts that were expurgated to meet the requirements of the Act of 1606 prohibit-

[1] '"Zounds" Revisited: Theatrical, Editorial, and Literary Expurgation', forthcoming.

ing the use of God's name on the stage. He points out that 'the Folio provides substitutes for seven examples of Quarto "God", while leaving nineteen intact, and actually adding another ["I pray God" (4.5.200)].' Moreover, such probable expurgation as there was occurs within the first thousand or so lines, the last instance of it being Polonius's 'With what, in the name of Heauen?' (2.1.76), and thus belongs to that part of the play, prior to the opening of 2.2, which was, we know, subject to editorial interference, since it was at this precise point that the abortive attempt to impose a division into acts and scenes on the play was abandoned. Four other variants are almost certainly editorial in origin: F's omission of Q2's *s'bloud* (2.2.362 and 3.2.352) and of its *s'wounds* (2.2.564 and 5.1.264). But both these expressions were oaths to which F was peculiarly sensitive, and, Taylor comments, 'All four, noticeably, fall in the latter portion of the text, where the complete tolerance of "God" gives us little reason whatever to suspect theatrical expurgation.'

The virtual absence of expurgation from the last three quarters of the Folio text means that the copy for F must have come into being before 1606, and so adds weight to the notion derived from Q1's use of it that it was put together very soon after Shakespeare wrote his first draft of the play in the form of Q2. A likely date for it, apart from the passage about the 'little eyases', would be the latter part of 1600. It also has its bearing on another question: had the fair copy on which F rests ever been used as a prompt-book at the Globe? The answer would seem to be that it could not have been so used after 1606. It is possible, however, to go further: another feature of F makes it most unlikely that it was ever employed as a prompt-book, namely, its stage directions. These are indeed (see pp. 114–16) more numerous and much fuller than those of Q2, but they still fall short of what would be required for performance, especially in the permissiveness so evident in many of them. The fair copy left ample work for the bookkeeper to do, but it did provide him with all the essential material he needed to put a prompt-book together. Representing the play substantially as Shakespeare left it, and not having been subjected to the wear and tear that the prompt-book of so popular a play as *Hamlet* had, one assumes, suffered by 1620 or thereabouts, it would naturally have seemed to Heminges and Condell the ideal 'copy' for inclusion in the First Folio.

The position adopted by Jenkins—and one must be grateful to him for spelling it out in so definite and uncompromising a fashion (pp. 5 and 19)—is an illogical one. He is ready and willing to trust Heminges and Condell when they say that Shakespeare was so fluent that his 'papers' were singularly free from 'blots', i.e. deletions and, presumably, the corrections accompanying them, yet he refuses to accept their other statement that the texts they print are the texts he wrote. A more logical and more consistent position is that of Ben Jonson. He states categorically in his eulogy of Shakespeare prefixed to the First Folio that Shakespeare did revise, and praises him for doing so:

> Yet must I not give Nature all; thy Art,
>   My gentle Shakespeare, must enjoy a part.
> For though the poet's matter Nature be,
>   His Art doth give the fashion; and that he,
> Who casts to write a living line, must sweat –
>   Such as thine are – and strike the second heat
> Upon the Muses' anvil, turn the same,
>   And himself with it, that he thinks to frame;
> Or for the laurel he may gain a scorn,
>   For a good poet's made as well as born.
> And such wert thou. Look how the father's face
>   Lives in his issue, even so the race
> Of Shakespeare's mind and manners brightly shines
>   In his well turnèd and true filèd lines.

Nor is this the end of the matter. In his *Timber, or Discoveries* Jonson virtually says that Shakespeare's revisions were a consequence of his fluency, of his having 'an excellent fancy, brave notions, and gentle expressions, wherein he flowed with that facility that sometime it was necessary he should be stopped' (Jonson, viii. 584, 656–9). One would dearly like to know who did the 'stopping' —the other sharers in the King's company seem the likeliest candidates—but, if these words mean anything, it is, surely, that some of Shakespeare's first drafts underwent cutting, and that the cutting was done by the playwright himself.

EDITORIAL PROCEDURES

In keeping with the hypothesis that F *Hamlet* is based on Shakespeare's fair copy and not, as many recent editors and textual critics have argued, on an annotated copy of Q2 or a manuscript that had been compared with Q2, F is used as the control text for the present edition. The passages peculiar to Q2, which were part of the play as originally drafted but then excised from it before it came to performance, are therefore relegated to Appendix A. Omissions from F which are obviously accidental, such as the loss of 'wrung ... consent' at 1.2.58–60, or of 'Alas ... worm' at 4.3.26–8, are, of course, supplied from Q2.

A further consequence of this hypothesis is that where indifferent readings are concerned that of F is normally preferred to that of Q2. Moreover, as Q1 derives from F, an agreement between these two texts, such as 'you spirits' (1.1.120), as against Q2's 'your spirits', or their assignment of 'What, has this thing appeared again tonight' (1.1.21) to Marcellus and not, as Q2 has it, to Horatio, is strong presumptive evidence that they represent accurately what was said and who said it on the stage at the Globe and elsewhere prior to the closing of the theatres in 1642.

The general principles governing the modernization of the text are those set out by Stanley Wells in his *Modernizing Shakespeare's Spelling* (Oxford, 1979); and, in keeping with them, passages from authors of the sixteenth and early seventeenth centuries, quoted in the commentary, have also been modernized even when they have been taken from an edition using old spelling. Within the text itself *my* is preferred to *mine* before a vowel, and *you* to *ye*, when either the Folio or the Second Quarto warrants it. Old spellings are, however, retained in documentary evidence, such as that provided by the Stationers' Register, for much of the matter in the Textual Introduction, and in the collations, where the lemma takes the modernized form but the rest of the entry is given in the original spelling.

Since directions such as 'aside' or 'to' another character, together with act and scene divisions, are all editorial, they are not attributed in the collations. Changes or variations in the punctuation are noted only where they are significant. Speech headings have been silently normalized.

Quotations from the Bible are taken, unless otherwise stated, from the Bishops' Bible of 1568; and references to other works by Shakespeare which have not yet appeared in the Oxford Shakespeare are keyed to Peter Alexander's edition of *The Complete Works* (1951).

Words are normally defined only when they first appear. All words that are glossed are listed in the index.

Abbreviations and References

The following abbreviations are used in the textual introduction, collations, and commentary. The place of publication is, unless otherwise specified, London.

EDITIONS OF SHAKESPEARE

Q1	*The Tragicall Historie of Hamlet Prince of Denmarke.* By William Shakes-peare. 1603
Q2	*The Tragicall Historie of Hamlet, Prince of Denmarke.* By William Shakespeare. Newly imprinted and enlarged to almost as much againe as it was, according to the true and perfect Coppie. 1604 (*uncorr.*), 1605 (*corr.*)
Q3	(As above), 1611
Q4	(As above), n. d. (1622?)
Q5	(As above), 1637
Q1676	*The Tragedy of Hamlet Prince of Denmark.* As it is now Acted at his Highness the Duke of York's Theatre. By William Shakespeare. 1676
Q1683	(As above), 1683
Q1695	*The Tragedy of Hamlet Prince of Denmark.* As it is now Acted at the Theatre Royal. By William Shakespeare. 1695
Q1703	*The Tragedy of Hamlet Prince of Denmark.* As it is now Acted by Her Majesties Servants. By William Shakespeare. 1703
F	The First Folio, 1623
F2	The Second Folio, 1632
F3	The Third Folio, 1663
F4	The Fourth Folio, 1685

Adams	Joseph Quincy Adams, *Hamlet* (New York, 1929)
Alexander	Peter Alexander, *Complete Works* (1951)
Boswell	James Boswell, *Plays and Poems*, 21 vols. (1821)
Cambridge	W. G. Clark and W. A. Wright, *Works*, The Cambridge Shakespeare, 9 vols. (Cambridge, 1863–6)
Capell	Edward Capell, *Comedies, Histories, and Tragedies*, 10 vols. (1767–8)
Clarendon	W. G. Clark and W. A. Wright, *Hamlet*, The Clarendon Press Shakespeare (Oxford, 1872)
Collier	John Payne Collier, *Works*, 8 vols. (1842–4)
Collier 1853	John Payne Collier, *Plays* (1853)
Dowden	Edward Dowden, *Hamlet*, The Arden Shakespeare (1899)
Dyce	Alexander Dyce, *Works*, 6 vols. (1857)
Furness	Horace Howard Furness, *Hamlet*, A New Variorum Edition, 2 vols. (Philadelphia, 1877)
Globe	W. G. Clark and W. A. Wright, *Works*, The Globe Edition (1864)
Hanmer	Thomas Hanmer, *Works*, 6 vols. (Oxford, 1743–4)
Jenkins	Harold Jenkins, *Hamlet*, new Arden Shakespeare (1982)
Jennens	Charles Jennens, *Hamlet* (1773)
Johnson	Samuel Johnson, *Plays*, 8 vols. (1765)
Keightley	Thomas Keightley, *Plays*, 6 vols. (1864)
Kittredge	G. L. Kittredge, *Hamlet* (Boston, 1939)
Knight	Charles Knight, *Works*, Pictorial Edition, 8 vols. (1838–43)
Malone	Edmond Malone, *Plays and Poems*, 10 vols. (1790)
Parrott–Craig	Thomas Marc Parrott and Hardin Craig, *The Tragedy of Hamlet. A Critical Edition of the Second Quarto* (Princeton, 1938)
Pope	Alexander Pope, *Works*, 6 vols. (1723–5)
Pope 1728	Alexander Pope, *Works*, 10 vols. (1728)
Riverside	G. B. Evans (textual editor), *The Riverside Shakespeare* (Boston, 1974)
Rowe	Nicholas Rowe, *Works*, 6 vols. (1709)
Rowe 1714	Nicholas Rowe, *Works*, 8 vols. (1714)

Spencer	T. J. B. Spencer, *Hamlet*, The New Penguin Shakespeare (Harmondsworth, 1980)
Staunton	Howard Staunton, *Plays*, 3 vols. (1858–60)
Steevens	Samuel Johnson and George Steevens, *Plays*, 10 vols. (1773)
Steevens 1778	Samuel Johnson and George Steevens, *Plays*, 10 vols. (1778)
Theobald	Lewis Theobald, *Works*, 7 vols. (1733)
Tschischwitz	Benno Tschischwitz, *Shakspere's Hamlet, Prince of Denmark* (Halle, 1869)
Warburton	William Warburton, *Works*, 8 vols. (1747)
White	Richard Grant White, *Works*, 12 vols. (Boston, 1857–66)
Wilson	John Dover Wilson, *Hamlet*, The New Shakespeare (Cambridge, 1934)

OTHER WORKS

Abbott	E. A. Abbott, *A Shakespearian Grammar*, second edition (1870)
Adams, *Chief Pre-Shakespearean Dramas*	*Chief Pre-Shakespearean Dramas*, ed. Joseph Quincy Adams (Boston, 1924)
Antonio's Revenge	John Marston, *Antonio's Revenge*, ed. Reavley Gair (Manchester and Baltimore, 1978)
Arber	Edward Arber, *A Transcript of the Registers of the Company of Stationers of London, 1554–1640*, 5 vols. (1875–94)
Arden of Feversham	*The Tragedy of M. Arden of Feversham*, in *The Shakespeare Apocrypha*, ed. C. F. Tucker Brooke (Oxford, 1908)
Bright	Timothy Bright, *A Treatise of Melancholy* (1586); facsimile reprint (New York, 1969)
Brook	G. L. Brook, *The Language of Shakespeare* (1976)
Browne	*The Works of Sir Thomas Browne*, ed. Charles Sayle, 3 vols. (1904–7)
Bullough	Geoffrey Bullough, *Narrative and Dramatic Sources of Shakespeare*, 8 vols. (1957–75)
Burton	Robert Burton, *The Anatomy of Melancholy*, ed. A. R. Shiletto, 3 vols. (1893)

Cercignani	Fausto Cercignani, *Shakespeare's Works and Elizabethan Pronunciation* (Oxford, 1981)
Chambers, *ES*	E. K. Chambers, *The Elizabethan Stage*, 4 vols. (Oxford, 1923)
Chambers, *William Shakespeare*	E. K. Chambers, *William Shakespeare*, 2 vols. (Oxford, 1930)
Chapman	*The Plays of George Chapman*, ed. T. M. Parrott, 2 vols. (1910–14), 4 vols. (New York, 1961)
Chaucer	*The Works of Geoffrey Chaucer*, ed. F. N. Robinson (Boston, 1933)
Cohn	Albert Cohn, *Shakespeare in Germany* (1865)
Dekker	Thomas Dekker, *Dramatic Works*, ed. Fredson Bowers, 4 vols. (Cambridge, 1953–61)
Dent	R. W. Dent, *Shakespeare's Proverbial Language: An Index* (1981)
Duthie	G. I. Duthie, *The 'Bad' Quarto of 'Hamlet'* (Cambridge, 1941)
Farmer	Richard Farmer, in *Works*, ed. Johnson and Steevens (1773)
Gollancz	Sir Israel Gollancz, *The Sources of 'Hamlet'* (1926)
Greene	*The Life and Complete Works . . . of Robert Greene*, ed. A. B. Grosart, 15 vols. (1881–6)
Hall	*The Collected Poems of Joseph Hall*, ed. A. Davenport (Liverpool, 1949)
Harvey Wood	*The Plays of John Marston*, ed. H. Harvey Wood, 3 vols. (1934–9)
Henslowe	*Henslowe's Diary*, ed. R. A. Foakes and R. T. Rickert (Cambridge, 1961)
Honigmann	E. A. J. Honigmann, *The Stability of Shakespeare's Text* (1965)
Jonson	*Ben Jonson*, ed. C. H. Herford and Percy and Evelyn Simpson, 11 vols. (Oxford, 1925–52)
Kyd	*The Works of Thomas Kyd*, ed. F. S. Boas (Oxford, 1901)
Malcontent, The	John Marston, *The Malcontent*, ed. G. K. Hunter (1975)
Marlowe	Christopher Marlowe, *Complete Plays*, ed. Irving Ribner (New York, 1963)
Marshall	Frank A. Marshall, *A Study of Hamlet* (1875)
Marston	*The Poems of John Marston*, ed. A. Davenport (Liverpool, 1961)

McKerrow   R. B. McKerrow, *Printers' and Publishers' Devices 1485–1640* (1913)

Mirror for Magistrates, The   *The Mirror for Magistrates*, ed. Lily B. Campbell (Cambridge, 1938)

More, Sir Thomas   For the text of the part of this play commonly attributed to Shakespeare, see Alexander, Appendix.

MSH   John Dover Wilson, *The Manuscript of Shakespeare's 'Hamlet' and the Problems of its Transmission*, 2 vols. (Cambridge, 1934)

Nashe   *The Works of Thomas Nashe*, ed. R. B. McKerrow (1904–10) ... With supplementary notes ... by F. P. Wilson, 5 vols. (Oxford, 1958)

OED   *The Oxford English Dictionary, being a corrected re-issue of A New English Dictionary on Historical Principles*, 13 vols. (Oxford, 1933), and Supplements 1–3 (1972, 1976, 1982)

Onions   C. T. Onions, *A Shakespeare Glossary*, second edition revised (Oxford, 1966)

RES   *Review of English Studies*

Schmidt   Alexander Schmidt, *A Shakespeare Lexicon*, fourth edition (revised by G. Sarrazin), 2 vols. (Berlin and Leipzig, 1923)

SFF   W. W. Greg, *The Shakespeare First Folio* (Oxford, 1955)

Shakespeare's England   *Shakespeare's England*, ed. C. T. Onions, 2 vols. (Oxford, 1932)

Sisson, New Readings   C. J. Sisson, *New Readings in Shakespeare*, 2 vols. (Cambridge, 1956)

Spanish Tragedy, The   Thomas Kyd, *The Spanish Tragedy*, ed. Philip Edwards (1959)

Sternfeld   F. W. Sternfeld, *Music in Shakespearean Tragedy* (1963)

Theobald, *SR*   Lewis Theobald, *Shakespeare Restored* (1726)

Tilley   M. P. Tilley, *A Dictionary of the Proverbs in England in the Sixteenth and Seventeenth Centuries* (Ann Arbor, 1950)

Tourneur   *The Works of Cyril Tourneur*, ed. Allardyce Nicoll (1930)

Walker   William S. Walker, *A Critical Examination of the Text of Shakespeare*, 3 vols. (1860)

Warning for Fair Women, A   *A Warning for Fair Women*, ed. Charles D. Cannon (The Hague, 1975)

Webster	John Webster, *Complete Works*, ed. F. L. Lucas, 4 vols. (1927)
WHH	John Dover Wilson, *What Happens in 'Hamlet'*, (Cambridge, 1935)
Woodstock	*Woodstock*, ed. A. P. Rossiter (1946)

The Tragedy of Hamlet

THE PERSONS OF THE PLAY

HAMLET, Prince of Denmark, son of the late King Hamlet and of Gertrude

HORATIO, a poor scholar, friend and confidant of Hamlet

GHOST of Hamlet's dead father

CLAUDIUS, King of Denmark, brother of the late King Hamlet

GERTRUDE, Queen of Denmark, widow of the late King Hamlet and now
the wife of his brother Claudius

POLONIUS, a member of the Danish Privy Council

LAERTES, his son

OPHELIA, his daughter

REYNOLDO, his servant

VOLTEMAND ⎱
CORNELIUS ⎰ Danish councillors, ambassadors to Norway

ROSENCRANTZ ⎱
GUILDENSTERN ⎰ courtiers, old schoolfellows of Hamlet

OSRIC, an affected courtier

FRANCISCO ⎱
BARNARDO ⎰ soldiers
MARCELLUS

FIRST CLOWN, a grave-digger

SECOND CLOWN, his crony

PRIEST

FORTINBRAS, Prince of Norway

CAPTAIN in Fortinbras's army

MESSENGERS

141

SAILORS

ENGLISH AMBASSADORS

LORDS

LADIES

GUARDS

DANES, supporters of Laertes

FIRST PLAYER, leader of the troupe, enacts the role of a king

SECOND PLAYER, enacts the role of a queen

THIRD PLAYER, enacts the role of Lucianus, nephew of the king

FOURTH PLAYER, speaks the Prologue to 'The Murder of Gonzago'

The Tragedy of Hamlet, Prince of Denmark

1.1   *Enter Francisco, a sentinel, who stands on guard.*
          Enter Barnardo, to relieve him

BARNARDO   Who's there?

FRANCISCO

Nay, answer me. Stand and unfold yourself.

BARNARDO   Long live the King!

FRANCISCO   Barnardo?

BARNARDO   He.

FRANCISCO

You come most carefully upon your hour.

BARNARDO

'Tis now struck twelve. Get thee to bed, Francisco.

FRANCISCO

For this relief much thanks. 'Tis bitter cold,
And I am sick at heart.

The Tragedy of Hamlet, Prince of Denmark] F (*title-page*); *The Tragedie of Hamlet* F (*running titles and Table of Contents*); THE Tragicall Historie of HAMLET, *Prince of Denmarke* Q2 (*title-page*); The Tragedie of HAMLET *Prince of Denmarke* Q2 (*head-title*); *The Tragedie of Hamlet Prince of Denmarke* Q2 (*running titles*); THE Tragicall Historie of HAMLET *Prince of Denmarke* Q1 (*title-page and head title*); *The Tragedie of Hamlet Prince of Denmarke* Q1 (*running titles*)

1.1.0 *Enter Francisco . . . him*] CAPELL (*subs.*); *Enter Barnardo and Francisco two Centinels* FQ2; *Enter two Centinels* Q1

1.1.0 *Francisco . . . him* All three of the earliest texts give the impression that the two sentinels enter at the same time; but even on the stage of the Globe Francisco almost certainly came on through one door *before* Barnardo came on through the other, because it is essential for the dramatic effect that the audience should know which of the two is on duty.

1 **Who's there** It is doubly significant that the challenge is given, as Francisco emphasizes in his counter-challenge, by the wrong man. First, it makes clear to the original audience, watching the play by daylight, that it is night on the stage; and, secondly, it suggests that Barnardo is jittery, and that things are not as they should be.

2 **me** Francisco asserts his right to make the challenge by stressing this word.
unfold identify (by giving the password)

6 **carefully upon your hour** punctually at your appointed time

8 **much** many. *Much* was 'used (where *many* would now be substituted) with a plural substantive taken collectively' (*OED*, A2d, citing this passage).

9 **sick at heart** thoroughly wretched. Macbeth's 'I am sick at heart, | When I behold —' (5.3.19–20) suggests that the phrase could mean 'filled with forebodings'. It is, in any case, the first of the play's many references to sickness.

BARNARDO

  Have you had quiet guard?

FRANCISCO   Not a mouse stirring.   10

BARNARDO Well, good night.

  If you do meet Horatio and Marcellus,

  The rivals of my watch, bid them make haste.

      Enter Horatio and Marcellus

FRANCISCO

  I think I hear them.—Stand! Who's there?

HORATIO

  Friends to this ground.

MARCELLUS   And liegemen to the Dane.

FRANCISCO

  Give you good night.

MARCELLUS   O farewell, honest soldier.

  Who hath relieved you?

FRANCISCO   Barnardo has my place.

  Give you good night.   *Exit*

MARCELLUS   Holla, Barnardo!

BARNARDO   Say—

  What, is Horatio there?

HORATIO   A piece of him.

BARNARDO

  Welcome, Horatio; welcome, good Marcellus.   20

MARCELLUS

  What, has this thing appeared again tonight?

BARNARDO I have seen nothing.

---

14 Stand! Who's] F; Stand ho, who is Q2   16 soldier] FQI; souldiers Q2   17 has] F (ha's);
hath Q2QI   21 MARCELLUS] FQI; Hora⟨tio⟩ Q2

---

10 **Not a mouse stirring** proverbial (Dent M1236.1)

13 **rivals** partners (the reading of Q1), sharers

15 **Dane** King of Denmark

16 **Give you** God give you (i.e. I wish you) —a stock phrase (Dent G185.1)

19 **A piece of him** All that's left of him. Compare Lychorida's description of the new born Marina as 'this piece | Of your dead queen' and as 'all that is left living of your queen' (*Pericles*, 3.1.17–18 and 20). Horatio humorously implies that he is shrinking away in the bitter cold.

21 MARCELLUS The agreement of F and Q1 in assigning this speech to Marcellus is strong evidence that it was Marcellus who spoke it on the stage, especially as his part in this first scene is very accurately reproduced in Q1. Those who follow Q2 in giving the line to Horatio attach great importance to the words 'this thing', which they interpret as sceptical mockery. But there is no dismissive mockery in Banquo's question, 'Were such things here as we do speak about?' (*Macbeth* 1.3.83), where the 'things' are the Witches. Moreover, it is natural that Marcellus, the last person addressed by Barnardo, should now take up the dialogue.

MARCELLUS

Horatio says 'tis but our fantasy,
And will not let belief take hold of him
Touching this dreaded sight twice seen of us.
Therefore I have entreated him along
With us to watch the minutes of this night,
That if again this apparition come,
He may approve our eyes and speak to it.

HORATIO

Tush, tush, 'twill not appear.

BARNARDO   Sit down awhile,   30
And let us once again assail your ears,
That are so fortified against our story,
What we two nights have seen.

HORATIO   Well, sit we down,
And let us hear Barnardo speak of this.

BARNARDO Last night of all,
When yon same star that's westward from the pole
Had made his course t'illume that part of heaven
Where now it burns, Marcellus and myself,
The bell then beating one—

*Enter the Ghost, clad in complete armour, with its visor
raised, and a truncheon in its hand*

26 along_A] FQI ; ~ ,Q2   33 two nights have] F; haue two nights Q2QI   39.1 *Enter the Ghost*]
Q2QI (*Enter Ghost*); *after off (40)* F   39.1–2 *clad . . . hand*] WILSON (*subs.*); *not in* FQ2QI

23 **fantasy** deceptive imagination. Compare
   Theseus' lines: 'Lovers and madmen
   have such seething brains, | Such shaping
   fantasies, that apprehend | More than cool
   reason ever comprehends' (*Dream*
   5.1.4–6).
26 **along** to come along. The verb of motion
   is often omitted in Elizabethan English
   (Abbott 30).
29 **approve** corroborate the evidence of
   speak to it See note to line 42.
33 **What** '*What* depends on a verb of speech,
   implied in either "assail your ears" or in
   "story," i.e. "let us tell you *what* we have
   seen," or "our story describing *what we*
   have seen"' (Abbott 252).
35 **Last night of all** Why, only last night
36 **yon same star** 'Barnardo presumably
   points to the sky at one side of the stage,
   guiding the eyes of the audience away
   from where the Ghost will enter' (Spencer).

pole pole-star
37 **his** its. In Shakespeare's day '*His* still
   represented the genitive of *It* as well as of
   He' (Abbott 228). *Its* is not found in any of
   Shakespeare's plays published during his
   lifetime.
   illume Like 'relume' (*Othello* 5.2.13), this
   word seems to be a Shakespearian invention. The reporter of Q1 misremembered it
   as 'Illumine', thus preserving the sense
   but ruining the metre.
39 **beating** striking. This use of 'beating' is
   very rare. The reporter of Q1 recalled the
   word as 'towling'.
39.1–39.2 **clad . . . hand** These details are
   derived from 1.2.200–29. There has
   been much debate about whether the
   Ghost was meant to come up through a
   trap or not. There is much to show that it
   does not, and nothing to suggest that it
   does. It 'comes again' (l. 40); 'it stalks
   away' (l. 50); 'With martial stalk hath he

MARCELLUS

Peace, break thee off. Look where it comes again.   40

BARNARDO

In the same figure like the King that's dead.

MARCELLUS

Thou art a scholar, speak to it, Horatio.

BARNARDO

Looks it not like the King? Mark it, Horatio.

HORATIO

Most like. It harrows me with fear and wonder.

BARNARDO

It would be spoke to.

MARCELLUS   Question it, Horatio.

HORATIO

What art thou that usurp'st this time of night,
Together with that fair and warlike form
In which the majesty of buried Denmark
Did sometimes march? By heaven, I charge thee speak.

MARCELLUS

It is offended.

BARNARDO   See, it stalks away.   50

41 figure_A] Q2Q1 ; ~ , F   43 Looks it] FQ1 ; Lookes a Q2   44 harrows] F (harrowes); horrowes
Q2; horrors Q1   45 Question] FQ1 ; Speake to Q2

gone by our watch' (l. 66); it 'Appears
before them, and with solemn march |
Goes slow and stately by them'
(1.2.201–2); and, at the end of its final
appearance, it goes 'out at the portal'
(3.4.131). For further discussion see Bernard Beckerman, *Shakespeare at the Globe*
(New York, 1962), pp. 201–3.

41 **same figure** i.e. same distinctive figure as
before

42 **Thou art . . . Horatio** It was widely
believed that ghosts could not speak until
spoken to; and this idea was still alive in
the days of Dr Johnson, who told Boswell:
'Tom Tyers described me the best: "Sir
(said he) you are like a ghost: you never
speak till you are spoken to."' It was
further thought desirable that the person
who did address a ghost should be a
scholar, because a knowledge of Latin
was needed to exorcise the ghost if it
proved to be an evil spirit and became
obstreperous. See Dover Wilson, *WHH*,
pp. 75–6.

44 **harrows** distresses, lacerates (*OED* 4).
According to *OED*, this is the earliest use
of the word in a figurative sense. Q2's
horrowes may be a variant spelling (*MSH*,
p. 428); but Q1's *horrors* looks like an
auditory error by the reporter.

45 **would be** wants to be

46 **usurp'st** Horatio means that the Ghost
has no right to be out at this time of night,
and no right to the form it has assumed. It
is not, therefore, surprising that this unfortunate victim of usurpation should be
offended (l. 50).

48 **buried Denmark** the buried King of Denmark

49 **sometimes** once, formerly

50 **stalks** a concealed stage direction. Shakespeare carefully spells out the Ghost's
characteristic movement for the benefit
of the actor, and he goes on doing
it, as though bent on making it crystal
clear that this ghost is not the traditional
figure of the sixteenth-century stage: 'a
filthy whining ghost, | Lapt in some foul

HORATIO Stay, speak, speak. I charge thee speak.

Exit Ghost

MARCELLUS 'Tis gone and will not answer.

BARNARDO

How now, Horatio? You tremble and look pale.
Is not this something more than fantasy?
What think you on't?

HORATIO

Before my God, I might not this believe
Without the sensible and true avouch
Of mine own eyes.

MARCELLUS   Is it not like the King?

HORATIO As thou art to thyself,

Such was the very armour he had on   60
When he th'ambitious Norway combated.
So frowned he once when in an angry parle
He smote the sledded Polacks on the ice.
'Tis strange.

---

61 he] Q2Q1; *not in* F   th'ambitious] F; the ambitious Q2Q1   63 Polacks] F (Pollax), Q2Q1
(pollax); Pole-axe ROWE; Polack POPE

sheet or a leather pilch, | [which] Comes
screaming like a pig half-stickt, | And cries
"*Vindicta!* revenge, revenge!" (*A Warning for Fair Women* (1598-9) Ind. 54-7).

52 **will not answer** because it has come to
speak to Hamlet not to Horatio

55 **on't** of it (Abbott 181)

56 **Before my God** God knows, by God

56-8 **I might . . . eyes** Two proverbial sayings have contributed to these words: 'I
will believe it when I see it' (Tilley B268)
and 'To believe one's own eyes' (Dent
E264.1).

56 **might** could (Abbott 312)

57 **sensible and true avouch** undeniable
confirmation provided by the senses. This
use of *avouch*, normally a verb, as a noun
seems to be peculiar to Shakespeare and
to this passage.

60-1 **Such was . . . combated** Furness
asks: 'Was this the very armour that he
wore thirty years before, on the very day
Hamlet was born (see 5.1.136-40)? How
old is Horatio?' However, the purpose of
the lines is not to tell us Horatio's age—
we can see that by looking at him—but to
take the story back to its beginnings: the
single combat between old Hamlet and

the King of Norway Horatio here is, as
befits a scholar, the voice of history.

61 Norway the King of Norway

62 **So frowned he** As Spencer points out, this
probably refers to the Ghost's reaction
when accused of usurpation, since
Horatio says later that the apparition's
behaviour during the encounter was expressed by 'A countenance more in sorrow than in anger' (1.2.231).

   an angry parle A useful gloss on these
words is provided by Leonard Digges in
the commendatory verses he wrote for the
1640 edition of Shakespeare's poems. He
tells there of how the audience 'Were
ravished' when 'on the stage at half-
sword parley were | Brutus and Cassius'
(ll. 42-3). The quarrel scene in *Caesar*
4.3, which leaves Cassius asking, 'How
scaped I killing when I crossed you so?'
(l. 148), shows vividly how easily a parley
might turn into a fight.

63 **He smote the sledded Polacks on the ice**
Two questions that have been the subject
of much debate arise here. First, does
'pollax' (Q2, Q1)/'Pollax' (F) mean 'pole-
axe', the weapon, or 'Polacks', i.e.
'Poles'; and, depending on the answer to

MARCELLUS

Thus twice before, and just at this dead hour,
With martial stalk hath he gone by our watch.

HORATIO

In what particular thought to work I know not,
But in the gross and scope of my opinion
This bodes some strange eruption to our state.

MARCELLUS

Good now, sit down, and tell me he that knows,   70
Why this same strict and most observant watch
So nightly toils the subject of the land,
And why such daily cast of brazen cannon
And foreign mart for implements of war,
Why such impress of shipwrights, whose sore task
Does not divide the Sunday from the week.
What might be toward that this sweaty haste
Doth make the night joint-labourer with the day,
Who is't that can inform me?

---

65 just] F; iump Q2Q1   68 my] FQ1; mine Q2   73 why] FQ1; with Q2   cast] F; cost Q2Q1

that question, what does 'sleaded' (Q2, Q1)/'sledded' (F) signify? 'He smote *the* sledded pole-axe on the ice' is un-Shakespearian and un-English. Normal usage demands *his*, as in '*His* falchion on a flint he softly smiteth' (*Lucrece* 176), the closest parallel to the passage at issue in all Shakespeare's work. The use of the definite article in 'the sleaded pollax' makes it clear that here we have the direct object of 'smote'—'the Polacks'. And, since those smitten are the Polacks, it follows that 'sledded' means 'equipped with sleds' or 'who travelled in sleds'. *OED* offers no other instance of 'sledded' in this sense; but Shakespeare was in the habit of making an adjective out of a noun by adding *ed* to it (see Schmidt, pp. 1417–18).

65 **dead** still as death, dark and dreary. Compare 1.2.198, 'the dead waste and middle of the night'.

67 **In what . . . not** i.e. I don't know exactly what line of thought to pursue

68 **gross and scope** general drift (hendiadys)

69 **strange eruption** extraordinary outbreak of evil or calamity. Compare *Caesar* 1.3.78, where Cassius describes the omens preceding Caesar's assassination

as 'these strange eruptions'.

70 **Good now** Now, my good friends. For the omission of the noun, see Abbott 13.
   tell me he that knows let him who knows tell me (Abbott 364)

71 **watch** state of constant vigilance

72 **toils** puts to toil (Abbott 290)
   subject people or subjects of a state viewed collectively. This use of *subject* appears to be peculiar to Shakespeare (see *OED* I.1b).

73 **cast** casting, founding. Like *avouch* (l. 57), this use of *cast* is found only in this passage. It is, therefore, not surprising that Q2 and Q1 replace it with the familiar *cost*.

74 **mart** trading

75 **impress** impressment, enforced labour in the service of the state. Compare *Antony* 3.7.34–6, 'Your ships are not well manned; | Your mariners are muleteers, reapers, people | Ingrossed by swift impress.' *OED* cites no example of this word prior to its appearance here in *Hamlet*.

76 **divide** distinguish

77 **might be toward** can be impending, can be afoot
   that so that, with the consequence that

148

HORATIO   That can I—
At least the whisper goes so: our last king,   80
Whose image even but now appeared to us,
Was, as you know, by Fortinbras of Norway,
Thereto pricked on by a most emulate pride,
Dared to the combat; in which our valiant Hamlet—
For so this side of our known world esteemed him—
Did slay this Fortinbras, who by a sealed compact,
Well ratified by law and heraldry,
Did forfeit, with his life, all those his lands
Which he stood seized on to the conqueror;
Against the which a moiety competent   90
Was gagèd by our King, which had returned
To the inheritance of Fortinbras,
Had he been vanquisher; as, by the same cov'nant

87 heraldry] FQI ; heraldy Q2   88 those] FQI ; these Q2   89 on] F ; of Q2QI   91 returned]
F (return'd); returne Q2   93 cov'nant] F (Cou'nant); comart Q2 ; compact Q1676

79 **That can I** Horatio is back here in his role
of historian or narrator.
80 **whisper** rumour—an under-theme in
the play as a whole
so thus, as follows
81 **image** visible form. The word is carefully
chosen to leave Horatio with the option
that the Ghost could, after all, be imaginary.
even but now only just now, a moment
ago (Abbott 130)
83 **pricked on** spurred on, incited
emulate emulous, envious. Shakespeare
does not use this word as an adjective
anywhere else in his writings; nor can
OED cite any other instance of it.
84 **the combat** single combat to the death,
'the combat that ends all dispute' (Abbott
92)
85 **this side of our known world** all Europe
86 **a sealed compact** a mutual agreement to
which each king set his seal. *Compact*,
with the accent on the second syllable,
appears to have been introduced into English by Shakespeare.
87 **heraldry** heraldic regulations governing
the conduct of a combat
88–9 **all those . . . seized on** Shakespeare is
thinking in terms of his own England. The
lands in question are not the whole of
Norway but those parts of the country,
the Crown lands, in which the king is his
own tenant in chief, and from which he

receives the revenues. These lands could be
sold, if the king so wished, or given away.
89 **Which he stood seized on** of which he was
the legal owner
90 **moiety competent** corresponding amount
of land
91 **gagèd** wagered, staked. There are
fascinating correspondences between the
way in which the story of the play begins,
with a single combat between old Hamlet
and old Fortinbras, and the way in which
it ends, with a duel between Hamlet and
Laertes which, like the initial combat, is
accompanied by wagers.
had returned would have fallen to
(Schmidt). Compare *Timon* 3.2.82–3, 'I
would have put my wealth into dona-
tion, | And the best half should have
returned to him.'
92 **inheritance** possession, ownership
93 **cov'nant** This is the reading of F
(Cou'nant), and makes good sense,
whereas *comart*, the reading of Q2, is a
nonce-word and an improbable one at
that, since any *mart* assumes at least two
participants. Glossed by Malone and later
editors who have adopted it as a *joint bargain*—can there be a bargain which is not
joint?—*comart* seems much more likely
to be a misreading of *Cou'nant* than vice
versa, especially as the Q2 compositor
could have been influenced by *foreign
mart* at line 74.

And carriage of the article designed,
His fell to Hamlet. Now sir, young Fortinbras,
Of unimprovèd mettle hot and full,
Hath in the skirts of Norway here and there
Sharked up a list of landless resolutes
For food and diet to some enterprise
That hath a stomach in't, which is no other—   100
And it doth well appear unto our state—
But to recover of us by strong hand

---

94 designed] F2; designe F; desseigne Q2   98 landless] F; lawelesse Q2Q1   101 And] F; As Q2

94 **carriage of the article designed** carrying
out of the article [in the compact]
designed to cover the point. *OED* glosses
carriage (21) as 'meaning carried by
words; burden, import, purport, bearing', but it was not until the article had
been fulfilled that the lands 'fell to Hamlet'.

96 **unimprovèd** untried, untested. This
word, apparently a Shakespearian
coinage, is not found elsewhere in his
work. *Improve* also occurs but once, at
Caesar, 2.1.158–60, where Cassius says
of Antony: 'his means, | If he improve
them, may well stretch so far | As to
annoy us all.' The usual explanation of
improve here is 'turn to good account', but
'put to the test' would serve equally well;
and 'untried' seems the right gloss on
unimprovèd because it allows for a pun on
metal/mettle, two words which were not
yet completely separated from one
another in Shakespeare's day. Compare
'Let there be made some more test of my
metal' (*Measure* 1.1.49). A number of
other possible explanations of *unimprovèd*
are given by Onions.

97 **skirts** outlying parts, places distant from
the capital

98 **Sharked up** picked up, gathered together
indiscriminately in the way a shark takes
other fish. *Shark up* appears to be a
Shakespearian coinage, as does *shark on*
which he uses in the passage he is
thought to have contributed to the play of
Sir Thomas More, where More tells the
rioting citizens of London: 'other ruffians
as their fancies wrought . . . | Would
shark on you, and men like ravenous
fishes, | Would feed on one another'
(ll. 84–7).

   list band, troop (literally 'catalogue of

soldiers'). This is the earliest example of
the word cited by *OED*. Its unfamiliarity at
the time when *Hamlet* was written probably explains the replacement of it in Q1
by the much older word *sight*, meaning 'a
multitude'.

   landless resolutes landless desperadoes.
F's *landless* is preferred to the *lawless* of Q2
and Q1 for several reasons: *landless*, occurring on one other occasion only, *K.
John* 1.1.177, is a rarer word in Shakespeare than is *lawless*; the Bastard Faul-
conbridge, the 'landless knight' of *K.
John*, has much in common with Fortinbras, who is also, one assumes, *landless*
after his father's defeat and death; and an
army made up of 'younger sons to younger brothers' would stand some chance of
being welded into the rather impressive
force that Fortinbras has at his command
in 4.4.

99–100 **For food . . . stomach in't** Shakespeare seems to have combined two
meanings into one. First, the 'landless
resolutes' are to serve as rations ('food
and diet') to the personified 'enterprise'
which has a challenge to their pride
('stomach') in it; secondly, in exchange
for their rations these men will take part
in any enterprise which promises something for the stomach to digest.

101 **doth well appear** is quite obvious
   state government

102 **But** than. '*But* in the sense of *except*
frequently follows negative comparatives,
where we should use *than*' (Abbott 127).
   of from (Abbott 166). Compare *Corio-
lanus* 5.6.14–15, 'we'll deliver you | Of
your great danger'.
   strong hand main force (with a pun on
the name Fortinbras)

And terms compulsative those foresaid lands
So by his father lost. And this, I take it,
Is the main motive of our preparations,
The source of this our watch, and the chief head
Of this post-haste and rummage in the land.

    Enter the Ghost

But soft, behold, lo where it comes again!
I'll cross it though it blast me.

    The Ghost spreads its arms

                Stay, illusion.

If thou hast any sound or use of voice,   110
Speak to me.
If there be any good thing to be done
That may to thee do ease and grace to me,
Speak to me,
If thou art privy to thy country's fate,
Which, happily, foreknowing may avoid,
O speak.
Or if thou hast uphoarded in thy life
Extorted treasure in the womb of earth,

---

103 compulsative] F; compulsatory Q2   109.1 *The Ghost spreads its arms*] Q2 (*It spreads his armes*); *not in* FQ1

103 **compulsative** compulsory. Both *compulsative* and *compulsatory* (Q2) appear to be Shakespearian inventions.
106 **head** well-head, source
107 For a passage following this line in Q2 but not in F, see Appendix A, l.
    post-haste feverish activity
    rummage bustle, commotion (not used elsewhere in Shakespeare)
108 **soft** stay, peace; 'used as an exclamation with imperative force, either to enjoin silence or deprecate haste' (*OED soft adv.* 8)
109 **cross it** cross its path. It was thought that anyone crossing the path of a ghost or demon became subject to its evil influence.
    The Ghost spreads its arms This direction, in the form of '*It spreads his armes*', appears only in Q2. Wilson, emending it to read '*he "spreads his arms"* ', thinks 'Horatio steps in the path of the Ghost and spreads his arms . . . so as to stop its passage.' It seems more natural, however, to regard *It* as the Ghost, whose spreading of its arms is interpreted by Horatio as preparation for flight and leads to his cry, 'Stay, illusion.' *His* (see note to

1.1.37) is the normal Shakespearian possessive of *it*.
110 **sound** the meaning seems to be 'means of making yourself heard', 'form of articulation'.
112-21 **If . . . speak** Horatio suggests three possible reasons, all well known around 1600, to account for the Ghost's appearance.
113 **to thee do ease and grace to me** i.e. give comfort and relief to you and reflect credit on me
116 **happily** perhaps (or possibly 'luckily')
    foreknowing may avoid prescience may prevent
118-20 **Or if . . . death** Compare Marlowe's *The Jew of Malta* 2.1.24-30: 'Now I remember those old women's words, | Who in my wealth would tell me winter's tales, | And speak of spirits and ghosts that glide by night | About the place where treasure hath been hid: | And now methinks that I am one of those; | For whilst I live, here lives my soul's sole hope, | And, when I die, here shall my spirit walk.'

For which, they say, you spirits oft walk in death,   120
Speak of it, stay and speak.

The cock crows

Stop it, Marcellus.

MARCELLUS
Shall I strike at it with my partisan?

HORATIO
Do if it will not stand.

BARNARDO   'Tis here.

HORATIO   'Tis here.   *Exit the Ghost*

MARCELLUS   'Tis gone.
We do it wrong, being so majestical,
To offer it the show of violence,
For it is as the air invulnerable,
And our vain blows malicious mockery.

BARNARDO
It was about to speak when the cock crew.

HORATIO
And then it started like a guilty thing   130
Upon a fearful summons. I have heard
The cock, that is the trumpet to the morn,
Doth with his lofty and shrill-sounding throat
Awake the god of day, and at his warning,
Whether in sea or fire, in earth or air,

---

120 you] FQ1; your Q2   121.1 *The cock crows*] Q2 *in the left margin opposite ll.* 120–1; *not in*
FQ1   122 at] F; *not in* Q2   123 *Exit the Ghost*] FQ1; *not in* Q2   132 morn] Q2; day F;
morning Q1

---

120 **you** The agreement of F and Q1 sup-
ports this reading; but the *your* of Q2 also
has its attractions, since Shakespeare
often uses *your* in the indefinite sense, as
in 'your water is a sore decayer of your
whoreson dead body' (5.1.162–3).

122 **partisan** 'weapon used by infantry in
the 16th–17th centuries, consisting of a
long-handled spear and a blade having
one or more lateral cutting projections'
(Onions)

123 **stand** stand still
'Tis here.... 'Tis here. By calling out thus
Barnardo and Horatio draw attention to
themselves and thus cover the Ghost's
exit.

127–8 **it is ... mockery** Compare *K. John*
2.1.251–2, 'Our cannons' *malice vainly*

shall be spent | Against th' *invulnerable*
clouds of heaven.' The two passages are a
fascinating example of the way in which
certain words were associated with one
another in Shakespeare's mind.

128 **malicious mockery** a futile mockery of
true ill-will

131 **Upon** at (Abbott 191)

132 **trumpet** trumpeter

133 **lofty** high-sounding. Compare *1 Henry
IV* 5.2.98, 'Sound all the lofty instruments of war.'

135 **Whether ... air** Robert Burton, among
others, divides spirits into 'Fiery spirits or
Devils . . . Aerial Spirits or Devils . . .
Water-devils . . . Terrestrial devils' (*Anatomy of Melancholy* i. 217–19).

Th'extravagant and erring spirit hies
To his confine; and of the truth herein
This present object made probation.

MARCELLUS

It faded on the crowing of the cock.
Some say that ever 'gainst that season comes   140
Wherein our Saviour's birth is celebrated,
The bird of dawning singeth all night long;
And then, they say, no spirit can walk abroad,
The nights are wholesome, then no planets strike,
No fairy takes, nor witch hath power to charm,
So hallowed and so gracious is the time.

HORATIO

So have I heard and do in part believe it.
But look, the morn in russet mantle clad
Walks o'er the dew of yon high eastern hill.

---

140 say] Q2Q1 ; sayes F   142 The] FQ1 ; This Q2   143 can walk] F ; dare sturre Q2 ; dare
walke Q1   145 takes] Q2Q1 ; talkes F   146 the] F ; that Q2Q1   149 eastern] F ; Eastward Q2

136 **extravagant** wandering out of bounds.
Compare *Othello* 1.1.137–8, 'an ex-
travagant and wheeling stranger | Of here
and everywhere.' This use of the word
appears to be peculiar to Shakespeare.
erring roaming, straying

137 **confine** place of confinement. Compare
Tempest 4.1.120–1, 'Spirits which by
mine art | I have from their confines
called.'

138 **object** i.e. something that causes a
strong emotional response, such as wonder, fear, admiration, and the like (*OED*
3b). Compare *Othello* 5.2.367–8, 'The
object poisons sight; | Let it be hid.'
probation proof

139 **It faded** These words appropriately
introduce a marvellous diminuendo as
the terrors of the night fade away with the
assertion of consoling superstitions and
the coming of daylight. No source has yet
been found for the belief that as Christmas
approaches the cock crows all night long.

140 **say** The rightness of this Q2 reading is
confirmed by *they say* at line 143; the
sayes of F could have come from the compositor's taking *Some* as a singular meaning 'someone'.
'gainst towards the time when (Abbott
142)

144 **wholesome** conducive to health, salu-

brious. *Wholesome*—compare 1.5.70;
3.2.244; and 3.4.65–6—is a very im
portant word in *Hamlet*, which pits the
wholesome against the unwholesome.
no planets strike According to the
astrological notions still prevalent in
Shakespeare's day, a planet in a 'malig-
nant aspect' was capable of striking and
blasting men and things. Compare
Coriolanus 2.2.111–12, 'with a sudden
re-enforcement struck | Corioli like a
planet.'

145 **takes** strikes with disease, bewitches.
Normally the verb takes an object, as in
Merry Wives 4.4.31, where Mistress Page
says of the legendary Herne the Hunter,
'he blasts the trees, and takes the cattle'.
Shakespeare's use of it here in an absolute
sense seems to be unique (*OED* 7).
charm practise magic

146 **gracious** full of divine grace

148 **russet** reddish-brown

149 **eastern** Shakespeare does not use *eastward*, the reading of Q2, elsewhere in his
work, whereas *eastern*, the normal adjec-
tival form, appears on seven other
occasions, four of them in connection
with the sunrise—*Dream* 3.2.391;
Richard II 3.2.42; *Romeo* 2.3.2; and
Lucrece 773.

Break we our watch up, and by my advice   150
Let us impart what we have seen tonight
Unto young Hamlet; for upon my life
This spirit, dumb to us, will speak to him.
Do you consent we shall acquaint him with it,
As needful in our loves, fitting our duty?

MARCELLUS
Let's do't, I pray, and I this morning know
Where we shall find him most conveniently.   *Exeunt*

I.2   *Flourish of trumpets. Enter Claudius, King of*
       Denmark, Gertrude the Queen, Prince Hamlet ⌐dressed
       in black,⌐ the Council, ⌐including Voltemand,
       Cornelius,⌐ Polonius and his son Laertes, with Lords
       Attendant

CLAUDIUS
Though yet of Hamlet our dear brother's death
The memory be green, and that it us befitted

155 duty?] FQI ; duty. Q2   156 Let's] Q2QI ; Let F   157 conveniently] FQI ; conuenient Q2
    1.2.0.1–3 Flourish . . . Lords Attendant] F (subs.) (Enter Claudius King of Denmarke, Gertrude the
    Queene, Hamlet, Polonius, Laertes, and his sister Ophelia, Lords Attendant); Florish. Enter Claudius,
    King of Denmarke, Gertrad the Queene, Counsaile : as Polonius, and his Sonne Laertes, Hamlet, Cum
    Alijs Q2 ; Enter King, Queene, Hamlet, Leartes, Corambis, and the two Ambassadors, with Attendants
    QI (beginning the scene at line 27)

150 **Break we** I suggest we break, let us
    break (Abbott 364)
155 **our loves** i.e. the love each of us feels for
    him. Shakespeare often uses the plural of
    an abstract noun when referring to a feel-
    ing or quality shared by more than one
    person.
157 **conveniently** The agreement of F and
    QI in this reading, as distinct from Q2's
    convenient, suggests that it is what was
    heard in the theatre. Moreover, *OED* does
    not recognize *convenient* as an adverb, nor
    does Shakespeare use it as such anywhere
    else in his work.
1.2.0 **Flourish . . . Attendant** See long note
    at p. 382.
0.2–3 **dressed in black** See 'nightly colour'
    (l. 68), 'inky cloak' (l. 77), etc.
0.3–4 **the Council, including Voltemand
    . . . Laertes** Wilson takes 'Council, as,
    (Counsaile : as)', the reading of Q2, to be a
    compositor's error for 'Councillors'. It
    seems simpler, however, to assume that
    Q2 follows the manuscript here, and to
    interpret its wording as 'Council, to wit'.

For 'as' in the required sense see *OED* 26 ;
and compare *Errors*, 1.2.97–8, 'They say
this town is full of cozenage; | As, nimble
jugglers that deceive the eye. . . .'
    Voltemand and Cornelius are given
their entry here, rather than at line 25
where F brings them in, on the assumption that their late entry in F was caused
by the doubling of the parts of Marcellus
and Voltemand. Rowe appears to be the
first editor to specify the ambassadors in
the initial entry.
    I **our** Here Claudius is using the royal
first person plural; but as the speech
develops the distinction between the royal
we and *we* meaning 'we Danes' is
deliberately blurred, thus giving the impression that his actions have received
general approval.
  2 **that** though. See *OED that conj.* 8, 'used
(like French *que*) as a substitute instead of
repeating a previous conjunction, or conjunctive adverb or phrase.'
    us befitted was right for us

To bear our hearts in grief, and our whole kingdom
To be contracted in one brow of woe,
Yet so far hath discretion fought with nature
That we with wisest sorrow think on him
Together with remembrance of ourselves.
Therefore our sometimes sister, now our queen,
Th'imperial jointress of this warlike state,
Have we, as 'twere with a defeated joy,   10
With one auspicious and one dropping eye,
With mirth in funeral and with dirge in marriage,
In equal scale weighing delight and dole,
Taken to wife. Nor have we herein barred
Your better wisdoms, which have freely gone
With this affair along. For all, our thanks.
Now follows that you know young Fortinbras,
Holding a weak supposal of our worth,
Or thinking by our late dear brother's death
Our state to be disjoint and out of frame,   20

8 sometimes] F; sometime Q2   9 of| F; to Q2   11 one auspicious and one] F; an auspicious
and a Q2   17 follows that you know] Q2; followes, that you know F

4 **contracted** in both the literal sense of knitting the brows by drawing them together and the figurative sense of the country's being united
6–7 **That we . . . ourselves** Claudius has two commonplaces in mind: 'He is not wise that is not wise for himself' (Tilley W532), and 'We should remember ourselves' (Dent R72.1).
8 **sometimes** former
9 **jointress** *OED* cites this as the first appearance of the word in English, and defines it as 'a widow who holds a jointure; a dowager'; but it derives *jointress* from *jointer*[1], which it defines as 'a joint possessor'. Subsequent events in the play do nothing to clarify the word's significance.
10 **defeated** frustrated (by grief)
11 **one auspicious and one dropping eye** proverbial—'To cry with one eye and laugh with the other' (Tilley E248).
13 **equal** impartial, precisely counterpoising. Compare *2 Henry VI* 2.1.199–200, 'poise the cause in justice' equal scales, | Whose beam stands sure'.

dole grief
14 **barred** excluded, failed to consult
15 **wisdoms** See note to 1.1.155.
15–16 **freely gone | With this affair along** unconstrainedly concurred with the conduct of this matter
17 **Now follows that you know** Now comes what you should know, that. Theobald's emendation to 'follows that [= that which] you know,' adopted by many editors in the form 'follows that you know:' is unnecessary and misleading. There is no point in Claudius's telling the members of the Council what they know already. The punctuation of Q2 makes it clear that 'follows' is impersonal, as it still is today in 'as follows', and that 'know' is subjunctive. See Sisson, *New Readings*.
18 **weak supposal** poor opinion (Shakespeare's only use of 'supposal')
19 **by** as a consequence of (Abbott 146)
20 **disjoint** out of joint, disordered
   out of frame out of shape, in a mess. Compare *Macbeth* 3.2.16, 'let the frame of things disjoint'.

Colleaguèd with the dream of his advantage—
He hath not failed to pester us with message
Importing the surrender of those lands
Lost by his father, with all bonds of law,
To our most valiant brother. So much for him.
Now for ourself, and for this time of meeting,
Thus much the business is: we have here writ
To Norway, uncle of young Fortinbras—
Who impotent and bed-rid scarcely hears
Of this his nephew's purpose—to suppress   30
His further gait herein, in that the levies,
The lists, and full proportions are all made
Out of his subject; and we here dispatch
You, good Cornelius, and you, Voltemand,
For bearing of this greeting to old Norway,
Giving to you no further personal power
To business with the King more than the scope
Of these dilated articles allow.
Farewell, and let your haste commend your duty.

---

21 Colleaguèd] F; Coleagued Q2; Co-leaguèd CAPELL   the] F; this Q2   advantage—] ALEXAN-
DER; Aduantage; F; aduantage_A Q2   24 bonds] F, Q2 (bands)   25 him.] Q2; him. | *Enter
Voltemand and Cornelius* F   35 bearing] F; bearers Q2Q1

21 **Colleaguèd with** allied to, united with.
The notion seems to be that Fortinbras is
impelled by two different considerations,
both illusory, yet lending support to one
another: on the one hand, his conviction
that Claudius is a weak king and Denmark is in disarray; on the other, his
belief in his own personal superiority to
Claudius—his 'dream of his advantage'.

22 **He** 'When a proper name is separated by
an intervening clause from its verb, then
for clearness . . . the redundant pronoun is
often inserted' (Abbott 242).

23 **Importing** about, dealing with, concerning

27 **Thus much the business is** Taking Claudius
at his word, Q1 begins the scene at this
point.

29 **impotent** weak, infirm

31 **gait** proceeding, going forward (*OED gate
sb.²* 6d)

32 **lists** See note to 1.1.98.
proportions numbers, forces. Compare
Henry V 1.2.304, 'let our proportions for

these wars | Be soon collected.'

33 **subject** See note to 1.1.72

34 **Voltemand** Voltemand, Valtemand, and
Voltemar are corruptions of the Danish
Valdemar, the name of several Danish
kings, including Valdemar I (1113–82),
who has a prominent place in Saxo's *History*.

35 **For** as, in the capacity of

37 **To** with regard to, for (Abbott 186)

38 **dilated** detailed, set out in full. Compare
All's Well 2.1.49–55, 'Use a more
spacious ceremony to the noble lords . . .
After them, and take a more dilated
farewell.'
  allow The verb has been attracted into
the plural by the proximity of the plural
noun 'articles' (Abbott 412)

39 **your haste commend your duty** 'i.e. your
haste rather than your words. Claudius
anticipates the usual parting formula'
(Jenkins). All the same, Voltemand and
Cornelius manage to work the formula
into their reply.

⌈CORNELIUS *and*⌉ VOLTEMAND
  In that and all things will we show our duty.   40
CLAUDIUS
  We doubt it nothing, heartily farewell.
                                        Exeunt Voltemand and Cornelius
  And now, Laertes, what's the news with you?
  You told us of some suit, what is't, Laertes?
  You cannot speak of reason to the Dane
  And lose your voice. What wouldst thou beg, Laertes,
  That shall not be my offer, not thy asking?
  The head is not more native to the heart,
  The hand more instrumental to the mouth,
  Than is the throne of Denmark to thy father.
  What wouldst thou have, Laertes?
LAERTES   Dread my lord,   50
  Your leave and favour to return to France,
  From whence though willingly I came to Denmark
  To show my duty in your coronation,
  Yet now I must confess, that duty done,
  My thoughts and wishes bend again towards France
  And bow them to your gracious leave and pardon.
CLAUDIUS
  Have you your father's leave? What says Polonius?

---

40 CORNELIUS *and* VOLTEMAND] Q2 (*Cor. Vo.*); *Volt⟨emand⟩* F; *Gent* Q1   41 *Exeunt Voltemand and Cornelius*] F (*subs.*); *not in* Q2Q1   45–6 Laertes, . . . asking?] F; *Laertes,? . . .* asking, Q2   50 Dread my] F; My dread Q2; My gratious Q1   55 towards] F; toward Q2

---

40 ⌈CORNELIUS *and*⌉ VOLTEMAND The use of 'we' in all three substantive texts strongly suggests that both ambassadors speak. The Folio's failure to give the name *Cornelius* in its speech heading can be simply explained: there is no room for it in a line that as it stands is a tight one.

41 **nothing** in no way, not at all (Abbott 55). Compare *Twelfth Night* 2.3.93, 'she's nothing allied to your disorders.'

45 **lose your voice** speak in vain

46 **That . . . asking** that I won't give you before you can ask for it

47–9 **The head . . . father** a reference to the well worn analogy, described at length in *Coriolanus* 1.1.94–152, between the body politic and the human body. 'The head'—'The kingly crownèd head' of *Coriolanus*—is, of course, the king himself; and 'the heart'—'The counsellor heart' of *Coriolanus*—is the Danish Council and, more specifically in this case, Polonius.

47 **native** naturally connected

48 **instrumental** serviceable

51 **leave and favour** favourable leave, kind permission (hendiadys)

55 **bend** turn, incline

56 **bow them** submit themselves
    pardon indulgence, permission. Compare *Antony* 3.6.59–60, 'whereon I begged | His pardon for return'. Shakespeare is thinking, as usual, about conditions in his own England, where anyone seeking to travel abroad needed 'a licence from the sovereign or the Privy Council' (*Shakespeare's England*, i. 212).

POLONIUS

He hath, my lord, wrung from me my slow leave
By laboursome petition, and at last
Upon his will I sealed my hard consent.   60
I do beseech you give him leave to go.

CLAUDIUS

Take thy fair hour, Laertes; time be thine,
And thy best graces spend it at thy will.
But now, my cousin Hamlet, and my son—

HAMLET

A little more than kin, and less than kind.

CLAUDIUS

How is it that the clouds still hang on you?

HAMLET

Not so, my lord, I am too much i'th' sun.

---

58 He] FQ1; *not in* Q2; A PARROTT–CRAIG   lord,] Q1; Lord: F; Lord꜀ Q2   58–60 wrung . . .
consent] Q2; *not in* F; wrung from me a forced graunt Q1   64 Hamlet,] FQ2; *Hamlet, Exit*
[*Laertes*] Q1   67 so] F; so much Q2   i'th' sun] F; in the sonne Q2

58–60 **wrung . . . consent** These two and a
half lines are omitted from F. They must
have stood in the original acting version
because Q1's version of the entire speech
runs thus: 'He hath, my lord, wrung from
me a forced grant, | And I beseech you
grant your highness' leave.' The 'forced
grant' implies that the reporter had a
vague recollection of more than 'my slow
leave'. He recalled that Laertes had put
pressure on his father by resorting to
'laboursome petition'. It therefore looks
as though F's omission is accidental and
not the result of an authorial cut.
59 **laboursome** assiduous
60 **Upon . . . consent** Polonius is quibbling.
Will = (1) wish (2) last will and testament; and *hard* = (1) reluctant, obtained
with difficulty (2) the hardness of the sig-
net-ring used in sealing a document.
62 **Take thy fair hour** enjoy yourself while
you are young
63 **thy best graces spend it** may your finest
qualities make use of it. Compare *Macbeth*
4.3.91–4, where 'the king-becoming
graces' are set out in detail.
64 **cousin** kinsman, relative by blood (ex-
cluding parent, child, brother, or sister)
son At this point Q1 gives Laertes an exit;
but neither Q2 nor F does so. He presum-

ably retires into the background.
65 **A little more than kin, and less than kind**
These characteristically riddling words,
the first that Hamlet speaks, are his own
version of the proverb 'The nearer in kin
the less in kindness' (Tilley K38), meaning 'the closer the relationship, the
greater the dislike'. Hamlet gives this saw
a personal application by saying, in effect,
'I am closer to you, now that you have
married my mother, than a mere kinsman
(*cousin*), but something less than your
son, since you are not my father and your
marriage to my mother is an unnatural
one; and, the more closely related to me
you become, the less I like it.' Most editors
since Theobald (1740) have marked the
speech as an *Aside*, but its barbed obscur-
ity strongly suggests that it is intended to
be heard by Claudius, to puzzle him, and
to disturb him.
67 **i'th' sun** in the sunshine of your favour.
This is the obvious meaning; but almost
equally obvious is the *sun/son* quibble,
which Shakespeare had already exploited
at the opening of *Richard III*: 'Now is the
winter of our discontent | Made glorious
summer by this sun of York' (1.1.1–2).
Hamlet pointedly refuses to take on the
role of Claudius's *son*.

GERTRUDE

Good Hamlet, cast thy nightly colour off,
And let thine eye look like a friend on Denmark.
Do not for ever with thy vailèd lids   70
Seek for thy noble father in the dust.
Thou know'st 'tis common—all that lives must die,
Passing through nature to eternity.

HAMLET

Ay, madam, it is common.

GERTRUDE   If it be,
Why seems it so particular with thee?

HAMLET

Seems, madam? Nay, it is, I know not 'seems'.
'Tis not alone my inky cloak, good mother,
Nor customary suits of solemn black,
Nor windy suspiration of forced breath,
No, nor the fruitful river in the eye,   80
Nor the dejected haviour of the visage,
Together with all forms, moods, shows of grief,
That can denote me truly. These indeed seem,
For they are actions that a man might play;
But I have that within which passeth show—
These but the trappings and the suits of woe.

68 nightly] F; nighted Q2   72 common—] ALEXANDER; common, F; common‚ Q2   77 good]
F; coold Q2   82 shows] F; chapes Q2; shapes Q3   83 denote] F; deuote Q2   85 passeth] F;
passes Q2

68 **nightly colour** night-like mourning garments and gloomy behaviour. The Queen
combines two meanings in one.
69 **let . . . Denmark** It is hard to say whether
Gertrude is asking her son to look on the
King of Denmark with a more friendly eye
—should the Prince be scowling at him?
—or to look on Denmark itself with a
more friendly eye, and not go back to Wittenberg. In the light of her request at lines
118–9, the latter seems the more likely.
70 **vailèd** lowered, downcast (*OED v.*² 1c).
Compare *Venus* 956, 'She vailed her eyelids'.
72–3 **'tis common . . . eternity** 'Death is
common to all' was proverbial (Tilley
D142), as Hamlet stresses in his answer
where *common* means 'commonplace'.

75 **so particular with thee** such a peculiarly
personal matter to you
77 **alone** only, simply
78 **customary** conventional, formal
79 **windy suspiration of forced breath** insincere constrained sighing. Hamlet's
elaborate way of expressing himself
mocks the empty show of grief he
describes. Shakespeare does not use *suspiration* anywhere else.
80 **fruitful** copious. According to *OED* 3, this
use of the word is chiefly Shakespearian.
81 **haviour** expression
82 **moods** external appearances (Schmidt).
Compare *Sonnets* 93. 7–8, 'In many's
looks the false heart's history | Is writ in
moods and frowns and wrinkles strange.'
85 **passeth** goes beyond, surpasses

CLAUDIUS

'Tis sweet and commendable in your nature, Hamlet,
To give these mourning duties to your father;
But you must know your father lost a father;
That father lost, lost his; and the survivor bound   90
In filial obligation for some term
To do obsequious sorrow. But to persever
In obstinate condolement is a course
Of impious stubbornness, 'tis unmanly grief,
It shows a will most incorrect to heaven,
A heart unfortified, a mind impatient,
An understanding simple and unschooled;
For what we know must be, and is as common
As any the most vulgar thing to sense,
Why should we in our peevish opposition   100
Take it to heart? Fie, 'tis a fault to heaven,
A fault against the dead, a fault to nature,
To reason most absurd, whose common theme
Is death of fathers, and who still hath cried,
From the first corpse till he that died today,

---

96 a mind] F; or minde Q2

87 **commendable** accented on the first syllable
89 **must know** should realize
90 **father lost** father who was lost (Abbott 246)
   bound was bound, was obliged
92 **do obsequious sorrow** mourn as obsequies (funeral ceremonies) demand. Compare *Titus* 5.3.152, 'to shed obsequious tears upon this trunk'.
   persever The accent falls on the second syllable.
93 **condolement** grieving, lamentation. Apparently introduced into English by Shakespeare and/or Marston in his *Antonio's Revenge* (5.6.58), this word does not appear in this sense elsewhere in Shakespeare, though it is misused by the Second Fisherman in *Pericles* (2.1.149).
95 **incorrect** recalcitrant, unsubdued (not found elsewhere in Shakespeare)
96 **unfortified** not strengthened against the assault of the emotions, lacking the stoic virtue of fortitude
   impatient unprepared to bear suffering
97 **simple** weak, ignorant
   unschooled undisciplined

98 **what** that which (Abbott 252)
99 **any the most vulgar thing to sense** most ordinary of the things we are aware of through our senses. See Abbott 419a; and compare *Cymbeline* 1.4.57, 'any the rarest of our ladies in France'.
100 **peevish opposition** perverse refractoriness
101 **fault** offence
102 **nature** the entire order of things in general
103–4 **whose . . . who** Since divine law, the law of nature, and the law of reason were inextricably involved with one another, the antecedent to *who* would appear to be all three regarded as a single entity. For the use of *who* to personify abstract antecedents, see Abbott 264.
105 **the first corpse** that of Abel. Critics notice the unconscious irony in Claudius's reference to the crime of Cain; but for the first audience to see the play it would not exist, because they had, as yet, no reason to think that Claudius had committed the same crime.
   till he to him, to the man (Abbott 184 and 205–6)

'This must be so'. We pray you throw to earth
This unprevailing woe, and think of us
As of a father; for let the world take note
You are the most immediate to our throne,
And with no less nobility of love   110
Than that which dearest father bears his son
Do I impart towards you. For your intent
In going back to school in Wittenberg,
It is most retrograde to our desire,
And we beseech you bend you to remain
Here in the cheer and comfort of our eye,
Our chiefest courtier, cousin, and our son.

GERTRUDE

Let not thy mother lose her prayers, Hamlet.
I prithee stay with us, go not to Wittenberg.

HAMLET

I shall in all my best obey you, madam.   120

112 towards] F, toward Q2   you.] F; you‸ Q2   119 prithee] F; pray thee Q2

106 **throw to earth** overthrow, get the better of. Claudius appears to have wrestling in mind.
107 **unprevailing** unavailing, unprofitable. Compare *Romeo* 3.3.60, 'It helps not, it prevails not.'
109 **most immediate** next in succession. Compare *All's Well* 2.3.130, 'to nature she's immediate heir'; and 2 *Henry IV* 5.2.71, 'Th' immediate heir of England'.
110–12 **And . . . you** And I offer a love for you no less free from all base considerations than that which the most devoted father feels for his son. This explanation assumes that *to impart with* can mean *to offer to share with*. It is possible, however, that Shakespeare, by the time he reached the end of the sentence, forgot that he had written 'with no less nobility of love', and concluded it as though he had written 'no less nobility of love'. The first explanation seems better, because the contorted syntax that gives rise to it could well be deliberate art. True love does not speak thus.
110 **nobility of love** love free from all base considerations
111 **dearest** the dearest, the most devoted (Abbott 82)
112 **For** as for (Abbott 149)
113 **school** university. This sense of the word, still current in North America,

seems to have become obsolete in England by the middle of the seventeenth century. See the passage from Hobbes's *Leviathan* (1651) quoted in *OED* (*sb.*[1] 7).
Wittenberg Well known in England as Luther's university and the birthplace of Protestantism, Wittenberg was also familiar to Elizabethan playgoers as the home of Dr Faustus. It seems to have been much frequented in Shakespeare's day by Danes studying abroad.
114 **retrograde** contrary. *OED* gives no earlier use of this figurative sense of the word, which was originally an astronomical term applied to the movement of stars which seemed to go backwards in the reverse direction to that of the signs of the Zodiac. Shakespeare plays with this other sense in his one other recourse to *retrograde* at *All's Well* 1.2.178–88.
115 **we beseech you bend you** we beseech you to incline yourself, submit yourself
116 **cheer and comfort** cheering and comforting influence—the antidote to melancholy and grief
eye almost equivalent to *presence*. Compare *Lear* 4.4.8, 'bring him to our eye'.
120 **in all my best** to the best of my abilities
obey you Hamlet stresses *you* to make it clear that it is Gertrude's request, not the King's, that he heeds.

CLAUDIUS

Why, 'tis a loving and a fair reply.
Be as ourself in Denmark. Madam, come.
This gentle and unforced accord of Hamlet
Sits smiling to my heart; in grace whereof,
No jocund health that Denmark drinks today
But the great cannon to the clouds shall tell,
And the King's rouse the heavens shall bruit again,
Re-speaking earthly thunder. Come away.
                                ⌈*Flourish.*⌉ *Exeunt all but Hamlet*

HAMLET

O that this too too solid flesh would melt,
Thaw and resolve itself into a dew,   130
Or that the Everlasting had not fixed
His canon 'gainst self-slaughter. O God! O God!
How weary, stale, flat, and unprofitable
Seem to me all the uses of this world!

---

127 heavens] F heauen Q2   128.1 *Flourish*] Q2; not in FQ1   129 solid] F; sallied Q2Q1;
sullied WILSON   132 self-slaughter] F; seale slaughter Q2   God! O God!] F; God, God,
Q2   133 weary] F; wary Q2   134 Seem] Q2 (Seeme), Seemes F

---

121 **'tis a loving and a fair reply** So far as
Claudius is concerned, the reply is
neither, but he tries to make the best of it
by treating it as a good excuse for having
a drink.
124 **Sits smiling to** delights. Contrast
Measure 5.1.387, 'Your brother's death, I
know, sits at your heart'.
   grace honour (*OED*, 1d). Compare *Dream*
4.1.131, 'Came here in grace of our
solemnity.'
125–8 **No jocund . . . thunder** Wilson aptly
quotes the following passage from Stow's
Annals (p. 1433), describing the events
that accompanied a royal christening and
the presentation of the order of the Garter
to Christian IV of Denmark in the summer
of 1603: 'That afternoon the King went
aboard the English ship [lying off Elsinore]
and had a banquet prepared for him upon
the upper decks, which were hung with
an awning of tissue; every health reported
[led to the firing of] six, eight, or ten shot
of great ordnance, so that during the
King's abode, the ship discharged 160
shot.'
127 **rouse** a full draught of liquor; a bumper
(*OED sb.*³). OED suggests that *rouse* is
'probably an aphetic form of *carouse*, due

to the phrase *to drink carouse* having been
apprehended as *to drink a rouse*', and
derives that phrase from the German '*gar-
aus trinken* to drink "all out", to empty
the bowl'. It also cites this as the earliest
occurrence of the word in English.
   bruit noisily proclaim. Compare *Macbeth*
5.7.21–2, 'By this great clatter, one of
greatest note | Seems bruited.'
129–30 **O that . . . dew** See long note at
p. 382–4.
129 **too too** altogether too, much too. The
reduplication of *too* for emphasis was very
common from about 1540 to 1660 (*OED*
4).
130 **resolve** dissolve (*OED v.* 1). Compare *K.
John* 5.4.24–5, 'even as a form of wax
| Resolveth from his figure 'gainst the fire.'
132 **His canon 'gainst self-slaughter** It was
taken for granted that suicide was
prohibited by the sixth commandment,
'Thou shalt not kill' (Exodus 20: 13).
Compare *Cymbeline* 3.4.74–6, 'Against
self-slaughter | There is a prohibition so
divine | That cravens my weak hand.' *Self-
slaughter* seems to be a Shakespearian
coinage.
133 **weary** wearisome, tedious
134 **uses** ways, activities

Fie on't! O fie, fie! 'Tis an unweeded garden
That grows to seed; things rank and gross in nature
Possess it merely. That it should come to this!
But two months dead—nay not so much, not two—
So excellent a king, that was to this
Hyperion to a satyr, so loving to my mother   140
That he might not beteem the winds of heaven
Visit her face too roughly. Heaven and earth,
Must I remember? Why, she would hang on him
As if increase of appetite had grown
By what it fed on, and yet within a month—
Let me not think on't; frailty, thy name is woman—
A little month, or ere those shoes were old
With which she followed my poor father's body,
Like Niobe, all tears, why she, even she—
O God, a beast that wants discourse of reason   150

135 O fie, fie!] F; ah fie Q2   136–7 nature . . . merely. That] F; nature, . . . meerely that
Q2   137 to this!] F (to this:); thus Q2   141 beteem] Q2; beteene F   143 would] FQ1;
should Q2   149 she, even] F; *not in* Q2   150 God] Q2Q1; Heauen F

135–7 'Tis . . . merely For Shakespeare, as
for his age in general, the properly ten-
ded garden was an image of the world
as it should be, ordered, productive,
wholesome. By the time he wrote *Hamlet*,
he had already painted two memorable
pictures of the uncared-for garden: in
Richard II 3.4.42–7, and in *Henry V*
5.2.38–55. These vivid descriptions
bring out the commonplace nature of the
proverbial saying, 'Weeds come forth on
the fattest soil if it is untilled' (Tilley
W241).
137 merely completely, entirely
139 to compared to (*OED* 18)
140 Hyperion to a satyr This phrase condenses into four words Hamlet's attitude
towards the two men. For him his father is
man in his god-like aspect, radiant as the
sun; whereas Claudius, the satyr, half
man and half goat, is man at his worst,
lustful and drunken, since satyrs were the
companions of Bacchus. This is the only
occurrence of *satyr* in Shakespeare.
141 might not beteem would not allow,
could not bring himself to permit (Abbott
312)
144–5 As if . . . fed on Compare 'Appetite
comes with eating' (Tilley A286); and
Antony 2.2.240–2, 'Other women
cloy | The appetites they feed, but she

makes hungry | Where most she satisfies.'
146 frailty . . . woman Compare 'Women
are frail' (Dent W700.1); and *Twelfth
Night* 2.2.29–30, 'Alas, our frailty is the
cause, not we | For such as we are made
of, such we be.'
147 or ere before (Abbott 131)
149 Niobe In Greek mythology Niobe is
the personification of bereavement. She
boasted that she was at least the equal of
Leto, because she had six (or seven) children of either sex, whereas Leto had but
one of each. In revenge of the slight,
Leto's two children, Apollo and Artemis,
killed all Niobe's children, leaving her to
grieve.
  even she These words, for which F is the
sole authority, are required for metrical
reasons and also for emphasis. Repetition,
so indicative of an obsessive preoccupation, is a feature of the entire speech.
Eye-skip, to which both compositors were
prone, would account for Q2's omission.
150 wants discourse of reason lacks the
capacity, peculiar to man, to reason logic-
ally from a premise to a conclusion. The
phrase *discourse of reason* was a common one (see *OED discourse sb.* 2b), and is
used again by Shakespeare in *Troilus*
(2.2.116).

Would have mourned longer—married with my
    uncle,
My father's brother, but no more like my father
Than I to Hercules; within a month,
Ere yet the salt of most unrighteous tears
Had left the flushing in her gallèd eyes,
She married. O most wicked speed, to post
With such dexterity to incestuous sheets!
It is not, nor it cannot come to good.
But break, my heart, for I must hold my tongue.
    Enter Horatio, Marcellus, and Barnardo

HORATIO
Hail to your lordship.

HAMLET   I am glad to see you well.   160
Horatio—or I do forget myself.

HORATIO
The same, my lord, and your poor servant ever.

HAMLET
Sir, my good friend, I'll change that name with you.
And what make you from Wittenberg, Horatio?
Marcellus.

MARCELLUS My good lord.

---

151 my] Q2; mine FQ1   155 in] Q2Q1; of F   159 break,] F4; breake‸ FQ2Q1

151 **married with** married (Abbott 194)
153 **I to Hercules** Does Hamlet mean that he
is not of heroic physical proportions; that
he is incapable, as Jenkins suggests, of
performing superhuman tasks; that he
does not share Hercules' appetite for
'weeding' monsters from the garden of
the world; or that he is not supremely
virtuous (see note to 1.3.47–51)?
154 **unrighteous** insincere
155 **left** ceased from leaving. Shakespeare
has, it seems, combined two senses of
leave—*leave off* and *leave behind*—into
one.
  flushing redness caused by the 'eye-
offending brine' (*Twelfth Night* 1.1.30) of
tears
  gallèd sore (from weeping). Compare
Richard III 4.4.53, 'galled eyes of weeping
souls'.
156 **post** hurry, rush
157 **dexterity** nimbleness (Schmidt)
  incestuous because marriage to a

deceased husband's brother was forbid-
den by the Church, whether Catholic or
Protestant
158 **nor it cannot** Shakespeare, like his con-
temporaries, often uses the double
negative for emphasis (Abbott 406).
159 **But . . . tongue** a very common sentiment. Compare the proverb 'Grief pent up
will break the heart' (Tilley G449), and
Macbeth 4.3.209–10, 'Give sorrow words.
The grief that does not speak | Whispers
the o'erfraught heart and bids it break.'
163 **change that name** exchange that name
'servant', or, possibly, that name 'friend'.
Compare 'A friend is one's second self'
(Tilley F696).
164 **make you from** has brought you from,
are you doing away from (*OED make v.*
58)
165 **Marcellus** F indents the word as though
it were a speech prefix; the catchword for
the previous page is '*Mar.*', the
abbreviated prefix for 1.2.166.

HAMLET

I am very glad to see you. (*To Barnardo*) Good even,
   sir.—
But what in faith make you from Wittenberg?

HORATIO

A truant disposition, good my lord.

HAMLET

I would not have your enemy say so,   170
Nor shall you do my ear that violence
To make it truster of your own report
Against yourself. I know you are no truant.
But what is your affair in Elsinore?
We'll teach you to drink deep ere you depart.

HORATIO

My lord, I came to see your father's funeral.

HAMLET

I pray thee do not mock me, fellow-student;
I think it was to see my mother's wedding.

HORATIO

Indeed, my lord, it followed hard upon.

HAMLET

Thrift, thrift, Horatio. The funeral baked meats   180
Did coldly furnish forth the marriage tables.
Would I had met my dearest foe in heaven

170 have] F; heare Q2   171 my] Q2; mine F   175 to drink deep] FQ1; for to drinke
Q2   177 pray thee] F; pre thee Q2Q1   178 see] FQ1; *not in* Q2

167 **Good even** a usual form of greeting at
   any time after midday
170 **have** This F reading avoids the jingle of
   Q2's *hear* followed by *ear*.
171–2 **that violence | To** such violence as to
   (Abbott 277)
175 **to drink deep** This F reading, with
   which Q1 agrees, is almost certainly due
   to authorial revision, since there is no
   other way of explaining how 'for to
   drink', the reading of Q2, could undergo
   such an alteration. Hamlet, with brilliant
   bitterness, suggests that Denmark can
   make one contribution to Horatio's education: it will teach him the *ars bibendi*.
180 **Thrift, thrift** Hamlet, the Renaissance
   Prince, has nothing but scorn for this
   middle-class virtue so much prized by
   Shylock.

baked meats pies and pastries in general
181 **coldly** in their cold state, when they had
   had time to cool
182 **dearest** most inveterate. Compare 1
   Henry IV 3.2.123, where the King
   describes the Prince as 'my nearest and
   dearest enemy'. *OED* suggests that
   'dearest friend' may have given rise to
   'dearest enemy' as its antonym (*dear a.*¹
   2e); but it also points to a likely connection between the phrase and another
   adjective *dear*, meaning *dire*, *grievous*, as
   in 'The dateless limit of thy dear exile'
   (*Richard II* 1.3.151); see *dear a.*² 2.
   Hamlet's strong dislike of the idea that
   any enemy of his should go to heaven is a
   fascinating anticipation of the reason he
   gives for sparing the praying Claudius in
   3.3.

Ere I had ever seen that day, Horatio.
My father—methinks I see my father—

HORATIO
O where, my lord?

HAMLET   In my mind's eye, Horatio.

HORATIO
I saw him once. He was a goodly king.

HAMLET
He was a man. Take him for all in all.
I shall not look upon his like again.

HORATIO
My lord, I think I saw him yesternight.

HAMLET Saw? Who?

HORATIO   My lord, the King your father.   190

HAMLET The King my father?

HORATIO
Season your admiration for a while
With an attent ear till I may deliver,
Upon the witness of these gentlemen,
This marvel to you.

HAMLET   For God's love let me hear.

HORATIO
Two nights together had these gentlemen,

183 Ere I had ever] F; Or euer I had Q2; Ere euer I had Q1   185 O where] F; Where
Q2Q1   186 He] FQ1; a Q2   187 He] FQ1; A Q2   190 Saw? Who?] F; saw, who?
Q2Q1   195 God's] Q2Q1; Heauens F

186 **once** It is a waste of time to try to fit
Horatio's various references not only to
old Hamlet but also to Denmark into a
coherent whole. No audience is likely to
notice that *once* is inconsistent with what
Horatio has already said about the old
King at 1.1.59 ff., or that his ignorance of
Danish customs at 1.4.7 is incompatible
with the knowledge of Danish history he
shows at 1.1.80–95. Horatio is essentially a piece of the dramatic mechanism,
a *Johannes fac totum* who will say or do
whatever the plot requires of him, even to
the extent of appearing from nowhere at a
call from Hamlet (3.2.48). What remains
constant in him is his fidelity to the
Prince.

187 **He was . . . in all** The punctuation here,
supported by that of F, is Jenkins's, who
argues convincingly that *all in all* means

'the epitome of all that a man should be',
'the sum and pattern of excellence'. He
also draws attention to the relevance here
of the proverb 'All in all and all in every
part' (Tilley A133).

190 **Saw? Who?** The Folio punctuation
brings out the importance of the moment.
Hamlet's *taedium vitae* disappears. From
now on he is all attention, probing the
mystery with question after question.

  Who Shakespeare often neglects to inflect
who (Abbott 274), as we still do in
colloquial speech today.

192 **Season** moderate, restrain. Compare
2.1.28.

  admiration wonder, amazement

193 **attent** attentive. Compare *Pericles* 3.
Prologue 11, 'Be attent', the only other
appearance of the word in Shakespeare.

Marcellus and Barnardo, on their watch,
In the dead waste and middle of the night,
Been thus encountered. A figure like your father,
Armed at all points exactly, cap-à-pie,   200
Appears before them, and with solemn march
Goes slow and stately by them. Thrice he walked
By their oppressed and fear-surprisèd eyes
Within his truncheon's length, whilst they, distilled
Almost to jelly with the act of fear,
Stand dumb and speak not to him. This to me
In dreadful secrecy impart they did,
And I with them the third night kept the watch,
Where, as they had delivered, both in time,
Form of the thing, each word made true and good,   210
The apparition comes. I knew your father;
These hands are not more like.

HAMLET   But where was this?

MARCELLUS
My lord, upon the platform where we watched.

198 waste] FQ2 (wast); vast Q1   200 Armed] F (Arm'd), Q2Q1 (Armed)   at all points
exactly,] F; at poynt, exactly_A Q2, to poynt, exactly Q1   cap à pie] F (*Cap a Pe*); *Capapea*
Q2Q1   202 stately by them.] Q2 (stately by them;); stately: By them_A F   204 distilled] Q2Q1;
bestil'd F   205 jelly . . . fear,] F; gelly, . . . feare_A Q2; gelly. With . . . feare_A Q1   209 Where,
as] Q1683; Whereas FQ2; Where as Q1, Q5   time,] F; time_A Q2   210 thing,] Q2; thing; F;
thing. Q1   213 watched] F (watcht) Q1 (watched); watch Q2

198 **dead waste** lifeless desolation. *Waste*
often appears as *wast*, the spelling of Q2
and F, in Shakespeare, and invariably so
in *Romeo*, *Venus*, and *Lucrece*. There is,
therefore, no reason whatever to reject
waste in favour of Q1's *vast*, which, in any
case, means much the same thing.

200 **Armed . . . cap-à-pie** Armed with exact
precision in every detail from head to foot.
Compare *Winter's Tale* 4.4.725, 'I am
courtier cap-a-pe'; and the commonplace, 'To be armed from top to toe' (Dent
T436.1).

202 **stately** majestically. Shakespeare's only
use of *stately* as an adverb.

203 **oppressed and fear-surprisèd eyes** eyes
overcome and taken prisoner by fear.
Compare *Richard II* 3.2.180, 'fear
oppresseth strength'; *Titus* 1.1.284,
'Lavinia is surprised', and 2.3.211, 'I am
surprised with an uncouth fear.' See also
OED surprise v. 2b.

204 **truncheon** military commander's staff

of office. Compare *Measure* 2.2.61, 'The
marshal's truncheon'.
   distilled melted, dissolved (OED 7). The
word was often spelt 'destil'd', which may
help to explain F's mistake.

205 **act** effect, operation. Compare *Cym-
beline* 1.5.21–2, 'apply | Allayments to
their act'.

207 **dreadful** awe-struck (Abbott 3).

209–10 **both . . . Form** For the omission of
the expected *and*, compare *Winter's Tale*
4.4.56, 'she was both pantler, butler,
cook'.

213 **platform** gun emplacement, level place
built for mounting cannon
   watched The reading of F, *watcht*, seems
preferable because it has the support of Q1
and because the past tense fits in naturally
with Hamlet's question. Moreover, the
speech comes from Marcellus, the reporter
of Q1, who usually gets his own part
right.

HAMLET
Did you not speak to it?

HORATIO   My lord, I did,
But answer made it none. Yet once methought
It lifted up it head and did address
Itself to motion like as it would speak.
But even then the morning cock crew loud,
And at the sound it shrunk in haste away
And vanished from our sight.

HAMLET   'Tis very strange.   220

HORATIO
As I do live, my honoured lord, 'tis true;
And we did think it writ down in our duty
To let you know of it.

HAMLET
Indeed, indeed, sirs, but this troubles me.
Hold you the watch tonight?

MARCELLUS *and* BARNARDO   We do, my lord.

HAMLET Armed, say you?

MARCELLUS *and* BARNARDO Armed, my lord.

HAMLET From top to toe?

MARCELLUS *and* BARNARDO My lord, from head to foot.

HAMLET Then saw you not his face.

HORATIO
O yes, my lord, he wore his beaver up.

HAMLET What looked he? Frowningly?   230

---

224 Indeed, indeed] FQI; Indeede Q2   225, 226, 227 MARCELLUS *and* BARNARDO] F (Both); *All*
Q2QI   228 face.] Q2; face? FQI   230 What looked he? Frowningly?] This edition; What,
lookt he frowningly? F; What look't he frowningly? Q2; How look't he, frowningly? QI; What
look'd he, frowningly? JENKINS

216 **it head** its head (Abbott 228)
  address prepare (*OED v.* 3). Compare
  Winter's Tale 4.4.53, 'Address yourself to
  entertain them'.
217 **to motion like as it would** for action just
  as if it wanted to (Abbott 107)
218 **even then** precisely at that moment
  (Abbott 38)
220–1 **strange . . . true** a conflation of two
  proverbial sayings: 'It is no more strange
  than true' and 'As true as I live' (Tilley
  S914 and L374)
225, 226, 227 MARCELLUS *and* BARNARDO
  F's 'Both' has the virtue of being more
  explicit than the 'All' of the two quartos.

228 **Then saw you not his face** This Q2 reading, without the question mark found in
  F, makes the better sense. Hamlet, sharp-
  witted as always, detects a seeming inconsistency in Horatio's account.
229 **beaver** visor, face-guard of a helmet
230 **What** How (*OED* A. 20). Compare
  Romeo 1.5.53–4, 'What dares the
  slave | Come hither'; and especially 'How
  look't he, frowningly', the reading of QI.
  The reporter recalled the meaning,
  though not the exact wording.
  Frowningly For a full description of
  how a warrior was supposed to look see
  Henry V 3.1.5–17.

HORATIO

A countenance more in sorrow than in anger.

HAMLET Pale or red?

HORATIO Nay, very pale.

HAMLET And fixed his eyes upon you?

HORATIO Most constantly.

HAMLET I would I had been there.

HORATIO It would have much amazed you.

HAMLET

Very like, very like. Stayed it long?

HORATIO

While one with moderate haste might tell a hundred.

MARCELLUS *and* BARNARDO Longer, longer. 240

HORATIO

Not when I saw't.

HAMLET His beard was grizzly, no?

HORATIO

It was as I have seen it in his life,
A sable silvered.

HAMLET

I'll watch tonight. Perchance 'twill walk again.

HORATIO I warrant you it will.

HAMLET

If it assume my noble father's person,
I'll speak to it though hell itself should gape

---

238 Very like, very like] F Q1; Very like Q2   240 MARCELLUS *and* BARNARDO] Q1 (Both); All
F; Mar⟨cellus⟩ Q1   241 grizzly] F (grisly); grissl'd Q2; grisleld Q1   242 was as...life,] Q1;
was, as...life, F; was‸ as...life‸ Q2   244 I'll] F; I will Q2Q1   walk] Q2Q1; wake F   245
warrant you] F; warn't Q2; warrant Q1

237 **amazed** astounded, bewildered, per-
plexed. Compare *Venus* 684, where the
origin of *amaze* in *a maze* is particularly
clear: 'like a labyrinth to amaze his foes'.
Horatio means that Hamlet himself would
not, to use a modern idiom, have known
what to make of it.
239 **tell** count
241 **grizzly** grey. F's *grisly* is merely a
variant spelling current in the 17th century. See *OED grizzly a.*
247 **though hell itself should gape** Hell-
mouth was a stage property well known
to the Elizabethan playgoer. Inherited
from the miracle plays of the Middle Ages,
it appears, for instance, at the end of Mar-

lowe's *Doctor Faustus*, causing the
protagonist to cry out with his last breath,
'Ugly hell, gape not.' Henslowe includes
'1 Hell mouth' in the inventory of the
properties of the Admiral's men which he
made on 10 March 1598 (*Henslowe's
Diary*, p.319).
Hamlet is facing the possibility that the
Ghost may, in accordance with the
Protestant thinking of the time, be a devil
which has *assumed* (i.e. appropriated) the
body of the dead King for its own wicked
purposes. Ben Jonson mockingly
describes the process of appropriation in
the first scene of his *The Devil is an Ass*.

And bid me hold my peace. I pray you all,
If you have hitherto concealed this sight,
Let it be tenable in your silence still,   250
And whatsoever else shall hap tonight,
Give it an understanding but no tongue.
I will requite your loves. So fare you well.
Upon the platform, 'twixt eleven and twelve,
I'll visit you.

ALL THREE   Our duty to your honour.

HAMLET
Your love, as mine to you. Farewell.

Exeunt all but Hamlet

My father's spirit, in arms! All is not well;
I doubt some foul play. Would the night were come.
Till then sit still, my soul; foul deeds will rise
Though all the earth o'erwhelm them to men's eyes.   260

Exit

1.3   *Enter Laertes and Ophelia*

LAERTES
My necessaries are embarked. Farewell.
And, sister, as the winds give benefit
And convoy is assistant, do not sleep

---

250 tenable] Q2Q1 (tenible); treble F   251 whatsoever] FQ1; what someuer Q2   253 you]
Q2Q1; ye F   256 love] F; loues Q2Q1   *Exeunt all but Hamlet*] Q1676 (*Exeunt. Manet Ham-
let.*); *Exeunt* FQ2Q1   257 in arms!] F (in Armes?); (in armes) Q2; in Armes, Q1   259 foul]
FQ1; fonde Q2
    1.3.0 *and Ophelia*] FQ1; *and Ophelia his Sister* Q2   1 embarked] F (imbark't), Q2 (inbarckt),
Q1 (inbarkt)   3 convoy is assistant,] F (Conuoy is assistant;); conuay, in assistant‿ Q2

---

249 **concealed this sight** i.e. kept your
  knowledge of what you have seen a secret
250 **be tenable in your silence** i.e. remain a
  secret. *OED* cites no earlier example of
  tenable in this sense, and glosses it as 'capable of being held'. Shakespeare does not
  use the word elsewhere.
256 **Your love** Hamlet insists that the
  relationship between him and the soldiers
  is one not merely of *duty* but of love.
258 **doubt** fear
259–60 **foul deeds . . . eyes** Compare *Macbeth* 3.4.122–6, 'It will have blood;
  they say blood will have blood. | Stones
  have been known to move, and trees to
  speak; | Augurs and understood relations

have | By maggot-pies and choughs and
  rooks brought forth | The secretest man of
  blood.'
1.3.1 **necessaries** luggage. Shakespeare
  seems to have associated this word with
  ships. Compare *Othello* 2.1.277, 'I must
  fetch his necessaries ashore', and *Two
  Gentlemen* 2.4.183–4, 'I must unto the
  road to disembark | Some necessaries'.
2 **as** according as, whenever (Abbott 109)
  give benefit are favourable. Compare
  Cymbeline 4.2.342–3, 'When expect you
  them? | With the next benefit o' th' wind.'
3 **convoy is assistant** means of transport
  are available
  sleep be remiss

But let me hear from you.

OPHELIA   Do you doubt that?

LAERTES

For Hamlet, and the trifling of his favour,
Hold it a fashion and a toy in blood,
A violet in the youth of primy nature,
Forward not permanent, sweet not lasting,
The perfume and suppliance of a minute,
No more.

OPHELIA   No more but so?

LAERTES   Think it no more.   10

For nature crescent does not grow alone
In thews and bulk, but as his temple waxes
The inward service of the mind and soul
Grows wide withal. Perhaps he loves you now,
And now no soil nor cautel doth besmirch

---

5 favour] Q2; fauours F   8 Forward] Q2; Froward F   8–10 lasting, | The perfume and
suppliance of a minute, | No more.] Q2 (lasting, | The . . . minute$_A$ | No more.); lasting$_A$ | The
suppliance of a minute? | No more. F   10 so?] ROWE; so. FQ2   12 bulk] F; bulkes Q2   his]
F; this Q2

---

5 **the trifling of his favour** his frivolous attention
6 **fashion** courtly accomplishment
   toy in blood ephemeral amorous impulse.
   A *toy* is a 'passing fancy', and the *blood* is
   regarded as the source of sexual passion.
   Compare *Much Ado* 2.1.158–9, 'beauty is
   a witch | Against whose charms faith melteth into blood'.
7 **primy** This word appears to be a Shakespearian invention. Onions glosses it 'that
   is in its prime'; Wilson, 'in its prime or
   springtime'. It may, however, be closely
   connected with a sense of *prime* that is to
   be found only in *Othello*, 'Were they as
   prime as goats, as hot as monkeys'
   (3.3.407), where *prime* obviously means
   'sexually excited'.
8 **Forward** (1) precocious, early-blooming
   (2) immodestly eager. Compare *Sonnets*
   99.1, 'The forward violet thus did I
   chide'.
9 **perfume and suppliance of a minute** perfume that serves as a momentary diversion. Shakespeare does not use *suppliance*
   elsewhere.
10 **No more but so?** No more than that? The
   phrase 'There is no more but so' was

proverbial (Dent M1158.1), and appears
in precisely this form at *Richard III* 4.2.82.
The question mark, supplied by Rowe,
seems necessary because Ophelia goes on
to offer more resistance to the idea that
Hamlet is merely trifling with her.
11 **nature crescent** i.e. man in his natural
    course of development
    alone only, simply
12 **thews and bulk** physical strength and
    size. Compare *2 Henry IV* 3.2.251–3,
    'Care I for the limb, the thews, the
    stature, bulk, and big assemblance of a
    man! Give me the spirit'.
    temple i.e. body as the temple of the soul.
    Compare 2 Corinthians 6: 16, 'ye are the
    temple of the living God'.
13 **inward service** spiritual duty
14 **wide withal** i.e. extensive along with it
15 **soil** stain, blemish
    cautel crafty intention, deceitful purpose.
    Shakespeare does not use *cautel*
    elsewhere; but he does employ the adjective *cautelous* in *Coriolanus* (4.1.33) and in
    Caesar (2.1.129).
    besmirch earliest example of the infinitive cited by *OED*; *besmirched* occurs in
    Henry V (4.3.111)

The virtue of his will; but you must fear,
His greatness weighed, his will is not his own,
For he himself is subject to his birth.
He may not, as unvalued persons do,
Carve for himself, for on his choice depends   20
The sanity and health of the whole state;
And therefore must his choice be circumscribed
Unto the voice and yielding of that body
Whereof he is the head. Then if he says he loves you,
It fits your wisdom so far to believe it
As he in his peculiar sect and force
May give his saying deed, which is no further
Than the main voice of Denmark goes withal.
Then weigh what loss your honour may sustain
If with too credent ear you list his songs,   30
Or lose your heart, or your chaste treasure open
To his unmastered importunity.
Fear it, Ophelia, fear it, my dear sister,

---

16 will] Q2; feare F   fear,] Q2; feare_A F   18 For . . . birth] F; *not in* Q2   21 sanity] HANMER,
conj. Theobald (*SR*); sanctity F; safty Q2   the] F; this Q2   whole] Q2F2; weole F   26 peculiar
sect and force] F; particular act and place Q2

16 **virtue of his will** honourable nature of his
   intentions
   must fear i.e. have every reason to be
   uneasy because
17 **his greatness weighed** when his high
   position is taken into account
19 **unvalued** unimportant
20 **Carve for himself** do as he likes, choose as
   he wishes. 'To be one's own carver' was
   proverbial (Tilley C110). Compare
   Richard II 2.3.144, 'Be his own carver
   and cut out his way'.
21 **sanity** soundness, well-being. Theobald's
   suggested emendation is adopted here
   because Q2's *safety* gives an unmetrical
   line and F's *sanctity* does not make good
   sense. Moreover, there is good evidence at
   2.2.209, where F correctly reads *Sanitie*,
   while Q2 wrongly reads *sanctitie*, that the
   two words could be easily confused with
   one another.
22 **circumscribed** restricted
23 **voice and yielding** expressly stated consent. Jenkins appositely quotes from Sir
   Thomas Smith's *The Commonwealth of*

England (1589), p. 121: 'The order of
proceeding to judgment is by assent of
voices, and open yielding their mind in
court.'
26 **in his peculiar sect and force** on account
   of his very special position of power. For
   sect, meaning 'rank' or 'class', see
   Measure 2.2.5.
27 **give his saying deed** make his promise
   good. Compare *Timon* 5.1.25–6, 'the
   deed of saying is quite out of use', and the
   proverb 'Saying is one thing and doing
   another' (Tilley S121).
28 **main voice** general consent. Compare
   Henry V 1.2.143–4, 'We do not mean the
   coursing snatchers only, | But fear the
   main intendment of the Scot'. See *OED*
   main a. 7b.
30 **credent** trustful. This rare word seems to
   be a Shakespearian coinage.
   list listen to
31 **your chaste treasure** the treasury containing your virginity. For this use of
   treasure compare *Sonnets* 136.5, 'Will will
   fulfil the treasure of thy love'.

And keep within the rear of your affection,
Out of the shot and danger of desire.
The chariest maid is prodigal enough
If she unmask her beauty to the moon.
Virtue itself scapes not calumnious strokes.
The canker galls the infants of the spring
Too oft before their buttons be disclosed,   40
And in the morn and liquid dew of youth
Contagious blastments are most imminent.
Be wary then; best safety lies in fear;
Youth to itself rebels, though none else near.

OPHELIA

I shall th'effect of this good lesson keep
As watchman to my heart. But, good my brother,

---

34 within] F; you in Q2   40 their] Q2; the F   45 th'] F; the Q2   46 watchman] Q2; watchmen F

34-5 **keep within . . . desire** Laertes, who seems to have picked up his father's addiction to figures of speech, is using military metaphors. His advice may be paraphrased thus: 'Do not advance into the exposed position where your affection would lead you, but stay well back from it, out of range of the dangerous gunshot of physical desire.' 'Out of gunshot' (Tilley G482) was a common expression for 'out of harm's way'.

36-42 **The chariest . . . imminent** In Q2 inverted commas are used at the beginnings of lines 36, 38, and 39 to show that the sentiments they introduce are of a proverbial and moralizing kind, commonplaces of the time.

36 **chariest** (1) shyest, most modest (2) most frugal (in displaying her charms). Compare *Merry Wives* 2.1.86-7, 'I will consent to act any villainy against him that may not sully the chariness of our honesty'.

37 **moon** the emblem of chastity

38 **Virtue . . . strokes** a version of the saying 'Envy (Calumny) shoots at the fairest mark (flowers, virtue)' (Tilley E175).
  scapes (old form of 'escapes') avoids, is spared from

39-40 **The canker . . . disclosed** a variant on

the saying 'The canker soonest eats the fairest rose' (Tilley C56). Compare *Two Gentlemen* 'And writers say, as the most forward bud | Is eaten by the canker ere it blow. . . .' (1.1.45-6).

39 **infants of the spring** i.e. young plants or shoots. Shakespeare uses the identical phrase at *LLL* 1.1.101.

40 **buttons** buds (*OED* 2)
  disclosed opened out, unfolded (*OED disclose v.* 1). Compare *Sonnets* 54. 8, 'summer's breath their maskèd buds discloses'.

42 **blastments** blights causing young growth to wither. Shakespeare associates blasting with the effects of scandal. Compare *Measure* 5.1.122, 'A blasting and a scandalous breath'. The word *blastment*, not found elsewhere in Shakespeare, seems to be a coinage of his.

43 **best safety lies in fear** Compare *Lear* 1.4.329, 'Well, you may fear too far.— Safer than trust too far.'

44 **to** against
  rebels i.e. feels the stirring of lust. The verb *rebel* often has strong sexual overtones in Shakespeare; compare 'Out upon it, old carrion! Rebels it at these years' (*Merchant* 3.1.31-2).

45 **effect** drift, tenor

Do not, as some ungracious pastors do,
Show me the steep and thorny way to heaven,
Whilst like a puffed and reckless libertine
Himself the primrose path of dalliance treads   50
And recks not his own rede.

LAERTES   O fear me not.

    Enter Polonius

    I stay too long—but here my father comes.
    A double blessing is a double grace;
    Occasion smiles upon a second leave.

POLONIUS

    Yet here, Laertes? Aboard, aboard, for shame!
    The wind sits in the shoulder of your sail,
    And you are stayed for. There—my blessing with thee;
    And these few precepts in thy memory
    See thou character. Give thy thoughts no tongue,

---

48 steep] FQ2 (*corr.*); step Q2 (*uncorr.*)   49 Whilst like] F; Whiles Q2   51.1 *Enter Polonius*] F; *after Ophelia's speech* Q2   57 for. There] THEOBALD (subs.); for there: F; for, there Q2Q1   thee] Q2Q1; you F   59 See] F; Looke Q2

47 **ungracious** wicked, devoid of spiritual grace (*OED* 1)

47–51 **pastors . . . rede** Shakespeare has lost control of his sentence. He has allowed 'the puffed and reckless libertine' of the comparison to take over the grammatical function of the true subject 'my brother'. For further examples of the same kind of grammatical shift, see Abbott 415.

    The whole passage is indebted to Matthew 7: 13–14: 'Enter ye in at the strait gate; for wide is the gate, and broad is the way, that leadeth to destruction, and many there be which go in thereat; because strait is the gate, and narrow is the way, which leadeth unto life, and few there be that find it.' It also seems to have been affected, however, by the story of Hercules' Choice, which goes back to Hesiod. In it Hercules has to choose between Vice and Virtue. Standing at a fork in the road, Hercules has to decide whether to take the smooth easy way that leads to wickedness or the long, steep, stony path that leads to virtue. See Erwin Panofsky, *Hercules am Scheidewege* (Leipzig, 1930). The proverbial 'Practise what you preach' (Tilley P537a) is also relevant.

49 **puffed** inflated (with pride). Compare

Timon 4.3.179, 'Whereof thy proud child, arrogant man, is puffed'.

50 **the primrose path** This familiar phrase appears to be a Shakespearian invention. He evidently liked it, for he went on to use it again in *All's Well*, where it is 'the flowery way that leads to the broad gate and the great fire' (4.5.48–9), and in *Macbeth*, where it is 'the primrose way to th' everlasting bonfire' (3.2.18–19).

51 **recks now his own rede** takes no notice of his own advice (to others). Shakespeare does not use *rede* elsewhere, though it was common enough in his time.

    fear fear for (Abbott 200). Compare *Richard III* 1.1.137, 'his physicians fear him mightily'.

54 **Occasion . . . leave** i.e. opportunity treats me kindly in granting me this second goodbye (Kittredge)

56 **sits in the shoulder** is at the back. Compare *Richard II* 2.2.123, 'The wind sits fair for news to go to Ireland'.

59 **character** engrave, inscribe (accented on the second syllable)

    Give thy thoughts no tongue Compare the proverbial saying, 'Wise men have their tongue in their heart, fools their heart in their tongue' (Tilley M602)

Nor any unproportioned thought his act.   60
Be thou familiar, but by no means vulgar.
The friends thou hast, and their adoption tried,
Grapple them to thy soul with hoops of steel,
But do not dull thy palm with entertainment
Of each new-hatched, unfledged comrade. Beware
Of entrance to a quarrel, but being in,
Bear't that th'opposèd may beware of thee.
Give every man thine ear, but few thy voice.
Take each man's censure, but reserve thy judgement.
Costly thy habit as thy purse can buy,   70
But not expressed in fancy; rich not gaudy;
For the apparel oft proclaims the man,

---

62 The] F; Those Q2Q1   63 to] FQ1; vnto Q2   65 new-hatched] Q2 (new hatcht); vnhatcht
F; new Q1   comrade] F; courage Q2Q1   68 thine] F; thy Q2

60 **unproportioned** Inordinate, unruly.
Lucrece bids night 'Make war against
proportioned [regular, normal] course of
time' (*Lucrece* 774).

61 **Be . . . vulgar** i.e. associate freely and
easily but never promiscuously with
others (*OED vulgar a.* 12).

62–5 **The friends . . . comrade** These lines
are a string of commonplaces. Compare
'Keep well thy friends when thou hast
gotten them'; 'Try your friends before
you trust'; and 'Give not your right hand
to every man' (Tilley F752, T595, and
H68).

62 **and** and also (very emphatic; see Abbott
95)
   their adoption tried i.e. their suitability
   for adoption as friends having been tested
   and proved. Compare *Romeo* 4.3.29, 'he
   hath still been tried a holy man'; and see
   OED try v. 13.

63 **Grapple** for a similar use of this word to
describe a close friendly relationship, see
Macbeth 3.1.105, 'Grapples you to the
heart and love of us.'

64 **dull** make callous

64–5 **with entertainment | Of** i.e. by giving
a friendly reception to

65 **comrade** The accent falls on the second
syllable, as it does in *1 Henry IV* 4.1.96.
The assumption behind this reading is
that *comrade* is Shakespeare's revision in F
of the unusual *courage*, meaning 'spirit'

(*OED* 1c), found in Q2 and Q1. A plausible
conjecture, first put forward in *Notes and
Queries*, 10th series, 1 (1904), 425–6, is
comrag(u)e, meaning 'comrade'.

67 **Bear't that** manage it so that

68 **Give . . . ear** Compare 'Hear much but
speak little' (Tilley M1177)

69 **Take . . . judgement** Compare 'A man
should hear all parts ere he judge any'
(Tilley M299).
   censure opinion

70–1 **Costly . . . gaudy** Compare 'Comely
not gaudy' (Tilley C541).

70 **habit** dress

71 **expressed in fancy** taking the form of fan-
tasticalness. Polonius here takes up a
stock complaint of Elizabethan satirists
and critics of society. William Harrison,
for example, writes: 'The fantastical folly
of our nation . . . is such that no form of
apparel liketh us longer than the first garment is in the wearing, if it continue so
long, and be not laid aside to receive some
other trinket newly devised by the fickle-
headed tailors, who covet to have several
tricks in cutting, thereby to draw fond
customers to more expense of money'
(quoted from *Life in Shakespeare's England*,
compiled by J. Dover Wilson (Harmondsworth, 1944), p. 129).

72 **the apparel . . . man** Compare 'Apparel
makes the man' (Tilley A283).

And they in France of the best rank and station
Are of a most select and generous chief in that.
Neither a borrower nor a lender be,
For loan oft loses both itself and friend,
And borrowing dulls the edge of husbandry.
This above all—to thine own self be true,
And it must follow, as the night the day,
Thou canst not then be false to any man.   80
Farewell—my blessing season this in thee.

LAERTES

Most humbly do I take my leave, my lord.

POLONIUS

The time invites you. Go; your servants tend.

LAERTES

Farewell, Ophelia, and remember well
What I have said to you.

OPHELIA   'Tis in my memory locked,
And you yourself shall keep the key of it.

LAERTES Farewell.   *Exit*

74 Are of a most select and generous chief] F (cheff); Or . . . generous, chiefe Q2 ; Are . . . generall
chiefe Q1 ; Are . . . generous choice COLLIER 1853   75 be] F; boy Q2   76 loan] F (lone); loue
Q2   77 dulls the] F; dulleth Q2; dulleth the Q3; dulleth th' *conj.* Parrott–Craig   83 invites]
F; inuests Q2   you. Go;] F (you, go); you goe, Q2

73–4 **And . . . that** ' "Chief," literally the
head, here signifies *eminence, superiority.*
Those of the best rank and station [in
France] are of a most select and generous
superiority in the indication of their dignity by their apparel' (Knight, as quoted
in Furness).

74 **Are** The *Or* of Q2, like its *or minde* for F's
a Minde at 1.2.96, is almost certainly a
misreading.
  generous truly aristocratic
  chief eminence, excellency (*OED sb.*
10)

76 **loan . . . friend** Compare 'Who lends to a
friend loses double' (Tilley and Dent
F725).

77 **dulls the edge of husbandry** The idea
behind this metaphor is that good husbandry, i.e. household management and
careful use of money, consists in paring
away, as with a sharp knife, all unnecessary expenditure. Compare *Macbeth*
2.1.4–5, 'There's husbandry in heaven: |
Their candles are all out.'

78 **to thine own self be true** be steadfast, be

constant (*OED true a.* 1c). See *Troilus*
3.2.169–79.

80 **false** injuriously faithless. Compare
Troilus 3.2.187–90, 'As false . . . As fox to
lamb, or wolf to heifer's calf, | Pard to the
hind, or stepdame to her son'.

81 **season** ripen, bring to maturity (as wood
is *seasoned* to make it fit for use).
Polonius's advice to his son, though
platitudinous, is not foolish. Had Laertes
given it better heed, he would not so
readily have led the revolt against
Claudius, or later trusted him, or, most
important of all, entered so rashly into his
quarrel with Hamlet, to whom he proves
false indeed.

83 **invites** Jenkins argues strongly for Q2's
inuests, meaning 'presses on', because it
'has the character of a Shakespearian
metaphor'; but unusual metaphors are
not part of Polonius's currency. *Invites*
has numerous parallels, including 'th' inviting time' (*Sonnets* 124.8), and 'The
time inviting thee' (*Cymbeline* 3.4.104).
  tend are waiting

POLONIUS

What is't, Ophelia, he hath said to you?

OPHELIA

So please you, something touching the Lord Hamlet.

POLONIUS Marry, well bethought.   90

'Tis told me he hath very oft of late
Given private time to you, and you yourself
Have of your audience been most free and bounteous.
If it be so—as so 'tis put on me,
And that in way of caution—I must tell you
You do not understand yourself so clearly
As it behoves my daughter and your honour.
What is between you? Give me up the truth.

OPHELIA

He hath, my lord, of late made many tenders
Of his affection to me.   100

POLONIUS

Affection, pooh! You speak like a green girl
Unsifted in such perilous circumstance.
Do you believe his tenders, as you call them?

---

88 **What . . . you?** It is typical of Polonius's attitude to Ophelia that, having heard her assure Laertes she will keep his advice secret, he should ask her what that advice was.

90 **Marry** to be sure (originally the name of the Virgin Mary used as an oath)

92 **private time** i.e. time spared from his public duties

93 **audience** i.e. time spent in listening to him
    free liberal. Compare *Othello* 1.3.265, 'to be free and bounteous to her mind'.

94 **put on** impressed upon, strongly suggested to (*OED put v.*[1] 27 (*b*)). Compare *Lear* 2.1.99, ' 'Tis they have put him on the old man's death'.

96 **understand yourself** know your place or how to conduct yourself properly (*OED v.* 1d). Compare 2.2.9, 'th' understanding of himself'.

101 **green** inexperienced. Compare *K. John* 2.1.472, 'yon green boy'.

102 **Unsifted** untried, untested. Compare Marlowe, *Dr. Faustus* 5.1.122–4 'Satan

begins to sift me with his pride. | As in this furnace God shall try my faith, | My faith, vile hell, shall triumph over thee.'
    circumstance affairs, circumstances. Shakespeare often uses this word without discrimininating between singular and plural (*OED sb.* 4b).

103 **Do you . . . them** Polonius's disapproval of and scepticism about Ophelia's use of *tender* is of some linguistic and social interest. The earliest example of *tender*, in the sense of 'an offer of anything for acceptance', dates only from 1577, according to *OED*, whereas the legal use of the word goes back to 1542–3. Shakespeare has Old Capulet say, 'I will make a desperate tender | Of my child's love' (3.4.12–13) as early as *Romeo* (*c*.1595). For Polonius, as for all men of position in Shakespeare's day, the only reliable 'tender of marriage' is a legal document, concerning dowries and the like. To him Hamlet's *tender* of *affection* is highly suspect. As it says nothing about money, it is not *true pay* (106) and not *sterling* (107).

OPHELIA

I do not know, my lord, what I should think.

POLONIUS

Marry, I'll teach you. Think yourself a baby
That you have ta'en his tenders for true pay
Which are not sterling. Tender yourself more dearly,
Or—not to crack the wind of the poor phrase,
Running it thus—you'll tender me a fool.

OPHELIA

My lord, he hath importuned me with love   110
In honourable fashion.

POLONIUS

Ay, 'fashion' you may call it. Go to, go to.

OPHELIA

And hath given countenance to his speech, my lord,
With almost all the holy vows of heaven.

POLONIUS

Ay, springes to catch woodcocks. I do know
When the blood burns, how prodigal the soul
Lends the tongue vows. These blazes, daughter,

---

105 I'll] F; I will Q2   106 his] F; these Q2   109 Running] COLLIER 1853; Roaming F; Wrong
Q2; tendring Q1; Wronging POPE   114 With almost all the holy vows] Q2; with all the vowes
F   115 springes] FQ1; springs Q2   117 Lends] Q2Q1; Giues F

107 **sterling** 'real' English money and, therefore, 'genuine', 'legal tender'
Tender yourself more dearly (1) offer yourself at a higher rate (2) show a more tender concern for yourself
109 **Running** Collier's emendation seems much the most satisfactory solution of the crux caused by three different readings, none of which makes sense. The metaphor derives from the common phenomenon in Shakespeare's day of the horse that has become broken-winded as a result of overwork. *OED* quotes John Fitzherbert, *A new tract . . . for all husbandmen* (1523): 'Broken winded is an ill disease, and cometh of running or riding over much . . . and will not be mended.' Shakespeare refers to a horse as a 'poor jade' twice: at *1 Henry IV* 2.1.6–7, and *2 Henry IV* 1.1.45. The similarity in sound between 'poor jade' and 'poor phrase' seems to clinch the matter.
tender me a fool show yourself a fool in my eyes (Onions). Compare *LLL* 2.1.242–3, 'jewels in crystal . . . tendering their own worth'.
111 **fashion** manner
112 **fashion** fashionable pretence. Polonius gives his own version of Ophelia's word.
Go to, go to Come, come (i.e. don't be silly)
113 **countenance** authority, confirmation
115 **springes to catch woodcocks** i.e. snares to catch simple-minded fools. The phrase was proverbial (Tilley S788), and appears again in a slightly different form, 'Now is the woodcock near the gin', in *Twelfth Night* 2.5.77. As the woodcock was supposedly an easy bird to catch, it became synonymous with gullibility.
116 **prodigal** prodigally, lavishly (Abbott 1)
117–20 **These blazes . . . fire** Compare the proverbial saying, 'The bavin burns bright but it is but a blaze' (Tilley B107).
117 **blazes** short-lived bursts of flame (as often in Shakespeare). Compare *Richard II* 2.1.33–4, 'His rash fierce blaze of riot cannot last, | For violent fires soon burn out themselves'.

Giving more light than heat, extinct in both
Even in their promise as it is a-making,
You must not take for fire. From this time   120
Be somewhat scanter of your maiden presence,
Set your entreatments at a higher rate
Than a command to parley. For Lord Hamlet,
Believe so much in him, that he is young,
And with a larger tether may he walk
Than may be given you. In few, Ophelia,
Do not believe his vows, for they are brokers,
Not of the dye which their investments show,
But mere implorators of unholy suits,
Breathing like sanctified and pious bawds   130
The better to beguile. This is for all—

120 From] Q2; For F   time] Q2; time Daughter F   121 somewhat] F; something Q2
123 parley] F; parle Q2   125 tether] F; tider Q2   128 the] F; that Q2   dye] Q2 (die); eye F
129 implorators] F; imploratotors Q2   130 bawds] POPE 1728 (conj. Theobald); bonds FQ2
131 beguile] F; beguide Q2

118 **extinct** extinguished, quenched. Compare *Richard II* 1.3.221–2, 'My oil-dried
   lamp and time-bewasted light | Shall be
   extinct with age and endless night'
119 **it is a-making** i.e. that promise is being
   made
120 **From this time** F's *For this time Daughter*
   where 'Daughter' has been caught from
   line 117, gives much less satisfactory
   sense than the Q2 reading, as well as
   producing a hypermetrical line.
122 **entreatments** negotiations, interviews.
   As Jenkins points out, the use of *parley* in
   line 123 suggests that there are military
   overtones to *entreatments*, a rare word not
   used by Shakespeare elsewhere.
124 **so** thus
126 **In few** in short. For the use of adjectives
   as nouns, see Abbott 5.
127 **brokers** Originally a retailer or
   middleman, a *broker* soon became
   synonymous, in some contexts, with a
   go-between, and thus a *bawd* or *pander*.
   This secondary sense is dominant in
   Shakespeare, and is the relevant one here.
   Compare *K. John* 2.1.582, 'This bawd,
   this broker'.
128 **investments** clothes, vestments. On the
   only other occasion when Shakespeare
   employs this word, *2 Henry IV* 4.1.45, it
   appears in the course of an extended
   diatribe against the evil of false appearances, especially as they are found in the
Archbishop of York 'Whose white investments figure innocence'. The *brokers*
Polonius has in mind would be dressed
soberly to figure rectitude.
129 **mere implorators** downright solicitors.
   Implorator, for which *OED* can cite no
   other example, seems to be a Shakespearian coinage.
   unholy suits wicked inducements (to
   illicit love)
130 **Breathing** speaking, whispering
   bawds This emendation, first proposed by
   Theobald in 1726, of the *bonds* of Q2 and
   F, is made almost certain by an echo of
   this passage in Dekker's *The Welsh Ambassador* (c.1623), where Armante says:
   'Away, I'll be a ghost and haunt this
   king, | Till want of sleep bids him run mad
   and die | For making oaths bawds to his
   perjury' (1.3.94–6). Reminiscences of
   Hamlet are fairly numerous in this play of
   Dekker's. The misreading of *bawds* as
   bonds can be accounted for on the
   assumption that Shakespeare wrote
   bauds, a spelling common enough at the
   time and found, for example, at *Romeo*
   2.4.126, where Q1, Q2, and F all read
   'A baud, a baud, a baud.'
131 **for all** once for all. Compare *Cymbeline*
   2.3.106–8, 'learn now, for all . . . I care
   not for you'.

I would not, in plain terms, from this time forth
Have you so slander any moment leisure
As to give words or talk with the Lord Hamlet.
Look to't, I charge you. Come your ways.

OPHELIA   I shall obey, my lord.   *Exeunt*

I.4   *Enter Hamlet, Horatio, and Marcellus*

HAMLET
The air bites shrewdly, it is very cold.

HORATIO
It is a nipping and an eager air.

HAMLET
What hour now?

HORATIO   I think it lacks of twelve.

MARCELLUS
No, it is struck.

HORATIO   Indeed? I heard it not.
Then it draws near the season
Wherein the spirit held his wont to walk.

        A flourish of trumpets, and two pieces of ordnance go off
What does this mean, my lord?

HAMLET
The King doth wake tonight and takes his rouse,
Keeps wassail and the swaggering upspring reels,

1.4.0.1 *and*] Q2; *not in* F   1 it is] Q2; is it F   2 a] F; *not in* Q2; An QI   5 Then it] F; it then
Q2   6.1 *A flourish ... off*] Q2; *not in* F; *Sound Trumpets* QI   9 wassail] Q2QI (wassell); wassels F

133 **slander** bring into disrepute
   moment leisure moment's leisure. See
   Abbott 22 and 430.
135 **Come your ways** come, come along
   (*OED way sb.*[1] 23b)
1.4.1 **shrewdly** sharply, keenly. With its
   emphasis on the cold and on the time, just
   after midnight, the opening of this scene
   deliberately and tellingly recalls the play's
   beginning. Now, however, Hamlet, missing from the first scene, is present, while
   Barnardo, no longer required, has been
   quietly dispensed with.
2 **eager** bitter. *OED* cites this as the first
   instance of *eager* used to qualify *air*.
3 **lacks of** is not yet
5 **season** time
6 **held his wont** has been accustomed
6.1 *A flourish ... off* The careful timing of
   this direction, omitted from F, deserves
   attention. Having aroused the interest of

his audience in the Ghost once again,
Shakespeare employs the most arresting
means available in his theatre to direct
that interest to another topic, so that the
appearance of the Ghost, when it happens, will still come as a surprise.
7 **What . . . lord?** Horatio, earlier so well
   informed about Denmark, asks this question, in his role of factotum, so that Hamlet can give his answer.
8 **wake** keep late hours, 'make a night of it'
   takes his rouse carouses. See note at
   1.2.127.
9 **Keeps wassail** holds a drinking-bout
   swaggering upspring reels blustering
   new-fangled revels. This gloss is substantially that of *OED*, and takes *upspring* as an
   adjective qualifying *reels*, meaning
   'revels', the sense it has in *Antony* 2.7.92,
   'Drink thou ; increase the reels.' The alternative possibility is to take *reels* as a verb,

And as he drains his draughts of Rhenish down,   10
The kettle-drum and trumpet thus bray out
The triumph of his pledge.

HORATIO   Is it a custom?

HAMLET Ay marry is't.
And to my mind, though I am native here
And to the manner born, it is a custom
More honoured in the breach than the observance.

Enter the Ghost

HORATIO Look, my lord, it comes.

HAMLET

Angels and ministers of grace defend us!
Be thou a spirit of health or goblin damned,
Bring with thee airs from heaven or blasts from hell,   20
Be thy intents wicked or charitable,
Thou com'st in such a questionable shape
That I will speak to thee. I'll call thee Hamlet,
King, father, royal Dane. O answer me!
Let me not burst in ignorance, but tell
Why thy canonized bones, hearsèd in death,

---

14 And] F; But Q2; and Q1   21 intents] Q2Q1; euents F   24 O] Q2Q1; Oh, oh F

---

meaning 'drunkenly dances', and *up-spring* as a noun, translating the German *hüpfauf*, a wild dance.

10 **Rhenish** Rhine wine

11 **kettle-drum and trumpet** instruments closely associated with the Danish march. Dekker's *The Magnificent Entertainment*, written to celebrate the entry of James I and his queen, Anne of Denmark, into the City of London on 15 March 1604, describes a scaffold, erected in the Poultry, 'where . . . to delight the Queen with her own country music, nine trumpets and a kettle-drum did very sprightly and actively sound the Danish march' (711–14).

12 **triumph of his pledge** i.e. his success in keeping his promise to drain the cup in one draught

15 **to the manner born** destined by birth to be subject to that custom (*OED manner sb.*[1] 3b)

15–16 **a custom . . . observance** Compare 'A bad custom is like a good cake, better broken than kept' (Tilley C931).

16 For a passage following this line in Q2 but not in F, see Appendix A, ii.

18 **ministers of grace** messengers of God. Compare *Measure* 5.1.115–16, 'O you blessed ministers above, | Keep me in patience'.

19–21 **Be thou . . . charitable** Hamlet balances two possibilities against each other: (1) that the Ghost is a good spirit (2) that it is an evil spirit.

19 **health** salvation
   goblin demon

20 **airs** pleasant breezes
   blasts destructive blighting winds

22 **questionable shape** form inviting questions (*OED questionable* 1a), not used elsewhere in Shakespeare

26 **canonized bones** consecrated bones, bones buried according to the rules of the Church
   hearsèd coffined. Compare *Merchant* 3.1.78–9, 'would she [Jessica] were hearsed at my foot, and the ducats in her coffin' A *hearse* is invariably 'a coffin' in Shakespeare.

Have burst their cerements, why the sepulchre,
Wherein we saw thee quietly inurned,
Hath oped his ponderous and marble jaws
To cast thee up again. What may this mean   30
That thou, dead corpse, again in complete steel,
Revisits thus the glimpses of the moon,
Making night hideous, and we fools of nature
So horridly to shake our disposition
With thoughts beyond the reaches of our souls?
Say, why is this? Wherefore? What should we do?
    The Ghost beckons Hamlet

HORATIO
It beckons you to go away with it,
As if it some impartment did desire
To you alone.

MARCELLUS (*to Hamlet*) Look with what courteous action
It wafts you to a more removèd ground.   40
But do not go with it.

---

28 inurned] F; interr'd Q2Q1   35 the] Q2Q1; thee; F   36.1 *The Ghost beckons Hamlet*] F (*Ghost beckens Hamlet*), Q2 (*Beckins*); *not in* Q1   40 wafts] F; waues Q2Q1

27 **cerements** grave-clothes. This word, meaning literally 'waxed wrappings for the dead', is a Shakespearian invention, derived from the normal *cerecloth* which he had used in *Merchant* (2.7.51).

28 **inurned** buried, entombed—another Shakespearian coinage. The use of *urn*, normally 'a receptacle for the ashes of the dead', to denote a *coffin* and thence, figuratively, a *grave* (*Henry V* 1.2.228 and *Coriolanus* 5.6.145) is not peculiar to Shakespeare. Dekker writes, 'The monumental marble urns of bodies | Laid to rest long ago, unreverently | Are turned to troughs of water now for jades' (*The Whore of Babylon* 1.1.166–8).

31 **complete steel** full armour (accent on first syllable of *complete*)

32 **Revisits** In verbs ending in *t* Shakespeare often replaces the normal *test* ending of the second person singular with *ts* to make it easier for the actor; see Abbott 340.
   glimpses of the moon flickering gleams of moonlight

33 **hideous** terrifying
   and we 'After a conjunction and before an infinitive we often find *I*, *thou*, &c.,

where in Latin we should have "me," "te," &c. The conjunction seems to be regarded as introducing a new sentence, instead of connecting one clause with another. Hence the pronoun is put in the nominative, and a verb is, perhaps, to be supplied from the context' (Abbott 216).
   fools of nature playthings, puppets of nature (because we have no idea of what nature is doing with us). Compare 'Death's fool' (*Measure* 3.1.11), and 'fortune's fool' (*Romeo* 3.1.133)

34 **horridly** dreadfully, horribly
   disposition normal mode of thought and behaviour

36 **Say . . . Wherefore** Compare 'The why and the wherefore' (Tilley W332).
   should must

38 **impartment** communication. The word, not found elsewhere in Shakespeare, appears here for the first time, according to *OED*.

40 **wafts** beckons
   removèd ground secluded place. Compare *As You Like It* 3.2.319, 'so removed a dwelling', the first instance cited by *OED* (*removed* *ppl. a.* 2a) of *removed* in this sense.

HORATIO   No, by no means.

HAMLET

It will not speak. Then will I follow it.

HORATIO

Do not, my lord.

HAMLET   Why, what should be the fear?

I do not set my life at a pin's fee,

And for my soul, what can it do to that,

Being a thing immortal as itself?

It waves me forth again. I'll follow it.

HORATIO

What if it tempt you toward the flood, my lord,

Or to the dreadful summit of the cliff

That beetles o'er his base into the sea,   50

And there assume some other horrible form

Which might deprive your sovereignty of reason

And draw you into madness? Think of it.

HAMLET

It wafts me still.—Go on, I'll follow thee.

42 will I] FQ1 ; I will Q2   48 lord] FQ1 ; *in some copies of* Q2, *missing from others*   49 summit]
ROWE; Sonnet F; somnet Q2   50 beetles] F; bettles Q2 ; beckles Q1   51 assume] Q2Q1 ; assumes F   54 wafts] F, waues Q2

43 **what should be the fear?** what is there to be afraid of?

44 **set** value, regard
   at a pin's fee as worth a pin. 'Not worth a pin' (Tilley P334) was, and still is, proverbial.

48–53 **What if . . . madness?** Horatio begins by voicing the idea, very common at the time when the play was written, that the devil sought to win souls for hell by tempting men into taking their own lives and by providing them with the means and the opportunities for doing so. See *The Faerie Queene* I.ix.21–54, and *Lear* 3.4.50–62; 4.6.57–72. The last of these passages is particularly relevant, because in it Edgar not only describes Dover Cliff but also the 'horrible form' taken on by his imaginary fiend who tempts Gloucester into attempting to commit suicide.

50 **beetles** projects itself, threateningly overhangs. Shakespeare seems to have made up this verb which occurs nowhere else in his work, and nowhere else in English

until the late 18th century, when writers began to borrow it from him. It comes, apparently, from the much older word *beetle-browed*, meaning 'having prominent eye-brows' (*OED beetle a.* and *beetle v.*[1]); compare 'beetle brows' (*Romeo* 1.4.32). That there was an intimate connection in his mind between a threatening brow and an overhanging cliff is evident from *Henry V* 3.1.9–14, 'Then lend the eye a terrible aspect . . . let the brow o'erwhelm it | As fearfully as doth a gallèd rock | O'erhang and jutty his confounded base, | Swilled by the wild and wasteful ocean.' With reference to the variant spellings of *beetles* in the three primary texts, Cercignani points out that 'a nonce-word . . . is particularly liable to textual corruption' (p. 321).

52 **deprive your sovereignty of reason** i.e. dethrone your reason from its proper sovereign place in your mind

53 For a passage following this line in Q2 but not in F, see Appendix A, iii.

MARCELLUS
   You shall not go, my lord.
HAMLET   Hold off your hand.
HORATIO
   Be ruled, you shall not go.
HAMLET   My fate cries out,
   And makes each petty artery in this body
   As hardy as the Nemean lion's nerve.
       The Ghost beckons
   Still am I called. Unhand me, gentlemen.
       He breaks away from them
   By heaven, I'll make a ghost of him that lets me.   60
   I say, away!—Go on, I'll follow thee.
                          Exeunt the Ghost and Hamlet
HORATIO
   He waxes desperate with imagination.
MARCELLUS
   Let's follow. 'Tis not fit thus to obey him.
HORATIO
   Have after. To what issue will this come?
MARCELLUS
   Something is rotten in the state of Denmark.
HORATIO
   Heaven will direct it.
MARCELLUS   Nay, let's follow him.   *Exeunt*

---

55 hand] F; hands Q2   59 called] Q2 (cald,); cal'd F   61.1 *Exeunt the*] *Exeunt* F; *Exit* Q2   62
imagination] FQ1; imagion Q2

---

57 **artery** In Shakespeare's day the arteries were thought of as conveyors, not of blood, since after death they do not contain any, but of an ethereal fluid known as 'vital spirits' or 'animal spirits', the source of sensation and motion, of nervous energy, and of courage. Compare *LLL* 4.3.301–2, 'universal plodding poisons up | The nimble spirits in the arteries'.

58 **Nemean lion's nerve** sinew of the Nemean lion, the supposedly invulnerable beast strangled by Hercules in the first of his labours

60 **lets** hinders, tries to stop

62 **imagination** delusions, fantastical ideas that have no basis in fact. Compare *2 Henry IV* 1.3.31–2, 'great imagination | Proper to madmen'.

64 **Have after** let's follow (*OED have v.* 20). The phrase was very common (Dent H218.1).
   issue conclusion

66 **it** i.e. the issue
   Nay i.e. let us do something instead of leaving it to heaven

1.5   *Enter the Ghost and Hamlet*

HAMLET
Where wilt thou lead me? Speak. I'll go no further.

GHOST
Mark me.

HAMLET   I will.

GHOST   My hour is almost come
When I to sulph'rous and tormenting flames
Must render up myself.

HAMLET   Alas, poor ghost!

GHOST
Pity me not, but lend thy serious hearing
To what I shall unfold.

HAMLET   Speak, I am bound to hear.

GHOST
So art thou to revenge, when thou shalt hear.

HAMLET What?

GHOST I am thy father's spirit,
Doomed for a certain term to walk the night,   10
And for the day confined to fast in fires,
Till the foul crimes done in my days of nature
Are burnt and purged away. But that I am forbid

1.5.1 Where] F; Whether Q2; whither Q1

1.5.0 *Enter Ghost and Hamlet* There is no break here in the action as it mounts to its first great climax. On Shakespeare's stage the Ghost and Hamlet, having made their exit through one of the two stage doors, move backstage across to the other while Horatio and Marcellus are still talking. Then, as Horatio and Marcellus go out through the first door, the Ghost and Hamlet return through the other. The main purpose of these manoeuvres is, of course, to get rid of Horatio and Marcellus, rather than to signal any change of location, though Hamlet's first words do suggest that there has been some shift.

2 **Mark me** having remained silent through two previous scenes, the Ghost speaks at last, taking complete control of the situation. Wielding the threefold authority of supernatural being, king, and father, he very appropriately begins with a command.

My hour is almost come i.e. dawn approaches

3 **flames** As lines 9–13 make clear, the *flames* are those of purgatory not of hell.

6 **bound** 'in duty bound' (Kittredge)

10 **walk the night** walk throughout the night. Compare *Lear* 4.6.13, 'the crows and choughs that wing the midway air', another example of what Schmidt, with specific reference to these and other passages, calls 'the accusative of space'.

11 **to fast** The notion that both in hell and in purgatory the punishment was made to fit the sin was widespread. See, for example, Nashe I. 218 and John Ford's *'Tis Pity She's a Whore* 3.6. Hamlet will say later that Claudius 'took my father grossly, full of bread' (3.3.80), a remark which accords well with the general impression the play gives of old Hamlet as one who enjoyed his mid-day meal and his post-prandial nap.

13 **But except**, if it were not

To tell the secrets of my prison-house,
I could a tale unfold whose lightest word
Would harrow up thy soul, freeze thy young blood,
Make thy two eyes like stars start from their spheres,
Thy knotty and combinèd locks to part,
And each particular hair to stand on end,
Like quills upon the fretful porcupine.   20
But this eternal blazon must not be
To ears of flesh and blood. List, Hamlet, O list!
If thou didst ever thy dear father love—

HAMLET   O God!

GHOST

Revenge his foul and most unnatural murder.

HAMLET   Murder!

GHOST

Murder most foul, as in the best it is,
But this most foul, strange, and unnatural.

HAMLET

Haste, haste me to know it, that I, with wings as swift
As meditation or the thoughts of love,   30
May sweep to my revenge.

18 knotty] F; knotted Q2Q1   20 fretful] FQ1; fearefull Q2   22 List, Hamlet, O list] F; list, list, ô list Q2; Hamlet Q1   list!] ~, F; ~ : Q2   24 God] Q2Q1; Heauen F   29 Haste, haste] F (Hast, hast); Hast Q2; Haste Q1   know it] FQ1; know't Q2   I] Q2; *not in* FQ1

17 **spheres** sockets. There was a close connection in Shakespeare's mind between stars, each enclosed within its sphere, and eyes, each enclosed within its socket. See *Romeo*, 2.2.15–17, 'Two of the fairest stars in all the heaven, | Having some business, do entreat her eyes | To twinkle in their spheres till they return.'

18 **knotty and combinèd locks** hair carefully and intricately arranged, possibly in curls. During the first act Hamlet should be 'The glass of fashion' (3.1.154).

19 **particular** individual, separate

20 **fretful** impatient, bad-tempered

21 **eternal blazon** revelation of the mysteries of eternity. Schmidt notes that Shakespeare sometimes uses *eternal* 'to express extreme abhorrence', and cites *Caesar*, 1.2.159–161, 'There was a Brutus once that would have brooked | Th' eternal devil to keep his state in Rome | As easily as a king.' A *blazon*, originally a heraldic shield, or the description of such a shield, is here equivalent to a publication or proclamation.

be i.e. be made

27 **in the best** at the best

29 **haste me to know it** i.e. let me know it at once

30 **meditation** thought. 'As swift as thought' was proverbial (Tilley T240).

31 **apt** quick to take the right impression

32–3 **duller . . . wharf** It is not clear which, if any, 'fat weed' Shakespeare has in mind. The asphodel, best known and most frequently mentioned of the plants connected with the underworld in Greek mythology, has often been suggested; but the word *asphodel* is not to be found in his works. *Poppy*, on the other hand, is (*Othello* 3.3.334), and with specific reference to its somniferous effects. It, therefore, seems the more likely of the two. Likeliest of all, perhaps, is the possibility that the Ghost conjures up a plant never seen by eyes 'of flesh and blood'.

GHOST   I find thee apt;
And duller shouldst thou be than the fat weed
That roots itself in ease on Lethe wharf,
Wouldst thou not stir in this. Now, Hamlet, hear.
It's given out that, sleeping in my orchard,
A serpent stung me. So the whole ear of Denmark
Is by a forgèd process of my death
Rankly abused. But know, thou noble youth,
The serpent that did sting thy father's life
Now wears his crown.
HAMLET   O my prophetic soul!   40
My uncle!
GHOST
Ay, that incestuous, that adulterate beast,
With witchcraft of his wit, with traitorous gifts—
O wicked wit and gifts that have the power
So to seduce!—won to his shameful lust
The will of my most seeming-virtuous queen.
O Hamlet, what a falling-off was there,
From me, whose love was of that dignity

---

33 roots] Q2Q1 ; rots F   35 It's] F ; Tis Q2Q1   my] Q2Q1 ; mine F   41 My] Q2Q1 ; mine F   43
Wit] POPE ; wits FQ2   with traitorous gifts—] Q2 (gifts,), hath Traitorous guilts. F ; with gifts,
Q1   45 to his] Q2Q1 ; to to this F   47 a] F ; *not in* Q2

---

32 **duller** slower, more indolent. Cordelia
gives a list of 'idle weeds' in *Lear*
(4.4.2–4).
 shouldst wouldst. Shakespeare often uses
should where modern English prefers
would (Abbott 322).
 fat gross, lazy (*OED a.* 11)
33 **roots** This Q2 reading is preferred to F's
rots because it offers a strong antithesis to
stir (l. 34), and it fits in perfectly with the
other instances of 'things rank and gross
in nature' which are so frequent in the
play.
 Lethe wharf banks of the Lethe (the river
of forgetfulness in the classical underworld). This sense of *wharf*, found again in
Antony (2.2.217), appears to be peculiar
to Shakespeare (*OED sb.*[1] 2c).
35 **orchard** garden for herbs and fruit-trees
(*OED* 1a)
37 **forgèd process** lying story, fabricated account (*OED process sb.* 4)

38 **Rankly abused** grossly deceived (*OED
abuse v.* 4). References to abusing the ear
of a person are frequent in Shakespeare.
40 **my prophetic soul** Hamlet does not mean
that he suspected his father had been
murdered by his uncle, but that his deep-
seated intuitive distrust and dislike of
Claudius have now been justified. He has
known all along that Claudius is 'a wrong
un'.
42 **adulterate** adulterous (the invariable
sense elsewhere in Shakespeare)
43 **traitorous gifts** 'Women are tempted
with gifts' was proverbial (Tilley W704).
47 **falling-off** (1) change for the worse (2)
revolt from allegiance. Compare *1 Henry
IV* 1.3.93–4, 'Revolted Mortimer! | He
never did fall off'.
48 **that** such (Abbott 277)
 dignity worthiness. Compare *LLL*
4.3.232, 'several worthies [= excel-
lences] make one dignity'.

That it went hand-in-hand even with the vow
I made to her in marriage, and to decline   50
Upon a wretch whose natural gifts were poor
To those of mine.
But virtue, as it never will be moved,
Though lewdness court it in a shape of heaven,
So lust, though to a radiant angel linked,
Will sate itself in a celestial bed
And prey on garbage.
But soft, methinks I scent the morning's air.
Brief let me be. Sleeping within my orchard,
My custom always in the afternoon,   60
Upon my secure hour thy uncle stole
With juice of cursèd hebenon in a vial,
And in the porches of my ears did pour
The leperous distilment, whose effect
Holds such an enmity wi'th' blood of man

49 hand-in-hand even] This edition; hand in hand, euen FQ2   55 lust] FQ1; but Q2   56
sate] F; sort Q2; fate Q1   58 morning's] FQ1 (Mornings); morning Q2   59 my] Q2Q1; mine
F   60 in] FQ1; of Q2   62 hebenon] F; Hebona Q2Q1   63 my] Q2Q1; mine F   65 wi'th']
This edition; with FQ2Q1

49 **went hand-in-hand even** accorded in perfectly matched agreement, was exactly in
step with. *To go even (OED adv.* 2) is 'to be
in agreement', and *hand in hand (adv. phr.*
1b) is 'to be in conjunction'. Compare
Twelfth Night 5.1.231, 'as the rest goes
even', and *Cymbeline* 1.4.65–6, 'As fair
and as good—a kind of hand-in-hand
comparison'.
50 **decline** sink down
53 **virtue as it** i.e. just as virtue. 'Sometimes
a noun occurs in a prominent position at
the beginning of a sentence, to express the
subject of the thought, without the usual
grammatical connection with a verb or
preposition' (Abbott 417).
54 **Though . . . heaven** Compare the 'sanctified and pious bawds' 1.3.130.
56 **sate** a Shakespearian coinage, explained
by *OED* as a 'pseudo-etymological alteration of *sade*, meaning "to become
satiated"'
57 **garbage** filth (literally 'entrails'). Compare *Cymbeline* 1.6.46–9, 'The cloyed
will— | That satiate yet unsatisfied desire,
that tub | Both filled and running—raven-
ing first the lamb, | Longs after for the

garbage.'
61 **secure** unsuspecting, over-confidently
free from apprehension
62 **hebenon** 'Hebenon, Hebon, Hebona.
Names given by Shakespeare and Marlowe to some substance having a
poisonous juice' (*OED*). It seems likely
that Shakespeare took the word from
Marlowe, who writes in *The Jew of Malta* of
'the blood of Hydra, Lerna's bane, | The
juice of hebon, and Cocytus' breath'
(3.4.97–8). Attempts to define *hebenon*
more specifically have been inconclusive.
63–70 **And in . . . blood** There is what looks
like another debt to Marlowe here. In *Edward II* the professional assassin, Light-
born, describes some of his methods. They
include these: 'whilst one is *asleep*, to take
a quill | And blow a little powder *in his
ears* : | Or open his mouth and pour *quick-
silver* down' (5.4.34–6).
64 **leperous distilment** distillation having
the effects of leprosy (i.e. covering the skin
with white scales). *Distilment* appears to
be a Shakespearian invention, like so
many other words in *Hamlet* that end in
ment.

That swift as quicksilver it courses through
The natural gates and alleys of the body,
And with a sudden vigour it doth posset
And curd, like eager droppings into milk,
The thin and wholesome blood. So did it mine;   70
And a most instant tetter barked about,
Most lazar-like, with vile and loathsome crust,
All my smooth body.
Thus was I, sleeping, by a brother's hand
Of life, of crown, of queen at once dispatched,
Cut off even in the blossoms of my sin,
Unhouseled, dis-appointed, unaneled,
No reckoning made, but sent to my account
With all my imperfections on my head.
O horrible, O horrible, most horrible!   80

68 posset] F; possesse Q2   71 barked] Q2 (barckt) QI (barked); bak'd F   75 of queen]
Q2QI; and Queene F   79 With all] FQI; Withall Q2

66 swift as quicksilver a common saying (Dent Q14.1) Compare *2 Henry IV* 2.4.219, 'The rogue fled from me like quicksilver.'

67 gates Onions suggests that 'there is perhaps an allusion to the "vena porta" (rendered "gate-vein" by 17th century writers)', the *vena porta* being the great vein formed by the union of the veins from the stomach, intestine, and spleen, conveying blood to the liver.

68 vigour efficacy. The word is again applied to poison in *Cymbeline*, where the Queen says, 'I will try the forces | Of these thy compounds . . . To try the vigour of them' (1.5.18–21).
posset curdle. A *posset* was a drink made of hot milk curdled with ale, wine, or the like, formerly regarded as a delicacy and as a cure for colds. Shakespeare, characteristically, turns it into a verb defining an effect that is neither comforting nor remedial.

69 eager sour, acid. Compare 'With eager compounds we our palates urge' (*Sonnets* 118. 2).

71 instant immediately occurring, instantaneous
tetter rash, eruption of the skin
barked about covered as with bark, encrusted (the only use of *bark*, in this sense, in Shakespeare)

72 Most lazar-like i.e. exactly as though I were suffering from leprosy

75 at once at one and the same time
dispatched deprived (*OED v.* 7b, citing no earlier instance)
76–9 Cut off . . . head Hamlet recalls these words at 3.3.74–95.
76 Cut off killed (but the literal sense, as in *cutting off a branch*, is still present, and leads on to *blossoms*)

77 Unhouseled not having received the *housel* (i.e. eucharist)—a word not used elsewhere by Shakespeare
dis-appointed unprepared (for death), not having made confession and received absolution (*OED ppl. a.* 2)—again a word Shakespeare does not use in this sense elsewhere
unaneled unanointed, not having the benefit of extreme unction. *Anele* and *anoil* were in frequent use from the beginning of the 14th century; but *unaneled* is yet another Shakespearian coinage. Line 77 as a whole makes one realize how much the strangeness and the impressiveness of the Ghost depends on the unusual language he is given.

78 reckoning i.e. rendering of an account to God of one's life and conduct, the process so vividly dramatized in *Everyman* (*c.*1495–1500)

If thou hast nature in thee, bear it not,
Let not the royal bed of Denmark be
A couch for luxury and damnèd incest.
But howsoever thou pursuest this act,
Taint not thy mind, nor let thy soul contrive
Against thy mother aught—leave her to heaven,
And to those thorns that in her bosom lodge
To prick and sting her. Fare thee well at once.
The glow-worm shows the matin to be near,
And gins to pale his uneffectual fire.   90
Adieu, adieu, Hamlet. Remember me.   *Exit*

HAMLET

O all you host of heaven! O earth! What else?
And shall I couple hell? O fie! Hold, hold, my heart,
And you, my sinews, grow not instant old,
But bear me stiffly up. Remember thee?
Ay, thou poor ghost, while memory holds a seat
In this distracted globe. Remember thee?

84 howsoever] FQ1; howsomeuer Q2   pursuest] F; pursues Q2   85 mind,] ~ ; F   91
Adieu, adieu, Hamlet] F; Adiew, adiew, adiew Q2; Hamlet adue, adue, adue Q1   91.1 *Exit*]
FQ1; *not in* Q2   93 O fie! Hold, hold] Q2; Oh fie: hold F   95 stiffly] F; swiftly Q2   96 while]
F; whiles Q2   97 thee?] FQ1; thee, Q2

81 **nature** natural feeling (such as a son
should have for his father). Compare *Lear*
3.6.85–6, 'Edmund, enkindle all the
sparks of nature | To quit this horrid act.'
83 **luxury** lust, lechery (as it always is in
Shakespeare), the deadly sin *Luxuria* of
the Middle Ages
85 **Taint not thy mind** don't allow your
mind to be corrupted (by contact with the
wickedness of Claudius). Compare *Cymbeline* 5.4.63–6, 'Why did you suffer
Iachimo, | Slight thing of Italy, | To taint
his nobler heart and brain | With needless
jealousy'. The quality of Hamlet's mind
that is insisted on throughout the play is
its nobility. What the Ghost says is in effect: 'Take revenge on Claudius, but on
no account stoop to his ignoble methods.'
He thus presents the hero with the dilem-
ma that is at the heart of revenge tragedy:
how is the nobility of the successful avenger to be preserved?
89 **matin** morning (*OED* 3)—not found
elsewhere in Shakespeare
90 **pale** dim, make pale—Shakespeare's
only use of the word as a verb
uneffectual fire i.e. fire that no longer

gives light. Compare *Pericles*, 2.3.43–4,
'a glowworm in the night, | The which
hath fire in darkness, none in light.'
Shakespeare does not use *uneffectual*
elsewhere.
91 **Adieu . . . me** The Ghost's lingering
farewell sounds far better suited to one
making his exit through a door than to
one about to disappear through a trap. He
has ample time in which to make his way
into the cellarage from backstage before
he has to speak again at line 156.
93 **fie** i.e. not to be thought of. Compare
Othello 4.2.135, 'Fie, there is no such
man; it is impossible.' Hamlet mentions
the possibility of the Ghost's infernal
origin only to dismiss it.
Hold be firm
94 **instant** immediately
95 **stiffly** strongly, firmly (*OED stiff* 8, 12).
Compare *Henry V* 3.1.7, 'Stiffen the
sinews'.
97 **distracted globe** confused head. Hamlet
is rather given to applying scientific terms
to himself; compare 'this machine'
(2.2.123).

Yea, from the table of my memory
I'll wipe away all trivial fond records,
All saws of books, all forms, all pressures past,   100
That youth and observation copied there,
And thy commandment all alone shall live
Within the book and volume of my brain,
Unmixed with baser matter. Yes, yes, by heaven!
O most pernicious woman!
O villain, villain, smiling damnèd villain!
My tables,
My tables—meet it is I set it down
That one may smile, and smile, and be a villain.
At least I'm sure it may be so in Denmark.   110
        He writes
So, uncle, there you are. Now to my word:
It is 'Adieu, adieu, remember me'.
I have sworn't.
HORATIO *and* MARCELLUS (*within*) My lord, my lord.
        Enter Horatio and Marcellus
MARCELLUS Lord Hamlet!
HORATIO Heaven secure him.
HAMLET So be it.

104 Yes, yes] FQ1; yes Q2   107–8 tables, | My tables] F; tables Q2Q1   110 I'm] F; I am
Q2Q1   114–114.1 HORATIO *and* MARCELLUS (*within*) My lord, my lord. | *Enter Horatio and
Marcellus*] F; *Enter Horatio and Marcellus.* | Hora⟨tio⟩ My Lord, my Lord Q2; Hor⟨atio⟩ My lord,
my lord. *Enter Horatio, and Marcellus* Q1   116 Heaven] F; Heauens Q2Q1   117 HAMLET] Q2;
Mar⟨cellus⟩ F

98 **table** tablet on which things could be in-
    scribed and from which they could, if
    necessary, be erased.
99 **fond** foolish
    records (accented on the second syllable)
100 **saws of books** maxims copied from
    books
    forms representations, likenesses (*OED
    form sb.* 2). Compare *Sonnets* 9.6, 'thou
    no form of thee hast left behind'.
    pressures impressions (*OED* 4). Compare
    3.2.23, the only other instance of *pressure*
    in Shakespeare.
103 **book and volume** voluminous book
    (hendiadys). Hamlet, in the manner typi-
    cal of Shakespeare's time, thinks of his
    mind as a memory bank.
105 **pernicious** wicked (the usual sense in
    Shakespeare)
107 **tables** small portable tablets for jotting

down notes and observations (*OED table
sb.* 2b)
109 **That . . . villain** Compare 'To smile in
one's face and cut one's throat' (Tilley
F16), and *3 Henry VI* 3.2.182, 'Why, I
can smile, and murder whiles I smile'.
111 **word** watchword
113 **sworn't** i.e. sworn to keep it
114 **within** This direction, found only in F,
makes good sense in preparing the
audience for the entry. Something is
needed to draw their attention to the door
of the stage from which Horatio and Marcellus will come.
116 **secure him** keep him safe. In the darkness or half-light that is still supposed to
envelop the stage, Horatio and Marcellus
have not yet seen the Prince, who is well
to the front of it.

HORATIO Hillo, ho, ho, my lord!

HAMLET Hillo, ho, ho, boy! Come, bird, come.

MARCELLUS How is't, my noble lord?   120

HORATIO What news, my lord?

HAMLET O wonderful!

HORATIO Good my lord, tell it.

HAMLET No, you'll reveal it.

HORATIO

   Not I, my lord, by heaven.

MARCELLUS   Nor I, my lord.

HAMLET

   How say you then, would heart of man once think it?
   But you'll be secret?

HORATIO *and* MARCELLUS Ay, by heaven, my lord.

HAMLET

   There's ne'er a villain dwelling in all Denmark
   But he's an arrant knave.

HORATIO

   There needs no ghost, my lord, come from the grave   130
   To tell us this.

HAMLET   Why, right, you are i'th' right.
   And so without more circumstance at all
   I hold it fit that we shake hands and part;
   You, as your business and desires shall point you,
   For every man has business and desire,
   Such as it is; and for my own poor part,
   Look you, I'll go pray.

118 HORATIO] FQ1 ; *Mar⟨cellus⟩* Q2   119 HAMLET] FQ2 ; *Mar⟨cellus⟩* Q1   bird] F ; and Q2 ; boy
Q1   120 is't] Q2Q1 ; ist't F   124 you'll] FQ1 ; you will Q2   127 heaven, my lord] FQ1 ;
heauen Q2   128 ne'er] F (nere); neuer Q2Q1   131 i'th' right] F ; in the right Q2Q1   134
desires] FQ1 ; desire Q2   135 has] F ; hath Q2Q1   136 my] Q2Q1 ; mine F   137 Look you, I'll]
F ; I will Q2 ; ile Q1

118 **Hillo** 'A call used to hail a distant or
   occupied person' (*OED*)
119 **Hillo . . . bird, come** Hamlet converts the
   halloo of Marcellus into a falconer's call to
   his hawk, bidding it return to his fist. He
   thus begins a train of imagery associated
   with hawks that has its place in the play.
126 **once** ever. Compare *Antony* 5.2.50–1,
   'If idle talk will once be necessary, | I'll not
   sleep neither.'
129 **But he's** i.e. that is not
   an arrant knave It looks as though Hamlet is on the point of revealing something

of what he has heard, and then changes
his mind.
130 **come** to come (Abbott 349)
132 **circumstance** ceremony. Compare *Win-
   ter's Tale* 5.1.89–90, 'His approach, | So
   out of circumstance and sudden'.
134 **point** direct
135 **every . . . desire** This phrase, first found
   in *1 Henry IV* 2.2.74 as 'every man to his
   business', became proverbial in the form
   'every man as his business lies' (Tilley
   M104).

HORATIO

These are but wild and whirling words, my lord.

HAMLET

I'm sorry they offend you, heartily—
Yes, faith, heartily.

HORATIO   There's no offence, my lord.   140

HAMLET

Yes, by Saint Patrick, but there is, Horatio,
And much offence too. Touching this vision here—
It is an honest ghost, that let me tell you.
For your desire to know what is between us,
O'ermaster't as you may. And now, good friends,
As you are friends, scholars, and soldiers,
Give me one poor request.

HORATIO   What is't, my lord?
We will.

HAMLET

Never make known what you have seen tonight.

HORATIO *and* MARCELLUS My lord, we will not.   150

HAMLET Nay, but swear't.

HORATIO In faith, my lord, not I.

MARCELLUS Nor I, my lord, in faith.

HAMLET Upon my sword.

MARCELLUS We have sworn, my lord, already.

HAMLET Indeed, upon my sword, indeed.

GHOST (*crying from under the stage*) Swear.

---

139 I'm] F; I am Q2Q1   141 Horatio] Q2Q1; my Lord F   142 too. Touching . . . here—]
ROWE; too, touching . . . heere: F; to, touching . . . heere, Q2; too, touching this vision,
Q1   145 O'ermaster't] F; Oremastret Q2; Or'emaister it Q1

138 **whirling** violently agitated. *OED* points
out that *whirling* was sometimes confused
with *hurling*, the reading of F.
141 **Saint Patrick** Compare Dekker, *2 The
Honest Whore* 1.1.42–3, 'Saint Patrick,
you know, keeps purgatory'.
143 **honest** reliable, trustworthy, genuine
144 **us** i.e. me and the Ghost
145 **as you may** as best you can

152 **not I** i.e. I will not reveal it
154 **Upon my sword** Oaths were often
sworn on a sword because the hilt is in
the form of a cross. Compare *Richard II*
1.3.179–82, where the King bids Mow-
bray and Bolingbroke: 'Lay on our royal
sword your banished hands; | Swear by
the duty that you owe to God . . . To keep
the oath that we administer.'

HAMLET

Ah, ha, boy, sayest thou so? Art thou there,
    truepenny?
Come on. You hear this fellow in the cellarage.
Consent to swear.

HORATIO   Propose the oath, my lord.   160

HAMLET

Never to speak of this that you have seen.
Swear by my sword.

GHOST Swear.

        ⌐*They swear*⌐

HAMLET

Hic et ubique? Then we'll shift our ground.
Come hither, gentlemen,
And lay your hands again upon my sword:
Never to speak of this that you have heard.
Swear by my sword.

GHOST Swear.

        ⌐*They swear*⌐

HAMLET

Well said, old mole. Canst work i'th'earth so fast?   170
A worthy pioneer! Once more remove, good friends.

HORATIO

O day and night, but this is wondrous strange.

---

158 Ah, ha] F; Ha, ha Q2Q1   sayest] F; say'st Q2   161 seen.] F; ~ ‸ Q2   163.1 *They swear*]
JENKINS; *not in* FQ2Q1   164 ubique?] F; *vbique*, Q2; *vbique*; Q1   our] Q2Q1; for F   169 Swear]
FQ1; Swear by his sword Q2   169.1 *They swear*] WILSON *subs.*; *not in* FQ2Q1   170 earth]
Q2Q1; ground F

---

158 **truepenny** trusty fellow—not elsewhere in Shakespeare
159 **cellarage** cellars (collectively)—earliest
instance of this sense in *OED*; not
elsewhere in Shakespeare. Could it have
been a theatrical name for the space
under the stage?
163 **Swear** Jenkins argues persuasively that
each time the Ghost utters this word it
coincides with a taking of the oath by
Horatio and Marcellus testifying to their
agreement to say nothing about three different things: what they have seen
(l. 161); what they have heard (l. 167);
and what they know about Hamlet's
behaviour (l. 186). Threefold oaths have,
he adds, a special binding power. As none

of the three texts has any direction about
the swearing of the oath, though there
must be such a swearing at line 189, it is
hard to be sure whether it also takes place
at lines 163 and 169, but it does seem
very likely.
164 *Hic et ubique* here and everywhere (a
Latin tag). The ability to be here and
everywhere at once was confined to God
and the devil. Compare *Twelfth Night*
5.1.219–20, 'Nor can there be that deity
in my nature | Of here and everywhere.'
171 **pioneer** military miner, sapper. Compare *Henry V* 3.3.29–30, 'have you quit
the mines? Have the pioneers given o'er?'
    remove move again, move to another
place

HAMLET

And therefore as a stranger give it welcome.
There are more things in heaven and earth, Horatio,
Than are dreamt of in our philosophy. But come,
Here as before, never, so help you mercy,
How strange or odd soe'er I bear myself—
As I perchance hereafter shall think meet
To put an antic disposition on—
That you, at such time seeing me, never shall,   180
With arms encumbered thus, or thus head shaked,
Or by pronouncing of some doubtful phrase,
As 'Well, we know', or 'We could an if we would',
Or 'If we list to speak', or 'There be an if they might',
Or such ambiguous giving out, to note
That you know aught of me—this not to do,
So grace and mercy at your most need help you,
Swear.

GHOST Swear.

They swear

---

175 our] F; your Q2Q1   177 soe'er] F (so ere) Q1; so mere Q2   180 time] F; times
Q2Q1   181 thus head shaked] This edition; thus, head shake F; this head shake Q2Q1; this
head-shake THEOBALD   183 Well] F; well, well Q2Q1   184 they] Q2Q1; there F   185 out, to
note‸| STEEVENS 1793 (*conj.* Malone); out, to note, Q2; out‸ to note, FQ1   186–8 this not to
do, | So . . . you, | Swear.] FQ1; this doe sweare, | So . . . you. Q2   189 *They swear*] KITTREDGE

---

173 **And . . . welcome** Compare the proverbial 'Give the stranger welcome' (Dent
S914.1).

179 **put an antic disposition on** assume a wild
fantastic manner of thought and
behaviour. It is also worth remembering
that an *antic* was a clown; for the part
Hamlet will now go on to play in his dealings with his opponents will have much in
common with that of the witty clown.

181 **encumbered** The precise meaning of
this word in this context is still to seek;
OED suggests *folded*. What is clear is that
the position of the arms signifies the self-
importance of one who has secrets which
he is eager to reveal.

 thus head shaked Neither Q2 nor F gives
satisfactory sense. Theobald's introduction of the hyphen results in a very odd
nonce-word; while F, as it stands, is
meaningless. The assumption behind the
present reading is that Shakespeare wrote
shakt, the form taken by *shaked* in Q1 of

Troilus (1.3.101), which the compositors,
mistaking *t* for *e*, set up as *shake*.

182 **pronouncing of** uttering. In Shakespearian English *of* naturally followed a
verbal noun (Abbott 178).
 doubtful ambiguous, likely to arouse
curiosity

183 **an if** if, if only

184 **There be an if they might** i.e. there are
people who if they were free (to speak)

185 **giving out** hinting, intimation. Compare *Measure* 1.4.54–5, 'His givings-out
were of an infinite distance | From his
true-meant design.'
 to note show, indicate (*OED note v.²* 5).
The *to* is redundant, since *note* is governed
by *never shall* (l. 180). See Abbott 350 for
further examples of this usage.

186 **this** i.e. everything Hamlet has said in
the previous ten and a half lines: 'Here as
. . . of me' (ll. 176–86).

187 **most** greatest, utmost (Abbott 17)

HAMLET

 Rest, rest, perturbèd spirit. So, gentlemen,   190
 With all my love I do commend me to you;
 And what so poor a man as Hamlet is
 May do t'express his love and friending to you,
 God willing, shall not lack. Let us go in together;
 And still your fingers on your lips, I pray.
 The time is out of joint. O cursèd spite,
 That ever I was born to set it right!
 Nay, come, let's go together.   *Exeunt*

2.1 *Enter Polonius and Reynoldo*

POLONIUS

 Give him this money and these notes, Reynoldo.

REYNOLDO I will, my lord.

POLONIUS

 You shall do marvellous wisely, good Reynoldo,
 Before you visit him, to make inquiry
 Of his behaviour.

REYNOLDO   My lord, I did intend it.

POLONIUS

 Marry, well said, very well said. Look you, sir,
 Inquire me first what Danskers are in Paris,

191 With all] F; Withall Q2; In all Q1 198 Nay, come,] Nay, come F; Nay come,
Q2 2.1.0.1 *Enter Polonius and Reynoldo*] F; *Enter old Polonius, with his man or two* Q2; *Enter
Corambis, and Montano* Q1 1 this] Q2Q1; his F 1, 3, 15 Reynoldo] F; Reynaldo Q2 3
wisely,] ~ : F; ~ᴧ Q2 4 to] Q2; you F inquiry] F; inquire Q2

193 **friending** friendliness—not elsewhere
in Shakespeare, and apparently a coinage
of his
195 **still** always
 your fingers on your lips i.e. keep silent.
'Lay thy fingers on thy lips', which goes
back to Juvenal's '*digito compesce labellum*'
(*Satires* i. 160), seems to have become
proverbial through Shakespeare's use of it
here (Tilley F239).
196 **out of joint** dislocated, disordered. 'To
be out of joint' (Tilley J75) was already a
common expression when *Hamlet* was
written.
196–7 **O cursèd spite . . . right** 'Alas that
ever I was born' (Dent B140.1) had been
in use since the mid-15th century. Hamlet has quickly come to realize the mag-
nitude and difficulty of the task the Ghost

has imposed on him.
2.1.0.1 *Reynoldo* This variant on 'Reynard'
is the name of the Fox in Spenser's *Mother
Hubberds Tale*.
3 **You shall do** i.e. you can be sure you
will be behaving. For this use of *shall*, see
Abbott 315, and compare *Macbeth*
3.4.56–7, 'If much you note him, | You
shall offend him'.
 marvellous very. Shakespeare often uses
marvellous in this sense; compare *Dream*
3.1.2, 'here's a marvellous convenient
place for our rehearsal.'
7 **me** An example of the so-called ethic
dative, and meaning originally 'for me',
this word is superfluous to the sense but
adds a touch of colour by drawing attention to the speaker (Abbott 220).
 Danskers Danes

And how, and who, what means, and where they keep,
What company, at what expense; and finding
By this encompassment and drift of question   10
That they do know my son, come you more nearer
Than your particular demands will touch it.
Take you, as 'twere, some distant knowledge of him,
As thus, 'I know his father and his friends,
And in part him'. Do you mark this, Reynoldo?

REYNOLDO Ay, very well, my lord.

POLONIUS

'And in part him, but', you may say, 'not well,
But if't be he I mean, he's very wild,
Addicted so and so', and there put on him
What forgeries you please. Marry, none so rank   20
As may dishonour him—take heed of that—
But, sir, such wanton, wild, and usual slips
As are companions noted and most known
To youth and liberty.

REYNOLDO   As gaming, my lord?

POLONIUS

Ay, or drinking, fencing, swearing,
Quarrelling, drabbing—you may go so far.

REYNOLDO My lord, that would dishonour him.

POLONIUS

Faith, no, as you may season it in the charge.

---

14 As] Q2; And F   24 lord?] ADAMS; ~. FQ2   28 no] F; *not in* Q2

8 **keep** lodge. Compare *Troilus* 4.5.278, 'In
what place of the field doth Calchas keep?'
10 **encompassment and drift of question** i.e.
roundabout and unobtrusive manner of
inquiry
11–12 **come you . . . touch it** i.e. make a
closer approach to touching on your main
concern than any specific questions
would allow you to do
11 **more nearer** nearer. Double comparatives, for the sake of emphasis, are
common in Shakespeare (Abbott 11).
13 **Take you** pretend you have
19 **put on him** ascribe to him, charge him
with
20 **forgeries** false accusations. Compare
Dream 2.1.81, 'These are the forgeries of

jealousy'.
22 **slips** errors in conduct
23 **noted** generally recognized
24 **youth and liberty** i.e. young men who are
free to do as they like
25 **fencing** Fencing was, of course, a much
admired accomplishment in Shakespeare's day, as Claudius makes plain at
4.7.83–91; but fencing schools had
rather a bad name as 'academies of man-
slaughter', and so had professional fencers. See John Webster's Character of 'An
ordinary Fencer' (Webster, iv. 27).
26 **drabbing** whoring—not elsewhere in
Shakespeare; earliest example in *OED*
28 **season** qualify

You must not put another scandal on him,
That he is open to incontinency—   30
That's not my meaning—but breathe his faults so
    quaintly
That they may seem the taints of liberty,
The flash and outbreak of a fiery mind,
A savageness in unreclaimèd blood,
Of general assault.

REYNOLDO   But, my good lord—

POLONIUS

Wherefore should you do this?

REYNOLDO   Ay, my lord,
I would know that.

POLONIUS   Marry, sir, here's my drift,
And I believe it is a fetch of warrant.
You laying these slight sullies on my son,
As 'twere a thing a little soiled i'th' working,   40
Mark you, your party in converse, him you would sound,
Having ever seen in the prenominate crimes
The youth you breathe of guilty, be assured

---

34 unreclaimèd] Q2; unreclaim'd F   38 warrant] F; wit Q2   40 i'th'] F; with Q2; wi'th'
ALEXANDER   41 you, . . . converse,] Q2; you . . . conuerse; F   42 seen_∧] Q2; seene. F

---

29 **another scandal** i.e. a very different and
    really scandalous fault. '*Other* was for-
    merly used to characterize things as of a
    different kind from those previously men-
    tioned: e.g. *other sinful men* = other men,
    who are sinful' (*OED other adj.* 7). Com-
    pare *Macbeth* 4.3.89–90, 'All these
    [deadly sins] are portable, | With other
    graces weighed.'

30 **incontinency** unrestrained sexual indul-
    gence. Polonius's distinction between
    drabbing and *incontinency* looks very like
    whore-splitting.

31 **quaintly** cleverly, artfully

32 **taints of liberty** i.e. stains resulting from
    freedom of action

34–5 **savageness . . . assault** i.e. natural
    wildness of undisciplined passion to
    which all young men are prone

34 **unreclaimèd** untamed, unsubdued
    (originally a technical term in falconry)

38 **fetch of warrant** justified stratagem, law-
    ful trick (*OED warrant sb.* 8b). Compare
    Othello 1.2.78–9, 'a practiser | Of arts in-
    hibited and out of warrant.'

39 **sullies** stains, blemishes (earliest instance
    cited by *OED*; not elsewhere in Shake-
    speare)

40 **as 'twere** i.e. as though you were dealing
    with
    working handling, making (i.e. contact
    with the world and its ways)

41 **party in converse** interlocutor
    him he whom (Abbott 208)

42 **Having ever** if he has ever. For this use of
    a participle to express a condition, see
    Abbott 377, and compare *2 Henry IV*
    4.4.39, 'But, being moody, give him line
    and scope'.
    prenominate crimes aforesaid mis-
    demeanours

198

He closes with you in this consequence:
'Good sir', or so, or 'friend', or 'gentleman',
According to the phrase and the addition
Of man and country.
REYNOLDO   Very good, my lord.
POLONIUS And then, sir, does he this—he does—what was
I about to say? By the mass, I was about to say something.
Where did I leave?   50
REYNOLDO At 'closes in the consequence', at 'friend, or so',
and 'gentleman'.

POLONIUS

At 'closes in the consequence', ay, marry!
He closes with you thus: 'I know the gentleman,
I saw him yesterday, or tother day,
Or then, or then, with such and such, and, as you say,
There was he gaming, there o'ertook in's rouse,
There falling out at tennis', or perchance
'I saw him enter such a house of sale',
Videlicet, a brothel, or so forth.   60
See you now,
Your bait of falsehood takes this carp of truth;
And thus do we of wisdom and of reach,
With windlasses and with assays of bias,

46 and] F; or Q2   addition] F; addission Q2   48 he this—he does—] F (he this? He does:);
a this, a doos Q2   49 By the mass] Q2; *not in* F   51–2 at 'friend, or so', and 'gentleman'] F;
not in Q2   54 closes with you] F; closes Q2; closeth with him Q1   55 tother] FQ1;
th'other Q2   56 and such] F; or such Q2   57 he gaming, there o'ertook] F; a gaming there,
or tooke Q2   62 takes] F; take Q2   carp] Q2; Cape F

44 **closes with you in this consequence** i.e.
takes you into his confidence to the
following effect
46 **phrase** form of expression
   addition manner of addressing another
49 **By the mass** probably omitted from F to
avoid the charge of profanity
57 **o'ertook in's rouse** i.e. overcome by
intoxication when engaged in a drinking-
bout (*OED overtake* 9)
58 **tennis** i.e. royal tennis, court tennis, *not*
lawn tennis. Nashe (i. 209. 31–3) links
tennis with dancing and fencing as
recreations of 'the unthrift'.
62 **Your bait . . . truth** Compare 'Tell a lie
and find a truth' (Tilley L237).
   takes catches
   carp Izaak Walton writes: 'The carp is
the queen of rivers: a stately, a good, and

a very subtle fish' (*The Compleat Angler* I.
ix). It is probably the carp's subtlety
Polonius has in mind.
63 **reach** far-ranging comprehension
64 **windlasses** roundabout manœuvres—
originally a *windlass* was 'a circuit made
to intercept the game in hunting' (*OED
windlass sb.*²). Compare *The Mirror for
Magistrates* (1578) 29. 316–7, 'Which
[the murder of Humphrey, Duke of
Gloucester] by sly drifts, and windlasses
aloof, | They brought about'.
   assays of bias indirect tests. The
metaphor derives 'from the game of
bowls, in which the player does not aim at
the Jack . . . directly, but in a curve, so
that the *bias* brings the ball round' (Furness).

199

By indirections find directions out.
So, by my former lecture and advice,
Shall you my son. You have me, have you not?
REYNOLDO My lord, I have.
POLONIUS God buy you, fare you well.
REYNOLDO Good my lord.   70
POLONIUS

Observe his inclination in yourself.
REYNOLDO

I shall, my lord.
POLONIUS And let him ply his music.
REYNOLDO Well, my lord.   *Exit*
          Enter Ophelia
POLONIUS

Farewell.—How now, Ophelia, what's the matter?
OPHELIA

Alas, my lord, I have been so affrighted.
POLONIUS With what, i'th' name of God?
OPHELIA

My lord, as I was sewing in my chamber,
Lord Hamlet, with his doublet all unbraced,
No hat upon his head, his stockings fouled,   80

69 buy you, fare you] F (buy you ; fare you); buy ye, far ye Q2   76 Alas, my lord] F ; O my Lord,
my Lord Q2   77 i'th' name of God] Q2 ; in the name of Heauen F   78 chamber] F ; closset Q2

65 **indirections** devious methods—first in-
    stance of *indirection*, in this sense, cited by
    OED
    directions real tendencies
66 **lecture** lesson. Compare *Shrew* 3.1.23,
    'His lecture will be done ere you have
    tuned.'
68 **God buy you** The origin of the modern
    goodbye, this phrase began as *God be with
    you (ye)*, which was then reinterpreted as
    God [be] by you and subsequently con-
    fused with *God buy you*, meaning 'God
    redeem you'. It was then reduced to *God
    buy*, and corrupted to *goodbye* through the
    influence of such formulas of leave-taking
    as *good-day* and *goodnight* (Cercignani,
    p. 365). It was commonly used, as it is here,
    as a polite way of dismissing someone.
69 **Good my lord** *Good* (*OED* 2b) was often
    used 'as a conventional epithet prefixed to
    titles of high rank'.
70 **Observe . . . yourself** 'do yourself as he is

inclined ; be serviceable to him, whatever
may be his disposition' (Schmidt)
73 **ply** work hard at. In Shakespeare's day a
    gentleman was expected to be proficient
    in music.
74.1 At this point the scene abruptly
    changes gear, as it were. The comedy of
    Polonius's elaborate efforts to find out
    what his son is doing in Paris gives way to
    the intense distress of Ophelia, already a
    victim, at least in part, of her father's
    interference in her life.
79 **unbraced** unfastened, unbuttoned. Com-
    pare *Caesar* 1.3.48–9, 'And, thus unbracèd,
    Casca, as you see, | Have bared my bosom
    to the thunder-stone'.
80 **No hat** Shakespeare and his contem-
    poraries, living in draughty houses, wore
    their hats indoors as well as out. More-
    over, the hat was essential to good
    manners (see 5.2.81–106).

Ungartered, and down-gyvèd to his ankle,
Pale as his shirt, his knees knocking each other,
And with a look so piteous in purport
As if he had been loosèd out of hell
To speak of horrors, he comes before me.
POLONIUS
Mad for thy love?
OPHELIA   My lord, I do not know,
But truly I do fear it.
POLONIUS   What said he?
OPHELIA
He took me by the wrist, and held me hard.
Then goes he to the length of all his arm,
And, with his other hand thus o'er his brow,   90
He falls to such perusal of my face
As he would draw it. Long stayed he so.
At last, a little shaking of mine arm,
And thrice his head thus waving up and down,
He raised a sigh so piteous and profound
That it did seem to shatter all his bulk
And end his being. That done, he lets me go,
And, with his head over his shoulder turned,
He seemed to find his way without his eyes,
For out o' doors he went without their help,   100
And to the last bended their light on me.

81 down-gyvèd] F2; downe gyued FQ2   92 As he] F; As a Q2   96 That] F; As Q2   98 shoulder] Q2Q1; shoulders F   100 help] FQ1; helps Q2

81 **down-gyvèd to his ankle** hanging down round his ankles like fetters—a typically Shakespearian compound coinage
82–5 **Pale . . . horrors** One recalls that the Ghost was, according to Horatio, 'very pale' (1.2.233); that it had been released from purgatory or the grave; and that it had spoken of horrors (1.5.2–20). Hamlet seems to be identifying himself with it and, simultaneously, reliving his encounter with it, whether deliberately or by imaginative compulsion it is hard to say.
82 **Pale as his shirt** Compare 'As pale as a clout' (Tilley C446).
86 **Mad for thy love** Polonius's deduction is a reasonable one, for Hamlet's appearance, as Ophelia describes it, is very close to that of the typical lover in Rosalind's mocking version of it: 'A lean cheek . . . a blue eye

and sunken . . . a beard neglected . . . Then your hose should be ungartered, your bonnet unbanded, your sleeve unbuttoned, your shoe untied, and every thing about you demonstrating a careless desolation' (*As You Like It* 3.2.346–53).
91 **perusal** close scrutiny—first instance cited by OED, though it also occurs at *Sonnets* 38.6. Compare *Lucrece* 1527, 'This picture she advisedly perused'.
93 **a little shaking of mine arm** giving my arm a little shake (Abbott 178)
94 **waving** moving (*OED* wave v. 8c)
96 **bulk** bodily frame, trunk. Clarence speaks of the sea smothering his soul 'within my panting bulk' (*Richard III* 1.4.40).
101 **bended** turned, directed

POLONIUS

Come, go with me. I will go seek the King.
This is the very ecstasy of love,
Whose violent property fordoes itself,
And leads the will to desperate undertakings
As oft as any passion under heaven
That does afflict our natures. I am sorry—
What, have you given him any hard words of late?

OPHELIA

No, my good lord, but as you did command
I did repel his letters, and denied   110
His access to me.

POLONIUS   That hath made him mad.
I am sorry that with better speed and judgement
I had not quoted him. I feared he did but trifle
And meant to wreck thee. But beshrew my jealousy!
By heaven, it is as proper to our age
To cast beyond ourselves in our opinions
As it is common for the younger sort
To lack discretion. Come, go we to the King.
This must be known, which, being kept close, might move
More grief to hide than hate to utter love.   *Exeunt*   120

---

102 Come] Q2; *not in* F   106 passion] F; passions Q2   107 sorry—] CAPELL; ~, FQ2
112 speed] F; heed Q2   113 feared] Q2; feare F   115 By heaven] Q2Q1; It seemes F
120 love.] F; loue, | Come. Q2

---

103 **ecstasy** madness
104 **Whose . . . itself** i.e. which has the
    peculiar effect, when it becomes violent,
    of destroying itself
106 **passion** painful suffering
110–11 **denied | His** refused to allow him
112 **speed** success, accuracy
113 **quoted** observed (*OED quote v.* 5b).
    Compare *Lucrece* 810–12, 'Yea, the il-
    literate . . . Will quote my loathsome tres-
    pass in my looks.'
114 **wreck** ruin. Compare *All's Well* 3.5.23,
    'the wreck of maidenhood'.
    beshrew curse
    jealousy suspicion (*OED* 5)
115 **proper to our age** i.e. natural to us old
    men

116 **cast beyond ourselves** 'overrun the
    trail' (Wilson), go too far. The metaphor is
    from hunting; to *cast about* is to 'search
    for a lost scent' (*OED cast v.* 70c)
119 **known** made known (to Claudius and
    Gertrude)
    being kept close if it were kept secret
    (Abbott 377)
119–20 **might move . . . love** i.e. this love
    affair could cause us more trouble and
    suffering, should we try to hide it, than
    any we may undergo (in the form of royal
    displeasure) for revealing it. Polonius, still
    casting beyond himself, thinks, quite mis-
    takenly, that the King and Queen are sure
    to disapprove of a match between the heir
    to the throne and his daughter.

2.2   *Enter Claudius, Gertrude, Rosencrantz, Guildenstern,
         and Attendants*

CLAUDIUS

Welcome, dear Rosencrantz and Guildenstern.
Moreover that we much did long to see you,
The need we have to use you did provoke
Our hasty sending. Something have you heard
Of Hamlet's transformation—so I call it,
Since not th'exterior nor the inward man
Resembles that it was. What it should be,
More than his father's death, that thus hath put him
So much from th'understanding of himself
I cannot deem of. I entreat you both,   10
That being of so young days brought up with him,
And since so neighboured to his youth and humour,
That you vouchsafe your rest here in our court
Some little time, so by your companies
To draw him on to pleasures, and to gather,
So much as from occasions you may glean,

2.2.0.1 *Enter Claudius . . . Attendants*] F (*Enter King, Queene, Rosincrane, and Guildensterne Cum
alijs*), *Flourish. Enter King and Queene, Rosencraus and Guyldensterne* Q2; *Enter King and Queene,
Rossencraft, and Gilderstone* Q1   1 *Rosencrantz*] F (*Rosincrance*); Rosencraus Q2   5 I] F; *not in*
Q2   6 Since not] F; Sith nor Q2   10 deem] F; dreame Q2   12 since] F; sith Q2   humour]
F; hauior Q2   16 occasions] F occasion Q2

2.2 After marking the beginning of this
scene as *Scena Secunda*, whoever was responsible for the attempt to divide the
Folio text into acts and scenes gave up the
unequal struggle. His tacit acknowledge-
ment of defeat is not surprising. From this
point onwards, until Fortinbras appears
at the opening of 4.4, there is no change
of location. Everything happens within
the palace at Elsinore; and, more important still, right up to the end of 4.4, the
action is almost continuous.

0.1 *Rosencrantz, Guildenstern* When Christian IV of Denmark came to the throne in
1588, Queen Elizabeth sent Daniel Rogers
to Elsinore to pay her respects to the new
king; and Rogers, in his report, specifically mentions 'George Rosencrantz, Master of the Palace, Axel Guildenstern of
Lyngbye, Viceroy of Norway, and Peter
Guildenstern, Marshal of Denmark'
(Bullough, vii. 184). The names are,
then, good Danish names. They are also
pretty names—'Rosy-wreath' and 'Golden-

star'. Most important of all, however, for
Shakespeare's purpose, they have the virtue of being, like Tweedledum and Tweed-
ledee, metrically identical, and so readily
transposable.

2 **Moreover** besides (*OED* 4)—no other
use, in this sense, cited

4 **sending** message (sending for you)

7 **that** that which, what
should can possibly (Abbott 325). Compare *Timon* 4.3.396, 'Where should he
have this gold?'

10 **deem of** judge, decide. Compare *2 Henry
VI* 3.2.65: 'What know I how the world
may deem of me?'

11 **of** from (Abbott 167)
so young days such an early age

12 **neighboured to** intimately familiar with
humour disposition, temperament

13 **vouchsafe your rest** consent to stay.
Compare *Pericles* 2. Prologue 25–6, 'And
that in Tarsus was not best | Longer for
him to make his rest.'

16 **occasions** opportunities

Whether aught to us unknown afflicts him thus
That, opened, lies within our remedy.

GERTRUDE

Good gentlemen, he hath much talked of you,
And sure I am two men there are not living   20
To whom he more adheres. If it will please you
To show us so much gentry and good will
As to expend your time with us awhile
For the supply and profit of our hope,
Your visitation shall receive such thanks
As fits a king's remembrance.

ROSENCRANTZ   Both your majesties
Might, by the sovereign power you have of us,
Put your dread pleasures more into command
Than to entreaty.

GUILDENSTERN   But we both obey,
And here give up ourselves, in the full bent,   30
To lay our services freely at your feet,
To be commanded.

CLAUDIUS

Thanks, Rosencrantz and gentle Guildenstern.

GERTRUDE

Thanks, Guildenstern and gentle Rosencrantz.
And I beseech you instantly to visit
My too much changèd son.—Go, some of you,
And bring these gentlemen where Hamlet is.

---

17 Whether . . . thus] Q2; *not in* F   20 are] FQ3; is Q2   29 But] Q2; *not in* F   31 services]
F; seruice Q2   36 you] Q2; ye F   37 these] Q2; the F

18 **opened** made known, revealed (*OED open
v.* 9)
21 **more adheres** is more attached
22 **gentry** courtesy (*OED* 1c)
24 **For . . . hope** i.e. by supplying what is
needed for the realization of our hope
(*OED supply sb.* 1)
27 **of** over (Abbott 174)
28 **dread pleasures** wills that we hold in awe
into i.e. into the form of
30 **give up** devote. Compare *Othello*
3.3.469–71, 'Iago doth give up | The
execution of his wit, hands, heart, | To

wronged Othello's service!'
in the full bent with the utmost willing-
ness. '"Bent" is used by Shakespeare for
the utmost degree of any passion or mental quality. The expression is derived from
archery; the bow has its *bent* when it is
drawn as far as it can be' (Dr Johnson).
Compare 'They fool me to the top of my
bent' (3.2.366).
31 **freely** unreservedly
36 **some** some one (*OED* A1). Compare
Richard II 4.1.268, 'Go some of you and
fetch a looking-glass.'

GUILDENSTERN

    Heavens make our presence and our practices
    Pleasant and helpful to him!

GERTRUDE   Ay, amen!

     Exeunt Rosencrantz, Guildenstern, ⌜and an Attendant⌝
     Enter Polonius

POLONIUS

    Th'ambassadors from Norway, my good lord,   40
    Are joyfully returned.

CLAUDIUS

    Thou still hast been the father of good news.

POLONIUS

    Have I, my lord? I assure you, my good liege,
    I hold my duty, as I hold my soul,
    Both to my God and to my gracious King.
    And I do think—or else this brain of mine
    Hunts not the trail of policy so sure
    As it hath used to do—that I have found
    The very cause of Hamlet's lunacy.

CLAUDIUS

    O speak of that, that I do long to hear.   50

POLONIUS

    Give first admittance to th'ambassadors.
    My news shall be the fruit to that great feast.

CLAUDIUS

    Thyself do grace to them, and bring them in.

                         Exit Polonius

    He tells me, my sweet Queen, that he hath found
    The head and source of all your son's distemper.

---

39 Ay,] Q2; *not in* F   *Exeunt Rosencrantz, Guildenstern,* ⌜*and an Attendant*⌝ JENKINS; *Exit* F (*after Guildenstern's speech*); *Exeunt Ros⟨encrantz⟩ and Guyld⟨enstern⟩* Q2   39.2 *Enter Polonius*] FQ2; *Enter Corambis and Ofelia* Q1   43 I assure you, my good liege] PARROTT–CRAIG; Assure you, my good Liege F; I assure my good Liege Q2; I assure your grace Q1   45 and] Q2Q1; one F   48 it hath] Q2; I haue F; it had Q1   50 I do] F; doe I Q2   52 fruit] Q2; Newes F   53 *Exit Polonius*] ROWE; *not in* FQ2   54 sweet Queen, that] F; deere Gertrard Q2

---

38 **practices** actions, activities

39 **Pleasant** pleasing, pleasurable

43 **I assure . . . liege** Parrott and Craig argue convincingly that Q2 omits *you*, while F omits *I* which appears in Q1.

44–5 **I hold . . . king** i.e. 'I regard my duty both to my God and to my gracious king as highly as I value my soul' (Kittredge).

47 **trail of policy** track or scent which requires a knowledge of men and affairs to follow it

48 **it hath used** it was wont. F's 'I haue v'sd' comes from 'I haue found'.

49 **very** true

52 **fruit** dessert

53 **grace** honour (with a quibble on the *grace* that precedes a meal)

GERTRUDE

I doubt it is no other but the main—
His father's death and our o'erhasty marriage.

CLAUDIUS

Well, we shall sift him.
           Enter Polonius, with Voltemand and Cornelius
                              Welcome, good friends.
Say, Voltemand, what from our brother Norway?

VOLTEMAND

Most fair return of greetings and desires.   60
Upon our first, he sent out to suppress
His nephew's levies, which to him appeared
To be a preparation 'gainst the Polack;
But, better looked into, he truly found
It was against your highness; whereat grieved
That so his sickness, age, and impotence
Was falsely borne in hand, sends out arrests
On Fortinbras, which he, in brief, obeys,
Receives rebuke from Norway, and, in fine,
Makes vow before his uncle never more   70
To give th'assay of arms against your majesty.
Whereon old Norway, overcome with joy,
Gives him three thousand crowns in annual fee

---

57 o'erhasty] F; hastie Q2   58.1 *Enter Polonius, with Voltemand and Cornelius*] F (*Enter Polonius, Voltumand, and Cornelius*); *Enter Embassadors* Q2   58 Welcome, good] F; welcome my good Q2   73 three] FQ1; threescore Q2

56 **doubt** fear
     main chief concern (*OED main sb.*¹ 6)
58 **sift him** examine Polonius closely
60 **return** reciprocation
61 **Upon our first** i.e. on our first raising the matter. Compare *Lear* 5.3.288, 'from your first of difference and decay'.
     sent out i.e. sent an order
63 **Polack** King of Poland
64 **better looked into** on closer inspection
64–5 **truly found | It was** i.e. found it truly was. Compare *Dream* 1.1.126, 'something nearly that concerns yourselves'.
65 **grieved** aggrieved, offended
67 **Was** Shakespeare uses the singular either because he looks on the King of Norway's infirmities as a collective whole or because he recognizes, rather belatedly, that it is the King who was 'falsely borne in hand' because of his infirmities.
     borne in hand deceived, 'led up the

garden-path', conned (*OED bear v.*¹ 3e). The expression was a very common one (Tilley H94).
     sends 'Where there can be no doubt what is the nominative, it is sometimes omitted' (Abbott 399).
67–8 **arrests | On Fortinbras** i.e. strict orders commanding Fortinbras to stop his military preparations and, it would seem from what follows, to appear before the King.
69 **in fine** finally, in conclusion
71 **give th'assay of arms** try to use armed force
73 **three thousand** Q2's *threescore thousand* is metrically awkward and financially excessive, whereas F's *three thousand* is metrically impeccable, financially reasonable, and has the support of Q1 which reports Voltemand's speech very well indeed.
     fee income

And his commission to employ those soldiers,
So levied as before, against the Polack,
With an entreaty, herein further shown,
              He hands a document to Claudius
That it might please you to give quiet pass
Through your dominions for his enterprise,
On such regards of safety and allowance
As therein are set down.

CLAUDIUS   It likes us well;   80
And at our more considered time we'll read,
Answer, and think upon this business.
Meantime, we thank you for your well-took labour.
Go to your rest; at night we'll feast together.
Most welcome home.
              Exeunt Voltemand and Cornelius ⌈and Attendants⌉
POLONIUS   This business is very well ended.
My liege and madam, to expostulate
What majesty should be, what duty is,
Why day is day, night night, and time is time,
Were nothing but to waste night, day, and time.
Therefore, since brevity is the soul of wit,   90
And tediousness the limbs and outward flourishes,

76.1 *He hands a document to Claudius*] MALONE subs.; *not in* FQ2Q1   78 his] F; this Q2   85 very well] FQ1; well Q2   90 since] F; *not in* Q2

74 **commission** authorization
77 **quiet pass** unmolested passage
79 **regards of safety and allowance** i.e. conditions ensuring the safety of the state and subject to your approval
81 **at our more considered time** i.e. when we have more time suitable for considering it. For this use of the past participle, see Schmidt, pp. 1147–8.
83 **well-took** well undertaken. 'Owing to the tendency to drop the inflection *en*, the Elizabethan authors frequently used the curtailed forms of past participles which are common in Early English: "I have spoke, forgot, writ, chid," etcetera. Where, however, the form thus curtailed was in danger of being confused with the infinitive, as in "taken", they used the past tense for the participle' (Abbott 343).
84 **at night** tonight
85 *and Attendants* it seems necessary to get the Attendants off stage at this point, since the business that follows is of too private a nature to be transacted in their presence.
86–104 **My liege . . . thus** The best comment ever made on Polonius's manner in his set speeches is Dr Johnson's: 'His mode of oratory is truly represented as designed to ridicule the practice of those times, of prefaces that made no introduction, and of method that embarrassed rather than explained.'
86 **expostulate** ask, inquire (*OED* 1b)
90 **brevity is the soul of wit** This *sententia*, which became proverbial (Tilley B652), almost certainly originated here in *Hamlet*.
   wit good sense, wisdom
91 **And . . . flourishes** i.e. and unnecessary extraneous matter and ornament make wisdom tedious

I will be brief. Your noble son is mad.
Mad call I it, for, to define true madness,
What is't but to be nothing else but mad?
But let that go.

GERTRUDE   More matter with less art.

POLONIUS

Madam, I swear I use no art at all.
That he is mad 'tis true; 'tis true 'tis pity;
And pity 'tis 'tis true—a foolish figure.
But farewell it, for I will use no art.
Mad let us grant him then; and now remains   100
That we find out the cause of this effect,
Or rather say the cause of this defect,
For this effect defective comes by cause.
Thus it remains, and the remainder thus.
Perpend.
I have a daughter—have whilst she is mine—
Who in her duty and obedience, mark,
Hath given me this. Now gather and surmise.

   He reads a letter

'To the celestial, and my soul's idol, the most beautified

---

97 he is] F; hee's Q2 98 'tis 'tis] Q2; it is F 104 thus.] F; thus_A Q2 106 whilst] F; while
Q2Q1 108.1 *He reads a letter*] Q1676 (*Reads*); *The Letter* F; *Letter* Q2 (*at* 115)

---

98 **figure** figure of speech
100 **remains** it remains, there remains. For
 the ellipsis of 'it' and 'there' see Abbott
 404.
103 **effect defective** i.e. consequence arising
 from lack of something (in this case lack of
 reason). Polonius appears to have in mind
 the theological notion of 'defective cause'
 for which OED quotes N. de Lawne's
 translation of *Du Moulin's Logick* (1624):
 'Under efficient cause we comprehend the
 cause which is called defective. As the
 want of sight is the cause of going astray'
 (*defective* A6).
 comes by cause must have a cause
105 **Perpend** listen and ponder. Shakespeare
 evidently found this Latinate word rather
 comic. He puts it into the mouths of three
 other characters, each of whom is seeking

to be impressive: Touchstone (*As You Like
It* 3.2.59); Feste (*Twelfth Night* 5.1.289);
and Pistol (*Merry Wives* 2.1.103, and
Henry V 4.4.8). He may well have picked
it up from *Cambyses* (l. 1018), where it
occurs shortly before the passage he
parodies in *1 Henry IV* (2.4.379–83).
108 **gather and surmise** i.e. make your own
 deductions
109 **beautified** beautiful, richly supplied
 with beauty. Nashe uses *beautified*, in this
 sense, in his dedication of *Christ's Tears*
 (1593) to Lady Elizabeth Carey (ii. 9.
 2–3): clear evidence that it did not always mean 'made beautiful by cosmetics', the sense in which Polonius seems to
 take it, though he may, of course, be ob-
 jecting to nothing more than its new-
 fangled quality.

Ophelia'— That's an ill phrase, a vile phrase, 'beautified'   110
is a vile phrase. But you shall hear—'these; in her
excellent white bosom, these.'
GERTRUDE Came this from Hamlet to her?
POLONIUS

Good madam, stay awhile, I will be faithful.
            'Doubt thou the stars are fire,
            Doubt that the sun doth move,
            Doubt truth to be a liar,
            But never doubt I love.
O dear Ophelia, I am ill at these numbers. I have not art
to reckon my groans. But that I love thee best, O most   120
best, believe it. Adieu.
        Thine evermore, most dear lady, whilst this
            machine is to him,   Hamlet.'
This, in obedience, hath my daughter showed me,
And, more above, hath his solicitings,
As they fell out by time, by means, and place,
All given to mine ear.
CLAUDIUS   But how hath she
Received his love?
POLONIUS   What do you think of me?
CLAUDIUS

As of a man faithful and honourable.
POLONIUS

I would fain prove so. But what might you think,   130

110–12 That's . . . bosom, these] *roman* F; *italic* Q2   111 hear—these: in] JENKINS; heare
these in F; *heare : thus in* Q2   112 these.] F; *these &c.* Q2   119–23 O dear Ophelia . . . him]
roman Q2; *italic* F   124 showed] F; showne Q2   125 above] F; about Q2   solicitings] Q2;
soliciting F

111 hear—'these The punctuation adopted
here is Jenkins's.
  these i.e. this letter. The plural, having
the singular sense, as in the Latin *litterae*,
is common in Shakespeare (*OED letter sb.*[1]
4b).
  in unto (Abbott 159)
112 excellent surpassingly, exceptionally
117 Doubt suspect
119 ill at these numbers i.e. a poor hand at
writing verse
120 reckon my groans (1) count my groans

(2) make my groans scan
123 machine bodily frame. This use of
machine, a word not found elsewhere in
Shakespeare, is the earliest cited by *OED*.
For the idea of the body as a complicated
mechanism controlled by the mind, compare *Venus* 367, where the tongue is
described as 'the engine of her thoughts'.
  is to him belongs to him, is his
125 more above besides, moreover
130 might you would you be likely to

When I had seen this hot love on the wing,
As I perceived it—I must tell you that—
Before my daughter told me, what might you,
Or my dear majesty your queen here, think,
If I had played the desk or table-book,
Or given my heart a winking mute and dumb,
Or looked upon this love with idle sight—
What might you think? No, I went round to work,
And my young mistress thus I did bespeak—
'Lord Hamlet is a prince out of thy star.   140
This must not be'. And then I precepts gave her,
That she should lock herself from his resort,
Admit no messengers, receive no tokens.
Which done, she took the fruits of my advice;
And he, repulsèd—a short tale to make—
Fell into a sadness, then into a fast,
Thence to a watch, thence into a weakness,
Thence to a lightness, and, by this declension,
Into the madness wherein now he raves,
And all we wail for.   150

132 it—I must tell you that—] Q2 (it (I must tell you that)); it, I must tell you that‸ F
136 winking] F; working Q2   139 And my young mistress] Q2; And (my yong Mistris) F
141 precepts] F; prescripts Q2   142 his] F; her Q2   145 repulsèd] F (repulsed); repell'd Q2
147 watch] FQ3; wath Q2   148 to a lightness] F; to lightnes Q2   149 wherein] Q2;
whereon F   150 wail] F; mourne Q2

131 **When** if when (OED *when* 8).
135 **played the desk or table-book** 'conveyed intelligence between them' (Warburton), both the *desk* and the *table-book* (= memorandum book) being used for writing.
136 **given . . . dumb** i.e. forced my heart to connive at what was going on and to say nothing about it. Compare *Romeo* 5.3.293–4, 'And I, for winking at your discords too, | Have lost a brace of kinsmen.' A *winking* is a 'deliberate closing of the eyes'.
137 **with idle sight** thoughtlessly, with no sense of its significance
138 **went round to work** i.e. did not mince matters
140 **out of thy star** i.e. beyond your reach (because of his rank). Compare *Twelfth Night* 2.5.130, 'In my stars I am above thee'.

141 **precepts** instructions
142 **resort** visits
144 **took the fruits of** profited by, i.e. did as I told her
147 **watch** state of sleeplessness (OED *watch sb.* 1)
148 **lightness** lightheadedness. Compare *Othello* 4.1.266, 'Are his wits safe? Is he not light of brain?'
     declension process of steady deterioration (with a pun on the grammatical sense of *declension*, as in *Richard III* 4.4.97–104, 'Decline all this . . . obeyed of none')
150 **all we** all of us. Abbott remarks: 'A feeling of the unemphatic nature of the nominatives *we* and *they* prevents us from saying "all we" . . . and "all they"' (240).
     wail This F reading is more absurd than Q2's *mourn*.

CLAUDIUS Do you think 'tis this?

GERTRUDE It may be—very likely.

POLONIUS
  Hath there been such a time—I'd fain know that—
  That I have positively said ''Tis so',
  When it proved otherwise?

CLAUDIUS   Not that I know.

POLONIUS (*touching his head and his shoulder*)
  Take this from this, if this be otherwise.
  If circumstances lead me, I will find
  Where truth is hid, though it were hid indeed
  Within the centre.

CLAUDIUS   How may we try it further?

POLONIUS
  You know sometimes he walks four hours together   160
  Here in the lobby.

GERTRUDE   So he does indeed.

POLONIUS
  At such a time I'll loose my daughter to him.

---

151 'tis] F; *not in* Q2   152 likely] F; like Q2   153 I'd] F; I would Q2   156 *touching ...
shoulder*] THEOBALD (*subs.*); *not in* FQ2   this, if this be otherwise.] Q2 (this, if . . . otherwise;);
this; if this be otherwise, F   161 does] Q2; ha's F

156.1 ***touching his head and his shoulder***
  Without this direction, the following line
  of Polonius, in which the first *this* means
  'my head', the second, 'My shoulders',
  and the third, 'my version of what has
  happened', is unintelligible. Yet it is found
  in none of the early editions, and makes
  its initial appearance in Pope's second
  edition of 1728. Up to that date there had,
  presumably, been a stage tradition for
  such a gesture.

157 **circumstances** relevant evidence. Compare *Othello* 3.3.410–11, 'imputation
  and strong circumstances | Which lead
  directly to the door of truth'.

159 **centre** centre of the earth. Polonius is
  improving on the proverbial 'Truth lies at
  the bottom of a well (pit)' (Tilley T582).
  try it i.e. test your theory

160 **four** several. Shakespeare and his con-
  temporaries often use *four*, much as we
  still use 'three or four', in an indefinite
  sense. Compare Webster, *The Duchess of
  Malfi* 4.1.10, 'She will muse four hours
  together'.

161 **lobby** 'passage or corridor connected
  with one or more apartments in a building . . . often used as a waiting-place or
  ante-room' (*OED*). The kind of place
  Shakespeare asks his audience to imagine
  is more fully described by Ben Jonson: 'Do
  you observe this gallery, or rather lobby,
  indeed? Here are a couple of studies, at
  each end one' (*Epicoene* 4.5.28–30).

162 **loose** let loose, set free. This is the obvious sense of the word, following on
  naturally from Polonius's account of his
  ordering his daughter to lock herself away
  from the Prince (l. 142). The idea, which
  has had a wide currency since Dover Wilson put it forward (*WHH*, pp. 103–4),
  that Polonius is consciously and
  deliberately using the language of stock-
  breeding is surely mistaken. His reference
  to 'a farm and carters', which Wilson
  regards as being 'in accordance with
  Shakespeare's habit of sustained imagery', is, in fact, a thoroughly contemp-
  tuous one, and makes it clear that
  Polonius would not dream of employing

Be you and I behind an arras then,
Mark the encounter. If he love her not,
And be not from his reason fallen thereon,
Let me be no assistant for a state,
But keep a farm and carters.
CLAUDIUS   We will try it.
        Enter Hamlet, reading on a book
GERTRUDE
But look where sadly the poor wretch comes reading.
POLONIUS
Away, I do beseech you both, away.
I'll board him presently. O give me leave.   170
        Exeunt Claudius and Gertrude
How does my good lord Hamlet?
HAMLET Well, God-a-mercy.
POLONIUS Do you know me, my lord?
HAMLET Excellent, excellent well. You're a fishmonger.

---

167 But] Q2; And F   167.1 *reading on a book*] F; *not in* Q2   174 Excellent, excellent] F;
Excellent Q2   You're] F (y'are) Q1; you are Q2

farm terminology about his own family.
This does not mean, of course, that
Shakespeare, as distinct from Polonius, is
unaware of the farmyard sense of *loose*,
which he exploits in *Merry Wives*
2.1.163–4. He makes Polonius's un-
awareness of the ambiguity of *loose* an
index of the old man's blind insensitivity
to what he is, in fact, proposing.
163 **arras** 'hanging screen of tapestry placed
    round the walls of household apartments,
    often at such a distance from them as to
    allow of people being concealed in the
    space between' (Onions)
165 **thereon** on that account
167.1 *Enter Hamlet* Dover Wilson's shifting
    of this entry to l. 159 is unnecessary and
    unwarranted. To have the Prince eaves-
    dropping on the plan is to obscure, almost
    to nullify, one of his most striking charac-
    teristics, insisted on by Saxo and
    Belleforest alike and emphasised by
    Shakespeare throughout the play: his
    keen sensitivity to nuances of tone and
    atmosphere. His ability to 'smell a rat' is,
    as Polonius will discover to his cost,
    almost uncanny.
168 **sadly** seriously
    wretch (a term of affection). Compare

'Excellent wretch! Perdition catch my soul
| But I do love thee' (*Othello* 3.3.91–2).
170 **board** accost, address
    presently immediately, forthwith
    give me leave i.e. please leave me alone
    (polite form of dismissal). Compare *Romeo*
    1.3.8–9, 'Nurse, give leave awhile, | We
    must talk in secret.'
172 **God-a-mercy** thank you. Meaning
    originally 'God reward you', this phrase
    had been reduced to a polite formula used
    in addressing an inferior in rank.
174 **fishmonger** As the response of every
    audience amply attests, Hamlet's reply, so
    beautifully designed to deflate Polonius's
    sense of his own importance and dignity,
    is gloriously funny. There may well, how-
    ever, be more than this in Hamlet's mind.
    A *fishmonger*, as well as meaning 'a seller
    of fish', could also signify 'a wencher';
    possibly 'a bawd', since Shakespeare
    refers to female flesh as *fish* in *Romeo and
    Juliet* (1.1.29–30); and, finally, 'one
    whose womenfolk are likely to be beauti-
    ful, wanton, and prolific'. That this last is
    the most important of the last three con-
    notations has been convincingly demon-
    strated by Harold Jenkins in his 'Hamlet
    and the Fishmonger' (*Deutsche Shake-*

POLONIUS Not I, my lord.

HAMLET Then I would you were so honest a man.

POLONIUS Honest, my lord?

HAMLET Ay, sir. To be honest, as this world goes, is to be one man picked out of ten thousand.

POLONIUS That's very true, my lord.   180

HAMLET For if the sun breed maggots in a dead dog, being a good kissing carrion—Have you a daughter?

POLONIUS I have, my lord.

HAMLET Let her not walk i'th' sun. Conception is a blessing. But not as your daughter may conceive—friend, look to't.

POLONIUS (aside) How say you by that? Still harping on my daughter. Yet he knew me not at first; he said I was a

---

179 ten] Q2Q1; two F   182 good] FQ2; God HANMER, WARBURTON   185 not as] F; as Q2 conceive—] MALONE; conceiue. F; conceaue, Q2

---

speare-Gesellschaft West Jahrbuch (1975), 109–20). Hamlet, having assumed an 'antic disposition', is playing the role of the natural fool with zest and bitterness, making remarks that seem quite mad, yet nevertheless point to truths. His main concern in the first part of this dialogue is not with Polonius but with Ophelia, now ripe for breeding.

176 **Then . . . honest a man** Hamlet now takes *fishmonger* in its primary sense, implying that a fishmonger's occupation is *honest* enough, which is more than can be said of Polonius's fishmongering activities.

178–9 **to be . . . ten thousand** Hamlet combines two proverbial sayings into one: 'A man among a thousand' (Tilley M217), and 'Thus goes the world' (Dent W884.1).

181–2 **For if . . . carrion** The idea that maggots and the like were produced by a process of spontaneous generation caused by the sun, the source of life, shining on dead matter was a commonplace of the time, which Shakespeare alludes to again in *Antony* 2.7.26–7, 'Your serpent of Egypt is bred now of your mud by the operation of your sun', and in *Timon* 4.3.1–2, 'O blessed breeding sun, draw from the earth | Rotten humidity'. What

Hamlet is about to say when he breaks off abruptly is almost certainly 'the corruption of the one is the generation of many another' (Tilley C667). Nashe develops this notion at some length in his *Pierce Penilesse* (i. 173.21–174.8).

182 **good kissing carrion** piece of flesh good for kissing. Schmidt compares *LLL* 1.1.65, 'too hard-a-keeping oath'. For the use of *carrion* to describe a loose woman, see *Troilus* 4.1.72–3, 'for every scruple | Of her [Helen's] contaminated carrion weight'.

Have you a daughter This unexpected question is prompted by the references to kissing and breeding that have preceded it, and, it seems likely, by Hamlet's understandable desire to disturb the complacency of the man who has locked Ophelia away from him.

184 **walk i'th' sun** (1) go about in public (2) run the risk of becoming pregnant by the sun/son

Conception (1) the ability to form ideas (2) becoming pregnant. The same quibble is carried further in *conceive*

185–6 **look to't** take care, be on your guard

187 **How say you by** what do you say about (OED *by* A26c)

harping 'To harp upon one string' (Tilley S936) was already proverbial.

fishmonger. He is far gone, far gone. And truly in my
youth I suffered much extremity for love, very near this.   190
I'll speak to him again.—What do you read, my lord?

HAMLET Words, words, words.

POLONIUS What is the matter, my lord?

HAMLET Between who?

POLONIUS I mean the matter you read, my lord.

HAMLET Slanders, sir; for the satirical rogue says here that
old men have grey beards, that their faces are wrinkled,
their eyes purging thick amber or plum-tree gum, and
that they have a plentiful lack of wit, together with most
weak hams—all which, sir, though I most powerfully   200
and potently believe, yet I hold it not honesty to have it
thus set down; for you yourself, sir, should be old as I am
—if, like a crab, you could go backward.

POLONIUS (aside) Though this be madness, yet there is
method in't.—Will you walk out of the air, my lord?

HAMLET Into my grave?

POLONIUS Indeed, that is out o'th'air. (Aside) How pregnant
sometimes his replies are! A happiness that often madness
hits on, which reason and sanity could not so prosperously
be delivered of. I will leave him, and suddenly contrive   210
the means of meeting between him and my daughter.
—My honourable lord, I will most humbly take my leave
of you.

188–9 he said . . . He is] F; a sayd . . . a is Q2   189 far gone, far gone] F; farre gone Q2   195
matter you read] Q1; matter you meane F; matter that you reade Q2   196 rogue] Q2; slaue
F   198 amber or] F; Amber, & Q2   199 lack] Q2; locke F   most] Q2; not in F; pittifull
Q1   202 you yourself] F; your selfe Q2Q1   should be] F; shall growe Q2; shalbe Q1   207
that is] F; that's Q2Q1   o'th'] F; of the Q2Q1   209 sanity] F; sanctity Q2   210–11 suddenly
. . . and] F; not in Q2   212 honourable] F; not in Q2Q1   most humbly] F; not in Q2Q1

189 **far gone** i.e. in a very bad way
190 **extremity** deep distress (OED 6). Com-
    pare Errors 5.1.306, 'O time's extremity'.
194 **Between who?** Hamlet deliberately and
    disconcertingly misunderstands matter
    (meaning 'substance') as 'cause of dis-
    pute'. Shakespeare often uses who for
    whom, especially in questions (Abbott
    274), much as we still do in colloquial
    speech today.
198 **purging** discharging, exuding
    amber resin
    plum-tree gum Compare Henry V

4.2.46- }, 'their poor jades . . . The gum
    down-r ing from their pale dead eyes'.
201 **hone...** decent behaviour, fair
202 **be old** become as old
205 **walk out of the air** go indoors (because
    fresh air was regarded as bad for anyone
    who was ill)
207 **pregnant** ingenious, witty (OED preg-
    nant a.² 3b)
208 **happiness** felicity (of expression)
209 **prosperously** successfully
210 **be delivered of** give birth to
    suddenly at once

HAMLET You cannot, sir, take from me anything that I will
more willingly part withal—except my life, except my
life, except my life.

Enter Rosencrantz and Guildenstern

POLONIUS Fare you well, my lord.

HAMLET These tedious old fools!

POLONIUS You go to seek the Lord Hamlet; there he is.

ROSENCRANTZ (*to Polonius*) God save you, sir.   220

Exit Polonius

GUILDENSTERN My honoured lord!

ROSENCRANTZ My most dear lord!

HAMLET My excellent good friends! How dost thou, Guildenstern? O, Rosencrantz! Good lads, how do you both?

ROSENCRANTZ
As the indifferent children of the earth.

GUILDENSTERN
Happy in that we are not over-happy,
On Fortune's cap we are not the very button.

HAMLET Nor the soles of her shoe?

ROSENCRANTZ Neither, my lord.

HAMLET Then you live about her waist, or in the middle of   230
her favours?

GUILDENSTERN Faith, her privates we.

HAMLET In the secret parts of Fortune? O most true—she is
a strumpet. What's the news?

ROSENCRANTZ None, my lord, but that the world's grown
honest.

214 sir] FQ1; *not in* Q2   214–15 will more] FQ1; will not more Q2   215–16 life, except my
life, except my life] Q2; life, my life F   216.1 *Enter ... Guildenstern*] Q2; *after* 219 F   219 the]
Q2; my F   220 *Exit Polonius*] CAPELL; *exit* Q1; *not in* FQ2   221 My] Q2; Mine F   223
excellent] F; extent Q2   224 O] F (Oh); A Q2   you] Q2; ye F   226 over-happy] F; euer happy
Q2   227 cap] F; lap Q2   228 shoe?] F (Shoo?); shooe. Q2   231 favours] Q2; fauour
F   234 What's the] F; What Q2   235 but that] F; but Q2

214–15 **will more** This F reading looks like
an authorial revision designed to get rid of
the awkward double negative in Q2's *will
not more*.
215 **withal** with. 'Withal, the emphatic
form of "with", is used for *with* after the
object at the end of a sentence. Mostly, the
object is a relative' (Abbott 196).
225 **indifferent** ordinary, middling
227 **button** knob at the top of a cap (and so
summit)
232 **privates** (1) private parts of the body (2)

private persons holding no office (*OED*
B1). Compare *Henry V* 4.1.226, 'And
what have kings that privates have not
too'.
233–4 **she is a strumpet** The idea was a
commonplace because Fortune gives and
withholds her favours indiscriminately.
Compare *Lear* 2.4.51–2, 'Fortune, that
arrant whore, | Ne'er turns the key to th'
poor'; and Dent F603.1.
235–6 **the world's grown honest** Possibly
proverbial; see Dent W893.1.

HAMLET Then is doomsday near. But your news is not true.
  Let me question more in particular. What have you, my
  good friends, deserved at the hands of Fortune, that she
  sends you to prison hither?   240

GUILDENSTERN Prison, my lord?

HAMLET Denmark's a prison.

ROSENCRANTZ Then is the world one.

HAMLET A goodly one, in which there are many confines,
  wards, and dungeons, Denmark being one o'th' worst.

ROSENCRANTZ We think not so, my lord.

HAMLET Why, then, 'tis none to you; for there is nothing
  either good or bad, but thinking makes it so. To me it is a
  prison.

ROSENCRANTZ Why, then, your ambition makes it one; 'tis   250
  too narrow for your mind.

HAMLET O God, I could be bounded in a nutshell and count
  myself a king of infinite space, were it not that I have bad
  dreams.

GUILDENSTERN Which dreams indeed are ambition; for the
  very substance of the ambitious is merely the shadow of
  a dream.

HAMLET A dream itself is but a shadow.

ROSENCRANTZ Truly, and I hold ambition of so airy and light
  a quality that it is but a shadow's shadow.   260

HAMLET Then are our beggars bodies, and our monarchs
  and outstretched heroes the beggars' shadows. Shall we

238–67 Let me . . . attended] F; *not in* Q2Q1

238–67 Let me . . . attended] F; *not in* Q2Q1

237 **Then is doomsday near** (because
  nothing but the threat of doomsday could
  convert this world to honesty)
238–67 **Let me . . . dreadfully attended** See
  Textual Introduction, pp. 110–12.
244 **goodly** (1) spacious (2) fine (used ironically). Compare *Othello*, 2.3.152, 'Here's
  a goodly watch indeed!'
  confines places of confinement (*OED confine sb.²* 5). This use of the word (compare
  1.1.137) appears to be original with
  Shakespeare.
245 **wards** large rooms in prisons where a
  number of prisoners lived together
247–8 **there is . . . so** See Tilley M254, 'A
  man is weal or woe as he himself thinks
  so', for many variants on this widespread

sentiment.
256–7 **the very substance. . . dream** i.e. in
  essence ambitious men themselves are
  merely the shadow of a dream.
261–2 **Then are . . . beggars' shadows** i.e. 'If
  ambition is a shadow, our monarchs and
  heroes, who are entirely composed of ambition, must be shadows, and our beggars, the only people in the world who
  have no ambition, must alone be composed of real substance. If, now, the beggars are the only real bodies, and the
  monarchs and heroes are shadows, then
  the monarchs and heroes must be the
  shadows of the beggars, since there
  cannot be a shadow without a real body
  to cast it' (Kittredge). Those who still find

to th' court? For, by my fay, I cannot reason.

ROSENCRANTZ *and* GUILDENSTERN We'll wait upon you.

HAMLET No such matter. I will not sort you with the rest of my servants, for, to speak to you like an honest man, I am most dreadfully attended. But, in the beaten way of friendship, what make you at Elsinore?

ROSENCRANTZ To visit you, my lord, no other occasion.

HAMLET Beggar that I am, I am even poor in thanks, but I thank you; and sure, dear friends, my thanks are too dear a halfpenny. Were you not sent for? Is it your own inclining? Is it a free visitation? Come, deal justly with me. Come, come; nay speak.   270

GUILDENSTERN What should we say, my lord?

HAMLET Why, anything but to the purpose. You were sent for, and there is a kind of confession in your looks, which your modesties have not craft enough to colour. I know the good King and Queen have sent for you.

ROSENCRANTZ To what end, my lord?   280

HAMLET That you must teach me. But let me conjure you by the rights of our fellowship, by the consonancy of our youth, by the obligation of our ever-preserved love, and

270 even] F; euer Q2   273 Come, deal] F; come, come, deal Q2   276 Why] F; *not in* Q2
anything but] Q2; any thing. But F   to the] F; to 'th Q2   277 of] Q2Q1; *not in* F

the passage puzzling are in good company; they can turn with relief to Coleridge's succinct comment on it: 'I do not understand this.'

262 **outstretched** elongated 'like late or early shadows'

263 **reason** i.e. argue according to the rules of logic

264 **wait upon** accompany, escort

265 **No such matter** i.e. I can't have that. 'No such matter' (Dent M754.1) was a well established phrase.
sort class, associate

267 **most dreadfully attended** very badly waited on (*OED dreadfully* 3): the earliest instance *OED* cites of *dreadfully* in this colloquial sense. But, while this is the meaning Hamlet intends and expects Rosencrantz and Guildenstern to attach to his remark, it seems more than likely that he himself also has in mind the Ghost

and the 'bad dreams' it has caused him.
beaten way well worn track (i.e. plain words)

268 **make you** are you doing, is your business

271-2 **too dear a halfpenny** (1) too dear at a halfpenny, i.e. not worth a halfpenny (Dent, H50.1) (2) too dear by a halfpenny, 'since what [the two] give in exchange is worth nothing' (Wilson). In support of his explanation Wilson quotes *As You Like It* 2.3.74, 'too late a week'.

273 **free** voluntary, unconstrained
justly truthfully

276 **anything but to the purpose** i.e. any lie you like

278 **modesties** sense of decency
colour disguise

282-3 **the consonancy of our youth** our harmonious relationship when we were young

by what more dear a better proposer could charge you
withal, be even and direct with me whether you were sent
for or no.

ROSENCRANTZ (*aside to Guildenstern*) What say you?

HAMLET (*aside*) Nay then, I have an eye of you—If you love
me, hold not off.

GUILDENSTERN My lord, we were sent for.   290

HAMLET I will tell you why. So shall my anticipation
prevent your discovery, and your secrecy to the King and
Queen moult no feather. I have of late—but wherefore I
know not—lost all my mirth, forgone all custom of exercise; and indeed it goes so heavily with my disposition
that this goodly frame, the earth, seems to me a sterile
promontory. This most excellent canopy, the air, look
you, this brave o'erhanging firmament, this majestical
roof fretted with golden fire—why, it appears no other
thing to me than a foul and pestilent congregation of   300
vapours. What a piece of work is a man, how noble in
reason, how infinite in faculty, in form and moving how
express and admirable, in action how like an angel, in
apprehension how like a god—the beauty of the world,
the paragon of animals! And yet, to me, what is this

284 could] F; can Q2   292 discovery, and] Q2; discovery of F   293 Queen_A] Q2; Queene:
F   294–5 exercise] F; exercises Q2   295 heavily] Q2; heauenly F   298 firmament] Q2; *not
in* F   299–300 appears no other thing] F; appeareth nothing Q2   300 than] F (then);
but Q2   301 a piece] F; peece Q2   302 faculty F (faculty?); faculties Q2   302–4 moving . . .
admirable, in action . . . angel, in apprehension . . . god—] F (mouing_A . . . admirable? in Action,
. . . Angel? in apprehension, . . . God?); moouing, . . . admirable_A . . . action, . . . Angell_A in
apprehension, . . . God: Q2

284 **proposer** maker of conditions, one who
sets out compelling reasons (*OED* 2):
earliest example in *OED*; not elsewhere in
Shakespeare
285 **even** straightforward (*OED a.* 4)
288 **have an eye of** have my eye on, am
watching
289 **hold not off** don't be backward, out with
your answer (*OED hold v.* 39b): earliest
instance of this use cited by *OED*
292 **prevent your discovery** forestall your
disclosure
   secrecy confidential relationship
293 **moult no feather** i.e. remain unim-
paired, look as good as new
295 **it goes . . . disposition** i.e. I am so
depressed
296 **frame** structure, fabric. Compare *1
Henry IV* 3.1.16, 'The frame and huge

foundation of the earth'.
297 **canopy** According to *OED*, this is the
earliest application of *canopy* to the air
298 **brave** splendid
299 **fretted** adorned 'with carved or em-
bossed work in decorative patterns' usually with reference to ceilings (*OED fret v.*[2]
2). Compare *Cymbeline* 2.4.87–8, 'The
roof o'th' chamber | With golden
cherubins is fretted'.
301 **piece of work** masterpiece of creative endeavour. Compare *Antony*
5.2.98–100, 'yet t'imagine | An Antony
were nature's piece gainst fancy, | Con-
demning shadows quite'.
302 **faculty** bodily and mental power
   form behaviour
   moving motion, movement
303 **express** fitted to the purpose

quintessence of dust? Man delights not me—no, nor woman neither, though by your smiling you seem to say so.

ROSENCRANTZ My lord, there was no such stuff in my thoughts. 310

HAMLET Why did you laugh then, when I said 'Man delights not me'?

ROSENCRANTZ To think, my lord, if you delight not in man, what lenten entertainment the players shall receive from you. We coted them on the way, and hither are they coming to offer you service.

HAMLET He that plays the King shall be welcome—his majesty shall have tribute of me; the Adventurous Knight shall use his foil and target; the Lover shall not sigh gratis; the Humorous Man shall end his part in peace; the Clown 320 shall make those laugh whose lungs are tickle o'th' sear; and the Lady shall say her mind freely, or the blank verse shall halt for't. What players are they?

306 no] FQ1 ; *not in* Q2   307 woman] FQ1 ; women Q2   311 you] FQ1 ; yee Q2   then] Q2Q1 ; *not in* F   318 of] FQ1 ; on Q2   320–1 the Clown . . . sear] FQ1 (*subs.*); *not in* Q2   321 tickle] CLARENDON (*conj.* Staunton); tickled FQ1   322 blank] FQ1 ; black Q2

306 **quintessence of dust** very essence of dust, dust at its dustiest. The *quintessence* is 'the "fifth essence" of ancient and mediaeval philosophy, supposed to be the substance of which the heavenly bodies were composed, and to be actually latent in all things, the extraction of it by distillation or other methods being one of the great objects of alchemy' (*OED*)

314 **lenten entertainment** a poor reception. Lent was not only a time of fasting but also a period during which the theatres were closed in Shakespeare's England.

315 **coted** caught up with and passed. Originally a term used in coursing to describe the action of a dog that outpaces its rival and turns the hare. Shakespeare's only use of *cote*.

318 **tribute** (concrete not abstract; compare *gratis*)
the Adventurous Knight this term and those like it that follow are capitalized to denote that the figures concerned are stage types.

319 **foil and target** sword and light shield. The inventory of the properties belonging to the Admiral's Men on 10 March 1598

includes one copper target, four wooden targets, and seventeen foils. (*Henslowe's Diary*, p. 320)

320 **Humorous Man** man controlled by some excessive humour, eccentric, such as Jaques in *As You Like It* or Kitely in *Every Man in His Humour*

321 **tickle o'th' sear** easy on the trigger, ready to explode on the slightest pretext. For *tickle*, meaning 'unstable', see *Measure* 1.2.165–7, 'thy head stands so tickle on thy shoulders that a milkmaid . . . may sigh it off'. The *sear* is the part of a gun that holds the hammer in position until it is released by the trigger: not used elsewhere in Shakespeare.

322–3 **the lady . . . shall halt for't** It is not clear what Hamlet has in mind here. The likeliest interpretation is 'the Lady shall be allowed to say her part without interruption, or, if she is not, the blank verse will fall to pieces'. The assumption behind this gloss is that the boys playing female roles were more likely to be put out by comments from the audience than the more experienced adult players.

ROSENCRANTZ Even those you were wont to take delight in
  —the tragedians of the city.
HAMLET How chances it they travel? Their residence, both
  in reputation and profit, was better both ways.
ROSENCRANTZ I think their inhibition comes by the means of
  the late innovation.
HAMLET Do they hold the same estimation they did when I   330
  was in the city? Are they so followed?
ROSENCRANTZ No, indeed, they are not.
HAMLET How comes it? Do they grow rusty?
ROSENCRANTZ Nay, their endeavour keeps in the wonted
  pace. But there is, sir, an aerie of children, little eyases,

---

324 take] F; take such Q2   332 they are] F; are they Q2   333–58 HAMLET How comes it
... load too] F; *not in* Q2   333 rusty] F; restie Q1

---

325 **tragedians** actors. Compare *All's Well*
4.3.248, where Parolles is said to have
'led the drum before the English
tragedians'.
326 **travel** are on tour
  residence i.e. remaining in the city
328–32 **I think . . . are not** There are no
solid grounds for thinking there are specific topical references in these lines. The
reasons Rosencrantz offers for the players'
being on tour are such as would have
occurred to anyone with some knowledge
of the fortunes of acting companies in the
1590s. Tours were undertaken when the
London theatres were closed on account
of the plague; or when the City
authorities managed to persuade the
Privy Council to ban plays, often on the
grounds that they led to disorders.
328 **inhibition** formal prohibition: not elsewhere in Shakespeare. See, for example,
the letter of 28 January 1593 from the
Privy Council to the Lord Mayor and
Aldermen of the City of London, ordering
them 'to inhibit within [their] jurisdiction
all plays' because of a fresh outbreak of
the plague. (Chambers, *ES*, iv. 313)
329 **innovation** disorder, disturbance.
Because Shakespeare uses *innovation* as a
synonym for *insurrection* in two places (*1
Henry IV* 5.1.78 and *Sir Thomas More* D
93) and *innovator* for *public enemy* once
(*Coriolanus* 3.1.174–5), it does not
necessarily follow that *innovation* had no
other meaning for him. When Cassio
speaks of the *innovation* drink has made in
his brains (*Othello* 2.3.36) it amounts to

no more than *disorder*. Chettle, in his *Kind-
Hart's Dreame* (1593), uses it to describe
squabbles among members of theatre
audiences deliberately provoked by 'lewd
mates' for their own felonious ends
(Chambers, *ES*, iv. 244). An even milder
meaning is apparent in the objection the
Merchant Taylors raised to the notion that
they should pay an annuity to the Master
of the Revels because it would be a
'precedent and innovation (enovacion)'
(ibid. 309). Within the context of *Hamlet*
itself, the frantic preparations for war,
described by Marcellus at 1.1.70–9, could
well qualify as an *innovation*.
330 **estimation** esteem
333–58 **How comes it . . . load too** See Textual Introduction pp. 110–12.
334 **keeps** continues
335 **aerie** literally 'nest of birds of prey', used
by Shakespeare to signify 'the brood in
the nest' of a bird of prey (*OED* 2)
  eyases young hawks. The *children*
referred to as 'little eyases' are the Children of the Chapel, the company of boy
actors who began to play at the Blackfriars Playhouse in 1600. They enjoyed a
considerable vogue and rapidly became
serious rivals to the adult companies. At
the end of 1600 they put on Ben Jonson's
Cynthia's Revels, and followed it up in
1601 with his *Poetaster*, probably in the
spring. In both these plays Jonson jeers at
the public theatres. Shakespeare's company retaliated with *Satiromastix* by
Dekker and, perhaps, Marston, in which
Jonson came under attack. But *Satiromas-*

that cry out on the top of question, and are most tyrannically clapped for't. These are now the fashion, and so
berattle the common stages—so they call them—that
many wearing rapiers are afraid of goose-quills, and dare
scarce come thither.   340

HAMLET What, are they children? Who maintains 'em?
How are they escoted? Will they pursue the quality no
longer than they can sing? Will they not say afterwards,
if they should grow themselves to common players—as
it is most like, if their means are no better—their writers
do them wrong to make them exclaim against their own
succession?

ROSENCRANTZ Faith, there has been much to-do on both
sides; and the nation holds it no sin to tar them to

---

338 berattle] F2 (be ratle); be-ratled F   345 most like] POPE; like most F; like most will
WILSON   no] F; not F2

---

tix was only part, though the main part,
of the 'storm of retaliatory abuse in pam-
phlets and satires' which 'broke upon
Jonson's head' (Jonson, i. 416).

336 **cry out on the top of question** i.e. make
themselves heard above all others involved in the controversy. See *OED top sb.*[1]
15).

336–7 **tyrannically** outrageously. Not
found elsewhere in Shakespeare, *tyrannically*, in this colloquial sense, also appears
in *Antonio's Revenge* 5.3.51–2, 'I am most
tyrannically hungry'. When *Poetaster*
was first played, 'A tumult of angry cries
broke out amid the excited plaudits; a
host of persons who had no concern in the
quarrel felt their withers wrung by the
large sweep of Jonson's satiric lash;
citizens of standing, professional persons,
lawyers and soldiers as well as players,
indignantly protested against the outrage
offered to their orders and to their persons' (Jonson, i. 416).

338 **berattle** noisily abuse, cry down—not
elsewhere in Shakespeare
common stages public theatres, such as
the Globe and the Fortune, as distinct
from the private theatres, such as Blackfriars. Jonson refers derisively to *common
stages* in *Cynthia's Revels* (Induction 182).

339–40 **many . . . thither** i.e. many

'fashionable gallants are afraid to visit the
common theatres, so unfashionable have
the writers for the children made them'
(Dowden); *goose-quills* are, of course,
pens; and there may well be a reference
here to the proverbial 'He cannot say bo
to a goose' (Tilley B481).

342 **escoted** supported, provided for: earliest
example cited by *OED*
pursue the quality continue in the acting
profession (*OED quality sb.* 5)

342–3 **no longer . . . sing** i.e. only until their
voices break

345 **means** opportunities (of earning a
living)

346 **exclaim against** rail at. Compare *Lucrece*
757,'Here she exclaims against repose
and rest', the earliest instance of *exclaim
against* cited by *OED*.

347 **succession** i.e. future employment as
adult actors

349 **tar** incite, hound on. This word was
closely associated in Shakespeare's mind
with a dog-fight. Compare *K. John*
4.1.116–7, 'And, like a dog that is com-
pelled to fight | Snatch at his master that
doth tar him on'; and *Troilus* 1.3.391–2,
'Two curs shall tame each other: pride
alone | Must tar the mastiffs on, as 'twere
their bone.'

controversy. There was, for a while, no money bid for   350
argument, unless the poet and the player went to cuffs in
the question.

HAMLET Is't possible?

GUILDENSTERN O, there has been much throwing about of
brains.

HAMLET Do the boys carry it away?

ROSENCRANTZ Ay, that they do, my lord—Hercules and his
load too.

HAMLET It is not strange; for my uncle is King of Denmark,
and those that would make mows at him while my father   360
lived give twenty, forty, fifty, a hundred ducats apiece for
his picture in little. 'Sblood, there is something in this
more than natural, if philosophy could find it out.

    A flourish of trumpets

GUILDENSTERN There are the players.

HAMLET Gentlemen, you are welcome to Elsinore. Your
hands. Come. The appurtenance of welcome is fashion
and ceremony. Let me comply with you in the garb, lest

359 not] F; not very Q2   my] Q2; mine F   360 mows] F; mouths Q2; mops and moes
Q1   361 fifty] Q2; *not in* F   a hundred] Q2; an hundred F   362 'Sblood] Q2; *not in* F   363.1
A flourish of trumpets] CAPELL (*subs.*); *Flourish for the Players* F; *A Florish* Q2; *The Trumpets sound*
Q1   366 come] F; come then Q2   The appurtenance] F; th'appurtenance Q2   367 the] F;
this Q2   367–8 lest my] F; let me Q2

350–2 **no money . . . question** i.e. acting
  companies would offer nothing for a play,
  unless it set the dramatists who wrote for
  the children and the actors of the public
  theatres against one another.
356 **carry it away** come off the better,
  emerge victorious. Compare *Othello*
  1.1.67–8, 'What a full fortune does the
  thick-lips owe, | If he can carry't thus!'
  See also Dent C100.1, and especially the
  reference to Nashe's *The Unfortunate
  Traveller* (Nashe, ii. 251) with its statement 'from all the world he carries it
  away', which may have helped to inspire
  Rosencrantz's answer.
357–8 **Hercules and his load too** According
  to Steevens and Malone, Hercules sup-
  porting the world on his shoulders was
  the sign of the Globe theatre. If it was,
  Shakespeare was admitting that his own
  company was beginning to feel the pinch
  caused by the success of the Children of
  the Chapel, much as 'the tragedians of the
  city' had done.
360 **make mows** pull faces

361 **ducats** The *ducat* was 'a gold coin of
  varying value, formerly in use in most
  European countries' (*OED*). Shakespeare
  uses the word frequently, but only in
  plays that are not set in England.
362 **picture in little** miniature. Brought to
  perfection by Nicholas Hilliard and Isaac
  Oliver, miniature painting was much
  prized and well patronized in Shakespeare's England.
363 **philosophy . . . out** the philosophers
  could discover what it is
363.1 *A flourish of trumpets* Acting companies used trumpets in the streets of
  towns and cities as a way of advertising
  their performances. The direction *Sound
  trumpets* heralds the arrival of the travelling players in *Shrew* (Induction 1.71.1)
366 **appurtenance** proper accompaniment:
  not elsewhere in Shakespeare
367 **comply** observe the expected forms
  (*OED comply v.*[1] 2): earliest instance of
  comply in this sense cited by *OED*
  garb recognized manner (by shaking
  hands)

my extent to the players, which, I tell you, must show
fairly outward, should more appear like entertainment
than yours. ⌈*He shakes hands with them*⌉ You are welcome.　370
But my uncle-father and aunt-mother are deceived.

GUILDENSTERN　In what, my dear lord?

HAMLET　I am but mad north-north-west; when the wind is
southerly, I know a hawk from a handsaw.

　　Enter Polonius

POLONIUS　Well be with you, gentlemen.

HAMLET　Hark you, Guildenstern, and you too—at each ear
a hearer: that great baby you see there is not yet out of his
swathing-clouts.

ROSENCRANTZ　Happily he's the second time come to them;
for they say an old man is twice a child.　　　　　　　380

HAMLET　I will prophesy he comes to tell me of the players;
mark it.—You say right, sir; for o' Monday morning
'twas so indeed.

POLONIUS　My lord, I have news to tell you.

---

369 outward] F; outwards Q2　　378 swathing-clouts] F; swaddling clouts Q2Q1　　379 he's]
F; he is Q2　　381 prophesy he] F (Prophesie. Hee); prophecy, he Q2　　382 for] F; *not in*
Q2Q1　　383 so] FQ1; then Q2

368　**extent** extension (of welcome) (*OED sb.*
　6a). Compare *Titus* 4.4.3–4.
369　**entertainment** favourable reception
370　**yours** l.c. my reception of you
371　**uncle-father and aunt-mother** These
　words are important for what follows.
　Hamlet has already made it clear,
　through his emphasis on formalities, that
　he no longer regards the two courtiers as
　friends. Now he succinctly points out to
　them who their employers really are: a
　king and queen who see nothing wrong in
　the monstrous and paradoxical relation-
　ship they have entered into, two people
　who have completely lost their moral
　bearings.
373–4　**I am . . . handsaw** Bringing out the
　contrast between the mental state of
　Claudius and Gertrude and of himself,
　Hamlet now explains that his mind is only
　a little out of true, no more so than a com-
　pass needle which points north-north-
　west when it should point north. He can,
　therefore, still distinguish between a *hawk*
　and a *handsaw*, which are as different

from one another as 'chalk from cheese'
or friends from enemies. It all amounts to
a very clear warning to Rosencrantz and
Guildenstern not to meddle in matters
that are no concern of theirs. The
ingenious attempts that have been made
to find further significance in *hawks* and
handsaws all suffer under the same disabil-
ity: it is hard to see how an audience in a
theatre can possibly have the time to pick
these significances up and work them out.
The fact that the phrase became proverbial (Tilley H226) does not help, since it
was its appearance in *Hamlet* that made it
so; but it does show that the general, as
distinct from the precise, significance it
bears has never been in doubt.
374　**handsaw** (1) a small saw that can be
　used with one hand (2) possibly a corrup-
　tion of *heronshaw* (heron)
377–8　**out of his swathing-clouts** The words
　were proverbial (Dent S1021.1).
379　**Happily** perhaps, it may well be
380　**an old man is twice a child** proverbial
　(Tilley M570)

HAMLET My lord, I have news to tell you. When Roscius was
  an actor in Rome—
POLONIUS The actors are come hither, my lord.
HAMLET Buzz, buzz.
POLONIUS Upon my honour—
HAMLET Then came each actor on his ass—   390
POLONIUS The best actors in the world, either for tragedy,
  comedy, history, pastoral, pastoral-comical, historical-
  pastoral, tragical-historical, tragical-comical-historical-
  pastoral, scene individable, or poem unlimited. Seneca
  cannot be too heavy nor Plautus too light. For the law of
  writ and the liberty, these are the only men.

385 was] Q2Q1; *not in* F   389 my] Q2; mine F   390 came] Q2; can F   392–3 pastoral-
comical, historical-pastoral] Q2 (*without hyphens*); Pastoricall-Comicall-Historicall-Pastorall
F   393–4 tragical-historical, tragical-comical-historical-pastoral] F; *not in* Q2   394 individ-
able] Q2; indivible F   Seneca] F; *Sceneca* Q2   395–6 light. For . . . liberty,] JOHNSON; light, for
. . . Liberty. F; light for . . . liberty: Q2

385 **Roscius** The most famous of Roman
actors, Roscius, whose death was recent
in 62 BC, was already something of a
legend in his own day. For the men of the
Renaissance he became the very type of
the actor. Henry VI describes Richard of
Gloucester, who is about to kill him, as
Roscius (3 *Henry VI* 5.6.10). Hamlet
deliberately spoils Polonius's 'news' by
getting in the word *actor* before Polonius
can.
388 **Buzz** an exclamation expressing contempt for stale news, the Elizabethan
equivalent of the modern 'raspberry'
390 **Then . . . ass** This could well be, as Dr
Johnson suggested, a line from a lost ballad. It certainly contains a rude quibble
—*ass* being a dialect form of *arse*—on
Polonius's 'Upon my honour'.
391–4 **tragedy . . . unlimited** Shakespeare is
making fun not only of Polonius but also
of the elaborate classifications of drama
produced by the theorists of the time. He
could also be taking a hint from John Marston, who, in his *Histriomastix, or The
Player Whipped* (1599), has the poet Post-
haste (Anthony Munday) give a list of his
plays which runs thus: '*Mother Gurton's
Needle* (a tragedy); *The Devil and Dives* (a
comedy); *A Russet Coat and a Knave's Cap*
(an infernal); *A Proud Heart and a Beggar's
Purse* (a pastoral); *The Widow's Apron-
strings* (a nocturnal)' (Harvey Wood, iii.
263).

394 **scene individable** The most probable
sense is 'plays with no breaks in the performance'. Shakespeare does not use *individable*, a word he appears to have
coined, elsewhere; but he does write of
dividable shores, meaning 'shores divided
and separated from one another', in
Troilus 1.3.105.
  poem unlimited As with *scene individable*,
the sense is not certain; but since *poem*,
which, oddly enough, does not occur
anywhere else in Shakespeare, obviously
means *dramatic poem* (i.e. play), the
crucial word is *unlimited*, which he uses
nowhere else. Fortunately *limit* and
limited, meaning 'confined in space and |
or time', are fairly common in the canon.
A reasonable gloss would therefore be
'plays not restricted as to their length,
and not conforming to the neo-classical
unities of time and place'.
394–5 **Seneca . . . light** The main influence
from the classical past on Elizabethan
drama was exerted by the Romans rather
than by the Greeks. Seneca was regarded
as the master of tragedy, and Plautus,
along with Terence, as the master of
comedy.
395–6 **the law of writ and the liberty** i.e.
(probably) plays that observe the rules
and plays that disregard them. The main
difficulty is *writ*, which normally means
'that which is written' not 'the art of composition'.

HAMLET

O Jephthah, judge of Israel, what a treasure hadst thou!

POLONIUS What a treasure had he, my lord?

HAMLET Why,

> 'One fair daughter, and no more,   400
> The which he loved passing well.'

POLONIUS *(aside)* Still on my daughter.

HAMLET Am I not i'th' right, old Jephthah?

POLONIUS If you call me Jephthah, my lord, I have a daughter that I love passing well.

HAMLET Nay, that follows not.

POLONIUS What follows then, my lord?

HAMLET Why,

> 'As by lot, God wot',

and then you know,   410

> 'It came to pass, as most like it was'—

the first row of the pious chanson will show you more; for look where my abridgements come.

Enter four or five players

---

412 row] FQ2; verse Q1   pious chanson| Q2; *Pons Chanson* F; godly Ballet Q1   413 abridgements come] F; abridgment comes Q2Q1   413.1 *four or five*] F; *the* Q2

---

397 **O Jephthah . . . Thou** This line is a 'fourteener', possibly a quotation from a religious ballad, or, perhaps, an extempore bit of pastiche from Hamlet himself. Jephthah, whose story is told in Judges 11, vowed to God that if he succeeded in defeating the Ammonites, he would sacrifice the first thing he met on returning home. He was victorious; but as he approached his house 'his daughter came out to meet him with timbrels and with dances; and she was his only child'. Nevertheless, he kept his vow and sacrificed her. Shakespeare had previously alluded to the story in *3 Henry VI* 5.1.91.

399–401 **Why . . . well** There appear to have been several ballads about Jephthah and his daughter of which only one has survived. Its first stanza is: 'I read that many years ago, | When Jepha, Judge of Israel, | Had one fair daughter and no more, | Whom he loved so passing well. | And as by lot, God wot, | It came to pass most like it was, | Great wars there should

be, | And who should be the chief, but he, but he.' The full text is printed by Harold Jenkins in his Arden edition of *Hamlet* (1982), 475–7.

401 **passing** surpassingly, very

406 **follows not** Hamlet's point is that Polonius's having a daughter is not a logical consequence of Hamlet's calling him Jephthah. But, having said this, he then switches the meaning of *follows* to 'the next line in the ballad'.

412 **row** stanza. This is a most unusual sense of *row*, which normally meant, in a context such as this, a *line* (*OED row sb.*[1] 3b).

pious chanson godly ballad, as Q1 has it. This is the first instance of *chanson*, a word Shakespeare uses nowhere else, cited by *OED*.

413 **abridgements** (1) those who cut me short (2) pastimes, entertainments. See *Dream* 5.1.39–40: 'Say, what abridgement | have you for this evening?/What masque? what music?'

You're welcome, masters, welcome all.—I am glad to see
thee well.—Welcome, good friends.—O, my old friend!
Thy face is valanced since I saw thee last. Com'st thou to
beard me in Denmark?—What, my young lady and
mistress? By'r lady, your ladyship is nearer heaven than
when I saw you last by the altitude of a chopine. Pray
God, your voice, like a piece of uncurrent gold, be not   420
cracked within the ring.—Masters, you are all welcome.
We'll e'en to't like French falconers, fly at anything we
see. We'll have a speech straight. Come, give us a taste of
your quality, come, a passionate speech.
FIRST PLAYER What speech, my good lord?
HAMLET I heard thee speak me a speech once, but it was
    never acted, or, if it was, not above once; for the play, I

414 You're] F (Y'are); *Ham⟨let⟩* You are Q2   415 my] FQ1; *not in* Q2   415–16 friend! Thy]
F; friend, why thy Q2   416 valanced] Q2 (valant) Q1 (valant); valiant F   418 By'r lady]
F (Byrlady); by lady Q2; burlady Q1   nearer] F; nerer to Q2   422 French] FQ1; friendly
Q2   425 good] Q2Q1; *not in* F

414–21 **You're welcome . . . all welcome**
Hamlet's exuberant welcome of the
Players stems, in part at least, from the
relief he feels in meeting a group of people
with whom he does not need to be on his
guard. For once he can be his own natural
self.

416 **valanced** provided with a draped edging
(i.e. bearded): first example of this
figurative sense cited by *OED*.

417 **beard** defy
my young lady i.e. the boy who played
female roles

418 **nearer heaven** taller

419 **chopine** 'a kind of shoe raised above the
ground by means of a cork sole or the like;
worn about 1600 in Spain and Italy, especially at Venice, where they were mon-
strously exaggerated' (*OED*).

420–1 **your voice . . . ring** The monarch's
head stamped on a gold coin was enclosed
within a ring. If a crack from the outward
edge of the coin extended beyond this
ring, the piece was no longer legal tender;
it had become *uncurrent*. Similarly a boy
actor, once his voice had broken, was no
longer available to play women's parts.
The saying was well established by 1600
(Dent R130.1).

422 **e'en to't** go to work at once. As *to*
originally implied motion towards some-

thing, a verb of motion is often understood before it in Shakespeare's English.

422–3 **French falconers . . . see** The general
sense of this remark is plain enough: 'let
us take a shot at the first thing that
springs to mind'; but it is less clear
whether the *French falconers* are objects of
scorn or praise. D. H. Madden takes the
first view, holding that Hamlet is decrying
them because they are indiscriminate in
their choice of a quarry for the hawk to fly
at (*The Diary of Master William Silence*,
1897, p. 140). Wilson, however, points
out that the French were regarded as the
experts on falconry and, following
Steevens, quotes Sir Thomas Browne's
opinion that they 'seem to have been the
first and noblest falconers in the western
part of Europe', together with his account
of how Julius Scaliger saw a gerfalcon,
belonging to Henry of Navarre, 'strike
down a buzzard, two wild geese, divers
kites, a crane and a swan' in a single day
(*Works of Sir Thomas Browne*, ed. Sayle, iii.
297, 299). As Hamlet thinks well of the
Players and pays them a compliment in
asking for an impromptu performance,
the second interpretation seems the more
appropriate.

424 **quality** acting ability

remember, pleased not the million, 'twas caviare to the
general. But it was—as I received it, and others whose
judgements in such matters cried in the top of mine—an   430
excellent play, well digested in the scenes, set down with
as much modesty as cunning. I remember one said there
were no sallets in the lines to make the matter savoury,
nor no matter in the phrase that might indict the author
of affectation, but called it an honest method, as
wholesome as sweet, and by very much more handsome
than fine. One speech in it I chiefly loved, 'twas Aeneas'
tale to Dido, and thereabout of it especially where he
speaks of Priam's slaughter. If it live in your memory,
begin at this line—let me see, let me see: 440

428 caviare] Q2Q1 (caviary), F (Caviarie)   430 judgements] Q2Q1; iudgement F   433 were]
Q2; was FQ1   435 affectation] F; affection Q2   435–7 as wholesome . . . fine] Q2; not in F;
as wholesome as sweete Q1   437 One] Q2; One cheefe F; a Q1   in it] FQ1; in't Q2   438 tale]
FQ1; talke Q2   where] FQ1; when Q2

428–9 caviare to the general i.e.
unappreciated by the general theatre-
going public. Introduced into England in
the late sixteenth century, caviare, not
mentioned by Shakespeare elsewhere,
was disliked by those who had not acquired a taste for it. John Bullokar, in his
An English Expositor (1616), describes it
as 'strange meat like black soap' (OED).
429 received it i.e. readily acknowledged
430 cried in the top of i.e. were of more
weight than
431 digested organized. Compare Troilus
Prologue 29, 'what may be digested in a
play'.
432 modesty restraint. Compare Shrew Induction 1. 65–6, 'It will be pastime pass-
ing excellent, | If it be husbanded with
modesty.'
   cunning professional skill
433 sallets salads (in the sense of highly
seasoned flavours such as those provided
by double entendre)
435 honest unpretentious
436–7 more handsome than fine i.e. perfectly adapted to the purpose rather than
showily ingenious
437 One speech . . . loved The speech Hamlet calls for is carefully chosen. It has its
bearing on his own position, since it deals

with the revenge taken by a son, Pyrrhus,
for the death of his father Achilles; and,
moreover, it describes the reactions of the
victim's wife, Hecuba, to the slaughter of
her husband, Priam.
437–8 Aeneas' tale to Dido The ultimate
source of the story is, of course, Aeneas's
account of the fall of Troy which he gives
to Dido and her court in Book II of Virgil's
Aeneid. The version of it that seems to
have been uppermost in Shakespeare's
mind when he wrote this scene was the
relevant part (2.1.213–58) of Marlowe's
Dido, Queen of Carthage, first published in
1594 as the joint work of Marlowe and
Nashe, though it is, in all probability, the
work of Marlowe alone and, perhaps, the
earliest of his plays (c.1586). By 1600,
the style of Dido, which Shakespeare
imitates and makes even more epic,
would have appeared somewhat stiff and
archaic, especially by comparison with
the flexibility and range of the manner of
Hamlet itself, and thus would serve to
mark off this bit of a play-within-the-play
from the play proper. Shakespeare is not
holding the old manner up to ridicule,
instead he is adapting it to his own
dramatic purpose.

'The rugged Pyrrhus, like th'Hyrcanian beast'—
It is not so. It begins with Pyrrhus—
'The rugged Pyrrhus, he whose sable arms,
Black as his purpose, did the night resemble
When he lay couchèd in the ominous horse,
Hath now this dread and black complexion smeared
With heraldry more dismal. Head to foot
Now is he total gules, horridly tricked
With blood of fathers, mothers, daughters, sons,
Baked and impasted with the parching streets,   450
That lend a tyrannous and damnèd light
To their vile murders. Roasted in wrath and fire,
And thus o'er-sizèd with coagulate gore,
With eyes like carbuncles, the hellish Pyrrhus
Old grandsire Priam seeks.'
So, proceed you.

POLONIUS Fore God, my lord, well spoken, with good accent
     and good discretion.

FIRST PLAYER   'Anon he finds him,
     Striking too short at Greeks. His antique sword,   460

442 It is] F; tis Q2; t'is Q1   445 the ominous] FQ1; th'omynous Q2   447 dismal. Head to
foot] F (dismall: Head to foote); dismall head to foote Q2; dismall, head to foote, Q1   448 total]
Q2Q1; to take F   451 damnèd] F; a damned Q2   452 vile murders] F (vilde Murthers); Lords
murther Q2   456 So, proceed you] Q2; *not in* F; So goe on Q1

441 **rugged** savage (literally 'shaggy').
Compare *Macbeth* 3.4.100–01, 'Approach
thou like the rugged Russian bear, | The
armed rhinoceros, or th'Hyrcan tiger'.
Hyrcanian beast Hyrcania, a region bor-
dering on the Caspian Sea, was famous in
classical antiquity for its ferocious tigers.
In her final speech to Aeneas, immediately before he leaves her, Marlowe's Dido,
translating three lines of Virgil's *Aeneid*
(iv. 365–7) into English, upbraids him
thus: 'Thy mother was no goddess, per-
jured man, | Nor Dardanus the author of
thy stock; | But thou art sprung from
Scythian Caucasus, | And tigers of Hyr-
cania gave thee suck' (5.1.156–9).
445 **couchèd** in ambush
   ominous fatal (Schmidt)
446 **complexion** general appearance (of
blackness)
447 **heraldry** heraldic symbolism. Compare
Lucrece 64, 'This heraldry in Lucrece' face
was seen'.
   dismal dire, disastrous

448 **total gules** red all over. Shakespeare
uses this heraldic term again in *Timon*
4.3.58, 'With man's blood paint the
ground, gules, gules.'
   tricked 'spotted and smeared' (Onions);
another heraldic term, meaning 'colours
indicated by certain arrangements of dots
or lines'
450 **impasted with** made into a crust by—
not used by Shakespeare elsewhere
   parching scorching (because on fire)
451 **tyrannous** cruel
452 **their vile murders** i.e. the vile murders
of 'fathers . . . sons'
453 **o'er-sizèd** (1) covered over as though
with size (2) looking even bigger than his
true size because of the clotted blood adhering to him. *O'er-sizèd* in the first sense
seems to be a Shakespearian invention.
454 **carbuncles** mythical gems of a fiery
colour supposed to give off light in the
dark
460 **antique sword** ancient sword, sword he
had used all his life

Rebellious to his arm, lies where it falls,
Repugnant to command. Unequal matched,
Pyrrhus at Priam drives, in rage strikes wide;
But with the whiff and wind of his fell sword
Th' unnervèd father falls. Then senseless Ilium,
Seeming to feel this blow, with flaming top
Stoops to his base, and with a hideous crash
Takes prisoner Pyrrhus' ear. For lo! his sword,
Which was declining on the milky head
Of reverend Priam, seemed i'th'air to stick.   470
So, as a painted tyrant, Pyrrhus stood,
And, like a neutral to his will and matter,
Did nothing.
But as we often see, against some storm,
A silence in the heavens, the rack stand still,
The bold winds speechless, and the orb below
As hush as death, anon the dreadful thunder
Doth rend the region; so, after Pyrrhus' pause,
A rousèd vengeance sets him new a-work;

462 matched] Q2 (matcht); match F   465 Then senseless Ilium] F; *not in* Q2   466 this] Q2;
his F   472 And] F; *not in* Q2   477–8 death,. . . region; so] Q2 (region, so); death:. . . Region.
So F   479 A rousèd] F (A ro wsed) Q2 (A rowsed); Aroused COLLIER

462 **repugnant to command** refusing duty
463–5 **Pyrrhus . . . falls** These words echo
  Marlowe. Aeneas tells how Priam 'would
  have grappled with Achilles' son, | Forget-
  ting both his want of strength and
  hands; | Which he [Pyrrhus] disdaining,
  whisked his sword about, | And with the
  wind thereof the king fell down' (*Dido*
  2.1.251–4).
463 **drives** rushes headlong
464 **whiff** puff of wind—not elsewhere in
  Shakespeare
465 **unnervèd father** strengthless old man
  —earliest instance of *unnerved* cited by
  OED
  senseless incapable of feeling, inanimate
  Ilium the royal palace or citadel in Troy,
  not the city itself. See *Troilus* 1.2.172–3.
469 **declining** descending (*OED decline v.* 7).
  Compare *Troilus* 4.5.188–9, 'When thou
  hast hung thy advancèd sword i'th'
  air, | Not letting it decline on the declined'.
  milky white. This gloss, which has the
  support of the proverbial 'As white as
  milk' (Tilley M931), seems preferable
  to *weak*, the gloss provided by Schmidt

and Onions, because elsewhere in
Shakespeare this latter sense of *milky*
refers to a person's disposition. Compare
Lear 1.4.342, 'This milky gentleness and
course of yours'.
471 **painted tyrant** tyrant in a painting (and
  so incapable of motion)
472 **a neutral to his will and matter** i.e. one
  who has lost all interest in a purpose he
  had set his heart on. A *neutral* is one who
  is indifferent; while *will and matter* is a
  hendiadys, meaning 'purposed business'.
474–83 **But as . . . Priam** The epic manner
  Shakespeare adopts in this part of his play
  is particularly evident in this elaborate
  long-tailed simile.
474 **against** preparatory to
475 **rack** clouds driven before the wind in
  the upper atmosphere
476 **orb** round earth
477 **As hush as death** proverbial (Dent
  133.1)
478 **region** sky, air. Compare *Romeo*
  2.2.20–21, 'her eyes in heaven | Would
  through the airy region stream so bright'.

And never did the Cyclops' hammers fall   480
On Mars his armour, forged for proof eterne,
With less remorse than Pyrrhus' bleeding sword
Now falls on Priam.
Out, out, thou strumpet Fortune! All you gods,
In general synod, take away her power,
Break all the spokes and fellies from her wheel,
And bowl the round nave down the hill of heaven,
As low as to the fiends!'

POLONIUS This is too long.

HAMLET It shall to the barber's, with your beard.—Prithee   490
say on. He's for a jig or a tale of bawdry, or he sleeps. Say
on, come to Hecuba.

FIRST PLAYER
'But who, O who had seen the mobled queen'—

HAMLET 'The mobled queen'?

POLONIUS That's good; 'mobled queen' is good.

481 Mars his] F; *Marses* Q2   armour] Q2; Armours F   488 to the] Q2Q1; to' th F   493 O
who] FQ1; a woe Q2   493–4 mobled … mobled] Q2Q1; inobled … inobled F   494 queen'?]
F (Queene?); Queene. Q2   495 good; 'mobled queen' is good] F (good: Inobled Queene is
good) Q1 (Mobled Queene is good); good. Q2

480 **the Cyclops** The Cyclopes, three one-
     eyed giants, were employed by Vulcan,
     the god of smiths (and of volcanoes), in
     making arms and armour for the gods and
     heroes.
481 **Mars his armour** 'In the *Iliad* it is
     Achilles' armour, in the *Aeneid* Aeneas's,
     that is forged by Vulcan and the Cyclops.
     Neither hero is suitable for mention in this
     context. So Mars is reasonably supposed
     as having a suit of Cyclopean armour too'
     (Spencer).
     for proof eterne i.e. to remain impene-
     trable for ever
482 **remorse** (1) pity (2) intermission. For
     the second sense, compare *Twelfth Night*
     2.3.88, 'without any mitigation or
     remorse of voice'.
485 **synod** Shakespeare uses this word six
     times in all. Only once (*Errors* 1.1.13)
     does it refer to an assembly of men. On the
     other five occasions it denotes an as-
     sembly of the gods.
486 **fellies** Also known as *felloes*, these are
     the curved pieces of wood, which, when
     joined together and held in place by an
     iron hoop, form the rim of a cart-wheel.
     wheel The emblem of Fortune standing

on a wheel was a commonplace of
mediaeval and Renaissance iconology.
Much of its significance is summed up in
the saying 'Fortune's wheel is ever turning' (Tilley F617). Shakespeare refers to it
frequently, and underlines its hackneyed
quality by having Ancient Pistol speak of
'giddy Fortune's furious fickle wheel'
(*Henry V* 3.6.26).
487 **nave** hub, 'all of the wheel that is left
     when the spokes and fellies are gone' (Jen-
     kins)
     hill of heaven Mount Olympus
491 **jig** 'a light performance or entertain-
     ment of a lively or comical character,
     given at the end, or in an interval, of a
     play' (*OED*)
493 **who, O who had** i.e. whoever had, any-
     one who had
     mobled muffled about the head and face.
     This unusual word, which, according to
     Onions, still survives in Warwickshire,
     has not been found in any English writing
     prior to Shakespeare's use of it here. The
     dramatist evidently meant it to be noticed,
     since he has Hamlet question it and
     Polonius approve of it.

FIRST PLAYER
　'Run barefoot up and down, threatening the flames
　With bisson rheum; a clout upon that head
　Where late the diadem stood, and for a robe,
　About her lank and all o'er-teemèd loins,
　A blanket in th'alarum of fear caught up—　　　　　500
　Who this had seen, with tongue in venom steeped,
　'Gainst Fortune's state would treason have pronounced.
　But if the gods themselves did see her then,
　When she saw Pyrrhus make malicious sport
　In mincing with his sword her husband's limbs,
　The instant burst of clamour that she made—
　Unless things mortal move them not at all—
　Would have made milch the burning eyes of heaven
　And passion in the gods.'
POLONIUS Look whe'er he has not turned his colour, and has　510
　tears in's eyes.—Pray you no more.
HAMLET (*to the First Player*) 'Tis well. I'll have thee speak
　out the rest soon.—Good my lord, will you see the players
　well bestowed? Do you hear, let them be well used, for
　they are the abstracts and brief chronicles of the time.
　After your death you were better have a bad epitaph than
　their ill report while you live.

496 flames] Q2; flame F　497 upon] Q2; about F; on Q1　500 th'alarum] F; the alarme Q2; the alarum Q1　505 husband's] F (Husbands) Q1 (husbandes); husband Q2　510 whe'er] FQ2 (where); if Q1　511 Pray you] F; prethee Q2　513 rest] F; rest of this Q2　514 you] Q2; ye F　515 abstracts] FQ1; abstract Q2　517 live] Q2Q1; liued F

496 **threatening** i.e. threatening to put out
497 **bisson rheum** blinding tears. *OED* lists *bisson v.*, but only in the form of the past participle *bissoned*; *rheum*, meaning 'tears', is common.
499 **all o'er-teemed** utterly worn out with child-bearing
500 **alarum** of excitement caused by
502 **state** rule, power
503–8 **But if ... did see ... would have made** In conditional sentences Shakespeare does not always make the antecedent and the consequent answer to one another in mood and tense (Abbott 371).
503 **But if** but if, if only. For the ways in which the position of *but* could be varied, see Abbott 129.
　did see i.e. had seen, could have seen
507 **Unless ... all** i.e. 'unless the Epicurean doctrine be true, that the gods live in un-

ruffled calm and are never disturbed by sympathy for mankind' (Kittredge).
508 **milch** milk-yielding, i.e. flow with tears of pity. For Shakespeare there is an intimate connection between the milk with which a mother feeds her child and the emotions of love and pity. Compare *Macbeth* 1.5.14, 'the milk of human kindness'.
　burning eyes of heaven i.e. sun, moon, and stars
509 **passion** overpowering grief
510 **whe'er** shortened form of *whether* (Abbott 466)
514 **bestowed** lodged and looked after
　Do you hear listen
515 **abstracts** epitomes, summaries. Compare *Richard III* 4.4.28, 'Brief abstract and record of tedious days'.

231

POLONIUS My lord, I will use them according to their desert.

HAMLET God's bodykins, man, much better. Use every man
after his desert, and who should scape whipping? Use   520
them after your own honour and dignity—the less they
deserve, the more merit is in your bounty. Take them in.

POLONIUS Come, sirs.

HAMLET

Follow him, friends. We'll hear a play tomorrow.
⌈*He detains the First Player while Polonius and the
other Players move to the rear, and then speaks
aside to him*⌉
Dost thou hear me, old friend, can you play *The Murder
of Gonzago*?

FIRST PLAYER Ay, my lord.

HAMLET We'll ha't tomorrow night. You could, for a need,
study a speech of some dozen or sixteen lines which I
would set down and insert in't, could you not?   530

FIRST PLAYER Ay, my lord.

HAMLET Very well. Follow that lord, and look you mock
him not.   *Exeunt Polonius and the Players*
My good friends, I'll leave you till night. You are welcome
to Elsinore.

---

519 bodykins] F; bodkin Q2   much] Q2; *not in* F; farre Q1   520 should] FQ1; shall
Q2   524.1–3 *He detains . . . him*] This edition; *Exit Polon* ⟨*ius*⟩ F; *exit* Q1 (*both after* 523); *not
in* Q2   528 for a] FQ1; for Q2   529 dozen] FQ1; dosen lines Q2   530 you] Q2; ye F   533
Exeunt Polonius and the Players] Q2 (*after* 535); *not in* FQ1

519 **God's bodykins** by God's dear body!
  Bodykin is the diminutive form, denoting
  endearment, of *body*; and the *bodykin* is
  the consecrated wafer used in the service
  of the Holy Communion. *God's bodkin*, the
  reading of Q2, is a recognized variant; but
  Body-kins is the spelling of *Merry Wives*
  2.3.40, the only other appearance of the
  word in Shakespeare.
520 **after** according to
524.1–3 **He detains . . . to him** The three
  primary texts do not agree about what
  happens at this point. F and Q1 give
  Polonius an *exit* immediately after 'Come,
  sirs' (l. 523) but ignore the Players. Q2,
  on the other hand, has no direction at
  all until after 'welcome to Elsinore'
  (l. 534–5), where it reads '*Exeunt Pol. and*

Players'. The editorial direction assumes
  that Polonius sets off with the Players at
  l. 523, then notices that the First Player is
  occupied with the Prince, and waits for
  him.
528 **for a need** if required
529 **study** get up, learn by heart. Compare
  Twelfth Night 1.5.167–8, 'I can say little
  more than I have studied, and that question's out of my part.'
  a speech . . . sixteen lines Kittredge's note
  says all that needs to be said about this
  matter: 'Much ingenuity has been wasted
  in identifying Hamlet's dozen or sixteen
  lines, as if we were to suppose that
  Shakespeare wrote *The Murder of Gonzago*
  without them, and then inserted them
  somewhere.'

ROSENCRANTZ Good my lord.

Exeunt Rosencrantz and Guildenstern

HAMLET

Ay, so, God buy you. Now I am alone.

O what a rogue and peasant slave am I!

Is it not monstrous that this player here,

But in a fiction, in a dream of passion,   540

Could force his soul so to his whole conceit

That from her working all his visage wanned,

Tears in his eyes, distraction in's aspect,

A broken voice, and his whole function suiting

With forms to his conceit? And all for nothing.

For Hecuba!

What's Hecuba to him, or he to Hecuba,

That he should weep for her? What would he do,

---

536 *Exeunt Rosencrantz and Guildenstern*| F (*Exeunt. Manet Hamlet*); *Exeunt* Q2; *Exeunt all but Hamlet* Q1   537 Buy you] F (buy'ye); buy to you Q2   541 whole] F; owne Q2   542 his| F; the Q2   wanned] Q2 (wand); warm'd F   543 in's] F; in his Q2   544 and] F; an Q2   547 to Hecuba] FQ1; to her Q2

536.1 **Exeunt Rosencrantz and Guildenstern** This direction marks the point at
which the two courtiers leave the Prince.
His farewell to them accompanies their
movement to one of the exit doors.

537–94 **Now I ... the King** The convention
of the soliloquy is employed in an unusual
and highly original fashion here. What
Hamlet does in this speech is to voice, in
their right sequence, the ideas that have
been going through his mind since he
asked for the speech about Pyrrhus at line
437. These ideas, culminating in the
decision to have *The Murder of Gonzago*
played before Claudius and his court,
could not, of course, be spoken aloud in
the presence of others, and so have to be
kept back until he is *alone*. The soliloquy
thus becomes 'in effect a dramatic reflection of what has already taken place'
(*WHH*, p. 142 n. 1).

538 **rogue and peasant slave** Hamlet sees
himself as a *rogue* because, like the 'sturdy
rogues and vagabonds' of Shakespeare's
day, he has been idle; and as a *peasant
slave* because he has behaved like a serf
not like a free man. *Peasant* was often used
as a term of abuse; and *rogue* and *slave* are
linked together in *Arden of Feversham*
2.1.5–6, 'For such a slave, so vile a rogue

as he | Lives not again upon the earth.'

539 **Is it not monstrous** i.e. does it not show
how outrageously unnatural my conduct
has been? As Schmidt (*monstrous* 3)
points out, it is not the Player's performance 'that Hamlet means to call monstrous, but his own lethargy so different
from it, which, however, by a kind of logical anacoluthon, he forgets to add.'

540 **But merely
dream of passion** i.e. violent outburst of
grief over a purely imaginary event

541 **force ... conceit** i.e. bring his innermost
being into such consonance with his conception of the part

542 **from her working** i.e. as a consequence
of the soul's control over the rest of him
(*her* because the soul, the *anima*, is
thought of as feminine)
wanned turned pale

544–5 **his whole ... conceit** i.e. 'all his
bodily powers responding with physical
expressiveness to these fictitious imagin-
ings' (Spencer)

547 **to Hecuba** Rejected by Jenkins as an
'actor's addition', *Hecuba* looks to this
editor very much like a case of authorial
revision, made to eliminate the repetition
of *her* in the Q2 version.

Had he the motive and the cue for passion
That I have? He would drown the stage with tears   550
And cleave the general ear with horrid speech,
Make mad the guilty and appal the free,
Confound the ignorant and amaze indeed
The very faculties of eyes and ears. Yet I,
A dull and muddy-mettled rascal, peak
Like John-a-dreams, unpregnant of my cause,
And can say nothing; no, not for a king
Upon whose property and most dear life
A damned defeat was made. Am I a coward?
Who calls me villain, breaks my pate across,   560
Plucks off my beard and blows it in my face,
Tweaks me by th' nose, gives me the lie i'th' throat
As deep as to the lungs? Who does me this?
Ha? 'Swounds, I should take it. For it cannot be
But I am pigeon-livered and lack gall
To make oppression bitter, or ere this
I should have fatted all the region kites
With this slave's offal. Bloody, bawdy villain!

549 the cue] F; that Q2   554 faculties] Q2; faculty F   562 by th'] F (by'th'); by the Q2   564
'Swounds] Q2; Why F; Sure Q1   567 have] F; a Q2Q1   568 offal. Bloody,] Q5 (offal: bloudy);
Offall, bloudy: a F; offall, bloody, Q2

549 **cue** imperative call (an actor must heed his cue)
551 **horrid speech** words that would make their hair stand on end
552 **free** innocent, guiltless
553 **Confound the ignorant** dumbfound those who know nothing (of such crimes)
    amaze bewilder, utterly confuse
555 **muddy-mettled** dull spirited: apparently a Shakespearian invention
    peak mope about (*OED peak v.*[1] 3)
556 **John-a-dreams** a dreamy fellow (*OED John* 4): probably a Shakespearian coinage: see Tilley J64.
    unpregnant of not quickened into action by: earliest citing by *OED*. Compare *Measure* 4.4.18–19, 'This deed unshapes me quite, makes me unpregnant | And dull to all proceedings.'
558 **property and most dear life** dearest possession—his life. The construction here is a kind of hendiadys, with a transference of the epithet from *property* to *life*. Compare *Macbeth* 1.4.10, 'the dearest thing he owed', i.e. his life.

559 **damned defeat** act of destruction deserving damnation. Compare *Much Ado* 4.1.46, 'made defeat of her virginity'.
560–3 **Who calls . . . the lungs** All these actions were deadly insults that would meet with immediate retaliation from a man of honour.
562 **Tweaks me** pulls me sharply. Not used elsewhere by Shakespeare, this is the earliest instance of *tweak v.* cited by *OED*.
562–3 **gives me . . . lungs** i.e. calls me an out-and-out liar. 'You lie in your throat' (Tilley T268) was a most insulting accusation.
564–5 **it cannot be | But I am** I must be. For this preventive use of *but* see Abbott 122.
565 **pigeon-livered and lack gall** Pigeons and doves were meek and gentle because, it was believed, their livers did not secrete *gall*, supposed to be the source of anger and resentment. Tilley (D574) offers many examples of this common notion.
567 **region kites** kites of the air. Compare l. 478.

234

Remorseless, treacherous, lecherous, kindless villain!
O, vengeance!   570
Why, what an ass am I! Ay, sure. This is most brave,
That I, the son of a dear father murdered,
Prompted to my revenge by heaven and hell,
Must, like a whore, unpack my heart with words,
And fall a-cursing like a very drab,
A scullion! Fie upon't, foh!
About my brain.—I have heard
That guilty creatures sitting at a play
Have by the very cunning of the scene
Been struck so to the soul that presently   580
They have proclaimed their malefactions;

---

570 O, vengeance!] F; *not in* Q2Q1   571 Why] Q2; Who? F   Ay, sure.] F (I sure,); *not in*
Q2   572 a dear father murdered] Q3; the Deere murthered F; a deere murthered Q2; my deare
father Q1   576 scullion] F; stallyon Q2; scalion Q1   577 brain] FQ1; braines Q2 *corr.*; braues
Q2 *uncorr.*   I] FQ1; hum, I Q2

569 **kindless** unnatural (both as a fratricide and as one guilty of incest): not used by Shakespeare elsewhere, and rare at any time

570 **O, vengeance!** The absence of this short line from Q2 has led many editors to omit it. Jenkins, following Parrott and Craig, rejects it as an actor's addition to his part, and argues that Hamlet does not begin to think about retribution until line 577. But the Prince has already said that he should have killed Claudius (ll. 567–8); and no one, to the best of this editor's knowledge, has questioned the authenticity of Posthumus's outburst, 'O, vengeance, vengeance!' (*Cymbeline* 2.5.8).

571 **most brave** i.e. a fine performance

572 **father** This word, omitted from both Q2 and F, is necessary for the sense, and, as its occurrence in Q1 shows, was being spoken on the stage by 1603.

573 **by heaven and hell** i.e. by my sense of natural justice (a good quality) and by my loathing and resentment of Claudius (a bad quality). The words can also be regarded as an anticipation of the Prince's doubts about the Ghost's 'honesty', expressed more fully in lines 587–92, 'The spirit . . . damn me.'

575 **drab** whore

576 **scullion** The lowest of kitchen servants and employed to do 'the dirty work',

scullions were notorious for their command of foul language. Nashe accuses Gabriel Harvey of being a 'kitchen-stuff wrangler' in his *Strange News* (1592), and offers some picturesque, though not entirely intelligible, examples of the 'rhetoric of Ram-Alley', as he calls it (Nashe, i. 299. 31–5).

577 **About** to work, get busy. Compare *Merry Wives* 5.5.53–4, 'About, about; | Search Windsor castle, elves, within and out'.

577–83 **I have heard . . . miraculous organ** A number of stories about malefactors who had been led to confess their crimes by seeing similar events in plays were current in Shakespeare's day, and were, of course, treasured and used by those seeking to defend the stage against the charge that it encouraged wickedness and immorality. If Shakespeare had a particular story in mind, the likeliest is one related in the anonymous *Warning for Fair Women*, published in 1599 and played by Shakespeare's company not long before that date. It tells of how a woman of 'Lynne, a town in Norfolk', saw a play in which a wife murdered her husband, and was so affected by it that she promptly confessed to having done the same thing herself (2036–48).

579 **cunning of the scene** i.e. skilful realism of the performance

For murder, though it have no tongue, will speak
With most miraculous organ. I'll have these players
Play something like the murder of my father
Before mine uncle. I'll observe his looks,
I'll tent him to the quick. If he but blench,
I know my course. The spirit that I have seen
May be the devil, and the devil hath power
T'assume a pleasing shape; yea, and perhaps
Out of my weakness and my melancholy,   590
As he is very potent with such spirits,
Abuses me to damn me. I'll have grounds
More relative than this. The play's the thing
Wherein I'll catch the conscience of the King.   *Exit*

3.1   *Enter Claudius, Gertrude, Polonius, Ophelia,*
        Rosencrantz, Guildenstern

CLAUDIUS
    And can you by no drift of circumstance
    Get from him why he puts on this confusion,

---

586 he but] F; a doe Q2   588 be the] F; be a Q2
    3.1.0.2 Guildenstern] CAPELL; Guildenstern, and Lords FQ2 (subs.)   1 circumstance] F con-
ference Q2

582–3 **murder . . . organ** a version of the
common saying 'Murder will out' (Tilley
M1315)
586 **tent** probe. A *tent* was a 'roll of lint used
to search and cleanse a wound' (Onions).
Compare *Troilus* 2.2.16–17, 'the tent
that searches | To th' bottom of the worst',
and Tilley Q13.
    blench flinch, start
588–9 **the devil . . . shape** In the form of 'The
Devil can transform himself into an angel
of light' (Tilley D231), this idea was a
commonplace of the time.
590 **Out of** making use of
    melancholy Bright says melancholy
causes 'fantastical apparitions' (p. 103);
and Burton lists the desire for revenge as a
contributory factor to the growth of
melancholy, since it leads us 'to
aggravate our misery and melancholy,
heap upon us hell and eternal damnation'
(i. 310–11).
591 **very potent with** i.e. possessed of great
power in exploiting
    spirits states of mind
592 **Abuses** deludes, deceives

    to **damn me** (by inciting me to kill an
    innocent man)
593 **relative** relevant, cogent (*OED* 3): first
    instance of *relative* in this sense cited by
    OED; not found elsewhere in Shakespeare
    this i.e. the Ghost's story
3.1.0 The *Lords* called for by Q2 and F have
    nothing whatever to do in this scene, and
    have, therefore, been omitted from this
    initial direction. Shakespeare seems to
    have begun it thinking he would need
    them, and then to have forgotten all
    about them.
1 **drift of circumstance** i.e. manipulation of
    the course of your talk. The *circumstance*
    of F looks very much like a 'second
    thought'. The *conference*, meaning 'con-
    versation', of Q2 makes excellent sense,
    but it does not carry the overtones of
    deliberately roundabout methods that *cir-
    cumstance* does. Compare *Merchant*
    1.1.153–4, 'You know me well, and
    herein spend but time | To wind about my
    love with circumstance'.
2 **puts on** assumes. Claudius is evidently
    becoming suspicious about the genuine-

Grating so harshly all his days of quiet
With turbulent and dangerous lunacy?

ROSENCRANTZ

He does confess he feels himself distracted,
But from what cause he will by no means speak.

GUILDENSTERN

Nor do we find him forward to be sounded,
But with a crafty madness keeps aloof
When we would bring him on to some confession
Of his true state.   10

GERTRUDE Did he receive you well?

ROSENCRANTZ Most like a gentleman.

GUILDENSTERN

But with much forcing of his disposition.

ROSENCRANTZ

Niggard of question, but of our demands
Most free in his reply.

GERTRUDE Did you assay him to any pastime?

ROSENCRANTZ

Madam, it so fell out that certain players
We o'er-raught on the way. Of these we told him;
And there did seem in him a kind of joy
To hear of it. They are about the court,   20
And, as I think, they have already order
This night to play before him.

POLONIUS   'Tis most true;
And he beseeched me to entreat your majesties
To hear and see the matter.

CLAUDIUS

With all my heart; and it doth much content me

6 he] F; a Q2   20 about] F; heere about Q2

ness of Hamlet's 'madness'.
  confusion mental disturbance
3 **Grating . . . quiet** i.e. making his life,
  which should be tranquil and harmonious, so harshly discordant and
  cacophonous. The analogy is a musical
  one. Compare *Antony* 1.1.18, 'Grates me!
  the sum'.
7 **forward** at all inclined
8 **crafty** (1) cunning (2) feigned. Compare
  K. John 4.1.53–4, 'you may think my

love was crafty love, | And call it cun-
ning.'
13 **disposition** real inclination
14 **Niggard of question** reluctant to start a
  conversation (*OED question sb.* 2)
  of our as regards our (Abbott 173)
15 **free** forthcoming
  assay tempt (Schmidt), woo (compare
  Merry Wives 2.1.22, 'that he dares in this
  manner assay me?')
18 **o'er-raught** overtook, came up with

To hear him so inclined.
Good gentlemen, give him a further edge,
And drive his purpose on to these delights.

ROSENCRANTZ
We shall, my lord.   *Exeunt Rosencrantz and Guildenstern*

CLAUDIUS   Sweet Gertrude, leave us too;
For we have closely sent for Hamlet hither,   30
That he, as 'twere by accident, may here
Affront Ophelia.
Her father and myself, lawful espials,
Will so bestow ourselves that, seeing unseen,
We may of their encounter frankly judge,
And gather by him, as he is behaved,
If't be th'affliction of his love or no
That thus he suffers for.

GERTRUDE   I shall obey you.—
And for your part, Ophelia, I do wish
That your good beauties be the happy cause   40
Of Hamlet's wildness; so shall I hope your virtues
Will bring him to his wonted way again,
To both your honours.

OPHELIA   Madam, I wish it may.

Exit Gertrude

POLONIUS
Ophelia, walk you here.—Gracious, so please you,
We will bestow ourselves.—Read on this book,

---

28 on to] F; into Q2   29 *Exeunt Rosencrantz and Guildenstern*] Q2 (*Exeunt Ros. & Guyl*); *Exeunt*
F   too] F; two Q2   31 here] Q2; there F   33 lawful espials] F; *not in* Q2   34 Will] F; Wee'le
Q2   43 *Exit Gertrude*] THEOBALD; *not in* FQ2   44 please you] Q2; please ye F

27 **edge** incitement, stimulus (*OED sb.* 2c)
30 **closely** privately (*OED* 3)
32 **Affront Ophelia** meet Ophelia face to face (*OED affront v.* 4): earliest instance of *affront* in this sense cited by *OED*
33 **espials** spies
36 **by ... behaved** i.e. from his behaviour. In this verbose expression *by* means 'about', and *behaved* means 'mannered, conducted' as it still does in *well-behaved* and the like. The construction is not pre-Shakespearian (Onions).
39–43 **And . . . honours** Gertrude offers Ophelia a plausible reason for taking part in the scheme, and, at the same time,

makes it clear that she has no objection to a union between Ophelia and Hamlet.
40 **beauties** 'the several parts and qualities which constitute the beauty of a person or thing' (Schmidt)
44 **Gracious** i.e. my gracious lord. This use of *gracious*, unaccompanied by a noun, as a vocative, though uncommon, is not unique. The Prologue Thomas Heywood wrote for the performance of *The Jew of Malta* before Charles I and his Court in 1633 opens thus: 'Gracious and great . . .'
45 **book** As the context shows, the *book* is a devotional work.

That show of such an exercise may colour
Your loneliness. We are oft to blame in this,
'Tis too much proved, that with devotion's visage
And pious action we do sugar o'er
The devil himself.

CLAUDIUS (*aside*)   O, 'tis too true.   50

How smart a lash that speech doth give my conscience.
The harlot's cheek, beautied with plast'ring art,
Is not more ugly to the thing that helps it
Than is my deed to my most painted word.
O heavy burden.

POLONIUS

I hear him coming, let's withdraw, my lord.

Claudius and Polonius ⌈hide behind the arras⌉.
Enter Hamlet

HAMLET

To be, or not to be—that is the question:
Whether 'tis nobler in the mind to suffer
The slings and arrows of outrageous fortune,

---

47 loneliness] F; lowlines Q2   49 sugar] Q2, surge F   50 too] Q2; *not in* F   56 let's| F; *not in* Q2   *Claudius and Polonius hide behind the arras*] *Exeunt* F; *not in* Q2Q1   56.1 *Enter Hamlet*] F; *before* 56 Q2

46 **exercise** religious exercise
46-7 **colour | Your loneliness** serve to explain your being alone
48 **too much proved** i.e. all too common an experience
49 **sugar o'er** give a sugar-coating to, set a deceptively pleasing appearance on
50-5 **O, 'tis . . . burden** This speech is the first sign that Claudius has a conscience.
52 **beautied** beautified: not elsewhere in Shakespeare
   plast'ring art skilful application of (1) cosmetics (2) curative plasters and ointments
53 **to the thing that helps it** when compared to the 'plaster' that improves its appearance
54 **painted** specious, deceptive (like the 'harlot's cheek')
56.1 **Claudius . . . behind the arras** Since they are following the plan outlined by Polonius at 2.2.163-4, the King and Polonius presumably go behind the arras at this point, instead of leaving the stage altogether, though none of the early texts

makes this clear. The direction in F is, however, sufficient to show plainly that, apart from the presence of Ophelia, the stage proper is unoccupied as Hamlet enters.
57-89 **To be . . . action** One thing can be said with some confidence about this much discussed and debated soliloquy: it is cast in general terms. Hamlet speaks of *we*, *us*, *who*, and *he*, without using *I* or *me* once.
58 **nobler in the mind** It is not evident whether *in the mind* is meant to go with *to suffer* or with *nobler*. The latter possibility seems more likely, for *nobler in the mind* can signify 'more magnanimous'; and *magnanimity* had two different but related senses, corresponding to the two courses Hamlet goes on to consider: 'fortitude in endurance' and 'courage in resistance'.
59 **slings** Shakespeare uses this word at one other place in his writings, *Henry V* 4.7.57, 'the old Assyrian slings', an allusion 'to Judith, 9: 7, "The Assyrians . . . trust in shield, spear, and bow, and

Or to take arms against a sea of troubles,   60
And by opposing end them? To die, to sleep—
No more; and by a sleep to say we end
The heartache and the thousand natural shocks
That flesh is heir to—'tis a consummation
Devoutly to be wished: to die, to sleep.
To sleep, perchance to dream. Ay, there's the rub;
For in that sleep of death what dreams may come,
When we have shuffled off this mortal coil,
Must give us pause. There's the respect
That makes calamity of so long life.   70
For who would bear the whips and scorns of time,
The oppressor's wrong, the proud man's contumely,
The pangs of disprized love, the law's delay,
The insolence of office, and the spurns
That patient merit of the unworthy takes,
When he himself might his quietus make

61–2 To die, to sleep— | No more] POPE (*subs.*); to dye, to sleepe | No more F; to die to sleepe
| No more Q2   65 wished: to] F (wish'd. To); wisht_∧ to Q2   72 The oppressor's] F;
Th'oppressors Q2   proud] Q2; poore F   73 disprized] F; despiz'd Q2   75 the unworthy] F;
th'vnworthy Q2

sling"' (Taylor). The linking of *bow* and
sling there may have suggested the linking of *slings and arrows* here.
60 **a sea of troubles** proverbial (Dent
S177.1)
61 **end them** 'Not by overcoming them but
(paradoxically) by being overcome by
them' (Jenkins).
61–2 **To die . . . more** i.e. dying is no more
than sleeping
63 **natural shocks** i.e. assaults by disease
and the like. Compare *Timon* 4.3.6–7,
'nature, | To whom all sores lay siege'.
64 **consummation** fitting end. Compare
Cymbeline 4.2.281, 'Quiet consummation have'.
66 **rub** obstacle, difficulty—a metaphor
derived from the game of bowls, in which
a *rub* is 'an obstacle or impediment by
which a bowl is hindered in, or diverted
from, its proper course' (*OED*). Shakespeare's use of it here seems to have made
'Ay, there's the rub' proverbial (Tilley
R196).
68 **this mortal coil** (1) this turmoil and
trouble of living (2) this mortal flesh, the
'too too solid flesh' of 1.2.129, which en-

closes within its coils or folds our essential
being and has to be *shuffled off* at death as
a snake sloughs its old skin. An extended
gloss on this second sense is provided by
Chapman in his *The Revenge of Bussy
D'Ambois* 5.5.168–75.
69 **give us pause** i.e. make us stop and think
    respect consideration
70 **makes calamity of so long life** 'makes
those afflicted by calamity willing to endure it for so long' (Spencer)
71–5 **For who . . . takes** Compare *Sonnets* 66
for a similar survey of the injustices of life.
71 **whips and scorns of time** i.e. lacerating
injuries and insults inflicted on us by the
world we live in
73 **disprized** undervalued, held in contempt.
Compare *Troilus* 4.5.74–5, 'disprizing the
knight opposed'.
74 **office** people in official positions
76 **his quietus make** secure his release from
life. *Quietus est* written on an account sig-
nified 'paid'. The debt in question here is
man's debt to God, who lent him life,
which he pays by dying. Compare *1 Henry
IV* 5.1.126, 'thou owest God a death',
and Tilley Q16.

With a bare bodkin? Who would these fardels bear,
To grunt and sweat under a weary life,
But that the dread of something after death,
The undiscovered country, from whose bourn   80
No traveller returns, puzzles the will,
And makes us rather bear those ills we have
Than fly to others that we know not of?
Thus conscience does make cowards of us all;
And thus the native hue of resolution
Is sicklied o'er with the pale cast of thought,
And enterprises of great pith and moment
With this regard their currents turn away
And lose the name of action.—Soft you now,
The fair Ophelia.—Nymph, in thy orisons   90

77 these] F, *not in* Q2   84 of us all] FQ1; *not in* Q2   86 sicklied] F; sickled Q2   87 pith] F;
pitch Q2   88 away] F; awry Q2

77 **bare bodkin** mere dagger
  fardels burdens, loads—often used with
  reference to 'sin, sorrow, etc.' (*OED sb.*[1]
  2b). In its literal sense of *bundle, fardel* is
  also found in *Winter's Tale* 4.4.697, 707,
  etc.
80–1 **The undiscovered country . . . returns**
  These words seem to owe something to
  Mortimer's farewell to Queen Isabella and
  the world in Marlowe's *Edward II*:
  'Farewell, fair queen: weep not for
  Mortimer, | That scorns the world, and, as
  a traveller, | Goes to discover countries yet
  unknown' (5.6.64–6). It has frequently
  been objected that this statement is inconsistent with Hamlet's own experience,
  since he has seen a returned traveller—
  the Ghost. Coleridge's answer to this
  point deserves quotation: 'If it be necessary to remove the apparent contradiction—if it be not rather a great beauty
  —surely, it were easy to say, that no
  traveller returns to this world, as to his
  home, or abiding place' (*Coleridge's Essays
  and Lectures on Shakespeare* [Everyman
  ed.] p. 150). In fact, Hamlet is stating one
  of the great commonplaces about death:
  that the road leading to it is a one-way
  street, or, as Horace puts it, *omnes una
  manet nox | Et calcanda semel via leti* (*Odes*
  1.28.15–16).
80 **bourn** frontier. See *OED bourne sb.*[2],
  where it is pointed out that the word first
  appears in Lord Berners' *Froissart* (1523),
  reappears in Shakespeare, who uses it

seven times, and then disappears once
more until the 18th century, 'the modern
use being due to Shakespeare, and in a
large number of cases alluding to [this]
passage in *Hamlet*.'
81 **puzzles** confounds, bewilders
82–3 **makes us . . . of** Shakespeare's version
  of the common saying 'Better the harm I
  know than that I know not' (Tilley
  H166).
84 **conscience** one's sense of right and
  wrong (the normal meaning of the word
  in Shakespeare)
85 **native hue** natural colour (ruddy or san-
  guine)
86 **sicklied o'er** covered all over with a sickly
  hue. This use of *sickly* as a verb is a
  Shakespearian invention.
  cast of thought tinge or shade of
  melancholy (*OED cast sb.* 35)—a usage
  introduced by Shakespeare in this passage
87 **pith and moment** gravity and importance. The Cambridge editors, while
  preferring Q2's 'pitch' to F's 'pith', point
  out that the Players' Quartos of 1676,
  1683, 1695, and 1703, 'have, contrary
  to their custom, followed the Folios,
  which may possibly indicate that 'pith'
  was the reading according to the stage
  tradition' (Note XVI).
88 **With this regard** because of this consideration
90 **Nymph . . . orisons** Wilson calls these two
  words 'pretentious', and thinks Hamlet is
  speaking 'ironically'. But Shakespeare

Be all my sins remembered.

OPHELIA   Good my lord,
How does your honour for this many a day?

HAMLET I humbly thank you, well, well, well.

OPHELIA
My lord, I have remembrances of yours
That I have longèd long to re-deliver.
I pray you now receive them.

HAMLET
No, no, not I. I never gave you aught.

OPHELIA
My honoured lord, I know right well you did,
And with them words of so sweet breath composed
As made the things more rich. Their perfume lost,   100
Take these again; for to the noble mind
Rich gifts wax poor when givers prove unkind.
There, my lord.

HAMLET Ha, ha? Are you honest?

OPHELIA My lord?

HAMLET Are you fair?

OPHELIA What means your lordship?

HAMLET That if you be honest and fair, your honesty should
admit no discourse to your beauty.

---

93 well, well, well.] F; well. Q2   96 you now] Q2; you now, F   97 No, no, not I. I] This
edition; No, no, I F; No, not I, I Q2   98 I know] F; you know Q2Q1
100 the] F; these Q2   rich.] Q4 (subs.); ~, FQ2   Their perfume lost,] Q2; then perfume left:
F   108 your honesty should] F; you should Q2

had used both, before writing *Hamlet*, in
contexts where they cannot possibly be
either pretentious or ironical. Valentine
thinks of Sylvia as 'Thou gentle nymph'
(*Two Gentlemen* 5.4.12); and Juliet says, 'I
have need of many orisons' (*Romeo* 4.3.3).
92 **for this many a day** all this long time
94 **remembrances** Ophelia's choice of this
word is a most unhappy one. To her it
means 'love-tokens', the sense it carries at
Othello 3.3.293, 'This was her first
remembrance from the Moor'. But to Hamlet, haunted by memories and sworn to
remember, it serves as a reminder—
another meaning of *remembrance*—of
how, according to the Ghost, Claudius
seduced Gertrude 'with witchcraft of his
wit, with traitorous gifts' (1.5.43). The
thought that his presents to Ophelia could
be regarded in the same light as Claudius's

gifts to his mother is anathema to Hamlet.
He therefore denies that he ever gave her
any, and then goes on to warn her against
following the example of Gertrude, whose
honesty was not strong enough 'to admit
no discourse to [her] beauty'. In fact, the
Prince's *remembrance* of his mother's fall
colours the rest of his dialogue with Ophelia and goes far towards explaining, and
so partly excusing, its bitterness.
100 **perfume** i.e. the perfume given to the
gifts by the 'words of so sweet breath composed'
101-2 **for to ... unkind** Compare the much
used and much varied saying, 'A gift is
valued by the mind of the giver' (Tilley
G97).
104 **honest** (1) speaking the truth (2) chaste
109 **admit no discourse to** permit no familiar
conversation with

OPHELIA Could beauty, my lord, have better commerce than   110
  with honesty?

HAMLET Ay, truly; for the power of beauty will sooner transform honesty from what it is to a bawd than the force of
  honesty can translate beauty into his likeness. This was
  sometime a paradox, but now the time gives it proof. I did
  love you once.

OPHELIA Indeed, my lord, you made me believe so.

HAMLET You should not have believed me. For virtue cannot so inoculate our old stock but we shall relish of it. I
  loved you not.   120

OPHELIA I was the more deceived.

HAMLET Get thee to a nunnery. Why, wouldst thou be a
  breeder of sinners? I am myself indifferent honest, but yet
  I could accuse me of such things that it were better my
  mother had not borne me. I am very proud, revengeful,
  ambitious, with more offences at my beck than I have
  thoughts to put them in, imagination to give them shape,
  or time to act them in. What should such fellows as I do
  crawling between heaven and earth? We are arrant

111 with] Q2Q1; your F   119 inoculate] F (innocculate); euocutat Q2   122 to] F; *not in* Q2
Why,] JENKINS; Why_A Q2Q1   127 in, imagination] Q2; in_A imagination F   129 heaven and
earth] FQ1; earth and heauen Q2

110–11 **Could . . . honesty** Ophelia brings
  Hamlet's explanation into line with the
  common saying 'Beauty and chastity
  seldom meet' (Tilley B163).
110 **commerce** (1) social intercourse (the
  sense Ophelia has in mind) (2) trade (the
  sense Hamlet gives it)
114 **translate** transform
115 **sometime** once, formerly
  paradox absurd statement, 'statement or
  tenet contrary to received opinion'
  (Onions)
  the time . . . proof the time we live in
  (which is 'out of joint') shows its accuracy
  (in the behaviour of Gertrude)
116 **once** once upon a time, i.e. in the golden
  age when my father was king and true
  love was possible
118–19 **virtue . . . of it** i.e. virtue, when
  grafted on to our original nature tainted
  by the sin of Adam, cannot so change that
  nature that we retain no flavour of it. The
  image is drawn from the practice of graft-
  ing a slip or bud (*oculus* in Latin) taken

from a good apple-tree on to the vigorous
  stock provided by a crab-tree, whose fruit
  has a bitter astringent taste. Compare
  Winter's Tale 4.4.92–3, 'we marry | A
  gentler scion to the wildest stock'.
119–20 **I loved you not** i.e. my love for you
  was not true love (how could it be, since I
  am the son of my mother?)
122 **Get thee to a nunnery** Hamlet means
  precisely what he says here. Only by
  entering a nunnery can Ophelia ensure
  that she will not become *a breeder of
  sinners*. The injunction makes it clear that
  nunnery is not being used here in the sense
  of 'brothel', as it is in *Christ's Tears over
  Jerusalem*, for example, where a *nunnery* is
  synonymous with *a college of courtesans*
  (Nashe, ii. 151–2).
  Why As Jenkins has pointed out, *Why*
  here is an interjection.
123 **indifferent honest** fairly virtuous, decent enough as men go
126 **at my beck** ready to be called on (like so
  many servants eager for work)

knaves all. Believe none of us. Go thy ways to a nunnery.   130
Where's your father?

OPHELIA At home, my lord.

HAMLET Let the doors be shut upon him, that he may play
the fool nowhere but in's own house. Farewell.

OPHELIA O help him, you sweet heavens!

HAMLET If thou dost marry, I'll give thee this plague for thy
dowry: be thou as chaste as ice, as pure as snow, thou
shalt not escape calumny. Get thee to a nunnery, go,
farewell. Or if thou wilt needs marry, marry a fool; for
wise men know well enough what monsters you make of   140
them. To a nunnery go, and quickly too. Farewell.

OPHELIA O heavenly powers, restore him.

HAMLET I have heard of your paintings too, well enough.
God has given you one face, and you make yourselves
another. You jig, you amble, and you lisp, and nickname

130 all] FQ1; *not in* Q2   134 nowhere] Q2 (no where) Q1; no way F   138 go] F; *not in*
Q2   142 O] F; *not in* Q2   143 paintings too] Q1; pratlings too F; paintings Q2   144 has] F;
hath Q2Q1   face] Q2Q1; pace F   yourselves] Q2 (your selfes) Q1; your selfe F   145 jig, you]
F (gidge, you); gig & Q2; fig, and you Q1   lisp,] F; list‸ Q2   and nickname] F; you nickname
Q2; and you nickname Q1

131 **Where's your father?** It has often been
suggested that this question is prompted
by a suspicion that Polonius is within ear-
shot; but there is no need for any such
assumption. Polonius himself virtually
anticipated some reaction of this kind
from Hamlet when he provided Ophelia
with a book to explain her *loneliness*
(ll. 45–7).

132 **At home, my lord** Ophelia's lie, like
Desdemona's lie (*Othello* 3.4.51), is an ex-
cusable one. What else can she say?

133–4 **Let . . . house** Ironically enough,
Hamlet's advice is even sounder than he
realizes. Had Polonius been locked up in
his own house, he would not have been
killed.

136 **plague** affliction

137 **as chaste . . . snow** These two conventional similes (Tilley I1, S591) make a fitting beginning to a diatribe that is, in essence, also conventional, though Hamlet
has the grace to admit that some of it may
be calumny.

138 **calumny** Compare *Measure* 3.2.174–5,
'back-wounding calumny | The whitest
virtue strikes.'

140 **monsters** (because cuckolds were supposed to sprout horns). Compare *Othello*
4.1.62, 'A horned man's a monster', and
Dent C876.2.

143–7 **I have . . . ignorance** Hamlet may
well say 'I have heard'; for charges such
as these were the stock in trade of the
Elizabethan satirist, and can be paralleled
in many works of the time. Ben Jonson
dramatizes face-painting, and its implica-
tions, in the most mordant and detailed
manner in Act 2 (53–136) of his *Sejanus*
(1603).

144 **you** i.e. women in general

145 **You jig . . . lisp** Compare Nashe's
portrait of 'Mistress Minx, a merchant's
wife' in his *Pierce Penilesse* (1592). She
'looks as simperingly as if she were be-
smeared, and jets it as gingerly as if she
were dancing the canaries. She is so fini-
cal in her speech, as though she spake
nothing but what she had first sewed over
before in her samplers; and the puling
accent of her voice is like a feigned treble
or one's voice that interprets to the puppets' (Nashe, i. 173).

  jig i.e. 'move with a rapid jerky motion'
(Onions)—earliest instance of *jig*, in this
sense, cited by *OED*

  amble i.e. move in an exaggeratedly
smooth and fluid fashion

  lisp Compare *Romeo* 2.4.28–9, 'such
antic, lisping, affecting fantasticoes'.

145–6 **nickname God's creatures** i.e. make
up fancy names for creatures that were

God's creatures, and make your wantonness your ig-
norance. Go to, I'll no more on't, it hath made me mad.
I say we will have no more marriages. Those that are
married already—all but one—shall live. The rest shall
keep as they are. To a nunnery, go.   *Exit*   150
OPHELIA
O, what a noble mind is here o'erthrown!
The courtier's, soldier's, scholar's, eye, tongue, sword;
Th'expectancy and rose of the fair state,
The glass of fashion and the mould of form,
Th'observed of all observers—quite, quite down!
And I, of ladies most deject and wretched,
That sucked the honey of his music vows,
Now see that noble and most sovereign reason
Like sweet bells jangled out of tune and harsh;
That unmatched form and feature of blown youth   160
Blasted with ecstasy. O woe is me
T'have seen what I have seen, see what I see.
      Enter Claudius and Polonius

146 wantonness your] FQ1; wantonnes Q2   148 more marriages] FQ1 mo marriage Q2
153 expectancy] F; expectation Q2   156 And] Q2; Haue F   157 music] F; musickt Q2
158 that] F; what Q2   159 tune] F; time Q2   160 feature] F; stature Q2   162 see.] FQ2
uncorr.; sec. *Exit.* Q2 *corr.* QI

given their proper names by Adam (Genesis 2: 19)
146-7 make . . . ignorance i.e. pretend that what you do out of sheer affectation is the result of simple ignorance
149 all but one The *one* is obviously Claudius; and, as Spencer observes, Hamlet's voicing this threat at this point makes it most unlikely that he suspects the King is listening.
151-5 O . . . observers These lines provide the one full-length portrait the play gives of Hamlet as he was—the ideal Renaissance prince—before his father's death.
152 The courtier's . . . sword Shakespeare lists the roles the prince was expected to fill, together with the prime attribute each role demanded, without bothering to preserve exactly the same order in the two parts of the list. *Lucrece* 615-6 offers a close parallel: 'For princes are the glass, the school, the book, | Where subjects' eyes do learn, do read, do look.'

153 expectancy 'that from which expectations are entertained' (*OED* 2c)—first instance of this sense cited by *OED*
   rose As the primate among flowers, the *rose* symbolized youth and beauty. Compare *Antony* 3.13.20-1, 'he wears the rose | Of youth upon him'.
154 glass model, ideal. Compare *2 Henry IV* 2.3.21.
   mould of form pattern of perfect behaviour (*OED mould sb.*¹ 5)
155 observed of all observers i.e. object of every true courtier's respectful attention (*OED observe v.* 4)
159 out of tune For the figurative use of this phrase, well established by Shakespeare's day, see Dent T598.1.
160 feature bodily proportion, complete physical appearance. Compare *Antony* 2.5.111-14, 'bid him | Report the feature of Octavia, her years, | Her inclination; let him not leave out | The colour of her hair.'
   blown youth youth in full bloom. Compare 3.3.81.

245

CLAUDIUS

    Love? His affections do not that way tend;
    Nor what he spake, though it lacked form a little,
    Was not like madness. There's something in his soul
    O'er which his melancholy sits on brood;
    And I do doubt the hatch and the disclose
    Will be some danger; which for to prevent,
    I have in quick determination
    Thus set it down; he shall with speed to England   170
    For the demand of our neglected tribute.
    Haply the seas, and countries different,
    With variable objects, shall expel
    This something-settled matter in his heart,
    Whereon his brain's still beating puts him thus
    From fashion of himself. What think you on't?

POLONIUS

    It shall do well. But yet do I believe
    The origin and commencement of this grief
    Sprung from neglected love.—How now, Ophelia?
    You need not tell us what Lord Hamlet said;   180
    We heard it all.—My lord, do as you please;
    But, if you hold it fit, after the play
    Let his queen mother all alone entreat him
    To show his griefs. Let her be round with him;

---

165 soul₍ₐ₎] Q2; soule? F   168 for] Q2; *not in* F   175 brain's] This edition; Braines FQ2   178 this] F; his Q2   184 griefs] F (Greefes); griefe Q2

---

163 **affections** inclinations, emotions. Compare *Caesar* 2.1.20–1, 'I have not known when his affections swayed | More than his reason.'
166 **sits on brood** sits brooding like a hen
167 **doubt** fear, suspect
    disclose disclosure, hatching-out (*OED disclose sb. Obs.* and *v.* 3c)
170 **set it down** resolved (*OED set v.* 143g)
171 **For . . . tribute** See Bullough, vii. 185 for the topical element in this reference to the Danegeld.
173 **variable objects** various sights
174 **something-settled matter** i.e. obsession that has taken rather a hold. Jenkins argues that *something* is an adjective meaning 'indefinite'; but had Shakespeare intended this, he would, presumably,

have written 'This something matter settled in his heart'.
175 **brain's** There is no way of deciding with certainty whether the *braines* of Q2 and F is nominative plural, genitive singular, or genitive plural. The genitive singular is preferred here because it gives the simplest construction.
    still beating constant hammering. For *still* signifying 'constant, unremitting', see *Richard III* 4.4.229, 'still use of grief makes wild grief tame'.
175–6 **puts . . . himself** i.e. makes him so unlike his usual self
178 **grief** troubled state of mind
184 **griefs** grievances
    round blunt, outspoken

And I'll be placed, so please you, in the ear
Of all their conference. If she find him not,
To England send him, or confine him where
Your wisdom best shall think.
CLAUDIUS   It shall be so.
Madness in great ones must not unwatched go.   *Exeunt*

3.2   *Enter Hamlet and two or three of the Players*
HAMLET Speak the speech, I pray you, as I pronounced it to
you, trippingly on the tongue. But if you mouth it, as
many of your players do, I had as lief the town-crier had
spoke my lines. Nor do not saw the air too much with
your hand, thus, but use all gently; for in the very torrent,
tempest, and, as I may say, the whirlwind of your passion,
you must acquire and beget a temperance that may give
it smoothness. O, it offends me to the soul to hear a robustious periwig-pated fellow tear a passion to tatters, to very
rags, to split the ears of the groundlings, who, for the most   10

185 placed, so please you,] Q2 (plac'd (so please you)); plac'd so, please you‸ F   189 unwatch-
ed] F; vnmatcht Q2
    3.2.0.1 *two or three*] F; *three* Q2   1 pronounced] F; pronoun'd Q2   3 your] FQ1; our
Q2   3–4 had spoke] F; spoke Q2   4 with] Q2Q1; *not in* F   6 the] F; *not in* Q2   your] Q2; *not
in* F   8 hear] Q2Q1; see F   9 tatters] F; totters Q2Q1

186 **find him not** i.e. does not find out what
is the matter with him (*OED find v.* 8)
3.2 In this scene the action moves to its
second climax, the first being the Prince's
encounter with the Ghost. At first sight,
the dialogue between Hamlet and the
leading Player, with which the scene
opens, appears unnecessary. It contributes
nothing to the action; and the advice it
gives the Players seems irrelevant to the
playing of *The Murder of Gonzago*, which
calls for rant rather than restraint. It does,
it is true, provide Hamlet with an opportunity to voice his views on the art of acting
and to express his disapproval of histrionic
excess; but this kind of interest can hardly
be cited as a valid reason for its inclusion in
the longest play Shakespeare ever wrote.
The case for excising it from performance
would seem to be strong. Nevertheless, it
appears in all three of the earliest texts, and
it still finds its place in most productions
today. Evidently producers feel, and have
the support of audiences in so feeling, that
this dialogue has its place in the total econ-
omy of the tragedy. Their instinct is a
sound one; for *acting*, in all its various senses, is at the heart of *Hamlet*.
  1 **pronounced** declaimed, recited. Compare
Merchant 1.2.9, 'Good sentences, and
well pronounced.'
  2 **trippingly** The earliest instance of this
word cited by *OED* is from *Dream*
5.1.384–5, 'And this ditty, after me |
Sing and dance it trippingly.'
  5 **use all** do everything
  7 **beget** get, obtain (*OED v.* 1)
8–9 **robustious** noisy, boisterous; applied to
the behaviour of mastiffs at *Henry V*
3.7.142
  9 **periwig-pated** wearing a wig (a typical
Shakespearian compound)
    passion passionate speech (*OED* 6d).
Compare *Dream* 5.1.307, 'her passion
ends the play.'
10 **groundlings** spectators who stood on the
ground in the yard of the public theatres,
the cheapest part of the house. First found
in this passage, and not used elsewhere in

part, are capable of nothing but inexplicable dumb shows
and noise. I would have such a fellow whipped for o'erdo-
ing Termagant. It out-Herods Herod. Pray you avoid it.

FIRST PLAYER I warrant your honour.

HAMLET Be not too tame neither, but let your own
discretion be your tutor. Suit the action to the word, the
word to the action, with this special observance, that you
o'erstep not the modesty of nature. For anything so overdone is from the purpose of playing, whose end, both at
the first and now, was and is to hold, as 'twere, the mirror   20
up to nature : to show virtue her own feature, scorn her
own image, and the very age and body of the time his
form and pressure. Now, this overdone or come tardy off,
though it make the unskilful laugh, cannot but make the

---

12 would] Q2Q1 ; could F   18 o'erstep] Q2 ; ore-stop F   18–19 overdone] F ; ore-doone
Q2   21 own feature] F ; feature Q2   24 it make] F ; it makes Q2

Shakespeare, *groundling*, in this sense,
appears to be an ingenious punning
variation on the 'name given to various
small fishes which live at the bottom of the
water' (*OED* 3 and 1). One cannot help
wondering how the groundlings at the
Globe responded to Hamlet's sally at their
expense. Q1, either through diplomacy
or, more probably, misremembering,
reads *ignorant*.

11 **capable** appreciative, susceptible to the
appeal (*OED* 3b). Compare *K. John*
3.1.12, 'I am sick and capable of fears'.

13 **Termagant** 'name of an imaginary deity
held in mediaeval Christendom to be
worshipped by Mohammedans: in the
mystery plays represented as a violent
overbearing personage' (*OED*)
   out-Herods Herod surpasses the excesses
of Herod. In the Coventry cycle, which
Shakespeare when young could have
seen, Herod, on hearing that the Magi
have returned to their own lands without
informing him of the whereabouts of the
infant Christ, breaks into a violent
passion, rants wildly, and goes on to rage
'in the pageant and in the street also'
(Adams, *Chief Pre-Shakespearean Dramas*,
p. 163).

19 **from** at variance with, contrary to
(Abbott 158)

19–23 **the purpose . . . pressure** This is
Shakespeare's version of a much quoted
definition of comedy, attributed to Cicero,
to the effect that comedy is an imitation of
life, a mirror of custom, and an image of
truth : *imitatio vitae, speculum con-
suetudinis, imago veritatis*. Ben Jonson,
characteristically, gives it in the original
Latin, and then adds: 'a thing
throughout pleasant, and ridiculous, and
accommodated to the correction of
manners' (*Every Man Out of His Humour*
3.6.203–9). Jonson's play was first acted
by Shakespeare's company in the last
weeks of 1599.

21 **scorn** objects of scorn, things that deserve
scorn (i.e. vice and folly). Compare *Errors*
4.4.100, 'To make a loathsome abject
scorn of me'.

22 **the very age and body of the time** the true
state of things as they are now. The *age* is
'the period we live in' and the *body of the
time* is the 'essential, substantial nature of
the time'.

23 **pressure** likeness, stamp (literally, 'impression made in wax'). Compare
1.5.100.
   come tardy off inadequately carried out,
falling short of what it should (*OED tardy
a. (adv.)* 3)

24 **unskilful** undiscerning, undiscriminat-
ing

judicious grieve; the censure of the which one must in
your allowance o'erweigh a whole theatre of others'. O
there be players that I have seen play, and heard others
praise, and that highly, not to speak it profanely, that,
neither having the accent of Christians, nor the gait of
Christian, pagan, nor no man, have so strutted and   30
bellowed that I have thought some of Nature's journeymen had made men, and not made them well, they
imitated humanity so abominably.

FIRST PLAYER I hope we have reformed that indifferently
with us, sir.

HAMLET O reform it altogether. And let those that play your
clowns speak no more than is set down for them; for there
be of them that will themselves laugh to set on some
quantity of barren spectators to laugh too, though in the

---

25 the which] F; which Q2   26 others'] This edition; others FQ2   28 praise] F; praysd
Q2   29 the accent] F; th'accent Q2   30 nor no man] This edition; or Norman F; nor man Q2,
Nor Turke Q1   35 sir] F; *not in* Q2

25–6 **censure . . . others'** Malone compares
Jonson's Address 'To the Reader' at the
end of his *Poetaster* (1601), where he announces his intention to turn to tragedy:
'Where, if I prove the pleasure but of
one, | So he judicious be, he shall be
alone | A Theatre unto me' (ll. 226–8).
25 **censure** judgement, opinion
    one solitary individual
25–6 **in your allowance** i.e. you are bound
    to admit (*OED allowance sb.* 3). Compare
    Troilus 1.3.377, 'Give him allowance for
    the better man'.
26 **others'** i.e. others' censure. This reading
    of *others* (Q2 and F) gives better sense than
    does taking it as accusative plural.
28 **not to speak it profanely** Hamlet apolo-
    gizes in advance for what might be
    regarded as the impiety of his statement
    that the actors he has in mind were not
    made in the natural way of creation.
29 **Christians** i.e. ordinary human beings.
    Compare *Twelfth Night* 1.3.79–80,
    'Methinks sometimes I have no more wit
    than a Christian or an ordinary man has'.
30 **nor no man** Q2's *nor man* is weak and
    anticlimactic; F's *or Norman* is patently
    wrong; Q1's *Nor Turke* has the right ring
    about it but cannot be reconciled with the
    readings of the two good texts. Shake-
    speare writes *nor no man* on at least four
    other occasions, including the superb

climax to *Sonnets* 116: 'If this be error,
and upon me proved | I never writ, nor no
man ever loved.' That Q2 should omit *no*,
especially after *nor*, seems likely; and
there is at least a resemblance of sorts between F's *or Norman* and the conjectured
nor no man.
31–3 **I have thought . . . abominably** Com-
    pare 'He is not a man of God's making'
    (Tilley M162).
31 2 **journeymen** hired workmen (not mas-
    ter craftsmen, such as nature herself)
33 **abominably** (1) execrably (2) brutishly.
    In both Q2 and F the spelling is *abhomin-*
    ably, reflecting the mistaken notion cur-
    rent at the time that the word was derived
    from the Latin *ab homine*, meaning 'away
    from man, inhuman, beastly'. Compare
    Measure 3.2.21, 'their abominable and
    beastly touches'.
34 **indifferently** fairly well
36–42 **And let . . . uses it** Commentators
    usually cite the name of Richard Tarlton,
    famous for his 'extemporal wit'. But Tarl-
    ton had been dead for twelve years when
    Hamlet was written; and the use of the
    plural suggests that Shakespeare had no
    specific target in mind. The passage is
    more important for what it tells us about
    Hamlet and his attitude to drama than for
    any topical bearing it may or may not
    have.

mean time some necessary question of the play be then to   40
be considered. That's villainous, and shows a most pitiful
ambition in the fool that uses it. Go make you ready.
                                          Exeunt Players
         Enter Polonius, Rosencrantz, and Guildenstern
How now, my lord? Will the King hear this piece of work?
POLONIUS And the Queen too, and that presently.
HAMLET Bid the players make haste.   *Exit Polonius*
Will you two help to hasten them?
ROSENCRANTZ *and* GUILDENSTERN   We will, my lord.
                       Exeunt Rosencrantz and Guildenstern
HAMLET What ho, Horatio!
         Enter Horatio
HORATIO Here, sweet lord, at your service.
HAMLET
Horatio, thou art e'en as just a man
As e'er my conversation coped withal.   50
HORATIO
O my dear lord—
HAMLET   Nay, do not think I flatter;
For what advancement may I hope from thee
That no revenue hast but thy good spirits
To feed and clothe thee? Why should the poor be flattered?

42.1 *Exeunt Players*] F (*subs.*) Q1 ; *not in* Q2   45 *Exit Polonius*] F ; *not in* Q2   46 ROSENCRANTZ
and GUILDENSTERN] F (*Both*); *Ros⟨encrantz⟩* Q2   We will] F ; I Q2   *Exeunt Rosencrantz and
Guildenstern*] Q2 (*Exeunt they two.*); *Exeunt.* F   47.1 *Enter Horatio*] Q2; *before* 47 F   51
HAMLET] F ; *not in* Q2 (*except as catchword*)

---

41 **villainous** i.e. cheap and objectionable
42 **uses it. Go** Between the end of the one
sentence and the beginning of the next Q1
inserts some examples of the kind of thing
the Prince is condemning. The passage
runs thus: 'And then you have some
again that keeps one suit of jests, as a man
is known by one suit of apparel; and
gentlemen quotes his jests down in their
tables, before they come to the play, as
thus: "Cannot you stay till I eat my por-
ridge?" and "You owe me a quarter's
wages", and "My coat wants a cullison
[i.e. badge]", and "Your beer is sour";
and blabbering with his lips, and thus
keeping in his cinquepace of jests, when,
God knows, the warm clown cannot

make a jest unless by chance, as the blind
man catcheth a hare. Masters, tell him of
it. | PLAYERS We will, my lord.'
48 **sweet** dear. *Sweet*, when used in addressing a person, conveyed respect as well as
affection (*OED adj.* 8b).
49 **just** (1) honest (2) well-adjusted,
balanced
50 **conversation** dealings with men (including but not restricted to 'talk') (*OED* 2)
coped withal met with, encountered (*OED
v.*² 5). Compare *Winter's Tale* 4.4.416,
'The royal fool thou cop'st with'.
53 **revenue** The accent falls on the second
syllable.
54 **Why . . . flattered** i.e. what point is there
in flattering the poor

No, let the candied tongue lick absurd pomp,
And crook the pregnant hinges of the knee
Where thrift may follow fawning. Dost thou hear?
Since my dear soul was mistress of her choice
And could of men distinguish, her election
Hath sealed thee for herself. For thou hast been   60
As one, in suff'ring all, that suffers nothing,
A man that Fortune's buffets and rewards
Hath ta'en with equal thanks; and blest are those
Whose blood and judgement are so well commingled
That they are not a pipe for Fortune's finger
To sound what stop she please. Give me that man
That is not passion's slave, and I will wear him
In my heart's core, ay, in my heart of heart,
As I do thee. Something too much of this.

55 tongue lick] Q2; tongue, like F   57 fawning] Q2 (fauning); faining F   58 her] Q2; my
F   59 distinguish, her election] F; distinguish her election, Q2   60 Hath] F, S'hath Q2   63
Hath] F; Hast Q2   64 commingled] F (co-mingled); comedled Q2

55–7 No . . . fawning As Walter Whiter (1758–1832) was the first to notice, the complex association of ideas in this passage recurs several times in Shakespeare. Commenting on these lines and on *1 Henry IV* 1.3.251–2, *Timon* 4.3.222–6, and *Antony* 3.13.165 and 4.12.19–23, he remarks: 'These passages are very singular. The curious reader will observe that the *fawning obsequiousness* of an animal, or an attendant, is connected with the word *candy*.' (*A Specimen of a Commentary on Shakespeare*, ed. Alan Over and Mary Bell [1967], p. 123 n. 1)

55 the candied tongue (1) the tongue of the dog that tries to make itself sweet to its master by licking his hand (2) the tongue of the courtier who tries to make himself sweet to his king by uttering honeyed words to him. Compare *K. John* 1.1.213, where flattery is described as 'Sweet, sweet, sweet poison for the age's tooth.'
absurd pomp i.e. the pompous man whose pretensions are empty and ridiculous

56 crook bend (for 'crooked' purposes)
pregnant readily inclined (to be so bent). This sense of *pregnant* (*OED a.*[2] 3d) seems to have been introduced into English by Shakespeare. Compare *Twelfth Night* 3.1.85–6, 'My matter hath no voice, lady, but to your own most pregnant and

vouchsafed ear.'

57 thrift profit (*OED sb.*[1] 2). Compare *Merchant* 1.3.45–6, 'my bargains, and my well-won thrift, | Which he calls interest.'

58 was mistress of her choice i.e. became capable of choosing for herself

60–9 For thou . . . do thee In these lines Hamlet equates Horatio with the Stoic ideal.

61 that suffers nothing (because he rises superior to suffering). Compare Samuel Daniel's assertion 'that unless above himself he can | Erect himself, how poor a thing is man' ('To the Lady Margaret, Countess of Cumberland', ll. 98–9).

64 blood and judgement passion and reason
commingled mingled together. Like *commedled*, the reading of Q2, this word appears to be a Shakespearian invention.

65–6 That they . . . please Hamlet makes a similar claim for himself at ll.346–54. The idea was a commonplace; compare 'He dances well to whom Fortune pipes' and 'Little wit serves to whom Fortune pipes' (Tilley F611 and W560).

68 heart's core . . . heart of heart The probability that *heart's core*, invented by Shakespeare (*OED core sb.*[1] 14b), involves word play on the Latin *cor* becomes a virtual certainty when it is noticed that *heart of heart* is a translation of *cor cordis*.

There is a play tonight before the King.   70
One scene of it comes near the circumstance
Which I have told thee of my father's death.
I prithee, when thou seest that act afoot,
Even with the very comment of thy soul
Observe my uncle. If his occulted guilt
Do not itself unkennel in one speech,
It is a damnèd ghost that we have seen,
And my imaginations are as foul
As Vulcan's stithy. Give him heedful note;
For I mine eyes will rivet to his face;   80
And, after, we will both our judgements join
To censure of his seeming.
HORATIO   Well, my lord.
If he steal aught the whilst this play is playing
And scape detecting, I will pay the theft.
HAMLET
They are coming to the play. I must be idle.
Get you a place.
> *A Danish March. A flourish of trumpets. Enter*
> *Claudius, Gertrude, Polonius, Ophelia, Rosencrantz,*
> *Guildenstern, and other lords attendant, with the*
> *King's Guard carrying torches*

74 thy] Q2 ; my F   75 my] Q2 ; mine F   79 stithy] Q2 ; Stythe F   heedful] Q2 ; needfull F   82
To] F ; In Q2   83 he] F ; a Q2   84 detecting] F ; detected Q2   86.1–4 *A Danish March . . .*
torches]   F   (subs.);   *Enter   Trumpets   and   Kettle   Drummes,   King,   Queene,*
Polonius, Ophelia Q2 ; *Enter King, Queene, Corambis, and other Lords* Q1 *(after l. 84* FQ2 ; *after l. 86*
Q1)   91 mine now. My lord, you] JOHNSON ; mine. Now my Lord, you F ; mine now my Lord, You
Q2 ; My lord, you Q1

71 **scene** i.e. part of the action
71–2 **the circumstance . . . death** This is the
    first intimation we have that Hamlet has
    confided the Ghost's story to Horatio.
73 **act** i.e. the *scene* of l. 71
74 **the very comment of thy soul** i.e. the
    most concentrated attention every faculty
    of your soul can bring to bear
75 **occulted** carefully concealed : not else-
    where in Shakespeare
76 **unkennel** reveal. Shakespeare thinks of
    Claudius's guilt as a fox that has to be
    dislodged from its hole. Compare *Merry
    Wives* 3.3.144, 'we'll unkennel the fox.'
79 **Vulcan's stithy** Vulcan's smithy. As Vul-
    can was the god of smiths, his smithy was
    thought of as being blacker than any
    earthly smithy, and as having affinities

with hell.
80 **mine eyes will rivet** This is the earliest
    example of the phrase cited by *OED* (*rivet
    v*. 4).
82 **censure of his seeming** i.e. decide on the
    significance of his reactions
83–4 **steal aught . . . detecting** i.e. manages
    to get away with anything unobserved
84 **pay the theft** i.e. take the blame (literally
    'pay for the thing that is stolen')
85 **be idle** (1) be mad, resume my antic dis-
    position (2) be unoccupied. For the first
    sense compare *Shrew* Induction 2.12,
    'Heaven cease this idle humour in your
    honour'
86.4 *carrying torches* (to make it clear to
    the audience that on stage it is now night)

252

CLAUDIUS   How fares our cousin Hamlet?

HAMLET Excellent, i'faith, of the chameleon's dish. I eat the
air, promise-crammed. You cannot feed capons so.

CLAUDIUS I have nothing with this answer, Hamlet; these
words are not mine.   90

HAMLET No, nor mine now. (*To Polonius*) My lord, you
played once i'th' university, you say?

POLONIUS That I did, my lord, and was accounted a good
actor.

HAMLET And what did you enact?

POLONIUS I did enact Julius Caesar. I was killed i'th' Capitol.
Brutus killed me.

HAMLET It was a brute part of him to kill so capital a calf
there.—Be the players ready?

93 I did] FQ1; did I Q2   95 And] F; *not in* Q2Q1

86 **fares** (1) is (the sense in which Claudius
means it) (2) well fed is (the sense in
which Hamlet takes it)

87–8 **Excellent . . . so** This speech is a rapid
series of pointed quibbles designed to give
Claudius the impression that thwarted
ambition is the cause of Hamlet's strange
behaviour.

87 **chameleon's dish** From '[chameleons']
inanimate appearance, and power of existing for long periods without food, they
were formerly supposed to live on air.
These attributes made the name famous
and familiar to many who knew nothing
else of the animal' (*OED*).

87–8 **I eat . . . so** Hamlet refers to the proverbial saying 'A man cannot live on air like
a chameleon' (Tilley M226); quibbles on
air and *heir*, to suggest that Claudius's
naming him 'the most immediate to our
throne' (1.2.109) has brought him no
material advantage; and concludes by
saying that even *capons*–castrated cocks,
regarded as types of stupidity because
they allow themselves to be *crammed* with
food in order to fit them for the table—
would not be taken in by such empty
promises as Claudius's have proved to be.
For this sense of *capon*, see *Errors* 3.1.32,
'Mome, malt-horse, capon, coxcomb,
idiot, patch!' *Promise-crammed* appears to
be a Shakespearian coinage.

89 **nothing with** i.e. nothing to do with

90 **not mine** i.e. bear no relationship to anything I said, are irrelevant to my question

91 **nor mine now** (because they have left my
lips and cannot be recalled). Compare
'While the word is in your mouth it is
your own, when it is once spoken it is
another's' (Tilley W776).

92 **i'th' university** Plays, usually though by
no means invariably in Latin, were performed by students at the universities during
the sixteenth and early seventeenth centuries.

96 **I did enact Julius Caesar** For the
likelihood of an 'in' joke here, see
Introduction, pp 3 4.
i'th' Capitol In fact, Caesar was
assassinated in the Curia Pompeii, not in
the Capitol; but the mistake, which
Shakespeare also makes in *Caesar* and in
Antony, was an old one, going back at
least as far as Chaucer's 'The Monk's
Tale' (ll. 713–15).

98 **brute part of** brutal action by
so capital a calf such a prize fool (a *calf*
being regarded as the type of mental and
physical imbecility). Compare the ironical
saying 'As wise as a calf' (Dent C16.1)
There also appears to have been some
peculiar connection in Shakespeare's
mind between *calves* and *the Capitol*; see
Coriolanus 3.1.238–40, where the hero
says of the plebs: 'I would they were bar-
barians, as they are | Though in Rome
littered; not Romans, as they are, |
Though calved i'th porch o'th'
Capitol.'

ROSENCRANTZ Ay, my lord, they stay upon your patience.   100
GERTRUDE Come hither, my good Hamlet, sit by me.
HAMLET No, good mother, here's metal more attractive.
      He joins Ophelia
POLONIUS (*to Claudius*) O ho! Do you mark that?
HAMLET Lady, shall I lie in your lap?
OPHELIA No, my lord.
HAMLET I mean, my head upon your lap.
OPHELIA Ay, my lord.
HAMLET Do you think I meant country matters?
OPHELIA I think nothing, my lord.
HAMLET That's a fair thought to lie between maids' legs.   110
OPHELIA What is, my lord?
HAMLET No-thing.
OPHELIA You are merry, my lord.
HAMLET Who, I?
OPHELIA Ay, my lord.
HAMLET O God, your only jig-maker. What should a man do
      but be merry? For look you how cheerfully my mother
      looks, and my father died within's two hours.
OPHELIA Nay, 'tis twice two months, my lord.
HAMLET So long? Nay then, let the devil wear black, for I'll   120
      have a suit of sables. O heavens, die two months ago, and

---

101 good] F; deere Q2   106-7 HAMLET I mean . . . lord] F; *not in* Q2   113 lord.] Q2;
Lord? F

100 **stay upon your patience** await your per-
    mission (to begin)
102 **metal more attractive** This is the con-
    ventional language of Elizabethan love
    poetry, in which the lady is thought of as
    a magnet. Hamlet plays the melancholy
    lover for the moment, but his purpose in
    doing so is a practical one: to avoid sitting
    beside Gertrude, where he would be un-
    able to watch Claudius, seated on the
    other side of her.
104 **lie in your lap** As well as carrying its
    normal sense, the phrase, as Ophelia
    realizes, brings sexual innuendo with it.
    Compare *Much Ado* 5.2.88–9, 'I will . . .
    die in thy lap', and *OED lap sb.*¹ 2b.
108 **country matters** sexual intercourse
    (quibbling indecently on the first syllable
    of *country*)
110 **fair** (1) pleasant (2) modest

112 **No-thing** (probably punning on 'thing'
    meaning 'penis')
116 **only jig-maker** i.e. unrivalled master in
    the art of composing pointless nothings.
    The *jig*, which often followed a play, was
    usually devised by the leading clown.
    Hamlet seems to be castigating himself for
    having done nothing, except play the fool.
118 **within's** within this
120-1 **let the devil . . . sables** Like so many
    of Hamlet's other remarks, this one is
    enigmatic. The Prince means, perhaps,
    'let the devil have my inky cloak, for,
    since my father is, amazing though it
    seems, not forgotten yet, I will wear more
    splendid mourning'. This gloss, which is
    substantially Jenkins's, rests on the recog-
    nition that the fur of the *sable* was gener-
    ally thought of as black.

not forgotten yet! Then there's hope a great man's memory may outlive his life half a year. But, by'r Lady, he
must build churches then, or else shall he suffer not
thinking on, with the hobby-horse, whose epitaph is 'For
O, for O, the hobby-horse is forgot'.

Oboes play. The dumb show enters.

*Enter a King and a Queen very lovingly, the Queen em-
bracing him and he her. She kneels, and makes show of
protestation unto him. He takes her up, and declines his
head upon her neck. He lays him down upon a bank of
flowers. She, seeing him asleep, leaves him. Anon comes
in a fellow, takes off his crown, kisses it, and pours poison
in the King's ears, and exits. The Queen returns, finds the
King dead, and makes passionate action. The Poisoner,*

123 by'r Lady] F (byrlady); ber Lady Q2   he] F; a Q2   124 he] F; a Q2   126.1 *Oboes play.
The dumb show enters*] F; *The Trumpets sounds. Dumbe show followes* Q2   126.2 *a Queen*] Q2;
Queene F   *very lovingly*] F; not in Q2   126.3 *and he her*] Q2; not in F   126.3–4 *She kneels
. . . him*] F; not in Q2   126.5 He] Q2; not in F   lays] F (Layes); lyes Q2   126.6–7 *comes in a
fellow*] F; *come in an other man* Q2   126.7 and] F; not in Q2   126.8 King's] F; sleepers Q2
exits] F; leaues him Q2   126.9 and makes] F; makes Q2

124–5 **suffer not thinking on** i.e. have to put
up with being forgotten
125–6 **the hobby-horse . . . is forgot** A
familiar figure in the morris dances which
were a prominent feature of May-games,
the *hobby-horse* was a male dancer wearing a paste-board representation of a
horse round his waist. The foot-cloth of
the horse reached to the ground, thus
concealing the dancer's legs and feet,
while false legs dangled from the saddle.
How the hobby-horse came to be equated
with 'that which is forgotten' is not
known; but the catch-phrase Hamlet
refers to was already in existence by about
1595, for *OED*'s first citation of it is from
LLL 3.1.25–6, where the love-sick Ar-
mado groans out 'But O—but O—', and
Moth completes the sentence by adding
'The hobby-horse is forgot.' Further
evidence provided by *OED* (*hobby-horse*
2b) shows that there was a ballad, now
lost, in which the words served as the
refrain. In frequent use for about forty
years, the phrase then seems, appropriately enough, to have disappeared
completely.
126.1 **dumb show** Dumb shows, i.e. mimes
portraying the action that is to follow in

allegorical terms, as in *A Warning for Fair
Women*, or actions that have taken place
elsewhere, were common in the dramatic
tradition Shakespeare inherited. By the
time he wrote *Hamlet*, however, they had
become old-fashioned and, consequently,
very suitable to accompany the deliberately outmoded *Murder of Gonzago*. There
has been much debate about the purpose
of this one. What is often forgotten is that
Claudius, unlike the audience for *Hamlet*
which is in the secret, has no suspicion to
begin with that *The Murder of Gonzago* is
anything other than what it purports to
be—a typical tragedy of the time. The
dumb show, which very significantly does
not reveal that the Poisoner is in any way
related to the Player King and Queen, is
designed to awaken his interest enough to
ensure that he will watch the play with
close attention, instead of falling asleep as
Polonius, according to Hamlet (2.2.491),
is prone to do.
126.3–4 **makes show of protestation** i.e.
uses the gestures appropriate to an
affirmation of love.
126.9 **passionate action** i.e. gestures expressive of deep sorrow

*with some two or three Mutes, comes in again, seeming
to lament with her. The dead body is carried away. The
Poisoner woos the Queen with gifts. She seems loath and
unwilling awhile, but in the end accepts his love.*

Exeunt

OPHELIA What means this, my lord?

HAMLET Marry, this is miching malicho. That means
mischief.

OPHELIA Belike this show imports the argument of the play.   130

Enter Prologue

HAMLET We shall know by this fellow. The players cannot
keep counsel; they'll tell all.

OPHELIA Will he tell us what this show meant?

HAMLET Ay, or any show that you'll show him. Be not you
ashamed to show, he'll not shame to tell you what it
means.

OPHELIA You are naught, you are naught. I'll mark the
play.

126.10 *two or three Mutes, comes*] F; *three or foure come* Q2   126.10–11 *seeming to lament*] F;
seeme to condole Q2   126.12–13 *loath and unwilling*] F; *harsh* Q2   126.13 *his*] F; *not in* Q2
Exeunt] F; *not in* Q2   128 *this is*] FQ1   *this* Q2   *miching malicho*] F (*Miching Malicho*);
munching Malico Q2; *myching Mallico* Q1   *That*] FQ1   *it* Q2   130.1 *Enter Prologue*] THEO-
BALD; *after 138* F; *after* fellow (*131*) Q2; *after 127* Q1   131 *this fellow*] Q2Q1; *these Fellowes* F
132 *counsel*] FQ1; *not in* Q2   133 *he*] Q1; *they* F; *a* Q2   134 *you'll*] FQ1; *you will* Q2

---

127 **this** i.e. the dumb show
128 **miching** lurking, skulking, waiting for
the chance to steal something. The verb
'to mich' (*OED* miche) was common
enough, and, in the sense of 'to play
truant', still survives in some parts of
England. Shakespeare does not use it
elsewhere, but he has the noun *micher* at
1 Henry IV 2.4.399.
 malicho The likeliest explanation of this
nonce-word is that it comes from the
Spanish *malhecho*, meaning 'wrong-
doing', to which Shakespeare has given a
general sense, making it the equivalent of
iniquity and thus bringing it into line with
one of the allegorical characters found in
the morality plays of the fifteenth and sixteenth centuries, a character he was
thoroughly familiar with. Compare
Richard III 3.1.82–3, 'Thus, like the for-
mal vice, Iniquity | I moralize two mean-
ings in one word.'

means (1) signifies (2) purposes
129 **mischief** bad trouble, wicked deeds (the
sense is much stronger than it is in
modern English)
130 **argument** story, plot
131–3 **this fellow . . . Will he** F's muddled
version of this passage is probably due to
Compositor B, misled by the reference to
'the Players' into thinking the plural was
intended throughout.
132 **keep counsel** keep a secret (*OED counsel sb.* 5d)
134 **Ay . . . show him** Wilson refers very
aptly to a passage in Ben Jonson's *Con-
versations with Drummond*: 'one other lay
divers times with a woman, who
shew[ed] him all that he wished except
the last act, which she would never agree
to' (Jonson i. 140. 292–4).
 Be not you i.e. if you are not
137 **naught** bad, offensive, indecent

PROLOGUE

> For us, and for our tragedy,
> Here stooping to your clemency, 140
> We beg your hearing patiently. *Exit*

HAMLET Is this a prologue, or the posy of a ring?

OPHELIA 'Tis brief, my lord.

HAMLET As woman's love.

Enter Player King and Player Queen

PLAYER KING

> Full thirty times hath Phoebus' cart gone round
> Neptune's salt wash and Tellus' orbèd ground,
> And thirty dozen moons with borrowed sheen
> About the world have times twelve thirties been,
> Since love our hearts, and Hymen did our hands,
> Unite commutual in most sacred bands. 150

PLAYER QUEEN

> So many journeys may the sun and moon
> Make us again count o'er ere love be done.
> But woe is me, you are so sick of late,
> So far from cheer and from your former state,

141 Exit] not in FQ2Q1 144.1 *Player King and Player Queen*] POPE (subs.); *King and his Queene* F, *King and Queene* Q2 | *the Duke and Duchesse* Q1 145, etc. PLAYER KING] FQ2 (subs.); *Duke* Q1 146 orbèd] F; orb'd the Q2 151, etc. PLAYER QUEEN] Q2 (Quee⟨ne⟩); Bap⟨tista⟩ F (Qu⟨eene⟩ at 213); *Dutchesse* Q1 154 your] F; our Q2 former] Q2; forme F

142 **posy of a ring** brief motto, usually in verse, inscribed on the inside of a finger-ring. Compare *Merchant* 5.1.147–50, 'a hoop of gold, a paltry ring | That she did give me, whose posy was | For all the world like cutler's poetry | Upon a knife, "Love me, and leave me not"'.

145–73 **Full thirty . . . in bed** Like the passage about Pyrrhus in 2.2, *The Murder of Gonzago* is sharply differentiated from the play proper by its style. But, whereas the manner in the first case is epic in its elevation, that in the second, at least up to line 173, is an exercise in the writing of fustian. The drumming couplets, mostly self-contained, the long-drawn-out sententious commonplaces, the repetition of ideas, the laboured periphrases, the references to classical mythology, and above all, the numerous inversions of normal sentence structure combine with one another to create a most telling criticism of dramatic writing as it was about the time when Shake-

speare left Stratford for London.

145 **Phoebus' cart** Apollo's chariot, the sun. Shakespeare had already made fun of this antiquated periphrasis by including it as 'Phibbus' car' in the tyrant's rant he gives to Bottom (*Dream* 1.2.29).

146 **Neptune's salt wash** 'a bombastic periphrasis for "the Sea"' (*OED wash sb.* 6)

Tellus' orbèd ground i.e. the earth (Tellus being the goddess of the earth, and the earth itself round or *orbèd*). *OED* can cite no pre-Shakespearian use of *orbèd*.

147 **borrowed sheen** borrowed radiance. Compare *Timon* 4.3.435–6, 'the moon's an arrant thief, | And her pale fire she snatches from the sun'. *OED*, citing this as the earliest occurrence of *sheen sb.*[1], notes that the word remained a rare one until the 19th century.

149 **Hymen** classical god of marriage

150 **commutual** reciprocal (earliest instance cited by *OED*)

257

That I distrust you. Yet, though I distrust,
Discomfort you, my lord, it nothing must;
For women's fear and love holds quantity,
In neither aught, or in extremity.
Now what my love is, proof hath made you know,
And as my love is sized, my fear is so.   160

PLAYER KING

Faith, I must leave thee, love, and shortly too;
My operant powers their functions leave to do.
And thou shalt live in this fair world behind,
Honoured, beloved; and, haply, one as kind
For husband shalt thou—

PLAYER QUEEN   O confound the rest!
Such love must needs be treason in my breast.
In second husband let me be accurst;
None wed the second but who killed the first.

HAMLET Wormwood, wormwood.

PLAYER QUEEN

The instances that second marriage move   170
Are base respects of thrift, but none of love.
A second time I kill my husband dead,
When second husband kisses me in bed.

---

157 For] F; For women feare too much, euen as they loue, | And Q2   holds] F; hold Q2   158
In] F; Eyther none, in Q2   159 love] F; Lord Q2   162 their] Q2; my F   164 kind_A] Q5;
kinde. F; kind, Q2   165 thou—] F; thou. Q2   169 Wormwood, wormwood] FQ1 (*subs.*);
That's wormwood Q2 (*in margin*)   170 PLAYER QUEEN] F (*Bapt⟨ista⟩*); *not in* Q2

155 **distrust** fear for, am worried about (not
    elsewhere, in this sense, in Shakespeare)
156 **Discomfort** distress, sadden (*OED v.* 2)
157 **holds quantity** i.e. are in exact propor-
    tion to one another (*OED quantity* 6)
158 **In neither . . . extremity** i.e. either love
    and fear are totally absent or both are
    present to an excessive degree
160 For a passage following this line in Q2
    but not in F, see Appendix A, iv.
    sized of a particular size
162 **operant** vital, active. Compare *Timon*
    4.3.25, 'thy most operant poison'. The
    word seems to be a Shakespearian
    coinage.
    leave to do cease to carry out
167 **In second . . . accurst** i.e. if I marry a
    second husband, let him prove a curse to
    me

168 **None wed . . . first** i.e. 'let no woman
    wed a second husband unless she has
    murdered her first husband' (Kittredge).
    Jenkins prefers to take *none* as plural and
    wed as indicative; but the structure of the
    sentence seems to call for the subjunctive.
169 **Wormwood** (literally, the plant
    Artemisia Absinthium, proverbial for its
    bitter taste, but used figuratively here)
170 **instances** reasons, motives
    move prompt, lead to
171 **respects of thrift** considerations of profit
    or advancement
172 **I kill my husband dead** 'To kill someone
    dead' was, and remains, an English
    idiom (*OED kill v.* 2c), comparable to
    the German *totschlagen*. Compare *Dream*
    3.2.269, 'What, should I hurt her, strike
    her, kill her dead?'

PLAYER KING

I do believe you think what now you speak;
But what we do determine oft we break.
Purpose is but the slave to memory,
Of violent birth, but poor validity;
Which now, like fruit unripe, sticks on the tree,
But fall unshaken when they mellow be.
Most necessary 'tis that we forget   180
To pay ourselves what to ourselves is debt.
What to ourselves in passion we propose,
The passion ending, doth the purpose lose.
The violence of either grief or joy
Their own enactures with themselves destroy.
Where joy most revels, grief doth most lament;
Grief joys, joy grieves, on slender accident.
This world is not for aye, nor 'tis not strange
That even our loves should with our fortunes change;
For 'tis a question left us yet to prove,   190
Whether love lead fortune, or else fortune love.

174 you think] Q2; you. Think F; you sweete. Q1   178 like] F; the Q2   184 either] Q2; other F
185 enactures] Q2 (ennactures); ennactors F   187 joys, joy grieves] F; ioy, loy griefes Q2

174–203 **I do believe . . . is dead** The style of
this speech is, as has often been noticed,
different from that of the rest of the play-
within-the-play. The clumsy inversions
and tautologies have given way to
weighty gnomic statements, which sound
like the fruit of experience and have a
bearing on the development and significance of the tragedy as a whole.

177 **Of violent . . . validity** i.e. strong at the
outset but weak in staying power

178 **Which** (referring to *Purpose*)

178–9 **Which now . . . be** 'The subject,
which is singular, is here confused with,
and lost in, that to which it is compared,
which is plural' (Abbott 415).

180–1 **Most necessary . . . debt** i.e. it is
inevitable that we should forget to carry
out an obligation we have laid on ourselves. Compare *Caesar* 2.2.36–7, 'death,
a necessary end, | Will come when it will
come', and 'Promise is debt' (Tilley
P603).

182–3 **What to . . . lose** i.e. to set oneself a
goal in a moment of passionate excitement is to ensure that the goal will
become meaningless as soon as the excitement subsides

184–5 **The violence . . . destroy** i.e. when
either grief or joy becomes extreme, it
destroys itself in the very process of
manifesting itself. Compare 'Nothing
violent can be permanent' and 'No extreme will hold long' (Tilley N321 and
E222)

185 **enactures** fulfilments (a Shakespearian
coinage; no other instance cited by *OED*)
destroy The verb has been attracted into
the plural by its proximity to *enactures*
(Abbott 412).

187 **slender accident** the slightest excuse

188 **This world . . . aye** proverbial (Tilley
W884)

190 **left us yet to prove** i.e. that we still have
to find the right answer to

191 **Whether . . . love** This very question is
discussed at considerable length in
Soliman and Perseda (*c.*1590), a play usually attributed to Kyd, where Love and
Fortune, together with Death, serve as the
Chorus and compete with one another for
recognition as the supreme arbiter of
human actions, or, as Death puts it, 'Let
the sequel prove | Who is [the] greatest,
Fortune, Death, or Love' (1.6.37–8)

The great man down, you mark his favourite flies;
The poor advanced makes friends of enemies.
And hitherto doth love on fortune tend,
For who not needs shall never lack a friend,
And who in want a hollow friend doth try,
Directly seasons him his enemy.
But, orderly to end where I begun,
Our wills and fates do so contrary run
That our devices still are overthrown;   200
Our thoughts are ours, their ends none of our own.
So think thou wilt no second husband wed;
But die thy thoughts when thy first lord is dead.

PLAYER QUEEN
Nor earth to me give food, nor heaven light,
Sport and repose lock from me day and night,
Each opposite, that blanks the face of joy,
Meet what I would have well, and it destroy,
Both here and hence pursue me lasting strife,
If, once a widow, ever I be wife!

HAMLET If she should break it now!   210

PLAYER KING
'Tis deeply sworn. Sweet, leave me here awhile.
My spirits grow dull, and fain I would beguile
The tedious day with sleep.

    He sleeps

---

192 favourite] Q2; fauourites F   204 me give] Q2; giue me F   209 once a widow, ever I be
wife] FQ1; once I be a widdow, euer I be a wife Q2; *once a widow, ever I be a wife* JENKINS   210
If she . . . now] *As* FQ1 (*subs.*); *in margin of 208 and 209* Q2   213 He sleeps] F (*Sleepes*) *after 213*
(brain); *not in* Q2

194 **hitherto** up to this point, thus far (in the
    argument)
    tend serve, follow
195–7 **For who . . . enemy** Compare the say-
    ing 'In time of prosperity friends will be
    plenty, in time of adversity not one among
    twenty' (Tilley T301).
195 **who not needs** i.e. the man who has no
    need of one
197 **seasons him** matures him into, hardens
    him into. The idea of a tree or piece of
    timber, implicit in *hollow*, is developed
    further here.
199 **contrary** in opposite directions to one
    another
200 **devices** plans, schemes

201 **ends** ultimate consequences
203 **die thy thoughts** i.e. your present inten-
    tions may well cease to exist. For this use
    of the subjunctive see Abbott 364.
205 For a passage following this line in Q2
    but not in F, see Appendix A, v.
    Sport . . . night i.e. let the day afford me
    no recreation and the night no rest
206 **opposite** opponent. Compare 'mighty
    opposites' (5.2.62).
    blanks blanches, makes pale (*OED v.* 1)
208 **here and hence** i.e. in this world and in
    the next. Compare *K. John* 4.2.89, 'This
    [the murder of Arthur] must be answered
    either here or hence.'

PLAYER QUEEN   Sleep rock thy brain,
And never come mischance between us twain!   *Exit*
HAMLET Madam, how like you this play?
GERTRUDE The lady protests too much, methinks.
HAMLET O, but she'll keep her word.
CLAUDIUS Have you heard the argument? Is there no offence
  in't?
HAMLET No, no, they do but jest, poison in jest. No offence   220
  i'th' world.
CLAUDIUS What do you call the play?
HAMLET *The Mousetrap.* Marry, how? Tropically. This play
  is the image of a murder done in Vienna. Gonzago is the
  duke's name; his wife, Baptista. You shall see anon. 'Tis
  a knavish piece of work. But what o' that? Your majesty,
  and we that have free souls, it touches us not. Let the
  galled jade wince, our withers are unwrung.

---

214 *Exit*] FQ1 (*exit Lady*); *Exeunt* Q2   216 protests] FQ1; doth protest Q2   223 how? Tropic-
ally] F, how tropically Q2; how trapically Q1; how tropically! JENKINS   226 o'] F; of Q2; A Q1

---

216 **The lady . . . methinks** Generalized to
the form 'Too much protesting makes the
truth suspected', this remark became
proverbial (Tilley P614).
218 **offence** (1) anything indecent or offensive to good manners (the sense Claudius
has in mind) (2) any criminal action (the
sense Hamlet gives it)
220 **do but jest** are merely playing
223 *The Mousetrap* The obvious thing Hamlet is thinking of when giving the play this
title is his plan to 'catch the conscience of
the King' (2.2.594); but *Hamlet* as a
whole is full of *traps*.
  Marry, how? This reading from F (Marry
how?) makes good sense. Hamlet
anticipates, and then answers, an
imagined query from the King.
  Tropically as a trope, figuratively speaking. Cercignani (p. 105) discounts 'the
dubious jingle *mousetrap–tropically*', often
thought to be reflected in Q1's *trapically*.
224 **image** precise representation
224-5 **a murder . . . Baptista** In October
1538 Francesco Maria della Rovere, Duke
of Urbino died after an illness that had

lasted some six weeks. It was rumoured
that he had been murdered by his barber-
surgeon, suborned to pour poison into his
ears by two of the Duke's enemies, Luigi
Gonzaga, Marchese di Castelgoffredo, and
Cesare Fregoso. Attempts were made to
bring these two men to justice, but with
no success. How Shakespeare picked up a
muddled version of this story, in which
the alleged murderer, Gonzaga, has been
transformed into the victim, is not
known. For details, see Bullough, vii.
28-34, 172-6, and his 'The Murder of
Gonzago', *MLR* 30 (1935), 433-44.
227 **free** innocent, guiltless
227-8 **Let . . . unwrung** 'Touch (Rub) a galled horse on the back and he will wince
(kick)' (Tilley H700) was a very common
saying.
228 **galled** sore from chafing, saddle-sore
  wince kick, lash out. The examples
quoted by Tilley, together with those cited
by *OED* (*wince v.*[1] 1 and *winch v.*[1] 2), make
it quite clear that there was no distinction
between *wince* (Q1) and *winch* (Q2, F).
  withers the highest part of a horse's back

Enter Player Lucianus

This is one Lucianus, nephew to the King.

OPHELIA You are as good as a chorus, my lord.   230

HAMLET I could interpret between you and your love, if I could see the puppets dallying.

OPHELIA You are keen, my lord, you are keen.

HAMLET It would cost you a groaning to take off my edge.

OPHELIA Still better, and worse.

HAMLET So you mis-take your husbands.—Begin, murderer. Pox, leave thy damnable faces and begin. Come —'the croaking raven doth bellow for revenge'.

228.1 *Enter Player Lucianus*] *As* F; *after* 229 Q2   230 as good as a] Q2Q1; a good F   234 my] F; mine Q2   236 mis-take] CAPELL; mistake FQ2; must take Q1   your] Q2Q1; *not in* F   237 Pox] FQ1 (a poxe); *not in* Q2

229 **Lucianus, nephew to the King** Hamlet's reason for putting on a play in which the poisoner is the nephew, not the brother, of the victim has been the subject of much speculation. There may, however, be a simple explanation: if Lucianus were announced as the brother of the Player King, Claudius would either stop the play at once, or, at least, prepare himself for the shock to come and give nothing away. In either case the Prince's experiment would fail.

230 **chorus** It was the function of the *Chorus* or *Presenter*, as he was also called, to narrate action that could not be staged, to supply necessary information, and to explain the meaning of dumb shows. Old Gower, in *Pericles*, is exactly the kind of *chorus* Ophelia is thinking of.

231 **interpret between** (1) provide suitable dialogue for (2) serve as a pander to. As in a Punch and Judy show today, so in a puppet-play in Shakespeare's day, the puppet-master or 'master of the motions', as he was called, ventriloquized for his puppets and was 'the mouth of 'em all', as Lantern Leatherhead puts it in Jonson's *Bartholomew Fair* (5.3.78–9). The same connection between lovers and puppets is made in *Two Gentlemen* 2.1.85–7, 'O excellent motion! O exceeding puppet! Now will he interpret to her.' Hamlet, at this point, thinks of himself as a puppet-master, because the stage audience as well as the Players are dancing to his tune; and, taking this role still further, he now proposes to give Ophelia an imagin-

ary lover and act as their go-between.

233 **keen** (1) bitterly witty, sharply satirical (the sense in which Ophelia means it) (2) sexually sharp-set (the sense in which Hamlet takes it)

234 **groaning** i.e. the cries of a woman losing her maidenhead
take off my edge i.e. satisfy my sharp sexual appetite. The expression was a fairly common one (Dent 57.1).

235 **better, and worse** wittier, and more offensively obscene—another proverbial saying (Tilley B333)

236 **mis-take your husbands** cheat your husbands (by deliberately mistaking, and substituting, one for another). Compare *Winter's Tale* 2.1.81–2, 'You have mistook, my lady, | Polixenes for Leontes', and Jonson's *Masque of Augurs* 34–6, where a Groom is accused of being accustomed 'To fetch . . . a parcel of invisible bread and beer for the Players (for they never see it) or to mistake six torches from the chandlery, and give them one' (Jonson, vii. 630). See also *OED mistake v.* 1. As Q1's *must take* makes especially clear, Hamlet relates Ophelia's remark to the marriage service in which the man and the woman *take* one another 'for better for worse' (Tilley M65), and then quibbles on it, aiming his shafts at Gertrude who *mistook* Claudius for Old Hamlet.

238 **the croaking . . . revenge** These words are a conflation of two lines from the anonymous *True Tragedy of Richard III* (c. 1591), published in 1594: 'The screeching raven sits croaking for

PLAYER LUCIANUS

Thoughts black, hands apt, drugs fit, and time
    agreeing,
Confederate season, else no creature seeing;   240
Thou mixture rank, of midnight weeds collected,
With Hecat's ban thrice blasted, thrice infected,
Thy natural magic and dire property
On wholesome life usurp immediately.

He pours the poison in the Player King's ears

HAMLET He poisons him i'th' garden for's estate. His name's
Gonzago. The story is extant, and writ in choice Italian.
You shall see anon how the murderer gets the love of
Gonzago's wife.

OPHELIA The King rises.

HAMLET What, frighted with false fire?   250

GERTRUDE How fares my lord?

POLONIUS Give o'er the play.

CLAUDIUS Give me some light. Away!

COURTIERS Lights, lights, lights!

Exeunt all but Hamlet and Horatio

---

240 Confederate| FQ1; Considerat Q2   242 ban] FQ2, bane Q1   infected] FQ1; Inuected Q2
244 usurp] F (vsurpe); vsurps Q2Q1   244.1 *He pours . . . ears*] F (*Powres the poyson in his eares*);
not in Q2; *exit* Q1   245 He] FQ1; A Q2   for's] F; for his Q2Q1   246 writ in choice] F; written
in very choice Q2   250 HAMLET What, frighted with false fire?| FQ1 (*fires*); *not in* Q2   254
COURTIERS| F (*All*); Pol⟨onius⟩ Q2   all but| Q2; Manet F

---

revenge | Whole herds of beasts comes
bellowing for revenge' (Bullough, iii. 339.
1892–3). 'The croaking raven bodes misfortune' (Tilley R33) was a well-worn
commonplace.

240 **Confederate . . . seeing** i.e. the occasion
itself conspiring to assist me, since there is
no one to observe me. Onions calls this
use of *confederate* 'strained'.

241 **of midnight weeds collected** i.e. distilled
from weeds gathered at midnight; *collected* seems to refer both to the time and the
process. It was widely thought that
poisonous herbs were most potent when
picked at midnight. Compare *Macbeth*
4.1.25, 'Root of hemlock digged i'th'
dark'.

242 **With Hecat's ban** by Hecate's curse.
Hecate, the tri-form goddess of the underworld and of witchcraft, seems to have

had a special place in Shakespeare's
imagination, probably because of the
large role she plays in Ovid's version of the
story of Jason and Medea (*Metamorphoses*,
vii).

  thrice Three was, of course, a magical
number. Compare the three witches in
Macbeth who chant 'Thrice to thine, and
thrice to mine, | And thrice again, to make
up nine' (1.3.35–6).

244 **On wholesome life usurp** let them
supplant wholesome life (*OED usurp v.*
9a). Compare *Pericles* 3.2.87, 'Death may
usurp on nature many hours'.

245 **estate** i.e. position and possessions

250 **false fire** fire-works (*feu d'artifice*) or
discharge of fire-arms loaded with blank
cartridges. Dent (F40.1) provides another
example of *false fire*.

HAMLET

>Why, let the stricken deer go weep,
>   The hart ungallèd play;
>For some must watch, while some must sleep,
>   So runs the world away.

Would not this, sir, and a forest of feathers—if the rest of
my fortunes turn Turk with me—with two Provincial   260
roses on my razed shoes, get me a fellowship in a cry of
players, sir?

HORATIO Half a share.

HAMLET A whole one, I.

>For thou dost know, O Damon dear,
>   This realm dismantled was
>Of Jove himself, and now reigns here
>   A very, very—pajock.

255 stricken] Q1; strucken F; strooken Q2   258 So] F; Thus Q2Q1   260 two] F; *not in*
Q2   262 sir] F; *not in* Q2   268 pajock] F (Paiocke); paiock Q2; Pajocke F2; Paicock Q1676;
Pecock Q1695; peacock POPE

255-8 **Why . . . away** These lines are usually considered to be a stanza from some
lost ballad; and, since *Hamlet* makes considerable use of popular poetry, the notion
seems a likely one.

255 **Why . . . weep** Compare 'As the stricken
deer withdraws himself to die' (Tilley
D189). Of the examples cited by Tilley,
only this and the description of the wounded stag in *As You Like It* (2.1.33-43)
refer to the deer's weeping.

257-8 **For some . . . away** Compare Dent
W884.1, 'Thus goes the world'.

257 **watch** stay awake

259 **this** i.e. this device of mine. Hamlet,
wildly elated by his success, congratulates
himself on his performance as playwright
and producer.

   a forest of feathers Feathers, prepared
and sold in the Blackfriars district of London, were much worn on the stage.

260 **turn Turk with me** desert me (like a
renegade deserting the Christian faith to
become a Moslem). A proverbial phrase
(Tilley T609).

260-1 **Provincial roses** large rosettes which
concealed the ties of shoes. Jenkins gives
some good reasons for thinking that
Provincial roses, so called because they
came from Provence, were cabbage roses.

   razed slashed (*OED race* v.[1] 1b)

fellowship partnership (*OED sb.* 1a), the
position of a *sharer*, i.e. a regular member
of an acting company who was not paid
wages but received a share, or *half a share*
(l. 263), of the takings

   cry pack (used contemptuously for 'company'). *Cry* is the technical term for 'a
pack of hounds' (*OED sb.* 13, 13b). Compare *Coriolanus* 3.3.122, 'You common
cry of curs'.

265 **Damon** Hamlet is probably alluding to
the often told story of Damon and Pythias,
the perfect friends. The tale has its place in
Sir Thomas Elyot's *The Governor* (II. xi),
and it had been dramatized by Richard
Edwards in his *Damon and Pithias*
(*c*.1565).

266 **dismantled** stripped, deprived. When
dismantle first appeared in English (1579,
according to *OED*) it did so as a military
term concerned with the dismantling
of fortifications and the like. Something
of that sense persists here. Denmark,
says Hamlet, has been deprived of its
bulwark—his father.

268 **pajock** The word Horatio expects to
hear is, of course, *ass*. The word Hamlet
speaks—*paiock* (Q2)/*Paiocke* (F1)—introduces an altogether more problematic
creature, utterly unknown elsewhere
in English. *Pajock* could be a nonsense

HORATIO You might have rhymed.

HAMLET O good Horatio, I'll take the ghost's word for a   270
thousand pound. Didst perceive?

HORATIO Very well, my lord.

HAMLET Upon the talk of the poisoning?

HORATIO I did very well note him.

Enter Rosencrantz and Guildenstern

HAMLET Ah, ha! Come, some music. Come, the recorders.
For if the King like not the comedy,
Why then, belike, he likes it not, pardie.
Come, some music.

GUILDENSTERN Good my lord, vouchsafe me a word with
you.   280

HAMLET Sir, a whole history.

GUILDENSTERN The King, sir—

HAMLET Ay, sir, what of him?

GUILDENSTERN Is in his retirement marvellous distempered.

HAMLET With drink, sir?

GUILDENSTERN No, my lord, rather with choler.

HAMLET Your wisdom should show itself more richer to
signify this to his doctor; for, for me to put him to his

274.1 *Enter Rosencrantz and Guildenstern*] F; *after 278* Q2; *after 277* JOHNSON   275 Ah, ha!]
Q2 (Ah ha,); Oh, ha? F   286 rather] F; *not in* Q2   288 his doctor] F; the Doctor Q2

word or it could be a corruption of some other word. In the latter case the possibilities come down to two: *peacock* or *patchcock/patchock*, a nonce-word used by Spenser in his *The State of Ireland* to describe the degenerate English living in Ireland, and apparently meaning 'clown', or something very like it.

270–1 **for a thousand pound** i.e. as absolutely reliable. The hyperbolical use of *a thousand pound* was well established (Dent T248.1).

275 **Ah, ha!** This interjection, expressive of suspicion, seems to be prompted by the arrival of Rosencrantz and Guildenstern.

276–7 **For if . . . pardie** This couplet is a neat and pointed bit of parody. In Kyd's *The Spanish Tragedy*, Hieronimo, having made all the arrangements for putting on his play-within-the-play, looks forward to its

performance, saying as he does so: 'And if the world like not this tragedy, | Hard is the hap of old Hieronimo' (4.1.197–8).

276 **comedy** For Hamlet *The Mousetrap* has indeed been a comedy, because it has had a prosperous outcome, having produced the effect it was designed to.

277 **pardie** indeed, assuredly (*pardieu*)

284 **retirement** withdrawal from public view

284 **distempered** (1) annoyed (Guildenstern's meaning) (2) drunk (the sense Hamlet puts on it). See *OED v.*[1] 3 and 4c; and compare *Othello* 1.1.100, 'Being full of supper and distempering draughts'.

286 **choler** (1) anger (*OED sb.*[1] 2) (2) bilious attack (1c)

287 **more richer** i.e. far more resourceful (double comparative for emphasis)

purgation, would perhaps plunge him into far more
choler.   290

GUILDENSTERN Good my lord, put your discourse into some
frame, and start not so wildly from my affair.

HAMLET I am tame, sir. Pronounce.

GUILDENSTERN The Queen your mother, in most great affliction of spirit, hath sent me to you.

HAMLET You are welcome.

GUILDENSTERN Nay, good my lord, this courtesy is not of the
right breed. If it shall please you to make me a wholesome
answer, I will do your mother's commandment. If not,
your pardon and my return shall be the end of my busi-   300
ness.

HAMLET Sir, I cannot.

GUILDENSTERN What, my lord?

HAMLET Make you a wholesome answer; my wit's diseased.
But, sir, such answers as I can make, you shall command;
or rather, as you say, my mother. Therefore no more, but
to the matter. My mother, you say—

ROSENCRANTZ Then thus she says: your behaviour hath
struck her into amazement and admiration.

HAMLET O wonderful son, that can so astonish a mother!   310
But is there no sequel at the heels of this mother's admiration? Impart.

ROSENCRANTZ She desires to speak with you in her closet ere
you go to bed.

HAMLET We shall obey, were she ten times our mother.
Have you any further trade with us?

289 far] F (farre); *not in* Q2   292 start] F; stare Q2   300 of my] F; of Q2   303 GUILDENSTERN]
F; *Ros⟨encrantz⟩* Q2   305 answers] F; answere Q2   306 as you] Q2; you F   310 astonish]
F; stonish Q2   312 Impart] Q2; *not in* F

289 **purgation** Hamlet quibbles on three different meanings of the word: (1) medical
purging, including blood-letting (2)
spiritual purging (3) legal purging, the
process of clearing oneself from the accusation of crime (*OED* 1b, 3, 4). Compare *Richard II* 1.1.153, 'Let's purge this
choler without letting blood'.
292 **frame** form, coherent shape (with, perhaps, a latent pun on the *frame*, also
known as a *trave*, in which a restive horse
was placed to be shod)
    start i.e. shy away like a startled horse
293 **Pronounce** i.e. say your piece

298 **breed** (1) kind (2) breeding in courtly
manners
    wholesome sensible, rational
300 **pardon** permission to leave you
309 **amazement and admiration** i.e.
bewildered astonishment
315–16 **We... our ... us** Hamlet's assumption of the royal *we* is intended to show the
two courtiers that he will stand no further
interrogation from them.
315 **were she ten times our mother** 'Ten
times' was a common form of hyperbole
(Dent T343.1).
316 **trade** business (used contemptuously)

ROSENCRANTZ My lord, you once did love me.

HAMLET So I do still, by these pickers and stealers.

ROSENCRANTZ Good my lord, what is your cause of distemper? You do freely bar the door of your own liberty if you   320
deny your griefs to your friend.

HAMLET Sir, I lack advancement.

ROSENCRANTZ How can that be, when you have the voice of
the King himself for your succession in Denmark?

HAMLET Ay, sir, but 'while the grass grows'—the proverb
is something musty.

Enter one with a recorder.

O, the recorder. Let me see. (*To Rosencrantz and Guildenstern whom he takes aside*) To withdraw with you. Why do
you go about to recover the wind of me, as if you would
drive me into a toil?   330

GUILDENSTERN O my lord, if my duty be too bold, my love is
too unmannerly.

HAMLET I do not well understand that. Will you play upon
this pipe?

---

318 So I] F; And Q2   320 freely] F; surely Q2   of] F; vpon Q2   325 sir] Q2; *not in* F   326.1
Enter one with a recorder] F; *Enter the Players with Recorders* Q2 (*after* 324)   327 recorder] F;
Recorders Q2   see] F; see one Q2

318 **pickers and stealers** hands. This picturesque periphrasis, apparently a
Shakespearian invention, is derived from
the Church Catechism in the Book of
Common Prayer, where the catechumen
promises to 'keep my hands from picking
and stealing, and my tongue from evil
speaking, lying and slandering'.

319–20 **your cause of distemper** the cause of
your mental disorder. The construction,
common in Shakespeare's work, can be
explained thus: 'two nouns connected by
"of" are often regarded as one. Hence
sometimes pronominal and other adjectives are placed before the whole compound noun instead of, as they strictly
should be, before the second of the two
nouns' (Abbott 423)

320 **freely** of your own accord. This F reading looks very like a 'second thought'
adding a touch of wit not present in Q2's
surely.

320–1 **bar . . . friend** Compare 'Grief is
lessened when imparted to others' (Tilley

G447). As Jenkins suggests, Rosencrantz
and Guildenstern regard the Prince as one
who has deliberately imprisoned himself
in his own misery.

325 **the proverb** i.e. 'While the grass grows
the horse starves' (Tilley G423)

326 **musty** (because it was already a saying
c.1440, the date of the earliest example
cited in *OED* [*grass sb.*¹ 1b])

328 **withdraw** be private, have a quiet word
(*OED v.* 12)

329 **go about** (1) busy yourself, conspire
(*OED about* A10) (2) take a roundabout
course
  recover the wind get to the windward (a
hunting term). Getting to the windward
of his quarry, so that it can smell him, the
hunter drives it down wind, so that it cannot pick up the scent of his fellow hunters
waiting to take it in their *toil*, i.e. 'net'.

331–2 **if my . . . unmannerly** i.e. 'if, in my
devotion to your interests, I am too bold in
questioning you, it is my love that causes
this breach of good manners' (Kittredge)

GUILDENSTERN My lord, I cannot.

HAMLET I pray you.

GUILDENSTERN Believe me, I cannot.

HAMLET I do beseech you.

GUILDENSTERN I know no touch of it, my lord.

HAMLET 'Tis as easy as lying. Govern these ventages with   340
your fingers and thumb, give it breath with your mouth,
and it will discourse most eloquent music. Look you, these
are the stops.

GUILDENSTERN But these cannot I command to any utterance of harmony. I have not the skill.

HAMLET Why, look you now, how unworthy a thing you
make of me. You would play upon me, you would seem
to know my stops, you would pluck out the heart of my
mystery, you would sound me from my lowest note to the
top of my compass; and there is much music, excellent   350
voice, in this little organ, yet cannot you make it speak.
'Sblood, do you think that I am easier to be played on than
a pipe? Call me what instrument you will, though you can
fret me, you cannot play upon me.

          Enter Polonius
God bless you, sir.

POLONIUS My lord, the Queen would speak with you, and
presently.

---

340 'Tis] F; It is Q2   341 fingers] Q2; finger F   thumb] F (thumbe); the vmber Q2; the thumb
Q3   342 eloquent] Q2; excellent F   349–50 the top of] F; *not in* Q2   351 speak] Q2; *not in*
F   352 'Sblood] Q2; Why F; Zownds Q1   that] F; *not in* Q2Q1   353–4 can fret me, you] F;
fret me not, you Q2; can frett mee, yet you Q1; fret me, you JENKINS   354.1 *Enter Polonius*]
after 355 FQ2

---

339 **know no touch of** i.e. have no notion of
how to play on. Compare *Richard II*
1.3.163–5, 'like a cunning instrument
cased up | Or, being open, put into his
hands | That knows no touch to tune the
harmony.'

340 **ventages** stops. Not found elsewhere in
Shakespeare, the word may well be a
Shakespearian coinage (*OED ventage²*).

349 **mystery** personal secret (*OED mystery¹*
5b)
    sound me (1) play on me, make me give
out sounds (2) fathom me. See *Romeo*

3.2.125–6, 'There is no end, no limit,
measure, bound | In that word's death;
no words can that woe sound.'

351 **organ** i.e. musical (especially wind) instrument, in this case the recorder (*OED
sb.¹* 1)

354 **fret** (1) irritate (2) furnish with frets—a
fret being formerly a ring of gut, and now
a bar or ridge of wood, metal, or the like,
placed on the fingerboard of a lute or
guitar to regulate the fingering. Compare
Shrew 2.1.151, '"Frets, call you these?"
quoth she "I'll fume with them"'.

HAMLET Do you see yonder cloud that's almost in shape of
  a camel?

POLONIUS By th' mass, and it's like a camel indeed.   360

HAMLET Methinks it is like a weasel.

POLONIUS It is backed like a weasel.

HAMLET Or like a whale?

POLONIUS Very like a whale.

HAMLET Then will I come to my mother by and by. (*Aside*)
  They fool me to the top of my bent.—I will come by and
  by.

POLONIUS I will say so.

HAMLET 'By and by' is easily said.   *Exit Polonius*
  Leave me, friends.   *Exeunt all but Hamlet* 370
  'Tis now the very witching time of night,
  When churchyards yawn, and hell itself breathes out
  Contagion to this world. Now could I drink hot blood,
  And do such bitter business as the day
  Would quake to look on. Soft, now to my mother.
  O heart, lose not thy nature. Let not ever

---

358 yonder] Q2Q1; that F   of] Q2Q1; like F   360 mass] Q2; Misse F   it's] F tis Q2; T'is Q1;
'tis—] JENNENS   363 whale?] F; Whale. Q2Q1   365 HAMLET] FQ1; *not in* Q2 (except as catchword)   will I] F; I will Q2; i' le Q1   368, 369 POLONIUS, HAMLET] F; *not in* Q2   369 *Exit*
Polonius] F (*Exit*) *at* 368; *exit Coram*⟨*bis*⟩ Q1 *at* 364; *not in* Q2   370 Leave me friends] F; *after*
367 Q2   *Exeunt all but Hamlet*] *not in* FQ2   372 breathes] F; breakes Q2   374 bitter business
as the] F; busines as the bitter Q2   375 Soft, now] Q2; Soft now, F

358–65 **Do you see . . . mother by and by**
Having warned Rosencrantz and
Guildenstern against trying to 'play upon'
him, Hamlet, giving his assumed madness
its full bent, now proceeds to 'play upon'
Polonius, a most responsive windbag.

362 **backed like a weasel** It would be hard to
find a back less like a camel's than a
weasel's is.

365 **by and by** soon, before long (as distinct
from its usual Shakespearian sense of 'at
once')

366 **fool me . . . bent** i.e. play along with my
fooling though I take it to the limit. The
metaphor comes from archery; a bow is
at its *bent* when it can be drawn no
further.

371 **witching time** i.e. time most suitable for
the activities of witches. The phrase appears to have originated in this passage

(*OED witching ppl.a.* 2b).

372 **yawn** open wide. Compare *Much Ado*
5.3.19, 'Graves, yawn, and yield your
dead.'

373 **Contagion** i.e. pestilential and poisonous influences. Compare *Caesar* 2.1.265,
'the vile contagion of the night'.
  drink hot blood The drinking of blood
was supposed to be an incitement to
homicide. See Jonson's *Catiline* 1.4,
where Catiline kills a slave, mixes his
blood with wine, and says as he drinks it,
'Be firm, my hand, not shed a drop, but
pour | Fierceness into me with it, and fell
thirst | Of more and more, till Rome be left
as bloodless | As ever her fears made her,
or the sword' (Jonson, v. 450).

374 **bitter** cruel (*OED a.* A5)

376 **nature** i.e. normal natural feeling of
affection a son has for his mother

269

The soul of Nero enter this firm bosom.
Let me be cruel, not unnatural.
I will speak daggers to her, but use none.
My tongue and soul in this be hypocrites—   380
How in my words somever she be shent,
To give them seals never my soul consent.   *Exit*

3.3   *Enter Claudius, Rosencrantz, and Guildenstern*
CLAUDIUS
    I like him not; nor stands it safe with us
    To let his madness range. Therefore prepare you.
    I your commission will forthwith dispatch,
    And he to England shall along with you.
    The terms of our estate may not endure
    Hazard so dangerous as doth hourly grow
    Out of his lunacies.

---

379 daggers] FQ1; dagger Q2   382 never my soul] FQ2; my soule shall ne're Q1; never, my soul, CAPELL   *Exit*] Q2Q1; *not in* F
3.3.6 dangerous] F; neer's Q2; near us Q1676   7 lunacies] F; browes Q2; lunes THEOBALD; braues PARROTT–CRAIG, *conj.* Wilson

---

377 **Nero** Nero had his mother Agrippina murdered. Shakespeare refers to the legend that Nero committed the murder himself and ripped open his mother's womb in order to see the place whence he came in *K. John* 5.2.152–3, where the Bastard upbraids the rebellious nobles as 'You bloody Neroes, ripping up the womb | Of your dear mother England'.
379 **speak daggers** The words became proverbial (Dent D8.1).
380 **My tongue . . . hypocrites** i.e. let my soul pretend a savage purpose it does not feel, and let my words express it
381 **shent** rebuked, rated
382 **seals** seals of approval, the confirmation that actions corresponding to the words would provide
    never my soul consent i.e. let my soul never consent
3.3 This scene is the play's centre. In 3.2 the advantage was with Hamlet. It does not remain with him long. The Claudius who enters now is already busy taking vigorous counter-measures. But the play-within-the-play is still working on his conscience, forcing him to kneel in prayer

and thus present the Prince, who enters unseen, with the perfect opportunity to take his revenge. Hamlet lets the opportunity slip. There are good dramatic reasons why he must. He cannot stab a kneeling opponent in the back and still remain a sympathetic hero. This is, of course, Shakespeare's reason, not Hamlet's, which is of a very different kind. But there can be no question that the Prince as he makes his exit has lost the advantage that was his when he entered. He has allowed the initiative to pass to the King.
1 **nor stands . . . us** i.e. it is not consistent with a proper regard for our own safety
2 **range** have unlimited scope
3 **commission** official orders
    dispatch prepare
5 **terms of our estate** i.e. responsibilities of our position (as King)
7 **lunacies** This F reading, replacing the troublesome *browes* of Q2, looks very like a bit of authorial revision. It is true that it produces a line with an extra foot, but such lines are not uncommon in *Hamlet*.
    provide equip. Compare *As You Like It* 1.3.83, 'You, niece, provide yourself'.

GUILDENSTERN   We will ourselves provide.
Most holy and religious fear it is
To keep those many many bodies safe
That live and feed upon your majesty.   10
ROSENCRANTZ
The single and peculiar life is bound
With all the strength and armour of the mind
To keep itself from noyance; but much more
That spirit upon whose weal depends and rests
The lives of many. The cease of majesty
Dies not alone, but like a gulf doth draw
What's near it with it. It is a massy wheel,
Fixed on the summit of the highest mount,
To whose huge spokes ten thousand lesser things
Are mortised and adjoined; which when it falls,   20
Each small annexment, petty consequence,
Attends the boisterous ruin. Never alone
Did the King sigh, but with a general groan.

---

14 weal] Q2; spirit F   17 It is] F; or It is Q2; O, 'tis WILSON   18 summit] ROWE; Somnet
FQ2   22 ruin] F; raine Q2   23 with] F; *not in* Q2

8-23 **Most holy ... groan** It is a nice touch
of irony that this orthodox statement of
16th-century political theory should be
made by a couple of sycophants to a king
who is a usurper and a murderer.
8 **fear** (1) apprehension (2) solicitude
11-13 **The single ... noyance** This is Rosencrantz's definition of the right to self-
preservation.
11 **single and peculiar life** i.e. private individual
13 **noyance** harm
14-15 **That spirit ... many** i.e. the king who
should embody 'The life, the right, and
truth of all [the] realm' (*K. John* 4.3.144)
14 **weal** well-being
depends and rests The verb often takes
the singular form when it precedes a
plural subject (Abbott 335).
15 **lives** livelihoods. At the time when *Hamlet* was first staged many of Elizabeth's
courtiers were wondering anxiously

about what would happen to them when
the old Queen died.
cease of majesty cessation of a king's
reign (at his death)
16 **Dies not alone** i.e. is not merely the death
of one man
gulf whirlpool
17-22 **It is ... ruin** The main idea here is
that of Fortune's wheel, also referred to at
2.2.484-8. The relation between kingly
power and the caprices of Fortune is
a common theme in Shakespeare. See
especially *Lear* 2.4.71-3 and *Timon*
1.1.66-97.
17 **massy** massive
20 **which** as to which, with the consequence
that (Abbott 272)
21 **annexment** adjunct (earliest instance of
this word recorded in *OED*)
petty consequence i.e. unimportant thing
connected with it
22 **boisterous ruin** tumultuous downfall

CLAUDIUS

Arm you, I pray you, to this speedy voyage;
For we will fetters put upon this fear,
Which now goes too free-footed.

ROSENCRANTZ *and* GUILDENSTERN   We will haste us.

Exeunt Rosencrantz and Guildenstern
Enter Polonius

POLONIUS

My lord, he's going to his mother's closet.
Behind the arras I'll convey myself
To hear the process. I'll warrant she'll tax him home.
And, as you said, and wisely was it said,   30
'Tis meet that some more audience than a mother,
Since nature makes them partial, should o'erhear
The speech of vantage. Fare you well, my liege.
I'll call upon you ere you go to bed,
And tell you what I know.

CLAUDIUS   Thanks, dear my lord.   *Exit Polonius*

O, my offence is rank, it smells to heaven.
It hath the primal eldest curse upon't—
A brother's murder. Pray can I not.
Though inclination be as sharp as will,
My stronger guilt defeats my strong intent,   40
And, like a man to double business bound,
I stand in pause where I shall first begin,

---

25 upon] F; about Q2   26 ROSENCRANTZ *and* GUILDENSTERN] F (*Both*); Ros⟨encrantz⟩ Q2   35
Exit Polonius] Q2 (*after* know); *not in* F   38 not.] This edition; not, FQ2   39 will, Q2; will: F

---

24 **Arm you** prepare yourselves. Compare
Dream 1.1.117–8, 'arm yourself | To fit
your fancies to your father's will'.
   speedy imminent, soon to be undertaken
25 **fear** cause of fear
28 **convey** i.e. conceal. *Convey* often carries
overtones of secrecy and stealth with it;
compare *Merry Wives* 3.5.78, 'they conveyed me into a buck-basket'.
29 **process** proceedings
30–3 **And . . . vantage** In fact, this 'brilliant
idea' was Polonius's own (3.1.182–6);
but he flatteringly gives the King the
credit for it while simultaneously
congratulating himself on its ingenuity.
33 **of vantage** besides, in addition. Compare

Othello 4.3.82–3, 'Yes, a dozen; and as
many to th' vantage as would store the
world they played for'; and see *OED vantage sb.* 2b and c.
37 **primal eldest curse** i.e. God's curse on
Cain for murdering his brother Abel
(Genesis 4: 10–12). This is the earliest
example of *primal*, in this sense, recorded
by *OED*. Shakespeare uses *primal* again at
Antony 1.4.41.
39 **Though . . . will** i.e. though my impulse
(to pray) is as strong as my determination
to do so
41 **to double business bound** faced with two
different tasks

And both neglect. What if this cursed hand
Were thicker than itself with brother's blood,
Is there not rain enough in the sweet heavens
To wash it white as snow? Whereto serves mercy
But to confront the visage of offence?
And what's in prayer but this twofold force,
To be forestallèd ere we come to fall,
Or pardoned being down? Then I'll look up.   50
My fault is past—but O, what form of prayer
Can serve my turn? 'Forgive me my foul murder'?
That cannot be, since I am still possessed
Of those effects for which I did the murder—
My crown, mine own ambition, and my queen.
May one be pardoned and retain th'offence?
In the corrupted currents of this world
Offence's gilded hand may shove by justice;
And oft 'tis seen the wicked prize itself
Buys out the law. But 'tis not so above.   60

---

50 pardoned] F (pardon'd); pardon Q2   58 shove] F, showe Q2

43–6 **What if . . . snow** Three well known
sayings seem to lie behind this sentence:
'To wash one's hands of a thing'; 'All the
water in the sea cannot wash out this
stain', and 'As white as snow' (Tilley
H122, W85, and S591). See also Dent
W85, and Isaiah 1: 10–20, where the
mere observance of ceremonies, unaccompanied by appropriate action in the
form of reformation, is condemned out of
hand. The following passage is especially
relevant: 'When you hold out your hands,
I will turn mine eyes from you: and though
ye make many prayers, yet I will hear
nothing at all, seeing your hands are full of
blood. Wash you, make you clean, put
away your evil thoughts out of my sight:
cease from doing of evil . . . though your
sins be as red as scarlet, they shall be as
white as snow' (15–18).
46–7 **Whereto . . . offence** what purpose
does mercy serve if not to oppose sin face
to face
48–50 **twofold force . . . down** i.e. 'Lead us
not into temptation, but deliver us from
evil' (Matthew 6: 13)
50 **look up** take heart, be cheerful (*OED look*

v. 45c). Compare *2 Henry IV* 4.4.113,
'My sovereign lord, cheer up yourself,
look up', and Dent L431.1.
51 **My fault is past** i.e. my sin has already
been committed
54 **effects** fruits, things acquired. This sense
appears to be peculiar to Shakespeare
(*OED sb.* 4).
55 **mine own ambition** i.e. everything I was
ambitious for
56 **retain th'offence** i.e. still keep what one
gained from the crime. 'He that does not
amend what can be amended retains his
offence' (Dr Johnson).
57 **currents** courses, conduct of things
58 **Offence's gilded hand** i.e. the hand of an
offender carrying a bribe of gold; but a
'gilded hand' can also be a hand covered
with blood. Compare *K. John* 2.1.316,
'Hither return all gilt with Frenchmen's
blood.'
     shove by push aside
59 **prize** booty, plunder (*OED sb.*[3] 2)
60 **Buys out** buys off. Compare *K. John*
3.1.164, 'Dreading the curse that money
may buy out'.
     above i.e. in heaven

There is no shuffling, there the action lies
In his true nature, and we ourselves compelled
Even to the teeth and forehead of our faults
To give in evidence. What then? What rests?
Try what repentance can. What can it not?
Yet what can it when one cannot repent?
O wretched state! O bosom black as death!
O limèd soul, that struggling to be free
Art more engaged! Help, angels! Make assay.
Bow, stubborn knees; and heart with strings of steel,   70
Be soft as sinews of the new-born babe.
All may be well.   *He kneels*

     Enter Hamlet

HAMLET
Now might I do it pat, now he is praying.
And now I'll do't.

     ⌈*He draws his sword*⌉
         And so he goes to heaven;

---

69 Help, angels!] THEOBALD; Helpe Angels, F; helpe Angels∧ Q2   70 Bow,] THEOBALD; Bow∧
FQ2   72 *He kneels*] Q1; *not in* FQ2   73 it pat,] F; it, but∧ Q2   he is praying] F; a is a praying
Q2   74 *He draws his sword*] *not in* FQ2Q1   he] F; a Q2

61 **shuffling** evasion, legal chicanery
61–2 **the action . . . nature** (1) the wicked
    deed appears in its true colours (2) the
    proceedings are conducted precisely as
    they should be
62–4 **and we . . . evidence** In English law, as
    distinct from the law of heaven, a man
    could not be forced to give evidence
    against himself, except when on trial for
    treason.
62 **compelled** i.e. are compelled. For the
    omission of the verb 'to be' after *and* see
    Abbott 95.
63 **to the teeth and forehead of** i.e. face to
    face with. Shakespeare often associates
    defiant opposition with bared teeth and a
    frowning forehead. Compare *Richard II*
    1.1.15–17, 'face to face | And frowning
    brow to brow, ourselves will hear | The
    accuser and the accusèd freely speak'.
64 **give in evidence** make our deposition
    What rests what remains, i.e. is there
    anything else I can do
65 **can** is capable of. For this absolute use of
    can see 4.7.72, and Abbott 307.

68–9 **O limèd . . . engaged** Compare 'The
    more the bird caught in the lime strives
    the faster he sticks' (Tilley B380).
68 **limèd** caught by bird-lime (a glutinous
    substance spread on twigs)
69 **engaged** entangled (*OED v.* 11a); earliest
    example of this sense cited in *OED*.
    Make assay make a determined effort
    (*OED assay sb.*14)
70 **heart with strings of steel** Claudius thinks
    of his heart as having hardened so much
    that the tendons (heartstrings), supposed
    to keep it in place, have turned to steel.
73 **pat** very conveniently. The word seems to
    have been associated in Shakespeare's
    mind with the perfectly timed stage
    entrance. See *Dream* 3.1.2 and 5.1.182;
    Lear 1.2.128.
74.1 *He draws his sword* As Jenkins notes,
    Hamlet must draw his sword if he is to
    sheathe it at line 88; and the reading of
    Q1, 'Ay so, come forth and work thy last',
    makes it plain that this is the point at
    which he draws it.

And so am I revenged. That would be scanned.
A villain kills my father; and for that
I, his sole son, do this same villain send
To heaven.
O, this is hire and salary, not revenge.
He took my father grossly, full of bread,   80
With all his crimes broad blown, as flush as May;
And how his audit stands who knows save heaven?
But in our circumstance and course of thought
'Tis heavy with him. And am I then revenged
To take him in the purging of his soul,
When he is fit and seasoned for his passage?
No.

He puts up his sword

Up, sword, and know thou a more horrid hint.
When he is drunk asleep, or in his rage,
Or in th'incestuous pleasure of his bed,   90

---

75 revenged.] F (reueng'd:) Q1 (reuenged:); reuendge, Q2   scanned.] SPENCER; scann'd, F;
scand_A Q2   77 sole] Q2; soule F   79 O] F; Why Q2   hire and salary] F (hyre and Sallery);
base and silly Q2; a benefit Q1; bait and salary WILSON   80 He] FQ1, A Q2   81 With all] F;
Withall Q2   flush] Q2; fresh F   89 drunk asleep] F; drunke, a sleepe Q2

---

75 **would be scanned** needs careful consideration (Abbott 329). The sense
'would be interpreted', countenanced by
Onions and *OED* (*scan v.* 4), seems less
likely, since it assumes a Hamlet more
concerned with what others might say
than with what he himself thinks.

77 **sole son** (and therefore the sole person on
whom the duty of taking revenge rests)

79 **hire and salary** i.e. 'as if I had hired him
to murder my father and am now paying
him his wages' (Kittredge). This F reading
is plainly superior to the *base and silly* of
Q2, since it provides a genuine antithesis
to *revenge*.

80 **grossly** in a state of gross indulgence
full of bread i.e. not in the state of
spiritual preparedness induced by fasting.
Hamlet is recalling the Ghost's statement
that he is 'for the day confined to fast in
fires' (1.5.11); and the rest of his speech is
shot through and through with recollections of the Ghost's story. It is these
recollections that determine the nature of
the revenge he plans.

81 **broad blown** in full blossom
flush full of lusty growth. This sense of
flush appears to originate in this passage;
but 'As fresh as May' was proverbial
(Tilley M763), which probably explains
Compositor B's recourse to it.

82 **audit** spiritual account; see 1.5.78.

83 **circumstance and course of thought** i.e.
our way of thinking (which is, of course,
limited)

84 **heavy with** i.e. a black outlook for

86 **seasoned** properly prepared

88 **Up** i.e. back into your scabbard
know experience
hint (1) opportunity, occasion (2) grasp.
Hint, meaning 'occasion', was sometimes
spelled *hent* (from which it seems to have
been derived) in the 17th century; while
hent could be spelled *hint* (*OED hent sb.*
and *hint sb.*). 'An occasion to be grasped'
would seem to be exactly what Hamlet
has in mind.

89 **drunk asleep** dead drunk
in his rage i.e. a prey to uncontrollable
sexual desire (*OED rage sb.* 6b)

At gaming swearing, or about some act
That has no relish of salvation in't—
Then trip him that his heels may kick at heaven,
And that his soul may be as damned and black
As hell, whereto it goes. My mother stays.
This physic but prolongs thy sickly days.   *Exit*

CLAUDIUS (*rising*)

My words fly up, my thoughts remain below.
Words without thoughts never to heaven go.   *Exit*

3.4   *Enter Gertrude and Polonius*

POLONIUS

He will come straight. Look you lay home to him.
Tell him his pranks have been too broad to bear with,
And that your grace hath screened and stood between
Much heat and him. I'll silence me e'en here.

---

91 gaming] F; (gaming,); game a Q2; game Q1
3.4.0.1 *Gertrude*] Q2 (*Gertrard*); *Queene* FQ1   1 He] F; A Q2   4 silence] FQ2; shrowde Q1; 'sconce HANMER   e'en] F; euen Q2

---

91 **at gaming swearing** The gambler's addiction to swearing was notorious; see Chaucer, 'The Pardoner's Tale' 651–5.
92 **relish** trace
93 **kick at** As well as having their literal sense, these words carry the connotation of 'spurning', 'treating with contempt'. Compare *Coriolanus* 2.2.122–4, 'Our spoils he kicked at, | And looked upon things precious as they were | The common muck of the world.'
94–5 **as . . . black | As hell** (a proverbial simile, Tilley H397)
95 **stays** awaits my coming
96 **This physic . . . days** This cryptic line, like so much else that Hamlet says, condenses two meanings into one. *This physic* is both the treatment the King is giving himself by praying and the treatment Hamlet is giving him by forbearing to kill him now.
97–8 **My words . . . go** The King's couplet endorses Hamlet's view that his wickedness is incurable; but it also contradicts Hamlet's belief that for the moment at least he is in a state of grace.
3.4 Act 3, scene 3 is the centre of the play's action; but 3.4 is its emotional centre. Having lost the initiative in his struggle with Claudius by being over-subtle in his plans to ensure the King's damnation,

Hamlet takes it and keeps it in his struggle with his mother in an effort to ensure her salvation. The scene, as Shakespeare makes abundantly clear (see 3.2.313, 3.3.27, and 4.1.34) is set in the Queen's *closet*, i.e. her own private apartment. A closet was not, it seems worth emphasizing, a bedroom. The bed, which has been so prominent in many productions over the last fifty years, made its first appearance in Gielgud's *Hamlet* as it was staged in New York in 1936, shortly after the publication of Dover Wilson's *What Happens in 'Hamlet'* where the scene is actually referred to as 'the Bedroom Scene'.
1 **lay home to him** Polonius repeats what he said to Claudius at 3.3.29.
2 **pranks** disgraceful and disorderly activities. Compare *1 Henry VI* 3.1.14–15, 'thy audacious wickedness, | Thy lewd, pestiferous, and dissentious pranks'.
   broad outrageous, unrestrained
   to bear with to be tolerated. For this use of the infinitive active where modern English calls for the passive see Abbott 359.
4 **heat** anger
   I'll silence me e'en here i.e. here is my last word. Ironically it is not.

Pray you be round with him.

HAMLET (*within*) Mother, mother, mother!

GERTRUDE

I'll warrant you. Fear me not.

Withdraw; I hear him coming.

> *Polonius hides behind the arras.*
> *Enter Hamlet*

HAMLET Now, mother, what's the matter?

GERTRUDE

Hamlet, thou hast thy father much offended.   10

HAMLET

Mother, you have my father much offended.

GERTRUDE

Come, come, you answer with an idle tongue.

HAMLET

Go, go, you question with a wicked tongue.

GERTRUDE

Why, how now, Hamlet?

HAMLET   What's the matter now?

GERTRUDE

Have you forgot me?

HAMLET   No, by the rood, not so.

You are the Queen, your husband's brother's wife,

But—would you were not so—you are my mother.

GERTRUDE

Nay, then I'll set those to you that can speak.

HAMLET

Come, come, and sit you down. You shall not budge,

You go not till I set you up a glass   20

Where you may see the inmost part of you.

---

5 with him] F; *not in* Q2   HAMLET (*within*) Mother, mother, mother!] F; *Ham⟨let⟩* Mother, mother Q1; *not in* Q2   7 warrant] F; wait Q2; war'nt WILSON   8.1 *Polonius hides behind the arras*] *exit Cor⟨ambis⟩* Q1 (*after 4*); *not in* FQ2   8.2 *Enter Hamlet*] F; *after* round (5) Q2   13 a wicked] Q2; an idle F   17 But—would you were not so—] F (But would you were not so.); And would it were not so, Q2   21 inmost] F; most Q2

5 **Be round with him** Polonius repeats what he said at 3.1.184. This F reading is entirely in character.

7 **Fear me not** i.e. have no doubt about that

13 **Go, go** *Go* in the imperative carries a rebuke with it.

15 **rood** Christ's cross

16 **your husband's brother's wife** Hamlet accuses his mother of incest.

18 **to** in opposition to, to work on. Compare *Troilus* 2.1.84, 'Will you set your wit to a fool's?'

19 **Come . . . down** Hurt and annoyed by her son's behaviour, Gertrude is evidently about to leave.

GERTRUDE

What wilt thou do? Thou wilt not murder me?
Help, help, ho!

POLONIUS *(from behind the arras)* What ho! Help, help, help!

HAMLET

How now, a rat? Dead, for a ducat, dead.
  He thrusts his sword through the arras

POLONIUS

O, I am slain.

GERTRUDE   O me, what hast thou done?

HAMLET

Nay, I know not. Is it the King?
  He lifts the arras

GERTRUDE

O, what a rash and bloody deed is this!

HAMLET

A bloody deed—almost as bad, good mother,
As kill a king and marry with his brother.   30

GERTRUDE

As kill a king?

HAMLET   Ay, lady, 'twas my word.—
Thou wretched, rash, intruding fool, farewell.
I took thee for thy better. Take thy fortune.
Thou find'st to be too busy is some danger.—
Leave wringing of your hands. Peace, sit you down,
And let me wring your heart. For so I shall

---

23 Help, help] F; Helpe Q2Q1   24 *from behind the arras*] *not in* FQ2Q1 Help, help, help] F; helpe
Q2; Helpe for the Queene Q1   25.1 *He thrusts . . . arras*] *Killes Polonius* F (*after* l. 26); *not in*
Q2Q1   31 'twas] F; it was Q2   33 better] Q2; Betters F

---

25 **a rat?** 'The rat betrayed herself with her
own noise' (Dent R30.1) and 'I smell a
rat' (Tilley R31) are both relevant here.
for a ducat i.e. I would stake a ducat on it
(*OED for* A9b)
29–30 **A bloody deed . . . brother** Shocked
by his mother's permitting a spy to over-
hear his interview with her, Hamlet
voices the most terrible of the suspicions
that have been weighing on his mind—
that Gertrude was privy to the murder of
his father. Her amazed incomprehension
clears his mind of that suspicion. He never

mentions it again.
33 **better** There may well be a quibble here.
As well as meaning 'social superior',
better could be the aphetic form of *abettor*,
a word Shakespeare uses at *Lucrece* 886,
where it signifies 'instigator'. *OED* cites
only one instance of the aphetic form,
dating from 1671; but aphesis 'has been
common in English since long before the
time of Shakespeare' (Brook, p. 145).
34 **to be . . . danger** Compare 'To be too busy
is dangerous' (Dent B759.1)
busy meddlesome, prying

If it be made of penetrable stuff,
If damnèd custom have not brassed it so
That it is proof and bulwark against sense.

GERTRUDE

What have I done that thou dar'st wag thy tongue   40
In noise so rude against me?

HAMLET   Such an act
That blurs the grace and blush of modesty;
Calls virtue hypocrite; takes off the rose
From the fair forehead of an innocent love,
And sets a blister there; makes marriage vows
As false as dicers' oaths. O, such a deed
As from the body of contraction plucks
The very soul, and sweet religion makes
A rhapsody of words. Heaven's face doth glow;
Yea, this solidity and compound mass   50
With tristful visage, as against the doom,
Is thought-sick at the act.

38 brassed] GLOBE (brass'd); braz'd F; brasd Q2   39 is] F; be Q2   45 sets] Q2; makes F
49 doth] F; dooes Q2   49–50 glow; | Yea] F (glow, | Yea), glowe | Orc Q2; glow, | And
WILSON   51 tristful] F; heated Q2

37 penetrable susceptible to feeling. This
figurative use of the word seems to have
originated with Shakespeare. Compare
Richard III 3.7.224–5, 'I am not made of
stones | But penetrable to your kind
entreaties'.

38 If . . . so 'Custom makes sin no sin' (Tilley
C934) and 'As hard as brass' (Dent
B605.1) both seem applicable.
    brassed it made it as hard as brass

39 proof and bulwark i.e. impregnably fortified
    sense proper feeling

40 wag i.e. use. '*Wag* was free from its
present trivial associations, and could be
used without incongruity in a serious
passage' (Brook, p. 64).

41 Such an act i.e. adultery joined to incest

42 That as (Abbott 279)

43 Calls virtue hypocrite i.e. makes any
semblance of virtue suspect
    rose The white rose symbolizes purity
and innocence. In *A Warning for Fair
Women* Anne Sanders wears a white rose
at her trial, 'In token,' she says, 'of my
spotless innocence: | As free from guilt as
is this flower from stain' (2313–14). As
the evidence against her mounts, how-

ever, the rose changes colour (2374–5),
convicting her of complicity in the murder
of her husband.

45 blister Branding on the forehead with a
red-hot iron was a common punishment
inflicted on malefactors, and especially on
whores. Compare 4.5.116–18.

47 body of contraction i.e. substance of the
marriage-contract, with word play on the
two bodies that become 'one flesh'

49 rhapsody stringing-together, mingle-
mangle (*OED* 3)—not used by Shakespeare elsewhere

49–52 Heaven's face . . . act The F reading
here has all the appearance of an
authorial revision made to clear up what
is something of a tangle in Q2.

49 glow blush with shame. Compare *K. John*
4.1.113–14, 'you will but make it
blush | And glow with shame of your pro-
ceedings'.

50 this solidity and compound mass i.e. this
earth (thought of as a solid body compounded of the four elements)

51 tristful sad
    as against the doom as though expecting
doomsday

52 thought-sick sick with thinking about

GERTRUDE   Ay me, what act,
That roars so loud and thunders in the index?

HAMLET
Look here upon this picture, and on this,
The counterfeit presentment of two brothers.
See what a grace was seated on this brow—
Hyperion's curls, the front of Jove himself,
An eye like Mars, to threaten or command,
A station like the herald Mercury
New lighted on a heaven-kissing hill;   60
A combination and a form indeed
Where every god did seem to set his seal
To give the world assurance of a man.
This was your husband. Look you now what follows.
Here is your husband, like a mildewed ear
Blasting his wholesome brother. Have you eyes?
Could you on this fair mountain leave to feed,

---

54 HAMLET] F; *before* 53 Q2   56 this] Q2; his F   58 or] F; and Q2   60 heaven-kissing] F; heaue, a kissing Q2   66 brother] Q2; breath F

53 **index** i.e. preface, prologue. The *index* to a book was, in Shakespeare's day, the table of contents, and so appeared at the beginning not at the end. Compare *Othello* 2.1.252–3, 'an index and obscure prologue to the history of lust and foul thoughts.'

54–5 **Look here . . . brothers** Perhaps the most useful comment on these lines is Arthur Colby Sprague's: 'traditional business accompanies the lines addressed to Gertrude . . . as the Prince forces her to examine actual miniatures . . . of the old King and the new. So he was accustomed to do through much of the 18th century if not before. Against his use of miniatures . . . only one piece of evidence is of much weight. In Rowe's Shakespeare is an engraving of the Closet Scene at the moment of the Ghost's return. Several details suggest that the artist was remembering the play as he had seen it acted. And on the wall two half-length portraits are partly visible, those presumably of the two kings. Hamlet, it is urged, had only to point at one of these as he spoke. But because some details in the engraving are theatrical in origin it does not follow that all must be. An illustrator of the scene might have been tempted to introduce the pictures, regardless of what was done on the stage. And one further detail, long overlooked, is curious. For Gertrude is certainly wearing a chain, on which is suspended what appears to be a locket, the locket containing, we may suppose, the picture in little of Claudius which Hamlet will snatch from her a moment later, to contrast with that of his father' (Arthur Colby Sprague and J. C. Trewin, *Shakespeare's Plays Today*, 1970, pp. 26–7).

55 **counterfeit presentment** portrayed representation (*OED counterfeit adj.* 5)

57 **front** forehead

59 **station** stance, way of standing

61 **combination** (of all the gods mentioned)

62 **set his seal** place his mark of approval

65–6 **a mildewed ear . . . brother** Mildew and blasting (i.e. blighting) are frequently associated with one another in the Bible. See 1 Kings 8 : 37, 'If there be in the land famine, if there be pestilence, blasting, mildew' (A. V.); and also Genesis 41 : 6–7; Amos 4 : 9; and Haggai 2 : 17.

67 **leave** cease

And batten on this moor? Ha? Have you eyes?
You cannot call it love; for at your age
The heyday in the blood is tame, it's humble,   70
And waits upon the judgement; and what judgement
Would step from this to this? What devil was't
That thus hath cozened you at hoodman-blind?
O shame, where is thy blush? Rebellious hell,
If thou canst mutine in a matron's bones,
To flaming youth let virtue be as wax
And melt in her own fire. Proclaim no shame
When the compulsive ardour gives the charge,
Since frost itself as actively doth burn,
And reason panders will.

GERTRUDE   O Hamlet, speak no more.   80
Thou turn'st mine eyes into my very soul,
And there I see such black and grainèd spots
As will not leave their tinct.

HAMLET   Nay, but to live
In the rank sweat of an enseamèd bed,

73 hoodman-blind] r; hodman blind Q2; hob-man blinde Q1   80 And] Q2; As F   panders]
F; pardons Q2   81 mine eyes into my very soul] F; my very eyes into my soule Q2   82
grainèd] F; greeued Q2   83 not leave] F; leaue there Q2   84 enseamèd] F; inseemed Q2

68 **batten** glut yourself
   moor fen, marshy ground (producing an
   abundance of rank grass)—*OED moor sb.*[1]
   ? The context shows that *OED* is wrong
   in citing this passage as an illustration of
   its first sense of *moor*: 'A tract of un-
   enclosed waste ground'.
70 **heyday in the blood** i.e. intense state of
   sexual excitement (typical of youth)
71 **waits upon** is subservient to
72 **to this** For a passage following these
   words in Q2 but not in F, see Appendix
   A, vi.
73 For a passage following this line in Q2 but
   not in F, see Appendix A, vii.
   cozened tricked, deceived
   hoodman-blind blind man's buff. Hamlet
   means that even a child would have
   known better.
74 **Rebellious hell** This phrase has pronounced sexual connotations Shakespeare
   employs the verb 'to rebel' to describe
   masculine erection (*Merchant* 3.1.31),
   and refers to the female genitals as *hell* at
   Lear 4.6.128. *Rebellious hell* is the sexual
   urge that revolts against the 'sovereignty
   of reason'.

75 **mutine** mutiny (the form the verb takes
   elsewhere in Shakespeare, though *mutine*
   was common enough at the time)
78 **compulsive** This is the earliest instance of
   compulsive cited by *OED*. Shakespeare
   uses it again in *Othello* 3.3.458.
   gives the charge makes the attack
79 **frost** i.e. age, matrons such as Gertrude.
   'To find fire in frost' was proverbial (Dent
   F383.1).
80 **reason panders will** i.e. reason, which
   should control lust, abets it. Compare
   Venus 791–2, 'O strange excuse, | When
   reason is the bawd to lust's abuse'.
81 **Thou . . . soul** 'To go into one's own
   bosom (turn one's eyes inward)' (Dent
   B546.1) is pre-Shakespearian.
82 **grainèd** deeply ingrained, dyed in grain.
   Compare *Twelfth Night* 1.5.222, ''Tis in
   grain, sir; 'twill endure wind and weather'.
83 **leave their tinct** give up their colour, i.e.
   cannot be removed (earliest instance of
   tinct in this sense cited by *OED*)
84 **enseamèd** soaked with grease (*OED en-
   seam v.*[2]). Compare *Troilus* 2.3.179–80,
   'the proud lord | That bastes his arrogance
   with his own seam'.

Stewed in corruption, honeying and making love
Over the nasty sty—
GERTRUDE   O, speak to me no more.
These words like daggers enter in my ears.
No more, sweet Hamlet.
HAMLET   A murderer and a villain,
A slave that is not twentieth part the tithe
Of your precedent lord, a vice of kings,   90
A cutpurse of the empire and the rule,
That from a shelf the precious diadem stole
And put it in his pocket—
GERTRUDE No more.
HAMLET A king of shreds and patches—
          Enter the Ghost in his night-gown
Save me and hover o'er me with your wings,
You heavenly guards!—What would you, gracious
          figure?
GERTRUDE Alas, he's mad.
HAMLET
Do you not come your tardy son to chide,

---

87 my] Q2; mine F   89 tithe] F (tythe); kyth Q2   95.1 *Enter the Ghost in his night-gown*] Q1;
Enter Ghost (after No more 94) FQ2   97 you] F; your Q2

---

85 **Stewed** (1) seethed, steeped (2) like the
inmates of a *stew* (brothel). Compare
Measure 5.1.316–7, 'I have seen corrup-
tion boil and bubble | Till it o'errun the
stew'.
    honeying calling one another 'honey',
using 'sweet' language
86 **sty** Compare *Pericles* 4.6.96, where Marina
calls the brothel she is living in 'this sty'
90 **vice** (1) epitome of all that is villainous
(2) the Vice, often called Iniquity, of the
Morality plays, whose language and
actions were both villainous and farcical.
See *Twelfth Night* 4.2.116–27.
91–3 **A cutpurse . . . pocket** The lines combine utter contempt with bitter resentment.
95 **of shreds and patches** i.e. made up of incongruous bits and pieces; and, as the
clown wore a motley garb, 'a clown of a
king'
95.1 **Enter the Ghost in his night-gown** It
seems right to preserve this direction from
Q1 for several reasons. It is the only in-

dication we have of how the Ghost appeared in this scene in Shakespeare's day.
Moreover, its precision leaves little room
for doubt that it represents what the
reporter recalled. Nor is there anything
incongruous about the *night-gown*, so
long as one remembers that what it signifies is a *dressing-gown* and, it can be assumed, a very splendid one at that, certainly not a thing 'of shreds and patches'.
Above all, however, the *night-gown* has at
least two functions: it reminds the
audience that it is night on the stage; and,
in its domesticity, it suggests that old
Hamlet is about to play a rather different
role from that of the martial figure of the
first act. In fact, our last glimpse of 'the
majesty of buried Denmark', showing him
'in his habit as he lived', modifies our
previous impression of him greatly by
bringing out his humanity.
98 **he's mad** It is abundantly plain that
Gertrude neither sees nor hears the Ghost.

That, lapsed in time and passion, lets go by   100
Th'important acting of your dread command? O, say!
GHOST
  Do not forget. This visitation
  Is but to whet thy almost blunted purpose.
  But look, amazement on thy mother sits.
  O, step between her and her fighting soul!
  Conceit in weakest bodies strongest works.
  Speak to her, Hamlet.
HAMLET How is it with you, lady?
GERTRUDE Alas, how is't with you,
  That you do bend your eye on vacancy,   110
  And with th'incorporal air do hold discourse?
  Forth at your eyes your spirits wildly peep,
  And, as the sleeping soldiers in th'alarm,
  Your bedded hair like life in excrements
  Start up and stand on end. O gentle son,
  Upon the heat and flame of thy distemper

---

110 you do] Q2; you F; thus you Q1   111 th'incorporal] Q2; their corporall F   114 hair]
FQ2; hairs ROWE   115 Start up and stand] FQ2; Starts up and stands Q3   on] POPE 1728; an
FQ2

100-1 **That, lapsed . . . command** The
meaning of these lines is disputed.
Schmidt connects *lapsed* with its use in
Twelfth Night 3.3.36-7: 'For which, if I
be lapsed in this place, | I shall pay dear',
where *lapsed* signifies 'surprised', 'apprehended'. He therefore construes the passage thus: 'who, surprised by you in a
time and passion fit for the execution of
your command, lets them go by'. Dr Johnson, on the other hand, taking *lapsed* to
mean 'having fallen into error', interprets
the lines: 'having suffered time to go by
and passion to cool'. This explanation is
the simpler and the one that fits the facts
better.
101 **important** urgent
104 **amazement** terrified bewilderment
105 **step between** interpose yourself between
106 **Conceit** imagination (of a morbid kind)
(*OED sb.* 11)
110 **vacancy** empty space (earliest use of
vacancy in this sense recorded by *OED*)
111 **incorporal** insubstantial, bodiless (not
elsewhere in Shakespeare)
112 **Forth . . . peep** It was thought that when

a man was excited his 'spirits' or 'vital
powers' would rise, as it were, to the
surface of his body. Compare *Troilus*
4.5.56-7, 'her wanton spirits look
out | At every joint and motive of her
body'; and Webster's *The Devil's Law-Case*
1.1.191-2, 'the soul | Moves in the super-
ficies.'
113 **the sleeping soldiers** The definite article
is used here to show that the case is a
typical one, it has the force of 'for example' (Abbott 92).
114 **bedded hair** i.e. hair that normally lies
flat like 'the sleeping soldiers' in their beds
like life in excrements as though out-
growths of the body had a life of their
own. The hair, beard, and nails, all of
which 'grow out of' the body, were, for
that reason, called *excrements*. Compare
LLL 5.1.92-3, 'dally with my excrement,
with my mustachio'.
115 **Start up and stand** There are two explanations for these plural verbs: (1) *hair*
is regarded as a collective noun; (2) they
have been affected by their proximity to
excrements.

Sprinkle cool patience. Whereon do you look?

HAMLET

On him, on him! Look you how pale he glares.
His form and cause conjoined, preaching to stones,
Would make them capable.—Do not look upon me,   120
Lest with this piteous action you convert
My stern effects. Then what I have to do
Will want true colour—tears perchance for blood.

GERTRUDE To whom do you speak this?

HAMLET Do you see nothing there?

GERTRUDE

Nothing at all; yet all that is I see.

HAMLET Nor did you nothing hear?

GERTRUDE No, nothing but ourselves.

HAMLET

Why, look you there. Look how it steals away.
My father, in his habit as he lived!   130
Look where he goes even now out at the portal.

Exit the Ghost

GERTRUDE

This is the very coinage of your brain.
This bodiless creation ecstasy
Is very cunning in.

HAMLET Ecstasy?

My pulse as yours doth temperately keep time,
And makes as healthful music. It is not madness

---

124 whom] Q2, F2; who F1   131 *Exit the Ghost*] Q2Q1; *Exit.* F   135 Ecstasy?] F (Extasie?);
not in Q2

---

118 **how pale he glares** Compare *Macbeth*
3.4.95–6, 'Thou hast no speculation in
those eyes | That thou dost glare with!'
119 **preaching to stones** See Luke 19: 40:
'And he . . . said unto them, I tell you that
if these hold their peace, then shall the
stones cry.'
120 **capable** capable of feeling, responsive
(*OED* 3c)
121–2 **convert | My stern effects** change the
course of my stern intentions. See *Macbeth* 1.5.42–4, 'That no compunctious
visitings of nature | Shake my fell purpose
nor keep peace between | Th'effect and it.'
123 **want true colour** i.e. will not be of the
kind it should (*OED colour sb.* 16) with a
pun on the literal sense of *colour*

126 **Nothing at all** Perhaps the closest parallel to the Ghost's being neither seen nor
heard by Gertrude is to be found in Tourneur's *The Atheist's Tragedy*, where the
Ghost of Montferrers appears to prevent
his son Charlemont from killing Sebastian
(3.2.43–5), who remains completely
unaware of the Ghost's presence.
130 **in his habit as he lived** i.e. the same in
dress and bearing as when he was alive.
Two senses of *habit* (*OED sb.* 1 and 4) are
combined into one. Compare *Twelfth
Night* 2.5.152–3, 'these habits of her
liking'.
133 **bodiless creation** i.e. tendency to
hallucinate
134 **cunning in** adept at

That I have uttered. Bring me to the test,
And I the matter will re-word, which madness
Would gambol from. Mother, for love of grace,   140
Lay not a flattering unction to your soul,
That not your trespass but my madness speaks.
It will but skin and film the ulcerous place
Whilst rank corruption, mining all within,
Infects unseen. Confess yourself to heaven;
Repent what's past; avoid what is to come;
And do not spread the compost o'er the weeds
To make them ranker. Forgive me this my virtue;
For in the fatness of these pursy times
Virtue itself of vice must pardon beg,   150
Yea, curb and woo for leave to do him good.

GERTRUDE

O Hamlet, thou hast cleft my heart in twain.

HAMLET

O, throw away the worser part of it,
And live the purer with the other half.
Good night—but go not to my uncle's bed.
Assume a virtue if you have it not.

---

139 I] F, not in Q2   141 a] F; that Q2   144 Whilst] F, Whiles Q2   147 o'er] F (or); on
Q2   148 ranker] Q2; ranke F   149 these] Q2; this F   154 live] F; leaue Q2   155 my] Q2,
mine F   156 Assume] F; Assune Q2

139 **re-word** repeat (apparently a Shakespearian coinage)
139-40 **which . . . gambol from** i.e. something madness would shy away from
  doing
140 **for love of grace** 'The was frequently
  omitted before a noun already defined by
  another noun, especially in prepositional
  phrases' (Abbott 89).
141 **Lay** apply (OED v.¹ 15)
  flattering unction i.e. ointment that
  soothes the pain without removing the
  cause of the pain
143-5 **It will . . . unseen** Compare Measure
  2.2.134-6, 'authority . . . Hath yet a kind
  of medicine in itself | That skins the vice
  o'th' top.'
143 **skin and film** i.e. cover over as with skin
  or membrane (earliest instance of film v.
  cited by OED)
144 **mining** undermining, sapping
146 **what is to come** i.e. further temptation
147-8 **spread . . . ranker** Compare

1.2.135-7.
148 **this my virtue** i.e. this sermonizing of
  mine
149 **fatness** grossness
  pursy (1) corpulent (2) purse-proud (emphasizing the moral laxity of the age).
  Compare Christ's Tears over Jerusalem:
  'How many cooks, apothecaries, confec-
  tioners, and vintners in London grow
  pursy by gluttony?' (Nashe, ii. 147).
151 **curb** bow, cringe (OED courbe v.)—not
  elsewhere in Shakespeare
152 **cleft my heart in twain** Some earlier
  examples of this figurative expression,
  which Shakespeare uses again in Measure
  3.1.64, are recorded by Dent (H329.1).
156 For a passage following this line in Q2
  but not in F, see Appendix A, viii.
  Assume (1) put on (2) pretend to. Virtue
  is regarded as a garment which may, in
  time, exert an influence on its wearer's
  behaviour.

Refrain tonight;
And that shall lend a kind of easiness
To the next abstinence. Once more, good night,
And when you are desirous to be blest,   160
I'll blessing beg of you. For this same lord,
I do repent. But heaven hath pleased it so,
To punish me with this, and this with me,
That I must be their scourge and minister.
I will bestow him, and will answer well
The death I gave him. So, again, good night.
I must be cruel only to be kind.
Thus bad begins, and worse remains behind.
One word more, good lady.

GERTRUDE   What shall I do?

HAMLET

Not this, by no means, that I bid you do: 170
Let the bloat King tempt you again to bed,
Pinch wanton on your cheek, call you his mouse,
And let him, for a pair of reechy kisses,
Or paddling in your neck with his damned fingers,

---

157 Refrain tonight] F; to refraine night Q2   168 Thus] F; This Q2   169 One word more,
good lady] Q2; *not in* F   171 bloat] WARBURTON; blunt F; blowt Q2

---

159 For the subsequent passage appearing
    in Q2 but not in F, see Appendix A, ix.
160–1 **And when . . . of you** i.e. 'and when
    you show some sign of wishing for the
    blessing of heaven [by repenting], I will be
    once more your dutiful son and ask your
    blessing at parting, as I used to do'
    (Kittredge).
162 **heaven . . . so** i.e. it has been the will of
    heaven (*pleased* is impersonal)
163 **this . . . this** i.e. the dead Polonius
164 **their** Shakespeare often treats *heaven* as
    a plural. See, for example, *Richard II*
    1.2.6–7, 'Put we our quarrel to the will of
    heaven; | Who when they see . . .'
    scourge and minister instrument of chas-
    tisement
165 **bestow** dispose of
    answer well make a satisfactory response
    to any charge concerning
168 **Thus . . . behind** i.e. the killing of
    Polonius is a bad beginning, and worse
    calamities will follow from it. The line

condenses three commonplaces into one:
'A bad beginning has a bad ending', 'To
go from bad to worse', and 'The worst is
behind' (Tilley B261, B27, and W918).
171 **bloat** bloated, flabby. 'The proper form
    is *blowt* (Qq), for which Warburton sub-
    stituted *bloat*. "Blowty" in the same sense
    is used in Lincolnshire' (Onions).
172 **Pinch wanton** i.e. 'leave marks of his
    fondling which proclaim you a wanton'
    (Jenkins)
    mouse This word was a common form of
    endearment, especially in exchanges be-
    tween husband and wife. Mistress Kitely,
    for instance, uses it time after time when
    speaking to Kitely in 2.3 of *Every Man in
    His Humour*.
173 **a pair of** a few (*OED pair sb.* 5)
    reechy filthy, rancid. The literal sense is
    'smoky'.
174 **paddling** fingering fondly. Compare
    Othello 2.1.249, 'Didst thou not see her
    paddle with the palm of his hand?'

Make you to ravel all this matter out,
That I essentially am not in madness,
But mad in craft. 'Twere good you let him know;
For who that's but a queen, fair, sober, wise,
Would from a paddock, from a bat, a gib,
Such dear concernings hide? Who would do so?   180
No, in despite of sense and secrecy,
Unpeg the basket on the house's top,
Let the birds fly, and like the famous ape,
To try conclusions, in the basket creep,
And break your own neck down.

GERTRUDE

Be thou assured, if words be made of breath,
And breath of life, I have no life to breathe
What thou hast said to me.

HAMLET

I must to England. You know that?

GERTRUDE   Alack,
I had forgot. 'Tis so concluded on.   190

HAMLET This man shall set me packing.
I'll lug the guts into the neighbour room.

---

175 ravel] F (rauell); rouell Q2   177 mad] Q2; made F   184 conclusions, in the basket] F2, Conclusions in the Basket, F; conclusions in the basket_A Q2

175 **ravel . . . out** disentangle—and so explain—all this matter. Compare *Richard II* 4.1.228–9, 'must I ravel out | My weaved-up follies?'

179 **from a paddock, from a bat, a gib** The toad, bat and tom-cat, all regarded as unclean or venomous, were supposed to be the familiars of witches, and so privy to their secrets. See *Macbeth* 4.1.1–15, where all three have their places in the Witches' incantations. Hamlet's contempt and loathing of Claudius unite here with his recollection of the Ghost's charge that Claudius seduced Gertrude 'With witchcraft of his wit' (1.5.43).

180 **Such dear concernings** matters of such vital concern to him (*OED dear a.* 4b and *concerning vbl. sb.*)

181 **sense and secrecy** i.e. the secrecy that reason would dictate

182–5 **Unpeg . . . down** The story has not survived, but it evidently combined two of the characteristics for which apes were *famous*: their addiction to mischief and to imitation. The ape steals a cage (*basket*) full of birds, and then carries it to the top of a house. Mischievously it opens the basket; and the birds fly away. Seeking to imitate them, the ape climbs into the basket, leaps out of it, and, instead of flying, breaks its neck in the fall. Hamlet warns his mother against the risk she will run if she opens the basket containing his secret.

184 **try conclusions** see what will happen. *To try conclusions* is 'to experiment' (*OED conclusion* 8b).

185 **down** i.e. at the bottom of your fall

190 For a passage following this line in Q2 but not in F, see Appendix A, x.
concluded on settled, decided (*OED conclude* 13)

191 **set me packing** (1) cause me to be sent off in a hurry (*OED pack v.* 10) (2) make me start plotting (*OED pack v.* 3).

192 **I'll . . . room** a practical response to the exigencies of the stage

Mother, good night indeed. This counsellor
Is now most still, most secret, and most grave,
Who was in life a foolish prating knave.
Come, sir, to draw toward an end with you.
Good night, mother.   *Exit Hamlet, lugging in Polonius*

4.1   *Enter Claudius*

CLAUDIUS

There's matter in these sighs, these profound heaves;
You must translate. 'Tis fit we understand them.
Where is your son?

---

193 good night indeed.] Q2 (good night indeed,); goodnight. Indeede F   195 foolish] FQ1;
most foolish Q2   197 *Exit Hamlet, lugging in Polonius*] JENKINS; *Exit Hamlet tugging in Polonius*
F; *Exit* Q2; *Exit Hamlet with the dead body* Q1
4.1.0.1 *Enter Claudius*] F (*Enter King*); *Eenter King. and Queene. with Rosencraus and Guyldensterne* Q2; *Enter the King and Lordes* Q1   1 matter] Q2; matters F   sighs, these profound
heaues,] Q2; sighes. | These profound heaues_A F

---

193 **indeed** in earnest
196 **draw toward an end with you** conclude
my dealings with you. 'To draw toward
an end' (Dent E128.1) was a common
phrase in the mouths of public speakers as
they began their peroration. It is an exquisitely
witty touch that Hamlet should
refer to Polonius as though he were a set
speech, while, at the same time, insisting
that he is now a corpse by quibbling on
another sense of *draw*, namely, 'drag'.
197 **lugging** Jenkins's emendation of F's *tugging*
seems obviously right. Hamlet does
what he said he would.
4.1.0.1 *Enter Claudius* While all three of the
earliest texts provide an *exit* for Hamlet,
none of them does for the Queen, who, as
Claudius's first words make plain,
remains on stage deeply distressed. Q2,
however, creates confusion by including
her in its direction for this entry. The
Quarto of 1676 sought to straighten out
the tangle by starting a fresh scene and a
fresh act, 4.1, at this point, though it
made no provision for getting Gertrude off
stage after Hamlet leaves her. The example
it set was, unfortunately, followed
by Rowe and most subsequent editors. Dr
Johnson recognized the absurdity, and
said of it: 'This modern division into Acts
is here not very happy, for the pause is
made at a time when there is more continuity of action than in almost any other
of the scenes.' Nevertheless, he kept the
division. It is retained here because it
makes for easy reference, and because it
serves to bring out the fact that all the
traditional divisions in the play are
editorial, and therefore have no authority.

In Q2 and in Q1 Claudius is accompanied
by Rosencrantz and Guildenstern
whom Q1 refers to as '*Lordes*'. But in Q2
the two courtiers are no sooner on stage
than Gertrude sends them away again.
Shakespeare may well have included
them in his foul papers version in order to
emphasize the King's eagerness to have
Hamlet on his way to England and to
bring out his frustration when, instead of
a chastened Hamlet, a distraught
Gertrude meets his gaze. If such was the
playwright's intention, he soon came to
recognize that the device was a clumsy
one and, therefore, dispensed with it in
the fair copy that lies behind F.
1 **matter** significance, matter of consequence
(*OED matter sb.*[1] IIc)
heaves i.e. heavy sighs from a heaving
breast
2 **translate** i.e. explain what they mean.
3 For a passage following this line in Q2 but
not in F, see Appendix A, xi.

GERTRUDE

Ah, my good lord, what have I seen tonight!

CLAUDIUS What, Gertrude! How does Hamlet?

GERTRUDE

Mad as the sea and wind when both contend
Which is the mightier. In his lawless fit,
Behind the arras hearing something stir,
He whips his rapier out, and cries 'A rat, a rat',
And in his brainish apprehension kills   10
The unseen good old man.

CLAUDIUS   O heavy deed!
It had been so with us had we been there.
His liberty is full of threats to all—
To you yourself, to us, to everyone.
Alas, how shall this bloody deed be answered?
It will be laid to us, whose providence
Should have kept short, restrained, and out of haunt
This mad young man. But so much was our love,
We would not understand what was most fit,
But, like the owner of a foul disease,   20
To keep it from divulging, let it feed
Even on the pith of life. Where is he gone?

GERTRUDE

To draw apart the body he hath killed;
O'er whom—his very madness, like some ore

4 Ah, my good] F; Bestow this place on vs a little while. | Ah mine owne Q2   6 sea] Q2Q1;
Seas F   9 He whips his rapier out, and] F; Whyps out his Rapier, Q2; whips me | Out his rapier,
and Q1   10 his] FQ1; this Q2   21 let] Q2; let's F   24–6 whom—. . . pure—] JENKINS;
whom . . . pure. F; whom, . . . pure, Q2

5 **What, Gertrude!** i.e. my poor Gertrude!
Claudius shows concern, but only as a
preliminary to the question that follows.

6–11 **Mad . . . man** Gertrude keeps the
promise she made to her son, not only by
stressing his 'madness' but also by 'translating' Polonius's cry for help into a mere
noise made by something or other stirring
behind the arras, and thus suggesting
that the *rat* Hamlet referred to was literal
not metaphorical.

6 **Mad as the sea** proverbial (Dent S170)

10 **brainish** brainsick, deluded

11 **heavy** grievous, fraught with consequences

16 **It will be laid** i.e. the responsibility for it
will be attributed

providence foresight, timely care

17 **short** tethered, under strict control
out of haunt secluded, away from the
society of others. Compare *As You Like It*,
2.1.15, 'this our life, exempt from public
haunt' (*OED haunt sb.* 2).

21 **divulging** becoming public knowledge
(*OED divulge v.* 4). Compare *All's Well*
2.1.170–1, 'a divulged shame, | Traduced
by odious ballads'.

22 **pith** essential substance, 'pith and marrow' of Appendix A, ii. 6.

24–6 **O'er whom . . . done** The punctuation
adopted here is Jenkins's.

24 **ore** vein of precious metal—probably
gold (*or* in French). Compare *All's Well*

Among a mineral of metals base,
Shows itself pure—he weeps for what is done.
CLAUDIUS O Gertrude, come away!
    The sun no sooner shall the mountains touch
    But we will ship him hence; and this vile deed
    We must with all our majesty and skill   30
    Both countenance and excuse. Ho, Guildenstern!
        Enter Rosencrantz and Guildenstern
    Friends both, go join you with some further aid.
    Hamlet in madness hath Polonius slain,
    And from his mother's closet hath he dragged him.
    Go seek him out, speak fair, and bring the body
    Into the chapel. I pray you haste in this.
                    Exeunt Rosencrantz and Guildenstern
    Come, Gertrude, we'll call up our wisest friends
    To let them know both what we mean to do
    And what's untimely done. O, come away!
    My soul is full of discord and dismay.   *Exeunt*   40

4.2   *Enter Hamlet*
HAMLET Safely stowed.
GENTLEMEN *(within)* Hamlet! Lord Hamlet!
HAMLET
    What noise? Who calls on Hamlet? O, here they come.
        Enter Rosencrantz, Guildenstern, and others
ROSENCRANTZ
    What have you done, my lord, with the dead body?

26 he] F; a Q2   31.1 *Enter Rosencrantz and Guildenstern*] *after* excuse (31) F; *after* skill (30)
Q2   34 mother's closet] Q2; Mother Clossets F   36 *Exeunt Rosencrantz and Guildenstern*] F
(*Exit Gent⟨lemen⟩*) Q1 (*Exeunt Lordes*); not in Q2   38 To] F; And Q2
4.2.0 *Enter Hamlet*] F; *Enter Hamlet, Rosencraus, and others* Q2   2 GENTLEMEN *(within)* Hamlet!
Lord Hamlet!] F; not in Q2   3 What] F; but soft, what Q2   3.1 *Enter Rosencrantz, Guilden-*
stern, and others] *Enter Ros⟨encrantz⟩ and Guildensterne* F; *Rosencraus, and others* Q2 (*at head of*
scene)

3.6.32–3, 'to what metal this counterfeit
lump of ore will be melted'.
25 **mineral** mine (*OED sb.* 3); not elsewhere,
in this sense, in Shakespeare. Joseph Hall
writes of 'fired brimstone in a mineral'
(*Virgidemiarium*, VI. i. 148).
31 **countenance** bear out, face out (*OED v.*
3)
39 **done** For a passage following this word in
Q2 but not in F, see Appendix A, xii.
4.2 The action is, of course, continuous, and

has more than a touch of the farcical
about it as the Prince taunts his pursuers
and then leads them on a wild chase
through the royal palace.
2 Not found in Q2, this line looks like something deliberately added in F to bring out
the farcical element mentioned above,
which provides a much needed contrast
to the emotional intensity of Hamlet's
scene with his mother.

HAMLET
Compounded it with dust, whereto 'tis kin.

ROSENCRANTZ
Tell us where 'tis, that we may take it thence
And bear it to the chapel.

HAMLET Do not believe it.

ROSENCRANTZ Believe what?

HAMLET That I can keep your counsel and not mine own.   10
Besides, to be demanded of a sponge—what replication
should be made by the son of a king?

ROSENCRANTZ Take you me for a sponge, my lord?

HAMLET Ay, sir, that soaks up the King's countenance, his
rewards, his authorities. But such officers do the King best
service in the end. He keeps them, like an ape an apple in
the corner of his jaw, first mouthed, to be last swallowed.
When he needs what you have gleaned, it is but squeezing
you and, sponge, you shall be dry again.

ROSENCRANTZ I understand you not, my lord.   20

HAMLET I am glad of it. A knavish speech sleeps in a foolish
ear.

---

5 Compounded] F; Compound Q2   16 like an ape an apple] PARROTT–CRAIG, *conj*. Farmer; like
an Ape F; like an apple Q2; as an Ape doth nuttes Q1

5 **Compounded it with dust** Compare *2
Henry IV* 4.5.116, 'Only compound me
with forgotten dust'.

10 **keep your counsel and not mine own** i.e.
follow your advice—to tell you where the
body is—and not keep my own secret—
my knowledge of the body's whereabouts
—to myself. Hamlet is quibbling on two
senses of *counsel*: (1) advice (2) secret;
and on two senses of *keep*: (1) follow, as in
Measure 4.5.3, 'keep your instruction' (2)
retain, keep to oneself, as in the proverbial
'The counsel thou wouldst have another
keep first keep thyself' (Tilley C682).

11 **to be demanded of** i.e. when questioned
by. For this use of the infinitive see Abbott
356.

   sponge This idea of flatterers being like
sponges comes ultimately from Suetonius,
who says, in chapter 16 of his *Life of
Vespasian*, that the Emperor gave high
offices to rapacious men 'so that the
common talk was that he used them as
sponges, letting them soak when they

were dry and squeezing them out again
when they were wet'. It became something of a commonplace in Shakespeare's
day. John Marston, for instance, writes:
'He's but a sponge, and shortly needs
must leese [lose] | His wrong got juice,
when greatness' fist shall squeeze | His
liquor out' (*The Scourge of Villainy*, vii.
58–60).

12 **the son of a king** Annoyed by Rosencrantz's insolence, Hamlet asserts himself. For the rest of the scene Rosencrantz
addresses him as 'my lord', something he
signally omitted to do at lines 6–7 and 9.

14 **countenance** favour, patronage

16 **like an ape an apple** The likelihood that
both F and Q2 are in error here is endorsed by Q1's *as an Ape doth nuttes*.

21–2 **A knavish . . . ear** 'a sarcastic remark
is wasted upon an unintelligent hearer'
(Spencer). Hamlet has, in fact, given the
pair a useful piece of advice: that Claudius
will discard them when they have served
his purpose.

ROSENCRANTZ My lord, you must tell us where the body is,
and go with us to the King.
HAMLET The body is with the King, but the King is not with
the body. The King is a thing—
GUILDENSTERN A thing, my lord?
HAMLET Of nothing. Bring me to him. Hide fox, and all after.
            Exit Hamlet hurriedly, pursued by the rest

4.3   *Enter Claudius*
CLAUDIUS
I have sent to seek him, and to find the body.
How dangerous is it that this man goes loose.
Yet must not we put the strong law on him.
He's loved of the distracted multitude,
Who like not in their judgement but their eyes;
And where 'tis so, th'offender's scourge is weighed,

28 Hide fox, and all after] F; *not in* Q2   Exit . . . rest] Exeunt FQ2
4.3.0 Enter Claudius] F (*Enter King*); *Enter King, and two or three* Q2

25–6 **The body . . . body** This pretty piece of chiasmus sounds impressive but is singularly reluctant to yield up a sense that can be apprehended by an audience in a theatre. Intended as a riddle, it remains a riddle.
26–8 **The King is a thing . . . Of nothing** Compare the Prayer Book version of Psalms 144: 4, 'Man is like a thing of nought: his time passeth away like a shadow.'
28 **Hide fox, and all after** Occurring in F only, these words, referring to the boys' game of 'fox and hounds' (*OED fox sb.* 16d), have often been regarded as an actor's interpolation. Yet they do give the scene a lively ending that is in keeping with Hamlet's *O, here they come* (l. 3) and with the 'savage comic humour' that is so characteristic of this scene and of the scene that follows. They may even anticipate the behaviour of the mad Lear when he issues his challenge to the Attendants in 4.6 and then runs off. Moreover, they fit in with the general tendency towards 'broader' effects which is so typical of F. The Prince's seemingly submissive *Bring me to him* puts his captors off their guard and gives him a good start over them. The sentence is, therefore,

accepted in this edition as part of the process of authorial revision which lies behind F.
4.3.0.1 *Enter Claudius* F's replacement of Q2's '*Enter King, and two or three*' with '*Enter King*' is very similar to its treatment of Q2's '*Enter King, and Queen, with Rosencrantz and Guildenstern*' at 4.1.0. In both cases it is tempting to regard the alteration as part of a deliberate though mistaken policy designed to reduce the number of supernumeraries (see Textual Introduction, pp. 114–15). On this occasion, however, there may be a better justification for the change. An audience could easily be puzzled and distracted by the appearance of 'two or three' whom they have not seen before, who are not identified in any way, and who say nothing whatever. None of these difficulties arises when Claudius's speech is converted, as it is in F, into a soliloquy.
3 **must . . . law** i.e. it is not fitting for me to bring the full rigour of the law to bear. For this use of *must* see Abbott 314.
4 **distracted** muddle-headed
5 **like not in** i.e. do not bestow their affection in accordance with
6 **scourge** punishment

But never the offence. To bear all smooth and even,
This sudden sending him away must seem
Deliberate pause. Diseases desperate grown
By desperate appliance are relieved,   10
Or not at all.
    Enter Rosencrantz
           How now? What hath befallen?

ROSENCRANTZ
Where the dead body is bestowed, my lord,
We cannot get from him.

CLAUDIUS   But where is he?

ROSENCRANTZ
Without, my lord, guarded, to know your pleasure.

CLAUDIUS Bring him before us.

ROSENCRANTZ
Ho, Guildenstern, bring in my lord.
    Enter Hamlet and Guildenstern

CLAUDIUS Now, Hamlet, where's Polonius?

HAMLET At supper.

CLAUDIUS At supper? Where?

HAMLET Not where he eats, but where he is eaten. A certain   20
convocation of politic worms are e'en at him. Your worm
is your only emperor for diet. We fat all creatures else to
fat us, and we fat ourselves for maggots. Your fat king and
your lean beggar is but variable service—two dishes, but
to one table. That's the end.

7 never] Q2; neerer F   11.1 *Enter Rosencrantz*] F; *Enter Rosencraus and all the rest* Q2   16 Ho,
Guildenstern] F; How, Q2   my] F; the Q2   16.1 *Enter Hamlet and Guildenstern*] F; *They enter*
Q2; *Hamlet enters guarded by soldiers* WILSON   20 he is] FQ1; a is Q2   21 politic] Q2Q1; *not
in* F   23 ourselves] Q2; our selfe F   24–5 service—two dishes, but to one table.] Q2
(seruice, . . . table,); seruice to dishes, . . . Table₄ F; seruices, two dishes to one messe: Q1

7 **bear all smooth and even** i.e. handle the matter with every appearance of composure and impartiality. Compare *Henry V* 2.2.3, 'How smooth and even do they bear themselves'.
9 **Deliberate pause** i.e. the result of careful deliberation
9–11 **Diseases . . . all** A version of the common saying 'A desperate disease must have a desperate cure' (Tilley D357), this idea is frequent in Shakespeare and is expressed with particular force in *Coriolanus* 3.1.154–5, 'To jump a body with a dangerous physic | That's sure of death without it'.
10 **appliance** remedies
21–2 **convocation . . . diet** Hamlet, very much the student from Wittenberg at this point, wittily alludes to the celebrated Diet of Worms of 1521, a meeting of the Reichstag of the Holy Roman Empire, summoned by the Emperor Charles V to hear Luther defend his new doctrine.
21 **politic** sagacious, shrewd. It will be recalled that Polonius prided himself on his ability to hunt 'the trail of policy' (2.2.47).
24 **service** dishes, food served up (*OED service*¹ 27b)

CLAUDIUS Alas, alas!

HAMLET A man may fish with the worm that hath eat of a
king, and eat of the fish that hath fed of that worm.

CLAUDIUS What dost thou mean by this?

HAMLET Nothing but to show you how a king may go a   30
progress through the guts of a beggar.

CLAUDIUS Where is Polonius?

HAMLET In heaven. Send thither to see. If your messenger
find him not there, seek him i'th' other place yourself. But
indeed, if you find him not within this month, you shall
nose him as you go up the stairs into the lobby.

CLAUDIUS (*to attendants*) Go seek him there.

HAMLET He will stay till you come.   *Exeunt attendants*

CLAUDIUS

Hamlet, this deed of thine, for thine especial safety—
Which we do tender as we dearly grieve   40
For that which thou hast done—must send thee
          hence
With fiery quickness. Therefore prepare thyself.
The bark is ready, and the wind at help,
Th'associates tend, and everything is bent
For England.

HAMLET For England?

CLAUDIUS Ay, Hamlet.

HAMLET Good.

26–8 Alas . . . that worm.] Q2; a man may fish with that worme | That hath eaten of a
King, | And a Beggar eate that fish | Which that worme hath caught. Q1 ; *not in* F   29 CLAUDIUS]
FQ1 (*King*.); *King. King.* Q2   35 indeed, if] F; if indeed Q2   *within*] Q2; *not in* F   37 *to
attendants*] *not in* FQ2Q1   38 He will] F; A will Q2; hee'le Q1   you] Q2Q1 ; ye F   *Exeunt
attendants*] *not in* FQ2Q1   39 of thine] F; *not in* Q2   42 With fiery quickness] F; *not in* Q2   44
is] Q2; at F   46 England?] F; *England.* Q2

26–8 **Alas . . . worm** The omission of these
words from F appears to be the result of
compositorial carelessness not of a deliberate cut, since they are represented in Q1
and are needed to prompt Claudius's
question at line 29.

31 **progress** state journey. Both Queen
Elizabeth and James I were in the habit of
making a royal progress through the land
each summer. Accompanied by an enor-
mous retinue of courtiers and servants,
they often ate their hosts 'out of house
and home'. The 'progress' Hamlet en-
visages is a marvellously ironical reversal

of that progress.

40 **tender** hold dear, are very concerned
about
dearly deeply

42 **With fiery quickness** Found in F only,
these words look like a piece of authorial
revision, designed to fill out a short line in
Q2.

43 **at help** favourable, in the right quarter to
help (*OED help sb.* 1c). For the derivation
and implication of *at* see Abbott 140 and
143.

44 **tend** are waiting (*OED tend v.*[1] 6b). Compare 1.3.83.

CLAUDIUS
So is it, if thou knew'st our purposes.

HAMLET I see a cherub that sees them. But come; for Eng-   50
land! Farewell, dear mother.

CLAUDIUS Thy loving father, Hamlet.

HAMLET My mother. Father and mother is man and wife;
man and wife is one flesh; and so, my mother. Come, for
England!   *Exit*

CLAUDIUS
Follow him at foot. Tempt him with speed aboard.
Delay it not. I'll have him hence tonight.
Away, for everything is sealed and done
That else leans on th'affair. Pray you make haste.
                              Exeunt all but Claudius

And, England, if my love thou hold'st at aught—   60
As my great power thereof may give thee sense,
Since yet thy cicatrice looks raw and red
After the Danish sword, and thy free awe
Pays homage to us—thou mayst not coldly set
Our sovereign process, which imports at full,
By letters conjuring to that effect,
The present death of Hamlet. Do it, England;
For like the hectic in my blood he rages,
And thou must cure me. Till I know 'tis done,
Howe'er my haps, my joys were ne'er begun.   *Exit*   70

---

50 them] Q2; him F   54 and so] FQ1; so Q2   59 *Exeunt all but Claudius*] Q1 (*exeunt all but the king*); *not in* FQ2   66 conjuring] F; congruing Q2   70 were ne'er begun] F; will nere begin Q2

---

50 **cherub** The cherubim, or second order of
angels, excelled in knowledge and keen-
ness of vision. Compare *Paradise Lost* xi.
128–31, 'watchful Cherubim; four faces
each | Had, like a double Janus, all their
shape | Spangled with eyes more numerous
than those | Of Argus'.
58–9 **everything . . . That else** i.e. everything else . . . that
59 **leans on** has a bearing on, appertains to
59.1 *Exeunt all but Claudius* This essential
direction, missing from F and Q2, is
supplied by Q1.
61 **thereof** i.e. of the value of my love
63 **free** unconstrained (since there is no
longer a Danish army in England)
64 **coldly set** coolly disregard (*OED set v.*
89c)
65 **sovereign process** royal command
imports at full calls in explicit terms for
66 **conjuring** making a solemn demand.
This F reading makes better sense than
Q2's *congruing*. The letters are designed to
put pressure on the King of England, as
distinct from merely spelling out the
details of Claudius's 'sovereign process'.
67 **present** immediate
68 **hectic** fever—not elsewhere in Shakespeare
70 **Howe'er my haps** i.e. no matter what my
fortunes have been or may be

4.4   *Enter Fortinbras with an army*

FORTINBRAS

Go, captain, from me greet the Danish king.
Tell him that by his licence Fortinbras
Claims the conveyance of a promised march
Over his kingdom. You know the rendezvous.
If that his majesty would aught with us,
We shall express our duty in his eye;
And let him know so.

CAPTAIN   I will do't, my lord.

FORTINBRAS Go safely on.   *Exeunt*

4.5   *Enter Gertrude and Horatio*

GERTRUDE

I will not speak with her.

HORATIO   She is importunate,
Indeed distract. Her mood will needs be pitied.

GERTRUDE What would she have?

4.4.0 *Enter Fortinbras with an army*] F ; *Enter . . . his Army ouer the stage* Q2 ; *Enter Fortenbrasse, Drumme and Souldiers* Q1   3 Claims] F ; *Craues* Q2Q1   8 safely] F ; *softly* Q2   *Exeunt*] F (*Exit*) Q1 (*exeunt all*) ; not in Q2
4.5.0 *Enter Gertrude and Horatio*] F (*subs.*) ; *Enter Horatio, Gertrard, and a Gentleman* Q2   1, 4 HORATIO] F ; *Gent⟨leman⟩*. Q2

4.4.0.1 **Enter Fortinbras with an army** Fortinbras and his forces enter by one of the two main doors to the stage ; march forward ; halt while Fortinbras gives the Captain his orders ; and then leave through the other main door.

3 **Claims** This F reading is more in keeping with Fortinbras's character and with the legalistic phrasing of the sentence than is Q2's *Craves*.

conveyance The word covers both the honouring of Claudius's promise and the provision of a Danish escort to make it clear that the Norwegian forces have the requisite *licence* to pass over Danish soil. Q1's *free passe and conduct* elucidates the position.

6 **eye** presence

8 For a passage following this line in Q2 but not in F, see Appendix A, xiii.

safely without fear of danger or offence (Schmidt)

4.5 It is here that the action enters its final phase. From the opening of 2.1 to the end of 4.4 the action is continuous, but after the end of 4.4 there is a break in it. The duration of this break is not clearly defined but it evidently covers several days (see Introduction, p. 36). Moreover, when the action does resume here, it is concerned with fresh matters : Ophelia's madness and Laertes' revolt. Both are, however, intimately related to the main business of the tragedy. Ophelia's madness is 'real', in contrast to the assumed madness of the Prince, while Laertes' over-eagerness to revenge his father's death makes one think again about Hamlet's tardiness in carrying out the Ghost's command.

0 **Enter Gertrude and Horatio** As at 4.1.0 and 4.3.0, F cuts out an unnecessary part. The Gentleman of Q2 is conflated with Horatio.

2 **distract** mad (*OED ppl.a.* 4)

HORATIO

She speaks much of her father, says she hears
There's tricks i'th' world, and hems, and beats her
    heart,
Spurns enviously at straws, speaks things in doubt
That carry but half sense. Her speech is nothing;
Yet the unshapèd use of it doth move
The hearers to collection. They aim at it,
And botch the words up fit to their own thoughts,   10
Which, as her winks and nods and gestures yield them,
Indeed would make one think there might be thought,
Though nothing sure, yet much unhappily.

GERTRUDE

'Twere good she were spoken with, for she may strew
Dangerous conjectures in ill-breeding minds.
Let her come in.

⌈*Horatio moves to the rear of the stage to admit*
    Ophelia⌉

(*Aside*) To my sick soul, as sin's true nature is,
Each toy seems prologue to some great amiss.
So full of artless jealousy is guilt,

---

9 aim] F (ayme); yawne Q2   12 might] Q2; would F   14 GERTRUDE] F (Qu⟨een⟩); Hora⟨tio⟩ Q2, *as continuation of previous speech* HANMER   16.1–2 *Horatio . . . Ophelia*] This edition; *not in* FQ2

6 **Spurns enviously at straws** i.e. takes offence and turns spiteful on the slightest pretext. These were recognized symptoms of melancholy. Burton writes of melancholics: 'they are commonly distrustful, timorous, apt to mistake, and amplify, *facile irascibiles*, testy, pettish, peevish . . .' (*Anatomy of Melancholy*, i. 449–50)
in doubt i.e. that make no obvious sense
7 **nothing** nonsense
8 **unshapèd use** incoherent manner
9 **collection** making something coherent of it; putting their own interpretation on it (*OED* 5). Compare *Cymbeline* 5.5.431–2, 'so from sense . . . that I can | Make no collection of it'.
aim at guess about (*OED v.* 3). Q2's 'yawn

at', meaning 'are bewildered by' (Schmidt) also makes good sense.
11 **Which** i.e. which words
yield affect their meaning (*OED v.* 12)
12 **thought** intended
13 **unhappily** The word seems to conflate two different senses: (1) mischievously, maliciously (*OED* 3) (2) unpleasantly near the truth (*OED* 4).
17–20 **To my . . . spilt** Q2 prefixes an inverted comma to each of these lines to show that they are *sententiae*.
18 **amiss** calamity, misfortune
19–20 **So full . . . spilt** i.e. the guilty are so full of irrepressible mistrust that they give themselves away by their obvious fear of doing so.

It spills itself in fearing to be spilt.   20

Enter Ophelia playing on a lute, and her hair down,
singing

OPHELIA

Where is the beauteous majesty of Denmark?

GERTRUDE How now, Ophelia?

OPHELIA (*sings*)

How should I your true love know
From another one?
By his cockle hat and staff,
And his sandal shoon.

GERTRUDE

Alas, sweet lady, what imports this song?

OPHELIA Say you? Nay, pray you, mark.

(*She sings*)

He is dead and gone, lady,
He is dead and gone,   30

20.1–2 *Enter Ophelia playing on a lute, and her hair down, singing*] Q1 *Enter Ophelia distracted* F;
Enter Ophelia Q2 (*after l. 16*)   23 *sings*] Q2 (*shee sings*) (*opposite l. 22*); *not in* F (*where songs are
printed in italic*)   29, 35, 37, 47, 57, 166, 190 *She sings/sings*] Q2 (*Song—to right of text*); *not
in* F

20.1 *Enter Ophelia playing on a lute, and
her hair down, singing* This full and explicit direction in Q1 probably reflects the
manner in which the part was played
when a boy who could play on the lute
—the Lucius of *Caesar*, for example—was
available. Jenkins's objection that the lute
is incongruous with Ophelia's songs is, in
fact, an argument for her using it, since
only a mad woman would think of doing
so.

23.1 *sings* The songs Ophelia sings are
not, with the single exception of lines
23–4, known elsewhere. However, they
smack very strongly of the traditional ballad, in which love—especially lost or
unrequited love—and death were the
leading motifs. The likeliest explanation of
their origin is that Shakespeare took
snatches, as the Queen calls them
(4.7.152), of old songs and wove them
together to fit his own purpose, for they do
render, in a manner which is both poignant and haunting, the two causes of
Ophelia's madness—Hamlet's rejection of
her love and the death of her father, killed
by his hand. Inextricably involved with
one another, her two losses compete for

attention in her mind, and thus, quite
literally, distract it, tear it apart.
    For the music to which these songs are
traditionally sung see Appendix D.

23–4 **How . . . one** These two lines are very
close in wording to the beginning of the
second stanza of the celebrated 'Walsingham' ballad often attributed to Sir Walter
Ralegh. In Agnes Latham's edition of *The
Poems of Sir Walter Ralegh* (1951), pp.
22–3, they run thus: 'How shall I know
your true love | That have met many one'.

25–6 **By his . . . shoon** This was the
traditional garb of the pilgrim. It then
became associated with the convention of
the lover making his pilgrimage to the
shrine of his 'saint'. See the sonnet which
Romeo and Juliet share at their first meeting (*Romeo* 1.5.91–104).

25 **cockle hat** A hat with a cockle-shell or
scallop-shell on it was worn by pilgrims to
show that they had been to the shrine of
St James of Compostella in Spain.

26 **shoon** The only other Shakespearian use
of this archaic plural of *shoe* is in *2 Henry
VI* 4.2.180, where Jack Cade speaks of
'clouted shoon'.

> At his head a grass-green turf,
>> At his heels a stone.

She sighs

GERTRUDE Nay, but, Ophelia—

OPHELIA Pray you, mark.

(*She sings*)

> White his shroud as the mountain snow—

Enter Claudius

GERTRUDE Alas, look here, my lord.

OPHELIA (*sings*)

>> Larded with sweet flowers,
>> Which bewept to the grave did not go
>>> With true-love showers.

CLAUDIUS How do you, pretty lady?   40

OPHELIA Well, God 'ild you! They say the owl was a baker's daughter. Lord, we know what we are, but know not what we may be. God be at your table!

CLAUDIUS Conceit upon her father.

OPHELIA Pray you let's have no words of this. But when they ask you what it means, say you this:

(*She sings*)

>> 'Tomorrow is Saint Valentine's day,
>>> All in the morning betime,
>> And I a maid at your window,
>>> To be your Valentine.'   50

32.1 *She sighs*] This edition; O ho Q2; *not in* F   35.1 *Enter Claudius*] Q2; *before* 33 F   37 Larded] FQ1; Larded all Q2   38 grave] FQ1; ground Q2   did not] FQ2Q1; did POPE   40 you] Q2; ye F   41 God 'ild] F (God dil'd); good dild Q2; God yeeld Q1   45 Pray you] F; Pray Q2

31 **grass-green** i.e. green with grass; earliest instance of this usage cited by *OED*

32.1 *She sighs* This seems to be the significance of *O ho*. Compare 5.2.311.1 and note.

35 **White . . . snow** This is a variant on the cliché 'As white as snow' (Tilley S591).

37 **Larded** bedecked, strewn over (originally a culinary term)

38 **not** As she sings Ophelia suddenly realizes that her father was *not* buried in the manner described by her song; hence the intrusive *not*.

41 **God 'ild you** may God yield (= reward) you. The phrase was a common form for rendering thanks (*OED* yield v. 7).

41–2 **the owl . . . daughter** The main reference is to a folk-tale in which Christ goes into a baker's shop and asks for food. The baker's daughter reprimands her mother for giving him too much. Thereupon Christ turns her into an owl. For other possible meanings see Dent B54.1.

42–3 **Lord . . . may be** This could be a reflection on the fate of the baker's daughter.

43 **God be at your table** This benediction of a meal, uttered by a guest, appears to have been triggered in Ophelia's mind by the story of the baker's daughter.

44 **Conceit upon her father** i.e. wild fancies caused by her father's death

47–64 **Tomorrow is . . . my bed** This song is based on the tradition that the first person of the opposite sex one sees on St Valentine's day will be one's sweetheart

50 **Valentine** sweetheart

> Then up he rose, and donned his clothes,
>> And dupped the chamber door;
> Let in the maid, that out a maid
>> Never departed more.

CLAUDIUS Pretty Ophelia—

OPHELIA Indeed, la, without an oath, I'll make an end on't.
  (*She sings*)
>> By Gis, and by Saint Charity,
>>> Alack, and fie for shame!
>> Young men will do't, if they come to't,
>>> By Cock, they are to blame.   60
>
>> Quoth she 'Before you tumbled me,
>>> You promised me to wed.'
>> 'So would I ha' done, by yonder sun,
>>> An thou hadst not come to my bed.'

CLAUDIUS How long hath she been thus?

OPHELIA I hope all will be well. We must be patient. But I
  cannot choose but weep to think they should lay him i'th'
  cold ground. My brother shall know of it. And so I thank
  you for your good counsel. Come, my coach! Good night,
  ladies. Good night, sweet ladies, good night, good night.   70

                                                          Exit

---

51 clothes] FQ1; close Q2   56 Indeed, la,] F (Indeede la?); Indeede Q2   63 So] FQ1; (He
answers.) So Q2   ha'] F (*ha*); a Q2Q1   65 thus] Q2; this F   67 should] F; would Q2   70
Exit] F; *not in* Q2

---

51 **clothes** pronounced *close* and so spelt in
Q2. By the eighteenth century *close* was
'widely accepted' and 'even taught as the
only correct pronunciation' (Cercignani
331–2).

52 **dupped** 'did up' the latch of, i.e. opened;
not elsewhere in Shakespeare

55 **Pretty Ophelia—** The punctuation adopted here is Jenkins's. Both F and Q2 read
'Ophelia.'. His view that the King tries to
divert Ophelia from her course is entirely
convincing; and, it may be added, her
refusal to let Claudius complete what he is
about to say increases the indecorum of
the scene.

57 **Gis** Often spelt *jis*, this is a form of *Jesus*
commonly used in oaths, though it ap-
pears nowhere else in Shakespeare.
  by Saint Charity Derived from the Old

French *par seinte charite* (by holy charity),
this phrase, often used in mild oaths,
came to be treated as though *charity* was
the name of a saint.

59 **do't** engage in sexual intercourse. Compare *Measure* 1.2.82–3.

60 **by Cock** by God—of which *Cock* is a perversion—but also with a quibble on *cock*
meaning 'penis'.

61 **tumbled me** made me fall backwards, i.e.
took my virginity. Compare *Winter's Tale*
4.3.12, 'we lie tumbling in the hay.'

69 **Come, my coach** These words look like a
reminiscence of another mad scene, the
suicide of Zabina in Marlowe's *1 Tambur-
laine* 5.2.242–56, where immediately
before she brains herself the Turkish Em-
press cries out, 'Make ready my coach,
my chair, my jewels'.

CLAUDIUS

Follow her close. Give her good watch, I pray you.

Exit Horatio

O, this is the poison of deep grief; it springs
All from her father's death. O Gertrude, Gertrude,
When sorrows come, they come not single spies,
But in battalions. First, her father slain;
Next, your son gone, and he most violent author
Of his own just remove; the people muddied,
Thick and unwholesome in their thoughts and
     whispers
For good Polonius' death; and we have done but
     greenly
In hugger-mugger to inter him; poor Ophelia   80
Divided from herself and her fair judgement,
Without the which we are pictures or mere beasts;
Last, and as much containing as all these,
Her brother is in secret come from France,
Feeds on this wonder, keeps himself in clouds,

---

71 *Exit Horatio*] *not in* F Q2   73 death. O] F; death, and now behold, O Q2   74 sorrows come]
Q2; sorrowes comes F   75 battalions] Q2; Battaliaes F   78 their] F; *not in* Q2   85 Feeds on
this] Q2; Keepes on his F

71.1 **Exit Horatio** Neither Q2 nor F has any
     stage direction at this point. Someone
     must, however, obey the King's com-
     mand; and it is essential that the stage be
     cleared of all but Claudius and Gertrude
74–5 **When sorrows . . . battalions** Compare
     'Misfortune never comes alone' (Tilley
     M1012).
74 **spies** i.e. soldiers in advance of the main
     body
76 **author** causer, instigator (*OED* 1c)
77 **remove** (1) dismissal, being sent away
     (the sense in which Claudius expects
     Gertrude to take it) (2) removal by death,
     murder (*OED remove sb.* 1b); compare *The
     Spanish Tragedy* 2.1.136, 'Her favour
     must be won by his remove.'
     muddied confused in mind, stirred up.
     Compare *Troilus* 3.3.303–4, 'My mind is
     troubled, like a fountain stirred; | And I
     myself see not the bottom of it.'
78 **Thick and unwholesome** i.e. clouded
     with uncertainty and dangerously sus-
     picious. As 'thin and wholesome blood'
     (1.5.70) is indicative of physical health,

so 'Thick and unwholesome. . . thoughts'
     are indicative of mental trouble.
79 **greenly** foolishly, like a novice; compare
     'like a green girl' (1.3.101)
80 **In hugger-mugger** secretly, clandestine-
     ly. The phrase was common enough
     (Tilley H805), though Shakespeare does
     not use it elsewhere; but he could have
     been reminded of it by its occurrence in
     North's *Plutarch*, where he would have
     read in the *Life of Brutus*: 'Then Antonius
     thinking good . . . [Caesar's] body should
     be honourably buried, and not in hugger
     mugger . . . Cassius stoutly spake against
     it' (Bullough, v. 104).
82 **pictures** i.e. imitations without a soul.
     See 4.7.94–5, 'are you like the painting
     of a sorrow, | A face without a heart?'
83 **containing** comprising
85 **Feeds on this wonder** i.e. nourishes the
     growth of this popular mood of astonish-
     ment mingled with perplexity and
     bewildered curiosity. See *OED feed v.* 6c
     and *wonder sb.* 7; also North's *Plutarch*
     (*Life of Publicola*): 'Publicola . . . was very

And wants not buzzers to infect his ear
With pestilent speeches of his father's death;
Wherein necessity, of matter beggared,
Will nothing stick our persons to arraign
In ear and ear. O my dear Gertrude, this,   90
Like to a murdering-piece, in many places
Gives me superfluous death.

    A noise within. Enter a Messenger

GERTRUDE Alack, what noise is this?

CLAUDIUS

Where are my Switzers? Let them guard the door.
What is the matter?

MESSENGER   Save yourself, my lord.
The ocean, overpeering of his list,
Eats not the flats with more impetuous haste
Than young Laertes, in a riotous head,
O'erbears your officers. The rabble call him lord;
And, as the world were now but to begin,   100

88 Wherein] Q2; Where in F   89 persons] F; person Q2   91 murdering-piece, in many places] THEOBALD (*subs.*); murdering Peece in many places, F; murdering peece in many places_∧ Q2   92.1 *Enter a Messenger*] FQ2; *after* 94 KITTREDGE   93 GERTRUDE Alack, what noise is this?] F; *not in* Q2   94 Where are] F; Attend, where is Q2   97 impetuous] Q3F2; impittious F; impitious Q2

diligent, not only to understand the original cause of [Appius'] sedition, but to feed on further and increase the same' (ed. George Wyndham (1895), i. 273).
  keeps himself in clouds remains inscrutable, does not reveal his motives. For the connection between 'walking in a cloud' and dissimulation see Dent C443.1 and C444.

86 **wants not buzzers** i.e. is well supplied with scandal-mongers. *OED* cites no other instance of *buzzer* in this sense; but compare *Titus* 4.4.6–7, 'these disturbers of our peace | Buzz in the people's ears'.

88–90 **Wherein . . . and ear** i.e. in these speeches of theirs they will not hesitate, in their need to make a strong case while having no facts to go on, to accuse me in whispers that come to everybody's ears.

90 **this** i.e. this 'sea of troubles'

91 **murdering-piece** Known also as a 'murderer', this was a small cannon or mortar loaded with a mixture of missiles instead of a single shot.

94 **Switzers** Swiss mercenaries were employed by many countries in Shakespeare's day, especially as royal guards.

95 *Messenger* This Messenger is very much the Nuntius of classical drama. He begins his description of what is happening with a long simile and finds a place in it for a brief disquisition on the importance of precedent in matters of government.

96 **overpeering of** rising above, towering over. For the now superfluous *of* see Abbott 178
  his list its bounds (the shore)

97 **impetuous** The spellings *impitious* (Q2) and *impittious* (F) serve to bring out the association with *pitiless*.

98 **head** insurrection (*OED sb.* 29). But Shakespeare also has in mind *head* 17c, meaning 'a high tidal wave'. In fact *riots* and *floods* that *o'erbear* authority are closely linked in his mind. Compare *Coriolanus* 3.1.248–50, where he writes of the mob 'whose rage doth rend | Like interrupted waters, and o'erbear | What they are used to bear'.

Antiquity forgot, custom not known,
The ratifiers and props of every word,
They cry 'Choose we! Laertes shall be king.'
Caps, hands, and tongues applaud it to the clouds,
'Laertes shall be king, Laertes king.'
    A noise within

GERTRUDE
How cheerfully on the false trail they cry!
O, this is counter, you false Danish dogs!
CLAUDIUS The doors are broke.
    Enter Laertes with his followers

LAERTES
Where is this king? — Sirs, stand you all without.
ALL HIS FOLLOWERS
No, let's come in.
LAERTES   I pray you give me leave.   110
ALL HIS FOLLOWERS We will, we will.
LAERTES I thank you. Keep the door.   *Exeunt Followers*
                        O thou vile king,
Give me my father.
GERTRUDE (*restraining Laertes*) Calmly, good Laertes.
LAERTES
That drop of blood that's calm proclaims me bastard,
Cries cuckold to my father, brands the harlot
Even here between the chaste unsmirchèd brow
Of my true mother.

105.1 *A noise within*] As SPENCER; *after* 107 F; *after* 106 Q2   108.1 *Enter Laertes with his followers*] SPENCER; *Enter Laertes* F (*after* 107); *Enter Laertes with others* Q2 (*after* 107)   109 this king?—Sirs] Q2 (this King? sirs); the King, sirs? F   110, 111 ALL HIS FOLLOWERS] SPENCER (subs.); *All* FQ2   112 *Exeunt Followers*] *not in* FQ2   114 *restraining Laertes*] *not in* FQ2   115 that's calm] Q2; that calmes F   117 brow] FQ2; brows Q1676

---

100 **as the world** i.e. as if social institutions
101–2 **Antiquity . . . word** Traditional precedent and custom are seen here as absolutely essential if what is said is to have any validity. The *words* of Laertes' followers have the sanction of neither. They are uttered in defiance of the *word* that does have such sanction—the civil contract between the King and his subjects.
106 **cry** give tongue (as hounds do)

107 **counter** i.e. following the scent backwards, in the direction opposite to that which the quarry has taken. The killer of Polonius has left the court, not come to it.
112 **Keep** guard
114.1 **restraining Laertes** This direction is required by the King's order at 120.
116–18 **brands . . . mother** See note to 3.4.45.
117 **Even here** 'i.e. in this of all places' (Jenkins)

303

CLAUDIUS   What is the cause, Laertes,
That thy rebellion looks so giant-like?—
Let him go, Gertrude. Do not fear our person.   120
There's such divinity doth hedge a king
That treason can but peep to what it would,
Acts little of his will.—Tell me, Laertes,
Why thou art thus incensed.—Let him go, Gertrude.—
Speak, man.

LAERTES Where's my father?

CLAUDIUS Dead.

GERTRUDE But not by him.

CLAUDIUS Let him demand his fill.

LAERTES
How came he dead? I'll not be juggled with.   130
To hell, allegiance! Vows to the blackest devil!
Conscience and grace to the profoundest pit!
I dare damnation. To this point I stand,
That both the worlds I give to negligence,
Let come what comes; only I'll be revenged
Most throughly for my father.

CLAUDIUS Who shall stay you?

LAERTES My will, not all the world;
And for my means, I'll husband them so well
They shall go far with little.

CLAUDIUS   Good Laertes,   140
If you desire to know the certainty
Of your dear father's death, is't writ in your revenge

126 Where's] F; Where is Q2   138 world] F; worlds Q2; world's POPE   142 father's death]
F; Father Q2   is't] Q2; if F

119 **giant-like** Schmidt sees an allusion here
to the revolt of the Giants against the
Olympian deities.
121–3 **There's such divinity . . . will** These
words are supremely ironical. Claudius
speaks with complete conviction; yet he
has himself done exactly what he says
cannot be done. No such divinity hedged
old Hamlet from his treasonous design.
His is true hypocrisy on the grand scale.
122 **but peep . . . would** merely peep (through
the hedge of divine protection) at its objective
132 **grace** God's grace
133 **To this point I stand** I adhere to, am
fixed in, this resolve (OED point sb.¹ 30).

134 **both the worlds** i.e. this world and the
next. Compare Macbeth 3.2.16, 'But let
the frame of things disjoint, both the
worlds suffer'.
     give to negligence disregard
135 **Let come what comes** a much used
phrase (Tilley C529)
136 **throughly** thoroughly
138 **world** This F reading seems a more suitable answer to a question beginning with
Who than does Q2's worlds, signifying
'world's will', a reading that might have
been influenced by worlds four lines
earlier.
142 **father's death** While this F reading

That, sweepstake, you will draw both friend and foe,
Winner and loser?

LAERTES None but his enemies.

CLAUDIUS Will you know them then?

LAERTES

To his good friends thus wide I'll ope my arms,
And, like the kind life-rend'ring pelican,
Repast them with my blood.

CLAUDIUS   Why, now you speak
Like a good child and a true gentleman.   150
That I am guiltless of your father's death,
And am most sensibly in grief for it,
It shall as level to your judgement pierce
As day does to your eye.

    A noise within

VOICES (*within*)   Let her come in.

    Enter Ophelia, with flowers in her hand, singing

LAERTES How now? What noise is that?

148 pelican] Q2; Politician F   152 sensibly] Q2 (sencibly); sensible F; peare
Q2; 'pear JOHNSON   154.1–55 *A noise within . . . LAERTES* How . . . *that?*] *essentially* F (*A noise
within. Let her come in.* | *Enter Ophelia* | *Laer ⟨tes⟩* How . . . *that?*); *A noyse within.* | *Enter Ophelia.*
Laer⟨tes⟩ Let her come in. | How . . . that? Q2; *Enter Ofelia as before.* | *Lear⟨tes⟩* Who's this,
Ofelia? Q1 ; [*A Noise within,* Let her come in. | *Laer⟨tes⟩* How . . . that? | *Enter* Ophelia THEOBALD;
A noise within. [Ophelia is heard singing.] *Let her come in. (As conclusion of Claudius's speech)* |
Laer⟨tes⟩ How . . . that? | *Enter* OPHELIA. JENKINS

results in a six-foot line, that line makes
better sense than its Q2 counterpart and
Q2 is plagued with omissions.

143 **sweepstake** indiscriminately. The King
asks Laertes if he intends to behave like a
gambler who sweeps all the money from
the board irrespective of whether it
belongs to losers or winners.

148–9 **like . . . blood** Laertes refers to the
fable, much overworked in Shakespeare's
day, of the pelican feeding its young with
its own blood and even bringing them
back to life with it. See Book v, chapter 1
of Sir Thomas Browne's *Pseudodoxia
Epidemica*.

149 **Repast** feed (*OED* v. 2); not elsewhere in
Shakespeare

152 **sensibly** feelingly

153–4 **It . . . eye** Shakespeare has combined
two proverbial expressions—'As swift as
an arrow' and 'As clear as the day' (Tilley
A322 and D56)—to convey the notion of
suddenly realizing something with pierc-

ing clarity. For 'level', meaning 'directly',
see Appendix A, xii. 3.

154 **Let her come in** Some interesting parallels to F are to be found in *The First Part of
the Contention* (1594), E3ᵛ–4, where 'the
Commons within' cry out in a similar
fashion.

154.1 **with flowers in her hand** None of the
primary texts contains this direction, but
Ophelia must bring the flowers with her,
so that she can distribute them later; and
she should be singing in order to prompt
Laertes' initial question.

155 **How now? What noise is that?** All three
early texts agree in not having Laertes
speak until *after* Ophelia has come in.
Moreover, in neither F nor Q2 are his first
words addressed directly to her, thus
making it clear that on first sight he
completely fails to recognize her. This
subtle and highly dramatic effect, endorsed by Q1's 'Who's this, *Ofelia*?', has been
obscured for centuries by Theobald's

O heat, dry up my brains! Tears seven times salt
Burn out the sense and virtue of mine eye!
By heaven, thy madness shall be paid by weight
Till our scale turns the beam. O rose of May,
Dear maid, kind sister, sweet Ophelia!   160
O heavens, is't possible a young maid's wits
Should be as mortal as an old man's life?
Nature is fine in love, and where 'tis fine
It sends some precious instance of itself
After the thing it loves.

OPHELIA (*sings*)
> They bore him barefaced on the bier,
>   Hey non nony, nony, hey nony,
>   And on his grave rained many a tear—
> Fare you well, my dove.

LAERTES
Hadst thou thy wits, and didst persuade revenge,   170
It could not move thus.

---

158 by] F; with Q2   159 turns] F; turne Q2   162 an old] FQ1; a poore Q2   163–5 Nature
. . . loves] F; *not in* Q2   167 Hey . . . hey nony] F; *not in* Q2   168 on] F; in Q2   rained] Q2;
raines F   169 Fare you well, my dove] Q2; *italic (as part of song)* F

shifting of the stage direction for Ophelia's
entry to make it follow Laertes' line, instead of preceding it.
157 **virtue** natural power
158 **paid by weight** atoned for in full
measure
159 **our scale turns the beam** i.e. the
balance (of the scales of Justice) tilts in our
favour
rose of May proverbial (Tilley F389)
163–5 **Nature . . . loves** i.e. 'Love . . . is the
passion by which [human] nature is most
exalted and refined; and as substances,
refined and subtilised, easily obey any impulse, or follow any attraction, some part
of nature, so purified and refined, flies off
after the attracting object, after the thing
it loves' (Dr Johnson).
164 **instance** illustrative example, specimen
167 **Hey . . . hey nony** This refrain, omitted
from Q2, is certainly incongruous, since it
relates, as Sternfeld remarks, 'more logic-
ally to lads, lasses and springtime than to
lamentation and tears' (p. 57); but, then,
incongruity is precisely what Ophelia's

state of mind demands.
169 **Fare you well, my dove** F makes these
words part of the song, while Q2 does not
distinguish them from it. Since the time of
Capell, however, most editors have
detached them from the song.
my dove It is not clear who it is Ophelia
has in mind when she uses this term of
endearment.
172 **A-down, a-down** a much used refrain in
popular songs of the time. Ophelia
evidently expects her hearers to join in.
172–3 **Call him a-down-a** Jenkins points out
that these words occur as a refrain to
Song 3 in Deloney's *The Garland of Good-
will* (*Works*, ed. F. O. Mann (Oxford,
1912), pp. 305–9). The song, which
could be obscurely connected in Ophelia's
mind with 'the false steward', tells how a
false knight, sent by King Edgar to woo
the beautiful Lady Estrild for him, wooed
for himself, won the lady, lied to the King,
and was eventually found out and killed.
The King then married the widow, who
had revealed her husband's lie to him.

OPHELIA You must sing 'A-down, a-down'; and you 'Call
him a-down-a'. O, how the wheel becomes it! It is the
false steward that stole his master's daughter.

LAERTES This nothing's more than matter.

OPHELIA (*to Laertes*) There's rosemary, that's for remembrance. Pray, love, remember. And there is pansies,
that's for thoughts.

LAERTES A document in madness—thoughts and remembrance fitted.   180

OPHELIA There's fennel for you, and columbines. There's

---

172 'A-down, a-down'] Q2 (a downe a downe); downe a-downe F   172–3 'Call him a-down
a'] JENKINS; *no quotes in* FQ2   173 it!] F (it?); it, Q2   177 Pray] FQ1; pray you Q2   pansies]
Q2; Pacuncles F; pansey Q1

---

173 **wheel** The context here almost dictates
that *wheel* be interpreted as 'refrain', even
though no precise parallel to such a
meaning has come to light. *OED*, after
defining the normal prosodic sense (*wheel
sb.* 16), quotes Edwin Guest's opinion that
a *wheel* signifies 'the return of some marked and peculiar rhythm' at the end of
each stanza (*A History of English Rhythms*
(1838), ii. 290).

173–4 **It is . . . daughter** No such ballad or
folk-tale is extant; but the very topic suggests there may well have been one.
Ophelia is haunted by the idea of betrayal.

175 **This . . . matter** i.e. this nonsense is
charged with significance beyond the
reach of common sense. Compare
'Though this be madness, yet there is
method in't' (2.2.204–5).

176.1 **to Laertes** In this case there can be no
doubt about the identity of the recipient.
Not only are the flowers appropriate, but
it is also Laertes who comments on what
Ophelia says.

176–85 **There's rosemary . . . died** The obvious parallel and contrast to this passage
is that in *Winter's Tale* (4.4.73–127)
where Perdita, the embodiment of health
and sanity, also distributes flowers but in
very different circumstances. Flower symbolism flourished in Elizabethan England;
and Shakespeare had already made use of
it in *Richard II* (3.4.104–7). Much of it is
conveniently gathered together in a poem
called 'A Nosegay Always Sweet', first
published in Clement Robinson's *A Hand-
ful of Pleasant Delights* (1584), and at the
beginning of Robert Greene's *A Quip for an
Upstart Courtier* (1592). But, while the

significances given to each flower in the
lyric are well authenticated and represent
popular traditions, those attributed to
them by Greene seem more idiosyncratic.

176–8 **There's rosemary . . . thoughts** Compare 'A Nosegay' in which the fourth
verse begins 'Rosemary is for remembrance between us day and night'. The
pansies are *for thoughts* because the word
comes from the French *pensées*. While the
speech echoes Laertes' 'remember well' of
1.3.84, Ophelia appears to be confusing
him with Hamlet.

179 **document in madness** i.e. lesson (*OED
document sb.* 2) from which a student of
madness might learn much. Compare *The
Faerie Queene* I. x. 19, 'and that her sacred
book . . . She unto him disclosed every
whit, | And heavenly documents thereout
did preach'.

181–5 **There's fennel . . . died** The problem
this passage raises is that of who receives
what. The most thorough discussion of it
is Jenkins's, to which the notes that follow
are much indebted.

181 **fennel** There is ample evidence (*OED
fennel* 3) that, as 'A Nosegay' puts it, 'Fennel is for flatterers'.
  columbines 'The horned nectaries suggested to an earlier age allusions to
cuckoldry' (*OED sb.*[2] 1). Malone thought
that the fennel and columbines were
given to Claudius; and he could still be
right, since Claudius won Gertrude 'With
witchcraft of his wit' and thus cuckolded
old Hamlet. Jenkins, however, pinning his
argument on Greene's remark that 'fennel . . . for flatterers' is 'fit generally for
that sex [women], sith while they are

rue for you; and here's some for me. We may call it herb-
grace o' Sundays. O, you must wear your rue with a
difference. There's a daisy. I would give you some violets,
but they withered all when my father died. They say he
made a good end.

(*She sings*)

            For bonny sweet Robin is all my joy.

LAERTES

Thought and affliction, passion, hell itself
She turns to favour and to prettiness.

OPHELIA (*sings*)

            And will he not come again?   190
            And will he not come again?
                No, no, he is dead,
                Go to thy death-bed,
            He never will come again.

182–3 herb-grace] F; herbe of Grace Q2; hearb a grace Q1   183 O, you] F; you Q2Q1   must]
FQ1; may Q2   185 he] F; a Q2   188 Thought and affliction] F; Thought and afflictions Q2;
Thoughts & afflictions Q1   190, 191 he] FQ1; a Q2

maidens, they wish wantonly; while they
are wives they will wilfully; while they are
widows, they would willingly; and yet all
these proud desires are but close dissemb-
lings', concludes that the right recipient is
the Queen, who certainly willed wilfully in
cuckolding her husband. The virtue of this
explanation is that it leaves *rue* for the King.
182 **rue** (1) the bitter plant so named (2)
regret, sorrow, repentance. The quibble
was almost irresistible; see *OED sb.*² 1b.
Rue is right for Claudius, the only one of
those present who has sought to repent. It
also fits Ophelia, but for a different
reason: she is filled with sorrow and her
'mood will needs be pitied'.
182–3 **herb-grace** another name for the
plant *rue* emphasizing its associations with
repentance. Compare *Richard II* 3.4.105,
'I'll set a bank of rue, sour herb of grace'.
183–4 **with a difference** The term is heraldic; but Ophelia seems to mean no more
by it than 'for a different reason'.
184 **daisy** Greene writes of the 'dissembling
daisy'; but there seems to be no reason
why Ophelia should see it or herself in this
light, unless she is thinking of the way in
which she was used as a decoy in 3.1. All
that can be said with any assurance is
that she is fond of the flower, the 'daisy
delectable' as it is so often called in lyrics
of the 16th century, since she finds a place

for it in her 'fantastic garlands' (4.7.143).
    violets According to 'A Nosegay', 'Violet
is for faithfulness'; but it is not obvious
why they should have *withered all* when
Polonius died. One would expect them to
have done so for Ophelia when Hamlet
rejected her love.
185–6 **he made a good end** proverbial (Dent
E133.1)
187 **For bonny sweet Robin is all my joy** According to Sternfeld, the music for this very
popular song survives 'in thirty contemporary sources, six of which were printed
between 1579 and 1621' (p. 68). Unfortunately, no text is extant, but in general
'"Bonny Robin" songs deal with lovers,
unfaithfulness and extra-marital affairs'
(p. 58). As *Robin* is a component part in the
names of a number of wild flowers, the
switch in Ophelia's interest may not be so
abrupt as it appears on first sight.
188 **Thought** sorrow, melancholy reflections (*OED thought*¹ 5)
    passion suffering (*OED sb.* 3). Compare
Antony 5.1.62–3, 'Give her what com-
forts | The quality of her passion shall
require'.
189 **favour** i.e. something charming and
attractive (*OED sb.* 8)
    prettiness i.e. something pleasant and
agreeable (*OED* 2); first instance of this
sense cited by *OED*

His beard as white as snow,
All flaxen was his poll.
    He is gone, he is gone,
    And we cast away moan.
    God ha' mercy on his soul.
And of all Christian souls, I pray God. God buy you.   200

                                                Exit

LAERTES Do you see this, O God?
CLAUDIUS
    Laertes, I must commune with your grief,
    Or you deny me right. Go but apart,
    Make choice of whom your wisest friends you will,
    And they shall hear and judge 'twixt you and me.
    If by direct or by collateral hand
    They find us touched, we will our kingdom give,
    Our crown, our life, and all that we call ours,
    To you in satisfaction. But if not,
    Be you content to lend your patience to us,   210
    And we shall jointly labour with your soul
    To give it due content.
LAERTES   Let this be so.
    His means of death, his obscure burial—
    No trophy, sword, nor hatchment o'er his bones,
    No noble rite nor formal ostentation—
    Cry to be heard, as 'twere from heaven to earth,
    That I must call't in question.

195 beard as] FQ1 ; beard was as Q2   196 All] FQ1 ; *not in* Q2   199 God ha' mercy] Q2Q1 (God
a mercy); *Gramercy* F   200 Christian] F ; Christians Q2 ; christen Q1   I pray God] FQ1 ; *not
in* Q2   buy you] Q2 ; buy ye F ; be with you Q1   *Exit*] F (*Exeunt Ophelia*) Q1 (*exit Ofelia*) ; *not
in* Q2   201 see] F ; *not in* Q2   O God] Q2 ; you Gods F   202 commune] Q2 ; common F
213 burial] F ; funerall Q2   217 call't] Q2 ; call F

198 **cast away** throw away pointlessly,
   waste (*OED cast v.* 72d)
202 **commune with** share in, participate in
   (*OED common v.* 3)
204 **whom** i.e. whomsoever among, any
   among
206 **by direct or by collateral hand** i.e.
   through any action taken directly by me
   in person or indirectly by any agent of
   mine
207 **touched** concerned, involved
213 **His means of death** the cause and
   manner of his death (Abbott 423)
   obscure burial F's substitution of *burial*

for the *funeral* of Q2 looks like an authorial
change made to get rid of the contradiction in terms presented by *obscure funeral*,
since *funeral* implies pomp and ceremony.
214 **trophy** memorial
   hatchment 'a square or lozenge-shaped
   tablet exhibiting the armorial bearings of
   a deceased person, which is affixed to the
   front of his dwelling-place' (*OED*). After
   the burial the tablet was usually placed
   over the tomb.
215 **ostentation** ceremony
217 **That** so that (Abbott 283)

CLAUDIUS   So you shall;
And where th'offence is, let the great axe fall.
I pray you go with me.   *Exeunt*

4.6   *Enter Horatio and a Servant*
HORATIO What are they that would speak with me?
SERVANT Sailors, sir. They say they have letters for you.
HORATIO Let them come in.   *Exit Servant*
I do not know from what part of the world
I should be greeted, if not from Lord Hamlet.
          Enter Sailors
FIRST SAILOR God bless you, sir.
HORATIO Let him bless thee too.
FIRST SAILOR He shall, sir, an't please him. There's a letter
for you, sir. It comes from th'ambassador that was bound
for England—if your name be Horatio, as I am let to   10
know it is.
HORATIO (*reads the letter*) 'Horatio, when thou shalt have
overlooked this, give these fellows some means to the
King. They have letters for him. Ere we were two days old
at sea, a pirate of very warlike appointment gave us chase.
Finding ourselves too slow of sail, we put on a compelled
valour. In the grapple I boarded them. On the instant
they got clear of our ship; so I alone became their prisoner.
They have dealt with me like thieves of mercy. But they
knew what they did: I am to do a good turn for them. Let   20
the King have the letters I have sent; and repair thou to
me with as much haste as thou wouldst fly death. I have

4.6.0 *and a Servant*] *with an Attendant* F; *and others* Q2   2 SERVANT] F (*Ser⟨uant⟩*; *Gent⟨leman⟩*
Q2   Sailors] F; *Sea-faring men* Q2   3 *Exit Servant*] *not in* FQ2   5 greeted, if] F; greeted. If
Q2   5.1 *Sailors*] Q2; *Saylor* F   6, 8 FIRST SAILOR] FQ2 (*Say⟨lor⟩*)   8 He] F; A Q2   an't] F
(and't); *and* Q2   9 comes] F; *came* Q2   ambassador] Q2 (Embassador); Ambassadours
F   12 HORATIO] Q2; *not in* F   *he reads the letter*] F (*subs.*); *not in* Q2   17 valour. In] F; valour,
and in Q2   20 good] F; *not in* Q2   22 haste] F; speede Q2

4.6 The value of Horatio as a piece of
dramatic machinery is particularly
evident in this scene. Through his
presence at the Danish court the audience
knows of Hamlet's return before Claudius
does so, and they are made aware of much
of his story that he does not choose to
reveal to Claudius.
  9 **th'ambassador** Hamlet has evidently

taken care to give the Sailors no hint as to
who he really is, and has assumed a false
identity for them.
13 **overlooked** read, looked over
      means means of access
15 **appointment** accoutrement
19 **thieves of mercy** merciful thieves
20 **I am . . . them** Compare 'One good turn
      asks another' (Tilley T616).

words to speak in thine ear will make thee dumb; yet are
they much too light for the bore of the matter. These good
fellows will bring thee where I am. Rosencrantz and
Guildenstern hold their course for England. Of them I
have much to tell thee. Farewell.

> He that thou knowest thine,
>
> Hamlet.'

Come, I will give you way for these your letters,   30
And do't the speedier that you may direct me
To him from whom you brought them.   *Exeunt*

4.7   *Enter Claudius and Laertes*

CLAUDIUS
Now must your conscience my acquittance seal,
And you must put me in your heart for friend,
Sith you have heard, and with a knowing ear,
That he which hath your noble father slain
Pursued my life.

LAERTES   It well appears. But tell me
Why you proceeded not against these feats,
So crimeful and so capital in nature,

---

23 thine] Q2; *your* F   24 bore] F; bord Q2   28 He] F; *So* Q2   30 give] F; *not in* Q2; make
Q3   32 Exeunt] Q2; *Exit* F
4.7.6 proceeded] F; proccede Q2   7 crimeful] F; criminall Q2

---

24 **much . . . matter** i.e. quite inadequate to
do the subject justice. The metaphor is
from gunnery: Hamlet's words will be like
small bullets in a large barrel.

30 **give you way** afford you the means of
access (*OED give v.* 49d)

4.7 In this scene, which prepares the way for
the catastrophe, Claudius is at his most
masterful. Rudely jolted out of the complacency he shows at its outset by the
receipt of Hamlet's letter, he regains his
control of things almost at once, turning a
temporary setback into an advantage.
The adroitness with which he works Laertes to his purposes throws its own light on
the earlier part of the tragedy. One sees
now how he won both Gertrude and the
crown.

3 **knowing** intelligent, knowledgeable

6 **proceeded not** took no legal proceedings

feats wicked actions (*OED sb.* 4). Compare *Macbeth* 1.7.80, 'this terrible feat',
i.e. the murder of Duncan, and *Henry V*
3.3.97, 'all fell feats | Enlinked to waste
and desolation'.

7 **crimeful** criminal. Wilson (*MSH* 163–4)
argues that *criminall* (Q2) is a vulgariza-
tion 'on the part of the printer'. But since
we now know that it was set by Y, the
more reliable of the two compositors, this
seems unlikely. The more tenable explanation is that Shakespeare wrote
criminall in his first draft, and then changed it to *crimefull* (F) in the process of
revision. He had used this very rare word,
which appears to be original with him,
once before at *Lucrece* 970, 'this cursed
crimeful night'.

capital punishable by death

As by your safety, wisdom, all things else,
You mainly were stirred up.

CLAUDIUS   O, for two special reasons,
Which may to you, perhaps, seem much unsinewed,   10
And yet to me they are strong. The Queen his mother
Lives almost by his looks; and for myself—
My virtue or my plague, be it either which—
She's so conjunctive to my life and soul
That, as the star moves not but in his sphere,
I could not but by her. The other motive,
Why to a public count I might not go,
Is the great love the general gender bear him,
Who, dipping all his faults in their affection,
Would, like the spring that turneth wood to stone,   20
Convert his guilts to graces; so that my arrows,

---

8 safety, wisdom] F; safetie, greatnes, wisdome Q2   11 And] F; But Q2   they are] F; tha'r
Q2   14 She's] F; She is Q2   conjunctive] F; concliue Q2   20 Would] F; Worke Q2   21
guilts] This edition; Gyues F; Giues Q2

---

8 **your safety** i.e. considerations concerning your safety
safety, wisdom The Q2 reading *safetie,
greatnes, wisdome*, resulting in a six-foot
line, looks like a first attempt which
Shakespeare then tidied up by omitting
greatness as redundant.

9 **mainly** forcefully, greatly (*OED adv.* 2)
special reasons The reasons are *special* in
a sense Claudius does not intend. Neither
is the true reason: the King's knowledge
that Hamlet can accuse him of fratricide.

10 **unsinewed** weak; earliest instance cited
by *OED* of the figurative use of the word

13 **be it either which** whichever of the two it
may be (Abbott 273)

14 **conjunctive** closely united (*OED* 2b).
Since *conjunction* carried the astrological
sense of apparent proximity between two
stars or planets, *conjunctive* leads on to the
simile that follows.

15 **the star . . . sphere** In the Ptolemaic cos-
mology the heavenly bodies were thought
to be carried round the earth by the
spheres, a series of concentric, trans-
parent, hollow globes.

17 **count** reckoning, account, i.e. legal in-
dictment (*OED sb.¹* 8)

18 **general gender** common sort of people
(*OED gender sb.* 1)

19–21 **Who . . . graces** A close parallel to the

idea expressed in these lines is provided by
Coriolanus 1.1.172–4, where the hero
tells the plebeians of Rome, 'Your virtue is
| To make him worthy whose offence sub-
dues him, | And curse that justice did it'.

20 **the spring . . . stone** As limestone
country, in which the springs soon
deposit a layer of lime on objects placed in
them, is common in England, it is not
possible to say which spring Shakespeare
had in mind. Dowden notes that William
Harrison, in his *Description of England* (ed.
Furnivall, p. 349), says that the baths of
King's Newnham in Warwickshire have
this petrifying effect.

21 **guilts** *gyves—Giues* (Q2), *Gyues* (F)—has
to be taken in a figurative sense to make it
at all acceptable. The justification for
guilts is threefold. It is graphically plausible. Shakespeare uses *guilts*, in the plural
and meaning 'crimes', 'faults', in *Lear*
(3.2.57), 'Close pent-up guilts'. *Guilts*
corresponds to *faults* (l. 19); and Shakespeare employs the idea of converting
faults to *graces* elsewhere. *Sonnets* 96
opens thus: 'Some say thy fault is youth,
some wantonness; | Some say thy grace is
youth and gentle sport; | Both grace and
faults are loved of more and less: | Thou
mak'st faults graces that to thee resort.'

> Too slightly timbered for so loud a wind,
> Would have reverted to my bow again,
> And not where I had aimed them.

LAERTES

> And so have I a noble father lost,
> A sister driven into desp'rate terms,
> Whose worth, if praises may go back again,
> Stood challenger, on mount, of all the age
> For her perfections. But my revenge will come.

CLAUDIUS

> Break not your sleeps for that. You must not think   30
> That we are made of stuff so flat and dull
> That we can let our beard be shook with danger,
> And think it pastime. You shortly shall hear more.
> I loved your father, and we love ourself;
> And that, I hope, will teach you to imagine—
> > *Enter a Messenger with letters*
> How now? What news?

MESSENGER   Letters, my lord, from Hamlet.

> This to your majesty; this to the Queen.

CLAUDIUS From Hamlet? Who brought them?

MESSENGER

> Sailors, my lord, they say. I saw them not.
> They were given me by Claudio. He received them.   40

CLAUDIUS Laertes, you shall hear them.—

> Leave us.   *Exit Messenger*

---

22 loud a wind] F; loued Arm'd Q2   24 And] F; But Q2   had] F; haue Q2   aimed] Q2
(aym'd); arm'd F   26 desp'rate] Q2 (desprat); desperate F   27 Whose worth] Q2; Who
was F   35.1 *with letters*] Q2; *not in* F   36 How now? What news?] F; *not in* Q2   Letters, my
lord, from Hamlet.] F; *not in* Q2   37 This] F; These Q2   40–1 them. | Laertes] F; them | Of
him that brought them. | *Laertes* Q2   42 *Exit Messenger*] F; *not in* Q2

---

22 **slightly timbered** lightly built, light in the
  shaft
  so loud a wind so strong a gale (of public
  opinion)
23 **reverted** returned (*OED v.* 2)
25 **have I** i.e. I find (Abbott 425)
26 **terms** circumstances, state (*OED term sb.*
  10)
27 **if praises . . . again** i.e. if I may praise her
  for what she once was
28–9 **Stood . . . perfections** i.e. offered a con-
  spicuous challenge to the entire age to

  equal her excellencies
28 **on mount** set up on high (Onions)
30 **Break . . . that** i.e. don't worry on that
  score. Claudius is quite sure that he has
  disposed of Hamlet.
32 **with** by
39–40 **Sailors . . . them** The roundabout
  route by which the letters reach the King
  testifies to Horatio's care in ensuring that
  Claudius knows no more than Hamlet
  wishes him to.

313

He reads

'High and mighty, you shall know I am set naked on your
kingdom. Tomorrow shall I beg leave to see your kingly
eyes, when I shall, first asking your pardon, thereunto
recount the occasion of my sudden and more strange
return.

Hamlet.'

What should this mean? Are all the rest come back?
Or is it some abuse, and no such thing?   50

LAERTES Know you the hand?

CLAUDIUS   'Tis Hamlet's character.

'Naked'—
And in a postscript here he says 'alone'.
Can you advise me?

LAERTES
I'm lost in it, my lord. But let him come.
It warms the very sickness in my heart
That I shall live and tell him to his teeth,
'Thus didest thou'.

CLAUDIUS   If it be so, Laertes—
As how should it be so, how otherwise?—
Will you be ruled by me?   60

LAERTES
If so you'll not o'errule me to a peace.

CLAUDIUS
To thine own peace. If he be now returned,

42.1 *He reads*] *not in* FQ2   45 eyes, when I shall, first asking your pardon, thereunto] Q2; *Eyes.*
When I shall (first asking your pardon thereunto) F   46 the occasion] Q2; *th'Occasions* F   and more
strange] F; *not in* Q2   48 Hamlet] F; *not in* Q2   50 abuse, and] Q2; abuse? Or F   54 advise] F;
deuise Q2   55 I'm] F; I am Q2   57 shall] FQ1; *not in* Q2   58 didest thou] F; didst thou Q2; he
dies Q1; diest thou WILSON (1964), *conj.* Marshall   61 If so you'll] F; I my Lord, so you will Q2

---

43 **naked** destitute of means
45–6 **pardon, thereunto recount** Since the
    Folio punctuation is obviously wrong in
    placing a full stop after *'eyes'*, it seems best
    to follow Q2 here also. For 'eyes' as almost
    equivalent to 'person' or 'presence' com-
    pare 'We shall express our duty in his eye'
    (4.4.6).
46 **more strange** i.e. even more strange than
    sudden (Abbott 6)
50 **abuse** deception (*OED sb.* 4) Compare
    Macbeth 3.4.142, 'My strange and self-
    abuse'.
    no such thing i.e. not at all what it seems

to be (*OED such* 27c)
51 **character** handwriting
58 **didest** This reading from F makes ad-
    mirable sense. It is an uncompromising
    statement of the *lex talionis* which matters
    so much to Laertes.
58–9 **If it . . . otherwise?** The *it* is am-
    biguous. It could refer to what Hamlet has
    written or to what Laertes has just said.
    The first alternative seems the more
    likely, since Laertes' desire for revenge
    has been so consistent as to leave no room
    for any question about its reality.

As checking at his voyage, and that he means
No more to undertake it, I will work him
To an exploit, now ripe in my device,
Under the which he shall not choose but fall;
And for his death no wind of blame shall breathe;
But even his mother shall uncharge the practice
And call it accident. Some two months since
Here was a gentleman of Normandy.   70
I've seen myself, and served against, the French,
And they can well on horseback; but this gallant
Had witchcraft in't. He grew into his seat,
And to such wondrous doing brought his horse
As had he been incorpsed and demi-natured
With the brave beast. So far he passed my thought
That I, in forgery of shapes and tricks,
Come short of what he did.

LAERTES   A Norman was't?

CLAUDIUS A Norman.

LAERTES Upon my life, Lamord.

CLAUDIUS   The very same.   80

LAERTES

I know him well. He is the brooch indeed
And gem of all the nation.

---

63 checking] F; the King Q2   69 Some] F; *not in* Q2   since| Q2; hence F   71 I've] F; I haue
Q2   72 can] Q2; ran F   73 into] F; vnto Q2   76 passed my] F; topt me Q2   80 Lamord] Q2;
Lamound F   82 the] Q2; our F

63 **As** as a result of, consequent on (Abbott 115)
    checking at stopping short in, shying away from (*OED check v.'* 5)
68 **uncharge the practice** i.e. exonerate our dirty trick from any suspicion of malicious intent (*OED uncharge* 1b)
69 **accident** For the subsequent passage appearing in Q2 but not in F, see Appendix A, xiv.
72 **can well** are very skilful, are masters (Abbott 307)
75 **As had he** as if he had (Abbott 107)
    incorpsed incorporated, made into a single body (a Shakespearian coinage)
    demi-natured i.e. taken on half the nature of (another Shakespearian coinage)

76 **passed my thought** surpassed anything I could imagine
77 **forgery** invention, fabrication
    shapes figures
    tricks feats of horsemanship (*OED sb.* 5)
80 **Lamord** This name, so suggestive of *La Mort*, looks the right name for the centaur-like Norman conjured up out of nowhere to usher in the last phase of the tragedy. F's *Lamound* seems more likely to be a misreading of it than a reference to the cavalier Peter Mount, as Hoby calls Pietro Monte in his translation of Castiglione's *The Courtier* (Everyman edn., p. 45).
81 **brooch** jewel, cynosure (*OED* 2b)

CLAUDIUS He made confession of you,
  And gave you such a masterly report
  For art and exercise in your defence,
  And for your rapier most especially,
  That he cried out 'twould be a sight indeed
  If one could match you, sir. This report of his
  Did Hamlet so envenom with his envy
  That he could nothing do but wish and beg   90
  Your sudden coming o'er to play with him.
  Now, out of this—
LAERTES   What out of this, my lord?
CLAUDIUS
  Laertes, was your father dear to you?
  Or are you like the painting of a sorrow,
  A face without a heart?
LAERTES   Why ask you this?
CLAUDIUS
  Not that I think you did not love your father,
  But that I know love is begun by time,
  And that I see, in passages of proof,
  Time qualifies the spark and fire of it.
  Hamlet comes back. What would you undertake   100
  To show yourself your father's son in deed
  More than in words?
LAERTES   To cut his throat i'th' church.
CLAUDIUS
  No place indeed should murder sanctuarize;
  Revenge should have no bounds. But, good Laertes,

---

86 especially] F; especiall Q2   88 sir. This] F; Sir, this Q2 (sir this)   91 him] F; you Q2   92
What] Q2; Why F   101 your father's son in deed] F4; your Fathers sonne indeed F1; indeede
your fathers sonne Q2; in deed your father's son MALONE

---

83 **made confession of** avowed concerning
  (*OED confession* 4)
85 **defence** fencing (*OED sb.* 4)
88 **one could match you** anyone could be
  found to make a match of it with you
  sir For the subsequent passage appearing
  in Q2 but not in F, see Appendix A, xv.
89 **his envy** envy of it
97 **time** circumstance (Onions)
98 **passages of proof** i.e. experiences that

bear out the truth of what I am saying
99 For a passage following this line in Q2 but
  not in F, see Appendix A, xvi.
  Time . . . it Compare 'Time wears away
  love' (Tilley T340)
  qualifies abates, diminishes (*OED v.* 12b)
103 **murder sanctuarize** i.e. afford sanctu-
  ary to a murderer (earliest example
  of *sanctuarize* cited by *OED*)

Will you do this?—Keep close within your chamber.
Hamlet returned shall know you are come home.
We'll put on those shall praise your excellence,
And set a double varnish on the fame
The Frenchman gave you; bring you, in fine, together,
And wager on your heads. He, being remiss,   110
Most generous, and free from all contriving,
Will not peruse the foils; so that with ease,
Or with a little shuffling, you may choose
A sword unbated, and, in a pass of practice,
Requite him for your father.

LAERTES   I will do't;
And for that purpose I'll anoint my sword.
I bought an unction of a mountebank,
So mortal that but dip a knife in it,
Where it draws blood no cataplasm so rare,
Collected from all simples that have virtue   120
Under the moon, can save the thing from death
That is but scratched withal. I'll touch my point
With this contagion, that, if I gall him slightly,
It may be death.

CLAUDIUS   Let's further think of this;

---

105 this?] Q5; this, FQ2   110 on] F; ore Q2   114 pass] F; pace Q2   116 that] F; not in Q2;
the Q3   118 that but dip] Q2; I but dipt F

105 **Will you do this?** The question mark is
required by Laertes' answer, 'I will do't'
(l. 115). The word *this*, used in an
anticipatory sense to mean 'this that I am
about to tell you', covers the entire plan
Claudius now sets out in detail.

107 **put on those shall** i.e. set agents to work
to

109 **in fine** finally

110–12 **He . . . foils** Compare 'They that
think none ill are soonest beguiled' (Tilley
T221).

110 **remiss** careless, negligent. The 'negligence' in question is the 'noble carelessness' or *sprezzatura* attributed to the hero
in *Coriolanus* (2.2.13).

111 **generous** noble-minded (*OED* 2b)

112 **peruse** examine carefully (*OED v.* 2)

113 **shuffling** sleight of hand, shifting
around (of the foils) (*OED vbl. sb.* 3)

114 **sword unbated** i.e. not blunted, as a foil
is (first instance of this sense of *unbated*
cited by *OED*). For *bate*, meaning 'to

blunt', see *LLL* 1.1.6, 'That honour
which shall bate his [Time's] scythe's
keen edge'.

    pass of practice either (1) treacherous
thrust, or (2) bout characterized by
deliberate treachery (on your part)

117 **unction** ointment. Webster, probably
influenced by *Hamlet*, refers to poison in
the form of a powder as an 'unction' (*The
White Devil* 5.3.28).

    mountebank itinerant quack, like Scoto
of Mantua, whom Volpone impersonates
in 2.2. of Jonson's play

119 **cataplasm** plaster, salve (not elsewhere
in Shakespeare)

120–1 **Collected . . . moon** See note to
3.2.241.

120 **simples that have virtue** herbs having
medicinal power

123 **contagion** poison that infects the blood
(*OED* 3b—no other instance of this sense
cited)

    gall graze

Weigh what convenience both of time and means
May fit us to our shape. If this should fail,
And that our drift look through our bad performance,
'Twere better not essayed. Therefore this project
Should have a back or second, that might hold
If this did blast in proof. Soft, let me see.   130
We'll make a solemn wager on your cunnings—I ha't.
When in your motion you are hot and dry—
As make your bouts more violent to that end—
And that he calls for drink, I'll have prepared him
A chalice for the nonce; whereon but sipping,
If he by chance escape your venomed stuck,
Our purpose may hold there.—

         Enter Gertrude ⌐in tears⌐

                         How now, sweet queen?

GERTRUDE
One woe doth tread upon another's heel,
So fast they follow. Your sister's drowned, Laertes.

LAERTES Drowned? O where?   140

GERTRUDE
There is a willow grows aslant a brook

---

126 shape. If this should fail,] ROWE; shape, if . . . faile; F; shape if . . . fayle, Q2   130 did] Q2;
should F   131 cunnings] Q2; commings F   133 that] Q2; the F   134 prepared] F; prefard
Q2   137.1 *in tears*] This edition; *not in* FQ2Q1   137 How now, sweet queen?] F2; how sweet
Queene. F1; but stay, what noyse? Q2; How now Gertred, Q1   139 they] Q2; they'l F   141
aslant a] F; ascaunt the Q2

126 **to our shape** for the role we are to play
(*OED shape sb.* 8)
127 **drift** scheme, plot (*OED sb.* 5). Compare
Two Gentlemen 2.6.43, 'As thou hast lent
me wit to plot this drift.'
   look become visible (*OED v.* 20b)
129 **back or second** stand-by (*OED back sb.*[1]
12) or second string (*OED second sb.*[2] 8c).
Claudius is now using military terminology.
   hold remain firm, prove effective
130 **blast in proof** i.e. blow up in our faces
when we put it to the test (Onions). The
metaphor, in keeping with those preceding it, appears to derive from the practice
of testing cannon by firing them; but
proof is lacking.
131 **cunnings** skills, proficiencies
136 **stuck** thrust or lunge (*OED sb.*[2]). Compare *Twelfth Night* 3.4.262–5, 'I had a
pass with him . . . and he gives me the

stuck in with such a mortal motion that it
is inevitable'.
137 **How now, sweet queen?** Although
these words, in the incomplete form *how
sweet Queene*, appear in F only, Q1's *How
now Gertred* shows that they were spoken
on the stage.
138–9 **One woe . . . follow** See note to
4.5.74–5, and Tilley M1012.
141 **willow** The tree is an appropriate one,
since the willow was the emblem of
mourning and of forsaken love; see *OED
willow sb.* 1d and 6d for numerous
examples, and Sternfeld's discussion
(pp. 23–52) of 'The Willow Song' in
Othello (4.3.25–55).
   aslant slanting across (as willows so often
do). Whereas *aslant*, the reading of F, is a
well authenticated word, *OED* can cite no
other instance of *askant* (Q2), a variant of
askance (*adv.*), being used as a preposition.

That shows his hoar leaves in the glassy stream.
There with fantastic garlands did she come
Of crow-flowers, nettles, daisies, and long purples
That liberal shepherds give a grosser name,
But our cold maids do dead men's fingers call them.
There on the pendent boughs her coronet weeds
Clambering to hang, an envious sliver broke;
When down the weedy trophies and herself
Fell in the weeping brook. Her clothes spread wide,   150
And mermaid-like awhile they bore her up;
Which time she chanted snatches of old tunes,
As one incapable of her own distress,
Or like a creature native and endued
Unto that element. But long it could not be
Till that her garments, heavy with their drink,
Pulled the poor wretch from her melodious lay
To muddy death.

LAERTES   Alas, then is she drowned.

142 hoar] F (hore), horry Q2   143 There with . . . come] F; There with . . . make Q2   146
cold] F; cull-cold Q2   147 coronet] F; cronet Q2; crownet WILSON   149 down the] F; downe
her Q2   152 tunes] FQI; laudes Q2   156 their] Q2QI; her F   157 lay] Q2; buy F   158
Alas, then is she drowned.] This edition; Alas then, is she drown'd? F; Alas, then she is drownd.
Q2; So she is drownde: QI

142 **hoar** greyish-white (the colour of the
underside of a willow leaf).
144 **crow-flowers . . . long purples** While the
precise designation of some of these wild
flowers has been the subject of dispute,
there seems to be general agreement that
all are flowers of the early spring and thus
suitable for Ophelia to pick and wear. It is,
perhaps, significant that the reporter of
QI was unable to remember the name of
a single one of them and, consequently,
lumped them all together as 'sundry sorts
of flowers'.
  crow-flowers ragged-robins (OED *crow-
flower* and *William*)
  nettles The plant referred to is probably
the *dead-nettle*, which has leaves like those
of the ordinary nettle but does not sting.
Some bear white flowers, others purple
flowers, thus fitting into the general pattern of colours—red, white, and purple
—in the garlands.
  long purples The flower intended is probably the *Orchis mascula* (OED *long a.*[1] 17c).
145 **liberal** free-spoken
  a grosser name Among the names given

in Lyte's *Herbal* (1578), all referring to the
appearance of the roots of the *Orchis
mascula*, are priest's-pintle, dog's cullions,
fool's ballocks, and goat's cullions.
146 **cold** chaste (and therefore reserved in
speech)
  dead men's fingers 'a local name for
various species of *Orchis* . . . in Shakespeare probably the Early Purple Orchis,
Orchis mascula' (OED *dead man*, citing this
as its earliest example)
148 **envious sliver** spiteful little branch
149 **trophies** i.e. garlands (Onions). Com-
pare *Caesar* 1.1.69–70, 'let no images | Be
hung with Caesar's trophies'.
152 **tunes** This F reading, supported by QI,
is preferred here to the *lauds* of Q2 on the
assumption that it is the product of
authorial revision, designed to replace a
rare word with a more immediately
intelligible one.
153 **incapable of** insensible to (OED *incapable* 2)
154–5 **endued . . . element** i.e. properly
equipped for living in water

GERTRUDE Drowned, drowned.

LAERTES Too much of water hast thou, poor Ophelia,   160
And therefore I forbid my tears. But yet
It is our trick; nature her custom holds,
Let shame say what it will.

     He weeps

                    When these are gone,
The woman will be out. Adieu, my lord.
I have a speech of fire that fain would blaze,
But that this folly douts it.   *Exit*

CLAUDIUS   Let's follow, Gertrude.
How much I had to do to calm his rage!
Now fear I this will give it start again;
Therefore let's follow.   *Exeunt*

5.1   *Enter two Clowns, ⌈the First carrying a spade and a*
      pickaxe⌉

FIRST CLOWN Is she to be buried in Christian burial that

---

163 He weeps] *not in* FQ2Q1   165 of fire] F; a fire Q2; o' fire WILSON   166 douts] F (doubts);
drownes Q2
    5.1.0 Enter two Clowns] FQ2; *enter Clowne and an other* Q1   *the First carrying a spade and a*
pickaxe] This edition; *not in* FQ2Q1   1 *(and throughout scene)* FIRST CLOWN] ROWE; *Clown*
FQ2Q1   that] F; when she Q2

---

162 **our trick** i.e. the natural response of us
mortals. Compare *2 Henry IV* 1.2.204–5,
'it was always yet the trick of our English
nation, if they have a good thing, to make
it too common.'
163 **these** i.e. these tears
164 **The woman will be out** i.e. the woman
in me will be over and done with
166 **folly douts it** i.e. foolish impulse (to
weep) extinguishes it
5.1 Between the death of Ophelia and her
funeral there comes what is, perhaps, the
most extraordinary scene in this extraordinary play. For the previous four acts
death has been a constant presence and a
constant preoccupation, brooding, as it
were, over the action. Apart from Hamlet's mordant comments on its reductive
powers in 4.3, the emphasis has been on
the terror and the mystery of it. It has
been treated with the seriousness usually
considered proper to tragedy. Now, however, the whole perspective undergoes a
radical alteration. To the Grave-digger
death is neither terrible nor mysterious. It
provides him with his living and with a
never failing source of conversation and
jest. It is no wonder that the Prince should
find him fascinating and engage in a
battle of wits with him. He tells Hamlet
much that Hamlet needs to know, and, in
doing so, he extends the whole scope and
significance of the tragedy.
0.1–2 *Enter . . . pickaxe* The First Clown, i.e.
rustic, is clearly a grave-digger, who will,
in due course, need his implements; but
there is nothing in what follows to indicate that the Second Clown is also a
grave-digger. He seems to be simply a
crony of the First Clown who has stopped
for a chat, unable to resist the fascination
that the digging of a hole still exerts on
Englishmen of all classes.
1 **Christian burial** i.e. burial in consecrated
ground, and with the full service and
ceremonies of the Church. The Book of
Common Prayer states explicitly that its
Office for the Burial of the Dead 'is not to
be used for any that . . . have laid violent
hands upon themselves'.

wilfully seeks her own salvation?

SECOND CLOWN I tell thee she is; and therefore make her
grave straight. The crowner hath sat on her, and finds it
Christian burial.

FIRST CLOWN How can that be, unless she drowned herself
in her own defence?

SECOND CLOWN Why, 'tis found so.

FIRST CLOWN It must be *so offendendo*, it cannot be else. For
here lies the point: if I drown myself wittingly, it argues   10
an act; and an act hath three branches—it is to act, to
do, and to perform. Argal, she drowned herself wittingly.

SECOND CLOWN Nay, but hear you, Goodman Delver—

FIRST CLOWN Give me leave. Here lies the water—good.
Here stands the man—good. If the man go to this water
and drown himself, it is, will he nill he, he goes. Mark you
that. But if the water come to him and drown him, he
drowns not himself. Argal, he that is not guilty of his own
death shortens not his own life.

3 *(and throughout scene)* SECOND CLOWN] ROWE; *Other* FQ2; 2 Q1   and therefore] F; therfore
Q2   9 *so offendendo*] This edition; *Se offendendo* F; so offended Q2   11 to act] Q2; an Act
F   12 do, and to] F (doe and to); doe, to Q2   Argal] F (argall); or all Q2   13 Goodman Delver]
F; good man deluer Q2   17 that.] F (that?); that, Q2

2 **salvation** Like Verges in *Much Ado*, who
says, 'it were pity but they should suffer
salvation, body and soul' (3.3.2–3), the
First Clown mistakes 'salvation' for
'damnation'.

4 **straight** (1) straightaway (2) narrow
(*strait*)
  crowner an obsolete by-form of *coroner*,
  now current only as an allusion to this
  passage
  sat i.e. held an inquest (*OED sit v.* 26)

4–5 **finds it Christian burial** i.e. finds Ophelia not guilty of suicide

9 *so offendendo* This reading is a combination of Q2's 'so offended' and F's '*Se offendendo*'. The assumption behind it is that
the Q2 compositor, Y, set *so* correctly but
then, merely glancing at the next word,
mistook it for *offended*. The F compositor,
I, on the other hand, knowing some Latin,
naturally read *so* as *se*, thus obscuring the
way in which the First Clown picks up *so*
from the Second's use of it in the previous
line. He means, of course, *se defendendo*.

10–19 **if I drown . . . life** As Sir John Haw-
kins, the friend and biographer of Dr Johnson, was the first to point out, this passage
of legal nonsense must allude to the

celebrated case of Sir James Hales, a Common Law judge, who killed himself by
walking into a river in 1554. His death
resulted in a lawsuit, turning on the question of whether he should or should not
forfeit a lease as a punishment for his
suicide. In the course of the hearing the
counsel for the defence divided 'the act of
self destruction' into three parts; and the
verdict of one of the judges was, 'Sir James
Hales was dead. And how came he by his
death? It may be answered by drowning.
And who drowned him? Sir James Hales.
And when did he drown him? In his
lifetime. So that Sir James Hales being
alive caused Sir James Hales to die, the act
of the living was the death of the dead
man. And for this offence it is reasonable
to punish the living man, who committed
the offence, and not the dead man.'

12 **Argal** therefore (a vulgar perversion of the
Latin *ergo*). The same word, in the form of
Argo, appears in *2 Henry VI* (4.2.28), and
in *Sir Thomas More* D, l. 5 in Alexander.

13 **Goodman Delver** *Goodman* was the normal prefix to designations of occupation.

16 **will he nill he** proverbial (Tilley W401)

SECOND CLOWN But is this law?   20

FIRST CLOWN Ay, marry, is't—crowner's quest law.

SECOND CLOWN Will you ha' the truth on't? If this had not been a gentlewoman, she should have been buried out of Christian burial.

FIRST CLOWN Why, there thou sayst; and the more pity that great folk should have countenance in this world to drown or hang themselves more than their even-Christian. Come, my spade. There is no ancient gentlemen but gardeners, ditchers, and grave-makers. They hold up Adam's profession.   30

        ⌈*He digs*⌉

SECOND CLOWN Was he a gentleman?

FIRST CLOWN He was the first that ever bore arms.

SECOND CLOWN Why, he had none.

FIRST CLOWN What, art a heathen? How dost thou understand the Scripture? The Scripture says Adam digged. Could he dig without arms? I'll put another question to thee. If thou answerest me not to the purpose, confess thyself—

SECOND CLOWN Go to.

FIRST CLOWN What is he that builds stronger than either the   40
mason, the shipwright, or the carpenter?

SECOND CLOWN The gallows-maker; for that frame outlives a thousand tenants.

FIRST CLOWN I like thy wit well, in good faith. The gallows does well. But how does it well? It does well to those that do ill. Now thou dost ill to say the gallows is built stronger than the church. Argal, the gallows may do well to thee. To't again, come.

---

23 of] F; a Q2   27–8 their even-Christian] F (their euen Christian); theyr euen Christen Q2;
other people Q1   28 Come,] F; Come₍ₐ₎ Q2   30.1 *He digs*] *not in* FQ2Q1   32 He] F;
A Q2   33–6 SECOND CLOWN Why . . . arms?] F; *not in* Q2   42 frame] F; *not in* Q2

21 **quest** inquest   32 **bore arms** had a coat of arms (the mark of
25 **there thou sayst** i.e. how right you are   a gentleman)
26 **have countenance** be privileged   37–8 **confess thyself** a reference to the com-
27–8 **even-Christian** fellow Christians (*OED*).   mon saying 'Confess thyself and be
    The word is used collectively.   hanged' (Tilley C587)
28–9 **ancient gentlemen** i.e. gentlemen   42 **frame** (1) a gallows (2) wooden frame-
    whose right to that title goes back to the   work of a house (*OED sb.* 7 and 10)
    remotest times   45 **does well** i.e. is a good answer
30 **hold up** carry on, keep up (*OED v.* 44b)

SECOND CLOWN Who builds stronger than a mason, a ship-
    wright, or a carpenter?   50
FIRST CLOWN Ay, tell me that, and unyoke.
SECOND CLOWN Marry, now I can tell.
FIRST CLOWN To't.
SECOND CLOWN Mass, I cannot tell.
        Enter Hamlet and Horatio, afar off
FIRST CLOWN Cudgel thy brains no more about it, for your
    dull ass will not mend his pace with beating. And when
    you are asked this question next, say 'a grave-maker'. The
    houses that he makes lasts till doomsday. Go, get thee to
    Yaughan; fetch me a stoup of liquor.   *Exit Second Clown*
    (*He digs and sings*)
            In youth when I did love, did love,   60
                Methought it was very sweet
            To contract-O-the time for-a-my behove,
                O, methought there was nothing meet.
HAMLET Has this fellow no feeling of his business that he
    sings at grave-making?
HORATIO Custom hath made it in him a property of easiness.

54.1 *Enter Hamlet and Horatio, afar off.* F; *Enter Hamlet and Horatio* Q2 (*after* 63) Q1 (*after* 59)   58 that] F; *not in* Q2Q1   lasts] FQ2; Last Q1   58–9 to Yaughan] F; in, and Q2   59 stoup] FQ1 (stope); soope Q2   *Exit Second Clown*] *not in* FQ2Q1   59.1 *He digs and sings*] *Sings* F; *Song* Q2   63 there was nothing meet] F; there a was nothing a meet Q2   64 business that he] F; busines? a Q2   65 at] F; in Q2

---

51 **unyoke** literally, unyoke your team of oxen, i.e. have done with the effort of thinking
55 **Cudgel thy brains** proverbial (Tilley B602)
55–6 **your dull ass . . . beating** Compare 'A dull ass must have a sharp spur' (Dent A348.1)
59 **Yaughan** One of the play's minor mysteries, Yaughan was, presumably, a tavern-keeper operating in or near the Globe.
60–92 **In youth . . . meet** The Clown's three snatches of song are a garbled version of some stanzas from Thomas Lord Vaux's very popular poem 'The Aged Lover Renounceth Love', which first appeared in *Songs and Sonnets*, or *Tottel's Miscellany*, as it came to be called, in 1557. The initial stanza of Vaux's poem runs thus in *Tot-*

tel's Miscellany: 'I loathe that I did love, | In youth that I thought sweet: | As time requires for my behove | Methinks they are not meet.' See Appendix D.
62 **contract** shorten. Jenkins suspects 'that in garbling the verse the Clown gives another instance of his penchant for replacing the required sense with its opposite. The point is not to *contract* the happy time of youthful love but to prolong it.'
    O . . . a The likeliest explanation of these interpolations is that they are meant to represent the grunts of the Grave-digger as he pauses for breath.
    behove behoof, advantage
66 **Custom . . . easiness** proverbial (Tilley C933)
    property of easiness i.e. something about which he has no qualms

HAMLET 'Tis e'en so; the hand of little employment hath the
      daintier sense.

FIRST CLOWN (*sings*)
            But age with his stealing steps
                Hath caught me in his clutch,   70
            And hath shipped me intil the land,
                As if I had never been such.

      He throws up a skull

HAMLET That skull had a tongue in it, and could sing once.
      How the knave jowls it to th' ground, as if it were Cain's
      jawbone, that did the first murder. It might be the pate of
      a politician which this ass now o'er-offices, one that
      would circumvent God, might it not?

HORATIO It might, my lord.

HAMLET Or of a courtier, which could say, 'Good morrow,

---

68 daintier] F; dintier Q2   69 sings] F (*Clowne sings*); *Song* Q2   70 caught] F; clawed Q2   71
intil] F; into Q2   72.1 *He throws up a skull*] not in FQ2; *he throwes vp a shouel* Q1   74 to th']
F; to the Q2   it were] F; twere Q2   75 It] F; this Q2   76 now] Q2; *not in* F   o'er-offices] F;
ore-reaches Q2   77 would] Q2; could F

67–8 **hath the daintier sense** i.e. is more sensitive
69–72 **But age . . . such** The Grave-digger
  combines Vaux's 3rd stanza with his
  13th, losing the rhyme at the end of his
  3rd line in the process. The relevant lines
  are: 'For age with stealing steps, | Hath
  clawed me with his crutch; | And lusty life
  away she leaps, | As there had been none
  such', and 'For beauty with her band |
  These crooked cares hath wrought, | And
  shipped me into the land, | From whence
  I first was brought.'
69 **age with his stealing steps** proverbial
  (Tilley A70)
71 **shipped** sent off, dismissed (*OED v.* 7d).
  Compare *Titus* 1.1.206, 'Andronicus,
  would thou were shipped to hell'.
  intil into (dialect)
  land earth (from which man came)
72 **such** i.e. such a thing as a young man in
  love
74 **jowls** slams, dashes (with a quibble on
  jowl meaning 'jawbone')
74–5 **Cain's jawbone, that** i.e. the jawbone
  of Cain, who. For this use of *that*,
  separated from its antecedent, see Abbott

262. According to a mediaeval legend
  which 'seems to have originated in England, where it is found as early as the
  ninth century in the Old English prose of
  Solomon and Saturn', Cain killed Abel with
  the jawbone of an ass; see A. C. Cawley's
  edition of *The Wakefield Pageants in the
  Towneley Cycle* (Manchester, 1958), p.
  93. But, as Jenkins shrewdly observes, 'it
  does not follow that the jawbone here is
  the ass's and not Cain's own. What does is
  the justice of Cain's being in his turn jow-
  led by an *ass*.'
76 **politician** Here, as always in Shakespeare, the word carries a pejorative sense
  —unprincipled schemer.
  o'er-offices i.e. lords it over by virtue of
  his office (*OED*)—a Shakespearian nonce-
  word. Jenkins compares *Coriolanus*
  5.2.61, 'a Jack guardant cannot office me
  from my son Coriolanus'.
77 **circumvent God** As Wilson observes,
  'Cain was the first "politician"; he denied
  that he was his brother's keeper, and
  when God asked him where Abel was he
  quibbled' (Genesis 4: 9).

sweet lord. How dost thou, good lord?' This might be my   80
Lord Such-a-one, that praised my Lord Such-a-one's
horse when he meant to beg it, might it not?

HORATIO Ay, my lord.

HAMLET Why, e'en so, and now my Lady Worm's, chapless, and knocked about the mazard with a sexton's
spade. Here's fine revolution, if we had the trick to see't.
Did these bones cost no more the breeding but to play at
loggats with 'em? Mine ache to think on't.

FIRST CLOWN (*sings*)

    A pickaxe and a spade, a spade,
      For and a shrouding-sheet;   90
    O, a pit of clay for to be made
      For such a guest is meet.

He throws up another skull

HAMLET There's another. Why, might not that be the skull of
a lawyer? Where be his quiddits now, his quillets, his
cases, his tenures, and his tricks? Why does he suffer this
rude knave now to knock him about the sconce with a
dirty shovel, and will not tell him of his action of battery?

---

80 thou, good] F; thou, sweet Q2   82 he meant] FQ1; a went Q2   84 chapless] F; Choples
Q2   85 mazard] F; massene Q2   86 if] F; and Q2   88 'em] F; them Q2   89 *sings*] F (*Clowne
sings*); *Song* Q2   92.1 *He throws up another skull*] *not in* FQ2Q1   93 Why,] JENKINS; why$_\Lambda$
FQ2   might] F; may Q2   of] Q2Q1; of of F   94 quiddits] F; quiddities Q2   quillets] FQ1;
quillites Q2; quillities Q3   96 rude] F; madde Q2

80–2 **This might . . . beg it** Compare *Timon*
   1.2.208–13, where Timon presents the
   Third Lord with 'a bay courser' of his
   which the Third Lord has praised.

84 **chapless** with the cheeks (chaps/chops)
   missing—the usual state of a skull. The
   word seems to be a Shakespearian
   coinage, the earliest instance cited by
   OED being at *Romeo* 4.1.83.

85 **mazard** head (a bit of Elizabethan slang
   for which Shakespeare seems responsible,
   a *mazard* or *mazer* being literally a cup or
   drinking vessel)

86 **revolution** change, alteration (brought
   about by time) (*OED sb.* 6)
   trick art, knack

87 **cost . . . play** i.e. cost no more to bring
   them to full growth than would warrant
   men's playing

88 **loggats** A game in which thick sticks (loggats) are thrown to lie as near as possible
   to a stake fixed in the ground or a block of
   wood on a floor (Onions).

89–92 **A pickaxe . . . meet** Vaux's 8th stan-
   za reads: 'A pickaxe and a spade, | And
   eke a shrouding sheet, | A house of clay for
   to be made, | For such a guest most meet.'

90 **For and** and furthermore (*OED for conj.* 5)

94 **quiddits** subtleties, captious arguments.
   The *quiddity* or *quiddit* of a thing was
   originally its essential nature, a much
   debated topic in scholastic logic.
   quillets quibbles (much the same things
   as *quiddits*, from which the word appears
   to derive). Compare *1 Henry VI* 2.4.17–18,
   'in these nice sharp quillets of the
   law, | Good faith, I am no wiser than a
   daw'.

95 **tenures** titles to property
   tricks sharp practices

96 **sconce** head (a jocular synonym of uncertain origin)

97 **action of battery** liability to prosecution
   for common assault. Compare *Twelfth
   Night* 4.1.33, 'I'll have an action of battery
   against him, if there be any law in Illyria'.

Hum! This fellow might be in's time a great buyer of land,
with his statutes, his recognizances, his fines, his double
vouchers, his recoveries. Is this the fine of his fines and the   100
recovery of his recoveries, to have his fine pate full of fine
dirt? Will his vouchers vouch him no more of his pur-
chases, and double ones too, than the length and breadth
of a pair of indentures? The very conveyances of his lands
will hardly lie in this box; and must the inheritor himself
have no more, ha?

HORATIO   Not a jot more, my lord.

HAMLET   Is not parchment made of sheepskins?

HORATIO   Ay, my lord, and of calf-skins too.

HAMLET   They are sheep and calves that seek out assurance   110
in that. I will speak to this fellow.—Whose grave's this,
sirrah?

FIRST CLOWN   Mine, sir.

(*He sings*)   O, a pit of clay for to be made
                          For such a guest is meet.

100–1 Is this . . . recoveries] F; *not in* Q2   102 his vouchers] F; vouchers Q2   103 double
ones too] F; doubles Q2   105 hardly] F; scarcely Q2   the inheritor] F; th'inheritor Q2   109
calf-skins] Calue-skinnes F; Calues-skinnes Q2   110 that] F; which Q2   112 sirrah] Q2; Sir
F   114 *He sings*] *not in* FQ2   O . . . made] *roman in* Q2; *italic in* F   O] F; or Q2   115 For
. . . meet] F (*in italic*); *not in* Q2

99   **statutes** bonds by which the creditor had
the power of holding the debtor's lands in
case of default (*OED sb.* 4a)
   recognizances bonds or obligations testifying that one party owes the other a certain sum of money (Onions)
   fines A *fine* was an 'amicable agreement
of a fictitious suit for the possession of
lands, formerly in vogue where the ordinary modes of conveyance were not available or equally efficacious' (Onions).

99–100 **double vouchers** *Vouchers* (l. 102)
and *double vouchers* were 'legal devices for
recovery or converting estate entail into
fee simple, involving fictitious actions,
and the summoning (vouching) of men of
straw to warrant titles which all parties
wished invalidated, and which became
invalidated by the vouchees defaulting'
(Wilson).

100   **fine of** end, net result of (*OED sb.*¹ 1).
Compare *All's Well* 4.4.35, 'the fine's the
crown'.

101   **recovery of his recoveries** profit from his
land transactions
   fine pate subtle head

101–2 **fine dirt** well powdered dirt

102   **vouch** assure, guarantee

103–4 **the length . . . indentures** i.e. a bit of
land (his grave) that is no bigger than one
of his legal documents

104   **a pair of indentures** a deed or covenant
between two parties taking the form of
two copies both of which were originally
written on one piece of parchment or
paper, and then cut apart in a serrated or
sinuous line, so that when brought
together again at any time, the two edges
exactly tallied and showed that they were
parts of one and the same original document.

105   **box** (1) deed-box (2) coffin. *OED* (*black a.*
1) has a citation for 'the black box (meaning the coffin)' that is dated 1674.
   inheritor owner

110   **sheep and calves** i.e. simpletons. Compare 'As simple as a sheep', and 'As wise
as a calf' (Dent S295.1 and C16.1).
   assurance (1) security (2) conveyance of
land

111   **that** i.e. a piece of parchment

HAMLET I think it be thine indeed, for thou liest in't.

FIRST CLOWN You lie out on't, sir, and therefore it is not
  yours. For my part, I do not lie in't, and yet it is mine.

HAMLET Thou dost lie in't, to be in't and say 'tis thine. 'Tis
  for the dead, not for the quick; therefore thou liest.   120

FIRST CLOWN 'Tis a quick lie, sir, 'twill away again from me
  to you.

HAMLET What man dost thou dig it for?

FIRST CLOWN For no man, sir.

HAMLET What woman, then?

FIRST CLOWN For none neither.

HAMLET Who is to be buried in't?

FIRST CLOWN One that was a woman, sir; but, rest her soul,
  she's dead.

HAMLET How absolute the knave is! We must speak by the   130
  card, or equivocation will undo us. By the Lord, Horatio,
  these three years I have taken note of it; the age is grown
  so picked that the toe of the peasant comes so near the
  heel of the courtier he galls his kibe.—How long hast
  thou been a grave-maker?

FIRST CLOWN Of all the days i'th' year, I came to't that day
  that our last king Hamlet o'ercame Fortinbras.

---

117 it is] F; tis Q2   118 and] F; *not in* Q2   119 'tis] F; it is Q2   132 these three] F; this three
Q2; This seauen Q1   taken] F; tooke Q2   134 heel] Q2Q1; heeles F   the] Q2Q1; our F   135
a] F; *not in* Q2   136 all] F; *not in* Q2   137 o'ercame] F; ouercame Q2

---

120 **quick** living

130 **How absolute** i.e. what a stickler for
  accuracy

130-1 **by the card** with absolute precision
  (*OED sb.*[2] 4c), much the same as 'by the
  book'

131 **equivocation** ambiguity

133 **picked** refined, over-concerned with
  fashion (*OED ppl.a.* 2). There seems to
  be a connection between *picked*, *tooth-
  picks*, and foreign travel; see *K. John*
  1.1.189-204.

134 **kibe** chapped or ulcerated chilblain
  especially on the heel

136 **Of all the days i'th' year** This expression
  is also used by the Nurse in *Romeo*
  (1.3.17), and she too connects it with a
  birthday—Juliet's. The resemblance may
  be significant; for whether the words
  spring from the poet's recalling his earlier
  tragedy or not, they lead into one of the

most remarkable moments in the entire
play, a powerful union of common experience and high art. The common experience is there in the common phrases:
'Of all the days i'th' year', 'It was the very
day', and 'man and boy, thirty years'. It is
thus that we all remember things that
happened in the past. But what do these
expressions authenticate? The first takes
us back to the beginning of the Hamlet
saga and to the opening scene. Also the
mention of old Fortinbras reminds us of
the existence of young Fortinbras with
whom the play will end. The second suggests that the paths of the Grave-digger
and the Prince have been converging ever
since Hamlet was born, even, perhaps,
that the next grave to be dug will be Hamlet's. And what of 'man and boy, thirty
years'? Like the other two expressions, it
authenticates matter of the first impor-

HAMLET How long is that since?

FIRST CLOWN Cannot you tell that? Every fool can tell that.
It was the very day that young Hamlet was born—he   140
that was mad and sent into England.

HAMLET Ay, marry. Why was he sent into England?

FIRST CLOWN Why, because he was mad. He shall recover
his wits there; or if he do not, it's no great matter there.

HAMLET Why?

FIRST CLOWN 'Twill not be seen in him there. There the men
are as mad as he.

HAMLET How came he mad?

FIRST CLOWN Very strangely, they say.

HAMLET How strangely?   150

FIRST CLOWN Faith, e'en with losing his wits.

HAMLET Upon what ground?

FIRST CLOWN Why, here in Denmark. I have been sexton
here, man and boy, thirty years.

HAMLET How long will a man lie i'th'earth ere he rot?

FIRST CLOWN I'faith, if he be not rotten before he die—as
we have many pocky corpses nowadays that will scarce
hold the laying in—he will last you some eight year or
nine year. A tanner will last you nine year.

HAMLET Why he more than another?   160

FIRST CLOWN Why, sir, his hide is so tanned with his trade
that he will keep out water a great while; and your water
is a sore decayer of your whoreson dead body. Here's a
skull now. This skull has lain in the earth three and
twenty years.

140 the] F; that Q2   141 was] F; is Q2   143–4 he...He...he] F; a...a...a Q2   144 it's] F;
'tis Q2Q1   146 him there. There] Q2 (him there, there); him, there F   153 sexton] Q2 (Sexten);
sixteene F   156 I'faith] FQ1; Fayth Q2   he...he] FQ1; a...a Q2   157 nowadays] F; *not in*
Q2Q1   158 he] FQ1; a Q2   162 he will] F; a will Q2   164 now. This skull has lain in the] F;
now hath lyen you i'th Q2   164–5 three and twenty] F; 23. Q2; this dozen Q1

tance: the detailed knowledge of dead
bodies, including Yorick's, which the
Clown now displays, and thus provides
the opening for a superb flash-back to
Hamlet's boyhood. The poet's concern is
not with arithmetic and Hamlet's age, but
with much larger matters.

146–7 **There . . . as he** Madness was often
attributed to the English by the social
satirists of the time. John Marston, for
example, writes: 'your lordship shall ever

find . . . amongst a hundred Englishmen,
four-score and ten madmen' (*The Malcon-
tent* 3.1.91–6).

157 **pocky** pox-ridden, syphilitic (not elsewhere in Shakespeare)

158 **hold the laying in** i.e. stand burial (*OED*
hold *v.* 3d)

163 **whoreson** used attributively here to express familiarity mingled with contempt
(*OED* b)

HAMLET Whose was it?

FIRST CLOWN A whoreson mad fellow's it was. Whose do
you think it was?

HAMLET Nay, I know not.

FIRST CLOWN A pestilence on him for a mad rogue! A poured   170
a flagon of Rhenish on my head once. This same skull, sir,
was Yorick's skull, the King's jester.

HAMLET This?

FIRST CLOWN E'en that.

HAMLET Let me see. (*He takes the skull*) Alas, poor Yorick. I
knew him, Horatio, a fellow of infinite jest, of most excellent fancy. He hath borne me on his back a thousand
times. And now how abhorred in my imagination it is!
My gorge rises at it. Here hung those lips that I have
kissed I know not how oft. Where be your gibes now,   180
your gambols, your songs, your flashes of merriment that
were wont to set the table on a roar? No one now to mock
your own grinning? Quite chop-fallen? Now get you to
my lady's chamber and tell her, let her paint an inch
thick, to this favour she must come. Make her laugh at
that. Prithee, Horatio, tell me one thing.

HORATIO What's that, my lord?

HAMLET Dost thou think Alexander looked o' this fashion
i'th'earth?

HORATIO E'en so.   190

HAMLET And smelt so? Pah!
          He throws the skull down

HORATIO E'en so, my lord.

---

171 This same skull, sir] Q2 ; This same Scull Sir, this same Scull sir F   172 was] F ; was sir Q2 ;
was one Q1   175 Let me see.] F ; *not in* Q2 ; I prethee let me see it, Q1   *He takes the skull*] *not
in* FQ2Q1   177 borne] F ; bore Q2   178 now] Q2Q1 ; *not in* F   in] Q2 ; *not in* F   it] Q2 ; *not
in* F   182 No] F ; not Q2   183 grinning] Q2 ; leering F   184 chamber] FQ1 ; table Q2   191 so?
Pah] Q5 ; so? Puh F ; so pah Q2   191.1 *He throws the skull down*] *not in* FQ2Q1

---

175 **Let me see** Q1's *let me see it* shows that
these words were spoken on Shake-
speare's stage.

182-3 **No one . . . grinning?** Is there no one
now to mock your grinning (as you used
to mock those you had set grinning)?

Compare 'Make her laugh at that'
(l. 185).

183 **chop-fallen** (1) with the lower jaw
hanging loose or fallen away (2) in poor
spirits, dejected

185 **favour** facial appearance

HAMLET To what base uses we may return, Horatio. Why,
may not imagination trace the noble dust of Alexander till
he find it stopping a bung-hole?

HORATIO 'Twere to consider too curiously to consider so.

HAMLET No, faith, not a jot; but to follow him thither with
modesty enough, and likelihood to lead it. As thus:
Alexander died, Alexander was buried, Alexander re-
turneth into dust. The dust is earth, of earth we make   200
loam, and why of that loam whereto he was converted
might they not stop a beer-barrel?

> Imperial Caesar, dead and turned to clay,
> Might stop a hole to keep the wind away.
> O, that that earth, which kept the world in awe,
> Should patch a wall t'expel the winter's flaw.

But soft, but soft. Aside.

Hamlet and Horatio stand aside.

Enter Claudius, Gertrude, Laertes, and other Lords,
with a Priest, all following Ophelia's coffin

> Here comes the King,
> The Queen, the courtiers. Who is that they follow?
> And with such maimèd rites? This doth betoken

---

193 Why,] JENKINS; Why∧ FQ2QI   195 he] F; a Q2   196 consider too] Q2; consider: to
F   198 As thus] FQI; *not in* Q2   200 into] F; to Q2   203 Imperial] F; Imperious
Q2QI   206 winter's] F; waters Q2   207 Aside] F; awhile Q2; stand by a while QI   207.1
Hamlet and Horatio stand aside] *not in* FQ2QI   207.2–3 *Enter Claudius . . . coffin*] QI (*Enter King
and Queene, Laertes, and other lordes, with a Priest after the coffin*); *Enter King, Queene, Laertes, and
a Coffin, with Lords attendant* F; *Enter K. Q. Laertes and the corse* Q2 (*in margin*)   208 that] F; this
Q2QI

---

196 **too curiously** i.e. with excessive and
misplaced ingenuity

203–6 **Imperial . . . flaw** Hamlet's shift into
verse at this point is reminiscent of his
similar shift from prose to verse after
Claudius has made his abrupt exit in the
play scene. Here he sums up what he has
learned from his exchanges with the
Grave-digger—the vanity of human ambition.

205 **that earth** i.e. Caesar's body, which Antony calls 'thou bleeding piece of earth' in
Caesar (3.1.255)

206 **expel** keep out, exclude (*OED v.* 4).
Compare *Two Gentlemen* 4.4.149, 'her
sun-expelling mask'.
flaw blast, gale

207 **Aside** stand aside. This F reading is
preferred to Q2's *awhile* because the

centre of the stage must be left clear for
the procession.

207.2–3 *Enter . . . coffin* Neither the direction in Q2 nor that in F is adequate, since
both omit the *Priest* or, as he is called in
his speech prefixes in Q2, *Doct.*, standing,
presumably, for 'Doctor of Divinity'. QI is
far more satisfactory because it provides
all the essential information, with a single
exception: it does not make clear whether
the *Priest* is of the Roman Catholic or of
the Protestant persuasion. Not that it
matters much which church Shakespeare
had in mind, since he clearly intended the
funeral to be shockingly bare of ceremony. Hamlet notices at once that the
rites are *maimèd*; and Laertes is outraged
by the truncated nature of the proceedings.

The corpse they follow did with desp'rate hand   210
Fordo it own life. 'Twas of some estate.
Couch we awhile, and mark.
LAERTES What ceremony else?
HAMLET That is Laertes, a very noble youth. Mark.
LAERTES What ceremony else?
PRIEST
    Her obsequies have been as far enlarged
    As we have warrantise. Her death was doubtful;
    And but that great command o'ersways the order,
    She should in ground unsanctified have lodged
    Till the last trumpet. For charitable prayers,   220
    Shards, flints, and pebbles should be thrown on her.
    Yet here she is allowed her virgin rites,
    Her maiden strewments, and the bringing home
    Of bell and burial.
LAERTES Must there no more be done?
PRIEST   No more be done.
    We should profane the service of the dead
    To sing sage requiem and such rest to her
    As to peace-parted souls.
LAERTES   Lay her i'th'earth,
    And from her fair and unpolluted flesh
    May violets spring. I tell thee, churlish priest,   230

210 desp'rate] Q2 (desprat); disperate F   211 of] Q2; *not in* F   216 PRIEST] FQ1; *Doct⟨or⟩* Q2   217 warrantise] F (warrantis); warranty Q2   219 have] F; been Q2   220 prayers] Q2; praier F   221 Shards] F; *not in* Q2   222 rites] F; Crants Q2   227 sage] F; a Q2

211 **Fordo** destroy
    it its (Abbott 228).
    estate rank
212 **Couch we** let us conceal ourselves, lie
    low (*OED v.*[1] 13)
217 **warrantise** official authorization
    doubtful i.e. of a questionable kind
218 **great command** i.e. the King's command
    o'ersways the order prevails over the
    established usage (*OED sb.* 15)
219 **She should . . . lodged** Q1 renders this,
    'She had been buried in the open fields',
    thus making the threat more specific.
220 **For** instead of
221 **Shards** bits of broken pottery
222 **rites** I take this to be, like *have* for *been*
    (Q2) in line 219, a piece of authorial

revision in keeping with the general
character of F. It replaces a rare word,
crants meaning 'garlands', in Q2 with a
more familiar one, just as the substitution
of *have* for *been* replaces an unusual construction
with a common one.
223 **strewments** flowers strewn on a grave
    (earliest instance of this rare word cited by
    OED)
    home i.e. to her last home—the grave
    (*OED adv.* 1c)
224 **Of bell and burial** with passing bell and
    funeral service
227 **sage** solemn (OED a. 3)
228 **peace-parted souls** souls that have
    departed this life in peace (a Shakespearian compound)

A minist'ring angel shall my sister be
When thou liest howling.

HAMLET   What, the fair Ophelia!

GERTRUDE (*scattering flowers*) Sweets to the sweet. Farewell.
I hoped thou shouldst have been my Hamlet's wife.
I thought thy bride-bed to have decked, sweet maid,
And not t'have strewed thy grave.

LAERTES   O, treble woe
Fall ten times treble on that cursèd head
Whose wicked deed thy most ingenious sense
Deprived thee of.—Hold off the earth awhile,
Till I have caught her once more in mine arms.   240

          He leaps into the grave

Now pile your dust upon the quick and dead,
Till of this flat a mountain you have made
To o'ertop old Pelion or the skyish head
Of blue Olympus.

HAMLET (*coming forward*) What is he whose grief
Bears such an emphasis, whose phrase of sorrow
Conjures the wand'ring stars, and makes them stand
Like wonder-wounded hearers? This is I,
Hamlet the Dane.

---

233 *scattering flowers*] not in FQ2Q1   Sweets to the sweet. Farewell.] Q2 (Sweets . . . sweet,
farewell,) Q1 (Sweetes . . . sweete, farewell:); Sweets, . . . sweet‸ farewell. F   236 t'have] F;
haue Q2   treble woe] Q2; terrible woe F   237 treble] F (trebble); double Q2   240.1 *He leaps
into the grave*] F (*Leaps in the graue*) Q1 (*Leartes leapes into the graue*); not in Q2   243 To o'ertop]
FQ1; To'retop Q2   244 *coming forward*] not in FQ2Q1   grief] Q2; griefes F   246 Conjures]
Q2; Coniure F

---

232 **howling** i.e. howling in hell. Compare
  Measure 3.1.128–9, 'those that lawless
  and incertain thought | Imagine howl-
  ing'.
238 **ingenious** quick of apprehension
241–4 **Now pile . . . Olympus** The allusion is
  to the war of the gods and the giants in
  Greek mythology. In the course of it the
  giants attempted to scale Olympus by
  piling Mount Ossa upon Mount Pelion.
  Virgil's mention of the story, *imponere
  Pelio Ossam* (*Georgics* I, 281), became
  proverbial (Tilley O81)
243 **skyish** lofty, sky-high (earliest instance

cited by *OED*)
244 **blue** Shakespeare is the first English
  writer cited by *OED* to use this adjective
  with reference to mountains, flames, and
  the veins of the body.
245 **emphasis** violence of utterance
246 **Conjures** puts a spell on (*OED v.* 7)
  wand'ring stars planets
  stand stand still
247 **wonder-wounded** wonder-struck (Shakespearian compound)
248 **Hamlet the Dane** In calling himself *the
  Dane*, i.e. King of Denmark, Hamlet asserts his right to the throne.

He leaps in after Laertes

LAERTES ⌈*grappling with him*⌉ The devil take thy soul!

HAMLET Thou pray'st not well.

    I prithee take thy fingers from my throat;   250

    For though I am not splenative and rash,

    Yet have I something in me dangerous,

    Which let thy wiseness fear. Away thy hand.

CLAUDIUS Pluck them asunder.

GERTRUDE   Hamlet, Hamlet!

ALL THE LORDS Gentlemen!

HORATIO   Good my lord, be quiet.

HAMLET

    Why, I will fight with him upon this theme

    Until my eyelids will no longer wag.

GERTRUDE O my son, what theme?

HAMLET

    I loved Ophelia. Forty thousand brothers

    Could not, with all their quantity of love,   260

    Make up my sum—What wilt thou do for her?

CLAUDIUS O, he is mad, Laertes.

GERTRUDE For love of God, forbear him.

HAMLET 'Swounds, show me what thou'lt do.

    Woo't weep? Woo't fight? Woo't fast? Woo't tear thyself?

    Woo't drink up eisel, eat a crocodile?

---

248 *He leaps in after Laertes*] Q1 (*Hamlet leaps . . . Laertes*); *not in* FQ2   *grappling with him*] *not in* FQ2   251 For] Q2Q1; Sir F   and] F; *not in* Q2   252 something in me] FQ1; in me something Q2   253 wiseness] F; wisedome Q2Q1   Away] F; hold off Q2Q1   255 ALL THE LORDS Gentlemen!] Q2 (*All.* Gentlemen); *not in* F   HORATIO] Q2; Gen⟨tleman⟩ F   264 'Swounds] Q2; Come F   thou'lt] F; th'owt Q2; thou wilt Q1   265 Woo't fast] Q2; *not in* F; wilt fast Q1

248.1 *He leaps in after Laertes* Q1 is very definite about what happens here; and so, in agreement with it, in the author of the elegy on Burbage quoted at p. 15. A 'grave' that was both shallow and wide would seem to have been essential.

251 **splenative** quick-tempered. The spleen was regarded as the source of anger.

253 **Which let . . . fear** i.e. which your own good sense should warn you to treat with caution

257 **wag** move. Movement of the eyelids is one of the last signs of life in a dying man.

263 **forbear him** leave him alone, i.e. don't take up his challenge

264 **'Swounds** F's *Come* is an evident case of 'purging'.

265 **Woo't** wilt (a colloquial form of the 2nd person singular of *will* (*OED v.*[1] A 3δ)). The form seems to have been associated with challenges and the like in Shakespeare's mind. Compare *2 Henry IV* 2.1.54–5; *Antony* 4.2.7.
    Woo't fast The omission of these words from F is the result of eye-skip.

266 **eisel** vinegar (regarded as the quintessence of bitterness). See *OED* for numerous examples and for the wide variety of spellings.
    crocodile (probably included here on account of the toughness of its skin, which, according to Nashe, 'no iron will pierce' —*Have With You to Saffron-Walden* iii. 96)

I'll do't. Dost thou come here to whine,
To outface me with leaping in her grave?
Be buried quick with her, and so will I.
And, if thou prate of mountains, let them throw   270
Millions of acres on us, till our ground,
Singeing his pate against the burning zone,
Make Ossa like a wart! Nay, an thou'lt mouth,
I'll rant as well as thou.

CLAUDIUS   This is mere madness;
And thus a while the fit will work on him.
Anon, as patient as the female dove
When that her golden couplets are disclosed,
His silence will sit drooping.

HAMLET   Hear you, sir,
What is the reason that you use me thus?
I loved you ever. But it is no matter.   280
Let Hercules himself do what he may,
The cat will mew, and dog will have his day.   *Exit*

CLAUDIUS
I pray you, good Horatio, wait upon him.   *Exit Horatio*
(*To Laertes*) Strengthen your patience in our last night's
          speech.
We'll put the matter to the present push.—

267 Dost thou come] F; doost come Q2; Com'st thou Q1   274 CLAUDIUS] F (Kin⟨g⟩) Q1 (King);
Quee⟨n⟩ Q2   275 thus] F; this Q2   277 couplets] Q2; Cuplet F   282 The . . . and] FQ2; A
. . . a Q1   Exit] F; Exit Hamlet Q2; Exit Hamlet and Horatio. Q1   283 you] F; thee Q2   Exit
Horatio] Q2 (and Horatio); not in F

271 **our ground** i.e. the earth beneath which
we are buried
272 **burning zone** orbit in which the sun
moves
274–8 **This is . . . drooping** Q2 assigns this
speech to the Queen; but the agreement of
F and Q1 in giving it to the King sems
decisive. Moreover, Claudius has earlier
employed much the same image when
referring to Hamlet's 'madness': 'There's
something in his soul | O'er which his
melancholy sits on brood; | And I do
doubt the hatch and the disclose | Will be
some danger' (3.1.165–8).
277 **golden couplets** Doves, like pigeons, lay
only two eggs; and their young, when
they hatch out, are covered with *golden*
down.

disclosed hatched. Compare 3.1.167.
281–2 **Let Hercules . . . day** This is one of
those enigmatic remarks that Hamlet so
often produces. It seems to say more than
logic can extract from it. However, as Hercules is sometimes associated with rant in
Shakespeare's mind and with 'a part to
tear a cat in' (*Dream* 1.2.23–4), it is
reasonable to assume that Hamlet sees
Laertes as Hercules. As for the *cat* and the
dog, both behave naturally; and nothing
Hercules can do will stop them. Moreover,
'Every dog has his day' (Tilley D464) is a
threat of revenge. So what Hamlet says is,
in effect, 'Let Laertes rant as much as he
likes, my day will come.'
284 **in** in the thought of (Abbott 162)
285 **present push** immediate trial

Good Gertrude, set some watch over your son.
This grave shall have a living monument.
An hour of quiet shortly shall we see;
Till then in patience our proceeding be.   *Exeunt*

5.2   *Enter Hamlet and Horatio*

HAMLET

So much for this, sir. Now, let me see, the other.
You do remember all the circumstance?

HORATIO Remember it, my lord!

HAMLET

Sir, in my heart there was a kind of fighting
That would not let me sleep. Methought I lay
Worse than the mutines in the bilboes. Rashly—
And praised be rashness for it; let us know
Our indiscretion sometimes serves us well
When our dear plots do pall; and that should teach us
There's a divinity that shapes our ends,   10
Rough-hew them how we will—

HORATIO That is most certain.

---

284 your] Q2; you F   288 shortly] F; thirtie Q2 (*uncorr.*); thereby Q2 (*corr.*)
5 2.1 let me] F; shall you Q2   5 Methought] F (me thought); my thought Q2   6 bilboes] F;
bilbo Q2   7 praised] Q2; praise F   8 sometimes] F; sometime Q2   9 dear] F; deepe Q2   pall]
F (paule) Q2 (*uncorr.*); fall Q2 (*corr.*); fail POPE   teach] F; learne Q2

287 **living monument** (1) lasting monument
(2) monument in the form of Hamlet, now
alive but soon to be dead
5.2 It is marvellously appropriate that the
keen and long drawn out duel of wits between the two 'mighty opposites', Hamlet
and the King, should end in a physical
duel between the Prince and the deadliest
of the King's instruments. It is also fitting
that this mortal combat, unlike that between old Hamlet and old Fortinbras,
which was absolutely fair and conducted
according to rules, should take the form of
a 'friendly' bout masking the deepest
treachery and defying every rule of the
game.
1 **So much . . . other** Hamlet and Horatio
are already deep in conversation as they
come on, with the Prince about to reveal
all that he did not put in his letter to his
friend.
6 **Worse . . . bilboes** i.e. worse than
mutineers in shackles are supposed to do.

The word *the* is used here to denote notoriety (Abbott 92), to show that this is a
recognized example of human discomfort
at its worst. *Mutine*, also found in *K. John*
2.1.378, was an older word than
mutineer, for which *OED*'s first citation is
Tempest 3.2.34. A third variant, *mutiner*,
appears in *Coriolanus* 1.1.248. A *bilbo* is
'a long iron bar, furnished with sliding
shackles to confine the ankles of
prisoners, and a lock by which to fix one
end of the bar to the floor or ground'
(*OED*).
Rashly on a sudden impulse
7 **know** recognize, acknowledge
9 **pall** become ineffectual (*OED v.*[1] 2). Compare *Antony* 2.7.81, 'I'll never follow thy
palled fortunes more.'
10–11 **There's . . . will** Compare 'Man
proposes, God disposes' (Tilley M298).
10 **our ends** our purposes and their final out-
comes

HAMLET Up from my cabin,
  My sea-gown scarfed about me, in the dark
  Groped I to find out them, had my desire,
  Fingered their packet, and in fine withdrew
  To mine own room again, making so bold,
  My fears forgetting manners, to unseal
  Their grand commission; where I found, Horatio—
  O, royal knavery!—an exact command,   20
  Larded with many several sorts of reason,
  Importing Denmark's health, and England's too,
  With ho! such bugs and goblins in my life,
  That on the supervise, no leisure bated,
  No, not to stay the grinding of the axe,
  My head should be struck off.
HORATIO   Is't possible?
HAMLET (*giving him a paper*)
  Here's the commission; read it at more leisure.
  But wilt thou hear me how I did proceed?
HORATIO I beseech you.
HAMLET
  Being thus benetted round with villains—   30
  Ere I could make a prologue to my brains,
  They had begun the play—I sat me down,

---

14 me, in the dark] Q5; me in the darke, F; me in the darke‸ Q2   18 unseal] F; vnfold Q2   20
O] F (Oh); A Q2; Ah WILSON   21 reason] F; reasons Q2   28 me] F; now Q2   30 villains]
FQ2; villainies CAPELL

14 **sea-gown** Defined by Cotgrave in 1611 as
  'a coarse, high-collared and short-sleeved
  gown, reaching down to the mid-leg', a
  sea-gown was, according to Dampier,
  writing in 1699, a sailor's 'covering in
  the night' (*OED sea sb.* 18j).
  scarfed loosely wrapped (*OED v.*[1] 2)
15 **find out** For this treatment of *find out* as a
  single word see Abbott 240.
  them i.e. Rosencrantz and Guildenstern
16 **Fingered** stole (*OED v.* 4). Compare *3
  Henry VI* 5.1.43–4, 'But, whiles he thought
  to steal the single ten, | The king was slily
  fingered from the deck.'
21 **Larded** garnished
  several separate, different
22 **Importing** relating to (*OED import v.* 7)
23 **such bugs and goblins in my life** i.e. such a
  mass of trumped up dangers and threats

  consequent on my being alive
  bugs bogies, imaginary terrors
24 **supervise** perusal. *OED* has no other
  example of *supervise* as a noun.
  no leisure bated i.e. with no loss of time
25 **stay** wait for
28 **me** This looks like an authorial revision
  made to get rid of the *now how* jingle of Q2.
  For the construction see Abbott 414.
30 **benetted round with** hemmed in by. The
  metaphor is from hunting deer and the like
  by driving them into nets; see note to
  3.2.329. For *with* meaning *by* see *OED
  with prep.* 40a and Abbott 193.
31–2 **Ere . . . play** i.e. before I could set my
  mind to work on evolving a logical course
  of action that mind was spontaneously
  busy in taking the right action. As the
  prologue to an Elizabethan play often con-

Devised a new commission, wrote it fair.
I once did hold it, as our statists do,
A baseness to write fair, and laboured much
How to forget that learning; but, sir, now
It did me yeoman's service. Wilt thou know
Th'effect of what I wrote?

HORATIO   Ay, good my lord.

HAMLET
An earnest conjuration from the King,
As England was his faithful tributary,   40
As love between them like the palm should flourish,
As peace should still her wheaten garland wear
And stand a comma 'tween their amities,
And many such like 'as'es of great charge,
That on the view and know of these contents,
Without debatement further more or less,
He should the bearers put to sudden death,
Not shriving time allowed.

HORATIO   How was this sealed?

---

38 Th'effect] Q2; The effects F   41 like] Q2; as F   should] F; might Q2   44 'as'es] ROWE
(As's); Assis F; as sir Q2   45 know] F; knowing Q2   47 the] F; thine Q2

tained the 'argument' or summary of the
action to follow, it is tempting to speculate
that Shakespeare is referring here to his
own manner of working, which may well
have been to start from a 'rough-hewn'
scenario and then allow things to take
their course, instead of adhering to any
fixed or predetermined plan. Hamlet certainly views his *play*, which is also deadly
earnest, with all the delight of an artist
who has seen his 'hunch' work out.

33 **fair** i.e. in an elegant legible hand
34 **statists** statesmen, politicians
37 **yeoman's service** (earliest instance of the
phrase cited by *OED*)
38 **effect** drift, purport
39–44 **An earnest . . . charge** Hamlet's
description of his letter is evidently meant
as a parody of Claudius's officialese.
41 **As love . . . flourish** See Ps. 92: 12, 'The
righteous shall flourish like the palm tree'.
42 **wheaten garland** one of the emblems of
peace; (see Jonson, vii. 97. 430–35)
43 **stand a comma 'tween their amities** *OED*
comma 2c, citing this passage, defines

comma as 'break of continuity, interval,
pause'. It also quotes a parallel from
Fuller's *Worthies*: 'Though a truce may
give a comma or colon to the war, nothing under a peace can put a perfect period
thereunto.' Hamlet's statement then
becomes ironical, implying that the *peace*
between the two 'friendly' nations is a
very precarious one and will be broken by
Denmark, unless England does what
Claudius requires of it. This interpretation
fits in with what Claudius himself has said
in his final speech in 4.3.

44 **'as'es** Hamlet quibbles on 'as' and 'ass'.
   of great charge (1) of great importance
   (referring to the *'as'es*) (2) heavily loaded
   (referring to the *asses*)
45 **know** knowledge (*OED sb.*[1])
46 **Without . . . less** without the slightest
   delay (for any argument over detail)
48 **Not shriving-time allowed** Hamlet seems
   to have his father's fate in mind
   (1.5.76–9) as well as the death Claudius
   planned to send him to (lines 23–5).

337

HAMLET
Why, even in that was heaven ordinant.
I had my father's signet in my purse,   50
Which was the model of that Danish seal;
Folded the writ up in the form of th'other,
Subscribed it, gave't th'impression, placed it safely,
The changeling never known. Now the next day
Was our sea-fight; and what to this was sequent
Thou know'st already.

HORATIO
So Guildenstern and Rosencrantz go to't.

HAMLET
Why, man, they did make love to this employment.
They are not near my conscience. Their defeat
Doth by their own insinuation grow.   60
'Tis dangerous when the baser nature comes
Between the pass and fell incensèd points
Of mighty opposites.

HORATIO   Why, what a king is this!

HAMLET
Does it not, think'st thee, stand me now upon—
He that hath killed my king and whored my mother,
Popped in between th'election and my hopes,
Thrown out his angle for my proper life,

49 ordinant] Q2; ordinate F   52 in the form of th'other] Q2; in forme of the other F   53 Subscribed] F; Subcribe Q2   55 sequent] Q2; sement F   56 know'st] F; knowest Q2   58 Why . . . employment] F; *not in* Q2   59 defeat] Q2; debate F   60 Doth] F; Dooes Q2   64 thinkst] F; thinke Q2; thinks't DYCE, *conj.* Walker   64–8 upon— . . . cozenage—] BOSWELL; vpon . . . coozenage; F; vppon? . . . cusnage, Q2

49 **ordinant** in control, ready with directions
51 **model** image, likeness (*OED sb.* 2b)
52 **writ** writing, document
54 **changeling** substitute (*OED sb.* 2)
57 **to't** to their deaths. Compare *Two Gentlemen* 4.4.3–5, 'one that I saved from drowning, when three or four of his blind brothers and sisters went to it'.
58 **Why, man . . . employment** The omission of this line from Q2 could be a compositorial oversight; but as its loss would be undetectable but for the evidence of F, the line seems more likely to be a 'second thought' designed to strengthen Hamlet's self-justification.
59 **defeat** destruction (*OED sb.* 1)
60 **insinuation** meddling, winding their way in
61 **baser nature** i.e. man of inferior rank and breeding
62 **pass** thrust (with a sword)
63 **opposites** adversaries (*OED sb.* 3)
64 **think'st thee** think'st thou. '*Thee* is probably the dative . . . or, at all events, there is, perhaps, confusion between "Thinks it *thee?*" i.e. "does it seem to *thee?*" and "thinkst *thou?*". Very likely "thinkst" is an abbreviation of "thinks it"' (Abbott 212).
   stand . . . upon become incumbent on me (*OED stand v.* 78q)
67 **angle** fishing-hook
   proper own

And with such cozenage—is't not perfect conscience
To quit him with this arm? And is't not to be damned
To let this canker of our nature come   70
In further evil?

HORATIO

It must be shortly known to him from England
What is the issue of the business there.

HAMLET

It will be short. The interim is mine;
And a man's life's no more than to say 'one'.
But I am very sorry, good Horatio,
That to Laertes I forgot myself;
For by the image of my cause I see
The portraiture of his. I'll count his favours.
But sure the bravery of his grief did put me   80
Into a tow'ring passion.

HORATIO   Peace! Who comes here?

Enter young Osric, ⌜*taking off his hat*⌝

OSRIC Your lordship is right welcome back to Denmark.

---

68 conscience,] F (conscience,); conscience? Q2   69–81 To . . . here] F; not in Q2   74
interim is] HANMER; *interim's* F   79 count] F; court ROWE   81.1 *Enter young Osric, taking off
his hat*] *Enter young Osricke* F; *Enter a Courtier* Q2; *Enter a Bragart Gentleman* Q1   82 OSRIC] F
(*throughout the scene*); *Cour*⟨*tier*⟩ Q2 (*to* 143); *Gent*⟨*leman*⟩ Q1 (*throughout*)

---

68 **cozenage** (1) trickery, deception (2) use of
the word *cousin* in talking to me. Compare
Richard III 4.4.222, 'Cousins, indeed;
and by their uncle cozened'.
  perfect conscience i.e. in perfect keeping
with the dictates of conscience (*OED conscience* 6)
69–81 **To quit . . . here** These lines, not
found in Q2, are probably an addition
made during the preparation of the text
that lies behind F. See Textual Introduction pp. 110–12.
69 **quit** repay, get even with (*OED v.* 10)
70 **canker** spreading ulcerous sore (*OED sb.*
1)
75 **a man's . . . 'one'** i.e. a man's life is no
longer than the time it takes to say 'one'.
Compare *Dream* 5.1.298–301, 'No die,
but an ace, for him; for he is but one.—
Less than an ace, man; for he is dead; he

is nothing.' See also 'Man (Life) is but a
figure of one' (Dent O50.1).
78–9 **For . . . his** Hamlet recognizes that he
and Laertes have the same motive for
action—the duty to avenge a father's
death.
79 **count his favours** take note of, think
about, his favourable characteristics
(*OED favour sb.* 8)
80 **bravery** bravado, ostentatious defiance
(*OED* 1)
81 **a tow'ring passion** (earliest instance of
this phrase cited by *OED*—*towering ppl.a.*
4)
82–144 This encounter between Hamlet
and Osric is reminiscent of that between
Woodstock and a foppish Courtier in the
anonymous play *Woodstock* (*c.*1592). See
Woodstock, ed. A. P. Rossiter (1946),
3.2.197–227.

HAMLET I humbly thank you, sir.—Dost know this water-
fly?

HORATIO No, my good lord.

HAMLET Thy state is the more gracious, for 'tis a vice to
know him. He hath much land, and fertile. Let a beast be
lord of beasts, and his crib shall stand at the king's mess.
'Tis a chough, but, as I say, spacious in the possession of
dirt.   90

OSRIC Sweet lord, if your friendship were at leisure, I should
impart a thing to you from his majesty.

HAMLET I will receive it, sir, with all diligence of spirit. Put
your bonnet to his right use; 'tis for the head.

OSRIC I thank your lordship, 'tis very hot.

HAMLET No, believe me, 'tis very cold. The wind is north-
erly.

OSRIC It is indifferent cold, my lord, indeed.

---

83 humbly] F; humble Q2   89 chough] F (Chowgh) Q2; chuff JENKINS   say] Q2; saw F   91
friendship] F; Lordshippe Q2   93 sir] Q2; *not in* F   Put] F; *not in* Q2   95 'tis] F it is Q2

83–4 **water-fly** Precisely which of the many
flies that frequent water Hamlet has in
mind it is hard to say. The dragon-fly
seems the most likely. In *Troilus* 5.1.32–3
water-flies are regarded as worthless
nuisances.

86 **Thy state . . . gracious** i.e. so much the
better for you

87–8 **Let . . . mess** i.e. if a man who is no
better than an animal owns large numbers of livestock, he will be welcome at
court.

88 **crib** manger
mess table

89 **chough** (1) chuff (of which it is a variant
spelling), i.e. churl, rustic (2) a kind of
jackdaw, much given to chatter and
imitation. Hamlet begins by calling Osric
a *water-fly*, alluding to his fashionable
appearance; then switches over at this
point to the first meaning of the word;
and then exploits the courtier's jackdaw-
like readiness to repeat whatever he is
told. Chuffs, usually referred to as *rich* or
fat—*rich choughs* are mentioned in *Woodstock* 3.3.2–3; and Falstaff describes
the men he robs at Gadshill as *gor-
bellied knaves* and *fat chuffs* (1 *Henry IV*
2.2.85–6)—were a very common object

of satire *c.*1600, because some of them
sought to use their wealth as a means of
rising in the social scale. Tourneur (or
Middleton?) puts the matter with characteristic incisiveness when he writes of far-
mers' sons who agreed 'To wash their
hands, and come up gentlemen' (*The
Revenger's Tragedy* 2.1.241). At the time
when Shakespeare wrote *Hamlet* his company had recently played Jonson's *Every
Man Out of His Humour*, in which rich
chuffs figure prominently. Three of the
leading characters are 'Sordido, a wretched hob-nailed chuff', his son Fungoso,
who extracts money from his father 'to
put him in the Courtier's cut', and Sog-
liardo, Sordido's brother, 'an essential
clown . . . yet so enamoured of the name
of a gentleman, that he will have it,
though he buys it.' And buy it he does,
paying good money in order to learn 'all
the rare qualities, humours, and comple-
ments of a gentleman' (1.2.22–3). There
is, therefore, no contradiction between
Osric the *chuff* 'spacious in the possession
of dirt', and Osric the *chough* who has 'got
the tune of the time'.

93 **diligence** assiduity

94 **bonnet** hat

HAMLET Methinks it is very sultry and hot for my com-
plexion.   100

OSRIC Exceedingly, my lord. It is very sultry, as 'twere—I
cannot tell how. But, my lord, his majesty bade me signify
to you that he has laid a great wager on your head. Sir,
this is the matter—

HAMLET I beseech you remember—

⌈*He motions Osric to put on his hat*⌉

OSRIC Nay, good my lord; for my ease, in good faith. Sir,
you are not ignorant of what excellence Laertes is at his
weapon.

HAMLET What's his weapon?

OSRIC Rapier and dagger.   110

HAMLET That's two of his weapons. But well.

OSRIC The King, sir, has waged with him six Barbary horses, against the which he has imponed, as I take it, six
French rapiers and poniards, with their assigns, as girdle,

---

99 Methinks] F; But yet me thinkes Q2   sultry] F (soultry); sully Q2   hot for] F; hot, or
Q2   102 But] F; *not in* Q2   103 he] F; a Q2   106 Nay, good my lord] Q2; Nay, in good
faith F   my ease] Q2; mine ease F   107–8 at his weapon] F; *not in* Q2   112 King, sir] Q2;
sir King F   has waged] F; hath wagerd Q2; hath layd a wager Q1   113 has] Q2; *not in* F
imponed] F (impon'd); impaund Q2

99–100 **complexion** constitution (*OED sb.* 2)

105 **remember** The polite formula, which
Hamlet completes with a gesture, is
remember your courtesy, i.e. put your hat
on again (*OED v.* 1d).

106 **for my ease** another polite formula
(Dent E35.1)

106 8 **Sir . . . weapon** For Q2's version of
this passage, see Appendix A, xvii.

112 **waged** wagered, staked (*OED v.* 6).
Compare *Cymbeline* 1.4.127, 'I will wage
against your gold gold to it.'

  Barbary horses The Barbary horse or
barb, as it was also called, was much
prized in Shakespeare's England. Impor-
ted originally from North Africa, the
breed was famous for its speed and endurance. Richard II's favourite horse is
'roan Barbary' (*Richard II* 5.5.78).

113 **imponed** So reads F (*impon'd*). Q2 reads
impawned (*impaund*), which most editors
adopt because, unlike *imponed*, it is a word
used elsewhere by Shakespeare (*1 Henry
IV* 4.3.108; *Henry V* 1.2.21; *Winter's Tale*
1.2.436), as well as by others. Meaning

'pawned', or 'pledged', *impuwned* has
nothing about it that would justify Hamlet's drawing attention to it, as he does at
line 127. *Imponed* is another matter. *OED*
can cite no other use of it in the sense of
staked, wagered. It looks very much like an
'inkhorn term' coined directly from the
Latin *imponere*, 'to pile on, to lay on', as in
Virgil's *Imponere Pelio Ossam* (compare
5.1.242–4), and would appeal to Osric's
taste for the affected.

114 **assigns** appurtenances (*OED sb.*² 3,
citing no other instance)

114–15 **girdle, hangers** The *rapier* was
attached by *hangers*, i.e. straps, to the
girdle, i.e. belt. Ben Jonson had already
made fun of the fuss about *hangers* in his
Every Man in His Humour (1598), where
the gull Matheo speaks of 'a hanger,
which I assure you, both for fashion and
workmanship was most beautiful and
workmanlike' (1.3.158–9). For further
details about the way in which *hangers*
were beautified and embroidered see the
note on this passage in Jonson, ix. 357.

hangers, or so. Three of the carriages, in faith, are very
dear to fancy, very responsive to the hilts, most delicate
carriages, and of very liberal conceit.

HAMLET What call you the carriages?

HORATIO (*to Hamlet*) I knew you must be edified by the
margin ere you had done.   120

OSRIC The carriages, sir, are the hangers.

HAMLET The phrase would be more germane to the matter
if we could carry cannon by our sides. I would it might be
hangers till then. But on. Six Barbary horses against six
French swords, their assigns, and three liberal-conceited
carriages—that's the French bet against the Danish.
Why is this 'imponed', as you call it?

OSRIC The King, sir, hath laid, sir, that in a dozen passes
between you and him he shall not exceed you three hits.
He hath laid on twelve for nine; and it would come to   130
immediate trial if your lordship would vouchsafe the
answer.

HAMLET How if I answer no?

OSRIC I mean, my lord, the opposition of your person in trial.

---

115 hangers] F; hanger Q2   or] F; and Q2   119–20 HORATIO I knew . . . done] Q2; *not in* F
121 carriages] F; carriage Q2   122–3 matter if] Q2; matter: If F   123 carry cannon] F;
carry a cannon Q2; carried the canon Q1   might be] F; be Q2 *uncorr.*; be might Q2 *corr.*
124–5 on. Six . . . French swords,] POPE (*subs.*); on sixe . . . French Swords: F; on, six . . . French
swords_Λ Q2   126 bet] Q2; but F   127 'imponed', as] F (impon'd as); all Q2; all 'impawned'
as WILSON; all impon'd, as KITTREDGE   128 laid, sir] Q2; laid F   129 you and] F; your selfe
and Q2   130 laid on] Q2; one F   nine] Q2; mine F   it] Q2; that F

115 **carriages** a fashionable word for *hangers*
(as Osric explains at line 121). *OED car-*
riage 30a, citing no other instance, suggests that this use was an affected one.
More affectation follows.

116 **dear to fancy** delightful to the fancy
very responsive to in perfect keeping with
(*OED responsive a.* 2)
delicate skilfully wrought (Onions)

117 **liberal conceit** tasteful design (Onions)

120 **margin** Explanatory and summarizing
notes were often printed in the *margins* of
books.

122–3 **The phrase . . . sides** an allusion to
gun-carriages

128–30 **The King . . . nine** 'This wager I do
not understand' (Dr Johnson). There has
been 'much throwing about of brains'
since Johnson's time; but the riddle posed
by the terms of the bet remains unsolved.
The initial stipulation is intelligible

enough. In order to win Laertes must take
at least eight of the twelve bouts. But
there is no way in which this stipulation
can be brought into line with 'twelve for
nine'. The odds are that Shakespeare himself was in a muddle about it all. But,
while the details of the wager are far from
clear, its purposes are plain enough: to
offer Hamlet odds that are an insult to his
skill, designed to sting him into acceptance of the challenge; and, even more
important, odds which will give Laertes at
least five opportunities, supposing that
Hamlet wins each of the first five bouts
and thus brings the match to an end, to
strike the blow that will be fatal.

128 **passes** bouts

132 **answer** (1) acceptance of the challenge
(which is what Osric means) (2) reply
(which is what Hamlet disconcertingly
makes it mean)

HAMLET Sir, I will walk here in the hall. If it please his
majesty, 'tis the breathing time of day with me. Let the
foils be brought, the gentleman willing, and the King hold
his purpose, I will win for him if I can. If not, I'll gain
nothing but my shame and the odd hits.

OSRIC Shall I re-deliver you e'en so?   140

HAMLET To this effect, sir, after what flourish your nature
will.

OSRIC I commend my duty to your lordship.

HAMLET Yours, yours.   *Exit Osric*
He does well to commend it himself; there are no tongues
else for's turn.

HORATIO This lapwing runs away with the shell on his
head.

HAMLET He did comply with his dug before he sucked it.
Thus has he—and many more of the same bevy that I   150
know the drossy age dotes on—only got the tune of the
time and outward habit of encounter, a kind of yeasty
collection, which carries them through and through the

136 'tis] F; it is Q2   137–8 brought, the . . . purpose,] THEOBALD; brought, the . . . purpose;
FQ2; brought. The . . . purpose, *conj.* Jenkins   138 if] F; and Q2   I'll] F; I will Q2   140
re-deliver] F; deliuer Q2Q1   e'en] F; *not in* Q2   144 yours] F; *not in* Q2   *Exit Osric*] Q1 ('exit',
opposite 140); *not in* FQ2   145 He] F; *not in* Q2 ; 'A RIVERSIDE, *conj.* Parrott–Craig   146 turn]
Q2; tongue F   149 He] F; A Q2   comply] F; sir Q2 *uncorr.*; so sir Q2 *corr.*   he] F; a Q2   150
has] Q2; had F   many] Q2; mine F   bevy] F (Beauy); breede Q2   152 outward] F; out of an
Q2   yeasty] F (yesty); histy Q2

136 **breathing time** time for taking physical
exercise (*OED breathe v.* 14a)
138 **I'll gain** I'm prepared to gain (Abbott
319)
139 **odd hits** i.e. the three hits Laertes makes
on Hamlet over and above those Hamlet
makes on him
140 **re-deliver you e'en so** take back those
words as your acceptance
141 **after what flourish** i.e. according to
whatever verbal affectation
143 **commend** (1) submit to your kind
regard (Osric's meaning) (2) praise (the
meaning Hamlet gives it)
145–6 **He does . . . turn** Compare 'He must
praise himself since no man else will'
(Dent P545.1).
147–8 **This lapwing . . . head** This proverbial synonym (Tilley L69) for 'foolish
precociousness' derives from the fact that
young lapwings do begin to run about
very shortly after they are hatched.
Another proverb, to much the same ef-

fect, 'His mother's milk is not out of his
nose' (Tilley M1204), may have served to
trigger off Hamlet's next remark.
149 **comply with** make polite address to, pay
compliments to (*OED v.*[1] *OED* sb. 2)
150 **bevy** company (*OED* sb. 2)
151 **drossy age** i.e. shoddy world we live in
which has no proper sense of values
151–2 **got the tune of the time** i.e. picked up
the jargon that is in fashion
152 **outward habit of encounter** exterior
show of politeness when meeting another
(*OED encounter* sb. 3)
152–3 **yeasty collection** frothy insubstantial
assortment (of fashionable tricks of speech
and behaviour)
153–4 **carries . . . opinions** i.e. brings them
safely through any trials they may face
when in the society of men whose
opinions have been tested and proved reliable. Compare *Troilus* 1.3.26–9, 'Distinc-
tion with a broad and powerful fan, | Puf-
fing at all, winnows the light away, | And

most fanned and winnowed opinions; and do but blow
them to their trials, the bubbles are out.

HORATIO You will lose this wager, my lord.

HAMLET I do not think so. Since he went into France, I have
been in continual practice. I shall win at the odds. But
thou wouldst not think how ill all's here about my heart.
But it is no matter.   160

HORATIO Nay, good my lord—

HAMLET It is but foolery. But it is such a kind of gain-giving
as would perhaps trouble a woman.

HORATIO If your mind dislike anything, obey it. I will forestall their repair hither, and say you are not fit.

HAMLET Not a whit. We defy augury. There's a special
providence in the fall of a sparrow. If it be now, 'tis not to
come. If it be not to come, it will be now. If it be not now,
yet it will come. The readiness is all. Since no man knows

---

154 fanned] HANMER, WARBURTON; fond F; prophane Q2; profound TSCHISCHWITZ, *conj.* Bailey
winnowed] F; trennowed Q2; trennowned Q3; renowned Q1676   155 trials] F; triall
Q2   156 this wager] F; *not in* Q2   158 But] F; *not in* Q2   159 ill all's] Q2; all F   162
gain-giving] F; gamgiuing Q2; game-giuing Q3   164 it] Q2; *not in* F   166 There's a] FQ1;
there is Q2   167 now] FQ1; *not in* Q2   169–70 knows aught of what he leaves,] JOHNSON;
ha's ought of what he leaues. F; of ought he leaues, knowes_Λ Q2; owes aught of what he leaves,
HANMER; knows of aught he leaves, SPENCER; of aught he leaves knows aught, JENKINS

---

what hath mass or matter by itself | Lies
rich in virtue and unminglèd.' The
metaphor in both cases derives from the
process of separating the wheat from the
chaff. F's *fond* can be explained as a
misreading of the spelling *fand*, for
fanned, which is to be found in Q1 of
Dream 3.2.142, 'Fand with the Easterne
winde'.

154 **and** do yet do (*OED conj.* 7b)

154–5 **blow them to their trials** i.e. test them
by blowing on them (which is what Hamlet has been doing to Osric)

155 **the bubbles are out** (1) the bubbles burst
(2) the impostors are at a loss for words.
Compare *All's Well* 3.6.5, where the
Second Lord says of Parolles, 'On my life,
my lord, a bubble'; and *Coriolanus*
5.3.40–42, 'Like a dull actor now | I have
forgot my part and I am out, | Even to a
full disgrace.'
    For a passage following this line in Q2
but not in F, see Appendix A, xviii.

162 **gain-giving** misgiving. Shakespeare
does not use this word elsewhere; and this

is the first instance of it, in this sense, cited
by *OED*.

165 **fit** ready (*OED a.* 5)

166 **defy** reject (*OED v.*[1] 5). Compare *K. John*
3.4.23, 'No, I defy all counsel, all
redress'.

166–7 **There's . . . sparrow** See Matthew
10: 29, 'Are not two little sparrows sold
for a farthing? And one of them shall not
light on the ground without your father.'

167 **it** death

169 **The readiness is all** The importance of
being ready to face death at any moment
had been central to the teaching of the
Church for centuries. See, for instance,
Chaucer's 'The Pardoner's Tale', 683–4,
'Beth redy for to mete him [Death] ever-
more. | Thus taughte me my dame, I sey
na-more.'

169–70 **Since no man . . . betimes** Since no
man has any knowledge or understanding of what he leaves behind him (i.e. the
world he has lived in and the future it
holds), what does it matter if he dies an
early death?

aught of what he leaves, what is't to leave betimes? Let be.   170

> *A table prepared. Trumpets, Drums, and Officers with*
> *cushions.*
> *Enter Claudius, Gertrude, Laertes, Osric, and all the*
> *State, and Attendants with foils and gauntlets*

CLAUDIUS

Come, Hamlet, come, and take this hand from me.

> *He puts Laertes's hand into Hamlet's*

HAMLET (*to Laertes*)

Give me your pardon, sir. I've done you wrong;
But pardon't as you are a gentleman.
This presence knows, and you must needs have heard,
How I am punished with sore distraction.
What I have done
That might your nature, honour, and exception
Roughly awake, I here proclaim was madness.
Was't Hamlet wronged Laertes? Never Hamlet.
If Hamlet from himself be ta'en away,   180
And when he's not himself does wrong Laertes,
Then Hamlet does it not, Hamlet denies it.
Who does it then? His madness. If't be so,
Hamlet is of the faction that is wronged;
His madness is poor Hamlet's enemy.
Sir, in this audience,
Let my disclaiming from a purposed evil
Free me so far in your most generous thoughts

---

170 Let be] Q2; *not in* F   170.1–4 *A table . . . gauntlets*] Enter King, Queene, Laertes and Lords, with other Attendants with Foyles, and Gauntlets, a Table and Flagons of Wine on it F; A table prepard, Trumpets, Drums, and officers with Cushions, King, Queene, and all the state, Foiles, daggers, and Laertes Q2; Enter King, Queene, Leartes, Lordes Q1   170.3 Osric] *not in* FQ2Q1   172 I've] F; I haue Q2   175 with] F; with a Q2   186 Sir, in this audience] F; *not in* Q2

170 **Let be** i.e. say no more (*OED let v.*[1] 20c)
170.4 **State** nobility, court (*OED sb.* 26a)
   gauntlets In F the *gauntlets* take the place of Q2's *daggers*. The alteration was probably made either before *Hamlet* was first staged or very soon after, since the Q1 direction at its equivalent of line 254 is 'They catch one anothers Rapiers'. Nor is the reason for it far to seek: the use of *gauntlets* to protect the hands would make the exchange of rapiers at line 254 easier and less dangerous. Unfortunately, no corresponding change was made in the dialogue at line 110, where all three of the earliest texts call for 'Rapier and dagger'.
174 **presence** assembly (*OED sb.* 3)
175 **distraction** pronounced as four syllables
177 **nature** i.e. natural feeling (for your father)
   exception disapproval, dislike (*OED sb.* 6b)
180–2 **If Hamlet . . . not** Compare 'To not be oneself' (Dent O 64.1)
184 **faction** party
187 **disclaiming from** i.e. disavowal of

That I have shot my arrow o'er the house
And hurt my brother.
LAERTES   I am satisfied in nature,   190
Whose motive in this case should stir me most
To my revenge. But in my terms of honour
I stand aloof, and will no reconcilement
Till by some elder masters of known honour
I have a voice and precedent of peace
To keep my name ungored—but till that time
I do receive your offered love like love,
And will not wrong it.
HAMLET   I do embrace it freely,
And will this brothers' wager frankly play.—
Give us the foils. Come on.
LAERTES   Come, one for me.   200
HAMLET
I'll be your foil, Laertes. In mine ignorance
Your skill shall, like a star i'th' darkest night,
Stick fiery off indeed.
LAERTES You mock me, sir.
HAMLET No, by this hand.
CLAUDIUS
Give them the foils, young Osric. Cousin Hamlet,
You know the wager?
HAMLET   Very well, my lord.
Your grace hath laid the odds o'th' weaker side.

---

189 my] Q2; mine FQ1   190 brother] Q2Q1; Mother F   196 keep] F; *not in* Q2   ungored]
Q2; vngorg'd F   till] F; all Q2   198 I do] F; I Q2   200 Come on] F; *not in* Q2   208 hath]
FQ1; has Q2

192 **in my terms of honour** i.e. where my
honour is concerned (*OED term sb.* 10).
Shakespeare is rather addicted to this
periphrastic use of *terms of*. See, for example, *Merchant* 2.1.13–14, 'In terms of
choice I am not solely led | By nice direc-
tion of a maiden's eyes'.
195 **voice and precedent of peace** i.e. firm
statement, based on precedent, in favour
of a peaceful arrangement
196 **name ungored** reputation uninjured (earliest instance of *ungored* cited by *OED*)
201 **foil** Originally the setting of a jewel, a *foil*
came to mean anything that sets off

another thing to advantage (*OED sb.*¹ 5b
and 6).
202 **like a star . . . night** Compare 'Stars
shine brightest in the darkest night' (Dent
S826.1).
203 **Stick fiery off** show to sparkling advantage (*OED stick v.*¹ 31, citing this as its first
instance)
208 **laid the odds o'** wagered on, backed
(*OED odds sb.* 5, citing as its first instance
2 Henry IV, 5.5.106–8, 'I will lay odds
that, ere this year expire, | We bear our
civil swords and native fire | As far as
France')

CLAUDIUS

I do not fear it; I have seen you both.
But since he is bettered, we have therefore odds.   210

Hamlet and Laertes choose foils

LAERTES

This is too heavy. Let me see another.

HAMLET

This likes me well. These foils have all a length?

OSRIC Ay, my good lord.

They prepare to play while Servants bring in stoups of wine

CLAUDIUS

Set me the stoups of wine upon that table.
If Hamlet give the first or second hit,
Or quit in answer of the third exchange,
Let all the battlements their ordnance fire.
The King shall drink to Hamlet's better breath,
And in the cup an union shall he throw
Richer than that which four successive kings   220
In Denmark's crown have worn. Give me the cups;
And let the kettle to the trumpet speak,
The trumpet to the cannoneer without,

---

210 bettered] F; better Q2   210.1 *Hamlet and Laertes choose foils*] not in FQ2Q1   213.1 *They prepare to play*] F (*Prepare to play [after 212]*); not in Q2Q1   213.1–2 *while Servants . . . wine*] not in FQ2Q1   219 union] F; Vnice Q2 *uncorr.*; Onixe Q2 *corr.*   221 worn. Give me the cups;] FQ2 (*subs.*); worn—give me the cups—JENKINS   222 trumpet speak] Q2; Trumpets speake F

---

210 **bettered** 'pronounced (by public opinion) to be the better' (Jenkins)
  odds i.e. odds that are in our favour. Claudius is doing his best to cover up the fact that the *odds* are designed to give Laertes as many opportunities as possible to kill Hamlet.
211 **Let me see another** It is here, of course, that Laertes sets about the business of picking out the unbated weapon.
212 **a length** i.e. the same length (Abbott 81)
216 **quit . . . exchange** repay Laertes (for winning the first two bouts) by making a return hit in the third
218 **better breath** increased staying power
219 **union** 'A pearl of large size, good quality, and great value, especially one which is supposed to occur singly' (*OED sb.*²). The business of drinking a pearl dissolved

in wine goes back as far as Pliny, who tells how Cleopatra made a bet with Antony that she could spend a hundred million sesterces on a single meal. She won it by putting a priceless pearl in her wine and then drinking it off (*Natural History* ix. 120–1). Ben Jonson refers to the story in *Volpone* 3.7.191–3, where Volpone says to Celia: 'See, here a rope of pearl; and each more orient | Than that the brave Egyptian queen caroused: | Dissolve and drink 'em.' Jenkins notes that according to a popular tradition, preserved in Thomas Heywood's *2 If You Know Not Me*, scene x, Sir Thomas Gresham was supposed to have drunk a pearl to the health of Queen Elizabeth when she visited the Royal Exchange in 1571.
222 **kettle** kettledrum

347

The cannons to the heavens, the heaven to earth,
'Now the King drinks to Hamlet'. Come, begin.—
            Trumpets the while
And you, the judges, bear a wary eye.

HAMLET (*to Laertes*) Come on, sir.

LAERTES Come, my lord.
            They play

HAMLET One.

LAERTES No.   230

HAMLET (*to Osric*) Judgement.

OSRIC A hit, a very palpable hit.

LAERTES Well, again.

CLAUDIUS
Stay. Give me drink. Hamlet, this pearl is thine.
Here's to thy health.
            ⌈*Drums and*⌉ *Trumpets sound, and shot goes off*
                        Give him the cup.

HAMLET
I'll play this bout first. Set it by awhile.—
Come.
            They play again
                        Another hit. What say you?

LAERTES A touch, a touch, I do confess.

CLAUDIUS
Our son shall win.

GERTRUDE   He's fat, and scant of breath.
Here, Hamlet, take my napkin, rub thy brows.   240
The Queen carouses to thy fortune, Hamlet.

---

224 heaven] FQ2; heauens Q3   225.1 *Trumpets the while* Q2; *not in* F   228 Come, my lord]
Q2; Come on sir F   228.1 *They play*] F; *not in* Q2   235 *Drums . . . off*] *Trumpets sound, and shot
goes off* F (*after* cup); *Drum, trumpets and shot. Florish, a peece goes off* Q2 (*opposite 232,
233*)   236 it] Q2Q1; *not in* F   237.1 *They play again*] Q1; *not in* FQ2   238 A touch, a touch,
I do confess] F; I doe confest Q2; I, I grant, a tuch, a tuch Q1   240 Here, Hamlet, take my]
Q2Q1; Heere's a F

---

234 **this pearl** The pearl is dropped into the
cup from which Hamlet is to drink in
order to identify that cup as Hamlet's. We
are not told how or when the poison was
mixed with the wine.

239 **He's fat, and scant of breath** This
remark has been the subject of much
debate because it has been taken as an

objective one. It looks more like a bit of
maternal solicitude. Gertrude is eager to
find an excuse for her son should he lose
the match; and her solicitude becomes all
the more evident if Hamlet is neither fat
nor scant of breath.

240 **napkin** handkerchief

HAMLET
  Good madam.
CLAUDIUS   Gertrude, do not drink.
GERTRUDE
  I will, my lord, I pray you pardon me.
      She drinks and offers the cup to Hamlet
CLAUDIUS (*aside*)
  It is the poisoned cup. It is too late.
HAMLET
  I dare not drink yet, madam—by and by.
GERTRUDE Come, let me wipe thy face.
LAERTES (*to Claudius*) My lord, I'll hit him now.
CLAUDIUS   I do not think't.
LAERTES (*aside*)
  And yet 'tis almost 'gainst my conscience.
HAMLET
  Come for the third, Laertes. You but dally.
  I pray you pass with your best violence.   250
  I am afeard you make a wanton of me.
LAERTES Say you so? Come on.
      They play
OSRIC Nothing neither way.
LAERTES Have at you now!
      Laertes wounds Hamlet. Then, in scuffling they change
      rapiers, and Hamlet wounds Laertes
CLAUDIUS Part them. They are incensed.
HAMLET (*to Laertes*) Nay, come again.
      Gertrude falls

243.1 *She drinks ... Hamlet*] *Shee drinkes* Q1 ; *not in* FQ2   248 'tis almost 'gainst] F ; it is almost against Q2 ; it goes almost against Q1   249 third, Laertes.] JOHNSON ; third. *Laertes,* F ; third‸ *Laertes,* Q2   but] F ; doe but Q2   251 afeard] F ; sure Q2   252.1 *They play*] F (*Play*); *not in* Q2   254.1–2 *Laertes wounds ... Laertes*] *In scuffling they change Rapiers* F ; *They catch one anothers Rapiers, and both are wounded, Leartes falles downe, the Queene falles downe and dies* Q1 ; *not in* Q2   256 Nay, come again] Q2 (Nay‸ come againe); Nay come, againe F   256.1 *Gertrude falls*] *not in* FQ2

250 **pass** make your thrust
  your best violence i.e. the utmost force you are capable of
251 **make a wanton of me** trifle with me, play with me as though I were a spoilt child
253 **Nothing neither way** i.e. things are (for some reason not stated) at an impasse with no advantage on either side
254 **Have at you now** Although these words are usually interpreted as the prelude to an unexpected and treacherous attack on a Hamlet who is off his guard, their normal purpose in Shakespeare is to serve as a warning to an opponent that he is about to be attacked. See, for instance, *Troilus* 5.4.21 ; 5.6.11 ; and 5.6.13. They could, therefore, be a sign that Laertes is being affected by his conscience.

349

OSRIC Look to the Queen there. Ho!

HORATIO
  They bleed on both sides. How is't, my lord?

OSRIC How is't, Laertes?

LAERTES
  Why, as a woodcock to mine own springe, Osric.   260
  I am justly killed with mine own treachery.

HAMLET How does the Queen?

CLAUDIUS   She swoons to see them bleed.

GERTRUDE
  No, no, the drink, the drink! O my dear Hamlet!
  The drink, the drink! I am poisoned.   *She dies*

HAMLET
  O, villainy! Ho! Let the door be locked.   *Exit Osric*
  Treachery! Seek it out.

LAERTES
  It is here, Hamlet. Hamlet, thou art slain.
  No med'cine in the world can do thee good.
  In thee there is not half an hour of life.
  The treacherous instrument is in thy hand,   270
  Unbated and envenomed. The foul practice
  Hath turned itself on me. Lo, here I lie,
  Never to rise again. Thy mother's poisoned.
  I can no more. The King, the King's to blame.

HAMLET
  The point envenomed too? Then, venom, to thy work.
        He stabs Claudius

ALL THE COURTIERS Treason! treason!

CLAUDIUS
  O, yet defend me, friends, I am but hurt.

---

258 is't] F; is it Q2   260 own] Q2; *not in* F   262 swoons] sounds FQ2   264 *She dies*] *not in*
FQ2   265 Ho!] How? F; how Q2; hoe Q3; ho, Q1   *Exit Osric*] *not in* FQ2Q1   267 Hamlet.
Hamlet,] F; *Hamlet*, Q2   268 med'cine] Q2 (medcin); Medicine F   269 hour of] FQ1; houres
Q2   270 thy] FQ1; my Q2   275.1 *He stabs Claudius*] F (*Hurts the King*); *not in* Q2   276 ALL
THE COURTIERS] FQ2 (*All*)

---

257 **Ho! Halt! Stop!** (*OED int.*²)
260-1 **Why . . . treachery** Compare 'The
  fowler is caught in his own net' and 'A
  springe to catch a woodcock' (Tilley F626
  and S788). The true son of his father (see
  1.3.115), Laertes combines two proverbs
  into one, recognizing his own would-be-

clever folly.
265 **Ho!** (*OED int.*¹—a cry calling for attention)
265.1 **Exit Osric** As Osric is to enter at line
  302, he has to make his exit first. He can
  do so here by going to lock the door.

HAMLET

Here, thou incestuous, murd'rous, damnèd Dane,
Drink off this potion.
> *He forces Claudius to drink*
                        Is thy union here?
Follow my mother.
> *Claudius dies*

LAERTES   He is justly served;   280
It is a poison tempered by himself.
Exchange forgiveness with me, noble Hamlet.
Mine and my father's death come not upon thee,
Nor thine on me!   *He dies*

HAMLET

Heaven make thee free of it! I follow thee.
I am dead, Horatio. Wretched Queen, adieu!
You that look pale and tremble at this chance,
That are but mutes or audience to this act,
Had I but time—as this fell sergeant Death
Is strict in his arrest—O, I could tell you—   290
But let it be. Horatio, I am dead;
Thou liv'st; report me and my cause aright
To the unsatisfied.

HORATIO   Never believe it.
I am more an antique Roman than a Dane.
Here's yet some liquor left.

HAMLET   As thou'rt a man,
Give me the cup. Let go. By heaven, I'll have't.

278 Here] F; Heare Q2   murd'rous] F; *not in* Q2   279 off] F; of Q2   *He forces Claudius to drink*] SPENCER; *not in* FQ2   thy union] FQ1; the Onixe Q2   280 *Claudius dies*] FQ1; *not in* Q2   284 *He dies*] FQ1; *not in* Q2   292 liv'st] F; liuest Q2   cause aright] Q2; causes right F   296 have't] F; hate Q2

279 **union** (1) the pearl (2) union with Gertrude. Characteristically, Hamlet is still punning with bitter irony.
281 **tempered** compounded, mixed (*OED* v. 4)
285 **make thee free** absolve you from the guilt
286 **Wretched** most unhappy (expressing both pity and affection)
288 **mutes** onlookers (literally, actors who have no words to speak)
   act (1) action, event (2) performance
289 **as** whereas (*OED* B8d, quoting this passage)

289-90 **fell sergeant . . . arrest** Compare *Sonnets* 74.1-2, 'When that fell arrest | Without all bail shall carry me away', and Dent D142.2.
289 **sergeant** officer of the law responsible for the arrest of offenders
292 **me and my cause** i.e. what I have done and my reasons for doing it
293 **unsatisfied** uninformed
294 **antique Roman** Many Ancient Romans, and, above all others, Cato Uticensis, chose suicide in preference to life on conditions they regarded as dishonourable.

O God, Horatio, what a wounded name,
Things standing thus unknown, I leave behind me!
If thou didst ever hold me in thy heart,
Absent thee from felicity awhile,   300
And in this harsh world draw thy breath in pain,
To tell my story.

> *A march afar off, and shot within*

What warlike noise is this?

> *Enter Osric*

OSRIC
Young Fortinbras, with conquest come from Poland,
To th'ambassadors of England gives
This warlike volley.

HAMLET   O, I die, Horatio.
The potent poison quite o'ercrows my spirit.
I cannot live to hear the news from England,
But I do prophesy th'election lights
On Fortinbras. He has my dying voice.
So tell him, with the occurrents, more and less,   310
Which have solicited—the rest is silence.

> *He gives a long sigh and dies*

HORATIO
Now cracks a noble heart. Good night, sweet prince,
And flights of angels sing thee to thy rest.
Why does the drum come hither?

297 God] Q2; good F; fie Q1   298 I leave] This edition; shall liue F; shall I leaue Q2; wouldst thou leaue Q1   302 *A march afar off, and shot within*] *March afarre off, and shout within* F; *A marche a farre off* Q2   302.1 *Enter Osric*] FQ2   304 th'ambassadors] FQ2; the ambassadors POPE   310 the occurrents] F; th'occurrants Q2   311.1 *He gives a long sigh and dies*] This edition, *interpreting* F (O, o, o, o. *Dyes*); Ham⟨let⟩ *dies* Q1; *not in* Q2   312 cracks] Q2; cracke F

298 **I leave behind me** The grounds for this emendation are: (1) it has a greater urgency than either the F or the Q2 reading; (2) it retains *leave* found in Q1 as well as Q2; (3) it is not metrically unsatisfactory as the Q2 reading is. The agreement of all three texts in their use of the future tense suggests that the trouble may well go back to an undeleted or inadequately deleted *shall* in the foul papers.

302.1 **shot within** (an order to the hands backstage to let off the 'warlike volley' referred to at 305)

306 **o'ercrows** triumphs over. The metaphor is from cock-fighting.

308 **th'election** i.e. the election of a new king of Denmark.

309 **voice** vote, support

310 **occurrents** occurrences, events (*OED sb.* 1)

311 **solicited** moved, urged. The sentence, which is broken off, would, presumably, have ended with some such words as 'me to support him'.

311.1 *He gives a long sigh* In thus 'translating' F's 'O, o, o, o.', which has been the object of unjustified derision, I follow the suggestion of E. A. J. Honigmann in *Shakespeare Survey* 29 (1976), 123.

313 **flights** companies

Enter Fortinbras, with the English Ambassadors, and
Soldiers with drum and colours

FORTINBRAS
Where is this sight?

HORATIO   What is it you would see?
If aught of woe or wonder, cease your search.

FORTINBRAS
This quarry cries on havoc. O proud Death,
What feast is toward in thine eternal cell,
That thou so many princes at a shot
So bloodily hast struck?

ENGLISH AMBASSADOR   The sight is dismal;   320
And our affairs from England come too late.
The ears are senseless that should give us hearing
To tell him his commandment is fulfilled:
That Rosencrantz and Guildenstern are dead.
Where should we have our thanks?

HORATIO   Not from his mouth,
Had it th'ability of life to thank you;
He never gave commandment for their death.
But since, so jump upon this bloody question,
You from the Polack wars, and you from England,
Are here arrived, give order that these bodies   330
High on a stage be placèd to the view;
And let me speak to th' yet unknowing world
How these things came about. So shall you hear
Of carnal, bloody, and unnatural acts,

314.1–2 *Enter Fortinbras . . . colours*] *Enter Fortinbras and English Ambassador, with Drumme, Colours, and Attendants* F; *Enter Fortenbrasse, with the Embassadors* Q2; *Enter Voltemar and the Ambassadors from England. enter Fortenbrusse with his traine* Q1   315 you] Q2; ye F   317 This] Q2; His F   proud] F; prou'd Q2   319 shot] Q2; shoote F   330 arrived,] Q2; arriued. F   332 th' yet] F; yet Q2

317 **quarry** pile of game at the end of a hunt (used metaphorically here for the corpses)
     cries on havoc i.e. unequivocally speaks of slaughter on a large scale. Compare *Othello* 5.1.48, 'Whose noise is this that cries on murder?'
318 **toward** being prepared, about to be made (*OED a.* 2b)
     eternal accursed, infernal (*OED a.* 7). Compare *Caesar* 1.2.160, 'Th'eternal devil', and *Othello* 4.2.131, 'some eternal villain'.
322 **The ears** i.e. Claudius's ears

325 **Where** whence (i.e. from whom). Compare *Antony* 2.1.18, 'Where have you this? 'Tis false'.
     his i.e. Claudius's
328 **jump upon** precisely apropos to
     question affair
331 **stage** platform, scaffold (*OED sb.* 4)
334–8 **Of carnal . . . heads** These lines are, in effect, a résumé of the play's action, similar to that at the end of *Romeo* (5.3.215–89.) But there is also a striking difference: what occupies some seventy lines in the earlier tragedy is here confined to five.

Of accidental judgements, casual slaughters,
Of deaths put on by cunning and forced cause;
And, in this upshot, purposes mistook
Fallen on the inventors' heads. All this can I
Truly deliver.

FORTINBRAS   Let us haste to hear it,
And call the noblest to the audience.   340
For me, with sorrow I embrace my fortune.
I have some rights of memory in this kingdom,
Which now to claim my vantage doth invite me.

HORATIO
Of that I shall have also cause to speak,
And from his mouth whose voice will draw on more.
But let this same be presently performed,
Even while men's minds are wild, lest more mischance
On plots and errors happen.

FORTINBRAS   Let four captains
Bear Hamlet like a soldier to the stage;
For he was likely, had he been put on,   350
To have proved most royally; and for his passage,
The soldiers' music and the rites of war
Speak loudly for him.
Take up the bodies. Such a sight as this
Becomes the field, but here shows much amiss.
Go, bid the soldiers shoot.

> *A dead march. Exeunt, bearing off the bodies, after the*
> *which a peal of ordnance is shot off*

---

336 forced] F; for no Q2   338 the inventors'] F; th'inuenters Q2   342 rights] Q2Q1; Rites
F   343 now] Q2Q1; are F   344 also] Q2; alwayes F   345 on] F; no Q2   347 while] Q2;
whiles F   351 royally] F; royall Q2   352 rites] F; right Q2; rite WILSON   354 bodies] Q2;
body FQ1   356.1–2 *A dead . . . off*] *Exeunt Marching : after the which, a Peale of Ordenance are
shot off* F; *Exeunt* Q2; *not in* Q1

336 **put on** instigated
    forced cause foul means
342 **rights of memory** 'rights living in the
    remembrance of men, traditional rights'
    (Schmidt)
343 **vantage** favourable opportunity (*OED
    sb.* 4b)
345 **whose voice will draw on more** i.e.
    whose support will attract further support
    from others
346 **this same** i.e. what I have suggested

347 **wild** wildly excited
348 **On** Two related senses of *on* are com-
    bined here: (1) on top of (2) in conse-
    quence of (Abbott 180).
350 **put on** put to the test, set to it (by
    becoming king)
351 **passage** passing, death
353 **Speak** For this use of the subjunctive
    with an imperative force see Abbott 364.
355 **field** battlefield

PASSAGES PECULIAR TO THE SECOND QUARTO

(i) After 1.1.107 Q2 reads:

BARNARDO

I think it be no other but e'en so.
Well may it sort that this portentous figure
Comes armèd through our watch so like the King
That was and is the question of these wars.

HORATIO

A mote it is to trouble the mind's eye.
In the most high and palmy state of Rome,
A little ere the mightiest Julius fell,
The graves stood tenantless, and the sheeted dead
Did squeak and gibber in the Roman streets

---

5 mote] moth Q2; mote Q4   9 *Omission marked after this line* JENNENS

(i) These eighteen lines were probably omitted from the text that lies behind F because they do not advance the action in any way. Moreover, if Horatio's speech was, as seems likely, intended to serve as an advertisement for *Julius Caesar*, there would be no point in including it when *Julius Caesar* was not being performed.

1 **be** can be. '*Be* is used with some notion of doubt, question, thought, etc . . . after verbs of thinking' (Abbott 299).

2 **sort** be fitting, be in accordance with your supposition
  portentous ominous, foreboding some calamity. Shakespeare employs this word on two other occasions only: *Romeo* 1.1.139, and *Caesar* 1.3.31, where Casca, having described the sights he has seen during the storm, remarks, 'I believe they are portentous things'. Did the playwright recall Casca's *portentous* because he had already decided to have Horatio speak of the same omens, or did the word trigger off Horatio's speech?

4 **question** cause

5 **A mote . . . eye** 'He is a mote in their eyes' is proverbial (Tilley M1189); but Shakespeare extends its meaning by changing

'eye' to 'mind's eye' in the first use of this pregnant phrase recorded by *OED* (*eye sb.* [1] 4d). Horatio does not mean that the Ghost is a trivial matter but that its appearance troubles his mind.

6–13 **In . . . eclipse** In this passage about the omens preceding the assassination of Julius Caesar Shakespeare draws, probably from memory, on the material he had used in *Julius Caesar*—primarily Plutarch's Life of Caesar, but also Ovid's *Metamorphoses* and Lucan's *Pharsalia*.

6 **palmy** flourishing (a Shakespearian coinage derived from Ps. 92: 11, 'The righteous shall flourish like a palm tree')
  state i.e. political entity

7 **mightiest** very mighty. 'The superlative inflection *est*, like the Latin superlative, is sometimes used to signify "very", with little or no idea of excess' (Abbott 8).

8 **graves stood tenantless** Compare *Caesar* 1.3.73–4, 'this dreadful night | That . . . opens graves', and 2.2.18 'graves have yawned and yielded up their dead'.
  sheeted in their winding-sheets

9 **Did squeak . . . streets** Compare *Caesar* 2.2.24, 'ghosts did shriek and squeal about the streets'.

At stars with trains of fire, and dews of blood,   10
Disasters in the sun; and the moist star,
Upon whose influence Neptune's empire stands,
Was sick almost to doomsday with eclipse.
And even the like precurse of feared events,
As harbingers preceding still the fates
And prologue to the omen coming on,
Have heaven and earth together demonstrated
Unto our climatures and countrymen.

(ii) After 1.4.16 Q2 reads:

This heavy-handed revel east and west

10 At] This edition; As Q2   14 feared] PARROTT–CRAIG, *conj*. Collier; feare Q2; fearce Q3
18 climatures] Q2; climature WHITE *conj*. Dyce
(ii)   1 revel] Q3 (reuelle); reueale Q2

10 **At** The assumption behind this emendation is that the *As* of Q2 comes from the
compositor's mistaking *t* for final *s*. Compare 1.5.68, where *posset* (F) appears as
possesse in Q2, and *LLL* 4.2.77, where
sapit is printed as *sapis* in all editions prior
to F2.
   stars with trains of fire the *comets* of
Caesar 2.2.30
   dews of blood Compare the battles in the
air 'Which drizzled blood upon the
Capitol' (*Caesar* 2.2.21).
11 **Disasters** malevolent influences (literally,
'unfavourable aspects')
   the moist star the moon; often referred to
as *moist* or *watery* because it was thought
to draw up water from the sea
12 **influence** an astrological term denoting
'the supposed flowing or streaming from
the stars or heavens of an etherial fluid ...
affecting sublunary things generally'
(*OED* 2). The *influence* here is the moon's
control of the tides.
   stands depends (Abbott 204)
13 **almost to doomsday** almost to death. The
allusion is to the prophecy (Matthew 24:
29) that at the second coming of Christ
'the moon shall not give her light'.
14 **even** exactly
   precurse heralding, premonitory signs
—earliest example in *OED*
   feared events i.e. events to be anticipated
with fear. Compare *Cymbeline* 2.4.6,
'these feared hopes'. Q2's *feare* is probably the result of the compositor's mistaking the *d* in *feard*, a likely Shakespearian
spelling, for an *e*. Q3 emended *feare* to
fearce, an emendation accepted by many
editors; but Q3 has no textual authority;

and *feared* makes better sense than *fierce*.
15 **still** always
   the fates both 'events that are fated to
happen' and 'the Fates that ordain them'
16 **omen** ominous events predicted. Shakespeare does not use *omen* elsewhere; but
the unusual sense he gives it can be paralleled. Furness quotes Farmer's observation that the frontispiece to Heywood's
Life of Merlin (1641) has a couplet which
runs: 'Merlin, well versed in many a hid-
den spell, | His country's omen did long
since foretell.'
18 **climatures** climes, part of the world (apparently a Shakespearian coinage)

(ii) The omission of the twenty-two lines
given here from F cannot be explained as a cut
made out of deference to the feelings of Anne of
Denmark, since Hamlet has already made his
disapproval of the King's addiction to drink
amply clear. The obvious reason for their
disappearance is that they slow the action
down. Eagerly awaiting a meeting between
the Ghost and his son, the audience is tan-
talized with a repetition of one of the stock
'complaints' of the Elizabethan satirist: the
drunkenness of the Danes. Nashe, for instance, describes them, in his *Pierce Penilesse*
(1592), as 'bursten-bellied sots, that are to be
confuted with nothing but tankards or quart
pots', and sums them up as 'this surly swinish
generation' (i. 180. 16–23). Furthermore, it
may well be no accident that this cut disposes
of the most notorious of all the cruxes in *Hamlet*, the 'dram of eale' passage with which the
lines peculiar to Q2 conclude.

1 **heavy-headed revel** i.e. revelling that
   makes men thick-headed

Makes us traduced and taxed of other nations.
They clepe us drunkards, and with swinish phrase
Soil our addition; and indeed it takes
From our achievements, though performed at height,
The pith and marrow of our attribute.
So, oft it chances in particular men,
That for some vicious mole of nature in them,
As in their birth, wherein they are not guilty,
Since nature cannot choose his origin,   10
By the o'ergrowth of some complexion,
Oft breaking down the pales and forts of reason,
Or by some habit that too much o'erleavens
The form of plausive manners—that these men,

---

3 clepe] Q5; clip Q2   11 the] POPE; their Q2

---

2 **taxed** of censured by
3 **clepe** call
swinish phrase i.e. the epithet 'swinish'.
'As drunk as a swine' was proverbial
(Tilley S1042).
4 **soil our addition** sully our name. Compare *Merry Wives* 2.2.270: 'they are devils' additions, the names of fiends.'
takes takes away from, detracts from
5 **at height** most brilliantly, to perfection
6 **pith and marrow** essential substance.
OED's illustrations (*marrow sb.¹* 2d) show how well established this phrase had become in the 16th century before Shakespeare adopted it here and gave it a still wider currency.
attribute reputation. Compare *Troilus* 2.3.111–12, 'Much attribute he [Achilles] hath, and much the reason | Why we ascribe it to him.'
7–22 **So . . . scandal** There is a marked resemblance between these lines and the following passage from Nashe's *Pierce Penilesse*: 'A mighty deformer of men's manners and features is this unnecessary vice [drunkenness] of all other. Let him [any man] be endued with never so many virtues, and have as much goodly proportion and favour as nature can bestow upon a man, yet if he be thirsty after his own destruction, and hath no joy nor comfort but when he is drowning his soul in a gallon pot, that one beastly imperfection will utterly obscure all that is commendable in him; and all his good qualities sink like lead down to the bottom of his carousing cups, where they will lie, like lees and dregs, dead and unregarded

of any man' (Nashe, i. 205. 23–33).
7 **particular men** individuals (as distinct from nations)
8 **for** because of
vicious mole of nature i.e. natural blemish constituting a defect of the kind described by Oberon as 'the blots of nature's hand' (*Dream* 5.1.398).
9 **As** namely, to wit
birth parentage (some defects being inherited)
11 **complexion** dominant element in a man's make-up. Shakespeare alludes to the old idea, still current in his time, that a man's temperament was determined by the combination in him of the four 'humours' or bodily fluids—melancholy, phlegm, blood, and choler. Whichever of the four was dominant controlled his disposition, and, if its dominance became excessive through *o'ergrowth*, led to an unbalanced personality and irrational behaviour.
12 **pales and forts** palisaded forts. A castle under siege was a common figure for the rational soul assailed by the forces of evil.
13–14 **some habit . . . manners** i.e. some once spontaneous touches of grace and charm that have been over-cultivated until they have become an annoying habit. The notion of excess, already present in *o'ergrowth*, is carried further in *too much o'er-leavens*, which suggests something so blown up that it has become insubstantial, a mere *form* of what it once was—a praiseworthy and pleasing attitude to others. The notion of *leaven* having a bad effect is clear in Imogen's

Carrying, I say, the stamp of one defect,
Being nature's livery or fortune's star,
His virtues else, be they as pure as grace,
As infinite as man may undergo,
Shall in the general censure take corruption
From that particular fault. The dram of eale   20
Doth all the noble substance of a doubt
To his own scandal.

(iii) After 1.4.53 Q2 reads:

The very place puts toys of desperation,
Without more motive, into every brain
That looks so many fathoms to the sea
And hears it roar beneath.

17 His] Q2; Their POPE 1728, conj. Theobald, SR   20 eale] Q2; ease Q3; base THEOBALD; ill
JENNENS; evil KEIGHTLEY, conj. Jervis; e'il KITTREDGE; ev'l RIVERSIDE   21 of a doubt] Q2; of
worth out THEOBALD; of worth dout MALONE; often dout STEEVENS 1793; to a doubt SISSON   22
To] Q2; Of SISSON

words, 'So thou, Posthumus, | Wilt lay the leaven on all proper men' (*Cymbeline* 3.4.59–60); and there is a close parallel to the unusual sense *plausive* has here in the King's praise of Bertram's father— 'his plausive words | He scattered not in ears, but grafted them | To grow there, and to bear' (*All's Well* 1.2.53–5).
    that picks up the previous *That* of l. 8
16 **nature's livery** i.e. the defects of ll. 8–14
    fortune's star the effect of a star influencing one's fortunes
17 **His** Probably influenced by 'the stamp of *one* defect', Shakespeare seems to have forgotten that his subject, 'these men', is plural, and to have continued the sentence as though it were 'this man'.
    else in all other respects
18 **undergo** bear the weight of. Compare *Measure* 1.1.23–5, 'If any in Vienna be of worth | To undergo such ample grace and honour, | It is Lord Angelo'.
19 **general censure** opinion of the public at large
19–20 **take corruption | From** undergo destructive perversion because of, be completely misrepresented through the influence of
20–22 **The dram . . . scandal** For the general sense, see Tilley C585, 'One ill condition mars all the good', and especially the

example given there from John Baret's *Alveary or Quadruple Dictionary* (1580): 'A proverb applied to those, which being indued with many good virtues, yet the vices that they are affected with do utterly stain and obliterate them . . . a little leaven leaveneth a whole lump.' But while there is no difficulty about the main drift of the sentence, its precise meaning remains elusive. Many emendations have been proposed, but none of them is thoroughly convincing.

22 **to his own scandal** This seems to mean 'to the shame and disgrace of the noble substance itself'.

(iii) Two things suggest that the absence of these four lines from F is the result of a deliberate cut. First, they have left no mark whatever on Q1; and, secondly, the excision is a neat one, affecting neither sense nor metre.

1 **toys of desperation** wild irrational impulses towards self-destruction. Compare *Othello* 3.4.156–8, 'Pray heaven it be state matters . . . And no conception nor no jealous toy | Concerning you.'
2 **more motive** further inciting cause (such as a demon); *OED motive sb.* 4b.

(iv) After 3.2.160 Q2 reads:

Where love is great, the littlest doubts are fear;
Where little fears grow great, great love grows there.

(v) After 3.2.205 Q2 reads:

To desperation turn my trust and hope,
An anchor's cheer in prison be my scope,

(vi) After 3.4.72 ('Would step from this to this?') Q2 reads:

                                    Sense, sure you have,
Else could you not have motion. But sure that sense
Is apoplexed; for madness would not err,
Nor sense to ecstasy was ne'er so thralled
But it reserved some quantity of choice
To serve in such a difference.

(vii) After 3.4.73 Q2 reads:

Eyes without feeling, feeling without sight,
Ears without hands or eyes, smelling sans all,
Or but a sickly part of one true sense
Could not so mope.

(v)   2 An anchor's] THEOBALD; And Anchors Q2   cheer] Q2; chair *conj.* Steevens

(iv) It is hard to be sure whether the disappearance of this wordy couplet from F is due to design or accident. But no matter what the reason for it may be, the loss of this 'copious' version of 'Love is never without fear' (Tilley L507) is no cause for regret.

(v) 'The Mousetrap' loses nothing by the excision of this couplet from F. The sense of the second line is far from clear, and has been disputed. As printed here, with Theobald's emendation of *An* for the *And* of Q2, it means 'let an anchorite's fare in prison be the limit of my desires'; but, as Steevens pointed out, Joseph Hall, in his *Virgidemiae* (1599), writes of fools who 'Sit seauen yeares pining in an Anchores cheyre' (IV. ii. 103). Unfortunately, OED offers no evidence that *chair* was ever spelled *cheere* (Q2).

(vi) Like the three passages peculiar to Q2 that follow it, this one appears to have been cut from F for good aesthetic reasons. All four run to excess. They smack of self-indulgence on the part of the hero and, possibly, of the author also. The play is stronger for their exclusion and far less open to the kind of attack

T. S. Eliot made on it in his essay of 1919.

1 **Sense** i.e. your senses
2 **motion** ability to move, to 'step from this to this'
3 **apoplexed** paralyzed, benumbed. This use of *apoplex* as a verb seems to be original with Shakespeare. It is certainly to the point, for *apoplexy* is defined by OED as 'a malady... which arrests more or less completely the powers of sense and motion.' **err** i.e. err so badly
4 **ecstasy** madness
5 **quantity of choice** slight portion of the ability to choose (OED *quantity* 8b). Compare *Shrew* 4.3.111, 'Away, thou rag, thou quantity, thou remnant.'
6 **To serve . . . difference** i.e. to enable you to see so great a difference

(vii) As the revising Shakespeare seems to have perceived, this catalogue merely elaborates on, without adding anything of substance to, what Hamlet has said already.

4 **mope** be impercipient, be unaware of the obvious

(viii) After 3.4.156 Q2 reads:

That monster custom, who all sense doth eat
Of habits vile, is angel yet in this,
That to the use of actions fair and good
He likewise gives a frock or livery
That aptly is put on.

(ix) After 3.4.159 ('To the next abstinence') Q2 reads:
                    the next more easy;
For use almost can change the stamp of nature,
And either shame the devil or throw him out
With wondrous potency.

(viii)   1–2 eat | Of habits vile,] This edition; eate | Of habits deuill, Q2; eat, | Of habits divell, Q5; eat | Of habit's devil, ROWE; eat | Of habits evil, THEOBALD, *conj.* Thirlby; eat | Of habits, devil, JOHNSON; eat, | Oft habits' devil STAUNTON   5 on.] Q5 (on:); on_A Q2
(ix)   3 either shame the] HUDSON 1879; either the Q2; Maister the Q3; either curb MALONE; either lodge JENKINS, *conj.* Clarendon

(viii) The general sense of this passage is conveniently summed up in two commonplace phrases: 'Custom makes sin no sin' (Tilley C934), and 'Custom is overcome with custom' (Dent C932.1). But it becomes contorted through Shakespeare's inability to resist the temptation to quibble held out by the word *habit*.

1–2 who . . . vile i.e. which destroys our ability to recognize bad habits for what they are
2 vile The assumption behind this emendation of Q2's *deuill* is that Shakespeare wrote *vilde* which Compositor X then muddled in much the same way as Compositor Y turned *thumbe* into *the vmber* (3.2.341).
3 use habitual practice
4 frock or livery uniform. The *frock* is the *habit* of a monk or priest; the *livery* that of a servant.
5 aptly is put on i.e. goes on easily and fits well

(ix) The excision of these words from F is remarkably adroit.

2 use . . . nature 'Use is another nature'

(Tilley C932) was a well worn saying.
stamp of nature i.e. innate qualities of the personality. Shakespeare often employs this metaphor, derived from coining, when referring to inherited characteristics. Compare *Cymbeline* 2.5.3–6, 'that most venerable man which I | Did call my father was I know not where | When I was stamped. Some coiner with his tools | Made me a counterfeit.'
3 shame Either the compositor has omitted the verb at this point, or, possibly, Shakespeare failed to supply one. Various conjectures as to what it should have been have been made, beginning with the *Maister* of Q3. The one adopted here seems appropriate for two reasons. 'Speak the truth and shame the devil' (Tilley T566) was proverbial, and so fits well into a context drawing heavily on common sayings. Furthermore, since a shamed devil would depart of his own accord, the conjecture provides the required antithesis to *throw him out*. See 1 *Henry IV* 3.1.59–61, 'tell truth, and shame the devil. | If thou have power to raise him, bring him hither, | And I'll be sworn I have power to shame him hence.'

(x) After 3.4.190 Q2 reads:

HAMLET

There's letters sealed; and my two schoolfellows,
Whom I will trust as I will adders fanged,
They bear the mandate, they must sweep my way
And marshal me to knavery. Let it work;
For 'tis the sport to have the engineer
Hoist with his own petard; and't shall go hard
But I will delve one yard below their mines
And blow them at the moon. O, 'tis most sweet
When in one line two crafts directly meet.

(xi) After 4.1.3 Q2 reads:

GERTRUDE

Bestow this place on us a little while.

Exeunt Rosencrantz and Guildenstern

(xii) After 4.1.39 ('And what's untimely done.') Q2 reads:

Whose whisper o'er the world's diameter,

(x) 6 and't] Q1676; an't Q2
(xii) 0 . . .] For, haply, Slander THEOBALD; So, haply, slander CAPELL; So viperous slander MALONE; So envious slander JENKINS

(x) The omission of these lines from F contributes to the suspense and surprise of what is to follow in Act 4 by making Hamlet's letters to Horatio and the King completely unexpected.

3 **They bear the mandate** Placed in a prominent position at the beginning of the line, *They* is heavily stressed because the orders for what the mission is to do should be in the hands of the most important member of it, Hamlet himself, not of two underlings. This breach of protocol is an immediate cause for suspicion.
4 **marshal me to knavery** i.e. ceremoniously conduct me into a trap
Let it work let things take their course
5 **engineer** maker of military engines such as bombs
6 **Hoist with his own petard** This phrase, which has itself become proverbial (Dent P243.1) is an ingenious variation on two older expressions: 'The fowler is caught in his own net' and 'To beat one at his own weapon' (Tilley F626 and W204).
Hoist hoisted, blown sky-high (*OED hoise v.* 2b)
petard Bomb, bell-shaped piece of metal filled with gunpowder and used to blow in doors and the like. The word, not found elsewhere in Shakespeare, was a very re-

cent loan from the French providing a new name for a new weapon.
6–7 **and't . . . delve** i.e. only very bad luck will prevent me from delving (*OED hard adv.* 2c)
9 **When . . . meet** i.e. when two exponents of the same skill or cunning device—in this case mining and counter-mining—meet one another head-on. The earliest instance of *craft*, signifying 'boat', cited by *OED* belongs to 1671–2, so there is little likelihood that Hamlet is quibbling.

(xi) Rosencrantz and Guildenstern, to whom the line is addressed in Q2, are not present in F.

(xii) These lines peculiar to Q2 were evidently marked for exclusion. The hiatus with which they begin, a hiatus that leaves the sentence without a subject, is almost certainly due to a careless marking of the manuscript. The hook above the missing words, denoting the start of the cut, was read by the compositor as a deletion sign. Various conjectures have been made as to what the missing words should be. The time honoured stopgap is Capell's 'So, haply, slander'.

1 **diameter** whole extent from side to side or from end to end (*OED* 2g)

As level as the cannon to his blank,
Transports his poisoned shot, may miss our name
And hit the woundless air.

(xiii) After 4.4.8 Q2 reads:

> *Enter Hamlet, Rosencrantz, Guildenstern, and Attendants*
> HAMLET Good sir, whose powers are these?
> CAPTAIN They are of Norway, sir.
> HAMLET How purposed, sir, I pray you?
> CAPTAIN Against some part of Poland.
> HAMLET Who commands them, sir?
> CAPTAIN
> The nephew to old Norway, Fortinbras.
> HAMLET
> Goes it against the main of Poland, sir,
> Or for some frontier?
> CAPTAIN
> Truly to speak, and with no addition,
> We go to gain a little patch of ground   10
> That hath in it no profit but the name.
> To pay five ducats, five, I would not farm it;
> Nor will it yield to Norway or the Pole
> A ranker rate should it be sold in fee.
> HAMLET
> Why, then the Polack never will defend it.

(xiii) 0.1 *Enter ... attendants*] *Enter Hamlet, Rosencraus, &c.* Q2   12 ducats, five,] Q2 (duckets, fiue₋); ducats—five—JENNENS

---

2 **level ... blank** directly as the cannon to its target at point-blank range. See *Lear* 1.1.157–8, 'let me still remain | The true blank of thine eye'.
4 **woundless** invulnerable (*OED* 2)—earliest instance cited of this sense

(xiii) The omission of this long passage from F and from the text that lies behind Q1, where there is no trace of it, cannot be accidental. The lines have been deliberately excised because, while they extend the speculative scope of the tragedy with their discussion of war and its causes, they do nothing to advance the action, nor do they reveal anything new about Hamlet and his state of mind. In spite of all that has happened since the end of 2.2, he is still very much where he was then. His soliloquy is a confession of failure, sum-

marizing what we have seen; and his determination to do better inspires little confidence, since we have heard it before, and at a time when circumstances were far more in his favour than they are now.

7 **main** main body (*OED sb.*¹ 4)
8 **frontier** 'fortress on the frontier, frontier town' (*OED sb.* 5)—earliest instance of this sense cited by *OED*
9 **addition** exaggeration
11 **name** fame (of conquering it) (*OED sb.* 7)
12 **farm** rent (*OED v.*² 1a)
13 **Norway or the Pole** i.e. the King of Norway or the King of Poland
14 **ranker** more excessive (*OED rank a.* 6c)
   in fee in fee simple, with absolute possession
15 **the Polack** the King of Poland.

CAPTAIN

Yes, it is already garrisoned.
Two thousand souls and twenty thousand ducats
Will now debate the question of this straw.

HAMLET

This is th'impostume of much wealth and peace,
That inward breaks, and shows no cause without   20
Why the man dies. I humbly thank you, sir.

CAPTAIN

God buy you, sir.   *Exit*

ROSENCRANTZ   Will't please you go, my lord?

HAMLET

I'll be with you straight. Go a little before.

                                        Exeunt all but Hamlet

How all occasions do inform against me,
And spur my dull revenge. What is a man,
If his chief good and market of his time
Be but to sleep and feed? A beast, no more.
Sure he that made us with such large discourse,

16 Yes, it is] Q2; Nay 'tis Q5, Yes, 'tis POPE; O, yes, it is CAPELL   17–18 Two . . . straw] (*as continuation of Captain's speech*) This edition, *conj* Anon., Ham⟨let⟩ Two . . . straw Q2   18 now] This edition; not Q?   21 Exit] not in Q2   23 Exeunt all but Hamlet] not in Q2

17–18 **Two thousand . . . straw** An anonymous contributor to the *Gentleman's Magazine* LX, 403 suggested that these lines belong to the Captain, who is knowledgeable about the war, not to Hamlet, who asks for information about it. The point seems a fair one. Moreover, there is mislineation at 3.4.53 in Q2, showing that Shakespeare was not very careful about his speech headings. It therefore seems reasonable to assign the lines to the Captain.

18 **now** This emendation of *not* fits in perfectly with the normal meaning of *debate*, i.e. *contest, fight over*, and obviates the necessity of giving it a sense such as *decide* or *settle*, for which there is no precedent.
straw proverbially worthless (Tilley S918)

19–21 **This is . . . dies** Compare 'Peace makes plenty, plenty makes pride, pride breeds quarrel, and quarrel brings war', cited by Tilley under 'By peace plenty' (P139). The entire cycle, which concludes with 'war brings penury, penury brings peace', is dramatized in Marston's *Histriomastix* (1599).

19 **impostume** abscess, purulent swelling.

Compare 'bladders full of imposthume' (*Troilus* 5.1.20).

24 **occasions** chance encounters
inform against denounce, bring a charge against

25–7 **What is . . . no more** There seems to be an echo here of some lines from Marston's *Histriomastix* : 'What [i.e. How] is a man superior to a beast | But for his mind? Nor that ennobles him | While he dejects his reason, making it | The slave unto his brutish appetite' (Harvey Wood, iii. 248). The idea was, of course, a commonplace of the time; but Shakespeare's phrasing of it is remarkably close to Marston's.

26–7 **If . . . feed** Nashe renders this notion, which goes back ultimately to Cicero's *De Natura Deorum*, i. 20.53, thus: 'Cicero saith, *summum bonum* consists in *omnium rerum vacatione*, that it is the chiefest felicity that may be, to rest from all labours' (*Summer's Last Will and Testament* 285–7—Nashe, iii. 242).

26 **market of his time** i.e. best use of his time, that for which he sells his time

28 **large discourse** capacious powers of reasoning

Looking before and after, gave us not
That capability and godlike reason   30
To fust in us unused. Now whether it be
Bestial oblivion, or some craven scruple
Of thinking too precisely on th'event—
A thought which, quartered, hath but one part wisdom
And ever three parts coward—I do not know
Why yet I live to say this thing's to do,
Sith I have cause, and will, and strength, and means
To do't. Examples gross as earth exhort me:
Witness this army, of such mass and charge,
Led by a delicate and tender prince,   40
Whose spirit, with divine ambition puffed,
Makes mouths at the invisible event,
Exposing what is mortal and unsure
To all that fortune, death, and danger dare,
Even for an egg-shell. Rightly to be great
Is not to stir without great argument,
But greatly to find quarrel in a straw
When honour's at the stake. How stand I, then,
That have a father killed, a mother stained,
Excitements of my reason and my blood,   50
And let all sleep; while to my shame I see
The imminent death of twenty thousand men
That, for a fantasy and trick of fame,

31 fust] Q2; Rust ROWE   46 Is not] Q2; Is not, not CAPELL

31 **fust** grow mouldy; not elsewhere in Shakespeare
33 **Of** resulting from (Abbott 168)
   event outcome
36 **to do** i.e. to be done (Abbott 359)
38 **gross** evident, obvious (*OED a.* 3)
39 **mass and charge** size and cost
40 **delicate and tender** carefully nurtured and sensitive (*OED delicate a.* 4). This description of Fortinbras is, at first sight, oddly out of keeping with the implications of his name and also with Horatio's characterization of him at 1.1.96; but see *K. John* 2.1.67–8, 'Rash, inconsiderate, fiery voluntaries, | With ladies' faces and fierce dragons' spleens'.
41 **puffed** inspired
42 **invisible** unforeseeable (Jenkins)
44 **dare** can do, may do (Schmidt)
45 **egg-shell** proverbially worthless (Tilley E95)
45–8 **Rightly . . . stake** i.e. true greatness does not consist in refraining from action when there is no compelling cause to act, but in finding a compelling cause in the merest trifle when one's honour is in question.
46 **not to stir** i.e. not not to stir. *Not* is a double negative.
   argument subject of contention (*OED* 5b)
48 **honour's at the stake** Appearing also in *Twelfth Night* (3.1.115), *Troilus* (3.3.227), and *All's Well* (2.3.147), this expression became proverbial (Dent S813.2). It is evident from the context in *Twelfth Night* and *Troilus* that the *stake* in question is that to which a bull or bear was fastened for baiting.
50 **Excitements** incentives, motives for action (*OED* 3a)
52 **twenty thousand** Shakespeare, casual about numbers, seems to have attached the figure for *ducats* (l. 17) to the *men*.
53 **fantasy and trick** i.e. insubstantial and deceptive trifle

Go to their graves like beds, fight for a plot
Whereon the numbers cannot try the cause,
Which is not tomb enough and continent
To hide the slain? O, from this time forth,
My thoughts be bloody, or be nothing worth.   *Exit*

(xiv) After 4.7.69 ('And call it accident') Q2 reads:

LAERTES   My lord, I will be ruled;
The rather if you could devise it so
That I might be the organ.
CLAUDIUS   It falls right.
You have been talked of since your travels much—
And that in Hamlet's hearing—for a quality
Wherein they say you shine. Your sum of parts
Did not together pluck such envy from him
As did that one; and that, in my regard,
Of the unworthiest siege.
LAERTES   What part is that, my lord?
CLAUDIUS
A very ribbon in the cap of youth,   10
Yet needful too; for youth no less becomes
The light and careless livery that it wears
Than settled age his sables and his weeds,
Importing health and graveness.

(xv) After 4.7.88 ('If one could match you, sir') Q2 reads:
The scrimers of their nation

54 **Go . . . beds** See Dent B192.1 for other
examples of this expression.
55 **Whereon . . . cause** i.e. which is not big
enough to hold the combatants
56 **continent** container (*OED sb.* 1)

(xiv) The omission of these lines from F is
evidently a deliberate cut, designed to speed
up the action by removing some of the 'indirections' Claudius has recourse to in his
approach to Laertes.

3 **organ** tool, instrument
9 **siege** rank (*OED sb.* 1). Compare *Othello*
1.2.22, 'men of royal siege'.
10 **very ribbon** mere ornament (*OED very*
9b)
11 **becomes** i.e. is suited by

12 **livery** literally 'clothes', 'uniform', but
here denoting 'the fashionable practice of
fencing'
13 **his sables and his weeds** i.e. its decorous
sober robes lined with dark fur
14 **health and graveness** i.e. a healthy concern about things that really matter
(such, Claudius implies, as Polonius
showed)

(xv) Shakespeare probably cut this sentence
because he realized that Claudius here is laying on the butter too thickly.

1 **scrimers** fencers. The word is an aphetic
form, for which Shakespeare appears responsible, of *escrimers* (from the French
escrimeur).

He swore had neither motion, guard, nor eye,
If you opposed them.

(xvi) After 4.7.99 Q2 reads:

There lives within the very flame of love
A kind of wick or snuff that will abate it;
And nothing is at a like goodness still;
For goodness, growing to a pleurisy,
Dies in his own too-much. That we would do,
We should do when we would; for this 'would' changes,
And hath abatements and delays as many
As there are tongues, are hands, are accidents,
And then this 'should' is like a spendthrift sigh
That hurts by easing. But to the quick of th'ulcer.   10

(xvii) After 5.2.106 ('Nay, good my lord; for my ease, in good
        faith') Q2 reads:

Sir, here is newly come to court Laertes. Believe me, an absolute
gentleman, full of most excellent differences, of very soft society

(xvi)   9 spendthrift] Q5; spend thirfts Q2; spend-thrifts Q3; spendthrift's POPE

2 **motion** i.e. disciplined movement of the body acquired by training (*OED sb.* 3c). Compare *Twelfth Night* 3.4.263–4, 'he gives me the stuck in with such a mortal motion that it is inevitable'.

(xvi) The excision of these lines from F is a gain. An audience eager to know Claudius's plan may well become impatient at his elaborate moralizing. He himself acknowledges it has gone on too long when he concludes by saying: 'But to the quick of th'ulcer.'

2 **snuff** that portion of a candle-wick which is only partially consumed as the candle burns and has to be removed at intervals if the candle is to continue giving light
4 **pleurisy** excess (*OED* 2). Owing to a mistaken etymological connection with *plus*, *pleurisy* meaning 'inflammation of the *pleura*' came to be regarded as a disease consequent on an excess of humours.
5 **too-much** over-abundance (*OED too adv.* 6a)—apparently a Shakespearian coinage
5–8 **That we . . . accidents** See Tilley N54, 'He that will not when he may, when he would he shall have nay.'
8 **tongues . . . hands** 'alluding to the words

and deeds of those who would dissuade or prevent' (Jenkins)
9–10 **'should' . . . easing** The reference is to the idea, fairly common in Shakespeare, that every sigh a man breathes costs him a drop of blood and thus wastes part of his life. Compare *Dream* 3.2.97, 'sighs of love that cost the fresh blood dear'.
10 **quick of th'ulcer** i.e. heart of the matter, real source of grievance

(xvii) Since F reduces this passage to the one sentence: 'Sir, you are not ignorant of what excellence Laertes is at his weapon', it seems plain that the excision was made to rid the play of a piece of over-elaboration. The difficulties Osric's praise of Laertes and Hamlet's parody of that praise gave both the compositor and the press-corrector of Q2 (see p. 108) also suggest that the lines may have been almost unintelligible to many in an Elizabethan audience.

1 **absolute** perfect
2 **differences** i.e. qualities and accomplishments that distinguish him from all other courtiers (*OED sb.* 4)
 soft society refined manners (*OED soft a.* 14c)

and great showing. Indeed, to speak feelingly of him, he is the card or calendar of gentry; for you shall find in him the continent of what part a gentleman would see.

HAMLET Sir, his definement suffers no perdition in you; though I know to divide him inventorially would dizzy th'arithmetic of memory, and yet but yaw neither, in respect of his quick sail. But, in the verity of extolment, I take him to be a soul of great article, and his infusion of such dearth and rareness as, to make   10 true diction of him, his semblable is his mirror, and who else would trace him, his umbrage, nothing more.

OSRIC Your lordship speaks most infallibly of him.

(xvii)   3 feelingly] U3; tellingly Q2 *corr*.; sellingly Q2 *uncorr*.   5 part] Q2; parts WILSON   7 dizzy] U3 (dizzie); dazzie Q2 *corr*.; dosie Q2 *uncorr*.   8 yaw] Q2 *uncorr*.; raw Q2 *corr*.

3 **great showing** distinguished appearance (Schmidt)

feelingly appropriately, in a way that will do him justice (*OED adv.* 2). Compare *Twelfth Night* 2.3.149, 'he shall find himself most feelingly personated'.

4 **card or calendar of gentry** i.e. 'general preceptor of elegance; the card by which a gentleman is to direct his course; the calendar by which he is to choose his time, that what he does may be both excellent and seasonable' (Dr Johnson). This paraphrase expresses admirably what Osric means, but does not deal fully with the mixed terms in which he says it. *Card*, meaning chart (*OED sb.* ² 3b), belongs to the language of seamanship; whereas *calendar*, meaning guide or directory, belongs to that of business, especially in the Latin *calendarium*, signifying an account book (*OED sb.* 3). Associating *card* with *sail*, and *calendar* with *sale*, Hamlet seizes on the opening Osric gives him here for some complicated quibbling.

4–5 **continent** (1) container (2) geographical continent

5 **what part . . . see** (1) whatever quality a gentleman would wish to see (2) whatever foreign country a gentleman would wish to see

6 **definement** description (earliest example cited by *OED*)

perdition in you loss or diminution in your mouth. *OED*'s first instance of this affected use of *perdition* (*sb.* 1b), which seems peculiar to Shakespeare, is Fluellen's 'The perdition of th'athversary

hath been very great' (*Henry V* 3.6.100–1).

7 **divide him inventorially** list his accomplishments one by one (earliest instance of *inventorially* cited by *OED*)

dizzy make dizzy, bewilder (*OED v.* 3)

7–8 **th'arithmetic of memory** This could be a reference to one of the memory systems described by Frances A. Yates in her *The Art of Memory* (1966).

8 **and yet . . . sail** and yet manage nothing better than an erratic course by comparison with his rapid sailing. The idea appears to be that Laertes, like a racing yacht, takes one course after another to demonstrate his versatility, so that it becomes impossible to keep up with him.

yaw deviate, fail to steer a straight course (not elsewhere in Shakespeare)

neither and nothing else (Abbott 128)

9 **extolment** eulogy (first instance cited by *OED*)

9–10 **great article** large scope (Onions)

10 **infusion** infused temperament, character imposed by nature (*OED sb.* 2c—no other instance of this sense cited)

10–11 **make true diction** give an accurate verbal description (*OED diction* 3)

11 **his semblable is his mirror** i.e. the only thing that really resembles him is his own image in a looking-glass (*OED semblable sb.* 2)

11–12 **who else . . . umbrage** i.e. anyone who tries to follow the path he takes can do so only as the shadow follows the substance (*OED umbrage sb.* 3)

HAMLET The concernancy, sir! Why do we wrap the gentleman in
our more rawer breath?
OSRIC Sir?
HORATIO (*to Hamlet*) Is't not possible to understand in another
tongue? You will to't, sir, really.
HAMLET What imports the nomination of this gentleman?
OSRIC Of Laertes? 20
HORATIO His purse is empty already. All's golden words are spent.
HAMLET Of him, sir.
OSRIC I know you are not ignorant—
HAMLET I would you did, sir. Yet, in faith, if you did it would not
much approve me. Well, sir?
OSRIC You are not ignorant of what excellence Laertes is—
HAMLET I dare not confess that, lest I should compare with him in
excellence. But to know a man well were to know himself.
OSRIC I mean, sir, for his weapon. But in the imputation laid on
him, by them in his meed, he's unfellowed. 30

(xviii) After 5.2.155 Q2 reads:

Enter a Lord
LORD My lord, his majesty commended him to you by young Osric,
who brings back to him that you attend him in the hall. He
sends to know if your pleasure hold to play with Laertes, or that
you will take longer time.

17 in another] Q2; in a mother TSCHISCHWITZ, *conj.* Johnson; in's mother *conj.* Staunton   18
to't] Q2 *uncorr.* (too't); doo't Q2 *corr.*   really] Q2; rarely THEOBALD   29 his] Q5; this Q2

14 **The concernancy** i.e. what business of
ours is it. Shakespeare seems to have invented *concernancy* for this occasion.
14–15 **Why do . . . breath** i.e. why do we
envelop this exquisite gentleman in our
words which are so much cruder than his
refined self
17–18 **Is't not . . . tongue** 'might not all this
be understood in plainer language' (Dr
Johnson).
18 **You will . . . really** you will be reduced to
it (plainer language), I assure you
19 **nomination** naming (*OED* 1). Compare
LLL 4.3.128–9, 'the nomination of the
party writing'.
25 **approve me** commend me, be to my credit
28 **to know . . . himself** i.e. before one can
know the true character of another one

must know oneself (proverbial Tilley
K175)
29 **imputation** estimate, reputation
30 **them in his meed** them in his pay. Osric is
probably thinking of Laertes' fencing-
masters.
unfellowed unequalled

(xviii) Even Dover Wilson admits that the excision of these lines, which serve no useful
purpose and require an extra speaking actor,
is 'a definite improvement' (*MSH* p. 32).

3 **that** if (Abbott 285)

HAMLET I am constant to my purposes. They follow the King's
  pleasure. If his fitness speaks, mine is ready, now or whenso-
  ever, provided I be so able as now.

LORD The King and Queen and all are coming down.

HAMLET In happy time.

LORD The Queen desires you to use some gentle entertainment to   10
  Laertes before you fall to play.

HAMLET She well instructs me.

Exit Lord

(xviii) 12 *Exit Lord*] *not in* Q2

6 **fitness** inclination, convenience (*OED sb.*
4). This sense of the word seems to be
confined to Shakespeare.

9 **In happy time** How opportune

10 **use some gentle entertainment** i.e.
behave courteously (as a gentleman
should)

ALTERATIONS TO LINEATION

THE principles governing what follows have been set out by Gary Taylor in his edition of *Henry V*. He writes:

> Since this list records only changes of verse to prose, of prose to verse, or of line-arrangement within verse, it differs from the textual collations in a few details of presentation. Both within the lemma and in the quotation of a rejected line-arrangement, punctuation at the end of the line is ignored, and spelling modernized. Attribution of an emendation or variant reading indicates only that the text or editor cited *arranges* the lines in a certain way; sometimes . . . not all the words of the text are identical with those printed in this edition (p. 303).

1.1.11–13	Well . . . haste] Q2; *as prose* F
40	Peace . . . again] Q2; Peace, break thee off: *Enter the Ghost.* | Look . . . again F
111–12	Speak . . . done] POPE; *as one line* FQ2
113–14	That . . . me] Q2Q1; *As one line* F
116–17	Which . . . speak] Q2; *As one line* FQ1 (*subs.*)
1.2.57	Have . . . Polonius] Q2; F *divides after* 'leave'.
87	'Tis . . . Hamlet] Q2; F *divides after* 'commendable'.
120	I . . . madam] Q2; F *divides after* 'best'.
160–1	I . . . myself] F; *as one line* Q2
162–3	The . . . you] Q2; F *divides after* 'lord', 'ever' *and* 'friend'.
244	I'll . . . again] FQ1; Q2 *divides after* 'tonight'.
1.3.113–14	And . . . heaven] ROWE; FQ2 *divide after* 'speech'.
1.4.4–5	Indeed . . . season] JENKINS; *as one* line FQ2Q1
54	It . . . thee] F; Q2 *divides after* 'still'.
1.5.29	Haste . . . swift] Q2; F *divides after* 'know it'.
52–3	To . . . moved] POPE; *as one line* FQ2
56–7	Will . . . garbage] Q2; *as one line* F
112–13	It . . . sworn't] Q2; *as one line* F
128–9	There's . . . Denmark] FQ1; Q2 *divides after* 'villain'.
130–31	There . . . this] Q2; *as prose* F
158–9	Ah . . . cellarage] Q2; *as prose* F
2.1.34–5	A . . . assault] Q2; *as one line* F
36–7	Ay . . . that] STEEVENS 1778; *as one line* FQ2
48–50	And . . . leave] MALONE; F *divides after* 'this' *and* 'say?'; Q2 *divides after* 'say?' *and* 'something'.
51–2	At 'closes . . . gentleman'] GLOBE; F *divides after* 'consequence'.
60–1	Videlicet . . . now] CAPELL; *as one line* FQ2
75	Farewell . . . matter] Q2; F *divides after* 'Farewell'.
86–7	My . . . it] Q2; *as one line* F
2.2.36	My . . . you] Q2; F *divides after* 'son'.
104–5	Thus . . . Perpend] Q2; *as one line* F
127–8	But . . . love] CAPELL; *as one line* FQ2
160–1	You . . . lobby] Q2; F *divides after* 'sometimes' *and* 'here'.

Appendix B

168	But . . . reading] Q2; F *divides after* 'wretch'.
170–1	I'll . . . Hamlet] Q2; F *divides after* 'presently'.
178–9	Ay . . . thousand] F; Q2 *divides after* 'goes'.
204–13	Though . . . you] Q2; F *divides after* 'madness', 'walk', 'lord', 'grave', 'air', 'are', 'happiness', 'on', 'not', 'of', 'him', 'meeting', 'daughter', *and* 'humbly'.
223–4	My . . . both] F; Q2 *divides after* 'Guildenstern'.
226–7	Happy . . . button] HANMER; *as prose* F; Q2 *divides after* 'cap'.
385–6	My . . . Rome] Q2; F *divides after* 'you'.
397	O . . . thou] POPE; *as prose* FQ2
399–401	Why . . . well] F; *as prose* Q2
409	'As . . . wot'] *as quotation* MALONE; *as prose* FQ2
411	'It . . . was'] *as quotation* POPE; *as prose* FQ2
441–2	'The . . . beast' . . . with Pyrrhus] CAPELL; *as prose* FQ2
443	'The . . . arms] FQ1; *as prose* Q2
455–6	Old . . . you] CAPELL; *as one line* Q2
472–3	And . . . nothing] Q2; *as one line* F
496	Run . . flames] Q2; F *divides after* 'down'.
575–8	And . . . play] JOHNSON; F *divides after* 'drab' *and* 'brain'; Q2 *divides after* 'foh', *and* 'heard'.
3.1.25–8	With . . . delights] POPE; F *divides after* 'me', 'gentlemen' *and* 'on'; Q2 *divides after* 'heart', 'me', 'inclined' *and* 'edge'.
32–3	Affront . . . espials] JOHNSON; *as one line ending* 'espials' F; *as one line ending* 'myself' Q2
110–11	Could . . . honesty] F; Q2 *divides after* 'commerce'.
133–4	Let . . . farewell] F; Q2 *divides after* 'him' *and* 'house'.
175–8	Whereon . . . grief] F, Q2 *divides after* 'beating', 'himself', 'on't' *and* 'well'.
3.2.43	How . . . work] Q2; F *divides after* 'lord'.
87–99	Excellent . . . ready] F; Q2 *divides after* 'i'faith', 'air', 'so', 'Hamlet', 'mine', 'lord', 'say', 'actor', 'enact', 'Capitol', 'me' *and* 'there'.
211	'Tis . . . awhile] Q2Q1; F *divides after* 'sworn'.
231–2	I . . . dallying] F; Q2 *divides after* 'love'.
236	So . . . husbands] Q2Q1; F *treats as a separate line.*
239	Thoughts . . . agreeing] Q2Q1; F *divides after* 'apt'.
266–7	This . . . here] Q2; F *divides after* 'himself'.
291–2	Good . . . affair] F; Q2 *divides after* 'frame'.
365–70	Then . . . friends] POPE; F *divides after* 'and by', 'bent', 'and by' *and* 'so'; Q2 *divides after* 'and by', 'and by' *and* 'friends', *concluding with* 'said'.
3.3.11	The . . . bound] Q2; F *divides after* 'single'.
78–9	To . . . revenge] Q2; *as one line* F
3.4.1	He . . . him] Q2; F *divides after* 'straight'.
52–3	Ay . . . index] Q2; *as prose* F
133–4	This . . . in] POPE; *as one line* FQ2
152	O . . . twain] Q2; F *divides after* 'Hamlet'.
156–7	Assume . . . tonight] This edition; *as one line* F
189–90	Alack . . . on] CAPELL; *as one line* F; Q2 *divides after* 'forgot'.
4.1.1	There's . . . heaves] Q2; F *divides after* 'sighs'.
4.3.50–5	I . . . England] F; Q2 *divides after* 'England', 'mother', 'Hamlet', 'wife' *and* 'mother'.
56	Follow . . . aboard] ROWE; FQ2 *divide after* 'foot'.

4.5.1–2	I . . . pitied] Q2; *as prose* F
14–16	'Twere . . . in] Q2; F *divides after* 'with' *and* 'conjectures'.
23–6	How . . . shoon] CAPELL Q1 (*subs.*); *as two lines divided after* 'one' FQ2
29–32	He . . . stone] CAPELL; *as two lines divided after* 'gone' FQ2
34–5	Pray . . . snow] F; *as one line* Q2
47–50	Tomorrow . . . Valentine] Q2Q1; *as two lines divided after* 'betime' F
51–4	Then . . . more] JOHNSON; *as two lines divided after* 'door' FQ2
61–2	Quoth . . . wed] FQ1; *as one line* Q2
71	Follow . . . you] Q2; F *divides after* 'close'.
72–3	O . . . death] F; *as prose* Q2
94–5	Where . . . matter] Q2 (*subs.*); F *divides after* 'Switzers'.
113–14	I . . . father] Q2; F *divides after* 'door'.
115	That . . . bastard] Q2; F *divides after* 'calm'.
140–1	Good . . . certainty] F; *as one line* Q2
170–1	Hadst . . . thus] Q2; *as prose* F
172–4	You . . . daughter] F; Q2 *divides after* 'a-down' *and* 'it'.
192–3	No . . . death-bed] JOHNSON; *as one line* FQ2
197–8	He . . . moan] JOHNSON; *as one line* FQ2
4.7.30	Break . . . think] Q2; F *divides after* 'that'.
36–7	Letters . . . Queen] THEOBALD; *prose* F
41–2	Laertes . . . us] F; *as one line* Q2
51–4	'Tis . . . me] JENKINS; *as prose* F; Q2 *divides after* 'Naked' *and* 'alone'.
58–60	If . . . me] Q2; F *divides after* 'should it be so'.
123–4	With . . . death] F; *as one line* Q2
5.1.113–14	Mine . . . made] F; *as one line* Q2
167–8	A . . . think it was] Q2; F *divides before* 'Whose'.
249–5	Thou . . . throat] F; *as one line* Q2
5.2.74–6	It . . . Horatio] HANMER; F *divides after* 'short' *and* 'more'.
83–4	I . . . water-fly] F; Q2 *divides after* 'sir'.
173–6	But . . . done] ROWE; F *divides after* 'gentleman', 'knows' *and* 'punished'; Q2 *divides after* 'knows' *and* 'punished'.
198–9	I . . . play] F; *as one line* Q2
206–7	Give . . . wager] Q2; F *divides after* 'Osric'.
209	I . . . both] Q2; F *divides after* 'it'.
211–12	This is . . . length] Q2 F *divides after* 'heavy', 'another', and 'well'.
221	In . . . cups] Q2; F *divides after* 'worn'.
234	Stay . . . thine] Q2; F *divides after* 'drink'.
243	I will . . . me] Q2; F *divides after* 'lord'.
245	I dare . . . and by] Q2; F *divides after* 'madam'.
249	Come . . . dally] Q2; F *divides after* 'third'.
260	Why . . . Osric] Q2; F *divides after* 'woodcock'.
263–4	No . . . poisoned] Q2; F *divides at* 'drink	O' *and* 'drink	I'.
267	It is . . . slain] Q2; F *divides after the first* 'Hamlet'.
275	The point . . . work] Q2 F *divides at* 'too?'.
278	Here . . . Dane] Q2; F *divides after* 'murd'rous'.
280–1	He . . . himself] F; *as one line* Q2
295–6	As . . . have 't] Q2; F *divides after* 'cup'.
312	Now . . . prince] Q2; F *divides after* 'heart'.
343	Which . . . me] Q2; F *divides after* 'doth'.
345	And . . . more] Q2; F *divides after* 'mouth'.
347	Even . . . mischance] Q2; F *divides after* 'wild'.
351	To . . . passage] Q2; F *divides after* 'royally'.

DER BESTRAFTE BRUDERMORD

In 1781 H. A. O. Reichard published a play entitled *Tragoedia. Der bestrafte Brudermord oder: Prinz Hamlet aus Dännemark* in his periodical *Olla Potrida*. The copy text for it was a manuscript, subsequently lost, dated 27 October 1710, which Reichard had obtained from the well known actor Conrad Ekhof, who died in 1778. The play was reprinted by Albert Cohn in his *Shakespeare in Germany* (1865), together with an English translation of it by Georgina Archer. Other translations followed: by E. G. Latham in 1870; by H. H. Furness in his *Variorum* of 1877, revised by Bullough (1973); and by E. Brennecke in his *Shakespeare in Germany, 1590–1700* (Chicago, 1964). Their number testifies to the interest this version of *Hamlet* has excited, an interest out of all proportion to any intrinsic value it may have, for *Der bestrafte Brudermord* or *Fratricide Punished*, as it came to be called in English, is a badly debased version of Shakespeare's tragedy, bearing eloquent witness to the damage a dramatic text could suffer from accretion as well as degeneration during the course of a century or more of playing.

The accretions are of two diametrically opposed kinds. On the one hand, someone has tried to pull the play into the classical mould; on the other, someone—not necessarily the same someone—has introduced a crude farcical element into it. Following classical practice, *Der bestrafte Brudermord* is divided into five acts, and a fresh scene begins whenever another character joins those who are on stage already. Furthermore, the play proper is preceded by a distinctly Senecan Prologue in which the allegorical figure of Night calls up the three Furies, tells them of the reigning King's murder of his brother, of his lust for that dead brother's wife, and then, without mentioning Hamlet, orders them to 'kindle the fire of revenge'. It is, in its own way, a rather impressive start, cast, apart from one speech, in verse. The play itself, however, is in prose; and within forty lines of its beginning knockabout comedy rears its head as the Ghost makes its first appearance, startles the sentry, and then gives him a smart box on the ear, causing him to drop his musket. Introduced early, this kind of thing continues late, becoming especially prominent in Act 3 and Act 4. In Act 3 Ophelia in her madness takes a foolish courtier, Phantasmo by name and Osric by derivation, for her lover, makes advances to him, and then, finding him unresponsive to them, strikes him. The farce reaches its climax in the first scene of Act 4, a scene that has no counterpart in any other version of the play. Here Hamlet, delayed on his voyage to England by adverse winds, has come ashore on an island not far from Dover.

Accompanied by two retainers who are really hired assassins, he proposes to take the air and enjoy a picnic lunch. The two *Banditen*, as the German text calls them, promptly disabuse him of this happy fantasy. Hamlet pleads for his life, but finding his pleas are of no avail, asks for permission to make his final prayer to God, adding that when he has made his peace with heaven he will give them the signal to fire at him. As he does so, however, he falls flat on his face, with the result that the two Ruffians, who have maladroitly positioned themselves on either side of him, shoot one another. The effect is ludicrous; yet the entire incident is curiously like the story of the Aloadae, the giants Otus and Ephialtes, who made war on the gods, sought to pile Ossa on Olympus, and Pelion on Ossa, and tried to seize Hera and Artemis. Artemis destroyed them by luring them to an island, standing between them in the form of a white deer, and then evaporating into thin air as they hurled their javelins at her and so killed one another. Perhaps the author of the Prologue was also responsible for the introduction of this bit of farce. The use of heightened language at this point, first for the 'pastoral' description of the island, and then again in the Prince's plea, certainly suggests that he could have been.

The hint for this accretion was probably the reference to the piling of Pelion on Olympus and of Ossa on Pelion in 5.1 of the authentic texts and in the First Quarto. The purpose of the addition is clear enough: to replace narrative with an action that can, unlike the business of the pirate ship, be staged; and this same emphasis on action accounts for the disappearance from the German text of all Hamlet's soliloquies, except his speech in 3.3 as he stands over the praying Claudius. This has to be retained because, without it, Hamlet's sheathing of his sword is not intelligible. There is, in fact, much in *Der bestrafte Brudermord*, including two references to the King's being closely guarded, to suggest that when it was first put on in Germany it was done in English. Action speaks a universal language.

Along with these alterations there go some changes in the ordering of the scenes. Especially noticeable in this connection is the shifting of the first part of 1.2, i.e. all that happens in it up to the entry of Horatio, Marcellus, and Barnardo, to the very end of the first act. A little reflection reveals the reason for the shift, and this, in turn, throws much light on the play as a whole. The court scene is moved to the end of the first act to bring that act within the compass of a small company made up of five men, two boys, and some supernumeraries. The boys had, it should be added, been replaced by women when the play finally took the form in which it has survived. It is true that the Prologue seems to require four female parts; but the allegorical figures concerned in it are supernatural, not human, and two of them could well be played by men. After that the whole thing becomes easy. The action begins with the two Sentinels. After telling the Second about the Ghost and about the way in which it has been plaguing him, the First makes his exit. In scene 2 the trumpets sound as the King drinks off stage; the Ghost appears and startles the Second Sentinel; drums and kettle-drums sound; the Ghost boxes the Sentinel's ears, causing him to drop his musket, and then makes its exit. At this point Horatio comes on. The Sentinel challenges him, and calls out the Guard, led by Francisco, who could well be played by the First Sentinel. Indeed, his being called Francisco, instead of Marcellus, implies as much. As Horatio, Francisco, and the Second Sentinel talk about the Ghost, it makes its second appearance; and after it has gone, Hamlet arrives on the scene. These four figures, together with the Ghost, who soon reappears, then proceed to enact what is left of 1.2, followed by 1.4 and 1.5, all much abbreviated. Some thirty-five lines before the end of this sequence, the Ghost makes its final contribution to the swearing, thus becoming free for other duties, and four lines later Hamlet dismisses Francisco, so that he can then confide the Ghost's story to Horatio. The first half of 1.2, the court scene, can now be staged, with the Ghost playing Claudius, and Francisco or the Second Sentinel playing Polonius. Significantly no Laertes is needed. We are told that he has already gone to Paris.

This pattern, established in the first act, persists through the rest of the play. No succeeding scene demands a larger speaking cast than five men and two women; and reasonable time is always allowed for the changes of costume that doubling entails. Taken in conjunction with the evident and sensible preference for action rather than dialogue, this economizing on actors explains the cuts, which are both large and numerous: all but one of the Prince's soliloquies; 1.3 in its entirety; the exchanges between Polonius and Reynoldo at the opening of 2.1; the Ambassadors to Norway; the activities of Rosencrantz and Guildenstern until, under the guise of Attendants, later transformed into Ruffians, they are given the task of escorting Hamlet to England; the Fishmonger scene between Hamlet and Polonius; the long excerpt from 'Aeneas' tale to Dido'; the reduction of the play-within-the-play to the Dumb Show alone; the whole of the graveyard scene, 5.1; and, finally, Fortinbras and all that is connected with him.

Considered in this way, *Der bestrafte Brudermord* emerges as a thoroughly professional job, a version of Shakespeare's play carefully designed to make the action of *Hamlet*, still being played in English to begin with, intelligible to a German audience, and, simultaneously, to bring it within the capacity of a small troupe. This initial adaptation could well be the work of the leader of that troupe. Soon, however, the need arose for a German version, and at this point, it seems reasonable to assume, a translator, probably a German, was employed; and he, having some pretensions to scholarship, was responsible for the division of the play into acts and scenes, the provision of the Prologue, and such bits of local colour as the substitution of a woman of Strasburg (2.8) for the 'guilty creatures sitting at a play'.

Exactly when the version of *Hamlet* that lies behind *Der bestrafte Bruder-mord* reached Germany we do not know. Nor do we know whether *Der bestrafte Brudermord* itself is or is not identical with the *Tragoedia von Hamlet einen Printzen in Dennemarck* played at Dresden on 24 June 1626. Cohn says on the title-page of his edition that it was 'Acted in Germany, about the year 1603', but gives no reason for this statement. Two can, however, be supplied. First, if the play was initially given in English, as seems likely, it must have reached Germany in the first decade of the seventeenth century, since there is, according to Brennecke (p. 5), 'no definite record of a performance in English after 1606'. Secondly, in so far as *Der bestrafte Brudermord* relies on a printed version of Shakespeare's play, that version is almost certainly the First Quarto of 1603. The crucial evidence in this regard is the agreement of the German play and the First Quarto in two mistakes on the part of the reporter responsible for concocting the text of the First Quarto. The initial error occurs at the very outset. In *Der bestrafte Brudermord*, exactly as in the First Quarto, the challenge is given by the soldier labelled '1', the sentry on duty, not, as in the two 'good' texts of *Hamlet*, by his relief '2'. The second agreement in error is in the misplacing of the 'Nunnery Scene' (see pp. 73 and 86–7), which in both texts follows immediately on Polonius's 'discovery' that Hamlet is mad for the love of Ophelia.

There are other significant agreements between *Der bestrafte Bruder-mord* and the First Quarto. In neither is Ophelia's father called Polonius. Named Corambis in the First Quarto, he appears as Corambus in the German play. Neither text contains the scene in which the Sailor brings Horatio Hamlet's letter telling of his escape from the vessel carrying him to England and of his return to Denmark. In the First Quarto its place is taken by Horatio's interview with the Queen to inform her of the King's treachery and of Hamlet's arrival; while in *Der bestrafte Brudermord* it is replaced by the farcical business of Hamlet's tricking the two *Banditen* into shooting one another. All the same, there is a link between these two versions clearly demonstrating that whoever was responsible for the making of *Der bestrafte Brudermord* certainly knew the corresponding scene in the First Quarto and deliberately substituted a scene of his own invention for it. In the First Quarto the Queen, having heard of Claudius's 'villainy', as she calls it, bids Horatio tell her son to take care. To this Horatio replies:

> Madam,
> Never make doubt of that. I think by this
> The news be come to court he [Hamlet] is arrived.
> Observe the King, and you shall quickly find,
> Hamlet being here, things fell not to his mind.
>   (H2ᵛ)

In *Der bestrafte Brudermord* Hamlet, in 5.2, gives Horatio an account of his escape from the assassins, and then adds: '*Meine Ankunft aber wird dem Könige nicht angenehm seyn* [I'm afraid my arrival won't exactly please the King]'. The resemblance between the two texts here is too close to be accidental. The scene peculiar to *Der bestrafte Brudermord* is simply the result of that play's preference for action over narration.

There are other substantial agreements between *Der bestrafte Brudermord* and the First Quarto. For instance, in both texts it is Claudius, not Laertes, who suggests that the unbated rapier be anointed with poison; and in both Hamlet expects the inset play to cause the King to 'turn pale'. Nevertheless, the First Quarto cannot be the sole source of the German adaptation, for on numerous occasions—Duthie finds no fewer than thirty-six, most, though not all, of them convincing—the latter corresponds with the 'good' texts either in wording that is different from that of the First Quarto or in containing matter that is ignored by it. How has this come about? The First Quarto is, it has already been argued (pp. 75–88), a memorial reconstruction of an abridged version of the Folio text and, consequently, a very imperfect representation of that abridgement. Now let us suppose that in the small troupe of English actors who took *Hamlet* to Germany there was one who had played in performances of the abridged version. Such a man might well be able to make good from memory some of the original reporter's errors and omissions, and thus produce the hybrid text on which the German play is based.

Duthie, who did far more than anyone else to clear up the relationship of *Der bestrafte Brudermord* to Shakespeare's play and to dispose almost entirely of the old idea that the German play goes back to the *Ur-Hamlet* of which so little is known, ran into one major obstacle: a curious correspondence, or seeming correspondence, between *Der bestrafte Brudermord* and the First Quarto for which there is no equivalent in either of the good texts. In the scene peculiar to Q1 where Horatio tells the Queen that Hamlet is back in Denmark he speaks of the letter he has just received from the Prince. In it Hamlet

> writes how he escaped the danger
> And subtle treason that the King had plotted.
> Being crossed by the contention of the winds,
> He found the packet sent to the King of England,
> Wherein he saw himself betrayed to death,
> As at his next conversion with your grace,
> He will relate the circumstance at full.

$$(H2^v-3)$$

That *conversion*, presumably a printer's error for *conversation*, never takes place, though it is badly needed, since the account the letter gives is anything but clear. It offers no explanation of how a fierce storm could have caused Hamlet to find 'the packet' or of how he made his way back to Denmark. All we have to go on is Horatio's answer to the Queen's question: 'But what became of Gilderstone and Rossencraft?' It runs, in the muddled fashion that is so typical of the First Quarto, thus:

> He being set ashore, they went for England,
> And in the packet there writ down that doom
> To be performed on them 'pointed for him;
> And by great chance he had his father's seal,
> So all was done without discovery.

In *Der bestrafte Brudermord*, on the other hand, we have Hamlet's escape from the two assassins, enacted in 4.1, and then recounted in 5.2. In 4.1 there is nothing to show where the island on which the scene takes place is, and no reason is given for the ship's anchoring there. However, when Hamlet tells the story to Horatio in 5.2 he makes good both these deficiencies by saying: *Nun begab es sich, dass wir eines Tages contrairen Wind hatten, und an ein Eyland, nicht ferne von Dovern anker setzen* [Now it so happened that one day we had an adverse wind, and so we cast anchor by an island not far from Dover].'

Are, then, this 'adverse wind' and the 'contention of the winds' one and the same phenomenon? If they are, it looks as though the First Quarto and *Der bestrafte Brudermord* are drawing on a version of the story that is different from that used in the Folio and in the Second Quarto. It can be said at once that an adverse wind is not the same thing as a violent storm. Secondly, *Der bestrafte Brudermord* is the only one of the four texts that mentions the island. Thirdly, this reference to a contrary wind is not the only one in the German play. In 2.7 the actors arrive at the court. Hamlet greets them, and then asks, 'What brings you here?' Carl, the leader of the troupe, replies that they set out hoping to put on a show for the King's marriage, but unfortunately they were delayed by '*contraire Wind*'. In fact, an adverse wind seems to be the translator's stock excuse for delay of any kind on a sea voyage. The similarity between *Der bestrafte Brudermord* and the First Quarto at this point in the play is not a genuine similarity at all, and so there is no need to drag in the *Ur-Hamlet* to account for it. The German play is an adaptation of the abridged version of *Hamlet* that lies behind the First Quarto.

THE MUSIC FOR THE SONGS

THE tunes that follow have been selected, with the generous permission of Dr Frederick W. Sternfeld, from those given in his *Songs from Shakespeare's Tragedies* (Oxford, 1964), where they are presented 'in a practical edition, suitable for the music rack and theatre rather than the library' (p. v). Further details about these and other versions are to be found in that volume and in his more extended study *Music in Shakespearian Tragedy* (1963)

How should I your true love know
Hamlet, Act IV

Shakespeare's text

Ballad tune: *Walsingham*
harmonized by Francis Cutting

```
OPHELIA
1. How should I    your—   true love  know  From a - no - ther    one?
2. He is dead   and —   gone, la - dy,  He is dead and      gone;
3. White his shroud  as  the  moun - tain  snow,*  Lar-ded all  with sweet flowers;

By his cock - le   hat  and   staff,—  And his san - dal  shoon.
At his head    a    grass - green  turf,—  At his heels   a    stone.
Which be - wept  to the grave  did not go—  With his true - love  showers.
```

*[*Singing interrupted:*](QUEEN) Alas, look here, my lord.

379

Tomorrow is Saint Valentine's day

Hamlet, Act IV

Shakespeare's text

Linley: *Shakespeare's Dramatic Songs*

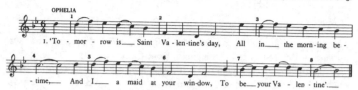

OPHELIA

1. 'To-mor-row is Saint Va-len-tine's day, All in the morn-ing be-time, And I a maid at your win-dow, To be your Va-len-tine'.

2. Then up he rose and donn'd his clothes
And dupp'd the chamber door,
Let in the maid, that out a maid
Never departed more.

3. By Gis and by Saint Charity,
Alack, and fie for shame!
Young men will do't if they come to't,
By Cock, they are to blame.

4. Quoth she, 'Before you tumbled me,
You promis'd me to wed.'
[He answers:] 'So would I ha' done, by yonder sun,
An thou hadst not come to my bed.'

They bore him bare-faced

Hamlet, Act IV

Shakespeare's text

Ballad tunes: *Walsingham*
and *Bandalashot* (adapted)

OPHELIA

They bore him bare-faced on the bier, Hey non non-ny, non-ny, hey non-ny; And in his grave rained ma-ny a tear,

[Singing stops:]
(OPHELIA) Fare you well, my dove.
(LAERTES) Hadst thou thy wits, and
didst persuade revenge,
It could not move thus.

You must sing, down a-down, and you call him a-down-a.

For bonny sweet Robin
Hamlet, Act IV

Shakespeare's text   Ballet Lute Book

For bon - ny sweet Ro - bin is all my joy.

And will he not come again?
Hamlet, Act IV

Shakespeare's text   Linley: *Shakespeare's Dramatic Songs*

1st stanza: And will he not come a - gain? And will he not come a -
2nd stanza: His beard as white as snow, All fla - xen was his
They bore him bare - faced on the bier, Hey non non-ny, non - ny, hey

- gain? No, no, -gain? No, no, no, lie is dead, Go
poll, He is poll, He is gone, he is gone, And we
non - ny, And non - ny, And in his grave rained

to thy death - bed, [and] He ne - ver will come a - gain.
cast a - way moan, Gra - mer - cy on his soul!
ma - ny a tear...

In youth when I did love
Hamlet, Act V

Shakespeare's text   Nott: *Songs and Sonnets*

FIRST CLOWN (GRAVEDIGGER)

1. In youth when I did love, did love, Me -
2. But age with his steal - ing steps Hath
3. A pick - axe and a spade, a spade, For

- thought it was ve - ry sweet: To con - tract O! the time for - a
claw'd me in his clutch: And hath shipp'd me in -
and a shroud-ing sheet; O! a pit of clay for

my be - hove, O! me - thought there - a was no - thing - a meet.
- til the land, As if there had ne - ver been such.
to be made, For such a guest is meet.

THE STAGE DIRECTIONS AT 1.2.0.1–4 AND
A NOTE ON 1.2.129–30

1.2.0.1–4 *Flourish* . . . *Attendant* F's inclusion of Ophelia in this entry is probably due to a slip by the revising Shakespeare who, having mentioned Polonius and Laertes, goes on to complete the family. Q1, which has the most business-like entry at this point, does not name her; nor does Q2; and if, as Q2 seems to imply, the occasion is a meeting of the Council, her presence is neither required nor appropriate.

The agreement of Q1 and F in having Hamlet enter immediately after the Queen almost certainly shows that this is what happened on Shakespeare's stage. The scene is a carefully orchestrated exercise in public relations, designed by the King to lead up to his proclamation that Hamlet is 'the most immediate to our throne' (l. 109). It is unthinkable in such circumstances that the second most important person in Denmark should come in at the tail-end of the procession, as Q2 makes him do. Moreover, it is not until line 64 that Hamlet is identified; but, if he follows Claudius and Gertrude, any audience that knows the rules of precedence, as an Elizabethan audience did, recognizes at once that he is more closely connected with the royal couple than is any of those who follow him. For the past fifty years editors and critics have allowed themselves to be too easily persuaded by Dover Wilson's brilliant but also misleading justification of the Q2 direction (*Hamlet*, p. 149; *MSH*, pp. 34–5; and *WHH*, pp. 28–32). The entry, as Q2 gives it, is not a true stage direction at all but something much more interesting: the playwright's scenario for what is to follow. As one reads it, one can almost hear Shakespeare thinking out how the scene can best be conducted. He knows what he wants to lead up to—the first confrontation of the hero and his antagonist, together with some exposition of the strange relationship created by the marriage of Hamlet's mother to his uncle. How is he to move towards this end? Q2 tells us. The process, as the 'stage direction' defines it, is one of narrowing down and sharpening up. Claudius begins by addressing his Council, first about domestic matters, and then about foreign affairs. The latter call for the sending of a mission to Norway. So at this point two of the characters hitherto thought of collectively as 'Council' acquire the names Voltemand and Cornelius. As they go, Claudius turns his attention to the next two characters in the scenario, Laertes and Polonius, and then comes round finally to its last named figure, Hamlet.

1.2.129–30 **O that . . . dew** Until 1932, when Dover Wilson gave four lectures at Cambridge, which he then expanded into his *MSH*, first published in 1934, the year in which his New Cambridge edition of *Hamlet* also appeared, editors had, with a rare unanimity, always preferred the *solid* of F to the *sallied* of Q2. Indeed, *solid* had taken the place of *sallied* before there was such a thing as an edited text at all. After five quarto versions of the play, including Q1, had printed *sallied*, the Players' Quarto of 1676 replaced it with *solid*, as did the Players' Quarto of 1703. We do not know who made the alteration; but his reason for making it was, presumably, that *sallied* no longer made sense, if it ever had. Wilson, however, having argued the case for Q2 as the most reliable of the three texts in his *MSH*, and, during the course of it, for *sallied*, of which he took *sallied* to be a misprint, as against F's *solid*, naturally adopted *sallied* in his New Cambridge edition of the play. Since then some evidence has come to light suggesting that *sallied* is, in fact, a variant spelling of *sullied*, with the result that most recent editions print either *sullied* or *sallied*. Nevertheless, *solid* is preferred in this edition for several reasons. First, if the origin of F, as set out in the textual introduction, is valid, *solid* is either what Shakespeare wrote in his first draft or a revision of what he wrote there. Secondly, the *sallied* of Q2 could well have come from the *sallied* of Q1, and is, therefore, suspect. Thirdly, Wilson, justifying his preference for *sullied*, says: 'Hamlet is thinking of snow begrimed with soot and dirt, as it often is in melting, and wishing that his "sullied flesh" might melt as snow melts in time of thaw.' There are two difficulties here: Hamlet says nothing whatever about snow, he refers to flesh; and, as anyone who has watched snow melting knows, when the snow goes the dirt remains. April is the dirtiest month in Ontario, until the rain comes to wash away what the snow leaves behind. Fourthly Wilson, backed astonishingly enough by Greg, holds that a reference by Burbage to his 'solid flesh' would have given rise to irrepressible mirth. In doing so he imports the twentieth-century anxiety about weight into Elizabethan England, and he gives *solid* overtones which it does not have. *OED* defines it, using these very lines from *Hamlet* as an example, thus, 'hard and compact'. Finally, the whole process of solid becoming liquid, becoming vapour seems to have interested Shakespeare. As early as *The Rape of Lucrece* he writes, 'For stones dissolved to water do convert . . . Melt at my tears, and be compassionate!' (592–4). Falstaff, the great antithesis to Hamlet, describes himself as 'a man of continual dissolution and thaw' (*Merry Wives*, 3.5.105) and goes on to say that the court 'would melt me out of my fat, drop by drop' (4.5.90). Most important of all, solidity is closely associated with earth. In *2 Henry IV* the King speaks of time making 'the continent, | Weary of solid firmness, melt itself | Into the sea' (3.1.47–9). In *Troilus and Cressida* Ulysses envisages the waters making 'a sop of all this solid globe' (1.3.113); and in *Hamlet* itself the Prince describes the world as 'this solidity and compound mass' (3.4.50). It is the flesh, the solid earthy part of himself that Hamlet wants to shed, and in doing so he comes very close indeed to the poet of *Sonnets* 44 and 45, wishing 'the dull substance of [his] flesh . . . so much of earth and water wrought' were turned to thought, and lamenting that because two of the elements in his make-up, 'slight air and purging fire', are already with his friend, his life, dependent on earth and water alone, 'Sinks down to death, oppressed with melancholy'.

INDEX

This is a selective guide to points in the Introduction and Commentary of more than routine note. Citations from other texts are not listed.

An asterisk indicates that the note supplements information given in *OED*. A = Appendix A.

galled jade, 3.2.228
gambol from, 3.4.140
gaming, 3.3.91
garb, 2.2.367
garbage, 1.5.57
gates, 1.5.67
gather and surmise, 2.2.108
gauntlets, 5.2.170.4
gender, 4.7.18
general (= general public), 2.2.429
generous, 1.3.74; 4.7.111
gentle, A.xviii.10
gentry, 2.2.22; A.xvii.4
Gertrude, pp. 44, 48, 51, 57-9, 63,
    73-4, 82-4, 86-7, 107, 116
ghost, pp. 27, 38-42, 47, 60
giant-like, 4.5.119
gib, 3.4.179
gibber, A.i.9
Gielgud, Sir John, p. 60
gilded, 3.3.58
girdle, 5.2.114
Gis, 4.5.57
give his saying deed, 1.3.27
give in evidence, 3.3.64
give me leave, 2.2.170
give th'assay of arms, 2.2.71
give to negligence, 4.5.134
give up, 2.2.30
give us pause, 3.1.68
give you, p. 80; 1.1.16
give you way, 4.6.29
gives the charge, 3.4.78
giving out, 1.5.185
glares, 3.4.118
glass, 3.1.154
glimpses, *sb.* 1.4.32
globe (= head), 1.5.97
glow, *v.* 3.4.49
go about, 3.2.329
go back again, 4.7.27
go hard, A.x.6
go to, 1.3.112
goblin, p. 40; 1.4.19; (plural) 5.2.23
God-a-mercy, 2.2.172
God be at your table, 4.5.43
God buy you, 2.1.68
God 'ild you, 4.5.41
God's bodykins, 2.2.519
God's creatures, 3.1.145
Gonzago, 3.2.224
good (= good friends), 1.1.70
good even, 1.2.167

good kissing, 2.2.182
good my lord, 2.1.69
good turn, 4.6.19
goodly, 2.2.244
Goodman, 5.1.13
goose-quills, 2.2.339
grace, *sb.* 1.1.113; 1.2.124; 2.2.53;
    3.4.140; 4.5.132
graces, 1.2.63; 4.7.21
gracious, 1.1.146; 5.2.86; (as form
    of address), 3.1.44
grainèd, 3.4.82
Granville-Barker, H., p. 35
grapple, *v.* 1.3.63
grass-green, 4.5.31
grating, 3.1.3
graveness, A.xiv.14
Gray, H. D., p. 76
great command, 5.1.218
green, 1.3.101
greenly, 4.5.79
Greg, W. W., pp. 18, 69, 76-7, 85,
    99-103, 107-9, 114, 120, 127-8
grief, p. 93; 3.1.178
griefs (= grievances), 3.1.184
grieved, 2.2.65
grizzly, 1.2.239
groaning, *sb.* 3.2.234
gross and scope, 1.1.68
gross, *a.* A.xiii.38
grosser name, 4.7.145
grossly, 3.3.80
groundlings, 3.2.10
Guildenstern, pp. 54, 55, 61, 72, 73;
    2.2.0
guilts, 4.7.21
gules, 2.2.448
gulf, 3.3.16

habit, 3.4.130
halfpenny, too dear a, 2.2.271-2
Halliwell, J. O., p. 75
halt, *v.* 2.2.323
Hamlet, pp. 24-7, 43-51, 54-66,
    73, 86-7, etc.
hand-in-hand, 1.5.49
handsaw, p. 31; 2.2.374
handsome, 2.2.436
hangers, p. 94; 5.2.114-15
haps, 4.3.70
happily, 1.1.116; 2.2.379
happiness, 2.2.208
hard consent, 1.2.60

Index

spirits, 2.2.591; 3.4.112
spite, p. 48; 1.5.195
splenative, 5.1.251
sponge, 4.2.11
sport, 3.2.205
spring that turneth wood to stone, 4.7.20
springe, 5.2.260; (plural), 1.3.115
spurns, v. 4.5.6
squeak, v. A.i.9
stage, 5.2.331
stage directions, pp. 20, 72, 97–8, 114–16, 121
staging, pp. 14–24
stake, A.viii.48
stalks, 1.1.50
stamp, sb. A.ix.2
stand, 1.1.123; 3.4.115; 5.1.246; 5.2.64
stands (= depends), A.i.12
stands it safe, 3.3.1
star, 2.2.140
start, v. 3.2.292
start up, 3.4.115
state, sb. 1.1.101; 2.2.502; 5.2.170.4; A.i.6
stately, adv. 1.2.202
station, 3.4.59
statists, 5.2.34
statutes, 5.1.99
stay, v. 5.2.25
stay upon, 3.2.100
stays, 3.3.95
stealers, 3.2.318
stealing steps, 5.1.69
step between, 3.4.105
sterling, 1.3.107
steward, 4.5.174
stewed, 3.4.85
stick, v. 4.5.89
stick fiery off, 5.2.203
stiffly, 1.5.95
still, a. 3.1.175
still, adv. 1.5.194; A.i.15
stir, A.xiii.46
stithy, 3.2.79
stock, 3.1.119
stomach, 1.1.100
straight, 5.1.4
strange, 4.7.46
straw, A.xiii.18; (plural), 4.5.6
strewments, 5.1.223
stricken deer, 3.2.255

strings of steel, 3.3.70
strong hand, 1.1.102
strong law, 4.3.3
strumpet, 2.2.234
Stubbes, George, pp. 24–5
stuck, sb. 4.7.136
study, v. 2.2.529
Sturlason, Snorri, p. 6
sty, 3.4.86
subject, sb. 1.1.72; 1.2.33
substance, 2.2.256
succession, 2.2.347
such, 4.7.50; 5.1.72
suddenly, 2.2.210
suffer, 3.2.124
sugar o'er, p. 118; 3.1.49
suits (= pleas), 1.3.129
sullies, sb. 2.1.39
sun, 1.2.67
supervise, sb. 5.2.24
supply, sb. 2.2.24
suppliance, 1.3.9
supply and profit, 2.2.24
supposal, 1.2.18
surmise, v. 2.2.108
survivor, 1.2.90
suspiration, 1.2.79
swaggering, 1.4.9
swathing-clouts, 2.2.378
sweepstake, 4.5.143
sweet, a. 3.2.48
swinish phrase, A.ii.3
Switzers, 4.5.94
'Swounds, p. 129; 5.1.264
synod, 2.2.485

table, 1.5.98, 107
table-book, 2.2.135
taint, v. 1.5.85
taints, sb. 2.1.32
take (= assume), 2.1.13
take off, 3.2.234
takes (= bewitches), p. 118; 1.1.145; (= detracts), A.ii.4
tar, v. 2.2.349
tardy, 3.2.23
target, 2.2.319
taxed of, A.ii.2
Taylor, Gary, pp. 116, 118, 122, 128
Taylor, Joseph, p. 17
teeth and forehead, 3.3.63
tell (= count), 1.2.237
tell me he that knows, 1.1.70